D0884076

AN ENCYCLOPEDIA OF THE BOOK

The Nuremberg 'Lederschnitt' bindings of the 15th century inspired this revival of the craft made for the author by Otto Wächter of the Österreichische Nationalbibliothek, Vienna. The calf was softened before being moulded, punched and pierced

GEOFFREY ASHALL GLAISTER

British Council Librarian

An Encyclopedia of the Book

TERMS USED IN PAPER-MAKING, PRINTING
BOOKBINDING AND PUBLISHING
WITH NOTES ON ILLUMINATED MANUSCRIPTS
BIBLIOPHILES, PRIVATE PRESSES
AND PRINTING SOCIETIES

Including Illustrations and Translated Extracts from

GRAFISK UPPSLAGSBOK

(Esselte, Stockholm)

THE WORLD PUBLISHING COMPANY

CLEVELAND AND NEW YORK

PUBLISHED BY THE WORLD PUBLISHING COMPANY
2231 WEST 110TH STREET, CLEVELAND 2, OHIO

LIBRARY OF CONGRESS CATALOG CARD NUMBER: 60-6660

FIRST EDITION

GBHC

Printed in Great Britain

To
Raoul Curiel

PREFACE

In the fifteenth century, when the bookcrafts as now practised may be said to have begun, the printer often combined the roles of typefounder, editor, printer, binder, publisher and seller of his productions; a time-consuming but surely very satisfying occupation. As the years passed, however, and the processes of making books grew into separate trades, each with its own master craftsmen, special terms were evolved to describe the technicalities particular to every stage of creating a book. This evolution has never ceased, yet an exhaustive search must be made in the many handbooks available before the interested bibliophile, the apprentice printer and binder, the publisher or the bookseller, the paper-maker or the librarian can find clear explanations of these terms and something of their history. Perhaps more disquieting than the absence of a comprehensive English glossary on the subject is the fact that in many works on book production, presumably written by authorities in their several branches, there is a perplexing failure to agree, not only on the spelling of names, the dates of an invention, or how fast a machine operates, but on such relatively simple matters as to whether an 'introduction' and a 'foreword' are synonymous (they are not). May this be offered as a reason why a librarian, although outside the book trade proper, has ventured to write a book for its use, claiming that the detachment of a broad general viewpoint is a not unsuitable qualification for doing so, even in an age when specialization discourages the polymath.

In the preface to his 'Dictionary of the English Language', 1755, Samuel Johnson states that 'to explain, requires the use of terms less abstruse than that which is to be explained, and such terms cannot always be found. For as nothing can be proved but by supposing something intuitively known, and evident without proof, so nothing can be defined but by the use of words too plain to admit of a definition.' I have taken this as a guiding principle in compiling this short glossary which aims at providing a reference-companion to be constantly available when studying or practising the processes of book-making.

The scope of the book is stated on the title-page, it merely remaining to add here that advertising, newspaper work, and other aspects of commercial printing have been excluded. To provide detailed technical information on printing machinery would have been to depart from the deliberately assumed limits of this work, and usurp the function of others; similarly, only short biographical notes on the more important personalities of the book world have been given. Entries for the various schools of manuscript illumination, and for individual manuscripts, should be read with the thought in mind that trends in painting which may have taken a century to develop can only be described in a general way in a work of this kind.

The form of alphabetical order used in dictionaries and other reference books can be one of two. Entries can be arranged word by word or letter by letter. The former, adopted here, is the recommendation of British Standard 1749: 1951 'Alphabetical arrangement', and is the practice of the 'British National Bibliography'. Yet seeming anomalies may occur, and, for example, the user must remember to look for 'photogravure' after 'photo-typesetting'.

It is doubtful if any one person could pronounce with certainty on the accuracy of all the terms in this book, and the publishers have therefore sent the typescript to several specialist and practising craftsmen for scrutiny and comment; without this assistance this book would not have been so complete, and their generous help is separately acknowledged. Not always were they in agreement with each other, so in making a decision between conflicting opinions I accept responsibility for controversial points which may emerge. The words of Thomas Watts in his 'Treatise of Mechanicks', 1716, seem particularly appropriate here, 'should there notwithstanding all the Care that has been taken be some Errata found in this Book, which we are persuaded are not many, it is hop'd the Publick will have the Goodness to pardon 'em, when they reflect what little Time I can have to spare from my daily Employment, and even what Interruptions must accompany those Moments.'

A technical work of this kind may be comprehensive, but will need constant revision to keep abreast of new developments, improved machinery, and other changes in the book-trade industries. Users of the book are invited to co-operate by sending me detailed suggestions or corrections: in particular, biographical notes on the world's publishing firms might be included in a future edition, and will be welcome.

The title-page announces that the Encyclopedia includes illustrations and translated extracts from the Swedish *Grafisk Uppslagsbok*. This excellent manual for the graphic trades was prepared under the auspices of the Sveriges Litografiska Tryckerier and published by Esselte, Stockholm, in 1951. The translations of extracts selected by me were made by E. Wesander (letters A to F) and Edward Birse, O.B.E. (letters F to Z.) Translated items which have been combined with my own previous notes are identified thus (With G.U.); translations merely edited by me are marked (G.U.).

'I have to acknowledge the benefits of a management at once businesslike and gentlemanlike, energetic and considerate' wrote Charlotte Brontë to her publisher in 1847. I wish to echo her words here; Sir Stanley Unwin believed in the possibilities of my first typescript when others were unable to see them, while his Production Manager, Ronald Eames, has guided my labours for eight years, encouraging me to continue when I would have gladly renounced the project for a less exacting task.

Dacca,
Pakistan
1960

G. A. G.

The griffin stamped on the front board is adapted from a design made for the author by Kurt Kierger of Vienna.

The wood engraving for the dedication was made by Reynolds Stone.

ACKNOWLEDGEMENTS

In the compilation, checking, and revision of this work the author and publisher gratefully acknowledge the assistance and suggestions of

Dr. Muriel Lock and Mr. Lewis G. Kitcat
(whose additions are marked M. L. and L. K.)

and also the following individuals and firms

J. C. Barnard
J. D. A. Barnicot
Charles Batey
Martin Bodmer
W. E. Bradford
Charles Butfield
Sydney Cockerell
Brooke Crutchley
Raoul Curiel
J. R. Dickens
H. Edmunds
H. C. Haycroft
Cyril Hayward
W. B. Hislop
Susan Hope-Jones
R. S. Hutchings
George Ingram
H. John Jarrold
A. Kirk
A. C. Larcombe
J. H. Macdonald
V. N. Perryman
Carl Pforzheimer
John Ryder
F. D. Sanders
Mortimer Shapley
R. G. Smith
Roy Stokes
Reynolds Stone
Dr. Josef Stummvoll
Beatrice Warde
David John Welsh
K. Whitworth

Bibliothèque Nationale, Paris; The Book Society, London;
The Booksellers Association, London; Bradford & Dickens, Ltd.;
British Federation of Master Printers;
British Standards Institution; W. S. Cowell Ltd., Ipswich;
Craske, Vaus & Crampton Ltd.; John Dickinson & Co. Ltd.;
Dorstel Press Leather Bindings Ltd.; Graphic Arts Foundation, Chicago;
Hazell, Watson & Viney Ltd.; Intertype Ltd.; Key & Whiting Ltd.;
Linotype & Machinery Ltd.; Percy Lund, Humphries Ltd., Bradford;
T. Mackrell & Co.; Maggs Bros.; The Monotype Corporation;
The Publishers Association, London; Bernard Quaritch Ltd.;
Sotheby & Co.; Stephenson Blake Ltd.;
The Typographical Association, Manchester;
Unwin Brothers Limited, Woking and London;
The World Publishing Company, Cleveland and New York.

CONTENTS

PLATES

à la cathédrale: see *architectural bindings.*

Abbey, John Roland, 1896– : a contemporary English bibliophile whose collection of bookbindings ranks as one of the finest in private hands today. He has bought extensively from famous libraries dispersed in the sale-room. Perhaps more important, Major Abbey has commissioned work from living craftsmen, seeking by his patronage to encourage a revival of interest in their skill.

No less outstanding is his collection of books with illustrations, mostly reproduced by aquatint or lithography and issued between 1770 and 1860. Excellent catalogues of these have been published.

Abbotsford Club: a Scottish book club founded in 1833 for the printing of 'miscellaneous pieces illustrative of [Scottish] history, literature, and antiquities'. Its activities ceased in 1866.

abbreviation: a shortened word form, made either by omitting certain portions from the interior of a word, or by cutting off part of it. A contraction is an abbreviation, but an abbreviation is not necessarily a contraction. (M. L.)

See also *publishers' and booksellers' abbreviations.*

abecedarium: a book containing the alphabet, spelling rules, tables, or an elementary Latin grammar. These primers were in use throughout Europe before the invention of printing. Those for learning Latin usually contained abstracts from the writings of *Aelius Donatus,* q.v.

The English abecedary was known in the 14th century; in the 16th century, the privilege for A B C books, as they became known, brought much profit to *John Day,* q.v.

See also *Costeriana, horn book.*

abridged edition: an edition of a work shortened by condensing the text or by omitting illustrations. This may be done for cheapness, or if preparing an edition for a particular class of reader. (With M. L.)

absorbency, absorption: the capacity of paper to take or retain ink or other liquid. (M. L.)

acanthus: the leaf of the plant *Acanthus spinosus* was much favoured as a decorative feature by illuminators of manuscripts, particularly by Carolingian artists in the 9th century, as still earlier by Greek and Roman sculptors. It became one of the principal leaf ornaments for borders, and a symbol for trees, used by artists of the *Winchester School,* q.v.

accents: diacritical signs placed over or under various letters in the alphabets of several languages, to show the nature or stress of the sounds they represent. While lower-case accent-bearing letters are cast as units, in display work it may be necessary to use separately cast, or *floating accents*; these are adjusted with leads.

Standard accents are:

acute	´	diaeresis or Umlaut	¨
cedilla	¸	grave	`
circumflex	^	tilde	~

e.g. áàâä éèêë íìîï óòôö úùûü ç ñ

See also *peculiars.*

acid blast: a method of etching half-tone and line plates by forcing sprays of acid on the face of the plate to obtain sharper lines. (M. L.)

Ackermann, Rudolf, 1764–1834: an Anglo-German inventor and publisher, born at Stolberg, removed to Schneeberg in Saxony in 1775. In 1795 he established a print-shop and drawing school in the Strand, London. He set up a lithographic press, and in 1817 used it for the illustration of his 'Repository of Arts, Literature, Fashions, etc.' (monthly until 1828). Rowlandson and Alken were regular contributors. Noteworthy were his annuals, e.g. 'Forget-me-not', 1825–47, and illustrated travel books such as 'The Microcosm of London', 1808–10. (M. L.)

Acme Colour Separator: an electronic machine, announced in 1954 by Acme Teletronix of Cleveland, U.S.A., for making sets of three or four colour-corrected continuous tone negatives from a coloured transparency. The latter is fitted about a transparent cylinder, illuminated from within, for scanning by a lens which transmits light through Wratten three-colour filters to three electronic light-sensitive tubes. The tubes control the light intensity reaching the separation films in a separate unit.

acrography: a method of producing relief surfaces on metal or stone by means of chalk tracery, for the making of electrotype or stereotype plates. (M.L.)

Acton, Lord John, 1834–1902: the English historian who formed at Aldenham, Herts, a library of some 60,000 volumes. This passed to Cambridge University Library in 1903. Among subjects included were French local history, biography, sociology, Italian and Spanish ecclesiastical history, works on the Society of Jesus, and English political history.

ad loc.: an abbreviation for the Latin 'ad locum', i.e. at (or concerning) the place (passage) cited.

Adams, Isaac: the inventor, in 1834, of mechanical *delivery*, q.v., from impression cylinders.

Adams press: a printing press invented by Isaac Adams of Boston, *c.* 1830, being a development of the principle of the hand press operated by mechanical power. Improved models of this machine were made up to 1875, but were then superseded by the cylinder press. (M.L.)

adaptation: a work which has been rewritten or modified for a special purpose.

addendum (pl. **addenda**): 1. matter to be included in a book after the body has been set. This is printed separately at the beginning or end of the text and is less extensive than a *supplement*, q.v.

2. a slip added into the finished book.

See also *appendix*, *erratum*.

additive colour synthesis: see *colour photography*.

adhesives: for joining materials by means of gluing, colloidal solutions are generally used which are converted (by removing the solvent, lowering the temperature, or internal combination) into a film of glue which has great power of adhering to any surfaces which are to be joined. Among *natural adhesives* gum arabic is chiefly used in the graphic industry. Various resins and rubber belong to this group; they are used in a benzol or other solution. Latex in the form of an emulsion in water can be preserved in this state by adding ammonia. Latex is used as an adhesive either by itself or combined with other adhesives (rubber size).

Artificial adhesives may consist of converted animal products (animal adhesives) or vegetable products (vegetable adhesives, paste). The former group includes skin glue, bone glue, leather glue, fish glue, etc. These contain glutin, a product of albumen, and are characterized by swelling in water; when heated they form a solution which jellifies on cooling. Casein glue is made by precipitating the casein in milk with lactic acid and then dissolving it in alkali: it is used as cold glue. Many adhesives are made of starch. 'Boiled paste' is made by heating flour in water up to about 212° F. Paste made by the action of various chemicals on starch (potato, maize, tapioca starch) is widely used as cold glue in pasting machines. Such pastes are often referred to as plant glues. By heating starch above boiling point dextrin is obtained for use in highly concentrated, quick-binding, and short adhesives.

Cellulose pastes are made from chemical woodpulp; these are used in a very diluted solution.

The multitude of adhesives made from artificial resins, which solidify and bind by heating or chemical treatment, are purely synthetic. Many other synthetic glues and pastes are in use. (G.U.)

advance copies: copies of a book bound up for use by salesmen 'subscribing' it; also given to reviewers and book-club selection committees. These copies may be final proofs or the earliest of the main printing, enclosed in plain or printed wrappers; alternatively, they may be bound, sometimes in a colour, fabric, or style differing in some way from the book as finally published.

See also *review copies*.

advance jackets: dust jackets of forthcoming books sent to booksellers and others as part of publishers' sales promotion material.

advance sheets: see *folded and collated copies*.

adversaria: a collection of notes or commentaries; originally referring to Roman works with the text written on one side of the parchment, the notes on the opposite side. The term was extended in scope, both by the Romans and later by the Humanists, to include collections of textual criticisms, also rough note books.

See also *association copy*, *scholium*.

advertisements: publishers' announcements of selected books; they may be printed at the end of the book (generally to use up blank pages at the end of a working) and on the back of the jacket, or they may be printed separately and included as an *insert*, q.v.

The earliest known printed advertisement of books was issued by Heinrich Eggestein at Strasbourg in 1466.

Aelfric Society: a printing society formed 'for the publication of Anglo-Saxon works, civil and ecclesiastical', in London. Various works were issued between 1843 and 1856. (M.L.)

Aethelwold, Saint: see *Benedictional of St Aethelwold*, *Winchester School*.

against the grain: across the direction of the lie of the fibres in paper.

See also *grain direction*.

agate: a former size of type, between pearl and nonpareil, approximating $5\frac{1}{2}$-point, measuring fourteen lines to an inch.

agent: see *literary agent.*

Agfacolor: see *colour photography.*

agreement, forms of: see *publishers' agreements.*

air buffer: a device for absorbing shock, retarding motion, or reversing a rectilinear movement. Such buffers are fitted, for example, to cylinder printing machines for reversing the bed in its movement to and fro. (G. U.)

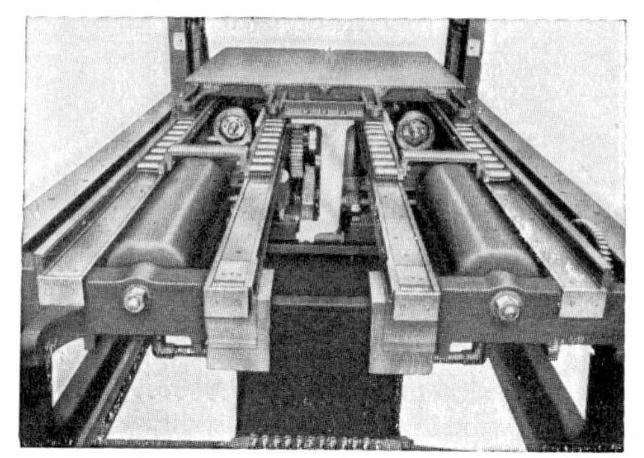

Roller courses and air buffers on a Swedish two-revolution press

air dried: said of hand-made, mould-made, or the better machine-made papers which, after sizing, have been dried by exposure to air at a controlled temperature on a series of drums. If the paper is coated it is passed through a heated chamber before reeling.

See also *loft dried, machine dried, relative humidity.*

airbrush: a retouching spray, invented in America about 1900, for use in spray painting and lithography, and introduced into Europe for the so-called American retouching of catalogue illustrations, also for lithographic work where fine-grain tones are required. The spray works by air pressure on the injector principle to deposit a cloud of fine drops on the material to be sprayed. In lithography a litho drawing ink is used, and by adjusting the size of the apertures, the air pressure, and the distance from the lithographic stone or plate, various tonal densities are obtainable. Both in retouching and spray lithography stencil plates or gum can be used to mask areas not requiring treatment. (G. U.)

Airbrush

The lithographic spray has a longer container

Aitken, Robert: the printer of Philadelphia, U.S.A., who in 1782 issued, in 12mo format, the first complete Bible in English to be printed in North America. Only twenty-five copies are known to survive.

ajouré: a style of decorating book covers practised in Venice in the late 15th century by craftsmen from the Near East. Features were patterns of cut-out leather, gilded arabesques, and a coloured ground.

Alaska seal: an imitation sealskin made from sheepskin or cowhide.

Albert, Joseph, 1825–86: a Munich photographer who sought to reproduce paintings in local museums. In attempts to make multiple copies of these he experimented with photolithographic methods, basing his work on that of Poitevin who had discovered the sensitivity of chromo-gelatine in 1855; the efforts of Poitevin had been improved by M. Tessié du Motay and C. R. Maréchal of Metz in 1865, but it was Albert who made these discoveries into a practical printing process. This is now known as *collotype*, q.v., but was at first named *albertype* after him.

His first collotype impression from a glass plate was a reproduction of Rubens's 'Früchtekranz', made in January 1868. As a result of the attention created by his display of collotypes at the Hamburg Exhibition of the same year he was awarded a gold medal; examples were printed on paper, leather, and silk.

Albert also made important contributions to the development of colour photography.

See also *Talbot, W. H. F.* (With G. U.)

Albert Schweitzer Buchpreis: a prize awarded by the Kindler Verlag of Munich to an author in any part of the world for an unpublished work, or for a work which has not been published in Germany.

Albert galvanos: hard-wearing electros, with a well-defined image, used in long runs, it being claimed that they are more durable than nickel electros. This process, in which a matrix of soft lead instead of wax is used, was devised by Eugen Albert in 1902. It can be used for colour printing.

Albert lead-moulding process: the method of making *Albert galvanos*, q.v. (M. L.)

albertype: see *collotype.*

Albion press: a hand printing press devised in 1823 by R. W. Cope of London. Type lay on a horizontal sliding bed, pressure being exerted by an elbow-shaped lever joint called a toggle which forced the platen on to the forme. Presses of this kind were used by William Morris in the *Kelmscott Press*, q.v., and are still occasionally found working.

albumen (ovalbumin): the chief protein content of egg white; soluble in water and coagulated by heating, it is an ingredient of *glair*, q.v.

albumen paper: see *printing-out paper*.

albumen process: a solution of albumen in water, with an addition of dichromate of ammonia or potassium, spread on a plate on which it is dried as a thin film; this provides a sensitive layer which, after exposure to light, becomes insoluble in water. The albumen processes employed in chemigraphy and lithography are based on this.

The best method of preparing the printing solutions is to mix the albumen and keep it separate, while the dichromate of ammonia is dissolved to a 20% storage solution. The albumen solution usually contains 5 to 20% of albumen, and immediately before use the two solutions are mixed in such proportions that the dichromate content does not exceed two-thirds of the albumen content. Enough ammonia is added to give the solution a straw colour.

The plate is prepared by pouring the liquid over the surface and distributing it evenly, preferably in a whirler, followed by heat drying.

Printing proceeds most rapidly in a bluish-violet light. After printing, the plate is inked with thick ink and developed in water. The image will consist of insoluble albumen with the attached ink. (G.U.)

Blackening an offset plate, printed by the albumen process, before developing

An offset plate, prepared by the albumen process, after developing

Alcophoto: a British photo-litho plate-making process for zinc, aluminium, anodized aluminium, tri-metal or electrolytic grain plates, announced by Algraphy Ltd., London, in 1956. In developing this new deep-etch process an attempt has been made to provide a range of chemicals which, while following orthodox technique, would not be so readily affected by humidity and temperature changes as, for example, the calcium chloride used in ordinary deep-etch processes. Alcophoto avoids calcium chloride.

The Alcophoto process comprises coating, developer, deep-etch, spirit wash, anti-humidity spirit wash, 'Patralac' lacquer base, inking-in and stop-off.

The coating solution gives thinner, tougher stencils; the contrast developer gives full tone range and resists high humidity; the deep-etch gives a grease-receptive image, and can be used on all types of plates; while the anti-humidity spirit-wash gives freedom from stencil penetration.

See also *deep-etch process*.

alcuinian script: see *Carolingian script*.

Aldine bindings: a name given to the various tooled morocco bindings made in Venice at the end of the 15th century for Aldus Manutius and his followers. Boards of thin wood or cardboard were covered with red or brown morocco, early examples being decorated in blind with an outer frame and a central device. The assumption is that since Aldus was then the leading printer of Venice he would actively supervise the binding of his work by the Greek binders he employed.

Aldine editions: books published between 1494 and 1515 by *Aldus Manutius*, q.v., and his family at Venice and Rome. The John Rylands Library in

Manchester has a unique collection of Aldines and many examples of the counterfeits. (M.L.)

Aldine leaves: small binders' stamps, bearing a leaf and stem design, used *c.* 1510 on books bound for Aldus. It is probable early printers were inspired to use them as *flowers*, q.v., on title-pages (e.g. De Tournes).

Aldus Manutius: the Latin name of Teobaldo Manucci (1450–1515), better known as Aldo Manuzio, the founder of the Aldine Press, who was born at Sermoneta, Italy. He studied in Rome and Ferrara, and became familiar with Greek. He aimed at using his printing press to revive the wisdom and culture of the ancients, especially of the Greeks, and by his enthusiasm he was able to persuade Alberto Pio, prince of Carpi, to finance his venture. Only in Milan, Venice, Vicenza, and Florence were Greek books produced when Aldus settled in Venice in 1494.

He invited Greek scholars and compositors to live in his house. He employed Francesco Griffo to cut for him a distinctive sloping roman type, tending towards the cursive, known today as *italic*. He popularized books of small size, especially the octavo. From 1494 to 1515 a steady stream of Greek texts issued from his press. In 1500 he formed an Academy at his house at which only Greek was spoken (members' names are given in A. F. Didot's 'Alde Manuce', Paris, 1875).

His dedication pages are interesting, while his device, the dolphin and anchor, was later used by *William Pickering*, q.v. (Illustrated under *device*, q.v.)

The first work to issue from the Aldine Press was an edition in Greek and Latin of Musaeus's 'Opusculum de Herone et Leandro', *c.*1495 (undated); the most important, his edition of Aristotle, 1495-97. Among scholars working with him was Erasmus, who supervised an edition of his 'Adagiorum Collectanea', 1508.

The greek type used by Manutius was modelled on the writing of his Cretan assistant, Marcus Musurus. When Jenson died in 1481 his punches, matrices, and types were acquired by Torresano, father-in-law and associate of Manutius. It was, however, the roman face which Aldus commissioned from Griffo (and not the Jenson) which was later to influence Claude Garamond's letter.

Between 1515 and 1533 the press was managed by his brothers-in-law, the Asolani, but as they dispersed the body of scholar-associates, the standards set by Aldus were not maintained. However, in 1533 *Paulus Manutius* (1512–74) youngest son of Aldus, took over the press. He concentrated on Latin classics, particularly on Cicero. He left for Rome in 1561, the affairs of the press passing to his son *Aldus II* (1547–97). (With M.L.)

See also *Aldine bindings, Aldine editions, chancery, Griffo, italic, Torresano.*

alfa grass: a variety of esparto used in paper-making.

algorism: the 12th-century name for the *arabic numerals*, q.v.

algraphy: see *aluminography*.

alignment: the exact correspondence at top and bottom of the letters and characters in a fount; the arrangement of type in straight lines; and the setting of lines of type so that the ends appear even up and down the page. (M.L.)

Alkuprint: see *offset reproduction.*

all along: the method of hand sewing the sections of a book on cords or tapes when the thread goes from kettle-stitch to kettle-stitch inside the fold of each section. Also used to describe a machine-sewn book in which each section has the full number of stitches.

See also *hand-sewing*.

All-purpose Linotype: a machine marketed by the American Linotype factory in 1932, in which matrices are hand-set in a specially constructed stick secured to the machine, where they are then cast. Matrices from Intertype, Linotype, or Ludlow machines can be used. Types, blanks, frames, and ornaments can all be cast, as also larger sizes of type, the moulds for this purpose being arranged at sufficiently large intervals to facilitate sawing the types apart after casting. (G.U.)

The All-purpose Linotype

All rights reserved: a statement formerly printed on the title-page verso to indicate that the book is copyright and that it is not permissible to reproduce it or any substantial part of it without the permission of the copyright holder.

See also *copyright notice.*

Allan, George, 1736–1800: a celebrated antiquary and topographer who acquired, among other treasures, the various collections known as Gyll's, Hunter's, Mann's, Hodgson's, and Swainston's MSS. About 1786 he set up a private press at Blackwell Grange, his residence near Darlington.

See also *Grange Press.* (M. L.)

Allde, John, fl. 1555–82: a London stationer and printer, the first person on the registers to take up the freedom of the Stationers' Company, January 1555. He printed first ballads and almanacs, later more books, chiefly of a popular nature. He lived 'at the long shop adjoining to St Mildred's Church in the Pultrie'. (M. L.)

allonym: the name of another person deliberately assumed by the author of a work; also the work published under such a name. (M. L.)

alluminor: an obsolete term for one who illuminated manuscripts. Later terms were *enlumineur* and *limner.*

almanac: a book containing the days, weeks, and months of the year together with information about festivals and holidays, ecclesiastical festivals, astronomical data, and often other information.

An early counterpart was the lists of days when work was allowed, known as *fasti,* made by the ancient Romans. The term *almanac* appears to have come into use in the 13th century, and it was thus used in 1267 by Roger Bacon in his encyclopaedia 'Opus maius' for a table giving the movements of celestial bodies. By the 15th century the term was generally given to calendars of astrological, astronomical and meteorological tables for a period of years, also to church and saints' days.

The production of almanacs in Europe has never ceased; in the 16th and 17th centuries almanacs of prophesies based on horoscopes had tremendous popularity in England and France. Richard Pynson issued the first printed almanac in England in 1502. Between 1557 and 1775 the privilege for almanacs was held by the Stationers' Company and the two universities. Dr. Francis Moore's almanac first appeared in 1700 as 'Vox stellarum', and is still issued as 'Old Moore's Almanack'. The important navigational aid the 'Nautical Almanac' was initiated in 1766 (for 1767) by the Astronomer Royal; while 'Whitaker's Almanack', which is widely accepted as an authoritative reference book, dates from 1868.

alphabet: see *letters—forms and styles.*

aluminium: a metal commonly used for lithographic plates as an alternative to zinc. Metal plates have for most purposes completely superseded lithographic stone.

aluminium leaf: see *Vapco* addendum, p. 433.

aluminography: the process of making and using aluminium plates for lithographic and offset printing. Also known as *algraphy.* (M. L.)

ambrogal printing: see *Galetzka, Ambrosius.*

American Book-Prices Current: established by Luther S. Livingston in 1895 (from September 1894) as an annual guide to sale prices, compiled from auctioneers' catalogues, of the more important sales of books in the U.S.A. The work has four main sections: books, autographs and manuscripts, broadsides, maps and charts. Occasional cumulative indexes have been issued.

American Book Publishers Council Inc.: a non-profit making corporation established in 1946 to further the interests of book publishers. Its objects include the encouragement of reading, the maintenance of credit information on bookstores and other outlets; the administration of a group insurance plan for the book trade; developing of sales outlets and publicity methods; the advising on copyright problems; the opposing of censorship; and liaison with government departments, library and educational organizations. Headquarters are in New York.

American Booksellers Association: founded in 1900. The oldest American organization for booksellers. Annual conventions are held at which there are trade exhibits by associate member publishers for store buyers, and at which trade methods and problems are discussed. The Association issues a monthly bulletin and also the annual 'Book Buyers' Handbook' which is one of the basic book trade reference books.

The address is 175 Fifth Avenue, New York 10.

American Institute of Graphic Arts: founded in 1914 by a group of members of the National Arts Club, New York. Its aims, briefly stated, were 'to do all things which would raise the standard and the extension and development towards perfection of the graphic arts in the United States'. These aims have been reached in many ways. In addition to occasional exhibitions featuring a single personality or aspect of graphic art there are two regular exhibitions: 'Printing for Commerce' (annually 1924–41, and since 1950), and 'The Fifty Books of the Year' (annually since 1923). A Trade Book Clinic was established in 1930, of which most of the participants are members of the production staffs of New York

Der Schrifftgieſſer. | Der Buchdrücker. | Der Buchbinder.

Type-founder

Printer

Bookbinder

Three of Amman's woodcuts to Hans Sach's stanzas in 'Eygentliche Beschreibung aller Stände auf Erden', printed in 1568 *by Sigmund Feierabend of Frankfurt. (Here reduced)*

publishers who meet for lectures and discussions at which the quality of their current publications is appraised.

In 1948 the Institute started a workshop where the office workers of printing and publishing firms can handle type and machines. In addition to occasional publishing, the Institute has issued the 'News-letter' (1922–45), which in 1947 was superseded by the 'Journal'.

At its annual meeting the Institute's medal is presented to some personality in the graphic art world. Among recipients have been W. A. Dwiggins, Frederic Goudy, Dard Hunter, Stanley Morison, Bruce Rogers, Carl Rollins, and D. B. Updike.

American joints: see *french joints.*

American russia: a strong, split cowhide, used for book covers. Also known as *imitation russia.*

Ames, Joseph, 1689–1759: notable as the author of 'Typographical Antiquities, being an historical account of printing in England, with some memoirs of our ancient printers, and a register of the books printed by them, from the year 1471–1600, with an appendix concerning printing in Scotland and Ireland to the same time'. London, 1749. Ames made use of notes supplied by his friend John Lewis of Margate and other antiquaries.

Amman, Jost, 1539–91: a Swiss engraver, etcher, and draftsman who, in 1563, took over the Nuremberg workshop of Virgil Solis. He was famous for his book illustrations, occasional etchings, and woodcuts. (G. U.)

Amos, Charles Edward: an English millwright and engineer who, in 1840, invented a consistency regulator, which he called a 'pulp regulator', for delivering a proper proportion of pulp and backwater according to the speed of the paper machine. He also invented a paper cutter. (M. L.)

ampersand: the sign &; the name being a corruption of 'and per se = and', i.e. '& by itself = and'. The sign derives from the scribes' ligature for the Latin *et*; in certain italic versions the letters *e* and *t* are clearly distinguishable.

anastatic printing: a relief printing process, first used by Rudolf Appel in Berlin about 1840. He employed etched zinc plates to produce facsimiles of writing, drawings, or letterpress.

Andersen Medal: see *Hans Christian Andersen Medal.*

Anderson, John, fl. 1800: a wood engraver and pupil of *Thomas Bewick*, q.v. Some of his work appears in the publications of *Thomas Bensley*, q.v.

Andrewe, Laurence, fl. 1510–37: a native of Calais, who worked in London and Antwerp as a translator and printer of scientific works. His first published translation was printed by *Jan van Doesborgh*, q.v., and the latter may have taught him the craft of printing.

Andrewe issued an undated edition of 'The myrrour & dyscrypcion of the world', taking Caxton's 1481 text and also some of the original blocks (STC 24764).

Angerer, Carl, 1838–1916: the founder, in 1870, of the Viennese firm of Angerer & Göschl, plate-makers and reproducers. Having acquainted himself while working with Firmin Gillot with the latter's process for making blocks, Angerer worked independently in 1865. In 1870 he developed the so-called Vienna process to which he gave the name 'chemigraphy'. He also contributed to the practical development of the half-tone block method. (G.U.)

Anglo-Saxon Chronicle: a chronological history of England which survives in six complete manuscripts, each devoted to a particular area and period: 1. from 891–1070, written in Winchester and Canterbury, now in Cambridge University Library; 2. up to 977, including a Mercian chronicle for 902–24, in the British Museum (Cotton, *Tiberius*, A. vi); 3. an Abingdon chronicle up to 1066 (B.M., Cotton, *Tiberius*, B. i); 4. begun in 1016, from Worcester and Northumbria, extends to 1079 (B.M., Cotton, *Tiberius*, B. iv); 5. a Peterborough chronicle, written from 1122–54, now in the Bodleian; 6. a Saxon and Latin manuscript from Canterbury, belonging to the 12th century (B.M., Cotton, *Domitian*, A. viii).

Other parts were lost in the fire which damaged the Cotton collection in 1731.

Anglo-Saxon illumination: see *Hiberno-Saxon illumination.*

aniline inks: cheaply made volatile printing inks consisting of a dye dissolved in methylated spirit and bound with a resin. Drying is almost immediate. Although all colours are available they have a tendency to fade, and in recent years pigmented inks or pigmented dyes have been introduced which do not fade.

aniline printing: 1. printing from rubber blocks with aniline printing inks; 2. a method of obtaining positive copies direct from original drawings.

animal-sized: paper which has been hardened or sized with animal glue or gelatine, by passing the finished sheet or roll through a bath of glue.

See also *tub-sized.*

annals: an historical record of the events of a year, published each year; the usage of the term dates to ancient Rome (the 'Annales Maximi').

annuals: 1. serial publications produced yearly.

2. in the 19th century, a variety of literary anthology illustrated usually by steel engravings, the latter being more important than the text.

See also *table book* (2).

3. in modern usage, a term used in juvenile publishing for anthologies for children, e.g. 'Chatterbox', 'Holiday Annual'.

anonymous: a publication of which the authorship is unknown or undeclared.

anopisthographic printing: a name for the manner of printing early block books on one side of the leaf and in writing ink.

See also *opisthograph.*

anthology: a collection of extracts from the writings of one or several authors. Early Greek examples date from the 2nd century B.C., and anthologies, particularly of poetry, have been continuously popular in most European countries.

See also *chrestomathy.*

anti-set-off sprayer: an apparatus attached to a printing press to prevent *set-off,* q.v. It is a spray gun which blows a mixture of resinous solution or powder by air on to each printed sheet as it falls on the delivery tray of the press; the tiny globules or grains keeping the sheets momentarily separate.

In modern usage either a dry powder such as limestone, starch, or hartshorn, or a solution of dextrin

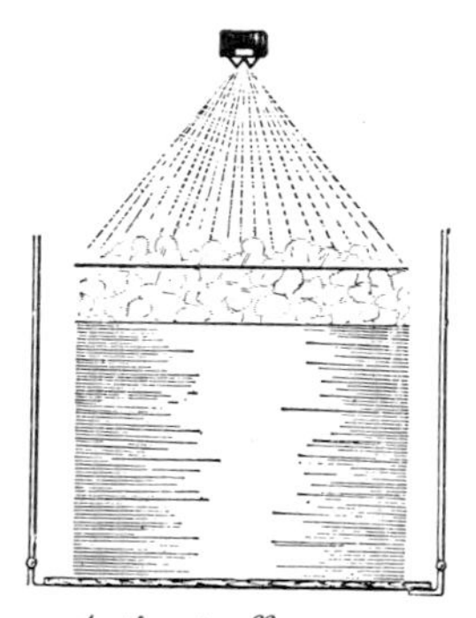

Anti-set-off sprayer

or gum arabic is used. Advantages claimed by the makers of powder sprays are that higher running speeds are possible; less escapes into the atmosphere, thus more reaches the sheet; and the equipment is easier to maintain. (With G.U.)

Antiphonary: one of the present liturgical books intended for use in choir. Generically includes antiphons and antiphonal chants sung at Mass and at the canonical Hours. Now refers only to the sung portions of the *Breviary,* q.v. (M.L.)

antiqua: 1. early types based on scripts developed by the Italians Niccoli and Poggio who modelled them on those used for manuscripts in North Italy during the 11th and 12th centuries.

2. the German name for roman type, as distinct from *Fraktur,* q.v.

antiquarian: the largest known size of hand-made paper, 53 in. by 31 in., introduced to the trade by James Whatman in the 18th century.

Antiquarian Booksellers' Association (International): the secondhand book trade association, founded in

London in 1906. Membership is open to any British or foreign bookseller dealing mainly in books no longer in print.

The aims of the Association are to promote and extend the sale of antiquarian and rare books, to improve the status of the trade, to promote honourable conduct in business, to provide funds to assist members or their dependants in distress, to promote exhibitions or co-operate with other organizations to further the distribution of books, and to act as an Association in matters where individual action would be less likely to succeed.

Antiquarian Etching Club: a London society, founded in 1848, which published between then and 1853 five volumes, each with descriptive index. (M.L.)

antique binding: see *monastic bindings.*

antique finish: applied to paper with a rough surface, such as was used before the invention of paper-making machinery which gives a smooth polished finish. (M.L.)

antique gold edges: said of the finish given to gilt edges which are either left unburnished, or burnished and washed over with water. When bound in stout or bevelled boards designs are sometimes tooled on book edges, a diapered pattern with centre tool being generally used.

Cf. *rough gilt.*

antique paper: a light bulky paper, rough surfaced, and of good quality. The finish is a matt or dull one, it being neither calendered nor coated. It is suitable for printing type and line engravings, but not half-tones, and is used for most books without blocks.

See also *featherweight paper, felt finish.*

Apocalypse: this was a favourite text for copying and illuminating in northern Europe during the 13th and 14th centuries. Most important were those of the *St Alban's School,* q.v. The text was often subordinated to the delicate, lightly tinted drawings, with tall slim figures for the virtuous, and ugly shapes for the powers of evil.

Among famous examples is the Douce Apocalypse (named after Francis Douce, d. 1834), now in the Bodleian Library, made prior to 1272 for Edward I.

apocryphal: of doubtful authenticity.

apograph: an exact copy of an original manuscript.

appendix (pl. **appendices**)**:** matter subordinate to the text of a work and printed immediately after it. An appendix differs from an addendum in that the need for the latter is only discovered when the book is set; the former is planned from the beginning as an integral part of the work.

Appledore Private Press: an American private press founded *c.* 1870 at Hamden, near New Haven, by William James Linton who had previously lived in England.

In addition to being a poet and champion for the freedom of the press Linton was a wood engraver of merit. Publications were mostly of verse.

Applegath press: an early rotary press invented by August Applegath of the London firm Applegath and Cowper. Their perfecting and rotary presses have been used all over the world for the past hundred years. (G.U.)

apud: the Latin for 'at [or obtainable at] the house of' (in the context described here). The word, followed by the name of the printer, publisher, or bookseller, appears occasionally on early title-pages. E.g. APVD SIMONEM COLINAEVM (Obtainable at the house of Simon Colines).

Aqua-trol: the trade name of an American device for the continuous removal of moisture from the inking system of a lithographic press. It is being developed by American Typefounders Inc.

This method of damping control uses an electric blower to flow heated air against one of the inking rollers, thereby collecting moisture from the entire inking system.

Advantages claimed are the obviation of frequent adjustment of ink-water balance; lengthened plate life, as after each transfer the plate receives a fresh layer of moisture-free ink; fewer spoils, as correct colour is attained with fewer run-in sheets; consistent colour throughout the run, with less ink control adjustment; and sharper transfer since the damping system can be regulated to the requirements of the plate without ink emulsification or roller stripping.

aquatint: 1. an intaglio process for reproducing illustrations which are normally tones (rather like black ink wash drawings), but often a combination of tones and etched lines. The design is first etched or engraved on a copper plate before the aquatint ground is applied. The design is one of varying degrees of tone, and these will be stopped out with varnish as etching proceeds, and the plate etched to different depths. The purpose of the *aquatint ground* is to divide the surface of the plate into microscopically small ink cells. The special granular effect of the ground is applied by either dry or wet methods. In the former case the plate is placed in a bitumen powder cupboard in which a fine dust of the powder is whirled about and allowed to settle uniformly on the upturned surface of the plate. This dust is melted by a gas or electric heater under the plate. The size of the granules depends on the time which passes between setting the dust in motion and laying up the plate in the cupboard, and its density on how long it is allowed to remain there. By the wet method liquid aquatint ground consisting of resin dissolved in alcohol is flowed over the plate, when after the evaporation of the alcohol the resin remains as a grain layer on it.

After laying on a ground by one of these methods and painting the back of the plate with varnish as a protection against the acid, etching is done with dutch mordant or perchloride of iron. The lightest grey tones will be etched first, and after the plate has been dried these areas are stopped out with varnish. The varying depths of tone are achieved by further controlled etching. If tones are etched too deeply they can be lightened with a burnishing tool. Aquatint and dry-point plates can be combined, the latter bearing the design in outline, the former the surface tinting.

A variant of the aquatint is the *aquatint wash*, when nitric acid of different strengths is painted with a brush on the copper plate in a manner similar to tinting in water colour painting.

Sugar or *reverse aquatint* is another etching method by which the plate is cleaned and the drawing is made on it with a pen or brush using a solution of sugar and indian ink (or a solution of gum arabic, sugar, and ox gall). After drying the plate is then given a thin coat of hard etching ground. This having dried (quickly) the plate is immersed in water which causes the sugar layer to swell and 'lift' the varnish off the design areas, exposing the metal. The remaining varnish acts as a resist to the etching acid in which the plate is now immersed. The etching is repeated if tones are required.

Another method consists in first laying on the hard ground and then painting on it with lavender oil, which dissolves the ground.

So that the artist can follow and control the etching more closely he often works with a plate sufficiently large to allow for a marginal key strip; on this he makes a number of tones corresponding to those of the main picture. When the plate is finished this strip is cut off. On completing the etching any remaining varnish and ground are washed off with benzol, after which printing takes place as in other copperplate printing. For specimens of aquatint surfaces see *etching*.

Claims for the invention of aquatint are made for Abbé St Non, 1750, and for J. B. Le Prince (1734–81): coloured aquatints were introduced by F. Janinet (1752–1814). The process achieved its finest results at the hands of Francesco de Goya (1746–1828) who combined etching and aquatint. Paul Sandby introduced it into England in 1775; and Thomas Malton (1708–1804) was an important worker in this medium, while the topographical books of *Rudolph Ackermann*, q.v., provide examples.

2. a print taken from the plates described above. (With G.U.)

aquatone: a method of printing by lithography from a gelatine surface on metal plates, using very fine screens (about 400 to the inch). Devised in 1923 by Robert John in the U.S.A.

arabesque: a pattern of lines, leaves, fruit or flowers (or an abstract from them), woven into graceful convolutions for book-cover and title-page decoration.

See also *flowers*.

arabic numerals: 1, 2, 3, 4, 5, 6, 7, 8, 9, 0. The system of numerals was reputedly brought to Europe by the Arabs from India in the 8th century. The numbers began to be used in foliation in the last quarter of the 15th century. As types, arabic numerals are cast as *hanging figures* and *ranging figures*, qq.v.

arabic type: the first book to be printed in arabic type was a book of Christian prayers 'Septem horae canonicae' ('Kitāb Ṣalat al-sawā'i'), printed at Fano in 1514 by Gregorius de Gregoriis. The letters were cast by Gersham Soncino.

Arber, Edward, 1836–1912: a London man of letters who, between 1868 and 1896, issued as cheap reprints the texts of famous and little known works written from the time of Caxton to Addison. He added notes and critical introductions.

More important to bibliophiles and librarians were the privately printed and published 'A transcription of the registers of the Company of Stationers of London, 1554–1646', 5 vols., 1875–94; and the 'Term catalogues, 1668–1709', 3 vols., 1903–6. The last work was edited from London booksellers' quarterly lists of new and reprinted books.

arbitraries: synonymous with *peculiars*, q.v.

archetypal novels: the earliest romances and novels on which later ones were modelled.

architectural bindings: a 16th-century style of book-cover decoration, of which only a few examples survive. Features were columns supporting an arch under which was a panel for the title to be lettered. The contents of the book only rarely related to architecture.

The 19th-century French binder Thouvenin revived the style as *à la cathédrale*.

archive: 1. the building in which public records or historical documents are kept.

2. as *archives*, the documents.

3. a title-word for scientific or academic periodicals, this being a usage dating from the early 18th century, particularly in Europe.

Arden Press: a private press founded in 1904 by Bernard Newdigate. It had its origins in his father's firm The Art and Book Company. In 1908 it was absorbed by W. H. Smith for whom Newdigate worked until 1914.

aristo paper: see *printing-out paper*.

Ark Press: a small private press established by Kim Taylor at Foxhole, Dartington, in 1954. In addition to printing pamphlets and jobbing work Taylor has issued small editions of well-designed illustrated books. The first to appear was an edition of St Matthew Passion limited to twenty-five copies printed on vellum. By close collaboration between author, artist, designer, and printer, and choosing materials with care Taylor has produced books of high standard to sell at low prices. Machining is done by Kenneth Worden, a commercial printer of Marazion, Cornwall.

armarian: the monk responsible for the care and maintenance of the books in a monastery library, of which he also made a catalogue. The scriptorium, and the supervision of the writing and copying done in it by other monks, were usually within his charge.

In ancient Rome an *armarium* was a bookcase: in the Middle Ages the usage of the word was extended to refer to a library, particularly in a monastery.

Armenian bole: a powdered red clay which is dusted on the edges of books before gilding as a base for the gold, to which it gives a greater depth and lustre. Bole is mostly obtained from Bohemia, Italy, and Silesia.

arming press: originally, a hand-press in which heated blocks were used to stamp arms on the sides of leather-bound books, an *armorial binding* being a book decorated in this way.

Such presses are adaptable to any sort of blocking and are much used today for single-copy work and short runs. (L. K.)

Arnoullet, Balthazar: a French pioneer of copper engravings. In 1546 he issued from his Lyons press a volume of portraits of the kings of France.

Arrighi, Ludovico degli, da Vicenza, fl. 1510–27: bookseller, scribe, and printer of Rome, where he was principally employed as 'scriptor brevium' in the Papal Chancery. He is remembered for his writing manual 'Operina', printed from engraved plates, and published in 1522. His work had a considerable influence on designers of italic type-faces.

See also *cursive*.

Arrivabene, Georgius, fl. 1483–1515: an early Venetian printer of the classics and also of legal works.

ars artificialiter scribendi: a Latin phrase, often found in the colophons of 15th-century printed books, indicating that the printer's craft was that of artificial writing.

Ars moriendi: literally, 'the art of dying'. This was a popular theme for 15th-century artists, the earliest illustrations being a block book, *c.* 1440 (now in the British Museum), and a series of eleven copper engravings by E. S. which appeared *c.* 1455, to be followed by block books, manuscripts and incunabula, the illustrations often being copied. As a subject for a book 'Ars moriendi' engaged the attention of late 15th-century printers in Germany, Holland, France, Italy, Spain, and England where 'Ars moriendi, that is to saye the craft for to deye for the helthe of mannes sowle', attributed to Caxton, appeared in 1491, to be followed by Wynkyn de Worde's dated edition in 1497.

art canvas: a rough-surfaced cloth used for book covers.

art paper: paper coated on one or both sides with casein, or glue, mixed with starch and china clay, after the paper has been made. The finest English art paper has an esparto base and is casein coated. If not calendered it has a matt surface; calendering gives a glossy or enamelled finish. In moist climates the surface will deteriorate. For the printing of text on art paper (which is also known as *coated paper*) such heavy faces as Plantin or Times New Roman should be used.

See also *cast coated paper*, *imitation art paper*.

Arundel MSS.: the collection of 550 manuscripts forming part of the library assembled by *Thomas Howard*, q.v., which in 1831 passed to the British Museum from the Royal Society (the recipient of most of his library). In addition to Biblical and ecclesiastical writings are works on French literature and English history.

Arundel Psalter: two Psalters bound together, each illuminated in a distinct style. The first, probably done by an early 14th-century Court artist, contains many small miniature-filled initials. The second was done earlier and has full-page scenes from the Passion, also a large number of allegorical scenes, all typified by rich and elaborate detail in the East Anglian manner. The work is now in the British Museum.

ascenders: the upper portion of lower-case letters above the x-height, i.e. b, d, f, h, k, l, t. The letters are known as *ascending letters.*

Ashbee, Charles Robert: see *Essex House Press.*

Ashbee, Henry Spencer, 1834–1900: an English bibliographer who is considered to have formed the finest Cervantic library outside Spain. He bequeathed his 16,000 volumes to the British Museum. (M. L.)

Ashburnham, Bertram, fourth Earl of, 1797–1878: a wealthy bibliophile whose library included some 3800 manuscripts and many incunabula, among which were a Gutenberg Bible, Caxtons, Shakespeare Folios, a block book Biblia pauperum, and the famous Pentateuch (see next entry). He bought an important group of nearly 2000 early Italian and French manuscripts from Guglielmo Libri; a second group of 700 French manuscripts from Joseph Barrois; and 996 manuscripts from the Stowe collection.

The Ashburnham library was dispersed by sale in 1897–98, the *Stowe MSS.*, q.v., being acquired by the Government for £50,000. It was later found that Libri and Barrois had stolen many of the items from French libraries.

Ashburnham Pentateuch: a famous illuminated manuscript of uncertain (but probably Spanish) origin, written in the 7th century. It passed to its present location in the Bibliothèque Nationale, Paris, from the collection of the great English bibliophile Bertram, fourth Earl of Ashburnham.

Ashendene Press: a private press founded in 1894 at Ashendene in Herts by C. H. St John Hornby, and in 1899 moved to Chelsea. Among other types Hornby used one designed by Sir Emery Walker modelled on that of Sweynheym and Pannartz of Subiaco (1465), which was cut by E. P. Prince.

The finest product of this press, which closed in 1935, was an edition of Dante.

Ashmole, Elias, 1617–92: an antiquarian whose collection of curiosities was given to Oxford University in 1682. In 1860 the Bodleian received the libraries of four antiquaries—Ashmole; John Aubrey, d. 1697; Sir William Dugdale, d. 1686; and Anthony Wood, d. 1695. These were the basis of the Ashmolean Library. The 706 manuscripts included scientific, medical, and heraldic works. The some 3000 books included an important group of works on astrology and astronomy, as well as pamphlets and official papers of the Civil War period.

Askew, Anthony, 1722–74: a physician, bibliophile, and classical scholar who collected an important library of Greek authors, including most printed editions of Aeschylus then available. After his death the library was sold, the British Museum buying some of the items.

Aslib: the short name for the 'Association of Special Libraries and Information Bureaux', founded in 1924 in London, for the benefit of business houses, industries, and learned societies. Not only are the librarians of these bodies brought into mutual contact, but translations, notes, and bibliographies on special subjects are published and circulated.

Asphodel Press: a hand-press established by Phyllis Gardner at Hampstead, London, in 1923. Several of the small editions of minor poetry printed have included wood engravings by the founder. It appears to have closed by 1927.

assembler box: the equivalent, on a Linotype machine, of a composing stick. To this the matrices and accompanying spacebands are conveyed automatically in response to the depression of keys by the operator.

assembling: see *gathering.*

assico: a probable corruption of the Latin phrase '*asse(ribus) corio*' meaning 'in boards [covered] with leather'. The word is used in the Day Book of John Dorne, a 16th-century Oxford stationer. [I am indebted to Strickland Gibson for this note.]

association copy: said of a copy of a book which belonged to the author and was probably annotated by him, or which belonged to a person who may be identified in some way with the subject-matter.

Association of Correctors of the Press: the only trade union in Britain composed entirely of printers' readers; it is confined to the London area, and was founded in 1854 as the 'London Association of Correctors of the Press', largely on the initiative of Henry Vernon, a reader employed by Bradbury & Evans; 'London' was later dropped. In 1908 it was registered as a trade union.

The membership card is only awarded to readers who pass an examination.

See T. N. Shane (pseud.) 'Passed for press: a centenary history of the Association of Correctors of the Press', n.d. (1954).

Association of Printing Technologists: a technical society for the printing and allied trades, formed in London in 1956, with the object of facilitating group discussion and the exchange of ideas among those interested in the application of scientific methods to production, research, and development in the industry. Closer liaison between research specialists and those engaged in printing will result. Membership is open to individual technologists in the printing and allied trades, to those in industries supplying raw materials and equipment, and to those using the products of the printing trades.

The secretary is F. W. Mackenzie, 58 Frith Street, London, W.1. The annual subscription is two guineas.

asterisk: a star-shaped sort, *, used as a reference mark in the text to draw attention to a footnote, to mark a word which is conjectural or obscure, to cover identity (Mrs S∗∗∗h), to make legally printable such words as s∗∗t, as a hiatus mark, or as a printer's flower.

Astrascribe: the trade name of a British process for accurately engraving fine line contours or stippling in positive or negative form. It was announced in 1955. Specially coated sheets of transparent Astrafoil are used as the drawing surface. Lines of uniform thickness are drawn with a stylus, which removes the coating, the width of line being varied by using a different stylus. Correction is by spot coating and re-scribing.

When the drawing is complete, each sheet of Astrafoil becomes a negative (or by dyeing the image and removing the coating, a positive) which can be used for printing down to metal for the making of printing plates.

The foil is dimensionally stable, ensuring perfect register, and is particularly suitable for mapmaking.

astronomical symbols:

♒	Aquarius	♆	Neptune
♈	Aries	☊	Node, ascending
♋	Cancer	☋	Node, descending
♑	Capricorn	☍	opposition
⚳	Ceres	⚴	Pallas
☄	Comet	♓	Pisces
☌	Conjunction	♇	Pluto
⊕ ♁	Earth	⚻	Quincunx
♊	Gemini	♐ ➳	Sagittarius
⚵	Juno	♄	Saturn
♃	Jupiter	♏	Scorpio
♌	Leo	⚺	semi-sextile
♎	Libra	∠	semi-square
♂	Mars	⚼	sesqui-quadrate
☿	Mercury	⚹	sextile
◍	Moon	✱	star, fixed
⊖	Moon, eclipse of	☉	Sun
☽	Moon, first quarter	☉̲	Sun, lower limb
○	Moon, full	☉̄	Sun, upper limb
☾	Moon, last quarter	♉	Taurus
☽̲	Moon, lower limb	♅	Uranus
●	Moon, new	♀	Venus
☾̄	Moon, upper limb	♍	Virgo

Athelstan Psalter: an early 10th-century Psalter of German origin, presented to King Athelstan about 925. Some illustrations were by Frankish painters, but the four full-page illuminations were added later by Saxon artists, the animal head initials being typical of the latter. A Syrian Christian influence is noticeable in some of their figure drawing.

The work is now in the British Museum (*Galba*, A. xviii).

atlas: a collection of maps published in book form. The name was first used in this connection by Gerard Mercator for his 'Atlas sive cosmographicae meditationes de fabrica mundi et fabricati figura', Parts I–III, Duisberg, 1585–95, although maps had been bound together from early times.

The figure of Atlas holding the globe, from which Mercator took the name, had appeared on the title-page of an earlier work, viz. 'Geographia, tavole moderne di geografia' by Antonio Lafreri, Rome, 1570.

See also *mappamondae, periplus, portolano, ruttier book*.

atlas folio: the largest folio size, 17 in. by 26 in.

attaching: the binding process of joining the boards to the body of a book, not to be confused with *casing-in*, q.v. A difference is made between attaching

Attaching

to a french joint or to a tight joint, single attaching or double attaching, made boards and whole boards. For the attaching joint a narrow strip of tough paper is introduced outside the end leaf to serve as a first connecting link with the boards when attaching these.

When using the *french joint*, q.v., the tapes are placed directly on the attaching joint. (G.U.)

Aubel print: a variety of lithographic print, for which the plates have been produced by transfer from collotype plates. In 1871, C. Aubel experimented with wet-plate negatives completely covered on the deposit side with chromate gelatine, which on drying was lit up from the uncoated side of the glass. The result was a kind of collotype plate which could be printed in a press or transferred to a lithographic plate. On modern dry plates there already exists a gelatine deposit which can be used in a similar way by bathing the developed negative in a dichromate solution and on drying be lit up from the reverse. (G.U.)

Auchinleck Press: a private press established at Auchinleck House, near Cumnock, Dumfriesshire. First publication, 1815. (M.L.)

Augustine Gospels: the two Latin versions of the Gospels, written in roman half-uncial script, which are thought to have been brought by St Augustine from Rome to Canterbury in 597. They are now in the libraries of Oxford and Cambridge Universities.

Aurispa, Giovanni, *c.* 1369–1459: a famous Italian scholar and collector of manuscripts which he gathered on journeys to the Middle East. His 300 Greek works included Aeschylus, the Iliad, Plato, Plutarch and Sophocles, and he did much to encourage the study of Greek in Italy.

Austin, Richard, fl. 1788–1830: a London punch-cutter and wood engraver who worked for John Bell's *British Letter Foundry*, q.v. He also cut punches for the Wilsons of Glasgow and for William Miller of Edinburgh.

He opened his own business under the name Imperial Letter Foundry, being assisted by his son George who succeeded him in 1824. They claimed that the use of a secret formula for casting made their punches the best in London.

authorized edition: an edition of a work published with the consent of the author or the copyright owner. It is thus distinguished from pirated or other editions which appear without this blessing.

author's binding: copies of a book bound to the specification of the author for presentation.

author's corrections: textual deviations from the original copy made by the author on his proof. As these are not printer's errors, the publisher and author are charged for their insertion or deletion.

author's proof: 'marked' proofs supplied to an author for correction. Printing errors are first corrected by the printer's reader, and the author's proof embodies these. The author returns the proof for any further corrections to be made. Revised page proofs, free from these errors, are then supplied.

autochrome process: an obsolete method of colour photography, using a layer of three colours of starch grains over an emulsion on glass, developed and reversed to a positive transparency.

autograph: 1. that which is written in a person's own handwriting: an author's own manuscript.

2. a person's own signature.

3. a copy produced by autolithography. (M.L.)

autolithographer: an artist who creates his original drawing directly on to the lithographic surface from which printing will be done. Cf. *lithographic artist*.

See also *Plastocowell*.

autolithography: the oldest and still the fundamental method of lithography is brush and pen drawing in which a lithographic artist draws directly on a stone or plate, using a brush or steel pen and liquid litho ink. For pen drawing it is best to use a yellow stone, ground beforehand with fine pumice stone, and treated with acetic acid of about 2%. Auxiliary key lines are transferred by tracing. Full covered surfaces are painted with a brush, which can also replace the pen in drawing lines. Shaded surfaces can be obtained by drawing a more or less regular network of lines, closer or further apart, or possibly crossing, and of varying thickness. A still more delicate scale of tones is obtained by dotting, a laborious task, though it gives a more durable forme than crayon-drawing in which dotted tones are obtained by drawing on a grained surface with soft or hard crayons. Crayon is deposited on the grains in coarse or fine dots according to its softness and the manner of its application. Crayon- and pen-drawing are often combined, and are the means of expression for actual autolithography by an original artist.

For shaded tones various means are used: a grained tone can be obtained on smooth surfaces by the splash manner. For this a hard brush is dipped into a solution of litho ink and drawn along the edge of a ruler or on a wire network so that the ink drops on to the stone or plate below. By varying the mesh of the network and the distance between the network or ruler and the stone differences in tone can be achieved. Still more delicate tones and shades result from *airbrush* spraying, q.v. Other means available are *Ben Day tints*, q.v., and the transfer of 'hatched tint' from original stones, which are similar in principle.

There are also many ruling machines and pantographs, though these are used chiefly in *stone engraving*, q.v., a method based more on the photogravure principle than on the principles of ordinary lithographic printing. On a grey or blue stone, the surface of which has been closed and made brilliantly smooth by treating it with oxalic acid solution, the desired image is engraved by hand or machinery to a slight depth, after which the stone is inked. In order to observe and check his work the lithographer usually gives the stone surface a thin, coloured ground. He can also use a real 'etching ground' which is only scored through in the engraving work, and then the deep engraving is done with nitric or acetic acid. After inking with a tampon or nap roller printing can be done directly from the stone on soft, preferably damped, paper. It is more usual, however, to transfer the engraving on to a yellow stone or plate. Cf. *letterpress machine*. (G.U.)

Lithographic drawing on a plate is perhaps more commonly practised than on stone, but as it is a difficult material to work on, similar drawing on plastic surfaces, plain or grained, is also used, the final printing surface being prepared by 'printing down' on to metal using light-sensitive coatings on the metal in the usual photo-lithographic manner.

See also *lithography*, *Plastocowell*, *transfer*.

automatic feeder: a general term applied to any of the many different mechanical sheet-feeding devices on platen and cylinder presses. (M.L.)

autonym: an author's real name.

autoplate machine: the moulding cylinder around which flong is placed in order to make a curved stereo for use on a rotary press.

See also *plate-boring machine*.

Autotron scanner: an electronic apparatus for maintaining accurate colour register on a reel-fed colour press, especially rotogravure, by controlling to within a thousandth of an inch the position of the web of paper. It is made by J. F. Crosfield, Ltd. of London.

One small line is printed by each colour cylinder, and the lines are scanned by pairs of photoelectric cells which compare the position of each colour with that of the colour printed before. Impulses from the cells are made to act upon electric motors coupled to the register mechanism of the press, automatically adjusting the paper web between colour printing units so as to maintain register. The 1955 Model Mark IV gives both circumferential and side register control.

autotype: 1. a process for photographically reproducing a picture in a carbon pigment. The Autotype Company supplies gelatine-coated papers used in the making of gravure cylinders, preparation of colour photographs (carbro), etc.

2. the German term for a half-tone engraving. (Die Autotypie.)

aux petits fers: the decorating of a book cover by impressing on it small individual tools to build up complete patterns.

See also *printer's flowers*.

azure: in the paper-making industry, azure refers to lighter tints of blue given to both laids and woves.

azure tooling: a manner of decorating book covers by tooling upon them a pattern of parallel lines or bars. The name is derived from the use in heraldry of thin horizontal lines to indicate blue. Azure tooling was practised at Lyons in 1530; later on books bound for Grolier.

See also *Grolier bindings*.

azured tool: a finishing tool with close parallel lines running diagonally across its surface.

ADDENDA

antique laid: 1. originally, descriptive of paper made on moulds which had the chain wires laced or sewed direct to the wooden ribs, or supports, of the mould. This caused the pulp to lie heavier along each side of every chain line in the sheet of paper.

2. now, any rough-surfaced laid paper. Better qualities have an esparto furnish; cheaper varieties may include sulphate or even mechanical wood.

Association Typographique Internationale: the name adopted in 1957 by the former *International Typographical Union.*

Astrafoil: the trade name for sheets of thin plastic used for mounting lithographic negatives or positives. The material has good dimensional stability.

Astralon: a German material similar to the British *Astrafoil*, q.v.

B

babery (or **babewynnery**)**:** the term used in the 14th century for illuminating with figures the margins of manuscripts. The term is of Italian origin (from babuino = monkey) and derives from the popularity of monkeys in contemporary decorative art; by extension it also included grotesque animals, or *babewynes*.

See also *bestiary*.

Back, Godefroy, fl. 1493–1511**:** an early printer and bookbinder of Antwerp, notable for the books he printed in his own language as distinct from the usual Latin classics.

back: the part of a book formed where and when the sections of it are united by sewing or stapling. The back may be left flat, but is usually given a convex shape by *rounding*, q.v. While *back* is also used to describe the portion of outer cover which encloses this, the term *spine* is to be preferred.

See also *flat backs*.

A firm flexible back gives a good opening

A firm stiff back is less satisfactory

A hollow back also gives a good opening

back cornering: the cutting away of a small chip off the boards of a book from their four inner corners. This is done by the forwarder before he attaches the leather cover. The easier opening of the boards is facilitated.

back knife: the knife fitted behind the mould wheel of a slug-casting machine. Its purpose is to cut off the jet from the cast slug. The sharpness and careful adjustment of this knife affect the accuracy of the base to paper height of the slug. (G.U.)

back margin: the inner page margin, parallel with the fore-edge or outer margin. See also *gutter*.

back mark: 1. the impression made in sheets of hand-made paper by the wire or cord on which they are hung to dry. It is smoothed out when glazing.

2. See *collating mark*.

back matter: another name for end-matter or *subsidiaries*, q.v.

back pages: see *verso*.

back-tenter: the operator of the dry end of a paper-making machine. Also known as *back-tender*.

backed: 1. said of a sheet in printing when it has been backed up, i.e. had the second side printed. See *backing-up* (1).

2. said of a book in binding after *backing*, q.v.

Backing by hand

backing: the bookbinding operation applied to the back of a book, which has been previously sewn and glued, whereby the backs of the sections are splayed outwards from the centre of the book. This adds to the permanence of the *rounding*, q.v., and provides an abutment for the boards.

See also *Steamset.*

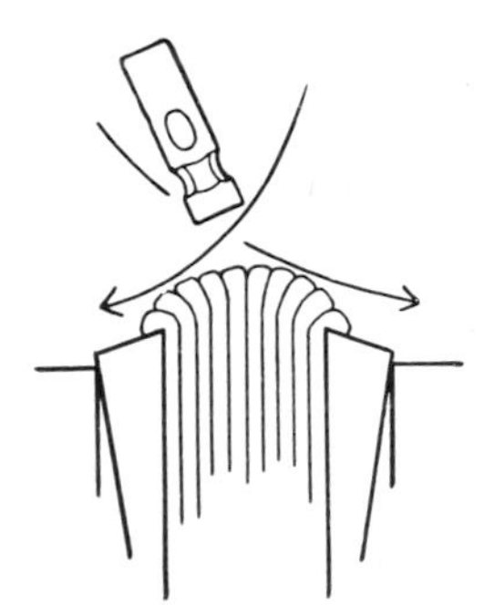

The correct angle for backing. Note the backing boards

backing boards: wedge-shaped boards between which an unbound book is held in the lying press for backing.

backing-up: 1. printing on the reverse of a printed sheet.

See also *perfecting.*

2. in electrotyping, the process of filling in the thin copper shell with metal in order to give the solid back.

backlining: an alternative name for *hollows*, q.v., in book cases.

backs: the back margins of pages, i.e. those next to the spine or hinge of a book.

See also *gutter, gutter margin.*

backwater: surplus water which drains off the wet end of a paper-making machine. The fibre, loading, and other substances suspended in it are extracted for re-use, e.g. to dilute the stuff, or in the Hollanders. Also known as *pulp water, size water, white water.* Cf. *retention.*

bad colour: a poorly printed impression due to the uneven distribution of ink.

See also *ink coverage.*

bad copy: manuscript or any other material which is to be set up in type, but is difficult to read. (M.L.)

bad sheets: see *imperfections.*

Badier, Florimond, fl. 1645–60: a Parisian bookbinder associated with the art of pointillé-tooled morocco covers and rich doublures. He also used a distinctive stamp bearing a man's head. Only three signed bindings of his are known, and many of those ascribed to him are possibly the work of imitators.

Badius Ascensius, Jodocus, 1462–1535: a scholar-printer of Ghent, and later (1503) of Paris, who printed over 700 books, and was noted for the accuracy of his classical Latin texts.

Bagford, John, 1650–1716: a notorious book collector who acted as agent for such bibliophiles as *Robert Harley*, q.v. His notoriety derives from his alleged destruction or mutilation of countless books in order to amass a collection in 216 volumes of title-pages, book-plates, paper specimens, etc., for a history of printing and the book crafts. It is probable, however, that some of the leaves so used were binder's waste.

bail: the metal band hinged on the edge of the platen on a job press, one at the upper and another on the lower edges, serving to hold the sheets of the tympan in place. (M.L.)

Bakalar, Nikolaus, fl. 1498: a Polish printer who worked in Pilsen at the end of the 15th century.

baked: said of type ready for distribution which, after rinsing, adheres closely together and cannot easily be separated. This probable trouble with new type may be prevented by soaking in a solution of soft soap and water before type is laid in case.

Bale, John, 1495–1563: the compiler of the first bibliography in England, 'Illustrium Majoris Britanniae scriptorum . . . summarium', Gippeswici, 1548.

ball: see *ink ball.*

Ballantyne, James, 1772–1833: the Scottish printer-publisher who founded his press in 1796 at Kelso, and is remembered for the high standard of his work. He was the publisher of Sir Walter Scott, the latter having a financial interest in the business.

See 'The Ballantyne Press and its founders, 1796–1908'. 1909.

Balligault, Félix, fl. 1492– early 16th century: a Parisian printer who worked for many booksellers and publishers including Gilles Gourmont, Claude Jaumar, and Antoine Vérard.

Balston, William, 1759–1849: one of England's leading paper-makers. In 1774 he was apprenticed to *James Whatman II*, q.v., at Turkey Mill near Maidstone. When the firm was sold to the Hollingworth brothers in 1794 Whatman lent Balston £5000 to buy a partnership, the firm being known as Hollingworths & Balston. This lasted until 1806 when Balston established his own business at Springfield Mill, Maidstone, installing there one of the earliest steam-power plants. He did not, however, acquire a Fourdrinier, and as in time printers came to find machine-made papers cheaper, it was the manufacture of writing and drawing papers, with the Whatman mark, that brought Balston fame and (much later) wealth. Financial difficulties led to a partnership in 1814, and the firm operated as Balston, Gaussen & Bosanquet until 1849, when it was re-named after William's sons who later assumed control; it became W. & R. Balston, by which name (plus Ltd.) it operates to-day.

See T. Balston, 'William Balston, paper-maker, 1759–1849', Methuen, 1954.

Bämler, Johannes, fl. 1472–95: a noted printer of Augsburg who lavishly illustrated his books with woodcuts. He is also remembered as a painter of miniatures and as a rubricator.

Bampton Press: a private press established at Bampton Vicarage, Oxfordshire, about 1848, by the Rev. J. A. Giles. The works issued from it were mostly of a religious or local character, many being written or edited by Dr. Giles. The best work, and perhaps the last to appear, was Joseph Bosworth's translation of King Alfred's 'Description of Europe', 1855. This was printed in an Anglo-Saxon letter, and was apparently set by a professional compositor. No work bears the name of the printer, the usual imprint being 'Printed at the author's Private Press'.

Bancroft, John S.: a collaborator with Tolbert Lanston in the development of the *Monotype* type-setting machine, q.v.

bands: the cords of flax or hemp to which the folded sheets of a book are attached by sewing across them. Sometimes the bands show on the spine of a book, but they are usually sunk into the back by sawing grooves across the folds of the collated signatures. Refers to hand-binding.

See also *flexible sewing, raised bands, sawn-in back*.

bank: a printer's bench on which sheets are placed as printed, or on which standing type rests. Also known as *random*.

Banks, Richard, fl. 1523–42: a London printer, few of whose thirty works are extant, who received from Henry VIII in 1540 a privilege for Epistles and Gospels.

Bannatyne Club: a club founded in Edinburgh in 1823 by Sir Walter Scott for the printing of works on the literature, history, and antiquities of Scotland. The name derives from a 16th-century scholar George Bannatyne. The last work published by the club was in 1867.

Sewing on unstranded bands

Sewing on flexible bands with frayed ends (slips)

bar: the long handle on a hand-press which is pulled over to give the impression. (M.L.)

Barber dried: said of paper which has been dried by means of Barber driers. The moist web of paper is tub-sized and passed over rolls for drying by hot air. (M.L.)

barge: a small wooden case having divisions. Used for holding spaces during the correction of type-matter.

Barker, Christopher, *c.* 1529–99: Bible printer to Queen Elizabeth I. He was succeeded by his son Robert, d. 1645, who printed the Authorized Version of the Bible in 1611 for James I.

Bartolozzi, Francesco, 1727–1815: an Italian painter and engraver who worked in London as a pioneer of *stipple engraving*, q.v.

Baryta paper: paper coated with barium sulphate gelatine which is used for text impressions on the Orotype and other photo-composing machines.

base line: the imaginary line on which the bases of capitals rest. Cf. *cap line*, *mean line*.

basil: a thin variety of sheepskin tanned in oak bark. It is of poor quality but is sometimes artificially grained to represent more costly leathers.

Baskerville, John, 1706–75: the English typefounder and printer of Birmingham who designed the famous transitional type which bears his name. After an early career as a writing-master and engraver, he made a fortune in japanning and began printing, building his own press in 1751–52. His first book was an edition of Virgil, 1757. His presswork was of the finest, and although not commercially successful he did much to improve the standards of his day. He had wove paper made to his requirements, probably at Whatman's mill. Printed sheets were finished by pressing them between hot copper plates. He made his own ink, 'shorter' than usual.

Baskerville's types were bought by Pierre Beaumarchais in 1779 for a ninety-two-volume edition of Voltaire (1780–89). The 2750 original punches were for many years lost in France; in 1953 they were presented by the French firm Deberny and Peignot to the Cambridge University Press (to which Baskerville had been Printer of Bibles and Prayer Books, 1758–63). His folio Bible, 1763, was his masterpiece.

Bassendyne, Thomas: a mid-16th-century printer, binder, and bookseller of Edinburgh. In 1575 he received a patent for printing the Bible, and in 1576 issued the first translation of the New Testament to be printed in Scotland.

Bassist process: 1. a process invented by E. Bassist for preparing retouchable screen transparent positives for offset reproduction. A glass plate coated with a layer of metal is provided with a preparation sensitive to light, and is copied under a screen negative. After developing, the separated metal is etched away, after which the remaining parts can be corrected by etching. He also suggested methods for colour reproduction by a combination of the Ben Day process and photo-litho, and has invented an apparatus for retouching by masking. (G.U.)

See also *Ambrosius Galetzka.*

2. a process whereby tonal values of half-tones are modified by slight moving of the camera screen in conjunction with supplementary exposure. (M.L.)

bastard: 1. a letter foreign to the fount in which it is found.

2. an obsolete paper size, 33 in. by 20 in.

3. any non-standard size paper.

bastard title: see *half-title.*

bastarda: a cursive gothic letter, later called secretary, with pointed descenders and often looped ascenders, used in the 15th century and introduced into England from Bruges by William Caxton. Modern German Schwabachers and Frakturs are later bastardas.

See also *letters—forms and styles.*

Batchelor, Joseph: a paper-maker of Little Chart, nr. Ashford, Kent, whose fine hand-made sheets were used by the Ashendene, Doves, Essex House, Gregynog, and Kelmscott presses. Watermarks were designed by his clients.

Bateman, Abraham & John: two London binders who in 1604 were appointed Court binders to James I. The use of small flowers, decorated corners, and the Royal arms as a centre-piece were features of their work.

batter: types which are damaged or worn so that defective impressions result.

battledore: a variety of school primer made of folded paper varnished on the inside and used in the late 18th century. When opened it resembled a *horn book*, q.v., which it superseded, but was without a handle.

Bauersche Giesserei: one of the largest firms of typefounders in Germany. It was founded at Frankfurt in 1835 by Johann Christian Bauer (1802–67) who between 1839–47 worked in England. In 1861 he introduced his 'Neue Kirchenschriften', modelled on 16th-century designs, in an attempt to popularize roman-face types in Germany. The firm's types were in use all over the world.

In the present century Emil Rudolf Weiss (1875–1942) designed several notable types for this firm, a Fraktur from 1911–14, a roman from 1924–31, a gothic in 1936, and a round gothic in 1937.

In 1940 the firm issued a sumptuous volume 'Aventur und Kunst: eine Chronik des Buchdruckgewerbes von der Erfindung der beweglichen Letter bis zur Gegenwart, bearbeitet von Konrad F. Bauer': this was to commemorate the 500th anniversary of the invention of printing.

Bauzonnet, Antoine, fl. 1830–48: a Parisian bookbinder and gilder who, with his son-in-law, *Georges Trautz*, q.v., had the leading bindery of 19th-century France. Many of their bindings were made in the manner of craftsmen of preceding times, and were collected by wealthy bibliophiles.

Baxter print: an illustration printed in colour by the method devised in 1835 by the wood engraver, George Baxter (1804–67). He used an aquatint foundation plate on which oil colours were superimposed with wooden blocks. It was found to be unsuited for book work, but examples may be seen in 'The Parlour Table-book' by Woodward, 1835.

bead-roll: a roll of parchment on which prayers and commemorative verses were inscribed to honour the dead. From about the 9th century such rolls were sent from monastery to monastery when an abbot died; further verses were added at each new place. Examples of the 16th century sometimes contain drawings depicting the abbot's life and death, with backgrounds of his Abbey.

Alternative names are *bede-roll* and *obituary roll.*

beard: 1. in Great Britain, the space on a type between the bottom of the x-height and the upper edge of the shank or body. This space comprises the shoulder on which the face rests and the bevel by which it is raised from it, and is the area in which the descenders of lower-case letters extrude.

2. in U.S.A., the bevel between the face of a type character and the shoulder.

bearers: 1. part of the printing press on which cylinders rest.

2. thin strips of type metal 0·918 in. high by $\frac{5}{8}$ in. wide, which are put in a forme to facilitate the smooth running of ink rollers.

beater: the paper-making machine in which the half-stuff passes from the *potcher*, q.v., to be formed into pulp. The most widely used beating machine is the *Hollander*, q.v.

See also *Jordan.*

beating: 1. converting half-stuff into paper pulp.

2. the original method of putting ink on type by means of ink balls.

3. the bookbinding process whereby the folded sheets are made to lie flat and solid by striking the folded edge with a beating hammer. (M.L.)

Beatty, Sir Alfred Chester, 1875– : a renowned book collector who acquired a series of manuscripts on papyrus of the Greek Bible written about the 2nd or 3rd century, and a series of ancient Egyptian papyri. The most important of these, written in hieratic characters on both sides of a roll, contains the mythological story of the Contendings of Horus and Seth, and, in addition, groups of love songs.

Sir Alfred has presented a collection of papyri to the British Museum, to which institution he has also loaned some important illuminated western manuscripts.

Beaumont Press: a private press founded in London in 1917, its purpose being to issue hand-printed editions of original work by contemporary writers. The books were quarter-bound in canvas with paper sides especially designed for each book by Cyril Beaumont.

Beckford, William, 1759–1844: a wealthy book collector who amassed a great library at Fonthill, Wilts. He spent large sums of money on binding. Most of his early collection he sold in 1822 when he moved to Bath, but between 1829 and 1844 he formed a second library. On his death, his son-in-law, the Marquis of Douglas, transferred the books to Hamilton Palace. The library was sold by Sotheby between 1882–84 for £86,000.

The collection included Jenson's Latin Bible, 1476; the Lactantius of Sweynheym and Pannartz; Greek and Latin classics from the press of Manutius; French and Italian literature, as well as Grolier, Maioli, Eve, and Padeloup bindings.

bed: the steel table of a printing press on which the forme of type is placed for printing. When the forme is secured it is sometimes described as having been 'put to bed'.

bede-roll: the earliest name for a *bead-roll,* q.v.

Bedford, Francis, 1799–1883: a London binder who worked for Charles Lewis until the latter's death in 1836, and then with John Clarke until 1850 when he opened his own bindery. For the bindings he made for wealthy collectors Bedford revived earlier Lyonnese and Italian styles, often copying the tools used. His *forwarding,* q.v., was reputed to be the best in England.

Bedford Missal: a superb example of 15th-century Parisian illumination commissioned by John, Duke of Bedford (1414–35) when Regent of France. Each page of text is bordered with leaves and flowers, interspersed with medallions showing scenes from the lives of the saints. There are in addition four full-page Biblical scenes.

The work is now in the British Museum (Add. MS. 18850).

Beebe, Murray: see *Neocol.*

begin even: an instruction to the compositor. When a compositor has a take of copy which ends in the middle of a paragraph, he must end his type even at the end of a line. The compositor having the next take must begin even, without indention at the beginning of the line. (M.L.)

Beka retouching methods: see *offset reproduction.*

Bekk apparatus: see *paper-testing.*

Beldornie Press: a private press set up about 1840 at Beldornie Tower, Ryde, Isle of Wight, by Edward Vernon Utterson. He issued several reprints of early

17th-century poetical tracts, usually in editions of from twelve to sixteen copies, carefully printed on good paper 'with the original woodcuts, headbands, and ornaments faithfully copied'. He added bibliographical notes. His press appears to have closed in 1843. (With M.L.)

Belin machine: an electronic photo-scanning machine, made in France by Etablissements Edouard Belin, the product of which is a photographic negative.

The original to be reproduced is fitted around a revolving drum. A beam of light is directed on to the picture, which, in revolving, reflects light of an intensity varying in proportion to the dark and light parts of the picture. This reflected light is received by a photoelectric cell which transmits impulses of related intensity to a drum containing a roll of sensitized film. This drum revolves at the same speed as that bearing the original, so that the film is exposed, in dots, to a beam of light having an intensity proportionate to that reflected by the original. The exposed film is printed on to a sensitized plate, and prepared by customary stages for use as a half-tone printing block.

See also *blockmaking*.

Bell, Andrew, 1726–1809: a Scottish engraver remembered now as the joint owner, with William Smellie and Colin Macfarquhar, of the first edition of 'Encyclopaedia Britannica', 1768–71, for which he engraved the plates.

Bell, John, 1745–1831: an enterprising London typefounder, publisher, and bookseller for whom, in 1788, Richard Austin cut the transitional types for which Bell is now remembered. It was in his edition of Shakespeare that the use of the long 's' was discontinued. He issued a library of poets in 109 illustrated 18mo volumes, 'The Poets of Great Britain complete from Chaucer to Churchill', Edinburgh, 1776–83. The series was reprinted in 1807 by Samuel Bagster.

Bell's type of 1788 was revived by Monotype in 1931–32 from the original punches, now at the Stephenson Blake foundry.

belles-lettres: the publishing term for literary studies, orations, essays, letters, criticism, etc.

bellows press: a small flat-bed platen press suitable for small jobbing work. An early model was the Parlour press of Edward Cowper, built in 1846. Maximum bed size was 15 in. by 10 in. The Adana flat-bed press, made since 1920, is based on this principle.

belly: the front or nick side of a type.

Ben Day tints: a series of mechanical tints in the form of celluloid sheets which, by the relief ruling or dots on them, are used in blockmaking and lithography to add texture, shading, and detail to line drawings. They may be applied to the drawing, the negative of it, or direct to the block before etching. They were originally conceived by Benjamin Day (1838–1916), an American, as an aid for lithographic draughtsmen.

An alternative name is *medium*.

Adding texture to a drawing on stone

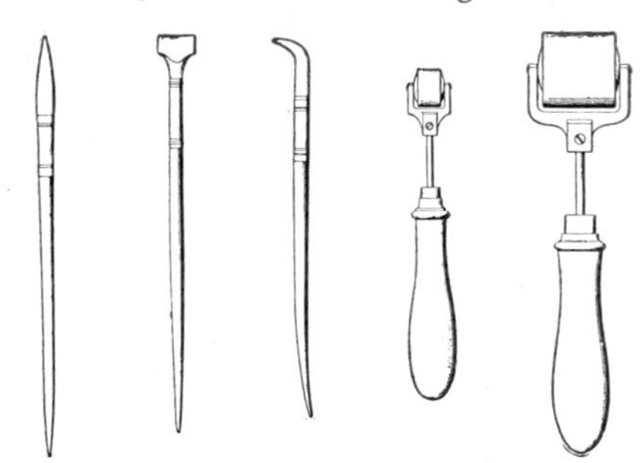

Tools for use in mechanical tinting

bench press: see *standing press*.

Benedictional of St Aethelwold: the finest example of the Winchester School of English manuscript painting. It dates from 975–80. The Carolingian minuscule text, written by Abbot Godeman, includes twenty-eight large illuminated pages, each a complete design, in which foliated borders, often terminating in corner rosettes of acanthus leaves, frame vividly coloured scenes from the Bible and lives of the saints which owe something in their presentation and lavish use of gold to continental iconography. (An influence probably transmitted by visiting monks from Rheims.)

The Benedictional was acquired by the British Museum in 1957.

Beneventan: a cursive minuscule used in Italy from the 8th–13th centuries for writing manuscripts. It is sometimes referred to as *Lombardic*.

Bensley, Thomas, 1785–1833: a distinguished London printer, noted for his careful presswork. He interested himself in Friedrich König's development of the first power-driven press. Of his many fine books he is best remembered for his 'History of England' by David Hume, 10 vols., 1806; and for the Macklin Folio Bible, 7 vols., 1800 (with the Apocrypha as an 8th vol. in 1816). He had types cut by Joseph Jackson and Vincent Figgins.

His working life ended in 1819 when fire largely destroyed his plant and premises.

Bentley, Richard, 1794–1871: a London printer-publisher who, with his brother Samuel, was noted for his careful work. He is remembered for 'Bentley's Miscellany' which began in 1837 and was for a time edited by Dickens, also for a fiction library of 127 volumes. Samuel was noted for his work of antiquarian interest.

Benton, Linn Boyd: the American inventor of the *punch-cutting machine*, q.v.

Berlin paper: see *transfer paper*.

Berne Convention: the international agreement first signed in 1887 (and subsequently revised) which secures copyright for an author in most countries of the world. The important exceptions among the original signatories were the U.S.A., Russia, Turkey, China, and certain South American republics (the latter having their own copyright convention).

See also *Copyright Act*, *Universal Copyright Convention*.

Berry, Jean Duc de, 1340–1416: a wealthy patron of French painting for whom were made several Books of Hours, notable being his 'Très riches heures' now in the Musée Condé, Chantilly. This was painted about 1416 and the splendour of its full-page scenes, painted by the Limbourg brothers, is generally accepted as the finest example of the illuminator's art in France. Other artists commissioned by the Duke were André Beauneveu and Jacquemart de Hesdin.

Berry Prize: see *David Berry Prize*.

Berte process: see *Jean Berte process*.

Berthelet, Thomas, fl. 1530–55: a London printer who, for a time, was King's Printer to Henry VIII. He was also binder to the King, but it has not been established whether any of the volumes he supplied from four if not five ateliers were actually his work.

He is specially remembered for the translations of Erasmus he issued, and the Latin dictionary of Sir Thomas Elyot, 1538. He is credited with the introduction into England of gold tooling.

Berthold, Hermann: the founder, in 1858, of a Berlin business known as 'Institut für Galvano-Typie'. In 1865 he opened a brass rule works which, as Hermann Berthold A.G., has developed into one of the world's largest type-foundries. In 1878 Berthold established a unit of measure for type which was adopted by all German founders; one point equals 0·376 mm. and there are 2660 per metre (one Anglo-American point equals 0·351 mm.).

The firm is noted for its extensive range of display types. Included are designs by Gunter Lange, Herbert Post, Imre Reiner, Georg Trump, and Martin Wilke. Founts are supplied in both Didot and Anglo-American point systems.

Besançon, Jacques de: a Parisian illuminator of the late 15th century. He worked for a time with Antoine Vérard for whom he painted initials in books the latter printed on vellum.

bestiary: a book containing myths and folk-lore about real or imaginary animals and places. The text was allegorical and the morals were made clearer by the inclusion of painted drawings of the strange beasts.

The earliest illuminated bestiary dates from the 10th century. Most surviving English bestiaries belong to the 12th century, a few to the 13th and 14th. They were a source of inspiration to wood carvers, illuminators, and stone-masons.

See 'The Book of Beasts' by T. H. White. Cape, 1954.

bevel: the sloping surface of a type rising from the shoulder to the face.

See also *beard*.

bevelled boards: strong boards with bevelled edges used for large books.

Bewick, Thomas, 1753–1828: the most famous of British wood engravers. For many years he worked in partnership with his brother John. His most famous works are perhaps 'A General History of Quadrupeds', 1790, and 'History of British Birds', 2 vols., 1797 and 1804. See *wood engraving*.

Bewoid: see *paper-making*.

Beyer, Albrecht: the discoverer, about 1839, of *reflex printing*, q.v.

B.F.M.P.: the customary abbreviation for the *British Federation of Master Printers*, q.v.

bibelot: an unusually small book.

Bible moralisée: a form of religious instruction popular in 13th- and 14th-century Europe. This was essentially a picture book, arranged with eight Biblical scenes to a page, each set in a square or roundel, interpreted by a Latin text. While often fully illuminated, some examples contain somewhat rough outline drawings.

Incipit epistola sancti iheronimi ad
paulinum presbiterum de omnibus
divine historie libris. capitulum primum.
Frater ambrosius
tua michi munus-
cula perferens detulit
sil et suavissimas
litteras que a principio
amicitiarum fidem proba-
te iam fidei et veteris amicitie nova:
preferebant. Vera enim illa necessitudo est.
et christi glutino copulata. quam non utili-
tas rei familiaris. non presentia tantum
corporum. non subdola et palpans adulatio.
sed dei timor. et divinarum scripturarum
studia conciliant. Legimus in veteribus
historiis. quosdam lustrasse provincias.
novos adisse populos. maria transisse.
ut eos quos ex libris noverant: coram
quoque viderent. Sicut pitagoras memphi-
ticos vates. sic plato egiptum. et archi-
tam tarentinum. eandemque oram ytalie. que
quondam magna grecia dicebatur: labo-
riosissime peragravit. et ut qui athenis
magister erat. et potens. cuiusque doctrinas

ingres
Appo
loqui
dunt.
alban
tissim
extren
tissimi
hyarc
tantal
discip
cursu
Inde p
os. m
pheni
ad all
ut gig
solis
venit
profici
sic sup
nibus.
Q
et ma

Part of a page of the 42-line Bible. Full size

Bible paper: a very thin, tough, opaque paper used mostly for printing Bibles and prayer-books. It is made from new cotton or linen rags with titanium dioxide or calcium carbonate as a loading agent. Bible paper, also called *Bible printing*, is widely and erroneously referred to as *india paper*, q.v., which was and is a thin soft paper imported from China for artists' proof work. *Oxford india paper*, q.v., is a proprietary article.

Bible printing: of all books the Bible has been issued in the largest number of editions. Already prior to 1500 there had appeared no fewer than ninety-four, most of which were in Latin. The 42-line, or Mazarin, Bible printed by Gutenberg was apparently begun about 1450–52 and completed about 1456. Its two volumes consist of 643 folio 2-column leaves. It is thought that thirty-five copies were printed on parchment and 165 on paper; of this total only forty-six are now known. Of similar importance is the 36-line Bible printed at Bamberg about 1459 by an unknown printer who may, however, have been Heinrich Keffer. Its 882 printed leaves, two columns to a page, are usually bound in three volumes. The 48-line Bible printed by Peter Schöffer of Mainz in 1462 is also important.

See also *Cracow fragments*.

Among Bibles printed in national languages may be mentioned the Low German versions printed by Quentell of Cologne in 1478 and by Arndes of Lübeck in 1498 (both famous for their illustrations); the first Bible in Italian appeared in 1471, in Catalan in 1478, in Bohemian in 1488, and in French in 1498. The original Hebrew text of the Old Testament was first printed at Soncino in 1488, and the Greek text of the New Testament by Froben in 1516. The complete Bible of Martin Luther was printed at Wittenberg by Hans Lufft in 1534, although the New Testament illustrated with woodcuts had appeared in 1522. It is said that Lufft sold 100,000 copies of Luther's Bible in forty years.

The Bible now exists in about 850 languages.

See also *polyglot edition*.

Bible printing in England: various portions of the Bible had been translated into English and printed, but no complete version appeared until 1535 (Coverdale's, printed abroad) and Matthew's Bible printed in England in 1538 by Richard Grafton.

Since 1504, when William Faques was the first to be appointed as King's Printer, the right to print the Bible has been restricted to holders of that office. Among Bible printers have been Richard Pynson, 1508; Richard Grafton and Edward Whitchurch, 1537–39; Thomas Berthelet, *c.* 1540–42; Anthony Marler, 1542–46; Richard Grafton, 1547; John Cawood, 1553, and with Richard Jugge, 1568–77; Christopher Barker and family, 1577–1709; Thomas Newcomb and Henry Hills, 1710–12; John Baskett, 1712–42, and his son Thomas, 1742–69; Charles Eyre, 1769–99, and his heirs, George Eyre, William Strahan, 1799; and with John Reeves, 1800–29. Andrew Spottiswoode, whose father married into the Strahan family, joined the partnership, and the firm of Eyre & Spottiswoode have held the office ever since. The two important versions of the Bible in English are:—

1. *Authorized Version*, 1611. The copyright for this and the Book of Common Prayer is vested in the Crown, authority to print in England being granted by charter to Oxford and Cambridge University Presses, and by licence to the Queen's Printer (Messrs Eyre & Spottiswoode). It was first printed by Robert Barker.

2. *Revised Version*, 1881–95. This is the joint property of the Oxford and Cambridge University Presses who financed it and by whom alone it may be printed.

Bible text: see *great primer*.

Biblia pauperum: a Latin name, meaning 'poor man's Bible', applied to those manuscript and block-book

Page from a German 'Biblia pauperum' Printed in 1471

versions of the Bible in which each page showed a scene from the New Testament, accompanied on either side by two antitype incidents from the Old.

A short Latin verse or simple explanatory text completed the page.

An early example, dating from *c.* 1325, was made at Klosterneuburg near Vienna: the nine folios now surviving in the Österreichische Nationalbibliothek, Vienna, comprise seventeen pen drawings, some coloured. Austrian and Bavarian scriptoria were centres for these Bibles.

Block-book versions date from *c.* 1440, and others were made during the next hundred years.

Bibliographical Society: founded in London in 1892 at the instigation of W. A. Copinger and Sir John MacAlister. The objects of the society are to promote and encourage bibliographical studies and research; to hold meetings at which papers are read and discussed; to form a bibliographical library; and to print books and papers dealing with different aspects of bibliography. The society's numerous publications are of considerable importance to librarians, scholars, and bibliophiles; perhaps the best known are A. W. Pollard and G. R. Redgrave's *Short-Title Catalogue*, q.v., and the journal 'The Library'.

Bibliographie de la France: the official bibliography of publications in French. It originated in 1811 as 'Bibliographie de l'Empire Français'. Currently issued weekly, it lists books entered in the copyright office of the Bibliothèque Nationale, and includes theses, periodicals, Government publications, and trade news. Supplementing the weekly parts are 'Les Livres du Mois', 'Les Livres du Trimestre', 'Les Livres du Semestre', and 'Les Livres de l'Année' (monthly, quarterly, half-yearly, and annual cumulations).

bibliography: 1. the history and systematic description of books as physical objects, their authorship, printing, format, publication, editions.

2. a list of books on a particular subject or written by a particular author. Bibliographies may be published separately or as part of a book or periodical, and either be limited to a specified period or appear serially in order to be up to date. They may include works published in several countries. Entries may be arranged chronologically, alphabetically by author, or by subdivisions of subjects, and be with or without notes. Forms of presentation within a book vary, alternatives are the end of the text, the ends of chapters, or footnotes to pages.

bibliology: the scientific description of books from the earliest times to the present, and including all the materials and processes involved in their making.

bibliomania: a mania or passion for acquiring books. (M.L.)

Bibliomites: the popular name for the *Society of Antiquarian Booksellers' Employees*, q.v.

bibliopegy: bookbinding viewed as a fine art.

bibliophile: literally, a friend of books, by which is now implied a collector of them. In the days of Plato and Aristotle (both of whom had libraries) books were collected to be read, and while later the Livres d'Heures so exquisitely illuminated for such patrons as the Duc de Berry were made to delight the eye rather than improve the mind, the great libraries of Sir Henry Savile and others of his day were collections of books to be studied by scholars and friends.

It was during the later 17th century and after, when increasing numbers of noblemen, statesmen, and the higher clergy developed their libraries, that a collection of books came to denote wealth and sometimes taste. Books were bought because they were rare, finely printed or sumptuously bound (and if they were not this would be rectified by rebinding, to the peril of an often important original cover).

By the 19th century a library of calf or morocco was the mark of success in business, and it was during this era, too, that another reason for collecting books developed: this was the limited edition from a private press (press books, as they are called).

The history of Quaritch (from 1847) or Sotheby (from 1744) shows how books were bought and sold for their incidental qualities rather than for their texts. The 19th century was not without tragedy for the British bibliophile since many great collections went to the sale-rooms, and while the Bodleian or British Museum occasionally benefited from a legacy or purchase, whole libraries were shipped across the Atlantic to a richer country anxious to acquire the cultural heritage of Europe. Thus it is that the greatest collections of the 20th century have developed in America.

bichromate process: see *chromate process*.

bill of fount: see *fount scheme*.

bill of type: see *fount scheme*.

bimetallic lithographic plates: printing plates made of two dissimilar metals, chosen for their wetting properties. Copper, brass, zinc, and silver are readily wetted by oils; aluminium, magnesium, lead, nickel, chromium, and stainless steel by water. Chemical treatment can, however, affect the receptivity of any metal to either fluid.

Although such plates require special electro-plating equipment, and are costly, there are certain advantages. The hardness of such metals as chromium permits long runs on high-speed offset presses; image areas on copper are more permanent than the albumen images on zinc; the plate may be used without graining to make it water-retentive (or with only a minimum grain) and will thus need less damping water than normal grained plates, thereby minimizing water-ink emulsification.

In most cases the image on these plates is formed by a combination of photomechanical stencil and electroplating, though chemical deposition is also possible, e.g. a deep-etched zinc plate can be copper-coated on its image areas by immersion in a copper sulphate-copper oxalate solution, or in the *Ahlen and Åkerlund* process where a chromium or stainless steel plate is coated with a light sensitive dichromated film, exposed under a positive, developed, and immersed in a copper solution.

There are two groups of electrolytic methods. In the first, negatives are used when exposing the plate. The finely-grained aluminium *Alkuprint* plate of M. Horn is given a copper deposit in an electrolytic bath. It is then given a light-sensitive coating and exposed under a negative. After development, the bared copper areas are etched off, and the non-image aluminium base thus exposed is treated with dilute nitric acid to make it ink-repellant. The difficulty of plating copper on aluminium limits the use of this process.

An iron base-plate coated first with lead (non-image) and then with copper (image) is the method of *W. A. Boekelmann and A. Elfers*. The printing rollers must be set with care when using these plates due to the softness of the lead.

In the *Electron intaglio plate* method of E. Blau a zinc or brass plate is coated with dichromated shellac. After exposure under a negative, it is developed in alcohol, washed, dried, and heated to harden the shellac. Nickel or zinc is then electroplated on to the non-image areas.

In the *Hausleiter* process a polished brass plate is sensitized, exposed, and developed; then the non-image areas are plated with nickel steel.

Positives are used in the second group of electrolytic methods.

In *C. Aller's* process a stainless steel base-plate (with a 12% chromium content) is coated with copper. It is then given a layer of dichromated gum arabic and exposed in contact with a half-tone positive. After development, the exposed copper image areas are protected with an electrically deposited resist, while the copper on the non-image areas is etched away with ferric chloride solution.

In the *Coates Bros.* process a grained copper plate is given a chromium layer. After coating with a dichromated colloid it is exposed under a positive and developed. Then chromium is removed electrolytically from the non-image areas (or by ferric chloride etching), leaving the copper image slightly recessed below the chromium.

In the *Nu-chrome* process, announced in Britain by Coates Bros. in 1957, a thin steel base is plated with copper and then chromium. The steel is solely for strength. A patent polyvinyl light-sensitive coating replaces the usual dichromated gum. After exposure, the image is dyed, dried, and retouched. Etching follows, leaving the exposed copper image slightly below the matt-finished water-absorbing chromium layer. Treatment with phosphoric solution enhances the ink receptivity of the copper and the water receptivity of the chromium.

Cheapness, stability, durability, and good definition are among advantages claimed for these plates.

There are other methods of preparing bimetallic plates, e.g. the *Pictograph bi-metal process*, q.v.

See R. A. C. Adams, 'The theory of bimetallic lithographic plates', B.F.M.P., 1950.

binder's boards: see *boards.*

binder's brass: a brass block bearing relief letters, or a design in relief, used for blocking the cover of a book. The binder or publisher sends the brass engraver a layout of his requirements. This layout may be a good pull, a sketch, or a careful reproduction in black and white. The lettering is set up in type, or drawn by hand, and photographed to the required size. The resulting negative is printed down on a 5-gauge brass plate of suitable size, the negatives from several jobs being printed at the same time. The plate is then shallow-etched.

It is next sawn into separate blocks which are given to a machinist who removes all the metal surrounding the design or lettering: this is where the brass gets its depth. Each block now receives the attention of a hand-engraver to take the burrs off, give shape and precision to the block, and give it the final finish. It is this hand craftsmanship which gives the brass block its superiority over the cheaper soft-metal zinco, cast from type, which is sometimes used as an alternative.

binder's cloth: see *book cloth.*

binder's title: the title as lettered on the binding. It may be contracted from that on the title-page, or original cover of a book being rebound. (L. K.)

binder's waste: surplus printed sheets used by hand-binders for lining end-papers and the like. (L. K.)

binding: 1. a difficulty arising when locking up type, caused by using furniture which is longer or wider than the type and 'binds' at the ends.

2. see *bookbinding.*

binding proof: see *witness* (2).

binding variants: differences of colour, fabric, lettering or decoration occurring between copies of the same edition as issued by the publisher. These may occur when not all copies are bound at one time or in one bindery.
See also *remainders, secondary binding.*

birthday book: a variety of book, popular in the Victorian Era, which gave a quotation for each day of the year, and had blank leaves for autographs. The first was published in 1866 by Mack of Bristol and was 'The Birthday Scripture Textbook'.

Bisticci, Vespasiano da, 1421–98: a Florentine scholar-bookseller who collected classical manuscripts for such wealthy patrons as Niccolo de' Niccoli and Cosmo de' Medici. He is said to have employed forty-five scribes to copy 200 works for the library of Fiesole Abbey which Medici founded *c.* 1440.

BL: a bibliographer's abbreviation, used in catalogues or lists, to indicate that an English book is printed in black letter. Cf. *GL.*

black: a blemish on a printed sheet made by a lead spacing which has risen to the height of type. Cf. *monk.*

black face: see *black letter.*

black letter: a term used to describe a script with angular outlines which superseded the lighter roman in the 12th century, also applied to types developed from it. Survivals are seen in types known as gothic, Old English, Fraktur, text, etc. In the early days of printing in Europe black letter was used for books printed in the vernacular, roman types for Latin.

Black Memorial Prizes: see *James Tait Black Memorial Prizes.*

Blackwell Prize: a prize of about £75 administered by the University of Aberdeen which makes the award in alternate years for an essay written on a subject selected by the University.

blad: a sample of a book, made up for the publisher's traveller to show to the trade. It usually consists of the first thirty-two pages, including prelims, bound up in the same cloth as the finished book.

Blado, Antonio, 1490–1567: printer to the Vatican from 1515–67. He acquired a cursive type-face, probably designed by Ludovico degli Arrighi in 1526. His use of it in 1539, for the 'Vita sfortiae' of Paolo Giovo, inspired its recutting in 1923 as the *Blado chancery italic* of the Monotype Corporation.

Blaeu press: a hand-printing press devised *c.* 1620 by Wilhelm Janszoon Blaeu (1571–1638), of Amsterdam. It had a suspended platen and was the first press to have a travelling carriage.

Blake, William, 1757–1827: one of the greatest English engravers, remembered particularly for his 'Prophetic Books','Milton', 'Dante', and 'Jerusalem'. He described his books of illustrated verse as 'illuminated printing'. Beginning in 1788 he experimented with printing from relief-etched copper plates on which illustration and text were outlined; some of the etched plates were finished off with a graver. He used a hand-press.
To increase the effect of an illuminated manuscript Blake varied during the printing the tints in which a plate was coloured, changed the order of plates, and transposed parts of the text; while to many impressions he and his wife added colour-washes by hand. Gold and silver further embellished some of his later work.
See G. Keynes and E. Wolf, 'William Blake's Illuminated Books: a Census', New York, Grolier Club, 1953.

Blakeney Press: a one-man private hand-press set up by E. H. Blakeney at Ely in 1908. Small editions of poetry were issued, not for public sale, in addition to occasional prose pamphlets.

blank line: a line which is filled with quads, leads, or blank slugs; a white line in which no letters or other type characters appear. (M.L.)

blanket: a woollen cloth or rubber sheet used in certain circumstances as part of the cylinder packing.

blanks: see *white out.*

bleaching: the process of whitening the fibrous materials of paper as a last stage in the final removal of certain remaining impurities.

bleaching paper: fox marks and certain apparently indelible stains on printed paper can be removed by bleaching. This operation is done in three stages: 1. immersion of the sheet in a weak solution of permanganate of potash and rinsing in clear water; 2. immersion in a hot weak solution of sulphurous acid and rinsing in clear water; 3. immersion in a solution of hypo-sulphate of soda followed by a final rinsing. The paper will now require re-sizing.

bled-off: said of illustrations which spread to the edge of the page, and allow no margins.

bleed: a page margin which has been overcut, thus mutilating the text, is said to bleed.

blind blocking: see *blocking.*

blind folio: any page in the prelims which, while not bearing a number, is included in the pagination.

blind-stamped panels: designs impressed on the leather cover of a book by means of an engraved metal stamp bearing a complete design. A blocking press was used to do this. The art originated in the Low Countries, being practised there from the 14th century. Characteristic designs were animals in circles or loops of foliage. In France the art flourished from 1488–1528; in Germany extensive use was made of blind-stamped panels on pigskin covers, mostly after 1550; in England the era was from 1485–1557, the Royal Arms and heraldic devices being popular motifs. Rectangular panels made with a single stamp continued in use until about 1623.

blind tooling: the impressing of a design on the cover of a book without the use of gold, ink, or foil. Heated tools are used, and pressed into the leather by hand. The amount of pressure directly affects the result, since on some leathers the skin is darkened in proportion to this. The tools are used at lower temperatures than when working with gold leaf.

The use of a die or stamp in a press is referred to as *blocking*.

blinding in: see *tooling*.

block: 1. an engraved or etched zinc or copper plate. Of modern blocks made by photographic processes *line blocks* and *half-tone blocks* are most important. The former gives a reproduction of an original image which consists only of lines, dots, and fully covered surfaces. For reproducing half-tones a screen must be used for dividing the tones into dots of varying extent according to the degree of density of the tone. A block reproduced by screen reproduction is called a *half-tone*; a *combined block* can be made from a line block and a half-tone. In a line block some areas can be coated with *block tone*, i.e. a screen tone of the desired density. This can be done by printing on the metal plate, by transferring, or by placing transparent films on the original image with screen tones imprinted in screen ruling adapted according to the scale of reproduction, for the screen ruling in the half-tone or block tone must be adjusted to the paper used for printing.

Half-tones are usually quadrangular, but are also supplied *vignetted*, the outer edges being milled away so that the main subject stands out. Screen tones can be vignetted. It was formerly common practice to frame the half-tone with a thin border line (block border).

See also *bled off*.

Two-, three-, or four-colour blocks are sets made for printing in the component colours of a coloured reproduction. A *duplex block* is a special two-colour block which is not intended to give a two-colour impression, but rather a mellower picture than an ordinary one-colour half-tone.

A block can be duplicated as an electro or a stereo. Blockmakers charge for blocks according to the surface area, a certain minimum price being fixed (a *minimum block*). For printing on paper with a dull or rough surface special deeply etched blocks are used (engraving blocks), or relief blocks which are more expensive. (G.U.)

See also *blockmaking*, *screen*.

2. a metal stamp, usually of brass, used to impress a complete design on a book cover with one movement, as distinguished from the building up of a pattern with single dies.

See also *binder's brass*.

3. to emboss a book cover with the block described in (2).

block books: books printed from woodcuts, usually of a religious nature. The text was normally limited to a description of the pictorial design. Whole books of text were also cut in wood and a print obtained by rubbing (see *frotton printing*). The date of origin is uncertain but extant examples in Europe belong to the era 1470–1510; the stamping of designs from wooden blocks on to paper is said to have originated in China about A.D. 700 if not earlier. Also known as *xylographs*.

For an illustration see *Biblia pauperum*.

block stitching: an alternative name for *wire stitching* q.v.

blocked up: composed type which cannot be printed off, probably because author's corrections, or special sorts, or paper are awaited.

See also *good*, *live matter*.

blocking: the impressing of a design or lettering on a book cover by machine. The blocking may be blind, ink, foil, or gold leaf.

See also *gold blocking*. Cf. *tooling*.

blocking foils: a foil in its strict sense is metal rolled or beaten to a thin leaf. Imitations of gold leaf, but using bronze powder as the colouring medium and made up in leaf form, are known as foils and used by bookbinders for blocking, as are similar leaves using aluminium or other white metals to imitate silver. White and coloured pigments and also coloured metal powders are made up in the same way. All are used as is gold leaf, the impression being obtained from a heated die and the surplus leaf brushed away. Modern practice, and especially with power-operated blocking presses, is to use foil made in the form of a transfer, the metal or pigment being held on a continuous web of thin paper or material of the cellophane type which is drawn over the heated

Reproduction of a line drawing on a line block

The same line drawing after the addition of mechanical tints

Line block made from an original drawing

Reverse line block from the same drawing

Line block greyed back with mechanical positive tint

Reversed line block with mechanical negative tint

blocks so as to present an unused portion for each impression. The use of any of the foregoing materials is known as *foil blocking* as distinct from blocking in real gold or other precious metals. (L.K.)

See also *blocking press*.

blocking press: a press in which heated blocks are used to stamp designs and lettering on book covers and cases. In machine bookbinding this is done mechanically, gold or pigment foil being fed through the machine on a plastic or paper ribbon which embodies its own size or adhesive. The press is also used for blind or ink blocking (for the latter heat being unnecessary). When gold leaf is used it is first laid on the book cover.

See also *glair*, *gold blocking*, *tip*.

blockmaking: as early as the first half of the 19th century attempts were made to etch copper plates in relief for producing printing blocks. Considerable use was made of a process, invented by the Dane Piil, for transforming a drawing etched in zinc into a relief printing forme (chemitype). Blasius Höfel of Vienna, however, is regarded as the man who introduced zinc as a material for blocks (1840). At first the art of producing an acid-resisting drawing directly on zinc was not known, transfers being used as in lithography. Firmin Gillot in Paris, who was considered to be the inventor of line etching, also worked in this way about 1850. At the same time he experimented with direct printing (asphalt printing) on zinc plates. The foundation of modern blockmaking was laid by Carl Angerer of Vienna in a process for making line blocks which he evolved in 1870. Ten years later Meisenbach and others invented screen process work for making half-tone blocks.

Blockmaking consists of three main parts: photographing, printing, and etching. In *direct reproduction* the negative is exposed in a reproduction camera (see *camera*) with or without a screen, the negative material consisting of wet plates (silver iodide collodion or silver bromide collodion), dry plates, or films (silver bromide gelatine), and is developed, fixed, intensified, and reduced in the way described in the entries dealing with the material concerned. As the image on ordinary blocks must be reversed laterally either the negative must be exposed with the use of a prism or mirror, or else be turned before printing. Wet plates, especially silver iodide collodion plates, afford good opportunities for this, as the light film can easily be removed from the glass base and be transferred by means of a damp sheet of paper to a new base (see *wet plate method*). In this way several exposures can be combined on one printing glass plate. If such a transfer is to be successful the glass supporting the sensitized layer in the camera must be thoroughly cleaned (with spirit and then with talcum) before being prepared. Furthermore, the developed negative must not be intensified with lead. A solution of rubber in benzine is poured over the dry negative, set aside to dry, and then collodion with an addition of castor oil is poured on it. When this coating, too, has dried, the layer round the image is cut through and is soaked in water. A thoroughly damped 'turning paper' is laid on the layer which is to be lifted, and after raising a corner of the layer carefully with a knife, it is pulled off by means of the paper which is readily accompanied by the layer. In the same way the layer is transferred to another damp paper and from it on to glass, where a thin solution of gum arabic has been poured. A rubber brush is used to smooth the transfer papers on their bases. If the pouring over the original negative is done with a thicker collodion layer or with a solution of gelatine which is allowed to solidify, while the glass lies horizontally, layers are obtained after pulling off which are strong enough to be used as film negatives.

In screen reproduction, especially in colour, the original image is often first exposed without a screen and then an 'intermediate copy' of this negative is made on paper or transparency material. Such indirect reproduction is used in order to facilitate retouching these half-tone negatives by reducing, intensifying, or masking.

Block printing aims at producing a copy of the line or screen negative on metal. The positive copy on metal should be capable of resisting the influence of an etching acid, so that the latter only attacks the metal on the exposed surfaces between the details of the image. In order to obtain a copy suitable for etching, the negative must have the greatest possible contrasts between the highlights and the dense shadows. The earliest known and used printing medium was asphalt (bitumen) which was dissolved in benzol and spread on the metal surface in a very thin coating. After drying, this was sensitive to light and could be exposed under a negative and developed with turpentine into a positive image.

The discovery of the sensitivity of chrome compounds in combination with gelatine, glue, and other substances laid the foundations for modern and quicker printing processes. The first of these, still much in use, is the *albumen process*, q.v. The printing solution is spread on a metal plate by a whirler and the dried layer is exposed through a negative in a printing frame, or in some cases in a step-and-repeat machine, usually with light from an arc or a mercury lamp. After developing, a positive copy in stiff ink is made on the plate. This is dusted with asphalt powder any loose powder being removed. The plate is heated and the powder melts into a layer which forms a strong etching resist. The albumen process was originally used for printing line drawings (line blocks) and

Lifting the wet plate layer from its glass base for turning

Etching the block in a bath

Inking up a line block

is still considered to be the best for fine line negatives. When half-tone printing was invented, screen negatives were also printed in this way at first. In Britain and America, where copper was largely used for making half-tone blocks, the *enamel process* which gives an acid-resisting layer lasting throughout the etching process was introduced. This method is less suitable for zinc, a metal in which the crystal structure changes and becomes brittle when heated to the temperature required by the process. By using a layer of shellac resistance to acid was achieved without heating to such high temperatures. At first these cold enamel processes were based on the principle of two layers, the one nearer the metal surface forming a film of resin soluble only in alcohol or oils, while the top layer was of chromate enamel which was exposed and developed in the usual way. After drying, the lower layer could be dissolved on the areas not protected by the enamel. This method of working was, however, very delicate and was completely superseded by the cold top enamel process introduced in 1922 and now predominating in blockmaking. Cold top enamel provides a protection against etching by heating to not more than 100° C (212° F), a temperature which all metals used in blockmaking will withstand.

Etching. The metals used in blockmaking are zinc, copper, and sometimes brass. Rolled zinc plates of specially pure quality, 2 mm. thick, are used. For bookbinding purposes zinc blocks are made up to a thickness of 7 mm. but brass is here the most usual metal. Copper blocks are made for printing long runs, especially for colour printing, but since the introduction of the cold top enamel process copper has lost some of its importance. Zinc is excellent for etching with nitric acid; for copper and brass, solutions of perchloride are used. The etching of line blocks is done in a slightly different manner from that of half-tone blocks. The lines in the former are generally separated by comparatively large non-image areas which must be etched to a considerable depth to avoid taking up ink from the rollers. Half-tones, consisting of minute dots separated by very small spaces, can be etched to a much shallower depth since the close dots prevent both the ink rollers and the paper from sinking into the cavities (coarse screens and coarse paper increase the need for deep etching). The deep etching required by line blocks cannot be completed in one operation, as the acid would then also attack the sides of the raised lines which correspond to the lines of the image. The etching must be done in stages, the side surfaces being protected by inking up the block in such a way that they, too, are covered. The albumen process can, therefore, be used for line blocks without much inconvenience in spite of its not providing permanent protection against acid, whereas the enamel process

Squared-up half-tone

Squared-up half-tone with rule added

Oval half-tone

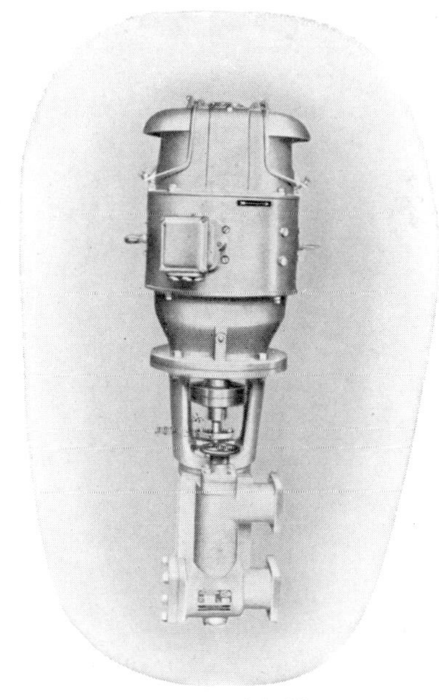

Soft vignetted half-tone

Cut out half-tone

Hard vignetted half-tone

(*Block*)

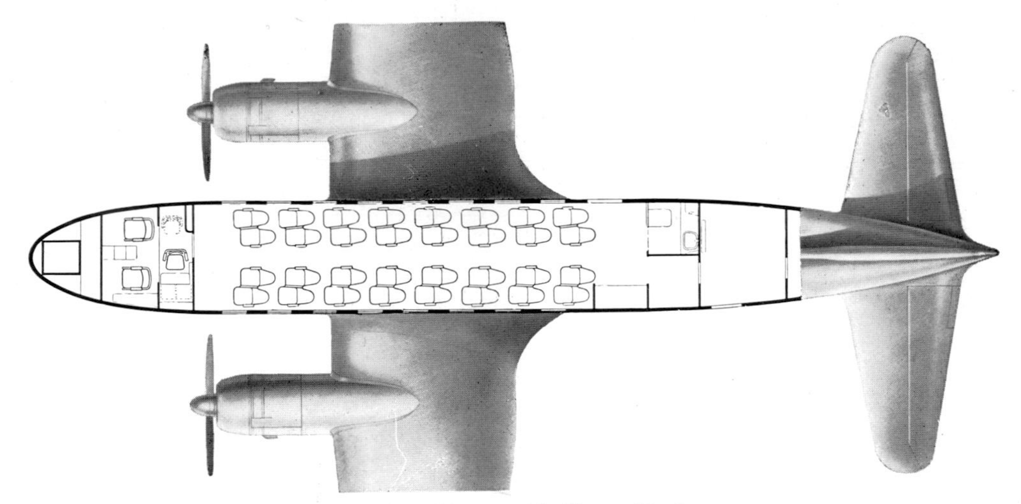

Combined line and half-tone block

Deep-etched half-tone

or the cold top enamel process are preferred for etching half-tones in order to avoid the need for repeated inking up as a protection against acid.

The etching of a line block begins by *rough etching* (sometimes preceded by a still weaker preparatory etching) which is done in an etching bath with about 4% nitric acid. The rough-etched block is dried and the stiff ink (from the albumen process) is washed off with turpentine. The block is inked up with a glazed roller and with ink of such consistency that it also settles on the sides of the etched lines. The layer of ink is sprinkled with powdered resin which is then melted by heating. If needed, further strengthening is done by sprinkling and melting powdered asphalt. Where the lines are very close to each other the intervals are filled in this inking up and are thus protected against further etching. Other intervals may also absorb ink, but this must be removed by scraping before the next *intermediate etching* which is done in 10–15% acid. By this the metal is etched to a depth of 1/20 mm. or slightly more. After the intermediate etching, inking up is repeated as before, but now a thinner ink is used which covers the more deeply etched side surfaces. Powdering and heating are done as before, if necessary with the addition of graphite. Finally comes the *deep etching* in about 25% acid. By this the deepest places are etched to about ½ mm. below the original level. This gradual etching gives the sides of the lines a number of distinct ledges which easily absorb ink in printing and must therefore be removed by *round etching*. This is usually done in two stages, first inking up, so that the ink reaches the lowest ledge which can then be etched away in about 15% acid. Then the process is repeated using stiffer ink and weaker acid. The last traces of the etching ledges are removed by clean etching in weak acid, and then inking up in such a way that only the surface of the image is covered. In using enamel-processed plates this inking up is unnecessary as the protecting layer has remained unaffected during the whole etching process.

The procedure described is adopted with numerous modifications in various blockmaking establishments. In Gillot's original etching method the etched metal surface was gummed and damped before being inked up (in much the same way as in lithographic printing), so that the scraping was unnecessary, and this 'French method' is still occasionally used in reproducing delicate line drawings, although it has been ousted to a great extent by Angerer's dry 'Vienna method'.

In etching a half-tone block with a comparatively close screen the necessary depth can often be attained by a single etching and without any precautions for protecting the sides of the picture dots. Nevertheless, the etching is often interrupted after a *rough etching*,

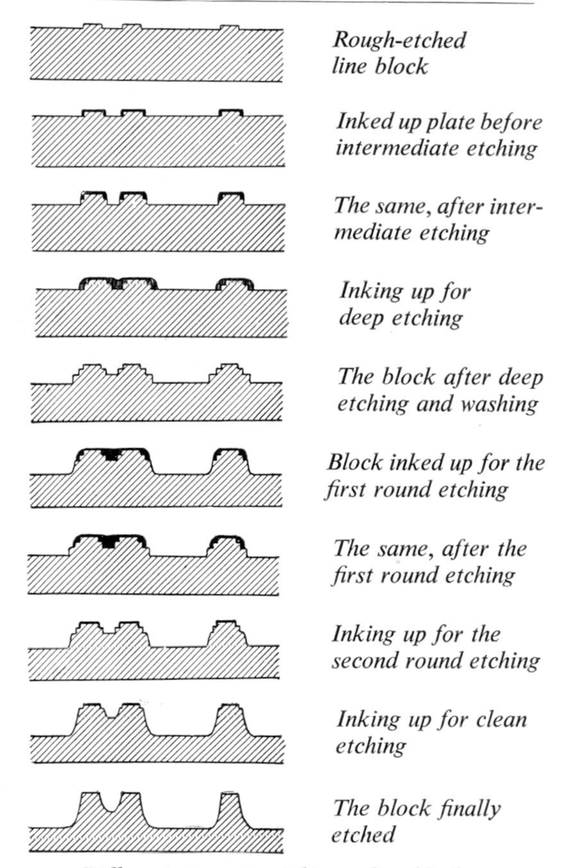

Different stages in etching a line block

Painting out a half-tone with acid-resisting varnish during tone etching

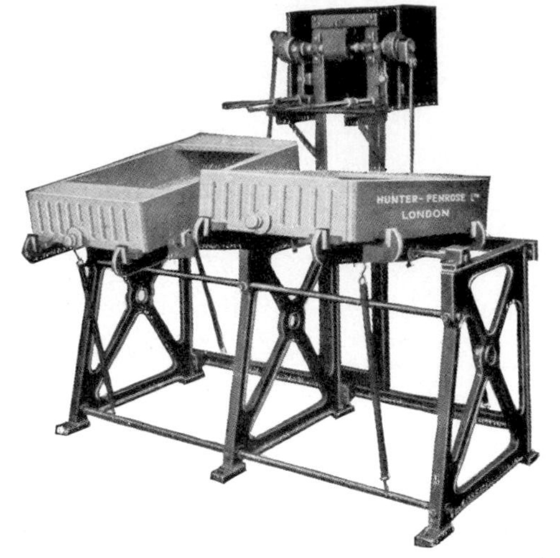

Hunter–Penrose etching bath with automatic rockers

Routing the block

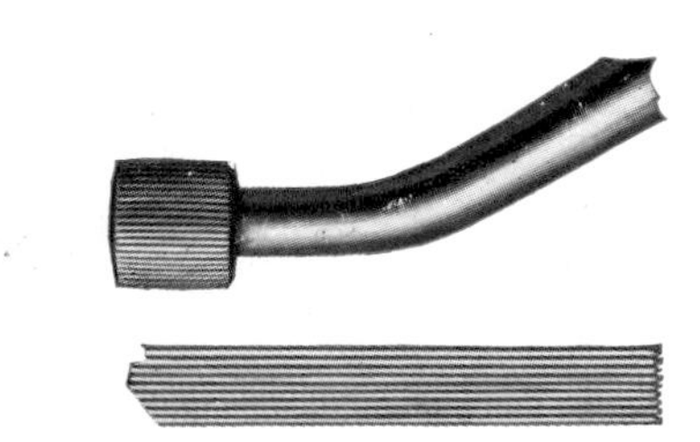

Enlargement of a roulette and screen burin

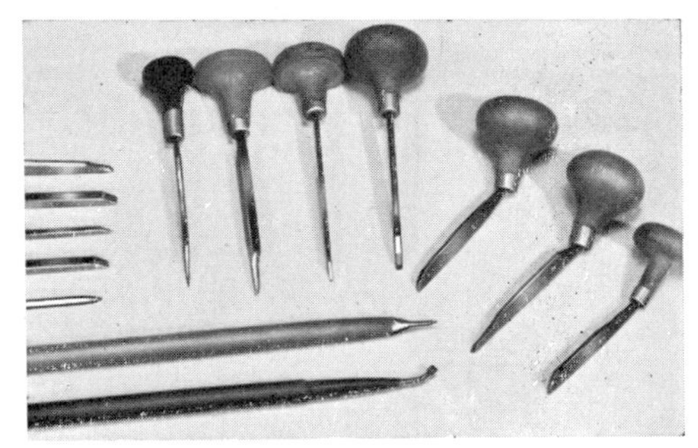

Some of the tools used in engraving and correcting blocks: burins of different kinds, burnisher, roulette, needle

When typesetting and casting by machinery parts of the slugs can be cast to such a height that they form a mount for a cut-in block

and the dark areas are painted out with asphalt varnish or thick chalk before continuing. This is repeated one or more times, and this *tone etching* can be renewed after proof-printing the block.

Etching can be done partly with a brush, in a rocking bath, or in an etching machine. In both brush etching and painting out the operator usually kneads chalk or magnesia into the half-tone block in order to see the image more clearly. The progress of the etching is checked through a magnifying glass. After taking a proof, especially in the case of colour work, various corrections are made. These may require renewed etching or mechanical treatment with different tools. These include engraver's tools with differently shaped edges (wedge-ended needle, round burin, flat burin, graver, screen burin, etc.; see illustration). With a screen burin, precisely fitted into the screen network of the half-tone, a tone can be 'drawn through', so that it becomes lighter, and the same procedure can be adopted with a dotting wheel, chiefly in order to smooth a tone surface. A tone can be intensified by flattening the dots with a burnisher. Any etching ledges in line blocks which have not disappeared in the round and clean etching are removed with a flat or round burin. In blockmaking establishments there is often a special engraver in charge of such work. By the skilful use of a graver any ragged or missing lines can be engraved higher and, if necessary, the metal can be punched up from the back for this purpose. In line blocks there are mostly large blank (non-image) areas, and in these places the remaining metal is lowered still further or removed entirely with a router, which can also be used for vignetting half-tones. Other blockmaking tools include the elliptograph for cutting out oval or circular border lines, jig saws, circular saws, guillotine cutters for sawing and dividing block plates, and trimmers for the rectangular cutting of blocks.

Mounting blocks. In most cases the blockmaking establishment supplies blocks mounted on a wooden base. On line blocks enough metal is left on the blank areas to allow for nailing, but on half-tone blocks a special bevelled edge must be provided round the image in which holes for nails can be made. This is done on a bevelling machine. The wooden mount on which the block is nailed must be of a definite height, and have perfectly smooth surfaces at right-angles to each other. Special trimming machines, smoothing planes, or planing trimmers are available, and there are Universal machines which embody combinations of all the auxiliary machines for completing blocks.

Mahogany and oak are stable woods, but if printing is done from the blocks themselves (and not from stereos) wooden mounts are unsuitable. Synthetic material (artificial resin) is also used for mounts, and successful experiments have been made with soft wood impregnated with artificial resin which is then hardened. Iron bases are preferable, but they require special mounting devices. (See *plate-dog*.) In some methods the block is fixed by means of slots cut in the base or sides. These are made in machines in blockmaking establishments or printing works, and offer the advantage of producing half-tone blocks without bevelled edges, so that the accompanying text can be placed flush with the image. This is the case, too, in mounting by pasting on masonite or lead plates, or in soldering on the latter. Recent British developments are honeycomb bases of duralumin or Elektron (magnesium) and special adhesives.

Blocks of copper, brass, etc., are produced in a similar way to zinc blocks, though with the use of other etching fluids. As already stated, ferric chloride is suitable for etching copper and brass, and can be used on steel.

Zinc blocks are often nickel-plated to increase their resistance to mechanical and chemical stresses; copper blocks can be chrome-plated or steel-faced for the same purpose.

See also *Astrascribe*, *Collobloc*, *Dow-Birmetals etching machine*, *electronic photoengraving machine*, *Formapex*, *Lithotex-Dirats etcher*.

Blooteling, Abraham, 1640–90: the inventor, about 1672, of the rocker used to give a pitted surface to plates for mezzotinting.

See also *mezzotint*.

Blower Linotype: the first Linotype in commercial use (1886). It was so named because matrices were carried to the assembler by a blast of air.

Blue Book: an official report of the Parliament of the United Kingdom and the Privy Council issued in a blue paper cover.

blueprint: a blue on white or white on blue print submitted as a rough proof by the blockmaker before blocks are available.

blurb: a colloquial term for the short note by the publisher describing and recommending a book or its author. This is usually printed on the jacket and sometimes at the beginning of the prelims.

See also *gutting*, *puff*.

B.N.B.: see *British National Bibliography*.

board covers: in bookbinding, a style of cover made from heavy cardboard, used for certain classes of school and other books, where an inexpensive yet fairly durable binding is required. (M.L.)

board glazed: a paper-finishing process in which boards are used instead of metal plates. The resulting surface is smooth but not highly glazed.

board paper: see *end-papers.*

boarding leather: the process of rolling dampened leather to emphasize the natural grain or to modify it in some way.

boards: 1. a general term for *millboards* and *strawboards* qq.v., when used for book covers. The substitution of these for the wooden boards previously employed is attributed to Aldus Manutius.

See also *liners, split boards.*

2. a term for certain types of card used in printing. *Bristol* boards are the best quality, and are made from rag. *Ivory* boards are good quality, made from wood. The term *pasted* indicates that the finished board has been laminated by the use of an adhesive (usually paste).

See also *fashion boards.*

Boar's Head Press: a private press founded by Christopher Sandford in 1931. He later acquired the *Golden Cockerel Press,* q.v.

bocasin: a fine quality buckram.

bodkin: a pointed steel tool secured in a wooden handle. It is used to lever up type when correcting.

Also known as a *spike.*

Bodley, Sir Thomas, 1545–1613: the diplomatist and scholar who financed the re-building between 1598 and 1602 of Oxford University Library which bears his name. From 1600 he solicited donations of books from wealthy and learned patrons, and he employed agents abroad to buy books and manuscripts. The library was opened in 1602 with a stock of about 2000 volumes, and may be considered the first semi-public library in Europe.

In 1610 Bodley concluded with the Stationers' Company an arrangement for the presentation of a copy of every book printed and published by members, a fore-runner of the *statutory copies,* q.v., still received.

See W. D. Macray, 'Annals of the Bodleian Library, Oxford, A.D. 1598–A.D. 1867', Rivingtons, 1868; and Sir Edmund Craster, 'History of the Bodleian Library, 1845–1945', O.U.P., 1952.

Bodmer, Martin, 1899–   : a Swiss banker, born in Zürich, who owns one of the world's finest private collections of Shakespeariana, forming part of his 'Bibliothek der Weltliteratur' at Grand Cologny, Geneva. Dr. Bodmer began collecting books after a trip to the U.S.A. in 1919, where he acquired his first English sets; but the kernel of his collection was formed around first editions of Goethe and the German classics and romantics of the same period. From Goethe came the idea of 'Weltliteratur', i.e. the great texts from Homer and the Bible to the present; in general poetry and literature in its proper sense, but including all important religious, philosophical, and scientific texts. All major languages are represented.

Dr. Bodmer writes 'I have always tried to have texts as near as possible to their origin. If this is not possible by manuscripts, I have the first prints, beginning with the Gutenberg Bible, about 500 incunabula, and all the important firsts from the 16th to the 20th century. From all eminent authors, from the Renaissance to our time, I try to have also an important or significant specimen in holograph MS. The collection contains over 1000.

'The "big five"—Homer, the Bible, Dante, Shakespeare, and Goethe—are specially developed. From Homer I have a very important papyrus scroll from the second century A.D., containing the 5th Canto of the Iliad, and also a 2nd-century papyrus with the almost complete Gospel of St John in Greek.'

The library contains about 70,000 items and is select rather than large.

The Shakespeariana is said to include the most perfect set in existence of the four Folios; an extensive group of quarto editions of the plays, and an uncut copy of 'Troilus and Cressida' (STC 22331) made unique as the only copy of any of Shakespeare's plays, printed during his lifetime, to survive in this state. This magnificent collection of folios and quartos was assembled over a period of years by the late Dr. A. S. W. Rosenbach, and sold to Dr. Bodmer in 1952.

Bodoni, Giambattista, 1740–1813: an Italian printer and punch-cutter born at Saluzzo, Piedmont. As a pupil of Abbot Ruggiero at the Congregation de Propaganda Fide, Rome, he printed his first book in 1762. Invited by Ferdinand of Parma to direct his newly established printing office, Bodoni became the most celebrated printer of his day. His finest books were Horace, 1791, Virgil, 1793, and Homer's Iliad, 1808. In his 'Inventory of Types' issued in 1788 (2nd ed. 1818 entitled 'Manuale tipografico') there are, inclusive of different sizes, 291 roman and italic typefaces. Most famous is the modern face he designed in 1790; under the name 'Bodoni' this is still supplied by most large foundries and matrix makers.

The Italian firm *Officina Bodoni,* q.v., founded in 1922, was granted sole rights by the Italian Government to use the original matrices of Bodoni.

body: 1. the shank of a type.

2. the measurement of thickness from back to front of a type, slug, lead, or rule, etc. The standard

measurements according to the British-American Point System are:—

5-point	0·0692 in.	14-point	0·1937 in.
6-point	0·0830 in.	16-point	0·2213 in.
7-point	0·0968 in.	18-point	0·2490 in.
8-point	0·1107 in.	24-point	0·3320 in.
9-point	0·1245 in.	30-point	0·4150 in.
10-point	0·1383 in.	36-point	0·4980 in.
11-point	0·1522 in.	48-point	0·6640 in.
12-point	0·1660 in.		

3. the main portion of a book, excluding the prelims, appendices, etc.

body-em: the em of any fount. The width is the same as the body, i.e. the em is square in section except in types cast on Monotype machines where the width of the em is related to the comparative width of the type design, e.g. in a 10-point fount of 9½ set the em will measure 10 points in body and 9½ points laterally.

body paper: the paper forming the base of coated stock.

body type: the type used for the main body of a work, excluding displayed matter.

Bohn, Henry George, 1796–1884: a London publisher and secondhand bookseller. In the mid-century he achieved fame and success as the publisher of several libraries (or series) totalling over 600 volumes. On retiring from business his copyrights were sold, Chatto & Windus acquiring many.

Bohn, John, 1757–1843: a German binder who opened premises in London in 1795. He was noted for such finishing details as gilded doublures, paper marbling, etc., and supplied these items to other binders.

boiler: the container in which such raw materials of paper as esparto, rags, straw, etc., are boiled. Cf. *digester*.

boiling agent: chemicals with which wood chips are boiled, or cooked, in a *digester*, q.v., as a preliminary stage of making *chemical wood* pulp, q.v.

bold face: type having a conspicuous black, heavy appearance, but based on the same designs as its *medium* weight in the same *fount*, qq.v. Bold can normally be set or tapped in the same line, as in the entry words of this book.

bole: 1. to reduce height of type by shaving the feet.
2. see *Armenian bole*.

bolts: three of the edges of a folded sheet in bookbinding. Hence, head bolts, fore-edge bolts, tail bolts. The folded edge at the back of a sheet is not referred to as a *bolt*; it is termed the *last fold* or *back fold*. Until the folds have been cut away by machine, or cut through by hand, the leaves cannot be opened. (L.K.)

See also *opened, uncut*.

book: for statistical purposes the British book trade assumes that a book is a publication costing sixpence or more. Other countries define a book as containing a minimum number of pages, but have not agreed on a standard number. At a UNESCO conference in 1950 a book was defined as 'a non-periodical literary publication containing forty-nine or more pages, not counting the covers'.

book auction: a place where books are sold to the highest bidder for them. It is believed that the selling of books by auction originated in Holland, where in 1599 the library of Philip van Marnix was sold in this way. The earliest English book auction of which a catalogue survives was held in 1676 by William Cooper in Little Britain: he sold the collection of Dr. Lazarus Seaman for about £3000. By 1700 London auctioneers were commissioned to sell collections in the provinces. Taverns and coffee houses were often used for the purpose of sales until well into the 18th century.

It was not until 1744 that Samuel Baker of Covent Garden founded the first auction room in England solely for the disposal of books, manuscripts, and prints. (For the subsequent history of this firm see *Sotheby & Co.*)

The earliest book auction in America appears to be the isolated example of Ebenezer Pembaton at Boston in 1717.

Book-Auction Records: first edited by Frank Karslake, and published by Stevens, as a quarterly record of London, New York, etc., book auctions, with annual cumulations. Vol. I appeared in 1903 (from June 1902), and the work continues. General indexes are issued periodically.

Book Buyers Guild: a company formed in London in 1957 to promote the sale of books by a credit scheme. A prospective member submits personal particulars to the Guild, and indicates the bookseller from whom he wishes to make future purchases. After accepting the member, the Guild informs the bookseller that in future Mr. X will buy books from him and has a credit rating of £Y. The member has credit with only one bookseller. When supplying books, the bookseller sends a copy of the order to the Guild, or if supplying from stock, he sends the Guild a record of the transaction. In either case a special form is used. The bookseller does not collect or account for money, his only responsibility being to keep the member's account within a set limit, of which he is notified monthly.

The member is invoiced monthly by the Guild, his account showing details of purchases made during the month and the total amount outstanding. Interest is added at the rate of $\frac{1}{2}$ per cent per month, and 11 per cent of the total outstanding is shown as due and payable. Thus the member is able to stagger his book purchases over nine months, paying interest at the annual rate of 6 per cent. There is no down payment.

The bookseller receives monthly an account of what is due to him for all Guild sales during the previous month. His account is discounted 10 per cent and he receives a monthly cheque for 90 per cent of his sales.

book case: see *case* (1).

book clamp: a device used by bookbinders to hold books together. (M.L.)

book cloth: dyed and treated calico used for book covers. This was introduced to the binding trade about 1822 by William Pickering of the *Chiswick Press*, q.v., and Leighton, the binder. A variety of canvas had occasionally been used for covering books in the late 18th century but it had not been developed. In modern usage there are two main groups of cloth:—thin, hard surface cloths which contain starch filling; and matt, unglazed cloths resembling heavy linen and having less starch than the former. The use of cloth for *edition binding*, q.v., increased during the 19th century, and thus became a charge to the publisher who in former times had issued books in folded sections, sewn or unsewn, and protected only by a wrapper.

See also *linson*.

book club: 1. a business organization which selects from current books a monthly choice for its subscribers, e.g. The Book Society.

2. a similar organization which publishes limited de luxe or cheap editions for members, e.g. Folio Society, Readers' Union.

book clubs and printing societies: bodies formed for the private printing of works which would not, because of their specialized nature, be published as commercial ventures. While often characterized by their scholarly editing, they are not always typographically remarkable. Notes on the following clubs and societies are given under their names: *Abbotsford, Aelfric, Antiquarian Etching, Bannatyne, Bibliographical, Border, Cambridge Bibliographical, Camden, Cavendish, Caxton, Chaucer, Chetham, Early English Text, Edinburgh Bibliographical, English Historical, Etching, First Edition, Fleuron, Galley, Gesellschaft der Bibliophilen, Grolier, Hakluyt, Hanserd Knollys, Harleian, Huguenot, Maitland, Malone, Manx, Motett, Musical Antiquarian, Newcastle on Tyne Typographical, Ossianic, Parker, Percy, Philobiblon, Pipe Roll, Ray, Roxburghe, Scottish Text, Spenser, Spottiswoode, Surtees, Sydenham, Verulam, Welsh Manuscript, Wernerian, Woodrow, Ye Sette of Odd Volumes.*

See also *private press*.

Book Clubs Group: founded in 1951, within the Publishers Association, to bring about co-operation between book clubs in their dealings with publishers, to ensure adherence to regulations drawn up for the conduct of book clubs, and to establish community of outlook towards other parties concerned with various subsidiary rights.

The Book Collector: since 1952, a quarterly journal for those interested in the collection and study of printed books and manuscripts. It incorporates 'Bibliographical Notes and Queries' and 'Book Handbook'.

Articles are specialized and of high standard. This elegant journal is printed at Hertford and published in London by the Shenval Press on Grosvenor Chater's Basingwerk Parchment, resulting in a most felicitous combination of scholarship and good taste.

book collector: according to Bernard Quaritch, who is quoted below, a *bibliophile*, q.v. In his 'Contributions towards a dictionary of English book-collectors', fourteen parts, London, 1892–1921, he states: 'The reader is a destroyer of books; he is undeserving of the title of book-collector, a title which connotes the idea of book-preserver. In order to preserve them, one must not read them. The man who reads his books does not expect to amass many, and is therefore devoid of that fine ambition which stimulates the bibliophile who knows that if he collects a sufficient number of rare and choice books, he is, provided he do not injure them by use, winning for himself a loftier distinction than knightage or even baronage could give. His name goes down to posterity with the library in which he has preserved things that future scholars will want to see; and in the far-off years it will receive semi-divine honours.'

There must, however, be many collectors of books who buy them to read or study, with no thought for posterity.

See Robert L. Collison, 'Book collecting: an introduction to modern methods of literary and bibliographical detection', Benn, 1957.

The Book-Collector's Quarterly: a periodical devoted 'wholeheartedly to the interests of those who collect books of any kind'. It was edited by Desmond

Flower and A. J. A. Symons, and was first published in London in December 1930 by Cassell & Co. Ltd. and The First Edition Club (whose official organ it was). The origin of this periodical lay in Flower's desire to revive the 'Bibliophile's Almanack', founded in 1920 by Harold Child and Oliver Simon, and printed at the Curwen Press. This had lapsed in the 1920's.

The Quarterly, also printed at the Curwen Press, maintained a high standard of production and editorial excellence. The final number, XVII, appeared in 1935.

book-fell: an obsolete term for a sheet or manuscript of parchment or vellum.

book form: said of a work which is issued within covers after having previously appeared in a journal, pamphlet, or newspaper. An example was Ernest Hemingway's novel 'Old Man and the Sea', issued in book form in the U.K. by Jonathan Cape after first publication in 'Life Magazine'.

book hand: any of several scripts used for manuscript books before the introduction of printing. Among examples are *black letter*, *cancellaresca formata*, *Carolingian script*, *cursive*, *half-uncial*, and *uncials*, qq.v.

See also *letters—forms and styles.*

Book Handbook: a periodical for book collectors, edited by Ronald Horrox, and first published in London in 1947. One volume was issued between then and 1950. The second and final volume, issued in 1951, was printed and published by the *Dropmore Press*, q.v. The 'Book Handbook' was then incorporated in *The Book Collector*, q.v., which until mid-1955 was also printed by the Dropmore Press.

Book Impositions 1956: a book setting forth diagrams of the impositions required for the various types of book-folding machine. It is published by the British Federation of Master Printers and is the standard work on the subject, containing full information for printing sheets for machine folding.

The 1956 edition is a revise of earlier editions, the first having been compiled by the Master Bookbinders Association (now the Master Binders Alliance of London) in 1927 'with the object of removing misunderstanding between Publishers, Printers and Binders on matters relating to machine folding'. (L.K.)

book jacket: see *jacket.*

book-mark: a piece of card, paper, ribbon, or other material slipped between the pages of a book to mark a particular place. (M.L.)

Book of Hours: a book of personal prayers for use by the laity. The usual contents were:

1. Calendar.
2. Four lessons from the Gospels.
3. Service for the Canonical Hours, the preparation and first few words of the Psalms, prayers, and hymns.
4. Seven penitential Psalms.
5. Choral portion of the Office for the Dead.
6. Miscellaneous meditations.

Such books were popular throughout Europe from the 12th to early 16th centuries and were usually illuminated. The most sumptuous specimen is 'Les très riches heures du duc de Berry', now in the Musée Condé, Chantilly, France.

The first version printed in Paris was issued by Antoine Vérard in 1487; the finest were issued by Philippe Pigouchet from 1491–1505: other editions appeared until 1568.

Also known as *Livre d'Heures* or *Horae.*

book papers: a generic term for all papers used in book production; *furnish*, q.v., may be anything from rag to wood pulp.

Book-Prices Current: first edited by J. H. Slater, published by Elliot Stock (1837–1911), 'being a record of the prices at which books have been sold at auction, the titles and descriptions in full, the names of the purchasers, etc.', London, 1888 (for 1887) to date. Occasional cumulative indexes are published.

book-ring: a group of persons, usually dealers, at an auction sale of books who have agreed in advance not to bid against each other. Sale prices are thus kept low. The dealers then meet for a private auction and divide among themselves the difference between the public and private sale prices.

book satchel: see *polaires.*

book shrine: see *cumdach.*

book sizes: these are standard sizes of British books with the usual abbreviations used in trade catalogues:

abbrev.	*name*	*inches*	*cm.*
Pott8	Pott Octavo	6¼ × 4	15·8
F'cap8	Foolscap Octavo	6¾ × 4¼	17·1
Cr.8	Crown Octavo	7½ × 5	19·0
L.Post8	Large Post Octavo	8¼ × 5¼	20·9
Dy8	Demy Octavo	8¾ × 5⅝	22·2
Med.8	Medium Octavo	9 × 5¾	22·8
Roy.8	Royal Octavo	10 × 6¼	25·4
SuR8	Super Royal Octavo	10 × 6¾	25·4
Imp8	Imperial Octavo	11 × 7½	27·9
F'cap4	Foolscap Quarto	8½ × 6¾	21·5
Cr.4	Crown Quarto	10 × 7½	25·4
L.Post4	Large Post Quarto	10½ × 8¼	26·6
Dy4	Demy Quarto	11¼ × 8¾	28·5
Med.4	Medium Quarto	11½ × 9	29·2
Roy.4	Royal Quarto	12½ × 10	31·7
F'cap fol	Foolscap Folio	13½ × 8½	34·2

(*The centimetre figure is for vertical height*)

It will be seen from this list that the word 'octavo' alone is not a definition of size since octavo volumes vary in vertical height from Pott Octavo, 6¼ in., to Imperial Octavo, 11 in. See also *folio, octavo, quarto.*

See also British Standard 1413: 1947, 'Book Sizes and Dating of Books'.

American book sizes are given next: in several instances there are minor differences between these and the British sizes with a common name, nor are the sizes absolute.

name	*inches*
Thirty-sixmo	4 × 3⅓
Medium Thirty-twomo	4¾ × 3
Medium Twenty-fourmo	5½ × 3⅝
Medium Eighteenmo	6⅔ × 4
Medium Sixteenmo	6¾ × 4½
Cap Octavo	7 × 7¼
Duodecimo	7½ × 4½
Crown Octavo	7½ × 5
Post Octavo	7½ × 5½
Medium Duodecimo	7⅔ × 5⅛
Demy Octavo	8 × 5½
Small Quarto (usually less)	8½ × 7
Broad Quarto (varies up to 13 × 10)	8½ × 7
Medium Octavo	9½ × 6
Royal Octavo	10 × 6½
Super Royal Octavo	10½ × 7
Imperial Quarto	11 × 15
Imperial Octavo	11½ × 8¼

(*The first column gives the vertical height*)

The Book Society: an organization founded in London in 1928 for distributing to its members recommended new books at the full published price. (It is thus not a book club in the normal sense of the term, since editions are neither printed specially for it nor offered as bargains.)

A company was formed under the management of Alan Bott (who later founded 'The Reprint Society' and Pan Books Ltd.), with an independent literary committee assembled by Sir Hugh Walpole to select books. Advance copies of likely titles were sent by publishers and the first 'choice' was Helen Beauclerk's 'The Love of the Foolish Angel', posted to the first 2000 members in April 1929. Members also received 'The Book Society News' which gave notes on new books.

The constitution of the selection committee has frequently changed since its inception, and has included many distinguished authors, but its terms of reference have not altered. The Book Society neither claims to find masterpieces, nor dictates to its members what they shall read. Membership is now world wide, and there are many among them who welcome the monthly recommendations of what will be worthwhile reading, and respect the standard implied by the book wrapper legend 'Recommended by the Book Society' or 'Chosen by the Book Society'.

Book Tokens Limited: a scheme devised in 1928 by Harold Raymond, a director of Chatto & Windus and the Hogarth Press. All shares are held by the *Booksellers Association*, q.v., for whom the National Book Council (now the *National Book League*, q.v.) managed the scheme until 1943 when it became a limited company. Book Tokens Ltd. exists to promote the sale of books by making the giving of them as presents more felicitous than was formerly always the case, since the recipient of a greetings card, bearing stamps worth 3/6, 5/–, 7/6, 10/6, 12/6, 21/–, or combinations of these, sent by its purchaser, can redeem it from any member bookseller for a book of his or her own choice.

Book Trade Benevolent Committee: an organization set up in 1955 to be responsible for the collection of donations for the benefit of the Booksellers Provident Institution, the National Book Trade Provident Society, the Booksellers Provident Retreat, and the Book Trade Hardship Fund. All of these are book trade charities, the Booksellers Provident Institution being the largest and oldest. The first two are mainly concerned with the relief of distress among members, former members (and their dependants) of the trade, and the Retreat offers accommodation for former members of the trade in homes at Abbots Langley, Herts. The Hardship Fund is a means of giving assistance to those deserving it who are not eligible for help within the rules of the other bodies.

Book Wholesalers Association: an association formed in 1957 by representatives of the British wholesale book trade. The address of the secretary is 13 Sackville Road, Bexhill, Sussex.

bookbinding: the hand or machine processes of fastening together the printed sheets of a work and enclosing them within a protecting cover. For comprehensive references see *bookbinding materials, bookbinding methods and processes, bookbinding styles and binding features, bookbinding tools.*

Historical. As a protection for medieval manuscript books thin wooden boards were used for covers, and during the early Middle Ages these were given a leather covering to join across the spine the back and front board, thereby giving rise to binding in the modern sense. Oxhide and pigskin were mostly used; calf was introduced in the 15th century, when parchment bindings also became popular. About 1500 cardboard was substituted for wooden boards in Italy where, at the same time, coverings of imported goatskin (morocco) were extensively employed. In

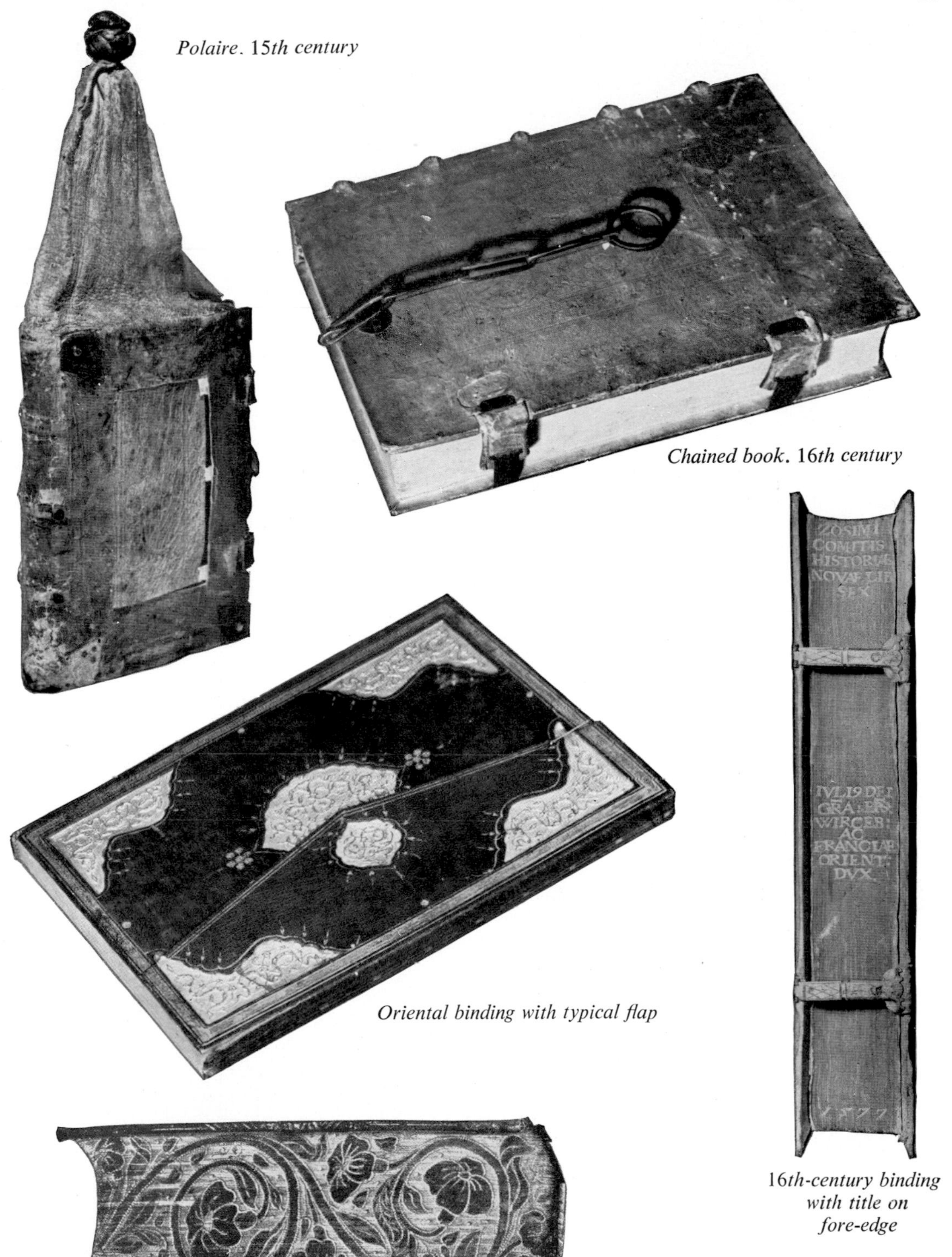

Polaire. 15*th century*

Chained book. 16*th century*

Oriental binding with typical flap

16*th-century binding with title on fore-edge*

Incised and painted edge of Jacob Krause (1526–85)

(*Bookbinding*)

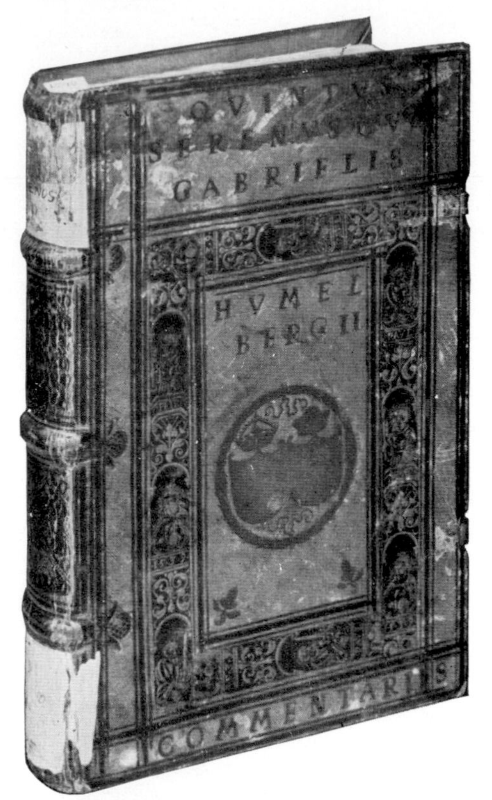

16*th-century blind stamped binding*

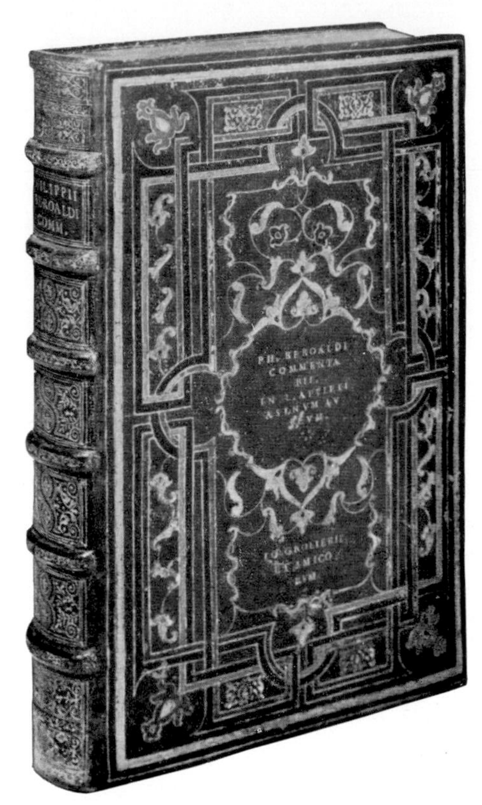

Grolier binding

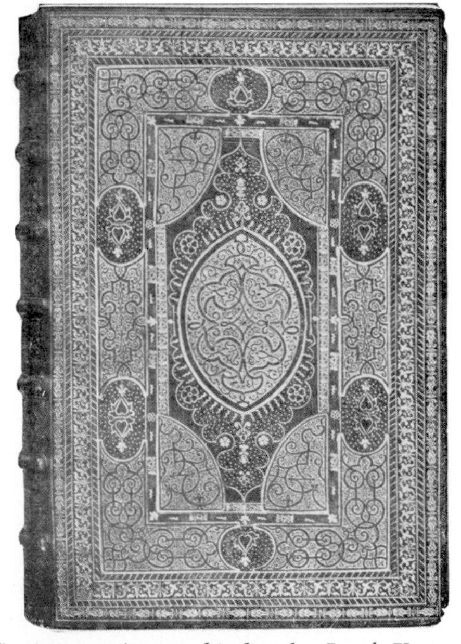

German renaissance binding by Jacob Krause

16*th-century fanfare binding attributed to Nicolas Eve*

Swedish embroidered binding. 17*th century*

17*th-century fan binding*

Derome dentelle binding. 18*th century*

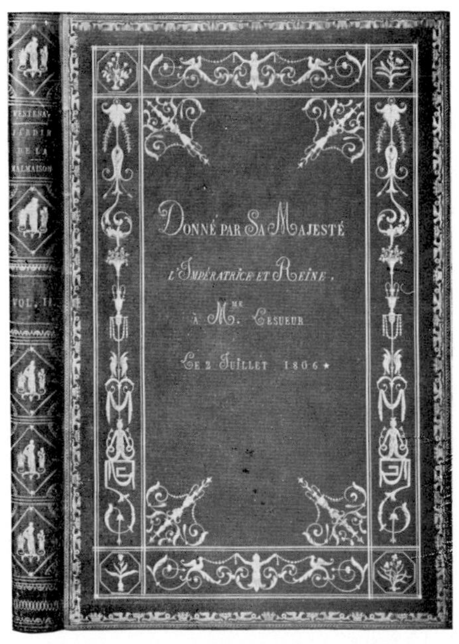

19*th-century French Empire binding*

(*Bookbinding*)

Roger Payne binding
18*th century*

Swedish binding
dated 1796

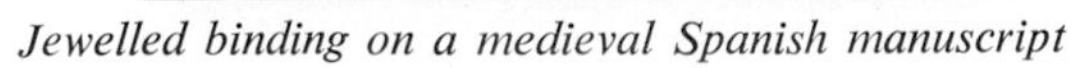

Jewelled binding on a medieval Spanish manuscript

Swedish binding of silver. 19*th century*

Germany, however, wooden boards continued in use until the 18th century. *Full leather* bindings, though modified to the requirements of modern bookbinding technique, maintain their superiority, but in more general use (particularly on the Continent) are *half-bound* books, and in England and America *cased books*.

If cloth is substituted for leather we have a *cloth* or *half-cloth* binding, and if only boards and paper are used the term *paper boards* is applied. If a book is provided only with a covering of paper we speak of *paper covers*.

Before the invention of printing books were relatively scarce and valuable, never to be found collected in large enough numbers to warrant their being shelved in vertical rows. The book was displayed in a lying position, and its ornamentation was thus concentrated on the front cover which often received the skilled attention of a jeweller. Leather bindings were often decorated in relief or stamped with dies or panel stamps. Before 1500, roll tools for impressing continuous patterns on borders were introduced. In southern Europe, where Venice was the chief centre of the trade, decorative taste showed an Oriental influence in gilded arabesques and interlaced strap-work used for corner and centre pieces. When the vertical shelving of books spread they were often placed with the spine innermost, the title being inscribed on the fore-edge. By 1600, however, books were generally shelved as now, and it was thus a natural consequence to extend the decoration of the binding to include the spine, and later to concentrate on its ornamentation.

Spinal lettering is thought to have been introduced by Jean Grolier whose influence on the art of book-binding in France was considerable. As the leather spine was attached direct to the back of the stitched sheets, the bands gave a raised appearance, dividing it into fields in which the decoration was contained. Through the years the decorative influence of the Orient was modified by local taste, but France and Italy retained a delicacy and elegance in sharp contrast to the heaviness of blind blocking which characterized the bindings of Germany and the Lowlands.

Practical. The main stages of edition binding are as follows: folding, gathering, sewing, cutting edges, rounding and backing, lining backs; casemaking is performed simultaneously and, after blocking, the cases are combined with the prepared books to provide the finished article. Printed matter is delivered to the binder in large flat sheets which are folded to book size. Each sheet usually comprises 16 or 32 consecutive pages but sheets of a lesser number of pages are used as convenient. A complete set of sheets comprises one book and it is necessary to arrange the sheets consecutively by *gathering* before the sewing is done. End-papers and single-leaf illustrations are tipped to the sheets where desired while four-page illustrations are wrapped round or placed in the centre of folded sheets so that they may be sewn in together with the sheets. After sewing the sheets together the book is pressed and the traditional method of binding calls for cutting the edges followed by coating the back with glue. When the glue is dry the book is rounded and backed, lined with mull and with paper and finally pasted into its case. The cases consist of a covering material, such as bookcloth or linson, which is glued to the boards with the edges turned in and subsequently blocked. Alternative methods of lining are by the use of *expandable cloth*, q.v., and there is some use of the *unsewn binding* method, q.v.

The books may be embellished by colouring the edges, the colour usually being applied by a spray gun, or more exceptionally one or more edges may be gilt. The back linings may be finished off with coloured headbands which, extending at the head and tail of the spine, enrich the finish.

When durability and appearance have to be sacrificed to extreme economy paper covers are stuck to the book after sewing and the book is subsequently cut, thus completing the simplest form of binding.

While today machines execute the great majority of the processes described these originated as hand processes and, where small quantities are dealt with, hand-binding remains the only practicable procedure.

Leather bindings, especially where thin leathers are concerned, may be achieved by much the same methods as used for cloth-bound editions. The finest leather binding, however, demands that the boards be laced to the sewing and the leather subsequently manipulated over the book and boards, while a wealth of small detail work adds to the beauty and longevity of the completed binding. Such work calls for hand craftsmanship of a high order.

Most books in Britain and America are sold in cased bindings, and while the custom is spreading in Europe many are sold there in paper covers to be bound according to the purchasers' wishes.

bookbinding materials: see *Alaska seal, Armenian bole, art canvas, bands, basil, bevelled boards, blocking foils, boards* (1), *bocasin, book cloth, bosses, buckram, buckskin, calf, canvas, case* (1), *cheveril, Cobb's paper, Cordovan leather, cords, cowhide, crash, cross-grained morocco, crushed Levant, deerskin, duck, dutch leaf, écrasé leather, end-papers, expandable cloth, extra cloth, fair calf, French Cape Levant, french shell, glair, glazed morocco, gold, grained leather, guards, hard-grain morocco, hollows, imitation leather, imitation morocco, jaconet, joints, jute board, lambskin, law calf, law sheep, leaf* (1), *leatherette, levant, library buckram, linen, liners, linson,* *manila, marbled calf, millboards, mordant* (1), *moroccos, mottled calf, mull, Niger morocco, oasis goat, ooze leather, oriental leaf, palladium, parchment, paste-grain, peccary, Rizzi paper, roan, russia cowhide, russia leather, Rutland, scratted paper, seal, sewing thread, sheepskin, size* (2), *skivers, smooth calf, Smyrna morocco, Spanish calf, split boards, sprinkled calf, stained calf, straight-grain morocco, strawboards, super, tree-calf, Turkey leather, Turkey morocco, vellum, watered silk.*

bookbinding methods and processes: see *all along, attaching, aux petits fers, azure tooling, back cornering, backing, beating, blind tooling, block* (3), *blocking, boarding leather, bundling, capping up, casing-in, chain stitch, craft bookbinding, creasing, cut in-boards, cut out-of-boards, edition binding, embossing, extra bound, finishing, flexible sewing, forwarding, gathering* (1), *giggering, gluing-up, gold blocking, gold tooling, guarding, hand-binding, hand-sewing, holing out, ink blocking, inlaying, kerfs, kettle-stitch, laced on, laying on, lining, lining up, machine binding processes, machine-sewing, marbling, marking up, meeting guards, miscellaneous binder, onlaying, overcasting, paring, pasting, pulling, rounding, saddle stitch, sawn-in back, sewing, side-stitch, siding, slips, smashing, stabbing, Steamset, stitching, sunken flexible, thread, tipped in, tooling, trimming, triple lining, turning-in corners, two sheets on, unsewn binding, warehousing, warping, whipstitching, wire stabbing, wire stitching.*

bookbinding styles and binding features: see *ajouré, Aldine bindings, antique gold edges, arabesque, architectural bindings, assico, author's binding, aux petits fers, azure tooling, back, backed, Bedford, Francis, binder's cloth, binder's title, binding variants, blind-stamped panels, board covers, bosses, Boyet bindings, Bradel binding, burnished edges, Cambridge-, cameo-, Canterbury bindings, caoutchouc binding, chamfered edges, champlevé, chased edges, chemise, circuit edges, clasps, cloisonné, cloth boards, cloth joints, coloured tops, corium, corners* (2), *Corvinus bindings, cottage binding, cuir bouilli, cuir ciselé, cut flush, dentelle bindings, Derome bindings, diapered, diced, divinity calf, dos à dos, doublures, drawn on, Ducali bindings, edge-rolled, Edwards of Halifax, embroidered bindings, end-papers, Etruscan bindings, Eve bindings, extension cover, extra bound, false bands, fanfare, fillet* (1), *flat backs, flexible binding, floriated, flush boards, fore-edge painting, forel bindings, french joints, french three-line, full bound, full gilt, gilt edges, gilt solid, goffered edges, gold, gótico-mudéjar, Grolier, groove, guinea edge, Günther, half-bound, half-cloth, half-leather, Harley, headband, headcap, hinges, hollow back, imbrication, in boards, in boards extra, inlaying, integral cover, interleaved, Irish bindings, Jansenist bindings, joints, labels, lace bindings, lacquered bindings, leather joints, Le Gascon bindings, Le Monnier bindings, lettering piece, library edition, limp binding, Little Gidding bindings, Lyonnese, Maioli bindings, marbling, Mearne bindings, Michel, mitred* (1), *monastic bindings, mudéjar bindings, one on and two off, onlaying, open back, padded sides, Padeloup bindings, palleted, panel* (1), *panel back, paper boards, paper covers, paste print, Payne, plaquette, pointillé, pot cassé, powdered, publisher's binding, publisher's cloth, quarter-bound, raised bands, re-backed, reinforced binding, reinforced signatures, Restoration bindings, Rivière, rough gilt, Roxburghe, rubber-back binding, run-up spine, Safavid bindings, sawn-in back, Scottish bindings, secondary binding, semé, shelf back, signet, slip case, slips, solander, spine, sprinkled edges, squares, stilted covers, sunk joints, tailband, tail cap, textile binding, three-quarter binding, ties, tight back, top edge gilt, trade binding, transparent bindings, Trautz-Bauzonnet, trimmed edges, two sheets on, unsewn binding, velvet bindings, wallet-edges, Yapp, yellow-backs, Zaehnsdorf.*

bookbinding tools: see *arming press, azure tooling, backing boards, block* (2), *blocking press, burnisher,*

A 16*th-century bookplate, now in the University Library, Graz, Austria*

cap, fillet (2), *floret, gilding rolls, gold-blocking press, gold knife, gouge, graining boards, guillotine, hand letters, key* (1), *lying press, machine-sewing, nipping press, pallet* (2 *and* 3), *panel stamp, plough, roll* (2), *standing press, tip.*

bookplates: printed labels of ownership pasted on the inside front cover of a book. The best known early examples are those of Bilibald Pirckheimer (1470–1530) which were designed by Albrecht Dürer. In addition to the owner's name the words 'ex libris' form part of the design, and it is by the latter that they are known on the Continent.

The Bookseller: one of the principal reference works for the British book trade. It was founded in 1858 by Joseph Whitaker, and now appears as a weekly journal giving trade news, and an alphabetical list in which new books of the week are entered under author and title. Some Government publications, and pamphlets costing 6d. or more, are included, but musical scores are not. Since 1924 cumulative editions of the bibliographical entries have been published quarterly and annually.

'The Bookseller' address is 13 Bedford Square, London, W.C.1.

See also *The Reference Catalogue of Current Literature, Whitaker's Cumulative Book List.*

booksellers' and publishers' abbreviations: see *publishers' abbreviated answers.*

Booksellers Association of Great Britain and Ireland: an association, founded in 1895, open to all bookselling establishments approved by *The Publishers Association,* q.v. It exists to further the sale of books, to protect the interests of booksellers, to provide classes and correspondence courses for the training of members and their assistants, to uphold the status of the trade, and to ensure adherence to the *Net Book Agreement,* 1957 q.v.

The address is 14 Buckingham Palace Gardens, London, S.W.1.

See also *Book Tokens Ltd., Booksellers' Clearing House.*

Booksellers' Clearing House: an organization founded by the *Booksellers Association,* q.v., in 1948 to enable bookseller members to pay their accounts with all publishers by one monthly or quarterly cheque. Similarly, publishers receive from the Clearing House a single cheque for the gross amount due from all bookseller members. The saving on postal and bank charges, also time, is considerable. Transactions are confidential. The Clearing House is operated on behalf of the Booksellers Association by *Book Tokens Ltd.,* q.v.

bookwork folding chases: see *folding chases.*

border: in bookwork, a border is a continuous decorative design arranged around matter on a page. Borders can be continuous cast strips of rule, plain or patterned, or they can be made up from repeated border units or *flowers,* q.v. An extensive range of proprietary borders is available.

Border Club: a printing society established in 1837 at Newcastle upon Tyne. (M.L.)

border decoration: the ornamentation of a page by surrounding the printed matter on it with a decorative border. This treatment of a page had long been a feature of the illuminator's art, and it was in imitation of this that Günther Zainer of Augsburg first used a woodcut initial with foliage trailing from it for a calendar he printed in 1472 (GKW 1292). He later developed the idea into a left marginal border and head border in which he included figures and birds. Other early printers did likewise, often adding gold and colours. Particularly fine examples embellished the Livres d'heures printed in Paris by Pigouchet at the end of the 15th century.

By the mid-16th century borders made up of type ornaments had appeared (see *flowers*), and the slavish imitation of the manuscript ceased.

boring machine: 1. a machine for shaving off the ribs on the inside of curved stereotype plates.

See also *plate-boring machine.*

2. a stamp-boring machine, being an engraving machine used in the manufacture of matrices for type-casting. (G.U.)

Börsenverein der Deutschen Buchhändler: the former principal association of the German book trade, founded in Leipzig in 1825, to organize, represent, and further its interests. The association had considerable influence in Austria and Switzerland. Publication of the trade news 'Börsenblatt für den Deutschen Buchhandel' began in 1834: after 1863 this was issued daily.

Since 1945 the Börsenverein for Western Germany has been established in Frankfurt. The 'Börsenblatt' now appears twice a week, and is a scholarly publication of use to bibliophiles and librarians as well as the book trade.

bosses: pieces of brass inset at the corners or elsewhere on a book cover for protection or decoration.

botanical symbols:

⊙ ① annual	♂-♀ monoecious
♂ antheridia	∞ number indefinite
◕ autumn flowering	♀ oogamia
② biennial	♃ perennial
∧ climbing plant	! personally checked
♂♀ dioecious	♂♀☿ polygamous
△ evergreen	◔ spring flowering
♀ female	◑ summer flowering
× hybrid	♄ tree
♂ male	◕ winter flowering
⊙ monocarpus	

bourgeois: the name for a former size of type, now standardized as 9-point. The name may derive from Bourges, the birthplace of Geofroy Tory, who mentions it in 'Champ Fleury', or from the writing used in commerce by the bourgeois of France. The type size was first used in 1498 by Andrea Torresano, the father-in-law of Aldus Manutius.

boustrophedon: literally 'in the manner in which an ox turns' when ploughing. An expression used to describe the early Greek manner of writing in which the first line was written from left to right, the second from right to left, the third as the first, and so on.

bow: to bend an imperfect type so that it cannot be used. It will then be put in the *hell-box*, q.v.

Bowdlerized: an edition of a work which has had the text expurgated by omitting words or passages which might give offence. The term derives from Dr. Thomas Bowdler who published an expurgated edition of Shakespeare in 1818.

Bowen, Emanuel, fl. 1740: map engraver to George II, best known for his county maps, often embellished with vignettes of towns, coats of arms, and historical notes. His son, Thomas, was also a map engraver of some merit.

bowl: the curved main strokes of a letter enclosing a *counter*, q.v. An alternative name is *cup*.

bowls: the non-metallic rolls of a *super-calender*, q.v. They may be made of compressed paper, cotton, linen or asbestos.

See also *crown* (2).

Bowyer, William, 1663–1737: the London printer for whom William Caslon designed the fount of roman and italic type which brought the latter fame. Bowyer, who was liveryman of the Stationers' Company and a leading printer, was a patron of Caslon.

His son William (1699–1777), 'the learned printer', entered the business in 1722, and worked for some years as corrector of the press. In addition to scholarly editorial activity he published several of his own writings. In 1761 he was appointed printer to the Royal Society.

See 'Anecdotes of William Bowyer'. Written, printed, and published by John Nichols, 1782.

box: see *hell-box*, *reader's box*.

box-in: to surround type matter with rule so that the printed result appears in a rectangular frame or box.

Boydell, John, 1719–1804: a London publisher who, with his nephew Josiah as partner, decided in 1786 to publish an illustrated folio edition of Shakespeare's works (at that time often spelled Shakspeare). He was assisted by George Nicol, later a partner, the King's bookseller who founded the Shakspeare Printing Office with William Bulmer as printer, William Martin as type-cutter and founder, and George Steevens as textual editor. The illustrations were stipple engravings from originals specially painted by such eminent artists as Reynolds, Romney, and Stothard. The plays were issued in parts from 1791–1802.

Boyet bindings: the manner of book decoration practised by Luc-Antoine Boyet, binder to Louis XIV from 1698–1733. His style was simple, consisting of a rectangular fillet of gold lines, ornamental corners, and a coat of arms in the centre of the front board. Other binding features he used were pointillé, leather doublures, and dentelles.

Boys, Thomas S., 1803–74: a London lithographer of distinction whose skill as a book illustrator may be assessed in his 'Original views of London as it is', 1842, and other works of the period.

Bozérian brothers: two eminent Parisian binders of the early 19th century. The elder bound whole libraries for wealthy patrons. The younger, who bound for Napoleon, favoured the use of contrasting leathers such as pale green or lemon yellow against navy blue or red.

B.P. chromo: see *proofing chromo*.

brace ends: type sorts, viz: ⏞.

See also *cock*.

bracket: a punctuation mark, used in pairs, [], to enclose words, phrases, figures, etc., to be separated from the text, and elsewhere for various purposes. (M.L.)

Bradel binding: a style of temporary binding, with uncut edges, the top sometimes gilded, and a spine of linen or leather. It was of German origin, but used in France by, it is thought, Alexis-Pierre Bradel, after whom it became known. There were, however, many binders of this name working in France.

Bradford, William, 1663–1752: a printer from Leicestershire who, in 1685, established the first press at Philadelphia. He printed many Quaker tracts. It was due to a difference with the local Quaker authorities that Bradford moved his press to New York in 1693, this being the first press there. Partnered by Samuel Carpenter, Bradford built the first American paper mill; this was erected in 1690 at Germantown, Pennsylvania, and was managed for them by *William Rittenhouse*, q.v.

The Bradford family were important Colonial printers for many generations.

Bradshaw, Henry, 1831–86: a scholar and bibliographer who for many years worked in the Library of Cambridge University. He is important for his researches into typographical history and the activities of early English and Continental presses.

His writings, edited by F. Jenkinson, were published in 1889 as 'Collected papers of Henry Bradshaw'.

Brailes, William de, fl. 1220–40: an illuminator, more unique for having signed his work than for any special excellence of it. He may have worked in London. His filling of medallions with miniatures shows a French influence, as does the careful figure drawing. Most accessible of surviving examples is a Psalter in New College, Oxford.

Braille: a system of embossed printing invented by Louis Braille of Paris in 1829, and used to print books for the blind. Cells of six dots are used for the alphabet and certain defined contractions. Printing is done with types, cast and composed as in ordinary typesetting, and also with thin plates or sheets of brass having the characters raised on the surface.

In 1952 an alternative to the above method of printing was announced, and given the name '*solid dot Braille*'. A transcribing machine, which interprets letters into dots, cuts a stencil. Liquid plastic ink is forced through the stencil holes on to paper. These solid dots of ink are then welded to the paper by an infra-red drying process. Advantages claimed for this process are greater sharpness of dot image, and thus legibility; increased life for the book; and reduced bulk and weight per volume since thinner paper is used.

Bramah, Joseph, 1748–1814: of Pimlico, the inventor of the first *cylinder machine*, q.v., for making paper. His patent (No. 2840 of 1805) was for the making of paper in 'endless sheets of any length'. A feeding cistern prepared with stuff was positioned above a gauze drum. From this any required quantity of stuff was let upon the drum as it turned. A felt-covered roller in gentle peripheral contact with the mould wheel took the paper as it formed. There were also squeezing rollers to assist drying.

This principle was considerably improved upon by John Dickinson in 1809.

branch out: an obsolete term for the insertion of leads or reglets between lines of type so as to extend the matter.

Branston, Robert, 1778–1827: a wood engraver working as a book illustrator and blockmaker in London where he was regarded as a rival of *Bewick*, q.v. His work is to be seen in 'History of England', Wallis & Scholey, 1804–10.

brass rule: strips of brass, type high, used to print lines and simple borders. They are also used as column rules in dictionaries, Bibles, etc.

See also *mitred* (2), *Oxford corners*, *rule*.

brayer: formerly, a wooden pestle of round shape, flat at one end and with a handle on the other, used to spread out ink to be taken up by the ink balls. Later, it became a small hand-roller used for distributing the ink before it is taken up by forme rollers. (M.L.)

break-line: the last line of a paragraph, where quads are required to fill out the last space. (M.L.)

See also *end a break*, *end even*.

break up: to unlock a forme and distribute the type.

breaker: a machine of *Hollander* type, q.v., being a large oblong vat with a central wall or mid-feather, in which rags or other ingredients of paper, in water, are propelled by a knifed roll; the knives break and separate the rags on a bedplate of standing knives. The half-stuff which results then passes to the *potcher* and *beater*, qq.v.

breaking length: an indication of the *tensile strength*, q.v., of paper, being the length at which a suspended strip of paper will break due to its own weight. (After G.U.)

Brehmer, August, b. 1846: a designer of Chemnitz who, with his brother Hugo, b. 1844, constructed machines for stitching and folding. In 1871 he emigrated to America where in Philadelphia he devised a machine for stitching cardboard by wire, to be followed by one for stitching books. In 1879 he returned to Leipzig to found the firm of Gebr. Brehmer, which became world-famous. In the 1880's they designed machines for thread-sewing. Their machines are made in Britain by British Brehmer Ltd., of London. (G.U.)

Bremer-Presse: a private press founded in 1911 in Bremen by Ludwig Wolde and Willi Wiegand: in

1921 it was transferred to Munich. Wiegand designed a roman and greek face, cut by Louis Hoell, for use in the series of translations of classical and modern poetry issued. Books were hand-bound by Frieda Thiersch. The press closed in 1934.

Breviary: the book of daily Divine Office used in the Roman Catholic Church. It properly contains:

1. Calendar.
2. Psalter.
3. Proprium de Tempore (collects and lessons).
4. Proprium de Sanctis (collects, etc., for Saints' Days).
5. Commune Sanctorum (collects, etc., for Saints without special services).
6. Hours of the Virgin, burial services, etc., i.e. Small Offices.

It does not contain the Communion Service or Mass.

breviate: an abridgement or summary of a work.

brevier: the name for a former size of type, now standardized as 8-point. In spite of the attractions of this theory, the name cannot derive from its use in Breviaries of the early Church, since larger sizes were mostly employed.

bridge: 1. a board for supporting the arm when lithographing by hand, etching, or doing other graphic work on a delicate foundation. It consists of a board elevated on supports to a convenient height for working.

2. an appliance for securing the matrix frame when casting on a Monotype machine.

3. in printing presses and other machines an appliance for supporting the moving sheets of paper through the machine.

4. in die-cutting, the narrow connecting strip of waste between stamped items which temporarily serves to hold the sheet of metal together. (G.U.)

Bright, Fred E.: the co-inventor of the *Typograph*, q.v.

brilliant: the name for a former size of type, 3½-point, now standardized as 4-point. See also *point*.

bring up: to underlay or interlay a block to make it correct printing height.

bristol board: fine cardboard, made in various qualities and thicknesses, usually of smooth finish, used for printing and drawing. It is so called because it is said to have been first made at Bristol. (M.L.)

British Book News: since September 1940, a monthly annotated list of the more important publications of Great Britain and (since January 1949) the Commonwealth, published by the British Council, 65 Davies Street, London, W.1.

The books are grouped by the Dewey classification scheme, the notes being short appraisals by specialists of each title. Fiction, reprints, and children's books are included, as well as authoritative subject 'reading-lists'. Musical scores are not entered.

British Federation of Master Printers: the voluntary national organization of employers in the general printing industry, including under this heading certain branches such as bookbinding, stationery manufacture, etc. It was founded in 1900 and now has over 4000 members representing over 90% of all printing production, wages paid, and labour employed in the industry. Membership is open to any individual, partnership, company, or other organization engaged in the printing industry which is the owner of an operating plant. Members belong to one of the 148 local Associations or thirteen regional Alliances, which the Federation comprises. Membership of an Association also means membership of an Alliance and the Federation. The Federation is governed by a Council which meets quarterly, and there is an annual general meeting of members at the time of the Annual Congress in May or June.

The Federation's objectives are to improve the status and progress of the industry, to take collective action on behalf of its members in labour negotiations and matters of legislation, to encourage the adoption of scientific costing, and to disseminate information regarding technical developments.

Historically, several Associations are older than the Federation. The London Master Printers held meetings in the late 18th century, and there are records of meetings of Edinburgh printers before 1792. The Association of Master Bookbinders of London—as it was then—met as early as 1786. The Manchester and Salford Association was formed in 1874, and printers in Glasgow were meeting in 1837. The Newcastle, Leeds, Bolton, Derby, N. Staffs, Leicester, Cardiff, Newport, and Norwich Associations were all founded in the 1890's.

The Alliances came into being in 1919, when a reorganization of 'The Federation of Master Printers and Allied Trades of Great Britain and Ireland', as it had been called since its foundation, took place. The Joint Industrial Council of the Printing and Allied Trades, of which the Federation is a constituent member, was founded in the same year.

The Federation adopted its present name in 1931. Its address is 11 Bedford Row, London, W.C.1.

See also *Printing, Packaging and Allied Trades Research Association.*

British Letter Foundry: a typefounding business started by *John Bell*, q.v., who employed the professional engraver *Richard Austin*, q.v., as punch-cutter. Monotype Bell Series 341, cut in 1930, is based on a type cut by Austin for this foundry, the original punches now being in the possession of Stephenson Blake of Sheffield. An American revival by *Bruce Rogers*, q.v., of the same face was given the name 'Brimmer' after the Boston writer Martin Brimmer, while *Updike*, q.v., based his 'Mountjoye' on Bell's original punches and matrices.

The foundry closed in 1797.

British National Bibliography: first issued January 1950, with the objects of listing every new work published in Great Britain, describing each in detail, and giving the subject-matter as precisely as possible; very brief annotations are occasionally included. It is based upon items deposited at the Copyright Office of the British Museum, and entries are grouped according to the Dewey Decimal Classification, with author, title, and subject indexes. Cheap novelettes, musical scores, maps, minor Government publications, and periodicals (except for first issues of new or revised titles) are excluded.

The B.N.B. is published by the Council of the British National Bibliography Ltd., British Museum, London. It appears weekly, with monthly author indexes, and four quarterly cumulations, the last being the cloth-bound annual volume.

British Standard letterpress inks: specifications in respect of the hue, saturation, and light fastness of inks for four- and three-colour letterpress printing, published as B.S. 1480: 1949 and B.S. 3020: 1959 by the British Standards Institution, London.

Colours are yellow, magenta, cyan, and black.

British Standard offset-lithographic inks: a specification in respect of the hue, saturation, and light fastness of five inks for offset lithography, published as B.S. 2650: 1955 by the British Standards Institution, London.

Colours are yellow (opaque), yellow (transparent), magenta, cyan, and black. The inclusion of transparent as well as opaque yellow permits the sequence in which the colours are printed down to be at the discretion of the printer.

broad: an obsolete term for wooden furniture four ems wide.

broadside: originally, a sheet of paper printed on one side only. Broadsides were used soon after the beginning of printing for royal proclamations and official notices. They were later a vehicle for political agitation and the expression of opposition to authoritarian rule. They were even used for the dissemination of scaffold speeches by criminals on the point of execution.

Early in the 16th century poems and ballads were printed in this form in England, and black letter fount continued to be used long after the introduction of roman for books.

Broadsides are also known as *broadsheets, single sheets, street- or stall-ballads*, and *black-letter ballads.*

The term broadside is now applied to a variety of large regular and special-fold sheets, printed on one or both sides. A broadside may also contain one job or a number of jobs. (B.E.S. & M.L.)

Brocar, Arnao Guillen de, fl. 1511–23: the Spanish printer of the first printed polyglot Bible.

See also *polyglot edition.*

brochure: a pamphlet or other short work which has its pages stitched and is not bound. The term derives from the French 'brocher', to stitch.

broke: that part of wet or dry paper, spoiled in the making process, which must be re-pulped.

broken matter: 1. type-matter out of order.

2. composition which has short paragraphs, headings, etc. (M.L.)

broken over: see *hinged.*

bronzing: the brushing of a fine metallic powder over a sheet freshly printed with ink, varnish, or sizing. This metallic dust, when applied to a smooth-finished surface that has been printed with sizing, gives a brilliant lustre. (M.L.)

bronzing size: printing ink made specially for bronzing. The ink must not dry too quickly on the paper nor be rapidly absorbed by it, but must give a very tacky surface to retain the metal powder.

The term is sometimes used for priming ink for subsequent printing with metallic ink. (G.U.)

Brotherton, Edward Allen, 1856–1930: a wealthy industrialist and book collector (created a baron in 1929) whose gifts totalling £200,000 provided for Leeds University the building known as The Brotherton Library. In 1935 his private library was presented to the University, on trust for the nation, and every facility for studying its contents is offered to accredited students.

Lord Brotherton began to form his collection in 1922, and at the time of its transfer to the University it included some 35,000 printed books and pamphlets, 400 manuscripts, and several thousand deeds and letters. Additions by gift and purchase are still made.

Among important manuscripts are an 11th- or early 12th-century copy of Bede's 'Expositio super septem epistolas canonicas' and a 14th-century German copy of Jacobus de Voragine's 'Legenda aurea sanctorum', as well as several French Livres d'heures.

The 251 incunabula include works from the presses of Jenson, Han, the da Spira brothers, Ratdolt, de Worde, and Pynson, while notable is a copy of Schedel's 'Liber chronicarum', 1493.

The greater part of the collection is devoted to English literature and history from the 16th to 19th century. There is also a virtually complete set of the Kelmscott Press books.

In 1950 an important collection of Romany literature was presented to the library by Mrs. McGrigor Phillips. This comprises some 700 books and pamphlets.

Brower press: a ball-bearing proof press. (M.L.)

Brown, John Carter, d. 1874: the most important of an American family of book collectors who greatly added to the library of Americana begun in the 18th century by Nicholas Brown. In 1904 the collection was given to Brown University, Providence, R.I., and is still being increased by members of the family.

bruising: a grey or mottled effect, most noticeable in coated papers, caused by undue heat or pressure in the calenders.

Brunet, Jacques Charles, 1780–1876: a French bookseller and bibliophile remembered for his 'Manuel du libraire et de l'amateur de livres', 3 vols., Paris, 1810. The fifth edition in six vols., with supplements, 1860–80, is best known. This gives particulars of some 40,000 rare and valuable books, especially in French and Latin.

buckle folder: see *folding machine.*

buckram: a strong fabric made of jute, cotton, or linen, stiffened by size or glue, and used for book covers. The term originally applied to woven cotton impregnated with starch. There are two varieties, 'single warp' and 'double warp'.

See also *book cloth.*

buckskin: deerskin prepared for covering books. Early English examples of books so covered have been traced to the 16th century.

buffing: the final polishing of a reproduction plate before etching.

building-in machine: a machine used for the rapid drying of cased books. By means of several applications of heat and pressure books are dried in a matter of seconds. This is an alternative to lengthy pressure in a *standing press,* q.v.

bulk: 1. the thickness of a book exclusive of its covers. The bulk will be less after binding than before.

2. the thickness of a sheet of paper related to its weight and measured in thousandths of an inch. Book papers are measured by the thickness of a number of pages.

Bullock press: a web printing machine, invented by William Bullock of New York in 1865.

See also *rotary press* for an illustration. (M.L.)

Bulmer, William, 1757–1830: a London printer in whose name was established the Shakspeare Press of *Boydell,* q.v. Bulmer also printed an edition of Goldsmith illustrated with woodcuts by his friend *Bewick,* q.v.

See also *Stanhope press.*

bumped out: 1. said of a line of letters to which extra spacing has been inserted in order to square it up with the measure of a longer line.

2. said of matter which is widely leaded.

bumping: see *smashing.*

bumping up: the making-ready of half-tone plates for printing on a rotary press. This is a form of interlaying the original plates, before stereos are cast, in which a sheet of paper, card or thin zinc is used to press the back of the original. This causes the deep tones to be raised higher than the mid tones or high lights.

bundling: the tying together in bundles of the folded sheets of a book to promote orderliness. Machines, called bundlers, are largely used for this work and

The Nidor bundler

exert considerable pressure upon the sheets thus expelling air from between the pages and producing compact bundles. (L.K.)

bundling machine: a machine, operated either by hand or mechanical power, for dry-pressing, smashing, bundling, or padding. (M.L.)

Burdett, Eric: a contemporary British teacher of bookbinding, and a double silver medallist of the City and Guilds of London Institute. In addition to lecturing on bookbinding he is a regular contributor to the monthly trade journal 'Print in Britain', and is a member of the *Guild of Contemporary Bookbinders*, q.v.

Burgkmair, Hans, 1473–1531: a German artist who, after Dürer, was the leading book illustrator of 16th-century Germany. He worked for, among other patrons, the Emperor Maximilian for whom he made as book illustrations a number of woodcuts. Burgkmair, or rather his cutter Jost de Negker, was an early worker in *chiaroscuro*, q.v. (G.U.)

burin: an engraving tool used by wood and metal engravers.

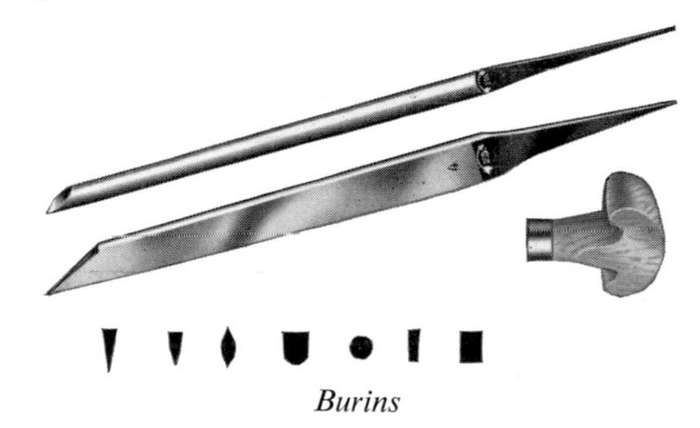

Burins

Burney, Charles, 1757–1817: a classical scholar whose important collection of some 13,000 works by Latin and Greek authors was bought by the nation in 1818 for placing in the British Museum. Equally valuable was a series of bound 17th-century newspapers, and some 525 manuscript volumes, mostly Greek and Latin (including the Townley Homer).

His father's music library had been acquired by the Museum in 1815.

burnished edges: the coloured edges of a book which have been smeared with wax and rubbed with a burnishing tool to impart a polished surface.

burnisher: 1. a costly hand-tool of agate or bloodstone used for polishing book edges.

2. a smooth, curved metal tool, used in photomechanical processes for removing rough spots from plates and half-tones. (M.L.)

burr: a rough edge left on a block by the routing machine. It must be removed before printing.

A burr is also characteristic of the surface of a *dry-point* plate, q.v.

Bury, Richard de, 1287–1345: (born Richard Aungerville of Bury St Edmunds) a bibliophile and patron of learning who, as Bishop of Durham, rescued countless classical manuscripts from oblivion or destruction. He employed agents in Europe to collect for him. The library he founded at Oxford was accessible to all students, and a model of its kind.

He is remembered for his 'Philobiblon' written in praise of books, learning, and libraries. The first printed edition of this appeared at Cologne in 1473. At the dissolution of the monasteries in 1537 his library was dispersed.

butted: said of slugs placed end to end to form a continuous line.

Byddell, John, fl. 1533–44: a London printer and bookseller, who held a patent for printing the English primer. His name sometimes appears as Bedel, and also with the appellation of Salisbury, thus the colophon of the 'Lyf of Hyldebrande', 1533, states that it was 'Imprinted by Wynkyn de Worde, for John Byddell, otherwise Salisbury'.

Bynneman, Henry, fl. 1566–83: one of the few English printers of distinction at work in 16th-century London. His presswork was careful, and his use of ornaments and borders on title-pages and elsewhere was often artistic. In 1559 he was apprenticed to Richard Harrison and their names occur on the title-page of Harrison's Bible of 1562. In addition to a printing shop in Knightrider Street, Bynneman had a bookseller's shop at St Paul's, but his main work was printing commissioned by others. In 1574 he appears to have acquired the types and ornaments of Reginald Wolfe (d. 1573). Both Archbishop Parker and Sir Christopher Hatton were among his patrons.

Bynneman printed editions of Latin and Greek classics, using good italic and greek founts. His most important work, issued without his name, was the printing of Raphaell Holinshead's 'Chronicles', 1577. The borders, ornaments, and types are considered sufficient proof that Bynneman was the printer.

Byzantine illumination: the art of manuscript illumination in Asia Minor originated before the 5th century when the form of a book was either a roll, where the illustration was a continuous picture, or a *volumen*, where single themes or incidents were depicted. Prior to the 6th century secular manuscripts were made (although the *Vienna Genesis*, q.v., may be cited as an exception), but the art subsequently flourished in the service of Christianity. By this time eastern mysticism, which stressed the inner meaning of a subject, and classical trends, which emphasized its delicacy and beauty, were the complements of Byzantine art.

In the iconoclast period (726–843) architectural and geometric designs predominated, the former being a feature of canon tables until a much later date. The most important survival is the Chloudov Psalter, now in Moscow.

Copies of the tetrevangelium were the chief works produced from 843–1261. Some included representations of Christ or the Emperor, while the Evangelists were depicted in most. Colours were now richer and much gold was used for backgrounds; elaborate borders were also common.

In later work (1261–1453) portraits of patrons and natural scenes were a new element. By this time the art was slowly declining, being eclipsed in importance by that of western Europe.

The work of Byzantine artists influenced in varying degrees that done in most European scriptoria.

See also *Vienna Dioscorides*.

ADDENDA

Bible printing in England (see also page 25): The appointment of Queen's Printers of Bibles and Prayer Books is by Letters Patent and is held during the Queen's pleasure. The current Patent was issued in 1901 to the then three partners of Eyre & Spottiswoode by name 'and each of them and each of their executors, administrators and assigns severally and respectively'. The appointment is not affected by the demise of the Crown, and consequently does not come up for renewal at the beginning of each reign. The appointment, being held during pleasure, can be at once revoked in the case of misconduct.

Interesting sequels to the foregoing are that Eyre & Spottiswoode came under Catholic control, and that the firm was sold in 1957 to Methuens. It will thus be seen that the right to print the Bible for the Church of England came into Roman Catholic hands, and that the right was subsequently sold, though technically Eyre & Spottiswoode still exist.

Book Design and Production: a quarterly journal edited by James Moran, and published by Printing News Ltd., London. It was established in 1958. Articles are illustrated, and describe practical ways in which improved methods of production can serve the book trade.

Books in Print: an American reference book, indexing by author and title separately the books listed in the 'Publishers Trade List Annual'. It is published annually by R. R. Bowker Company, New York.

Brightype: a method of converting letterpress printing material into a photographic image for use in litho or gravure, announced in 1958 by the Ludlow Typograph Company of Chicago.

Briefly, a complete forme of type and line or half-tone blocks is placed in a spraying cabinet where it is coated with a quick-drying black lacquer. The coating is then removed from the printing surface making the latter reflective while the background is light absorbent.

A special same-size camera and a unique system of shadowless lighting over the whole forme are other features of the process which, it is claimed, gives reproductions of excellent quality.

British Books: since 1959, the title of the former *Publishers' Circular*, q.v.

C

©: the symbol for copyright. See *copyright notice.*

cabinet: an enclosed rack for holding type-cases, etc., formerly in wood, now also of pressed sheet steel.

Cabinet des Poinçons: one of the most important collections of historic types in the world, being part of the French Imprimerie Nationale. Garamond, the Didots, Grandjean, and Le Bé are among the many whose punches and types are preserved.

caddying: the adding of fibrous materials, sizing, and loading to paper pulp. The word is particular to paper-makers in southern England and is elsewhere replaced by *furnishing.*

Café Royal Book Prize: an annual award of £500, established in 1956 by Mr. Charles Forte, of Forte & Co. Ltd., the present owners of the Café Royal in London. The prize is administered by a committee set up jointly by the Café Royal and the National Book League. Each year the prize books will be chosen from different fields, and for the first year of the award the subject was London entertainment. In 1956 Laurence Irving won £300 for 'Henry Irving', Faber, 1951; while £100 each were received by Mary Clarke for 'Sadler's Wells Ballet', Black, 1955, and Willson Disher for 'Melodrama', Rockliff, 1954.

calamus: a sharpened reed used for writing on papyrus or parchment.

Caldecott Medal: since 1938, an annual award made by the American Library Association to the illustrator of an outstanding picture-book for children.

calender: part of the dry end of a paper-making machine, being a column of iron or steel rolls (usually five). When paper is passed under pressure through these the action closes the pores and smooths the surface.

See also *finish, super-calender.*

calender crush: a fault in paper-making seen as hard discolorations in the sheet: caused when the calender rolls crush a thickening of the web.

calendered paper: paper which has been finished in a calender. The varying degrees of gloss may be characterized as *low machine finish* or *high machine finish.*

See also *machine finish.*

calf: calfskin with a smooth finish used for book covers, for which it is known to have been employed at least as early as 1450.

See also *fair calf, law calf, mottled calf, Spanish calf, sprinkled calf, stained calf, tree-calf.*

calipers: compasses-type calipers are used by finishers for marking out the position of lettering and ornamentation before commencing tooling. (L.K.)

calligrapher: one who writes elegantly, especially a skilled transcriber of manuscripts.

calligraphy: literally (from the Greek) beautiful handwriting, penmanship. From Roman times to the 16th century such scripts as half-uncial, Carolingian, humanistic, and their derivatives attained their finest forms in the service of religion, law, and commerce.

Printing did not immediately eclipse interest in calligraphy, especially in 16th-century Italy where such writing masters as Arrighi, Tagliente, Cresci, and Palatino were famed, as were their English contemporaries Baildon and Ascham, and later, Billingsley and Bickham.

See also *letters—forms and styles.*

calotype: a process made public in 1841 by W. H. Fox Talbot for producing negatives on silver iodide paper by developing with gallic acid. Positive copies were afterwards made by contact printing on silver chloride paper. Also known as *Talbotype.* (G.U.)

Cambridge Bibliographical Society: a society founded in 1949 to encourage an interest in all forms of the printed book, with a particular emphasis on Cambridge books and men. The annual dues of one guinea include the yearly volume of the 'Transactions', as well as extra monographs which are issued free to members from time to time.

A regular programme of lectures, meetings, and visits is also arranged.

Cambridge bindings: bindings done by a group of craftsmen working in Cambridge from 1610–30. The main features of their designs were double panels with a flower tool at the four outer corners, on brown calf.

Cambridge india paper: the trade name of a *Bible paper*, q.v., of high quality, made at Bury, Lancs, by J. R. Crompton & Bros. In 1945 it was selected for the airmail edition of 'The Times'.

Cambridge University Press: the second oldest learned press in Britain, which originated in 1521 with John Siberch as the first printer. The 'Oration' of Henry Bullock was the first book published. Siberch was not actually appointed by the University, which did not receive a Royal Charter permitting the appointment of a printer until 1534. The first genuine University Printer was Thomas Thomas, who took office in 1583. Mr. Brooke Crutchley, the University Printer, has kindly supplied the following annotated list of printers; an asterisk precedes the names of those to whom patents were issued but who are not known to have printed anything.

Cambridge Printers

1521	John Siberch	He disappears after 1522
1534	*Nicholas Speryng	
	*Garrett Godfrey	
	*Segar Nicholson	
1539	*Nicholas Pilgrim	
1540	*Richard Noke	
1546	*Peter Sheres	
1577	*John Kingston	
1583	Thomas Thomas, M.A.	d. 1588
1588	John Legate	d. 1620
?	*John Porter (before 1593)	
1606	Cantrell Legge	d. 1625
?	Thomas Brooke, M.A. (before 1608)	Resigned (?) 1625
1622	Leonard Greene	d. 1630
1625	Thomas Buck, M.A.	At least till 1668
	John Buck, M.A.	At least till 1668
1630	Francis Buck	Resigned 1632
1632	Roger Daniel	Patent cancelled 1650
1650	John Legate, jun.	Patent cancelled 1655
1655	John Field	d. 1688
1669	*Matthew Whinn	
1669	John Hayes	d. 1705
1680	*John Peck, M.A.	
1682	*Hugh Martin, M.A.	
1683	*James Jackson, M.D.	
1683	*Jonathan Pindar	
1693	*H. Jenkes	
1697	*Jonathan Pindar	At least till 1730
1705	Cornelius Crownfield	Pensioned 1740
1730	William Fenner, Mary Fenner, Thomas James, John James	Lease relinquished by Mrs. Fenner in 1738
1740	Joseph Bentham	Resigned 1766
1758	John Baskerville	Nothing after 1763
1766	John Archdeacon	d. 1795
1793	John Burges	d. 1802
1802	John Deighton	Resigned 1802
1802	Richard Watts	Resigned 1809
1804	Andrew Wilson	1811 (?)
1809	John Smith	Pensioned 1836
1836	John William Parker	Resigned 1854
1854	George Seeley	Retired 1856
1854	Charles John Clay, M.A.	Retired 1895
1882	John Clay, M.A.	d. 1916
1886	Charles Felix Clay, M.A.	Retired 1904
1916	James Bennet Peace, M.A.	
1923	Walter Lewis, C.B.E., M.A.	Retired 1945
1946	Brooke Crutchley, C.B.E., M.A.	

See also *Bible printing in England*, *Curatores Praeli Typographici*, *Pitt Press*, *Siberch, John*, *Syndics*.

Camden Society: a society founded in 1838 for the printing of inedited manuscripts and the reprinting of rare works on the 'civil, ecclesiastical or literary history of the United Kingdom'. In 1897 it was affiliated to the Royal Historical Society.

cameo bindings: book covers decorated with an inset or stamped cameo, especially important being those made in Italy from 1500–60. Damp vellum was pressed on a design-bearing die, coloured lacquer paste being applied to fill up the cavities and preserve the outline. In the books so embellished which were thought to have belonged to *Canevari*, q.v., the centre of the cover bears a cameo depicting Pegasus on Mount Helicon with Apollo driving towards him on a chariot drawn by two horses.

French examples done in the 16th century for Henry II and for *Grolier*, q.v., bore a central medallion stamped with an intaglio cut die. The design was embossed on a gilded and coloured background. *Roger Payne*, q.v., revived the style in England in the 18th century. Cf. *plaquette*.

cameo coated paper: an American brand of dull-finished coated paper, presenting a delicate surface, for printing half-tones, etc. Its advantage is in giving a non-lustrous surface, offering a rich and soft background for artistic engravings. (M.L.)

Its English counterpart is *matt finished art*.

camera: in principle, a lightproof enclosed space in one wall of which a lens is fixed, while the sensitive material on which a photograph is taken is on the opposite wall.

The *process camera* is generally constructed as a very large stand camera with solid front and back parts joined by strong bellows. Easily changeable lenses can be fixed in the front, and a focusing screen or dark slide in the back. Both parts are movable and

Process camera (Littlejohn & Co., London)

Vertical camera with automatic focusing (Klimsch & Co., Frankfurt)

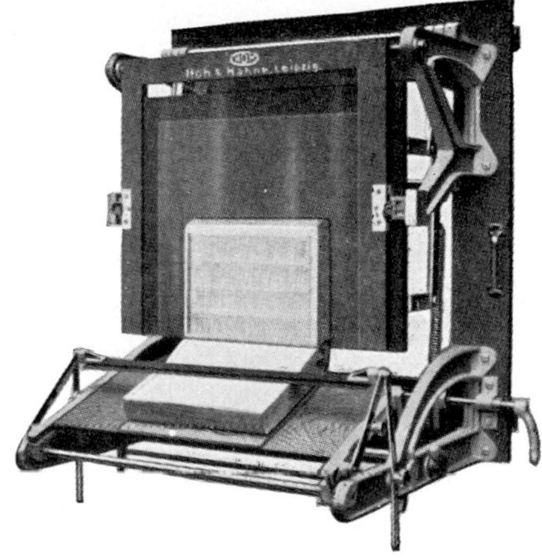

Device for reproducing books (Hoh & Hahne, Leipzig)

can be turned as needed. The base rests on a horizontal stand, along which it can be moved on rails (hence the former name *travelling camera*). The stand is suspended or rests on strong springs. A copyboard is also installed on the stand which, in its normal position, is at a right-angle to the optical main axis, and is intended for mounting the originals to be reproduced. The copyboard can be placed at an angle if required, e.g. when reproducing maps. The camera can be turned parallel to the copyboard, which is necessary when photographing through a prism (mirror). In order that the centre of the copyboard should be exactly in front of the lens, the copyboard must be movable laterally. In some circumstances, however, this lateral movement may be inconveniently large and therefore devices are often used by which both the copyboard and the camera can be placed

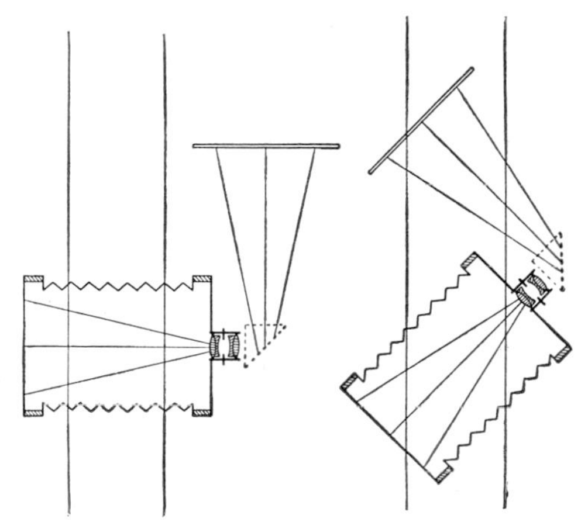

Process camera in prism position with copyboard moved sideways; or camera and copyboard turned at an angle of 45°

at an angle of 45° to the stand, though still parallel to each other. In some cases the copyboard can be exchanged for a transparency stand. The rear of the camera has a holder for the dark slide into which the sensitized material can be inserted. In the back, immediately in front of the plate holder, there is also a screen holder into which different screens can be inserted. Their distance from the plate can be varied, being adjusted by a lever. All movable parts of a process camera can usually be controlled from the rear. The lens is usually provided with a shutter, and sometimes with a built-in iris diaphragm.

Modern *dark-room cameras* are constructed with the back built into the wall of the dark room. This ensures great rigidity. (The prism problem can be solved by a 'double prism'.)

The prism position is so common when photographing in a reproduction studio that special cameras have been built with a fixed prism position, i.e. the camera always has the dark slide positioned at right-angles to the copyboard. Some cameras of this kind are made (to save floor space) in the form of *vertical cameras* in which the lens is placed vertically above the horizontal copyboard. The latter can be raised or lowered, the lens is fixed, and the back part is movable in relation to it. The action has been made more or less automatic so that the movements of the copyboard and the position of the dark slide are synchronized while the image at the focal plane is always in focus. As a rule process cameras are equipped with special lighting devices, formerly with arc lamps, but now often with mercury vapour tubes or incandescent bulbs. (G.U.)

See also *Chemco dark-room camera.*

camlet: to marble.

See also *marbling.*

Campbell press: a cylinder machine made by Andrew Campbell, for typographic and lithographic work.

cancel: a leaf containing an error or errors which is removed and replaced by another, suitably amended. If the need is discovered before printing is completed the cancel leaf may be set up with the prelims, being later cut and inserted in its appropriate place. If the new leaf bears a signature an asterisk should precede the signature letter. While 'cancel' applies to both leaves, in bibliographical cataloguing the old is referred to as 'cancellandum' and the new as 'cancellans'. There are also MS. cancels for individual words or letters.

See also *stub* (2).

cancel-title: a new title-page, often showing alterations to the imprint; such a page is usually inserted when a book printed in England is prepared for the American market.

cancellaresca corsiva: a cursive, informal script adopted in 1450 by the Papal chancery for use in Briefs. Cut for Aldus Manutius as a type in 1500 and known as italic in England, italique in France, corsivo in Italy, and Kursiv in Germany. It was not based on Petrarch's handwriting (a popular misconception due to a misreading of a statement in the Aldine Petrarch, 1502, that the *text* was based on the manuscript in Petrarch's hand).

cancellaresca formata: a stylized version of humanistic cursive script, used in Italy during the 15th and 16th centuries. It was adopted by the Papal Chancery for diplomatic documents and other official purposes, while *cancellaresca corsiva* (also a humanistic cursive) developed as a smaller, quickly written literary script.

When the spread of printing meant that fewer texts were copied by hand, scribes could devote more time and care to the embellishment of the single documents for which writing was still used—briefs, poems, letters, etc. The writing of cancellaresca formata became a skilled accomplishment, technically polished but lacking freshness: it reached its finest development in Rome at the hands of the calligrapher Giovanbattista Palatino, whose writing manual 'Libro nuovo d'imparare a scrivere' was engraved and published in 1540.

See also *cursive.*

Candle Press: a private press founded in Dublin by Colm O'Lochlain in 1917. Books issued were mostly Irish ballads, verse, and folk-lore, some being printed in Gaelic.

Canevari Library: a collection of books having the front covers decorated with cameos of Apollo and Pegasus. They reputedly belonged to the library of Demetrio Canevari (1559–1625) who was physician to Pope Urban VII. Present-day bibliophiles seek to disprove this by pointing out that the *cameo bindings,* q.v., were made before 1550, and that the subjects of the books were not of Canevari's known interests; furthermore, he would be unlikely to collect a library of volumes printed so long before his birth. It is now generally accepted that the books were part of the library of Pier Luigi Farnese (1503–47.)

canon: the name for a former size of type, about 48-point. The name may derive from the use by early printers of this size for printing the Canon of the Mass.

Canterbury bindings: a group of 15th-century bindings (of which some ten survive) probably made in the monastery of Canterbury. The main decorative feature of the front panel was a circle, or two interlaced squares, filled with repetitions of a small tool; a feature probably deriving from Italy.

Canterbury School: an important centre of manuscript illumination in England from the 8th to 13th centuries was at Canterbury. Such foreign developments as the 11th-century Rheims ink-drawing technique influenced the limners, many of whom came from Winchester. Distinctive features at this time are capitals in red, green, and blue, interlaced foliage borders, occasional figures in line, and a predominantly deep colour scheme. The main works written were Apocalypses, Bibles, and bestiaries; many examples are to be seen in various College libraries at Cambridge.

See 'Canterbury School of Illumination' by C. R. Dodwell, C.U.P., 1954.

canting mark: a printer's *device*, q.v., in which the design is based on a pun on the printer's name. Two famous examples are those used by Androw Myllar of Edinburgh (a windmill) and John Day (a sunrise and the legend 'Arise for it is Day').

canvas: heavy cotton binding cloth firmly woven. It is used for binding cheaper grades of books. Also called *duck*. (M.L.)

caoutchouc binding: a method of binding books by securing their pages into a unit with rubber solution. No thread was used. The process was devised by Hancock about 1838, and can be regarded as a precursor of *unsewn binding*, q.v.

cap: the protecting cover of brown paper with which the binder encloses the whole book except the boards during finishing.

See also *capping up*.

cap line: 1. a line of type set in capital letters.

2. an imaginary line which rules across the top of capital letters. Cf. *base line*, *mean line*.

capitals: large letters, e.g. Z, I, A, etc. The name derives from the inscriptional letters at the head, or capital, of Roman columns. Their use in proof corrections and manuscripts is indicated by three lines under the letter or letters concerned. Abbreviated as *c*. or *caps*.

See also *small capitals*.

capping up: the fitting of a thin paper cover around the body of a book but leaving the back exposed. This is done after sewing, edge trimming and gilding are finished, and serves to protect the edges while covering, headbanding, and finishing processes are carried out.

caps and smalls: words having the first letter set as a large capital and the following letters of the same word set in small capitals. The first word of a chapter is often set in this way. The use of caps and smalls is indicated in manuscripts by three lines under the first letter and two under the remaining letters of each word concerned. E.g. WATERLOO BRIDGE.

capsa: the cylindrical container in which papyrus rolls were kept.

caption: strictly, descriptive matter printed as a headline above an illustration. The custom of the composing room, however, is to refer to descriptive matter printed underneath an illustration as a caption.

See also *legend*.

Caradoc Press: a private press founded in 1899 by H. G. Webb. He was a wood engraver and used this medium for initials, borders, etc. Printing was hand done.

carbon black: see *gas black*.

carbon print: one of the chromate methods of copying in photography. Carbon tissue (sold in various shades) is used which is sensitized by bathing it in a solution of potassium dichromate or ammonium dichromate, and then dried in darkness without heat. The chromate bath should be 2 to 5% with the addition of sufficient ammonia to produce a yellowish colour. The stronger the chromate bath, the softer the pictures. Copying is done in daylight or with an arc lamp, and takes a few minutes in the case of normal negatives. In copying, the gelatine in the carbon tissue is hardened in proportion to the action of light, and becomes insoluble in lukewarm water to a greater or lesser depth. As the hardening progresses from the surface of the carbon tissue, while the lowest layers of gelatine next to the paper backing remain soluble, the gelatine base would become entirely or partly detached when directly developing the copied carbon tissue in lukewarm water, and would run off the backing. Consequently a transfer is first made to fresh paper, a *transfer paper* treated with hardened gelatine. Both the pigment copy and the transfer paper are softened in cold water and brought together below the surface of the water with the gelatined surfaces towards each other, whereupon the two papers are lifted and lightly pressed by a roller against a glass plate, and finally laid between sheets of blotting paper to dry off the surplus water. The two papers are then 'developed' by immersing them in a bowl of water at 100 to 120° F. The unexposed gelatine dissolves and the original paper backing can be pulled off, developing being continued for a few more minutes, so that the picture is clear when taken out to dry. Single transfers can be used but these produce a picture reversed left to right. To overcome this it is usual to make a double transfer. Carbon print was formerly known as *charcoal print* because finely powdered charcoal was often used as a black pigment.

The carbon process has been applied extensively in reproduction work, especially for *intaglio*, q.v.

See also *photogravure*. (G.U.)

carbon tissue: paper coated with gelatine which is made semi-opaque by the addition of pigment. The gelatine usually contains some sugar and glycerine to preserve its flexibility. Such carbon tissue is used for various methods of photographic reproduction based on the sensitivity to light of gelatine treated with alkali dichromate. (See *photogravure*.)

Carbon tissue is sensitized immediately before use by bathing it in a 2 to 5% solution of potassium dichromate or ammonium dichromate with the addition of a little ammonia. While the paper is wet its sensitivity to light is slight. In a dry state it is sensitive, above all, to blue and violet light, through the action of which on the dichromate it is rendered insoluble in water of not more than 105° F. The object of the pigment is to act as an absorber of light, so that the penetration of light into the layer depends on its intensity. In this way, after copying and developing, a gelatine relief is obtained from the layer of pigment built up from the upper side of the base. In developing, it would therefore run off the backing paper if, in the process referred to, the base were not transferred to a new backing by spreading the paper over it with the damped side of the base reversed before developing.

Carbon tissue and carbon print were invented by Poitevin in 1855, but were perfected by Joseph Wilson Swan in 1862–64. The latter also established the first factory, still in existence, for manufacturing tissue. (G. U.)

card fount: the smallest complete fount of type stocked and sold by a typefounder.

cardboard: see *boards*.

caret: the symbol ⁁ used in proof correcting to indicate that something is to be inserted at that point. This symbol was first used by scribes in the early 13th century.

Carmelite Missal: an illuminated Missal, of Carmelite use, made for the London Whitefriars. It was probably written in London prior to 1391, and illuminated by five artists during the next seven years. In the 19th century the Missal was cut up and pasted into scrap-books which were acquired by the British Museum in 1874. From 1933–38 Margaret Rickert of Chicago skilfully reconstructed the surviving portions: these are large initials decorated in various styles, some with grotesques in the East Anglian manner of the early 14th century, others being finely drawn Biblical scenes.

Carnegie Medal: an annual award made by the Library Association of London for an outstanding book for children by a British author published in England during the preceding year. It dates from 1936.

Caroline minuscule: see *Carolingian script*.

Carolingian illumination: the Carolingian renaissance in the 8th century led to the development of Frankish illumination. Many cultures met and fused in the court of Charlemagne, the influence of Byzantium being seen in the arcaded Canon-tables and the use of gold and silver lettering on purple grounds; the large initial page designs appear to be of Celtic origin, while the inclusion of exotic birds is Syrian. Important centres, with stylistic differences particular to each, were Tours, Rheims, Aachen, Trier, Metz, and Hautvillers.

It was at Trier that the Gospel-book of Ada (Charlemagne's sister?) was made in the early 9th century (now Cod. 22, Trier Library). This, and other works of the *Ada-group*, shows rich colouring and greater fantasy in the lively figure representations of the Evangelists and their symbols, deriving, it is suggested, from the pictorial tradition of Italy and England. The Golden Psalter (c. 783–95), written in gold minuscules with gold or silver capitals by the scribe Dagulf, is the finest example of this group. It is now in the Österreichische Nationalbibliothek, Vienna.

In Bibles written and decorated at the *Tours School* the Anglo-Saxon influence is especially marked.

The *Metz School* perfected the historiated initial. From *Rheims* came the *Utrecht Psalter*, q.v., held to be the most splendid example of Carolingian illumination.

The *Palatine School* of Aachen saw the revival of pure classical tradition.

Carolingian script: a 9th-century script developed at the Abbey of St Martin at Tours under the direction of Abbot Alcuin (Albinus Flaccus), formerly head of the Benedictine monastery at York, for the Emperor Charlemagne's revision of grammars, Bibles, church books, etc. It was probably developed from Anglo-Saxon half-uncial script or early Merovingian, though present-day scholars disagree as to the precise origin. The influence of Alcuin extended across Europe; he developed punctuation and the division of words into sentences. For the first time sentences began with an initial capital. Carolingian was revived in the 15th century by Italian humanistic (renaissance) scholars and known as neo-caroline or scrittura umanistica. From these forms our present-day roman lower-case letters derive. Alternative names for Carolingian are *alcuinian script* and *caroline minuscule*.

carriage: the part of a printing machine on which the forme moves backwards and forwards during printing.

cartouche: the space on a map, enclosed by an elaborate drawing of human figures, plant life, animals, or heraldic devices, in which the name or title is printed. Alternatively, the cartouche may be in the form of a scroll with rolled ends and the title in the centre. Splendid examples of the former are contained in the atlas of Abraham Ortel (Ortelius), 'Theatrum Orbis Terrarum', which was printed in 1570 by Christopher Plantin of Antwerp.

cartridge paper: a rough-surface printing paper, often tub-sized, and used for a variety of purposes, such as drawing, envelopes, jackets, offset printing, wrapping, etc. Offset-cartridge may include esparto-fibres to assist stability when printing.

cartulary: see *chartulary.*

Cary, John, *c.* 1754–1835: an English mapmaker who, in his county maps, did much to improve the craft of map engraving and printing.

case: 1. a cover, made by hand or machine, consisting of two boards, a hollow, and a binding material. This case is subsequently attached to the book, providing the style in common use by most British and American publishers.

See also *book cloth.*

2. the compositor's case, divided into many compartments, in which individual letters, numerals, and spaces are kept. Cases may be used in pairs, an upper and lower, or the whole fount may be in a double case, i.e. one unit.

In the U.S.A. a post-war alternative to the traditional case is a space-saving set of coloured plastic boxes laid out on a steel tray: it is known as the 'Rob Roy' system. The British adaptation of this is described under *Multifont*, q.v.

See also *frame, lay of the case.*

case lot: a quantity of flat paper, usually wrapped in packages, and enclosed in a wooden box. The term is indeterminate, but means, in the custom of the paper trade, a quantity of about 500 lb. (M.L.)

cased books: books bound in cases. Usually done by machine. The first book in England to be issued by its publisher in a cloth case, with spinal lettering in

Smyth case-maker

Cases ready for use

Casing-in by hand

Smyth casing-in machine

gold, was volume two of 'The Works of Lord Byron', London, John Murray, 1832.
See also *case* (1).

casein: a substance obtained from curdled milk. It is used as an adhesive in the manufacture of coated papers.

Casement Award: an annual award of £50 provided by Marquis MacDonald (U.S.A.) and granted by the Irish Academy of Letters, Dublin, for the best book of verse or play by an Irish author. The award, named after Roger Casement, was first made in 1933 but has now lapsed.

casing-in: the final stage in the production of cased books. After the cases are attached the books are pressed for several hours while they dry out.

Caslon, William, 1692–1766: an eminent English typefounder, who cut his version of old-face letters between 1720–26 for the printer William Bowyer; the punches were based on a type by Christoffel van Dijk (1601–69) of Holland and on other Dutch types then popular in England. His first specimen sheet was issued in 1734.
The lightness of Caslon type makes it unsuitable for printing on coated papers.

cassie: a derivation of the French word 'casser'= to break; said of damaged sheets at the top and bottom of a ream.
See also *cording quires, outsides.*

cast: see *electrotype* and *stereotype.*

cast coated paper: an art paper with an exceptionally high finish, developed in America about 1950. Body paper unwinds from the reel and receives an application of coating. While still in a plastic state the surface is brought into close contact with a highly polished metal drum, and there dried. It thus differs fundamentally from orthodox coated art papers, where, after application to the body paper, the coating dries uninfluenced by any other surface and has a natural polish with characteristics dependent on the coating. The surface will fracture unless the paper is handled with care at all stages.
The soft, absorbent, and uniformly flat surface of cast coated paper is suitable for letterpress, offset litho, and gravure. For half-tone, screens of 120 to 150 lines give the best results. The choice of ink needs special care: for a high gloss in the printed result, quick drying inks with a high gloss varnish content are used. For letterpress printing, types with fine hair lines and great contrast between their thick and thin strokes, e.g. Bodoni, are unsuitable.
The high cost of this paper has limited its use in books, but the 'Connoisseur Year Book, 1956' offers an opportunity to examine its possibilities for high-class colour work.
Cast coated paper is made in America, Canada, and Belgium, and in Britain under licence by the Clyde Paper Company of Rutherglen.
See also *art paper.*

cast-off: the estimating by the printer of the number of pages that copy will occupy when set up in type. The cast-off is the basis of the printer's estimate of production costs which he submits to the publisher. The number of words in the copy is counted, or averaged by a recognized method, and the total converted into its equivalent in printed pages, the extra pages needed for prelims, etc., being added.
Users of *Monotype*, q.v., should consult 'Scientific Copyfitting for Composition on Monotype Machines', 1952.

cast-up: the computing by the printer of the cost of setting up matter in type. He makes calculations to determine the number of characters, ens, or words which have been accommodated in an average page. From the cost per thousand ens, plus charges for display setting or any extras, a total for composing the whole work, including author's corrections, is reached.

casting: to found type by pouring molten type-metal (an alloy of lead, tin, and antimony) into an adjustable mould to the upper orifice of which is brought a matrix of a letter or character.
See also *stereotype.*

casting box: a device for casting stereos, the mould being connected to the melting pot. There are two main types of casting box for curved stereos, different in principle. In one, the plate is cast in a horizontal position, usually without any jet; in the other the plate is cast vertically and has a jet (see illustration). The former was first built by the Swiss firm Winkler, Fallert & Co. In the smaller models the melting pot contains no more than 1000 kg (2204 lb), in the larger ones not more than 2500 kg of metal. In gas-heated pots the sloping base is exposed to the direct flame of the burner, and the flue gases escape round the upper part of the pot. Near the base there is a narrow exhaust opening, its length being equal to the width of the plate. It is opened and shut by a shutter of the same material as the pot. The illustration shows the casting flask in the casting position with the shutter catch open. Cooling water is supplied to both the core and the outer casting bowl. Most of the heat is drawn off through the core, for the matrix insulates the plate from the outer bowl. The shutter is opened automatically when the flask is in position, and closes automatically before the metal has time to solidify. The plate has no jet and need only be bored

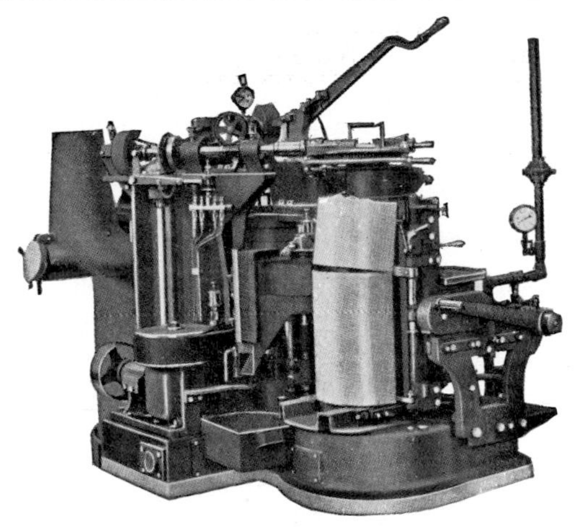

The Junior Autoplate machine casts vertically with a large jet which is automatically cut off. Boring is done in a separate machine. Capacity—two plates a minute. (*L & M*)

(see *plate-boring machine*) before being put on the press. In some works the plates are not bored, but are placed directly on the printing press. Such a casting box delivers two plates a minute, but special models will deliver four plates a minute. The casting box takes up little space, and the temperature in the pot can be kept low due to its direct contact with the mould. It is worked by one man and a plate-layer who attends to two boxes at the same time. This type is used extensively in Europe.

Modern boxes of the vertical type were developed with the help, among others, of König & Bauer of Würzburg, and Vomag of Plauen, and were made automatic by the American H. Wise Wood. The pot and the mechanical parts are placed independently of each other, and the metal is pumped through a pipe to the mould. The latter is almost twice the height of the completed plate, and, in casting, is entirely filled with metal. The jet is sawn off before the plate leaves the machine. Cooling is done by spraying the inside of the cylinder with water from a stationary central pipe, and by means of water between the double walls of the outer flask. A light signal indicates when cooling has proceeded

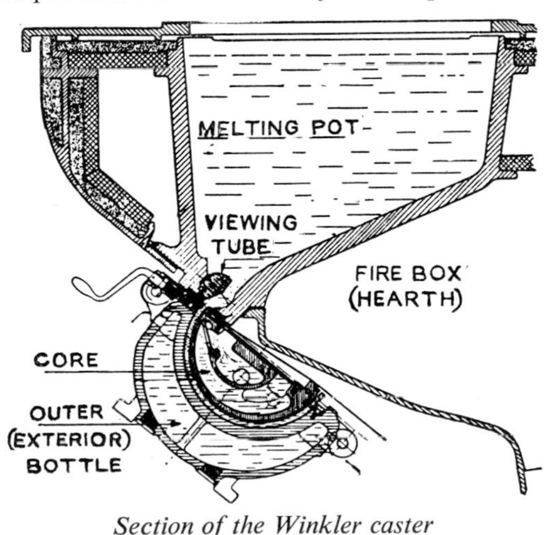

Section of the Winkler caster

Winkler casting box for horizontal plates

sufficiently for the mould to be opened. When this has been done, the core makes half a revolution, the jet being cut off. The jet and an old plate are thrown into the pot for each casting, so that the level of the metal is kept constant. The normal output is two plates in about fifty seconds. Here, too, there is an entirely

Gas-heated caster for vertical plates

automatic type which produces four plates a minute. The vertical machine, the most generally used in Britain and the U.S.A., occupies more space than the Winkler and requires a larger crew (2–3 men).

Special casting boxes for cylindrical plates are made in the U.S.A. (Scott, Goss, see illustration under *rotary press*). Models with centrifugal casting are also in existence.

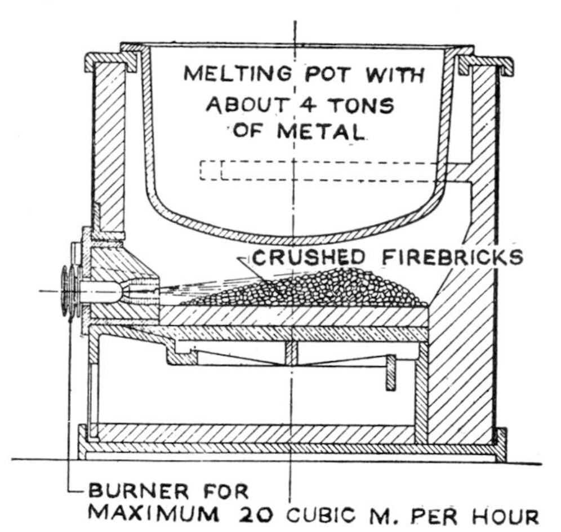

Section of the gas-heated metal pot

The melting of the metal is now often done by heating the pot electrically, either by means of resistance coils placed in grooves of special bricks in the space under the pot, or immersion heaters (see illustrations). The power required in casting two normal plates a minute is 100 kw. Automatic quick-casting boxes are equipped with heating devices for a maximum of 250 kw. The temperature of the pot is controlled thermostatically. (G.U.)

casting-off: see *cast-off*.

casting-up: see *cast-up*.

Catalan bindings: see *gótico-mudéjar*.

catalogue: 1. a list of names, titles, persons or things, usually in alphabetical or classified order, with explanatory additions, as in a catalogue of books.

2. a commercial catalogue is a list of goods or merchandise, with relevant description. (M.L.)

catalogue raisonné: a classified book-list in which a brief appraisal of the subject-matter follows each entry.

catch-letters. See *catchword* (2).

catchline: the temporary headline printed on proofs.

catchword: 1. the word written underneath the last line of each page or section in a manuscript which was also the word with which the next page or section commenced; its purpose was to guide the binder in assembling. The use of catchwords in European printed books varied and was never consistent; in Italian books of the era 1470–1500 they first appeared at the end of a section, later at the end of every page. Their use in England was from *c.* 1530–1800 and usually on each page.

2. the word printed in bold type or capital letters at the top of each page in a dictionary or encyclopaedia to serve as a guide to use. The first three letters of a word are sometimes used as an alternative; these are *catch-letters*.

catenati: *chained books*, q.v.

Cathach Psalter: the earliest surviving Irish manuscript, probably written towards the close of the 6th century, and traditionally attributed to St Columba (521–97). The script is a round Insular majuscule, and pen-drawn outline initials surrounded by dots are the decorative feature.

The name derives from the curious use to which it was put. A cathach, protected in a *cumdach*, q.v., was carried into battle to ensure victory. The Cathach Psalter was credited with this magic power long after the death of Columba, and Irish refugees took it to France. In 1842 it passed to the Royal Irish Academy; the cumdach was taken to the National Museum, Dublin.

Catholicon: a Latin dictionary written by Johann Balbus, a Dominican, in the late 13th century. It was first printed at Mainz, in 1460, on 373 folio leaves. Although dated, the printer is not named, and it has been ascribed, without proof, to Gutenberg, to whom is attributed the colophonic inscription of its completion 'non calami, stili aut pennae, sed mira patronarum formarumque concordia, proportione et modulo. . . .' that is, 'not with a reed, stylus or pen, but by the wonderful accord, proportion, and harmony of punches and types' has it been finished.

Wherever printed, the stock passed to Peter Schöffer by 1469, as, of course, did Gutenberg's equipment.

Catnach, John, 1769–1813: a printer who established himself at Alnwick, Northumberland, in 1790. His importance now derives from the publication, *c.* 1790, of 'Beauties of Natural History' in which were sixty-seven small cuts by *Thomas Bewick*, q.v., to be followed by other books with wood engravings by Bewick and Luke Clennel. From 1807–9 Catnach took William Davison as a partner. The latter later published independently many works illustrated by Bewick, and remained in business until 1858.

Catnach moved to Newcastle in 1808, and to

London in 1813. He was here succeeded by his son James (1792–1841). From the Catnach Press at Seven Dials he issued between 1813 and 1838 countless ballads, chap-books, cheap books for children, and sensational broadsides, mostly of murders, real or fictitious. There was no special typographical merit in these productions.

Cavendish Society: a printing society established in London, 1846–54, 'for the promotion of chemistry and its allied sciences'. It was named after the English chemist and physicist Henry Cavendish (1731–1810) whose biography by Wilson the Society published in 1851. (With M.L.)

Caxton, William, *c.* 1422–91: the first English printer and publisher, who also translated many of the works he issued, and had a considerable literary influence.

In 1438 he was apprenticed to a wealthy London merchant, Robert Large, who in 1439 was Lord Mayor of London. The precise date when Caxton went abroad is uncertain, but by 1446 he was in business at Bruges, an important city where commerce and literature flourished. In 1453 he was admitted to the Livery of the Mercers' Company. By 1462 Caxton was head in Bruges of the 'Merchant Adventurers' or 'English Nation' which had been formed by the Mercers' Company. This meant that Caxton was governor of a guild of English merchants, with powers of magistrate and judge; an office he held for about seven years.

In 1469 Caxton began writing his translation of 'Le Recueil des Histoires de Troyes' of which he completed about forty pages before tiring of the labour. It was at the suggestion of Margaret of Burgundy (whose adviser he now was) that Caxton resumed his translation, and completed it at Cologne in 1471. By this time he had learned to print, though from whom is not known. That it may have been from Ulrich Zell in Cologne is suggested by the close similarity of several letters used by both printers. It was, however, at Bruges that he printed the first book in English, 'Recuyell of the Historyes of Troye' by Raoul Le Fèvre, about 1475.

On establishing in 1476 the first press in England, at Westminster, Caxton printed an Indulgence and probably other small undated works before he issued the first book printed in England to bear a date: this was 'Dictes or Sayengis of the Philosophres', 1477, to be followed by nearly a hundred other works before he died. His 'Mirrour of the World', 1481, was the first illustrated book printed in England. The use of eight gothic types is attributed to Caxton.

He was succeeded in business by his assistant, *Wynkyn de Worde*, q.v.

Caxton Society: a society founded in 1845 for the publication of Latin and Anglo-Norman chronicles and biographies. It closed in 1854.

Cayme Press: a printing press founded in London by P. A. L. C. Sainsbury in 1923, with the aim of printing 'in pleasant form . . . any work that was not merely commercial, or which involved no departure from good typographical standards. . . . Particular attention was given to the designing, engraving, and printing of Heraldic and Genealogical books and Tabular Pedigrees.'

The Cayme Press also installed an etching press for artists to pull their own prints.

See also *Favil Press.*

cellulose: the fibrous substance obtained from wood, cotton, hemp, flax, and other plants. It is used in paper-making, the quality of the paper depending on the quality of its cellulose base.

Celtic illumination: see *Hiberno-Saxon illumination.*

centre head: synonymous with *cross-head,* q.v.

centre notes: notes set between columns.

centre-stitching: in pamphlet binding, stitching with thread by working it through the fold or centre, in a manner similar to wire saddle-stitching. (M.L.)

centred: type lines which are placed in the centre of a sheet, or in the centre of a type measure. (M.L.)

Cerne, Book of: an illuminated manuscript of the Passion and Resurrection portions of the Gospels, written at Lichfield in the early 9th century. Decoration is in a severely calligraphic style and the colours used are light shades with only occasional gold; small beasts enliven some pages.

The name comes from its former location at Cerne Abbey, Dorset, but it is now in Cambridge University Library.

cerography: engraving on wax spread on a sheet of copper; this plate is used as a mould from which an electrotype is made. The process is used in making maps. Hence, *cerograph* or *cerotype*, a print made by this process. (M.L.)

cf.: the abbreviation for 'confer', i.e. compare, or refer to.

chain lines: the vertical lines on laid paper, about 1 in. apart.

See also *turned chain lines.*

chain stitch: the stitch made by the binder at the head and tail of a section before beginning to sew the next.

chained books: books secured by chains to a horizontal bar which extended above the reading desk on which they rested, or to a shelf over it. This method of securing books was used in monastic and other libraries from the early 15th century until, in English church libraries, the early 18th century. Also known as *catenati*.

chalcography: the art of engraving on copper or brass.

chalk overlay: see *mechanical overlay*.

chalk plate engraving: a simple and inexpensive method of making a relief printing plate, where there is a stereotyping plant. The design is drawn on a smooth steel plate coated with a chalk preparation. The success of the method depends largely on the skill of the engraver, who must do his work freehand. (M. L.)

chalking: a printing fault caused by using an over-reduced ink or one unsuited to the paper; thus the ink vehicle soaks into the paper leaving the pigment deposited on the surface.

Challenge press: a small job-press of the Gordon style, made in several sizes. (M. L.)

chamfered edges: bevelled edges. When heavy boards are used for large books the top, fore, and bottom edges are sometimes bevelled.

champlevé: enamelled book-covers made by craftsmen from the 11th to 13th centuries. Designs were cut into a thin sheet of gold or copper which formed the cover, the cavities being filled with enamel. On other bindings the enamelling was limited to the subsidiary decoration of borders and corners. Limoges was a centre of this art. Cf. *cloisonné*.

chancery: the name given by Aldus Manutius to the narrow italic type based on the cursive chancery script, or *cancellaresca corsiva*, q.v. It was first cut as a type by Francesco Griffo, in 1500, for Aldus (who in 1495 used a cursive form of greek), to save lateral space in his series of pocket editions of the classics. See also *cursive*.

chancery hand: see *cancellaresca corsiva*.

Channel School: the name sometimes given to the interdependent north French and south English schools of art in the 13th century, and particularly to manuscript painting of the time.

See *Gothic illumination*.

chap-book: a pamphlet or ballad of the kind hawked by chapmen, or pedlars, from village to village during the Middle Ages, and reaching the height of its popularity in the 16th century.

chapel: the term applied to a group within a printing works; thus to 'call a chapel' is to hold a chapel meeting of the journeymen. The elected leader is known as the Father of the Chapel.

There is a popular belief that the term originates from the setting up of a press in the almonry of Westminster Abbey by William Caxton.

Chapter books: books published by members of the Chapter Coffee House, an association of London booksellers formed in the 18th century, whereby they paid for shares in a book and its printing costs, receiving in return a proportion of the books at cost price. They were later known as *Trade books*.

chapter heading: the displayed heading at the beginning of every chapter. It is set to uniform height for each chapter of the book and may be embellished with a head-piece or illustration.

character: any single letter, number, punctuation mark or symbol cast as a type. Synonymous with *sort*.

character book: a volume of literary exercises or essays, based in their form on the character sketches of Theophrastus, and popular, in England, in the 17th century.

The well-known 'Microcosmographie, or a peece of the world discovered; in essayes and characters', first printed by William Stansby, 1628, has been printed in various editions until the 20th century. It was written by John Earle whose name did not appear as the author until E. Say's edition of 1732.

See G. Murphy, 'A bibliography of English character-books, 1608–1700', Bibliographical Society, 1925.

charcoal paper: a soft, rough-finished paper used for making illustrations with a charcoal crayon or pencil. (M. L.)

charcoal print: see *carbon print*.

chargeable time: in the *Standard Cost-finding System*, q.v., chargeable time is designated as the number of hours or hour-units (six minutes each) necessary for the production of any work or job. In composition, the chargeable time may include preparation of the copy or layout, setting up the type, proof reading, revising, correcting, making up of formes and locking up. In presswork, bookbinding, or any of the graphic arts, similar systems of cost-finding are used. (M. L.)

See also *Federation Costing System*.

chart: a sheet of cardboard, paper, or other material containing information in tabulated form, written or printed; a graphic drawing or map. (M. L.)

See also *tabular work*.

chart paper: a good-quality paper with a strong furnish, often tub-sized or wet-strengthened, which is suitable for the lithographic printing of maps.

charter: a deed or document by which a sovereign grants privileges to a person or corporate body, e.g. when founding a university or corporation.

chartulary: 1. a collection or set of charters, especially the volume in which were copied out by hand the charters, title-deeds, etc., of the land and property of a monastery.

2. a modern printed version of such a volume.

chase: a steel or cast-iron frame into which type and blocks are locked by means of wooden wedges or small metal expanding boxes called quoins. Chases vary in size. The term 'in chase' describes a book which is imposed ready for printing.

chased edges: the gilded edges of a book which have been decorated by the finisher with heated tools known as goffering irons. A wavy or crimped effect results. Also known as *goffered edges.*

Chaucer Society: a society founded in 1868 by F. J. Furnivall for the publication of parallel texts of Chaucerian manuscripts.

cheeks: the two main vertical timbers forming the frame of a hand-printing press. They normally extended from floor to ceiling.

Chemco dark-room camera: a modern American camera, made in Britain by Pictorial Machinery Ltd., for the photoengraver and photo-lithographer. The copyboard and bellows are mounted on rails, but all controls are outside the dark room. The camera is loaded with three rolls of film, of different width. A strip is positioned, held flat by a vacuum, and exposed. Exposure is controlled electronically. The strip is then cut off and drops into a box for subsequent development. Thus a number of exposures can be made and developed together. The copyboard will take an original 24 in. by 30 in. Accurate focusing is done according to scale readings; setting the scales aligns lens and copyboard. For half-tone work built-in screens are held below the camera.

The camera is claimed to be fast and accurate, since the possibility of human error or miscalculation is largely obviated.

chemical printing: the name given by Senefelder to his invention of *lithography*, q.v.

chemical wood: pulp obtained by the chemical treatment of wood. It differs from *mechanical wood* pulp, q.v., by the fact that the resin, ligneous matter and oils contained in the wood are removed by boiling with acid or alkaline solution. This leaves the wood cellulose fibre isolated so that these dissolved impurities can be washed out preparatory to the bleaching and other processes of paper-making.

See also *sulphite pulp*, *wood free*.

chemigraphy: the name given to any process of mechanical engraving depending upon the action of chemicals; a method of etching on metal in which photography is not employed. (M.L.)

chemise: a cover of silk or chevrotain sometimes used in the 15th century as a protection for embellished leather-bound books. Also, the extended covering of the boards in early bindings.

chemitype: 1. a process for producing maps, etc., by etching lines on a zinc plate covered with wax, filling them with fusible metal, and then eating away the zinc with acid, leaving the lines in relief.

2. a plate made by this method. (M.L.)

Chepman, Walter, *c.* 1473–*c.* 1538: the associate of Androw Myllar in establishing, in 1508, the first printing press in Scotland. They had a joint licence and monopoly from James IV for printing and selling all books in Scotland. The first work they issued was 'The Complaint of the Black Knight' by Lydgate, also known as 'The Maying or Disport of Chaucer'.

chessmen: the pieces used in games of chess are represented in printing by standard symbols cast as separate types.

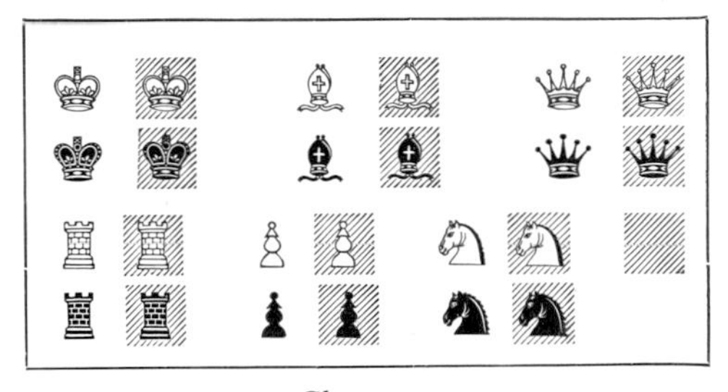

Chessmen

Chetham Society: a society founded in Manchester in 1843 for the printing of local records, memorials, chartularies, etc.

cheveril (or **chevrotain**): leather made from the skins of small guinea deer; used in the Middle Ages for *chemises*, q.v.

chiaroscuro: a method of printing wood engravings in which successive blocks of wood are used to print lighter and darker shades as solid masses. This method, which was used in Italy and Germany in the 16th and 17th centuries, traces its origins to a German wood engraver Georg Lucas Cranach in 1507. In the late 18th century it was revived in England, notably in the 1820's by George Baxter.

See also *Baxter print*.

Childs, John, 1783–1853: a printer of Bungay, now remembered for his cheap editions of standard authors and annotated editions of the Bible.

china clay: an important ingredient of the surface coating of some *art papers*, q.v.

china paper: a thin hand-made paper of silky texture made from bamboo and used for proofing wood engravings. Its modern machine-made substitute is more accurately termed *Japanese paper*, q.v.

chinese transfer: a proof taken with stiff ink on transfer paper (formerly prepared china paper) for use as a lithographic transfer. (G. U.)

chirograph: a formal handwritten document.

Chiswick Press: the printing press founded in 1811 by *Charles Whittingham*, q.v., and from 1840 controlled by his nephew of the same name who printed for *William Pickering*, q.v. It was noted for its fine typography and careful presswork at a time when these were not universally a feature of book production. Notable was the series of Aldine poets.

Chodowiecki, Daniel Nikolaus, 1726–1801: a German artist-engraver who lived in Berlin. He is remembered for his illustrations to the works of Goethe, Shakespeare, Cervantes, Voltaire, Sterne, Lessing, Le Sage, and others. His influence on contemporary illustrators in Germany was very great.

chrestomathy: a collection of extracts from the writings of one or more authors, especially from a foreign language, used as specimens of a literature or language.

chromate process: any of several very important photographic or reproduction methods based on the fact that a combination of chromate and a suitable colloid (gelatine, glue, albumen, gum arabic, etc.) is sensitive to light in such a way that the colloid loses its solubility or its ability to swell under the influence of light; it is said to be *tanned* or *case-hardened*. This phenomenon was discovered by Fox Talbot in 1852.

Different groups of methods are distinguished according to the way in which they are utilized. 1. The colloidal substance unaffected by light is dissolved, so that a relief is formed by the light-affected parts. If the colloid embodied a finely distributed insoluble pigment, the relief will be coloured. On this fact carbon printing, rubber printing, and other delicate methods of printing are based. In the *absorbing process* the relief obtained is, indeed, colourless at the beginning, but later it absorbs a solution of, for example, aniline dye. If the relief obtained is coated with stiff ink the latter only adheres to the paper in the colloid-free areas. The colloidal relief can also be produced on a metal surface where it serves as an etching resist, so that a metal relief can be obtained by etching. In this way, as well as by utilizing the difference in properties between freely exposed metal and the picture layer, formes of various kinds can be made.

See also *albumen process*, *carbon tissue*, *enamel process*, *photogravure*.

2. The colloidal substance which is unaffected by light (as a rule, gelatine) absorbs more liquid (as a rule, water), so that it swells to a greater degree than the parts tanned by the light. If stiff ink is spread with a roller or brush on a printed chromate-gelatine layer it adheres in varying degress according to the degree of dampness of the layer, i.e. it adheres most on the strongly tanned areas and least (or not at all) on the most swollen and watery. From a gelatine relief inked up in this way the ink can be transferred to paper pressed against it, a principle utilized in *collotype*, q.v. Finally, dry ink powder can be sifted over the swollen gelatine layer, in which case the powder adheres best on the most swollen and viscous areas.

However, the properties of the chromate colloids can be utilized in another way, namely, in a number of *indirect* chromate processes. In 1893 H. E. Farmer discovered that chromate gelatine became insoluble in the presence of finely distributed silver, even without the influence of light. Due to this an ordinary photographic silver picture can be produced, and by placing this in contact with a gelatine layer in the presence of chromate the gelatine layer can be tanned. It is thus possible, starting for example with a silver bromide enlargement, to produce pictures of a character corresponding to those obtained by the direct chromate methods already referred to. (G. U.)

chromatic type: type made so that it will print part of a character in one colour; then a second type is inserted in its place to print another colour until the character is complete. Rarely used. (M. L.)

chromium plating: a means of protecting blocks and other printing formes of copper, brass, or other metals, in the latter cases usually after previous copper depositing or nickel plating. The galvanically precipitated chrome film is very resistant to mechanical influence and chemical attack, but not to hydrochloric acid or concentrated sulphuric acid. Chromium plating is done in galvanic baths in which the electrolyte consists chiefly of pure chromic acid in water. The anodes consist of lead or other material insoluble in chromic acid. The chromium is thus taken from the bath itself, and thus fresh chromic acid must be added regularly. The bath should have a specific gravity of 30–35° Bé, and a temperature of 40° C (105° F).

Poisonous gases develop during the work, so that a suction device must be fitted to the bath. Chromium plating can be removed by hydrochloric acid or galvanically. (G.U.)

chromo-paper: paper which is more heavily coated than art paper. The surface can be dull or glazed. It is used for colour lithography.

chromograph: an apparatus for reproducing multiple copies of plans, manuscripts, etc., using an aniline dye instead of ink. The impressions are taken from a gelatinous substance to which the material to be copied has been transferred.

chromolithography: lithographic printing in several colours. The term has been in use since 1837 when Gottfried Engelmann obtained a French patent for stone engraving in colours, the component colours being produced in crayon drawing. He called his process 'chromolithographie'. Illustrations made in this way first appeared in English books about 1839, such names as Day, Humphreys, Hullmandel, and Boys being important.

Present-day workers often use a large number of colours. The chromolithographer first makes an outline drawing with border lines for all the coloured areas. This is engraved on gelatine foil, or is drawn on a material from which it can either be traced on a number of plates or transferred on to stone from which the required outline offsets can be made. The work is generally done on grained stones or plates on which the autolithographic artist can use crayon. Crayon lithography is often combined with pen drawing and airbrush spraying. The photo-litho method is also combined with chromolithography. (G.U.)

See also *autolithography, colour printing, Plastocowell.*

chromorecta process: see *offset reproduction.*

chronicles: a detailed record of events arranged in order of time but without any attempt at literary style.

chronogram: a sentence or inscription, printed on the title-page of a book, in which certain typographically stressed letters denote by their numerical values the publication date.

E.g. (from the O.E.D.):

LorD haVe MerCIe Vpon Vs = 1666
i.e.: 50 + 500 + 5 + 1000 + 100 + 1 + 5 + 5 = 1666

chrysographer: an artist who embellished manuscripts in gold. Early examples date from the 4th century.

See also *gold, illumination.*

chuck: the small wheel on the end of the forme roller on a job press. Sometimes called *roller collar* or *roller truck.* (M.L.)

Church, William, *c.* 1778–1863: a native of Vermont, U.S.A., where he was a practising doctor of medicine before emigrating to England *c.* 1820 and settling in Birmingham. Here he took up mechanical engineering with some success, notable being his inventions of a type-caster, a printing press, and a composing machine (patented 1822). The caster discharged the types into a magazine from which they were selected and set up by keyboard operation. When printing was completed the types were thrown back into the casting pot.

The Church press of 1821 was a flat-bed hand-press of iron with vertically applied pressure, a new feature being roller ink distribution. Writing in his 'Typographia' Hansard stated that the pressman 'has only to lay the sheet on the tympan, and immediately apply his hand to the rounce, by the turning of which the forme is inked, the frisket and tympan turned down, the press run in, and the impression given'.

cicero: a Continental unit for measuring the width or 'measure' of a line of type and the depth of a page. One cicero equals 4·511 mm. or 12 Didot points. The name is said to derive from the size of type cut and cast for Schöffer's edition of Cicero's 'De Oratore' in the late 15th century.

See also *Didot point, point.*

circuit edges: limp-backed Bibles and prayer-books are sometimes bound with projecting covers turned over to protect the edges. The cover is split at the corners, allowing it to fold closely to the edges like a box. Also known as *divinity circuit.*

See also *Yapp.*

circular: printed or duplicated advertising matter used to announce new publications.

circulating library: a subscription library of fiction or other popular works. One of the largest of Victorian England was that established in 1842 by Charles Edward Mudie; this, like its imitators, gave a great impetus to the publishing of fiction, particularly in the form of the *three-decker novel,* q.v.

City and Guilds of London Institute: the organization, founded in 1878 and granted a Royal Charter in 1900, which, by means of examinations, issues certificates of craft proficiency recognized throughout the printing industry (and other trades).

civilité: a cursive type-face originated about 1557 by Robert Granjon of Lyons, and based on a current French manuscript hand because he considered italic as essentially Italian. The first work he printed with it was 'Dialogue de la Vie et de la Mort' by Innocent Ringhière, 1558.

The name is thought to derive from a work of Erasmus, translated by Jean Louveau as 'La civilité puérile', printed in the new type in 1559.

Clairouin Translation Prize: see *Denyse Clairouin Translation Prize.*

Clarendon: 1. a thick-faced, narrow type with angular, semi-Egyptian serifs, designed in England about 1845.

2. Edward Hyde, first Earl of Clarendon (1607–59) author of 'History of the Rebellion'. The profits of the copyright of this were used by the owners, Oxford University, to found the Clarendon Press in 1713.

Clarke, John: a 19th-century binder associated with Charles Lewis in the use of *tree-calf* covers, q.v.

clasps: ornamental clasps of brass, or of a precious metal, were a feature of bookbindings from the late 14th to the early 17th centuries. They were fitted to the boards of books at the fore-edge, over which they fastened, their purpose being to prevent warping of the boards. This was a practical feature of bookbinding when books were stored flat on shelves or chained to a stand. The metal was often elaborately chased.

Claudin, Anatole, 1833–1906: a Parisian bookseller who made extensive researches into the history of French printing and typography. These were issued as 'Histoire de l'imprimerie en France au XVe et au XVIe siècle', 4 vols., Paris, 1900–14 (the last volume by Paul Lacombe); and the posthumously published 'Documents sur la typographie et la gravure en France au XVe et XVIe siècles', 1926.

Clavell, Robert, d. 1711: a London bookseller and sometime Master of the Stationers' Company. He is now remembered for his *Term Catalogues,* q.v., of the years 1668–1709.

clay-coated paper: see *art paper.*

Claybourn process: a method introduced by the Claybourn Process Corp., U.S.A., to bring the height of a type forme to an exact level. Copper or nickel electros of the forme are pressed in a hydraulic press to make the printing surface level, while allowing any uneven places to appear on the back where they can be smoothed off later.

For multi-colour work the firm also make proofing presses for printing off all four colours in a set of blocks. (G.U.)

See also *Cottrell-Claybourn.*

clean proof: a printer's proof which is free from errors. See also *proof.*

clearing: see *distribute.*

clearing the stuff: the paper-making post-beating process in which any knots or clumps remaining in the stuff after beating are brushed out. This action takes place as the stuff is passed through a refiner.

Clennell, Luke, 1781–1840: a draughtsman and engraver who was an apprentice of *Thomas Bewick,* q.v. He collaborated in the cutting of blocks for Ackermann's 'Religious Emblems', 1809.

cliché: the French word, used elsewhere on the Continent, for a block or a stereotype or electrotype.

Clichograph: an alternative spelling of *Klischograph,* q.v.

clicker: the foreman of a companionship of compositors who distributes copy among them.

The Clique: since 1890, the weekly journal of the Antiquarian Booksellers' Association. Only available to bona fide antiquarian booksellers.

clogged: a printing fault, seen as a smudged impression, caused by the filling with ink of the spaces separating the image elements. This may be due to the presence of dust, over-inking, or the incorrect damping of a lithographic plate. (G.U.)

Also known as *filling in.*

cloisonné: enamelled book covers made mostly by Greek and Italian craftsmen during the 11th century. The design was first outlined by soldering thin strips of metal on to a metal plate; coloured enamels were filled in the compartments formed. Cf. *champlevé.*

close: the second of a pair of punctuation marks, e.g. ")].

closed up: when work is divided among several compositors and each has completed his part, the matter is closed up. (M.L.)

cloth: see *book cloth.*

cloth boards: stiff cloth binding, as distinct from limp or flexible covers.

cloth joints: reinforcement with cloth of the fold of an end-paper. The cloth is visible as an embellishment in the joint of the book. (L.K.)

Clover Hill Press: a private press established in the 1930's by Douglas Cleverdon at Bristol where he had a publishing and bookselling business. He used an Albion press for the production of a few limited editions, as well as for catalogues of the rare books he offered for sale.

clumps: interlinear spacing material used in whiting out, and for footlines at the foot of pages. They are made of lead and are usually from 6- to 12-point thick. If made of wood they are called *reglets*.

coated papers: a general term for art, chromo, enamel, and similar groups of paper on the surface of which a mineral (e.g. china clay) is applied after the body paper has been made. Also known as *surface papers*.

coating machine: a machine which deposits a layer of mineral on the web of partly finished paper. Brushes distribute this evenly and the paper is then dried and calendered.

coating paper: synonymous with *body paper*, q.v.

Cobb's paper: a variety of thin, matt, self-coloured paper sometimes used for the sides of half-bound books or for end-papers. It was invented by Thomas Cobb in 1796.

Cobden-Sanderson, Thomas James, 1840–1922: a famous English bookbinder and founder, with Emery Walker, of the *Doves Press*, q.v.

Cochin: 1. a celebrated French family of printers and engravers of whom the best known was Charles Nicolas Cochin (1715–90). He established a reputation for his engraved title-pages.

2. the name of a series of types produced by the Parisian typefounders Gustave Peignot & Fils (since 1923 Deberny & Peignot). In the Cochin type, 1912 (Monotype, 1927), it was sought to embody the spirit of 18th-century engraved lettering; the Nicolas Cochin type, 1913, was cut from a design by Gustave Peignot.

Coci, Georg, fl. 1500–37: an important German printer working at Saragossa, Spain. With two partners, L. Hutz and W. Appentegger, he acquired in 1506 the press founded there by Paul and Johann Hurus.

His printing was of a high standard, and he issued classical, poetical, and liturgical works. His Livy, 1520, included a title-page printed in three colours.

cock: the middle portion of a *brace end*, q.v., when cast in three pieces, viz.: ⌒ ^ ⌒

cock-robin shop: a London epithet for a small printing shop where the work is poor and the labour badly paid. (M.L.)

cock-up initial: an initial that extends above the first line of the text and aligns with the foot of it.

Cockerell, Douglas, 1870–1945: one of the most influential teachers of the craft of bookbinding in Britain. He served his apprenticeship in the Doves Press bindery of T. J. Cobden-Sanderson. From 1896 he taught in the London Central School for Arts and Crafts, and is remembered for his classic handbook 'Bookbinding and the Care of Books' (Pitman).

His son, Sydney M. Cockerell, has carried on the traditions of his father. See also *marbling*.

cockled: said of paper which has its surface marred by wavy or puckered areas, due to incorrect drying. It may be improved by *conditioning*, q.v.

cockroach: a colloquial expression for display matter set entirely in lower-case type.

codex: 1. a volume of manuscripts; generally applied to Scriptures. Abbreviated as *cod.*

See also *illumination*.

2. see *codices*.

Codex Alexandrinus: a Greek text of the Bible, written in uncial letters on vellum, probably dating from the 5th century. It was given to Charles I in 1627 by the Patriarch of Constantinople, who was formerly Patriarch of Alexandria. Since 1757 it has been in the British Museum.

See 'The Codex Sinaiticus and the Codex Alexandrinus', 2nd ed., British Museum, 1955.

Codex Amiatinus: a copy of the Vulgate written at Monkwearmouth or Jarrow about 715, and intended by the Abbot Ceolfrid as a gift for Pope Gregory II. The decoration is entirely Italian in derivation, bearing no trace of contemporary Northumbrian styles, and was probably influenced by works brought from Rome by ecclesiastical pilgrims: it may even have been written by emigrant Italian scribes.

The name derives from its sometime preservation at Monte Amiata in the Abruzzi mountains, but it is now in the Laurentian Library, Florence.

Codex Argenteus: a 6th-century Italian manuscript of the Bible. The work is a translation into Gothic, originally made by Bishop Ulfilas about 350, written mostly in greek characters with some roman and runic. The writing is done in gold and silver on purple-stained parchment.

The main portion of the New Testament, on 187 leaves, has been in the Library of Uppsala University, Sweden, since 1669; the silver binding is 17th-century work. Other fragments survive in Milan and Wolfenbüttel.

codex aureus: a manuscript volume in which the letters are written in gold on leaves of parchment stained with murex. Examples belong to the 9th and 15th centuries. The two famous examples written at

Canterbury, and now in the British Museum and the Stockholm Library may, however, date from the mid-8th century. Decoration is usually restrained, rich and organized, owing more to continental origins than English art.

Codex Bezae: a 6th-century manuscript of the Gospels and Acts of the Apostles, written in uncial letters on vellum, with text in Latin and Greek. In 1581 it was presented to Cambridge University Library by Theodorus Beza who had acquired it from the monastery of St Irenaeus at Lyons.

Codex Friderico-Augustanus: the portion now in the Leipzig Library of the *Codex Sinaiticus*, q.v.

Codex Laudianus: a manuscript of the Acts of the Apostles, written in Greek and Latin, and brought from Italy to England in the 7th century, probably by Benedict Biscop. It is now in the Bodleian.

codex rescriptus: another name for a *palimpsest*, q.v.

Codex Rescriptus Aphraëmi: a 5th-century palimpsest manuscript of the Bible, on which, in the 12th century, some works of Ephrem Syrus were written. The surviving fragments are in the Bibliothèque Nationale, Paris.

Codex Rossanensis: a Greek manuscript of the Gospels of Matthew and Mark, probably originating in Antioch in the 6th century. The silver uncial letters of the text are written on pages stained with murex. The name derives from its discovery in 1879 at Rossano Cathedral, Calabria.

Codex Sinaiticus: a manuscript of the Bible in Greek, written in uncials, four 48-line columns to a vellum page, probably dating from the 4th century. The place of its origin has not been determined. It is the oldest extant Greek vellum codex. In 1844 it was discovered at a monastery near Mount Sinai by Constantine Tischendorf. He secured at that time forty-three leaves of the Old Testament, taking them to the Leipzig Library (where they now are) and giving them the name *Codex Friderico-Augustanus*.

In 1859 he secured a larger portion of the Old Testament and all the New, presenting them to the Russian Czar at St Petersburg (who was patron of the monastery). Part of the Old T. and all the New T. (347 leaves from an estimated original of 730) were acquired by the British Museum in 1933 for £100,000.

See 'The Codex Sinaiticus and the Codex Alexandrinus', 2nd ed., British Museum, 1955.

codices (sing. *codex*): originally, wax-covered wooden or ivory writing tablets which were hinged together like the pages of a book, the writing on them being done with a stylus. Later, codices were made of vellum and used for manuscript purposes. Abbreviate as *codd.*

cods: glass, porcelain, or steel marbles used for graining printing plates.

coffin: 1. an ornamental box for the safe keeping of books.

2. the frame of wood which encloses the bed of a *joiner's press*, q.v.

3. the carriage or bed of a cylinder or platen press.

Coke, Sir Thomas, 1697–1759: a bibliophile who bought books and manuscripts, largely from Italian collections, for the library he established at Holkham Hall, Norfolk. This was further enriched by his great-nephew Thomas William Coke (1752–1842), first Earl of Leicester. From this library, which exists today, the British Museum acquired twelve important manuscripts in 1952.

cold enamel: a dichromated shellac used as a photo-engraving resist for line or half-tone blockmaking.

cold pressing: an operation employed in the better grade of books. After sheets are printed and dried they are placed under pressure in a screw press or hydraulic press to take out the indentations made by the type. (M.L.)

Colines, Simon de, 1475–1547: a distinguished French printer who pioneered in 1528 the use in France of italic types, and furthered the use of the roman letter. In 1520 he took over the press of Henri Estienne, whose widow he married, printing more than 700 works.

He developed a trade in 16mo editions, and printed numerous Books of Hours with woodcut borders by Geofroy Tory.

A legal work, 'Praxis criminis persequendi', by J. Millaeus, which he issued in 1541, contained in its thirteen large illustrations perhaps the finest French woodcuts of his era.

collate: 1. to put the sections of a book in order. In modern practice, collating is the checking by the binder of the sections after gathering. The work will be easier if the printer has used *collating marks*, q.v.

2. to compare one copy of a printed and bound book with another copy of the same impression.

See also *collating machine*.

3. to describe in terms of a standardized formula the physical make-up of a book. This gives a bibliographer a precise description of how the book was gathered when given to the binder by the printer, i.e. the number of leaves to each quire, the presence of unsigned leaves, cancels, extra leaves, and so forth.

collating machine: a bibliographer's aid, of American origin, for comparing different copies or impressions of a book, map, etc. Differences in material to be compared must be limited to minor corrections and changes made to an author's text while a sheet was being printed off: different editions cannot be compared by the machine.

Two copies of a book are placed open on the machine. By means of strong lamps and a series of mirrors the text is superimposed page by page on a final mirror and there magnified. The two images are displayed alternately. If the two pages are identical, a single motionless image will be reflected. If they are not, the place where type has been disturbed will appear as a disturbed reflection.

The British Museum announced the acquisition of a machine in 1957.

collating mark: a quad mark, having a printing surface usually about 12-point deep by 5-point wide, which is printed in the back, between the first and last pages of each section when in the forme. After folding and gathering the marks appear in descending order on the back of each section, a mistake in gathering being easily seen.

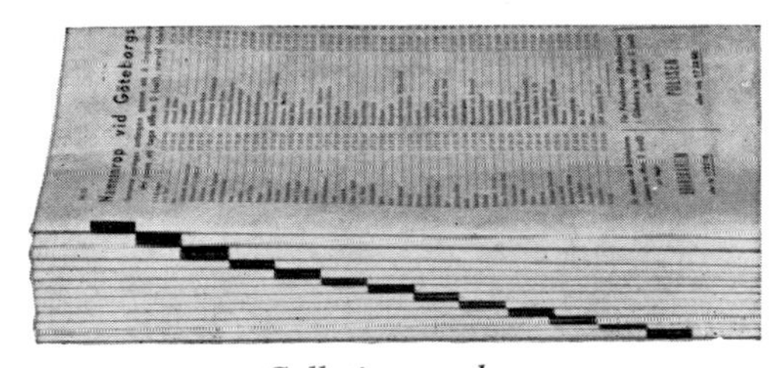

Collating marks

Collectarium: a book of short prayers, lessons, and their collects to be used on particular days.

collected edition: the publication in uniform format, and under one imprint, of the works of an author. Cf. *definitive edition.*

collecting drum: a revolving drum fitted to high-speed printing presses and paper-making machines to catch copies or sheets coming out of the machine and collect them in stacks of five or ten before delivery so that final delivery can proceed at a slower rate. They are then delivered together as a flat layer which can be passed on with only one-fifth of the speed otherwise required. (G.U.)

Collobloc: the trade name of a letterpress half-tone process which eliminates etching and metal printing surfaces. It was announced in 1954 by Koch Processes Ltd., a member of the Photogravure & Allied Holdings Ltd. Group, and derives in principle from the largely experimental washout gelatine relief processes of the 1870's, which failed to give an image of sufficient depth.

The basic material of the printing surface is a three-layer laminated foil comprising a paper backing sheet; a black pigmented separation layer; a brown relief layer; and a clear layer of compounded colloids, blended to be hard yet not brittle, and of adequate printing depth. The foil is sensitized in a potassium or ammonium dichromate bath, dried by warm air, and is then ready for printing down. Other equipment needed is a patent vignette contact screen (65 or 133 ruling) instead of the usual cross-line glass screen, a vertical reproduction camera with vacuum back, a printing-down frame with arc illumination, a simple transfer mangle, and a hot-water development system.

The negative must be an authentic rendering of all the tone values of the original; the shadow areas require pinpoint dots, and highlights the smallest open dot possible.

The original is photographed in a vertical camera, through the contact screen, using such process material as Kodalith or Formalith.

The foil should be sensitized in batches prior to printing down. It can be stored in a refrigerator. Foil varies in thickness according to screen rulings; that used for 120 lines or more is 0·1 mm., that for coarser screens is 0·22 mm.

Several negatives are put in a printing-down frame and covered with a sheet of sensitized foil. Exposure in front of an arc lamp takes place. The exposed foil is transferred via the mangle to the supporting material: this may be a sheet of offset zinc, previously coated with a special adhesive to bind the colloidal surface to the metal. The block is developed in warm water, dried, cut and mounted. Collobiocs transferred to 16 gauge zinc, instead of offset sheeting, can be used on normal plate mounts and bevelled.

Dot formation is the same as that obtained by etching and fine etching, and depth equals that of normal photoengraving standards. Colloblocs incorporate photographic interlays in exact relation to the tonal values of the original: this is one of the major features of the process.

Colloblocs are very durable—150,000 impressions during test, and electrotypes or cold-moulded stereotypes can be made.

For colour work colour-corrected negatives are needed as originals. Experiments with the Collobloc process for line originals are being made, the problem being principally that of routing away large blank areas.

The process is not (1957) in use for bookwork.

collodion: the vehicle on which the photographic image is deposited in the *iodized collodion process*, q.v. Collodion is a solution of pyroxylin in alcohol and ethyl ether, e.g. 50 gm. pyroxylin with 1000 c.c. each of ether and alcohol (95%). This is allowed to stand for some time before being iodized with a mixture of halide salts, e.g. ammonium iodide, cadmium iodide, cadmium bromide, strontium chloride in alcohol. The proportion of 1 of iodizer to 20 of collodion is recommended, but different ingredients and proportions may be used to influence as desired the sensitivity and viscosity of the collodion film. Before being used for coating a glass plate the collodion should be filtered and allowed to stand until it has a reddish colour. Collodion is usually supplied ready for use.

The plate is covered with a film of albumen. The collodion solution should be used at a temperature of 65–70°F. When the film has set, the plate is sensitized in a bath of silver nitrate (below 70°F), and it is then ready for exposure in the camera while still wet.

Colloplas: the trade name of a process for making non-etched gravure cylinders. It substitutes a rubber surface on which the printing image is impressed hydraulically for the copper-coated etched cylinders used in photogravure, and was announced in 1954 by Koch Processes Ltd., a member of the Photogravure & Allied Holdings Ltd. Group.

Instead of the continuous tone positive of normal photogravure, a continuous tone negative of the original, in the size finally required, is joined with a contact positive screen and printed down on a special Colloplas foil. The foil is sensitized in the same way as carbon tissue, and printed down after drying. The exposed foil is next transferred to a polished sheet of brass and developed in hot water. This results in a matrix relief on which the screen lines appear as blank metal, and the actual image as square-shaped mounds. The latter represent the ultimate cells, in depths varying according to the grey values of the original.

The printing cylinder is covered with a special unvulcanized rubber compound, and the brass matrix, when dried, is wrapped round it. The cylinder, as then prepared, is put in a Colloplas vulcanizing press which heats it to the 300° F necessary for vulcanization, and at the same time hydraulically presses the matrix into the rubber.

The narrow ridge, caused by the join of the matrix sheet, is ground away and polished, resulting in a seamless cylinder with a smooth glazed surface, but with the printing image impressed as an exact replica of the matrix. Duplicate cylinders can be made from the same matrix.

It is claimed that the Colloplas process saves time and cost; also 1. the use of a negative instead of the usual positive obviates retouching; 2. printing down is a single operation as negative and screen are combined; 3. etching is eliminated; there is no expensive copper depositing of cylinders, and duplicates of the matrix can be made quickly and easily. Any type of photogravure ink can be used.

collotype: a planographic, photo-mechanical, non-screen printing process suitable for fine detail reproductions in monochrome or colour. Printing is done from a glass plate prepared by printing a negative on a gelatine film containing dichromate. Fox Talbot discovered in 1852 that a chromate gelatine layer was case-hardened by exposure to light. The first to employ this principle for the direct production of printing plates (lithographic stone) was A. L. Poitevin (1855) and sheets printed by him were exhibited in Paris in 1855. The method was given its practical adaptation mainly by Joseph Albert of Munich during 1867–71, who introduced the glass plate. In 1869 Jakub Husník of Prague issued an edition printed by Albert's process. Collotype came into general use under various names: glass printing, gelatine printing, albertype, etc. In 1871 Albert had the first collotype cylinder printing press built by Faber & Co. of Offenbach; the first satisfactory coloured collotype impression was made in 1875, and the first three-colour collotype was made in 1898.

Various materials have been tried as a base plate for the chromate gelatine layer, but the only one of great practical use is glass. Plates are usually ½ to 1cm. thick, and must be completely smooth. In order that the gelatine layer should adhere to the glass surface, the latter must be given preparatory treatment; for this Albert used chromate albumen which was exposed to light and soaked before the main preparation was begun. Nowadays silicate of soda (water-glass) is used universally for this purpose, an idea said to have been suggested by J. Obernetter. A solution of water-glass, which is flowed over the plate and allowed to dry, produces a strongly adhesive layer insoluble in cold water. By adding certain substances to the solution of water-glass a film is obtained which forms a suitable base for the gelatine layer; either organic substances soluble in water can be added, so that the surface becomes porous, or gelatine which remains blended with the water-glass is added, making a close combination possible between the latter and the main preparation. The glass plate, dully ground with emery powder or etched with hydrofluoric acid, is washed, e.g. with a solution of water-glass (about 10%), gelatine (about 4%), and some chrome alum in water. When this layer dries the actual preparation is

COLLOTYPE

On examination through a magnifying glass the grain which typifies collotype can be seen; to the naked eye the picture appears grain free.

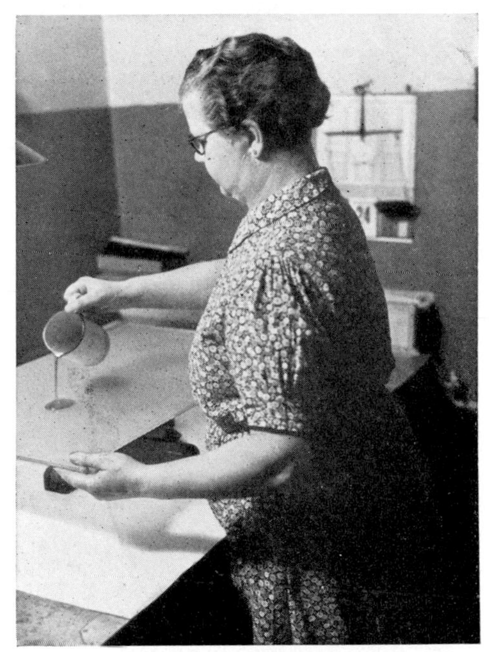

Preparing a collotype plate

Prepared plates in the drying oven

Cleaning the back of the plate before laying it in the press

done with a layer solution, or upper preparation, consisting of distilled water, gelatine, potassium dichromate, and chrome alum or formalin. The solution, which must contain dichromate, gelatine, and water in the approximate proportion 2:10:100, is prepared in a bath of water at about 160° F. After filtering, a weighed quantity of the solution is spread over the glass plate placed in the drying stove, and levelled to a horizontal position by set-screws. The quantity of liquid should be calculated so that the solution will form a layer about ⅓ mm. thick. The plate is then heated slowly to a temperature ranging from 105 to 140° F, at which it should remain for half an hour before being allowed to cool in the stove. The whole drying process takes about two hours. While drying, the reticulated skin or 'grain' is formed, or at least begun, which characterizes the collotype film. When the layer dries, the plate is sensitive mainly to blue and violet, so that it can be manipulated in a yellow or red light.

The negatives to be printed consist of ordinary continuous tone negatives without screens, in general a film or films taken off glass negatives: they are reversed, and mounted before printing on glass plates where they are surrounded in the margins between the pictures with tinfoil or some opaque material.

The printing plate is tightly wedged in a frame with the layer side towards the negative, and then printing is done by the light of an arc lamp, mercury vapour lamp, or by daylight. Printing takes a fairly long time and its progress can be followed on the back of the plate, due to changes in colour which appear in the layer. In exposure to light the chromate disintegrates, and the chrome oxides formed tan the gelatine which thereby loses its capacity to absorb water. It would seem as if the formation of grain affects this procedure in such a way that the tanning starts with the points of the grain, while the intervals only become hardened by degrees. On completing the printing, the plate is soaked for two hours, during which the remaining chromate is dissolved and the plate ceases to be sensitive to light. At the same time the unexposed parts of the gelatine absorb water with the result that they begin to swell. Tanning is greatest and penetrates most deeply in the exposed parts, i.e. the dark parts of the image, while it is insignificant in the lightest parts. The result of the graining, tanning, and swelling is that the surface of the collotype plate displays an irregular grain pattern of case-hardened gelatine in which the grains are larger and lie deeper the stronger the exposure has been, i.e. the darker the picture is. The grain structure is affected by the thickness of the layer, and the length and temperature of the drying after preparation, but also by the length of exposure and the temperature of the rinsing water. Fine grain is desirable, especially for pictures with

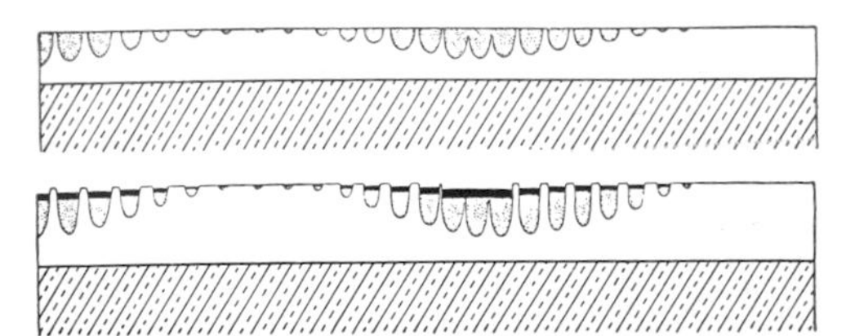

Sectional drawing of the collotype layer. This has been tanned (hardened) to varying depths by exposure. After damping, the least tanned parts have absorbed most water and are swollen, while the strongly tanned parts lie higher and absorb more ink during the inking in

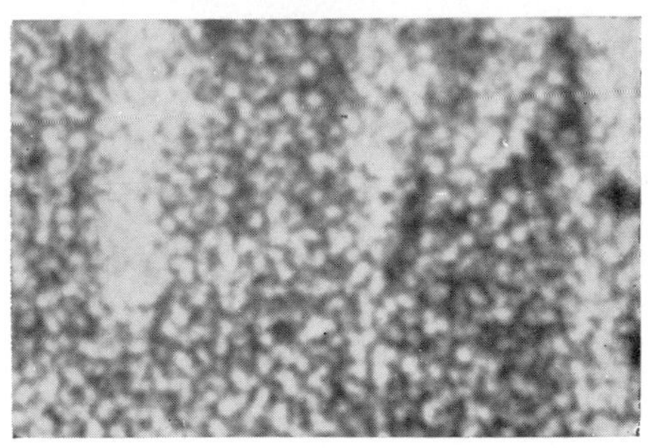

When highly magnified the variation of the irregular grain formation, both in size and density, is clearly visible

The first proof pulled gives a somewhat negative picture

After further treatment of the plate the quality of the impression improves and correct tone values result

Damping the plate in the damping trough (table)

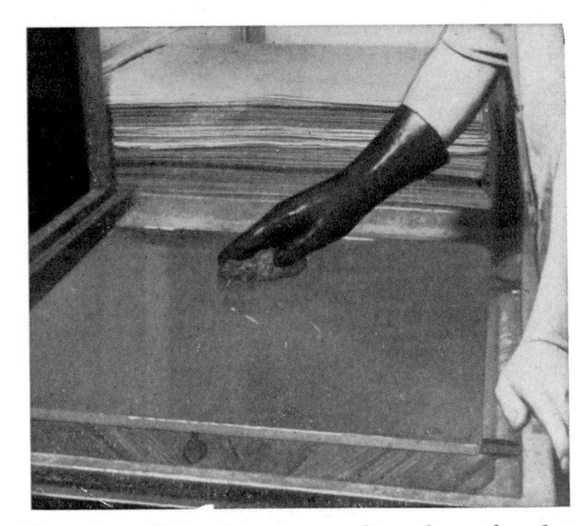

Sponging off the damping medium from the plate

Partial damping with a brush when the collotype plate is on the press

many details. After soaking, the plate is left to dry, usually for a night.

Before being placed in the printing press the plate is damped once more, this time with a mixture of about two parts of glycerine and one part of water, with the addition of a little ammonia, if necessary. For this, the plate is laid horizontally on a couple of levelling irons in a damping table, a trough provided with an outlet, whereupon the glycerine solution is poured out and spread evenly over the plate. After a time, determined by experience, the solution is removed with a sponge, and the plate is wiped with some sheets of tissue-paper. It is then ready to be placed in the press.

Proofing begins, an impression being pulled to serve as a guide to the printer in his further work. This first impression shows a picture which is rather uneven, as the darkest parts of the picture, which are most tanned and therefore lie deepest, have not come into contact with the inking rollers and have consequently not absorbed any ink. After washing the ink off the plate it is repeatedly damped with different strengths of solution, i.e. glycerine mixtures with increasingly large proportions of ammonia, or even soda, potassium hydroxide, or ox-gall. At this point the printer has an excellent opportunity for influencing the picture by touching up its various details. By this strong damping the layer is made to swell sufficiently for printing to begin. This is done with thick ink which is absorbed by the tanned gelatine, but is repelled by the swollen parts containing water. On a correctly treated plate this absorption of ink occurs in proportion to the amount of exposure, and an impression can be obtained with

The printer awaits the right moment for using his blowpipe with which he can affect the gelatine layer without stopping the press

a gradation corresponding closely to that of the negative. In regard to quality this impression is not much below the photographic silver copy. In printing in a cylinder press a double inking device with an inking slab and rollers is generally used, the forme rollers in one of them consisting of raw leather rollers which serve mainly to ink in the deeper shadowy parts, while the rollers in the other have a synthetic surface. The ink must be very stiff and is put on the rollers by hand. The press is equipped with arrangements for double or treble inking in of the plate between impressions. As the dampness of the plate changes during printing, fresh damping and proofing on waste paper must be done after 50 to 100 impressions before the printing of the edition continues. It may also be necessary for the printer to treat individual parts of the picture with a blowpipe while the press is running. All this makes the speed of printing low (500 to 1000 impressions a day), and the result depends on the printer's skill more than in any other printing process. The process is expensive but capable of the finest results.

As a modern alternative to the glass plate, from which only about 1500 good impressions can be taken, a film base fitted to flexible aluminium plates is used on a rotary offset machine, enabling long runs to be made; this variant of collotype is known on the Continent as *collography*. (G. U.)

collotype inks: soft, highly concentrated pigments in a medium of wax and lithographic varnish.

colonial editions: originally, editions of novels bought in sheets from English publishers by exporting firms who issued them in cheap bindings for sale in the Colonies. Subsequently, publishers produced their own colonial editions, bound in cheap boards, and with a title-page indicating that they were solely for export sale. They were retailed at a sum below the English net price.

It is not now usual to prepare special editions for oversea sale, but merely to supply copies of the home edition on special terms.

Colonna, Francesco: the Dominican monk remembered for his 'Hypnerotomachia Poliphili', Venice, 1499. This was written in a mixture of Latin and Italian of his own devising, and related the love affair of Poliphilo and Polia, set in a background of classical archaeology. It was printed by Aldus Manutius.

Its importance and influence throughout Europe derived from the initial letters and some 168 woodcuts, by an unknown designer, which were included. These inspired craftsmen, artists, and decorators seeking models.

colophon: 1. the inscription formerly placed at the end of a book giving the title, printer's name, place and date of printing. The 'Psalter' of Fust and Schöffer, published in 1457, is believed to be the first printed book to have a colophon.

2. in modern times, a publisher's decorative *device*, q.v., or trade mark, printed on the title-page, the last page of text, or elsewhere. This is a wrong usage of the term.

colour: when light reaches the retina of the eye it produces there an irritation which is conveyed by the optical nerve to the brain where the impression of *colour* arises. This depends not only on the wavelength of the incoming light but also on the organs of vision conceiving it. A normal eye is sensitive to a range of wavelength between approximately $\frac{380}{1,000,000}$ and $\frac{760}{1,000,000}$ mm. The longest waves are conceived as *red*, followed by *orange*, *yellow*, *green*, *blue*, *indigo*, and *violet*. These make up Newton's *spectral colours* which are obtained when a ray of sunlight is divided into its composite parts by passing it through a prism. A definite limit for any single colour is not possible as the spectrum shows a continuous transition through the series. If the eye is met with the seven kinds of light contained in the spectrum, and in the same proportions as in it, the impression received is *white*. However, white is also formed by blue and orange light, as by yellow and indigo, and generally by the primary colours in pairs; the colours forming such pairs are called *complementary colours*. Green, however, lacks a complementary colour and in order to form white with it a mixture of violet and red, i.e. purple, is necessary. Mixed or *composite colours* are generally obtained by mixing the simple colours. Such a mixture of coloured light is called an *additive colour mixture*. The colour of an object usually depends on the white light striking its surface being wholly or partly absorbed in the surface layer whilst the remaining light is reflected from it. Thus when we say that the surface of a paper is coloured yellow we mean that all the rays of incoming white light have been absorbed except those which are capable of giving the eye the impression of yellow. If the light reflected from the paper is allowed to pass through a further coloured layer before it reaches the eye, e.g. through a transparent blue layer, more light will be absorbed. The result will become a mixed colour, in this case green, by *subtractive colour mixture*: this means the colour obtained by successively subtracting light of different wavelengths from white light.

The colour impression conceived by the eye is affected by *colour tone*, *lightness*, and *saturation*. The colours obtained by additive mixture are less saturated than the most saturated part colour, frequently even less so than the least saturated. The colour tone appears more diluted, the colour usually becomes lighter, and by mixing two complementary colours neutral grey to white is obtainable. A subtractive mixed colour is always darker than the darkest part colour, but on the other hand the saturation may be either greater or less than that of the part colours. Subtractive mixture of complementary colours can give neutral grey to black.

The conception of colours may also be grouped into *luminous colours* deriving from light sources and their reflections, and *object colours* which are illuminated from a certain light source. Luminous colours (sunlight, daylight, mercury light, etc.) are always conceived as *clear*; although object colours can be clear they are usually less so. The brightness (light intensity) has no upward limit, whereas object colours can never be lighter than white. White as an object colour is characterized by colour tone saturation = 0 and maximum lightness. Black has both colour saturation and a maximum of brightness, while neutral grey is the name given to colours between white and black. As regards luminous colours grey does not occur because a luminous colour lacking tone is always conceived as white, even should the degree of brightness vary. (G. U.)

colour engraving: a sheet printed in several colours by an intaglio method (copperplate engraving, etching). The term is also used incorrectly for wood engravings and lithographs in colour. Copperplate printing combined with some means of colouring (or hand-colouring) has been known since the 17th century. Both then and in the 18th century engravings were made by colouring different parts of the same plate in different colours.

In actual colour engraving with several plates printed in succession the soft ground method (see *etching*) allows the picture to be drawn in coloured crayon on paper laid over the ground, the paper being removed to a new plate when changing the coloured crayon (*colour crayon printing*). A disadvantage is that during printing the first coloured reliefs printed are flattened by the succeeding ones. (G. U.)

colour gravure: the process of reproducing coloured illustrations in colour by *photogravure*, q.v. In contrast to colour work in letterpress and lithographic printing the colour picture in colour gravure is usually of almost continuous tone character, the dark and light colours being obtained by varying depth of the etched cells. In conventional gravure cylinder wear will reduce the depth of the shallow high light cells proportionately much more than the deeper shadow cells, causing colour changes. The use of varying area dots something on the lines of half-tone letterpress or lithography has the advantage of better colour control. Attempts have been made to combine the rich colour range of variable depth with the control possible with variable dot area. The best known is the *Dultgen*, much used in coloured journals. Others are the *Henderson* and the comparatively new *McCorquodale-Gresham process*. The technical problems are still much greater than in colour letterpress and colour lithography. The principal uses of colour gravure are in mass circulation colour magazines and packaging materials. Progress in other fields of printing awaits technical improvements in cylinder and plate making. (H. J. J.)

See also *Autotron scanner*.

colour guides: 1. small marginal marks placed on each of the three negatives used in making blocks for colour printing so that the printer can superimpose them in register when building up the picture.

2. the set of progressive proofs supplied by the plate- and blockmaker as a guide to the printer.

colour key: a process for reproducing coloured line drawings. A line block is made of the original drawing and pulls are taken from this, printed in light blue ink; on these the colours are drawn and etched, a separate sheet for each printing.

colour lithography: see *chromolithography*.

colour photography: the photographic depiction of a subject in its natural colours.

As early as 1810 the German physicist J. Seebeck showed that in certain circumstances silver chloride took on colour to some extent according to the light in which it was exposed; the colour has, however, little brilliance and cannot be fixed. On the other hand the *bleaching out process* (Wiener 1895, Worel 1899, and others) was more promising.

Interference methods. Here, too, there are several old methods of producing 'photochromes' on chlorided silver papers (E. Becquerel 1847, C. Niepce de St Victor 1851–66), but only one important method, the *Lippmann process* (1891), for which the French inventor Gabriel Lippmann was awarded the Nobel prize for physics in 1908. He used very fine-grained silver bromide gelatine plates ('Lippmann plates') placed in a dark slide, the glass side being in front and the layer side in contact with a mercury reflector. When light passes from the subject through the plate with its transparent emulsion layer it is reflected on to the mercury surface, by which means so-called standing waves are formed in the emulsion layer. After developing, the silver forms thin films in the layer and these films lie at a distance of half a wavelength from each other. The distance between the films is therefore slightly larger in the case of red light, the wavelengths of which are about 0·0006–0·0007 mm., than, for example, in the case of blue light in which the wavelengths are not much more than 0·0004 mm. If such a plate is exposed to ordinary white light, only light of the same wavelength as in the exposure will be reflected from its various points owing to the influence of interference. In some circumstances Lippmann plates give a good colour rendering, but their sensitivity is slight, involving long exposure times, and there are other difficulties.

Three-colour methods. The different shades of nature are formed by the light of the spectral colours being mixed in different proportions. (See *colour.*) The *three-colour principle* was proclaimed in 1860 by James Clerk Maxwell in his paper 'On the theory of compound colours' ('Phil. Trans.', 1860). In order to utilize this principle in colour photography three negatives of the subject are made with an identical adjustment of the camera. One exposure is made through a blue-violet filter which only admits light of wavelengths corresponding to the blue-violet third of the visible spectral area. The blue-violet content of the different parts of the subject is thus registered on the first negative. The second negative is exposed through a green filter which allows the green part of the spectrum to penetrate from blue-green through green to yellow, while the third negative is similarly exposed through a red filter. In this way a *three-colour analysis* of the subject is made and its proportions of blue, green, and red are recorded separately. (See *colour separation.*) Then it becomes a matter of arranging by a *colour synthesis* for mixing the light of the three colours of the analysis on the retina so that the impression of the original colours is obtained. This can be done in two ways differing in principle, viz. by *additive* or *subtractive* colour mixing.

In *additive colour processes* the image may consist of projected positives of each of the three colours, but more usually of a division of the image into minute dots of approximately one-third for each of the colours. When viewed from a distance the colours combine to give a visual colour photographic effect.

The first of these processes was the autochrome plate with coloured starch grains acting as filters over a silver emulsion. After exposure the silver bromide was processed to a positive giving a full colour photograph of the original scene. An early Agfacolor plate was similar. In the Finlay plate (also the Thames plate) the colour was in regular lines of green, red, and blue as a separate filter used in contact with a panchromatic plate. The Dufaycolor system had similar lines ruled on the panchromatic film itself.

Such methods have been almost entirely superseded by the *subtractive methods* which absorb much less light and are normally free of any dot or line pattern. In subtractive methods advantage is taken of the fact that fully coloured images can be obtained by the superimposition of the three colours yellow, magenta, and cyan. In the basic process three negatives are made using respectively blue, green, and red filters: from these three positives a yellow absorbing blue, magenta dye absorbing green, and cyan absorbing red. Cyan superimposed over yellow absorbs the blue and red ends of the spectrum transmitting only the central green position. Other superimpositions work similarly.

In 1935 Kodak introduced Kodachrome, and shortly after Agfa introduced Agfacolor. Both processes consisted of three emulsions on a single film sensitised to the three colours, and developable by suitable processing direct to a three-colour transparency. Since then many similar processes have been introduced, such as Ektachrome (Kodak), Ilfordcolour, Gevacolor (Gevaert), Ferraniacolor (Ferrania). In a more recent extension of this process the film is developed to a negative (in complementary colours, e.g. green is red, black is white, and so on). This can be printed on to a similar film or paper to give colour positive transparencies or colour prints. This negative-positive process has the advantage of greater latitude, better quality, and the possibility of paper prints. It is, of course, more expensive and takes twice as long to carry out as there are two materials to expose and process. Agfacolor negative-positive was the first example, followed by Kodacolor and Ektacolor (both Kodak). There are now several such processes, e.g., Pakocolor in England.

The production of colour prints by earlier processes is still carried out, and it is probable that they still provide better quality. Foremost is carbro which makes use of tanned coloured gelatine films. Duxochrome is a somewhat similar German process. Dye transfer, sometimes known as wash-off relief, makes use of tanned gelatine reliefs from which soft gelatine has been washed away with hot water. The gelatine image is dyed with the appropriate cyan, magenta, or yellow dye and transferred to gelatine-coated paper. The process has the advantage that it can be repeated to give a number of prints. The process used in making technicolour films is similar in principle. These old processes, in spite of their high quality, are very tedious to carry out and require much skill. It seems certain that they will soon be superseded by the new colour-negative processes which are improving rapidly, especially with the new use of colour-correcting (masking) layers in the colour negative. (H. J. J.)

colour printing: printing in inks other than black. As regards printing on paper this usually means the image obtained by impressing on one sheet a succession of formes bearing different colours.

The earliest colour printing was done from woodcuts, and actual coloured prints made from several blocks date from 1482 when Erhard Ratdolt issued astronomical illustrations in up to four colours. In 1485 he also printed the first more purely artistic woodcut; this was the coat of arms of the Bishop of Augsburg, and appeared in a Breviary.

In the early 16th century chiaroscuro engraving from successive blocks was introduced, a method used by Baldung, Burgkmair, Cranach, Dürer, among others. The oldest dated print made in this way was printed by Ugo da Carpi in 1518. It was not, however, until the 18th century that attempts at actual colour printing were renewed. Cornelius Bloemaert (d. *c.* 1680) did, indeed, print some sheets with outlines in copperplate engraving, colouring them with wooden blocks, but otherwise hand-colouring was usual. Two methods were used: either the copperplate engraving was coloured after printing, or the un-inked plate was impressed on the sheet, when the faintly visible outlines served as a guide for the colours, a final impression from the inked plate completing the picture. A similar method was used with wooden blocks.

It was only when mezzotint, aquatint, and crayon engraving had provided better technical conditions that there was any actual colour printing and attempted colour reproduction. Sometimes different parts of a plate were inked up in different colours, a method probably first used by the Dutchman Herkules Seghers (1585–*c.* 1650) and adopted in England and Germany during the 18th century. This method was perfected by William Wynne Ryland who worked with Bartolozzi on stipple engraving, and who developed a technique combining etching and engraving. With the help of his printer Seigneur, Ryland printed in colour by first inking the plate with a ground colour which was then dried hard, after which various parts of the plate had different colours ground into them by means of small colour pelts called 'dolls' (Fr. poupées). From this the method took its name 'gravure à la poupée' (also 'manière anglaise', a term also applied to mezzotint). The plate was heated before printing so that the colours ran into one another to some extent. Ryland was hanged in 1783 for forging banknotes, but his method survived and such single-plate coloured prints made by the stipple or mezzotint processes were made in large numbers at the end of the 18th century and later, particularly in England. Constable's coloured reproductions of his own paintings are also celebrated.

Colour reproduction in its present sense may be said to have been born in the workshops of Le Blon. Inspired by Newton's theory of light and colour he tried to reproduce natural colours by printing with several plates, at first with seven for the seven colours of the spectrum, later with only three, for yellow, red, and blue. The experiments appear to have begun in 1711, but it was not until 1720 that he found sleeping partners in London who formed a company ('Picture Office') for reproducing in colour the works of the Italian masters. The company was liquidated in 1723. A second venture begun in 1731 also went bankrupt and Le Blon had to flee the country. In 1737 he obtained a licence in Paris for colour printing which prevented his successor and competitor Dagoty from experimenting until after Le Blon's death in 1741. The work done in Amsterdam by Le Blon's pupil Jean Ladmiral was technically of a higher standard than that of his master or Dagoty.

A new epoch was inaugurated by Janinet who issued coloured engravings in the 1770's, technically excellent reproductions in aquatint with from four to seven colours. In the 1780's the aquatints of Louis XVI's court painter Philibert Louis Debucourt (1755–1832) were very popular, as were his artistically and technically elegant coloured engravings of Parisian life.

In the 19th century lithography predominated in colour reproduction. Among early coloured lithographs may be mentioned those printed by J. A. Barth of Breslau in 1816, and Wilhelm Zahn of Berlin in 1829. The term chromolithography occurs for the first time in connection with Gottfried Engelmann's French patent in 1837. Other prominent workers were Lemercier in Paris, William Day in London, Arnz in Düsseldorf, and the State Printing House in Vienna.

Present-day colour printing is governed entirely by the process work which originated at the end of the 19th century and is used both in letterpress, lithography, and photogravure. (G.U.)

colour printing (technical note): for good work the forme must be securely locked, the cylinder dressing taut, the sheets accurately laid, and the machine run at a constant speed for each colour. The paper should be matured in the printing room, thus assisting good register by avoiding stretch; it should have the grain direction the narrow way of the sheet.

See also *Idotron.*

colour reproduction (process work): colour printing from formes made by photographic means is based on the same principles as are observed in modern colour photography. In those printing processes in which the reproduction or printing requires the use of a screen the possibility of *moiré* formations, q.v., should be borne in mind. Among those who developed screen reproduction work in colour were E. Albert of Munich and Ives of New York, who was probably the first to introduce the turning of the screen between exposures in order to avoid moiré (*c.* 1881). Ives's system of 'composite heliochrome' was completed in 1890. The Heliochrome Engraving Co., New York, was the first establishment making colour-blocks in the U.S.A.; its manager, Stieglitz, opened his own business in 1892. In Sweden the first coloured blocks were made about 1900. (G.U.)

See also *colour photography*, *colour printing.*

colour sensitivity: a typical silver bromide photographic emulsion is only sensitive to violet and ultra-violet light and could not, of course, be used for colour photography. By the addition of suitable dyes the sensitivity can be extended. The emulsion without added dyes is known as 'ordinary'. 'Orthochromatic' film has the sensitivity extended to green, but is not sensitive to red. If the emulsion is sensitive to the whole of the visible spectrum it is known as 'panchromatic'. It is also possible to make emulsion sensitive to infra-red.

Each of these emulsions has many uses. The panchromatic emulsion can only be processed in darkness or in a very dim green light. Ordinary emulsions, on the other hand, can be processed in yellow light, but orthochromatic emulsion only in a red light. (H. J. J.)

colour separation: photographic three-colour analysis, especially in connection with the production of printing plates. It is here mostly a question of smooth originals: paintings, coloured photographs (transparencies or prints), etc. As in all three-colour analysis, the separating is done by exposing through filters, and mostly by taking three negatives in succession, changing the dark slides and filters between exposures which are made in an ordinary process camera. For separating small pictures (transparencies 24 × 36 mm.) in particular, a special colour-separation apparatus is used. In this the filters are often placed between the original and the source of light, but in process cameras in front of or inside the lens. The lenses used for colour separation must be high-class apochromats, and matched sets should be used.

As colour reproduction is often done in four colours it is usual, in addition to the negatives for blue-green, yellow, and magenta, to make a fourth for black, though one of the negatives for blue-green or magenta can often be used for this purpose. If more than four colours are required for printing it is usual to produce the 'additional' colours from standard negatives. It is sometimes of advantage to separate individual negatives through differently coloured filters, this often depending on the nature of the original picture. Colour separation by infra-red radiation is occasionally used in some establishments as normal procedure for making the 'black' negative.

As colour separation has certain defects, the negatives obtained and the positives made from them must often be adjusted and retouched before the work of reproduction can continue. According to the method of printing employed this retouching is done in various ways. (See *blockmaking*, *masking*, *offset reproduction*.) In some cases the retouching can be done on the original picture; for example, it may be desirable when reproducing water-colours to avoid the black outlines in the coloured prints, in which they would otherwise appear automatically in all colours with subsequent register difficulties. There are methods of painting the outlines over with covering colours of shades matching the surrounding colour surface, this painting being done on a thin transparent film which is removed when exposing the 'black' negative.

The negatives obtained by means of colour separation are known as *colour-separation sets.* (G. U.)

colour systems: colour can be described by three terms, which can be three colours. This, the international system, is closely related to methods of colour printing. It has the disadvantage that it is difficult to visualize a colour in terms of its three colour co-ordinates, e.g. the relation between a pale green, a bright green, and a duller version of the same hue would not be visually obvious. So for everyday use three different terms are preferable, i.e. *hue* (the content of yellow, red, etc., which gives it its name), *saturation* (the strength with which the hue emerges after dilution by white light), and *luminosity* (in comparison with the grey scale, the ends of which are black and white). The two principal systems are the Munsell and the Ostwald: both are American.

The *Munsell* system defines colour in terms of hue, chroma (= saturation) and value (approximately = luminosity). The usefulness of the Munsell chart of numbered colours has been limited in Europe by its cost.

The somewhat similar *Ostwald* system is available in an excellent colour atlas issued by the Container Corporation of America.

The British Colour Council produces a cheaper and useful, if less systematic, chart. Tintometer Limited also have a method of colour measurement. (H. J. J.)

colour vision: a factor which is not yet fully understood, although the generally accepted theory is in accordance with our normal experience and with the practice of colour printing. Physically visible light covers a very small band of the vast range of wavelengths of electromagnetic radiation, ranging from wireless waves of about 30,000 metres down to a few centimetres, through heat waves, infra-red light, and X-rays, to the even shorter gamma rays of atomic radiation. The light of our daily experience —sunlight, incandescent light, or candle light, contains the entire range of visible light wavelengths, but in varied proportions. By use of a prism or a diffraction grating a pencil of white light can be split into its component wavelengths, ranging from short-wave blue-violet through blue, green, yellow, orange, to long-wave red.

(*Colour printing*)

see page 79

Reproduction in two-colour half-tone of a painting, 'Siberian Tigers' by W. Kuhnert
(Below) Enlargement of the yellow and blue screen dots which build up the picture
See *two-colour reproduction*

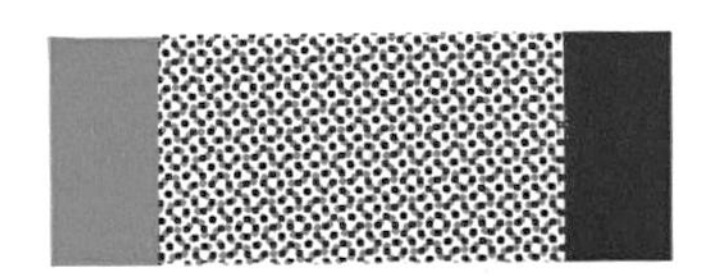

COLOUR PRINTING

Reproduction in four colours printed in letterpress on coated stock. Photograph from Söderberg, 'Garden Flowers'. The picture is built up of screen dots in yellow, red (magenta), blue (cyan), and black as shown (enlarged) in the panel below

By the use of coloured dyes, for example in the form of dyed gelatine, certain of the wavelengths may be absorbed: a typical yellow dye absorbs the blue of the spectrum; a typical bright blue-green (cyan) dye absorbs the red end of the spectrum; while a red (magenta) dye absorbs the centre green part of the spectrum yet still transmits both the blue and the red ends of the spectrum. If light is passed through any two of the filters mentioned above it is obvious that less of the spectrum is transmitted: for example, the yellow filter superimposed over the blue-green dye which removes the red leaving only the centre (green) part of the spectrum. The yellow and the magenta together absorb all but the red end of the spectrum. The blue-green and the magenta filters together will remove red and green, leaving only the blue-violet end of the spectrum. This is all consistent with the theory that our eyes have three types of sensitive reception, one each for green, red, and blue, and they are the true primary colours. In looking at a spectrum at the red end only the red receptor is in action, for yellow both red and green receptors are effective and the green receptor is even more stimulated than the red, so that the yellow overlap region of the spectrum seems extremely bright. The blue receptor, on the other hand, is less stimulated, and this part of the spectrum appears much darker. This is particularly so in the case of candlelight or incandescent light owing to the fact that the emitted light in each case contains a comparatively small proportion of blue light.

Most coloured objects appear so not because they emit light, but because they absorb a portion of the light falling on them. If the object absorbs all the light and reflects none it is called black. In fact, absorption and reflection are quite complex. For example, an object may appear green because it reflects green light and absorbs a large part of the rest of the light. Another object may also appear green even if it absorbs the green portion of the spectrum, provided that it reflects the yellow and blue-green. If, however, the same two objects which appear to match in sunlight are examined in artificial light, one will probably appear darker and even of a different hue.

It has not yet been possible to discover in the eye receptors sensitive to the three primary colours, and although the mechanism of colour vision must be of this type it is possibly rather more complex.

Fluorescent colours differ from ordinary colours in that the light falling on the colour is absorbed and re-emitted always at a longer wavelength. Thus some brilliant red dyes not only transmit red light falling on them, but convert the blue light falling on them into additional red light.

No satisfactory method of describing visual colour has yet been devised. This is partly because the apparent colour is influenced by its surroundings. For example, a green patch surrounded by a red patch will appear much brighter than an identical green patch surrounded by a darker green. A similar effect is obtained with other so-called complementary pairs of colour, i.e. blue and yellow and black and white.

coloured tops (or **edges**)**:** book tops (or all three edges) tinted with a dye or pigment, usually applied with a spray gun. Much used for publishers' binding. The edges may be brushed with wax, after colouring, to provide a gloss, and a still higher gloss is obtained by rubbing them with an agate burnisher. For books of reference, e.g. directories, bands of contrasting colours may be used on the fore-edge to facilitate reference, further aid being given by rubber-stamping sub-titles in ink on the sections. (L.K.)

column-face rule: a rule used to separate adjacent columns of text.

Combe, Thomas, 1797–1872: a manager of the Clarendon Press, Oxford, who, on behalf of the University, purchased the paper mill at Wolvercote where Oxford india paper is still made by a secret process, no workman being allowed to know details of more than one stage of its manufacture.

combined half-tone and line: see *blockmaking*.

combing wheel: part of the mechanical device on a printing machine which, with the forwarding sucker, passes sheets of paper singly from the stock pile to the feed board and thence to the impression cylinder.

come-and-go: the name for an imposition scheme whereby one set of type is imposed with the head of the first page laid to the head of the last page, and so on throughout the forme. The signatures are delivered *two-up*, q.v., so that the last signature is head-to-head with the first. If a book consists of an even number of sections the gathering of one of each will make a set, with another set turned upside down. This method gives two copies, one running from beginning to end, and the other from end to beginning and upside down. The two copies are not separated until final trimming.

comma: a punctuation mark, which was already in use in 9th-century Greek manuscripts.

Command Papers: sessional papers printed by Command of Her Majesty and presented to either or both Houses of Parliament. A Treasury directive recommends that they should be 'limited to the cases of documents likely to be the subject of early legislation or which may be regarded as otherwise essential to Members of Parliament as a whole to enable them to discharge their responsibilities'. The serial numbers they bear run (theoretically) from 1 to 9999; the present (5th) series began in 1956.

commission agreement: a contract between an author and a publisher by which the former assumes full financial responsibility for the production and advertising costs of his book and owns the stock: the publisher, in return for an initial cash payment plus commission on sales, publishes and sells the book.
See also *publishers' agreements.*

companionship: a group of compositors working together under a foreman. He is known as a *clicker.*

compendium: a condensation of a larger work giving briefly the important matter of it.

compensation guards: narrow guards, in the form of page-length stubs of paper, bound up, to balance at the back, in a book having bulky folding plates or maps. Also known as *filling-in guards.*

compiler: one who assembles or arranges for publication a collection of the writings of others, e.g. an anthology of plays, poetry, or prose. Whereas an *editor*, q.v., may also assemble a collection of the writings of others, he may alter, amend, delete, or annotate portions of the texts; a compiler usually presents exactly as written the writings he brings together.

Complutensian Polyglot: see *polyglot edition.*

compose: to set up type according to copy.
See also *composing rule*, *composing stick*, *copy* (2), *piecework*, *setting rule.*

composing: the placing together of typographic material into a forme for letterpress printing in a printing press. Typographical material consists of type, the printed image of which is visible in the impression, and of non-printing blanks or whiting out material. The latter, also called spacing, is lower than type height so that it does not come into contact with the inking rollers or paper. Its object is to separate the characters so that they are legible, and at the same time to hold them together in the units of which lines and pages consist. To facilitate this all typographical material must be dimensioned according to a definite system (see *point*). Letters which are to form words and lines of a given measure must have the same body size, as also the spacing material used between the words to justify the lines. For filling larger spaces *quads*, q.v., are used. For interlinear spacing leads of standard thickness and various lengths are used. Larger blank areas and margins are filled with *furniture*, q.v. For securing the forme firmly in the chase quoins are used. Composing is done from a manuscript, either by hand or machine. Machine composition must also be prepared for printing by hand compositors. See also *hand composition.*

In most cases composing is first done in galleys or slips, which means that type set up to a given measure continues in unbroken sequence in long columns for pulling *proofs*, q.v. After various proofs have been pulled and corrected the matter can be made up into pages, imposed in correct order for printing and subsequent folding, and locked up in a *chase*, q.v. When printing is completed, type (if not required for stereos or to be left standing) should be distributed, which means that typographical material is returned to the case or sent to the metal box (mechanically cast types are melted down for re-use in the composing machine).

Composing in many printing establishments is done to rules known as the *style of the house*, q.v. This term includes the physical setting up of matter, the use of spaces, headings, rules, marginal proportions, etc., and also orthographical style so that punctuation, word division, abbreviations, capitalization, etc., will be uniform even if a long manuscript is set up by several compositors. As a general guide to authors preparing their copy, and printers working without house rules, 'Rules for Compositors and Readers at the University Press, Oxford' by Horace Hart, 36th ed., O.U.P., 1952, and 'Authors' and Printers' Dictionary' by F. H. Collins, 10th ed., O.U.P., 1956, should be used. (G.U.)

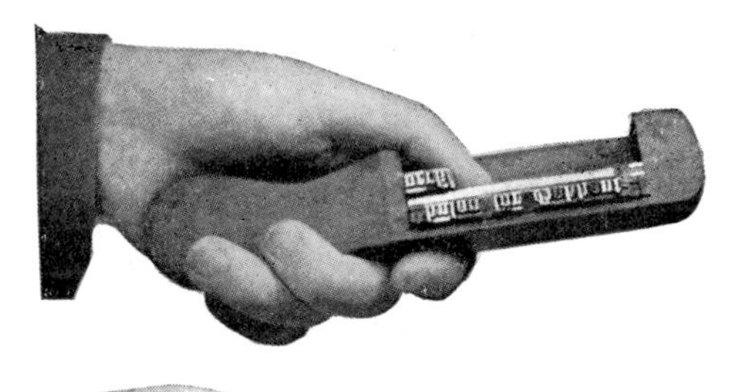

Two types of composing stick. In the upper illustration the setting rule is clearly visible

composing rule: a piece of steel or brass, put in a composing stick, and against which the types are placed in setting. (M.L.)

composing stick: a metal holder in which the compositor sets up type in words and lines. The stick is

adjusted to the required measure before setting. The compositor reads type upside down and from left to right.
See also *setting rule*.

composite block: a combined half-tone and line block; also a plate made up of two or more originals.

composite book: a book made up of distinct parts, either different subjects or the works of several authors, collected by an editor and bound in one volume.
See also *fly-title*.

composite negative: a negative intended for printing on plates and made up of a number of small negatives arranged side by side. The negatives can be made by the exposure of different images, or can be multiples of one made by repeated exposure in a camera or printing apparatus. (G. U.)
See also *step-and-repeat machine*.

composite work: a book written by several authors in collaboration.

composition: see *composing*.

composition fount: a loose description for any type-face used for book printing, as distinct from display, which is 'tapped' on a type-composing machine in sizes not larger than 14-point.

composition roller: a lithographic roller suitable for use at the highest speeds. Such rollers are marketed under various trade names, e.g. Mintite, Gestite, etc.
See also *glazed roller*, *nap roller*.

compositor: a craftsman whose work consists of setting up type by hand or machine, correcting machine-set composition, making up pages, imposing them, and performing all the necessary assembling of the type forme. In the 16th and early 17th centuries it was not unknown for a compositor to set up a take of copy in his own home, delivering it to the printer who employed him for printing off.

concordance: an alphabetically arranged index which shows where any selected word appears in the collected writings of an author, e.g. 'Concordance to Shakespeare' by Bartlett.

condensed face: a type-face having an elongated or narrow appearance, e.g.

GILL BOLD CONDENSED Gill Bold Condensed

conditioning: the maturing of paper by the drying out or addition of moisture to it. This is done in a conditioning plant which consists of a series of vertical compartments into which conditioned air is blown while rolls of paper are fed through.
See also *relative humidity*.

Conditioning hand-made paper

conditions for the sale of books: see *terms* (2).

conducting roller: a roller for ferrying the paper through a rotary press. Such rollers must run freely and be in static and dynamic balance; they usually have ball-bearings and are driven solely by friction with the paper. (G. U.)

Congreve print: a coloured print made by a process invented in 1820 by Sir William Congreve (1772–1825), which in its essentials had already been adopted in 1457 for the printing of initials in the Mainz Psalter.
The printing plate was divided into separate pieces which were removed for colouring, after which they were re-assembled and printed as one forme. Congreve also built a press in which the colouring as well as the printing could be done mechanically. (G. U.)

conjugate leaves: any two leaves of a book which together form one piece of paper.

Constance Lindsay Skinner Award: an annual award made by the American Women's National Book Association for an outstanding contribution by a woman to the world of books.

Constance Missal: the English name for the *Missale speciale Constantiense*, q.v.

contact screen: a half-tone screen made on a film base and having a graded dot pattern. It is used in direct contact with a film or plate to obtain a half-tone negative from a continuous tone original. Contact screens give better definition than the conventional glass screen, and excellent gradation. They can also be used for silk screen work.

Experiments with silver contact screens were made at the beginning of this century, but the problem of light scatter (which caused loss of detail) was first satisfactorily overcome when Kodak introduced their orange and magenta screens which permitted contrast control without light-scatter. The orange screen was designed for screen positive making, the magenta for screen negatives. It having been shown by tests in the trade that satisfactory negatives or positives can be made with the Kodak magenta screen, the orange screen is now obsolete. The magenta contact screen is supplied in two types, one for photo-lithography, the other for photoengraving, the gradation in the dot being slightly different on the two screens to give the best tone reproduction for the particular process to be used.

Kodak Magenta Screen for photo-litho. A contact screen with various screen rulings which has a dye rather than a silver dot pattern. The screen can be used in vacuum contact in a camera for making screen negatives on Kodalith products from a black and white print. The same screen can be used for the preparation of screen positives from a continuous tone negative. This can be achieved either in the camera, the enlarger, or the vacuum frame. The dye pattern makes it possible to control half-tone contrast by the use of colour filters. With the camera or enlarger techniques, contrast control can also be achieved by a flash exposure to yellow light. An exposure using white light is made of the subject, and a flash exposure to an 0B safelight, made in the darkroom, controls the shadow areas. The flash exposure varies with the contrast range of the original. A Kodak Graphic Arts Exposure Computer facilitates the handling of contact screens.

When used in a vacuum frame the best definition results from using a point source light.

Kodak Magenta Screen for photoengraving. This screen also has a dyed dot pattern designed to give the best results for screen negative making for photo-engraving. Contrast control is achieved with rose and yellow filters, or with the white light and yellow flash exposure.

Kodak Grey Contact Screen. This can be used for direct screen negatives on Kodalith Pan for photo-lithography. Contrast control is achieved by a flash exposure to yellow light.

Kodalith Autoscreen Ortho film. A film which embodies the equivalent of a screen in its emulsion coating. When exposed to a continuous-tone image this film produces a lithographic dot pattern automatically, just as if a half-tone screen had been used in the camera.

contents: part of the prelims where the separate divisions of a book are listed in the order in which they appear. Often set in type two points smaller than that used for the text, to a narrower measure, and printed on the next recto page after the preface or foreword.

continuation: a book begun by one author but concluded by another. The second is a continuator.

continuous feed: a term used to describe the action of an automatic sheet feeder attached to a printing press, folder, or other machine, so constructed that the supply of sheets can be renewed without interrupting the action of the machine.

See also *feeder.*

continuous guard: a method used when sewing sections of vellum or other material which would be damaged by the glue or paste used for binding. A long strip of hand-made paper, as wide as the book is high, is either folded like a concertina before sewing, or creased to about $\frac{1}{2}$ in. round the back of each section as sewing proceeds. A flat wooden blade is used for creasing. The needle must pass centrally through the fold, and even tension is important. When gluing-up, the book itself remains untouched by the mucilage.

continuous tone: said of photographs, negatives of photographs, or coloured originals in which the subject contains shades between the lightest and darkest tones. Such originals as maps may be a combination of line (including type) and continuous tone: their reproduction may involve the preparation of separate negatives (masking), later combining the negatives in printing.

See also *half-tone process.*

continuous tone negative: a photographic negative. The tone variation is inversely proportional to the subject. Dark areas (shadows) in the original are represented with minimum density in the negative; light areas (highlights) have a high density, and in-between tones vary according to the light reflected from the subject.

contract, forms of: see *publishers' agreements.*

contraries: such harmful impurities as pins, buttons, string or rubber which are found when sorting rags in the paper mill.

copal: a resinous substance exuding from various tropical trees, used as a vehicle in the making of printing inks. (M.L.)

Cope, R. W.: see *Albion press.*

Copland, Robert, fl. 1508–48: a bookseller-printer who, until about 1515, worked for Wynkyn de Worde. Few of his works remain.

Copland, William, fl. 1548–*c.* 69: a London printer and original member of the Stationers' Company. He worked with his relative *Robert,* q.v., whom he succeeded in 1548.

copper depositing: the precipitation of copper in the form of a thin surface layer on an object placed as a cathode in a galvanic bath. Copper depositing on a large scale is done in treating the printing forme material for photogravure printing. (G.U.)

See also *electrotype.*

copper engraving: an impression taken from an engraved copper plate. The work is done on a brightly burnished copper plate (16 or 18 gauge) which is first coated with a ground on which the design is traced with a needle, then the ground is washed off. Guided by the lines, the artist engraves by cutting away metal shavings with a *burin* (graver), a narrow steel tool of varying section (oval, triangular, square, etc.) cut obliquely at the point, while the other end is fixed in a wooden handle. The 'burr' lifted out of the metal may remain on the edge of the line, and this may be removed with a *scraper*, a three-edged cutting tool. The strength of the inked impression is in proportion to the depth of the line. In order to control the plate more easily during engraving the artist rests it on a rounded cushion of sand. The finished plate is warmed, inked, and together with the sheet to be printed, passed through a roller press. For direct printing such plates should be steel-faced.

See also *copperplate printing, dry-point, etching.*

Early examples of copper engravings in Germany and Italy date from *c.* 1440, but this graphic method was certainly used in the 14th century and may be even older. It has been suggested that it originated from the metal-engraved patterns used by the armourers, but it is not known when it became an independent art-form in which the impression was the main object. Copper engraving was first used for making playing cards and religious pictures.

Its use for book illustrations began with Boccaccio's 'Du dechiet des nobles hommes et femmes' printed by Colard Mansion, Bruges, 1476 (GKW 4432), which probably had ten engravings pasted in, though no copy with more than nine survives. In Italy Antonio Bettini's 'Monte Santo di Dio' printed by Nicolaus Laurentii, Florence, 1477 (GKW 2204), was the first book to include engravings from copper plates. Among copperplate engravers of the 15th century may be mentioned Andrea Mantegna (1431–1506) with a few, but skilfully done sheets, Martin Schongauer, and several unknown artists now referred to as 'Meister des Hausbuches', 'Meister mit den Bandrollen', etc. About 1500 Albrecht Dürer and others contributed considerably to the development of this medium, both technically and artistically. In the 16th century the art was particularly flourishing in Italy, while the most important work in the 17th and 18th centuries was done in France, Holland, and Belgium.

The first English book to be illustrated in this way was 'Byrth of Mankynde', a translation by Richard Jonas of a German treatise on childbirth, 1540. The first English copperplate title-page was engraved for Thomas Gemini's 'Compendiosa totius anatomiae delineatio', London, 1545. (Gemini's real surname was Lambert or Lambrit.)

In the mid-17th century, in the Netherlands, colour work was introduced; only one plate was used (often a combination of etching and engraving), bearing various colours, and requiring fresh inking after each impression; Bartolozzi later developed this idea for his *stipple engravings*, q.v. Colour printing from three plates was devised by Jakob Christoffel Le Blon of Amsterdam in 1711; he worked on Newton's theory that all colours stem from the primaries blue, yellow, and red.

The workshop of the copperplate engraver Wolfgang Kilian of Augsburg (1581–1662), *after an engraving of* 1623

Copperplate engraving was extensively used for illustrating books during the 17th and 18th centuries, but when wood engraving developed, it lost its popularity. An attempt to revive engraving as a means of illustration was made with *steel engraving* early in the 19th century; such plates were more durable than copper, but the method is no longer used for book work. Copperplate engraving is still in occasional use for map work, security printing, book plates, visiting cards, etc., the plates often being made by mechanical means or process work. (With G.U.)

copperplate printing: printing in a hand-press from plates made on an intaglio principle. In such plates the image lies below the otherwise level surface. Ink is distributed over the whole surface by manual inking up, after which the surplus is dried off, so that only the sunken image remains filled. A soft, absorbent paper is then pressed against the plate, the ink being transferred to it. In this way the printing of etchings is done, whether they are made in zinc or copper, of copperplate engravings, photogravures, heliogravures, etc. The stiff copperplate printing ink must be warmed to make it pliable before inking up. This is done by letting the plate lie on a heater, an iron plate heated from below. The heater is often combined with a cooler, i.e. a base of the same height as the heater, but with no source of heat. Ink is spread on the warmed plate by a hand-roller or a dabber, and is wiped off with a piece of canvas folded into a small pad. Wiping is often done in stages with rags of different softness, and finally with the palm of the hand, sometimes rubbed with powdered chalk. Lye is used, when the last traces of ink are to be removed from the margins. Drying can be done on a hot or cold plate and in several ways which give a different character to the impression. Subsequent treatment may be done with *retroussage*, which means that the heated plate is gone over with the edge of a folded piece of gauze, causing the ink in the lines to spread slightly.

Paper for printing must be of good quality, soft, and with a smooth surface sufficiently absorbent to take up the ink. Special copperplate printing paper is sold, being a slightly sized, pure rag paper which is damped prior to use, preferably the day before so that the sheets can lie and 'draw' overnight. Immediately before printing, the paper is brushed so that its surface is sufficiently softened. Japanese or china paper (thin sheets made from the bark of the mulberry tree or of rice) can be used for copperplate printing, combined with thicker backing. Such paper is sold with a coating of paste on one side; the other side is damped and laid on the inked plate, being covered there by a larger sheet of thick backing paper. In passing through the press the Japanese paper adheres to the backing, while the impression is made at the same time. (G.U.)

copperplate printing ink: a pliable and 'short' ink made of pure weak linseed oil with a high pigment content. (G.U.)

copperplate printing press: a press which through the years has changed its appearance very little, with the sole difference that the first presses were made entirely of wood, whereas now they are made of iron and steel and are often power-driven. A strong iron plate

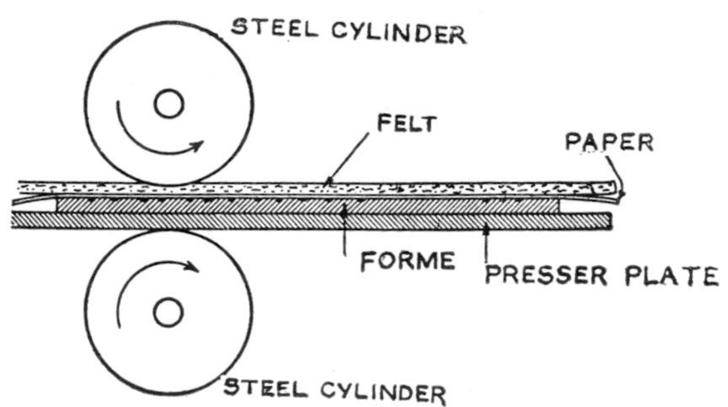

Diagram to show the passage of paper and plate through a hand-press

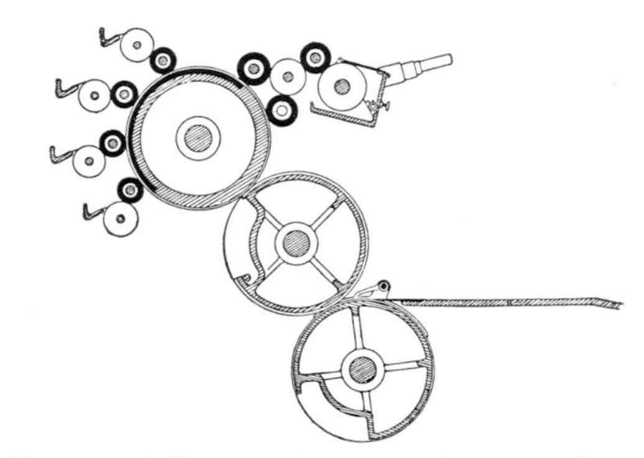

Diagram of offset press for printing from curved copperplates. Built in 1877 *by Guy, Paris*

forms the bed for the printing plate which, however, does not generally rest on it, but on an intermediate, softer zinc plate. Above the paper laid on the printing plate there are felts on which an upper cylinder presses when the bed with the plate, paper, and felt is driven forward between two revolving cylinders. Under this strong pressure the paper is pressed into the cavities of the plate, but also into the margins which extend beyond it. The bevelled edge of the plate stands out clearly on the paper as a 'bevelled border', a characteristic of printing in a hand-press which is often reproduced artificially. The impressions taken on damp paper must first dry between sheets of cardboard, after which they are again slightly damped and dried in a press. In former times not only copperplate printed sheets but any sheets printed in a hand-press were hung on cords to dry as a means of preventing mould. (G.U.)

See also *intaglio, photogravure.*

copy: 1. a single example of a book.

2. matter to be set up in type by the printer. The

author should prepare his typescript on one side of the paper, double spaced, and with the same number of lines on each page; the typing should all be done on one machine. A good left-hand margin is necessary.

Apart from the index, which cannot be compiled until page proofs are run off, the copy should be complete with title-page, dedication, appendices, etc., and an indication must be given of any item which is to follow.

Illustrations should be numbered, and the legends (with corresponding numbers) should be typed together on a separate sheet. Marginal numbers in the typescript will show where the illustrations are to be printed.

Words which are to be printed in italic should be underlined with a straight line, words in bold type are indicated by a wavy underline, those in bold italic with a wavy line under a straight. Other typographical styling will normally be done by the printer who will submit a specimen page for the author's approval.

3. an illustration for reproduction. Various points require attention when submitting copy for the process worker. Photographs should be glossy, at least half-plate size, and in any case larger than the reproduction, with a full range of tones. Line drawings should be on blemish-free white board, and be drawn twice the size of the ultimate negative, preliminary or layout lines should be in light blue pencil. Copper or steel engravings used as lithographic copy must be in rich black ink on good white paper; pencil sketch originals reproduce best when photographed to the same size or only slightly reduced. Colour prints and transparencies should not be too contrasty, while hand-coloured photographic prints require bleaching before colouring or the silver deposit will affect the three-colour negatives. Wash-drawings should be on smooth paper, and be made with brown or red-grey pigments rather than blue-grey. Water-colours and oil paintings make good copy, as do pastel crayons if the colours have not been overlaid too much by the artist.

copy money: the sums of money paid to printers' workmen in the 17th century in lieu of free copies of the books they produced to which they were formerly entitled by custom.

copyholder: one who reads aloud from copy as the printer's proof corrector follows the reading in the proof.

copying machine: 1. an apparatus for making photographic contact copies on an endless web with automatic exposure, developing, fixing, washing, and drying.

2. a machine for photoprinting.

3. a *step-and-repeat machine*, q.v. (G.U.)

Copyright Act: an Act first introduced in 1709 to protect authors from the illicit printing of their works, either in whole or in part. In 1911 the scope of the Act was extended to include music, paintings, drawings, etc. In general an author's works are protected for his lifetime and for fifty years after his death, which protection extends via the *Berne Convention*, q.v., throughout most countries of the world.

A new British Copyright Act was enacted in 1956. According to the new law 'copyright subsisting in a work shall continue to subsist for a full fifty years from the end of the calendar year in which the author dies, and shall then expire'. The provision made in the 1911 Act whereby during the last twenty-five years of the copyright life of a work, that work could be published as of right on payment of a statutory royalty, was repealed. In the case of a work of joint authorship, the reference to author means the author who dies last.

In the case of works which have been commissioned, and works made under contract of service, the 'commissioner' or 'employer' shall be entitled to copyright unless an agreement has been made to the contrary.

Provision is made for the copying of certain copyright material by libraries which are not established or conducted for profit. Such copies are only to be supplied to persons proving that they are required solely for research or private study.

One section relates to the use of extracts from a copyright work used for 'fair dealing'. Fair dealing covers extracts made for the purpose of conveying news of current events to the public, literary criticism and reviews, extracts published for schools, and the reading of extracts in public. Such usage is to be accompanied by a 'sufficient acknowledgement'. This is elsewhere defined as one 'identifying the work in question by its title or other description and, unless the work is anonymous or the author has previously agreed or required that no acknowledgement of his name should be made, also identifying the author'.

Welcomed by the Publishers Association was the section which granted the publisher for twenty-five years the copyright of the typographical arrangement of a published edition of a work. This includes reproduction by photographic or similar process.

See J. P. Eddy, 'Law of Copyright', Butterworth, 1957.

See also *outright sale of copyright*, *statutory copies*, *Universal Copyright Convention*.

copyright in America: (for non-U.S. citizens) is secured for publications of adherents to the *Universal Copyright Convention*, q.v., which, from the time of first publication of a work, bear the encircled ©, the name of the copyright proprietor, and the date.

See Philip Wittenberg, 'The Law of Literary Property', *World*, 1957.

copyright notice: intimation of a book's copyright usually appears on the verso of the title-page and in the following words:

'This book is copyright under the Berne Convention. Apart from any fair dealing for the purposes of private study, research, criticism or review, as permitted under the Copyright Act, 1956, no portion may be reproduced by any process without written permission. Enquiry should be made to the publisher.'

To meet the requirements of the signatories to the Universal Copyright Convention a publisher must ensure that the first edition of a work bears the symbol © (for copyright), the date of publication, and the name of the copyright owner.

cording quires: a 16th-century term for the outside quires of a ream of paper.

See also *cassie, outsides.*

Cordovan leather: goatskin, originally tanned and dressed at Cordova in Spain. It was often dyed red.

See also *mudéjar bindings* for which it was used.

cords: lengths of flax or hemp (usually five) placed across the back of a book; to these the sections are sewn.

cordwain: the English name for *Cordovan leather*, q.v.

cored type: large-size types and spacing of which the feet have been hollowed to reduce weight. (G.U.)

corium: the Latin for leather. The term 'in corio' is found in some 16th-century documents to denote a book bound in leather.

corners: 1. in printing, material for setting corners in ruled frames, or connecting ornamental borders.

See also *Oxford corners.* (G.U.)

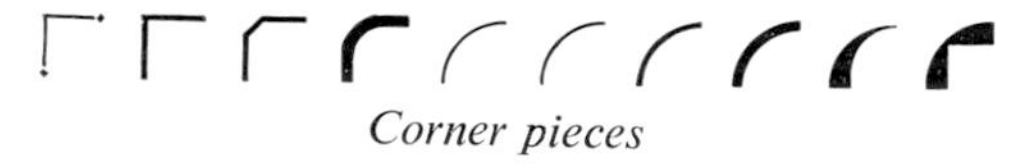

Corner pieces

2. in binding, the triangular pieces of leather or cloth which cover the corners of half- or three-quarter bound books.

See also *mitred* (1), *turning-in corners.*

correcting: the alteration of errors or defects in printing formes, whether text, plates, or blocks; also reproduction negatives, etc. (G.U.)

See also *proof corrections.*

Correcting composed type. The wrong letter is removed with a bodkin. A pair of tweezers lie on one side of the galley; a composing stick on the other. If an error is found in a Linotype setting the slug must be taken out, re-set and re-cast

corrigendum (pl. **corrigenda**)**:** a slip of paper giving corrections of mistakes in the text which were not noticed until the book was printed. Also known as *erratum.*

Corvinus bindings: bindings done for Matthias Corvinus, King of Hungary, 1458–90, by craftsmen who are believed to have come from Naples. Features were elaborate tooling in gold, and decoration with blue paint. Many manuscripts were bound in brocade with bosses and clasps of silver, while others were bound in stamped leather or red velvet. In 1526 the King's library, variously estimated at from 1500 to 3000 volumes, was sacked by the Turks and has never been recovered; some examples may be seen in the Österreichische Nationalbibliothek, Vienna.

Corvinus Press: a modern private press founded by the late Viscount Carlow. Editions were small and the work largely experimental.

In 1945 the equipment was acquired by the *Dropmore Press*, q.v.

Costeriana: the name given to editions of Latin grammars (Aelius Donatus) printed in Holland in the early 15th century, and, it is suggested, from movable letters of wood. These letters are thought to have been cut by Laurens Janszoon Coster of Haarlem, *c.* 1370–1440.

Tradition demands mention of this here, but it is difficult to believe that each letter could be cut with mathematical precision, or that, if this were achieved, subsequent usage with ink and pressure would not warp them.

cottage binding: a 17th-century style of book decoration, widely practised in England (especially in the workshops of *Mearne* and *Payne*, qq.v.), in which the framework of the design tooled on the cover may be said to resemble a gable.

Cotton, Sir Robert Bruce, 1571–1631: an eminent bibliophile whose library of books and manuscripts was enriched by his son and grandson. In 1753 the collection was acquired by the British Museum. At one time it had been stored at Ashburnham House, Westminster, where in 1731 a fire had damaged over 200 of the English State Papers, deeds, and abbey chartularies.

Among the treasures of Cotton's library were the *Lindisfarne Gospels*, q.v., a copy of Beowulf (*c.* 1000), and two copies of Magna Charta.

Cottrell-Claybourn: a name for printing presses of various kinds constructed by C. B. Cottrell & Sons Co., Claybourn Division, Milwaukee, U.S.A. Among others are rotary sheet presses for one or more colours. (G. U.)

A Cottrell-Claybourn rotary sheet press

Cottrell, Thomas, fl. 1757–85: a London typefounder who served his apprenticeship with the first Caslon before opening his own foundry. In his day he was notable for a fount of two-line Engrossing, in imitation of the law hand used for legal documents; for a fount of Domesday characters; and for his refurbishing, on behalf of William Bowyer the elder, of the Anglo-Saxon types (cut from drawings by Humphrey Wanley) which had been used in 1715 for Mrs. Elstob's 'Anglo-Saxon Grammar'.

Nine years after Cottrell's death his foundry was bought by *Robert Thorne*, q.v.

couch: 1. the board on which sheets of leaf are pressed in hand-made paper-making. See *leaf* (2). To couch is thus the action of lifting the sheets on to the board.

2. the felt blanket on to which sheets of partly dried leaf are transferred for drying into sheets of paper.

3. the roll from which the wet web on the paper machine is transferred unaided from the wire to the next section.

coucher: 1. the craftsman who lifts the newly formed (and still wet) sheet of paper from the mould in which it has been made, and skilfully transfers it to the couch board on which he builds up a *post*, q.v.

See also *upper end boy*.

2. an obsolete term for a large book meant to rest on a table or stand, especially a chartulary, register, or antiphonary.

counter: 1. the inside area of a type-face, e.g. the centre of an 'o', the space between the vertical strokes of an 'n', etc. This is so called because the steel punch used to stamp the matrix is often counter-punched to form these areas.

2. an automatic device incorporated with printing and folding machines and the like for the purpose of recording the quantity of sheets produced. (L. K.)

counter-etching: a stage in the preparation of lithographic printing plates, immediately after graining, and before transferring the image, whereby the plates are sensitized or counter-etched. A zinc plate is washed in running water, and then put in a solution of alum (4 oz.), nitric acid ($\frac{1}{2}$ oz.), and water (80 oz.). The nitric acid will attack the metal and break up the film of zinc oxide, while the alum deposits a layer of water-insoluble aluminium sulphate. This aluminium salt is more sensitive to the image-forming materials than the original zinc surface.

counter-mark: a watermark embodying the paper-maker's initials which is placed in the second half of the sheet opposite the normal *watermark*, q.v.

Court hand: a general term for all handwriting, other than *book* and *text hands*, qq.v., used in England from 12th–17th centuries for business, accounts, proceedings, memoranda, etc. In the 18th century the term applied only to legal hands. (A Court was an English administrative department.)

See also *calligraphy*.

courtesy terms: special discounts off the published prices of books allowed by publishers, wholesalers, and booksellers to their own employees, to the press and to members of allied trades. Such discounts should not exceed those granted to the retail trade except in the case of publishers' employees purchasing the publications of their own firms.

cover: the paper, board, cloth, or leather (used singly or combined) to which the body of a book is secured by glue and thread. The cover of a machine-bound book is called a *case*.

See also *bookbinding styles and binding features*.

cover papers: papers for the covers of books, pamphlets, etc., made from almost every kind of paper-making material, and of endless variety in colour and finish. (M. L.)

cover title: the title of a book as stamped or lettered on the cover of a book. This may be an abbreviation of the full title.

cowhide: leather made from unsplit cowhide or its grain split. Also similar leather from any bovine animal hide.

Cowper, Edward, 1790–1852: the inventor, about 1818, of a perfecting machine which influenced the design of most subsequent models, and, in 1827, of a four-cylinder machine for newspaper printing. In the latter he was partnered by *August Applegath*, q.v., with whom he also had for some time a printing business.

crabs: a colloquialism for copies of a book returned by the bookseller to the publisher.

Crabtree: the trade mark of letterpress machines, offset machines, rotary newspaper presses, etc., manufactured by R. W. Crabtree & Sons Ltd., of Leeds and London, founded in 1895. Their all-size rotary press for book printing, which is reel fed, will print and deliver sections from eight to thirty-two pages, cut and folded to size, with a total of 256 pages, in one revolution of the cylinders. (G. U.)

Cracherode, Clayton Mordaunt, 1730–99: a bibliophile of wealth and taste who formed a library of 4500 volumes. Included were many first printed editions of classics, the Mainz Catholicon, Dante's 'Divine Comedy' (Florence, 1481), etc. Roger Payne was commissioned to re-bind many of his books.

Cracherode bequeathed his library to the British Museum.

crackle: a desirable sound produced in a sheet of good paper when held by the fingers and moved quickly. (M. L.)

Cracow fragments: portions of five printed leaves, belonging to the University Library of Cracow, Poland. In the catalogue of the library's incunabula (1900) they appeared simply as 'Donati fragmenta'. They attracted considerable attention in 1937, however, when loaned to Dr. Carl Wehmer, principal editor of the 'Gesamtkatalog der Wiegendrucke', for documentation.

Wehmer found the fragments were printer's proofs, all pulled on leaves taken from an account book which had been used by a cloth merchant of Mainz for business transacted between 1383 and 1393. This book had apparently turned up as waste in a Mainz printing shop. The five leaves were printed in an early state of the 36-line Bible type: three were from a Donatus grammar; the fourth was from a Bible, apparently 40-line; while the fifth was part of an astrologer's planetary table for January and February of an unspecified year. This last proved to be identical with fragments of an astronomical calendar discovered at Wiesbaden in 1901. The Berlin Astronomische Rechen-Institut had declared the Wiesbaden fragments to be planetary tables for 1448, leading one to infer that they were printed in 1447. If this were so, then the Cracow leaves belonged to the same year. This had upset all theories that Gutenberg's invention was dated 1454.

Now Gutenberg's 42-line Bible was completed by 1456, and the 36-line Bible by 1461 (or a little earlier). The Cracow Bible fragment was apparently set from an independent manuscript, and judged from its type vis-à-vis the 36-line version must have been printed about 1458. Experts also assigned the Donatus fragments to 1458. There remained the calendar.

Dr. Wehmer, aided by authorities on medieval astrology, concluded that such tables were not intended for scientists, but for popular travelling astrologers to whom it would matter little that their tables were ten years out of date. Thus 1454 may still be considered as the earliest date when printing from movable type began.

See Carl Wehmer, 'Mainzer Probedrucke in der Type des sogenannten Astronomischen Kalenders für 1448', Munich, Leibniz Verlag, 1948.

cradle: a bow-shaped steel rocker, with a toothed edge, used to roughen the surface of a copper mezzotint plate, so that an even and deep grain is given to the entire surface. The cradle is drawn over

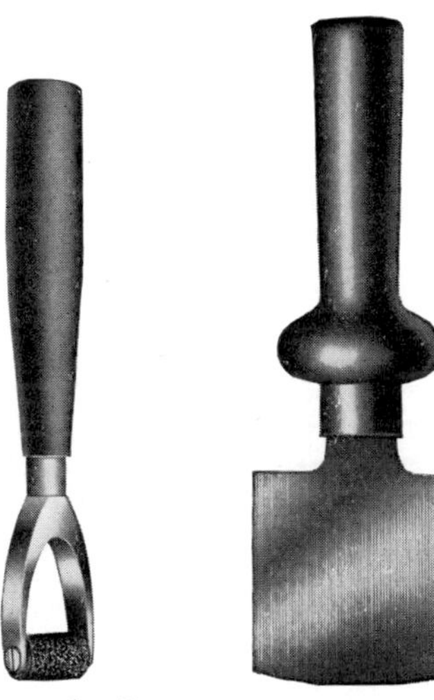

Graining roller *Mezzotint cradle*

the plate in one direction until the whole has been treated. The rocking is then repeated in another direction, and continued in several directions, determined by means of a special composing stick.

The invention of the cradle is attributed to Abraham Blooteling, 1672, who in any case perfected the technique of its use. Before this time graining was done in a more primitive way, and even today an artist will do the preliminary roughening of the plate with sandpaper, a roulette, or a sand jet blower.

See also *mezzotint*. (G. U.)

cradle book: see *incunabulum*.

craft bookbinding: the binding of individual books for individual customers. The craft bookbinder's work includes restoring valuable manuscripts, repairing old bindings, and sentimental work of all kinds. All processes are largely by hand. Sometimes known as *miscellaneous binding*. (M. L.)

Cramoisy, Sebastien, 1585–1669: a Parisian printer and publisher who was appointed first director of the Imprimerie Royale upon its establishment in the Louvre in 1640.

Cranach, Lucas, 1472–1553: a German painter, also a wood-cutter. His real name was Müller or Sunder, but he was called Cranach after his Bavarian birthplace Kronach. He worked in Bavaria and Austria before settling in Wittenberg where he employed a number of assistants, among others being his sons Hans (1500–37) and Lucas, jun. (1515–86). His work was mostly for religious books, some of which bear his mark of a winged serpent with a ring in its mouth. Cranach was one of the most important and influential book illustrators of his day. He experimented with colour printing, and also in copperplate engraving, a medium he chose for two portraits of Luther (1520–21) which were extensively circulated in pamphlets. (With G. U.)

Cranach Presse: a private press founded in 1913 at Weimar by Harry Graf von Kessler, a German diplomatist. Hand-presses were used for the small editions issued, some works being illustrated by, among others, Eric Gill and Edward Gordon Craig. J. H. Mason, a Doves Press compositor, and Gage Cole, a Doves Press pressman, both spent a short time working for Kessler. The press closed in 1933.

Crantz, Martin: associated with Friburger and Gering in establishing the first press in France at the Sorbonne, Paris. The first book issued was the 'Epistolae' of the Italian Gasparinus Barzizius. The work was undated but is known to have appeared in 1470. The types used were modelled on early founts of Rome.

crash: a loose-weave binding cloth.

crash finish: a variety of paper having a surface like coarse linen; it can be used in offset printing.

Crawford, Alexander William, 1812–80: a Lancashire bibliophile who, by 1860, had established a library of 100,000 volumes at Haigh Hall. Many were acquired by the John Rylands Library in 1900, but some of the incunabula, rare books, and works on fine arts remain.

Crawshay Prize: see *Rose Mary Crawshay Prize*.

creasing: 1. a linear indentation made by machine in thick paper to provide a hinge.

2. a printing fault, seen as deep creases, which may occur when paper is not stored at the correct humidity, or through other causes.

criblé: minute punctures or depressions made in surfaces of wood or metal. De Vinne describes the process as being intended partly to offset the impossibility of obtaining a solid black background due to the imperfections of early presswork. Criblé backgrounds can be used to lighten borders which would appear too dark in relation to the text area of a page were they printed solid black.

criblé initials: decorated initials used at the beginnings of chapters, notably by the 16th-century French printer Geofroy Tory, in which the capital appears on an all-over ground of small dots or sieve-like pattern.

Cromberger, Jakob, fl. 1503–37: a German printer of Seville, who worked for a time in Evora and Lisbon. He was noted for the fine books he issued, mostly essays, romances, poetry, etc. In 1527 his son Johann (or Juan) succeeded him. In 1539 the latter sent a press and a printer, Juan Pablos, to Mexico where he printed eight works: one of these, 'Ordinarium sacri ordinis heremitarum Sancti Augustini', 1556, contained the first music printed in America.

Cromer Greek Prize: a prize founded by the late Lord Cromer as an annual award of £40 for the best essay on the culture of ancient Greece. It is administered by the British Academy, all British subjects under 26 years the December preceding the award being eligible.

Crompton Bequest: a fund established by the late R. H. Crompton to assist the publication of works of merit and permanent worth which would not otherwise be published, due to the unlikelihood of their being financially profitable. Awards are made by the trustees, the Society of Authors.

cropped: said of a book which has had its margins unduly trimmed. They are said to *bleed.*

Cropper: a small platen printing machine, named after its maker.

cross: the following forms of cross are available as types:

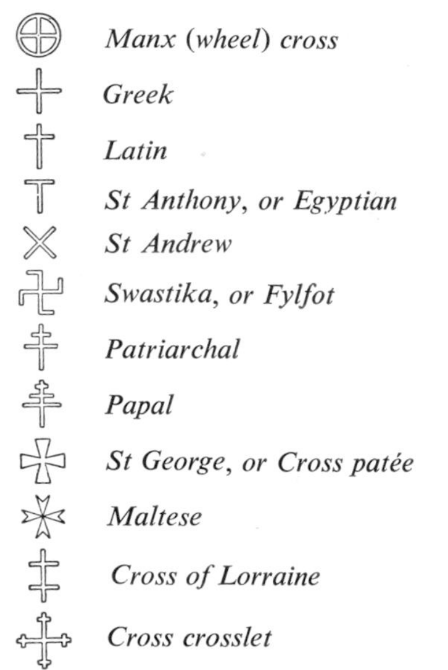

cross-bars: bars used to divide a chase into sections so as to lock up the pages more securely.

cross-grained morocco: goatskin, used for book covers, having diagonally crossed lines produced artificially.

cross-heads: subsection or paragraph headings or numerals printed across the page and centred in the body of the text from which they are separated by one or more lines of space. They normally mark the first subdivision of a chapter.
See also *sub-heads.*

cross reference: a reference from one part of a book to another.

crown: 1. a standard size of printing paper, 15 in. by 20 in.
2. the camber from the centre to the ends of a calender roll.
See also *bowls.*

crown octavo: a book size, $7\frac{1}{2}$ in. by 5 in.
See *book sizes.*

crushed Levant: large-grained goatskin, used for book covers. The surface is crushed before use, and after covering the book is polished until smooth.

crystallization: a printing fault, seen as a mottled or uneven effect, which may occur when using two or more colours on a letterpress working. This indicates that the first ink has been allowed to dry so hard by oxidation that it will not properly receive a subsequent impression. The trouble may be overcome by adding an ink solvent to the overprinting ink which will soften the crystallized first impression.

Cuala Press: an Irish private press founded by Elizabeth C. Yeats in 1902, being until 1908 known as the *Dun Emer Press,* q.v. In 1924 the press was moved from Dundrum to Dublin.
The press was largely concerned with encouraging the continuance of Irish literature. Writing in 1933 W. B. Yeats said 'My sister's books are like an old family magazine. A few hundred people buy them all and expect a common theme.'
Elizabeth Yeats died in 1940, and the press was then managed by Mrs. W. B. Yeats.

cuir bouilli: leather which has been soaked in very hot water and resins; it can then be moulded and sets very hard. (In spite of the name it is not boiled.) In the 9th century it was found suitable, without boards, for covering books. The outline of a design was lightly cut into the leather while damp: it was then hammered into relief. Hot wax was poured behind the relief to preserve the design. In the 14th century the background was punched, making it slightly sunk, and leaving the design in relief. Motifs were mythical animals and interlaced foliage. Leather treated in this way was used by craftsmen working at Nuremberg and Bruges.

cuir ciselé: a manner of decorating leather-bound books widely practised in 15th-century Germany. The design was outlined on dampened leather by cutting it with a sharp tool or knife. A relief effect was then obtained by punching and deepening the leather round the outline. Sometimes the design was hammered from the back, giving an embossed effect. More recent, and superb, were examples made in France by Henri Marius Michel, *c.* 1866.
For an illustration see the frontispiece.

cul-de-lampe: the French term for a *head-* or *tail-piece.*

cum licentia: a Latin phrase appearing on the title-page of a book (or on a *licence leaf,* q.v.) to indicate that it is published by permission of some secular or ecclesiastical authority.
See also *imprimatur, nihil obstat.*

cum privilegio: see *privilege.*

cumdach: a jewelled and elaborately decorated box used in late 9th-century Ireland for keeping manuscript books. Also known as a *book shrine*.
See also *Cathach Psalter*.

Cumulative Book Index: one of the most important bibliographical works for the American book trade. This was established in 1898 by the H. W. Wilson Co. of New York as a monthly list of U.S. publications; since 1929 it has claimed to list all books printed in English wherever issued. The annual volumes are cumulated over periods of years, entries being arranged in one alphabetical sequence of author, title, and subject.

cumulative list: a list of books which combines material previously published in separate lists.

cuneiform script: wedge-shaped letters in which Sumerian, Assyrian, Babylonian, and Old Persian inscriptions were stamped into clay tablets. They belong to the era 4000–100 B.C.

cup: an alternative name for *bowl*, q.v.

Cura Pastoralis: a copy of the 'Regulae' of Pope Gregory I in a version translated from Latin into Old English. This was thought to be the work of King Alfred, but is more probably that of scholars at his court. It is now in the Bodleian Library, Oxford.

Curatores Praeli Typographici: the body formed at the instigation of Richard Bentley (1662–1742), in 1698, to direct the affairs of the Cambridge University Press. This control is now exercised by a University committee; its members being known as the *Syndics*, q.v.

curiosa: a bibliophile's term for works in some degree indecent.
See also *erotica, pornography*.

Curll, Edmund, 1675–1747: a London bookseller, publisher, and pirate. His occasionally unethical publishing activities brought him into conflict with many in the literary world, particularly Pope, in whose 'Dunciad' he is satirized. In 1716, 1721, and 1735 he was ordered to appear at the bar of the House of Lords. It was as a result of his publishing the works of the Duke of Buckingham that a resolution was passed making it a breach of privilege to print, without permission, 'the works, life, or last will of any lord of this house' (i.e. House of Lords). This remained in force until 1845.

Curll was also prosecuted for libel, pilloried, and publicly reviled for some of his actions.

See R. Straus, 'The Unspeakable Curll', Chapman & Hall, 1927.

cursive: a running script, with letters formed without raising the pen. The humanistic script which was used in Italy in the middle of the 15th century was usually, but not necessarily, sloped. Its use developed in two ways. One was for the class of diplomatic document written in the Papal Chancery, the Brief. The Brief began its formal existence some time before 1390, and was written in gothic cursive. The earliest humanist Brief on record is dated 1446. The script became relatively formal and generous in size. During the same period, humanistic cursive was also used by scholars, but their version was small, quick, and ligatured wherever possible. The first typographic form followed the literary, and was cut in 1500 for Aldus Manutius, who called it *chancery* (known elsewhere as italic). It was copied by other Venetian printers.

When italic type was first used in Rome, the Venetian literary form was abandoned in favour of the older diplomatic cursive. Ludovico degli Arrighi, alias Vicentino, was a 'scriptor brevium' in the Papal Chancery. His italic type was cut by Lautizio de Bartholomeo dei Rotelli of Perugia, and appeared in 1524. The several versions made for Arrighi have had considerable influence on present-day italic faces cut for use with old-face romans. Indebted to him are Antonio Blado, Robert Estienne, Simon de Colines, Granjon, and Garamond.

Monotype faces based on chancery cursive are Bembo italic, 1923; Blado italic, 1924; Arrighi (hand), 1925, (machine), 1929.

See S. Morison, 'A tally of types cut for machine composition, and introduced at the University Press, Cambridge, 1922–32'. (Privately published.) C.U.P., 1953.

Curwen Press: a commercial printing establishment, mentioned here because of the good taste and faultless workmanship of its productions. It was founded in 1863 by the Rev. John Curwen of Plaistow for the printing of Tonic Sol-fa music. His grandson, Harold Curwen, assumed control in 1916, and with Claud Lovat Fraser laid the foundation of the present high standards. In 1921 Oliver Simon joined the press and later directed it until his death. Among important publications on typography printed by the Curwen Press were Vols. I–IV of 'The Fleuron', and 'Signature', edited by *Oliver Simon*, q.v.

cut: 1. a wood, copper, or steel plate bearing a design cut or engraved. While formerly restricted to woodcuts, the term has been loosely used for half-tone, zinc etching, or other illustrative letterpress material.

2. an illustration printed from such plates.

3. an instruction to the blockmaker that part of an original must not be reproduced.

cut edges: the three edges of a book which have been cut solid by a cutting machine so that all pages on each are flush. Cf. *trimmed edges.*

cut flush: said of a book which has its cover and page edges quite even, the cutting being done after the cover is attached. Also known as *flush boards* or *trimmed flush.*

cut in-boards: said of a book which has its head, tail, and fore-edge trimmed after the boards have been laced on by the sewing cords. Cf. *cut out-of-boards.*

cut-in heads: paragraph or section headings set in a bold or otherwise distinguishing type in the text, i.e. not in the margin.

cut-in side notes: notes to a work which are set in the text, the type being built around them on three sides.
See also *marginal notes.*

cut out half-tone: synonymous with *outline half-tone,* q.v.

cut out-of-boards: said of a book which has its edges cut or trimmed before affixing the boards. The latter are used for positioning during the cutting of head and tail edge. This method is used when boards are not laced on, but fit closely in the grooves. (A hollow back is needed.) Cf. *cut in-boards.*

cut the line: a former printing-trade expression which meant that if a member of a *companionship,* q.v., ran out of copy or type the whole companionship stopped work until fresh supplies enabled him to continue.

cut to register: said of watermarked paper which has been cut so that the watermark appears in the same position in each sheet. Applicable to expensive hand-made paper.

Cuthbert Gospels: a name sometimes given to the *Lindisfarne Gospels,* q.v.

cutting cylinder: a cylinder bearing a knife and forming part of a rotary press. It is used for cutting each copy from the web.
See also *cutting stick* (2).

cutting machine: see *guillotine.*

cutting off: a stage in *machine-sewing,* q.v., whena row of books sewn as a unit must be separated to permit subsequent binding processes to be continued. (G. U.)

cutting stick: 1. the strip of wood on which a guillotine knife descends when cutting.
2. the strip of wood, rubber, or composition fitted to the folding-roller of a rotary web press. When cutting each copy from the web the knife presses against the stick.

cyan (blue) ink: the correct name for the shade of blue ink used in four-colour printing as established by British Standard 1480: 1949.

cylinder dried: said of paper that has been dried on the paper-making machine in distinction from other methods of drying. (M. L.)

cylinder machine: a standard paper-making machine invented in 1805 by Joseph Bramah, and considerably improved by John Dickinson in 1809. The sheet is formed on the surface of a cylindrical wire mould which revolves in a vat of stuff, the water draining through the mesh. The partly-formed sheet is then transferred to a felt with the aid of a roll which rides on the surface of the felt and presses it against the sheet, the subsequent stages of its manufacture being similar to those employed in making paper on the *Fourdrinier machine,* q.v.

cylinder press: a printing press in which the forme is carried on a flat bed under a paper-bearing cylinder for an impression to be made at the point of contact. The cylinder revolves against the forme with the same peripheral speed as the lateral speed of the forme. The first cylinder machine in Britain was built in 1812 by Friedrich König.
Designs vary, and include principally the *stop-cylinder machine* in which the cylinder is stationary during the return of the bed; the *two-revolution machine* in which the cylinder revolves continuously at a constant speed, making one revolution during the forward movement of the bed and one during its return (for the latter the cylinder is raised to clear the forme and the sheet is delivered); the *single-revolution machine* in which the cylinder revolves at a constant speed, making half a turn for each of the movements of the bed. (G. U.)
See also *letterpress machines.*

ADDENDA

Caxton Club: a club for bibliophiles, established in Chicago in 1895. Occasional works of interest to book collectors are published.

The Colophon: an 'American Book Collectors' Quarterly', established in February 1930 and now discontinued. A final one-volume collection of bibliophilic essays was published in 1950, entitled 'The New Colophon'.

colour printing—paper condition: the age, quality, and condition of paper are of considerable importance in colour printing. Large sheets, fresh from the mill, may shrink in the pressroom, affecting register. It is of assistance, therefore, if a relative humidity of 60 to 65 per cent is maintained, thereby reducing in addition a tendency to wave or produce static.

If a paper-conditioning plant is installed sheets are held for some time before printing on a hanging conveyor while room air is circulated. The maintainance of condition during the run is also important, since each printing adds moisture to it. It is useful to check the paper after running off ream batches. Batches should be numbered and covered with a few sheets of interleaving to prevent dimensional changes in the top sheets. The batches will then be reloaded in the press in the order of emergence.

colour sequence: the accepted order of letterpress printing in four colours is yellow, red, blue, black. It was suggested in Germany in 1957 that to print yellow as the third colour would help to make *moiré*, q.v., less noticeable, since blue, usually printed third, is very intense. If yellow is not printed first a transparent yellow ink should be substituted for the normal near-opaque trichromatic yellow ink.

The engraver will, however, require notice of any departure from the normal sequence.

coloured printings: a cheap quality of paper, with a high content of mechanical wood pulp, used, among other things, for the covers of pamphlets.

conger: a group of from ten to twenty wholesale booksellers who combined to share the publishing and selling of a work, and to use their power as wholesalers to protect the sale of their books from undercutting and piracy. Congers were a feature of the London book trade in the late 17th and early 18th centuries, when such famous men as Lintot, Longman, Rivington, and Tonson were among those co-operating in this way.

The number of shares held by individual members of a conger was not always equal, and the whole conger might own only part of a work, e.g. an encyclopaedia. A member could sell his rights, while on his decease they might be disposed of by legacy or auction. Thus title-pages of a work which appeared in several editions through the years would list different proprietors.

D

dabber: see *ink ball.*

dagger (or **obelisk**): a printer's sign † used in the text of a work, as part of a recognized sequence of alternatives to superior letters or numbers, to draw the reader's attention to a footnote. If placed before a person's name it denotes 'deceased'.
See also *reference marks.*

Daguerre, Louis Jacques Mandé, 1787–1851: a French artist and inventor who interested himself in photography. In the 1820's he became well known as a result of a diorama he built in Paris. His efforts at photography were not really successful until 1829 when he entered into partnership with J. N. Niepce. After the latter's death in 1833 Daguerre invented the process which bears his name, *daguerreotype*. This was a means of making photographs on silver plates, and is considered the first really practicable photographic method. (G. U.)
See H. & A. Gernsheim, 'Daguerre', Secker, 1956.

daguerreotype: a method of making and fixing a photographic image, invented in 1833 by L. J. M. Daguerre.
A silver plate or silvered copperplate exposed to iodine or bromine vapour is transformed on the surface into silver iodide or silver bromide respectively, thereby becoming light-sensitive. On exposure in a dark room the picture is developed in vaporized mercury which is deposited on the different parts of the plate in proportion to the amount of light influencing them. The plate is fixed in a solution of carbonate of soda, and is often toned by gold chloride. Such daguerreotypes are unique in that they cannot be copied. The process was made public in 1839. In the 1850's it was superseded by a negative-positive process by which any number of copies can be made. The few genuine daguerreotypes extant are considered fairly valuable. They are recognizable by the metal plate being reflecting, thus the picture with its soft and fine details appears positive only under certain light conditions; also the image is usually turned sideways. The image is very sensitive to any rubbing, for which reason it is always kept mounted under glass with sealed airtight edges. (G. U.)

dammar: a resin derived from certain pine trees and used as a varnish in the manufacture of printing inks. (M. L.)

damping: 1. the moistening of paper before using it in a hand-press to make the surface softer and more receptive to the ink. The paper is laid between moist blotting or waste-paper, or sprinkled with water, the damping being followed by brushing. In earlier rotary presses damping was done by guiding the paper course over perforated steam rollers and then between smoothing rollers before printing.
2. see *collotype.*
3. the keeping moist of a lithographic plate. In a hand-press this is done with a sponge; in a machine press by means of damping rollers similar in construction to the inkers. The fluid used, known as damping mixture, varies in composition according to the material used for the forme (stone, zinc, aluminium, steel, etc.).
4. the damping, with a sponge dipped in water, of hand-set formes prior to distribution of the type. (G. U.)

damping paper: sheets of hand-made paper are normally slightly damped before printing takes place. Among reasons for this are the hardness of the size, making the paper less receptive to ink and liable to set-off; while the roughness and inevitable variations of thickness found in dry hand-made paper call for much greater pressure to obtain good sharp impressions than is the case with damped sheets.
When preparing for the press, piles of paper are interleaved with moistened waterleaf, one piece between every twenty sheets of paper, and allowed to stand for a few hours. They are then pressed flat in a standing press. Printing should take place immediately, water being sprinkled on the pressroom floor so that the paper will not dry before the sheets have been perfected. On completion of the work the sheets must be thoroughly and quickly dried to avoid the growth of mould.

damping solution: the liquid used in the damping unit of a lithographic press. The composition of this is of particular importance in offset printing from zinc or aluminium plates. Formulas vary. The acidity content must be kept low (pH approximately 3·8) but must be sufficient to maintain the precipitation obtained by the etching of fine-grained, damp-absorbing products on the surface of the plate. (G.U.)

damping unit: an appliance for maintaining the supply of the quantity of damping solution necessary to the printing forme on a lithographic press. (G.U.)

Damping unit in an offset press

dandy roll: a light cylindrical frame covered with wire gauze used for solidifying the partly formed web of paper by pressing on it. The dandy roll is usually placed between the first and second suction boxes of the Fourdrinier. According to the weave of the wire gauze the impression left on the moving paper is either the ribs with parallel cross-lines for laid papers, or the uniform woven effect of wove papers. Devices or monograms are also worked into the gauze, being made of wire which is soldered or sewn to it; these impress the watermark and countermark respectively.

A *spiral-laid dandy roll* is one where the wires round the circumference run spirally.

Early models of the dandy roll were patented in England by Phipps in 1825 and John Wilks in 1830.

Daniel Press: a precursor of the Victorian Private Press movement. It was established by the Rev. C. H. O. Daniel in 1845 at Frome, then in 1876 at Oxford. Daniel revived the Fell types of the Oxford University Press. The Daniel Press ceased its activities in 1919, and is now being used for the instruction of students in the Bibliography Room in the New Bodleian Library.

See 'Memorials of C. H. O. Daniel, with a bibliography of the Press, 1845–1919', Oxford, Daniel Press, 1921.

dark-room camera: a reproduction camera with the back portion let into the wall of a dark room, so that dark slides are unnecessary. Modern dark-room cameras are automatic and mechanized, so that they can be manoeuvred entirely from within the dark room. Although, due to its construction, the camera cannot be swung into the 'prism position' it is possible by means of mirrors to obtain reproductions turned laterally. (G.U.)

With the Huebner Reverser the image in the dark-room camera can be reversed

Darlington Press: a private press established about 1768 at 'The Grange' (i.e. Blackwell Grange, near Darlington), the seat of George Allan (1736–1800). He was an enthusiastic printer and issued many pamphlets of antiquarian and topographical interest, in addition to publishing the poetry and miscellaneous writings of his friends. (With M.L.)

dash: 1. for decoration, a short strip of rule which may be plain or ornamented in several ways.

See also *border*, *french rule*, *rule*, *swelled rules*.

2. for punctuation, a short strip of rule cast in the following lengths: the two-em dash ——; the one-em dash —; the en rule –; and the hyphen -. (Collins gives guidance on their usage.)

David Berry Prize: a prize of a gold medal and the sum of £50 awarded for a work dealing with Scottish history within the reigns of James I to James VI, the subject to have been previously approved by the Royal Historical Society, London.

Dawson, William: see *Wharfedale machine*.

Day, Benjamin, 1838–1916: of New Jersey, the inventor of a mechanical tinting process.
See also *Ben Day tints.*

Day, John, 1522–84: a London printer and typefounder who was an original freeman of the Stationers' Company, and Master in 1580. He is remembered for his almanacs, ABC primers, Psalms, and the first English edition of Foxe's 'Book of Martyrs', 1563 (entitled 'Actes and Monuments of these latter and perillous Dayes'), in addition to early efforts at music printing and woodcut initials.

He worked with roman and gothic types, and introduced a fount of roman with matching italic.

Day also printed 'De antiquitate Britannicae ecclesiae Cantuariensis' for Archbishop Parker on the latter's private press at Lambeth, in 1572.

Dayco Color Separator: see *split-duct printing.*

Daye, Stephen, fl. 1638–48: an Englishman who worked the first press to be set up in America. This had been taken from England by the Rev. Jose Glover (of Sutton, Surrey) who died on the voyage, and Daye had been engaged as pressman. The press was erected at Cambridge, Mass., in late 1638. The first publication of the press was 'The Oath of a Free-man', 1639, but no copy of this is known. The first book to be issued of which a copy survives was 'The whole Booke of Psalmes, faithfully translated into English Metre', 1640. There is a copy in the Bodleian Library, Oxford. (The book is also known as the 'Bay Psalm Book'.)

From 1649 until it closed in 1692 the press was managed by Samuel Green.

dead: said of fibres which, due to excessive action in the beater, have had their strength and resilience destroyed.

dead line: a short line incised on the bed of a flat-bed cylinder press to guide the positioning of the forme. Should the latter be pushed over the line the grippers may damage the matter.

dead matter: set up type which has been printed and is to be distributed. Cf. *standing type.*

Deberny and Peignot: the largest type-foundry in France, established in 1923 by the amalgamation of Deberny & Cie with G. Peignot & Fils. In 1827 Honoré de Balzac, in partnership with Barbier and Laurent, founded a company which was to be a combined foundry, printing office, and bookseller's. It was unsuccessful, but soon after Laurent and Deberny, with money from Balzac, formed a new type-founding company. Laurent resigned in 1840, and in 1877 the company amalgamated with the firm of Tuleu. Among well-known letter designers who worked for the firm was Carlègle.

Gustave Peignot acquired a type-foundry in 1862, incorporating with it a number of others. He was succeeded by his second son Georges who gave a new impetus to French type-designing; this began with a face by Eugène Grasset, 1899, and one by Georges Auriol, 1902. In 1912 the firm purchased the original matrices of Firmin Didot. Among type-faces well known outside France is the series 'Les Cochins' which was begun in 1912. (G.U.)

See also *Cochin* (2).

decimo-sexto: see *sixteenmo.*

deck: the feed board on cylinder presses. (M.L.)

deckle, deckle strap: on the paper-making mould, the frame or border, usually of wood, which confines the paper pulp to the mould. On the paper-making machine, the strap on either side of the moving web which limits the lateral flow of the pulp and also controls the contour of the edge of the paper web.
See also *deckle edge.* (M.L.)

deckle edge: 1. the rough uneven edge of hand-made paper, caused by the pulp flowing between the frame and deckle of the mould. In machine-made papers this effect can be produced mechanically on the edges of the paper.

2. in bookbinding it is usual to leave the deckle edges of hand-made paper uncut as in the bound book they are thought to have a beauty of their own. As dust collects on them they are not very practical.

dedication: in the 16th and 17th centuries, an inscription by the author in which he commended his book to the favour or patronage of some nobleman or eminent person. Now, usually an inscription of a less fulsome nature in which the author records his esteem for some person. The dedication is printed on the leaf following the title-page.
See also *impensis, patron.*

deep-etch half-tone: a half-tone plate from which the screen dots of any unwanted areas have been routed completely away. These areas appear as plain paper on the printed sheet. (Illustrated under *block.*) Cf. *deeply-etched half-tone.*

deep-etch process: a method of making a lithographic plate by photo-mechanical means. It involves the printing on to metal of a photographic positive, and the very slight (in spite of the name) etching of the plate so that the image is slightly recessed below the general level, making it durable and capable of giving richer effects.

The positive can be an original line-drawing, or a print made on paper or other translucent material. A lithographic plate is coated with a dichromated colloid, e.g. gum arabic, fish glue. It is then exposed to light under the positive. Washing the plate leaves the metal bare in the image areas, while the rest of the plate is covered by the colloid, now hardened by exposure so that it forms a stencil about the image. At this stage the bare metal is etched slightly. Greasy ink is applied and the colloid stencil removed, leaving the inked image on an otherwise clear metal plate.

See also *Alcophoto*. (With G.U.)

deep-etching: the removal by etching of the unwanted metal on half-tone plates to give a white background.

deeply-etched half-tone: a half-tone plate in which the spaces between the dots have been etched to extra depth, but without removing the highlights. This is done to enable rougher paper to be used with the block. Cf. *deep-etch half-tone*.

deerskin: a book-covering material used as long ago as 774, when examples were made for Charlemagne. In the Middle Ages it was superseded by calf, sheep, or goatskin.

See also *forel bindings*.

definition: 1. as applied to a photographic layer, definition means its ability to reproduce clearly the delicate details of a picture; as the layer is composed of silver grains, there is a limit to this. The larger the grains the less the definition, while the thickness of the layer also affects the result. Definition is tested by printing a test object on the layer, e.g. lines of different thickness and density, etc.

2. Similar considerations apply to definition in regard to a screen picture; in this case the coarseness of the *screen*, q.v., is decisive.

3. In micro-photography definition is defined as the shortest distance separating two small objects when seen in the microscope. There is a limit to 'useful' enlargement beyond which no new details will appear. The limit is determined, among other things, by the wavelength of the light used (the lower this is the better the definition) and the aperture angle of the microscope (the larger the angle the better the definition). (G.U.)

definitive edition: the final authoritative edition of an author's complete writings.

Degener, Friedrich Otto: see *Liberty press*.

dele: the symbol ₰ representing the letter d, the initial letter of the Latin 'deleatur', delete. This is used marginally when correcting proofs to indicate that a word or words scored through with a line must be deleted.

Delegates: the governors of the *Oxford University Press*, q.v., being persons appointed by the Vice-Chancellor and Proctors of the University for a period of years.

In 1584 the University appointed a delegacy to consider the question of printing, and allowed a printer to establish himself in the city and call himself 'Printer to the University'. The first acquisition of printing equipment was a fount of greek matrices, bought in 1619, and by 1652 the University owned sufficient matrices to warrant their housing in a special room called the 'printing-house'.

The committee of Delegates of the Press was first appointed in 1653 to supervise printing and publishing in the name of the University, but the present University Press is perhaps best regarded as descending from a venture of John Fell, Bishop of Oxford, who undertook in 1669, with three partners, to lease the University's right, granted by Royal Charters of 1632–36, to print all manner of books. Fell and his partners were granted the use of University premises and the equipment from the 'printing-house'. Fell made further purchases, and under his will the printing business and all the equipment and plant became the property of the University. This was in 1691 since which date the Delegates have controlled it.

The Delegates, who give their services free, are responsible to the University for the successful conduct and development of the Press, and they direct its policy. They appoint the principal officers, control finance, and supervise the selection and production of the learned and educational books chosen for publication.

See also *Oxford imprints*.

delivery: the disposal of sheets immediately after they have been printed. There was originally no special equipment, even on cylinder machines, for delivering the sheets, and they were taken by hand from the cylinder. (See *delivery flies*.) Mechanical delivery from impression cylinders was introduced in 1834 by Isaac Adams of Rochester, and is now standard on cylinder and automatic platen machines though in different forms (see illustrations of stop-cylinder and

Extended pile delivery on a Miehle two-revolution press

High feeder and pile delivery on the Miehle

two-revolution presses). Apart from speed, the object is to prevent the newly printed surface from coming into contact with parts of the press and smearing. Modern delivery arrangements work with movable grippers, entirely without tapes, and such equipment is usual on offset machines and intaglio machines for sheet work. On these presses delivery is often combined with high feeders (see illustration). Modern two-revolution machines may have feeding equipment supplied as a separate apparatus, connected to the press after removing the usual delivery table. (G. U.)

delivery flies: the delivery tapes of a printing press along which the printed sheet, impression side uppermost, is conveyed to the delivery table. Before the automatic flyer was invented by R. Hoe in 1846 the boy who removed the sheets was called a *fly*.

In *extended delivery* extra long tapes allow several successively printed sheets to be in simultaneous process of delivery. This allows the ink to dry off slightly before reaching the pile, and lessens set-off troubles. (With G. U.)

See also *printer's devil*.

de luxe edition: an edition of a work printed on higher-grade paper than the standard edition, often from specially cast type, and usually expensively bound. The lavish use of illustrations is a feature of French books of this type.

demonym: a pseudonym for which a quality or qualification is used, e.g. 'First Nighter', 'Theatre-goer', etc.

demotic: a form of Egyptian writing used by the people (as its name implies) as distinct from the priestly hieratic (of which it was a cursive derivative, and which it later superseded), and the stone-cut hieroglyphics used for monumental inscriptions. Demotic script belongs to the era 700 B.C.–A.D. 476 and is the middle script on the Rosetta Stone.

See also *letters—forms and styles*.

demy: a standard size of printing paper, 17½ in. by 22½ in.

demy octavo: a book size, 8¾ in. by 5⅝ in.

See *book sizes*.

dendritic growths: small discolorations in a sheet of paper caused by the oxidation of minute particles of copper or brass present in it. The metal may not have been removed from the rags, or may have entered the stuff if this has been beaten with bronze roll bars. With the passage of time irregular fern-like designs radiate from the particles, sometimes for as much as ¼ in.

Denham, Henry, fl. 1559–91: a London printer and official of the Stationers' Company, remembered now as the printer of the first edition of the New Testament in Welsh, 1567, and the second edition of Holinshed's 'Chronicles'.

densitometer: an instrument used for measuring the density of a photographic layer by the process worker who requires to know the density (or degree of blackness) of a photographic image. There are also instruments for measuring the density of an opaque surface (print) before setting the camera and screen for half-tone exposure: a reflection-densitometer is used for this. Measuring the optical density of ink films during the run is done with a similar instrument.

density: the density of a developed photographic plate (or film) is determined by measuring the amount of light which will penetrate it. For this a logarithmic scale is used; if light penetrates the plate unhindered the density of the latter is said to be 0; if one-tenth of the incident light passes through the density is 1; if one-hundredth passes through the plate the density is 2; if one-thousandth penetrates the density is 3, and so on. Measurements are usually made with diffused light as direct light produces higher degrees of density (Callier effect); the instrument used is called a densitometer.

The foregoing refers to diascopic measurements; for episcopic pictures the quantity of light reflected by a blackened area, compared with the quantity of reflected light from a blank area, is determined. If the former is one-tenth of the latter, the density is 1, and so on. In comparisons between an original picture and a reproduction a density diagram can be drawn, preferably in a system of co-ordinates, in which the density values of the original are disposed along one axis, and those of the corresponding parts of the reproduction along the other. A faithful reproduction of the original will be represented by a 45° line through origo. However, the constructed density curve usually deviates considerably from the ideal. (G.U.)

dentelle bindings: the manner of decorating book covers believed to have been devised in the 17th century by the Frenchman Padeloup 'le jeune'. He used broad borders having an effect of lace edging tooled on the covers. Dentelles were later used to embellish *doublures*, q.v.

See also *Derome bindings.*

Denyse Clairouin Translation Prize: a prize founded by 'Les amis de Denyse Clairouin' in memory of the Parisian literary agent of this name who died in a concentration camp in 1945. It is awarded annually to a translator whose work is of high quality and most usefully furthers literary exchanges between France, the U.S.A., and the U.K. The amount varies.

deposit copies: see *statutory copies.*

De Ricci, Seymour: see *Ricci, Seymour de.*

Derome bindings: the bindings of Nicolas Denis Derome (1731–88), the best known of a large family of binders in France. He was famed for his dentelle borders which often featured a bird and were known as 'dentelle à l'oiseau' (although other binders are known to have used this motif). His work sometimes resembles that of Padeloup 'le jeune'.

De Roos, S. H., 1877– : one of Holland's leading type-designers of whose types known in England are Egmont, 1937, and De Roos Roman, 1947, originally made for the Amsterdam Typefoundry.

About 1928 he founded the Heuvel Press, this being the second private press in Holland.

descenders: the portion of lower-case letters below the main body, i.e. g, j, p, q, y. In setting to measures of twenty-one or more picas a face with short descenders will have its appearance and effect improved if longer descenders are used, the whole type being cast on longer bodies.

desensitization: the treatment of a lithographic printing plate, after an image has been transferred to it, by applying a solution of nitric acid and gum arabic (for stone); or gum arabic, chromic acid, and phosphoric acid (for zinc); or gum arabic and phosphoric acid (for aluminium). This solution, called an *etch*, desensitizes the non-image areas, removes stray traces of grease from them, and increases the moisture-retaining capacity.

designation marks: letters corresponding to the initial letters of the title of a book which are occasionally printed near the signature letter of each section and help the binder to identify the particular title.

De Thou, Jacques Auguste, 1553–1617: a French historian, statesman, Royal librarian, and bibliophile who in 1583 inherited his father's library of rare books. (His father had been a friend of Grolier.) While many of the books were simply bound in morocco with a coat of arms on the front panel and a monogram in the compartments formed by the bands on the spine, others were in the celebrated *fanfare* style, q.v. De Thou had copies of books pulled on paper specially made for him, and it is not surprising to learn that his library was one of the glories of Paris. By the time of his death he possessed about 1000 manuscripts and 8000 books.

After an interim period (1617–43) in which the library was administered by Pierre and Jacques Dupuy it passed to Jacques De Thou, jun., the French Consul at The Hague, who greatly enriched it. On his death in 1677 the collection went to Jacques Auguste De Thou, abbé de Souillac, but due to the demands of creditors it was sold in 1679, most of the books being bought by the Marquis de Menars.

Other subsequent owners were Cardinal de Rohan (from 1706) and his nephew the Prince de Soubise (until 1787). Between January and May 1789 the library was dispersed in a series of sales.

De Tournes, Jean, 1504–64: an important scholar-printer of Lyons, whose printing and publishing business survived in the family until 1780 (after 1585 in Geneva). De Tournes was trained by Sebastian Gryphius, and set up his own press in 1540. His books were carefully printed, being noted both for their scholarship and elegance, and in the last decade of his life he was probably the leading French printer. He used delicate woodcut borders and headpieces of arabesque fleurons, later to be cast as types by Robert Granjon.

Among his major works were Petrarch, 1545; Dante, 1552; and Froissart's 'Chronicles', 1559–61.

His son of the same name succeeded him and effected the move to Geneva in 1585.

See A. Cartier, 'Bibliographie des éditions des De Tournes', 2 vols., 1937–38.

developing: 1. developing photographic material by the reduction of silver salts has for its purpose the production of black metallic silver in proportion to the quantity of light previously cast upon the emulsion in the camera, enlarger, or contact printer. A substance capable of reducing the silver salts to silver is called a reducing agent, and it is obvious that the chief ingredient of the developer must be one having these properties. Owing to their fundamentally different effects the developing solutions may be divided into two main types, *chemical developers* and *physical developers*. The difference is that by chemical developing the silver is reduced direct from the silver bromide granules affected by light, whilst by physical developing the silver is reduced from soluble silver salts added, whereupon the silver is deposited on the 'spots' formed in the silver bromide granules affected by light.

In the case of dry plates or films (silver-bromide gelatine) *chemical developers* are mostly used. The developing substance itself is an organic reducing agent of special composition; among the best known are metol, glycin, hydroquinine, amidol, pyrocatechin, pyrogallol, etc. In addition an alkaline accelerating substance will usually be added to obtain full offset; an exception in this respect is amidol which is active even in an acid solution. Most developers are used with soda or potash. (In connection with soda it should be noted whether the formula contains anhydrous soda or soda crystals; one part anhydrous soda equals $2\frac{3}{4}$ parts of soda crystals.) The more alkali added the quicker the developer works. Approximately the following amounts of alkalis are equivalent: sodium hydroxide 6, potassium hydroxide 8, potash 60, anhydrous soda 40. Excessive amounts of alkali will injure the gelatine in the plate. A third group of substances present in chemical developers are the protecting substances, of which only sodium sulphite is generally used. The sulphite is thought to protect the developer from oxidation by the oxygen in the air, although, in fact, its importance is of a more complicated nature. Finally the developer may contain a checking substance, potassium bromide, in very small quantities. This has the effect of making the negative clearer by preventing the appearance of a grey veil. A difference is often made between rapid and slow developers, where the nature of the developing substance and alkali content determine to which group a developing solution belongs. Raising the temperature also has an accelerating effect.

Perhaps a more rational division would be surface developers and deep developers (the former being quicker). Their effect is very different. In the case of a surface developer the shaded as well as the light parts, that is to say the least as well as the most exposed, are developed almost simultaneously. The longer developing continues, the more density or blackness is added to all details of the picture, and at the same time the contrast between them increases.

In the case of deep developing the lighter parts of the negative become dense first, but as development proceeds this includes by degrees the less exposed (or shadow) parts. This depends on the slower speed of these developers resulting in the liquid beginning to work in the deeper parts of the layer before the surface itself has been completely developed. On the other hand, in the case of surface developing, the greater part of the reduced picture silver is to be found at or near the layer surface. There are, of course, all kinds of intermediate forms between the two types of developer.

Physical developers, where the reduced silver is not taken from the silver bromide or silver iodide of the layer, but from soluble silver salts added during the developing or present from the beginning in the sensitized layer, generally work very slowly, but afford exceedingly fine grain (the silver deposit is often very light). Gelatine plates or films are seldom developed physically. The so-called fine grain developers are sometimes intermediary forms between physical and chemical developers.

2. The developing in chromate processes is usually done by water, and consists in dissolving an unaffected colloid. When producing blue-prints the developing (or rather 'fixing') takes place by water; in diazotype processes by amines or phenols in alkaline solutions; and in the ozalide process by ammonia only. (G. U.)

developing paper: the material mostly used for the production of photographic copies. For a sensitive substance it has either silver bromide or silver chloride (or both mixed); the sensitive layer consists of a dried-on emulsion of the silver salts in gelatine. It is supported by a layer of barytes, consisting of barium sulphate in gelatine, spread on paper of a thickness which varies in accordance with its intended purpose. In order to obtain a visible image on such paper after copying, it must be developed rather like a dry photographic plate or film by using similar developers.

After developing the picture is fixed in an acid fixing bath.

Silver bromide paper can be made highly sensitive and is particularly suited for enlargement paper. *Silver chloride paper* is slower, and normally used for contact printing. By a combination of various proportions of the two, *silver chloro-bromide paper* is obtained with some of the properties of each; it usually gives a warmer-tone picture suitable for portraits and pictorial effects.

Papers are made in several contrast grades with a great variety of surface textures. (G. U.)

device: a trade-mark or design introduced by a printer or publisher on the title-page, or at the end of the text, to distinguish his productions. Their use dates from the 15th century at which time the printer was usually the publisher of his books, and early devices passed from one printer to another, often with only slight modification. The orb and cross was the basis of several 15th-century marks.

The earliest known device is the twin shields of Fust and Schöffer who first printed it in their 'Biblia latina' of 1462 (GKW 4204). The Vienna copy of the

Fust and Schöffer

Nicolas Jenson, succs

Aldus Manutius

Johann Froben

Lucantonio Giunta

Erhard Ratdolt

Christopher Plantin

William Caxton

Bernhard C. Breitkopf

Firmin Didot

William Morris

Joaquim Ibarra

FAMOUS DEVICES

Mainz Psalter, 1457, is the only one of this work extant to bear the device, and it is assumed that this was stamped in by hand at a later date. The Fust and Schöffer shields were adopted by Gerhard Leeu (Antwerp), Peter Drach (Speyer), Johann Veldener (Lyons), Bernhard Richel (Basle), and Wolfgang Stöckel (Leipzig) with only slight variations.

In 1539 Francis I of France issued a decree forbidding printers and booksellers to make use of a device which had been originated by another printer.

As the craft of printing became independent it was the publisher who retained the trade-mark. After 1700 their use became rarer, but was revived towards the end of the last century by printers as well as publishers.

See also *canting mark*.

devil: see *printer's devil*.

devil's tail: the lever of a hand-press. (M. L.)

De Vinne, Theodore Low, 1828–1914: a distinguished American printer whose work was careful and skilled if not always inspired. He is also known for his writings on the craft, especially 'The Invention of Printing', Hart, 1876. De Vinne was a co-founder in 1884 of the *Grolier Club*, q.v., and printed its first publication, a reprint of the Star Chamber Decree of 1637.

About 1860 he encouraged New York printing-house owners to form a union known as 'Typothetae': such groups from several cities merged as 'United Typothetae' in 1887 with De Vinne as first president.

Devonshire, Dukes of: a family notable, within the scope of this book, for the library they established at Chatsworth. The second Duke, William (1672–1729), laid the foundations with a collection of incunabula. The sixth, William (1790–1858), made the most important additions by buying whole collections in the sale-rooms. In 1914 the Caxtons and the former drama library of John Kemble were acquired by *Henry E. Huntington*, q.v.

The *Benedictional of St Aethelwold*, q.v., was among the treasures preserved at Chatsworth.

Dewey Classification: the scheme of library classification based on the decimal system devised by Melvil Dewey in 1876. It is in extensive use in the English-speaking world.

dextrin: an adhesive substance, obtained from the sap of plants, and also manufactured artificially, used in bookbinding. (M. L.)

diacritical marks: signs used to denote the different sounds or values of a letter.

See also *accents*.

diamond: the former name for a size of type, about 4½-point.

diapered: 1. said of the gold- or blind-tooled cover of a book on which the decoration consists of a panel divided by a small uniform geometric pattern, e.g. a diamond. Each compartment of the pattern may bear a design or be left blank.

2. said of cloth for book covers which has a grained pattern of diamonds or squares: the style was first popular about 1840.

3. the uniformly patterned background for pictorial scenes in illuminated manuscripts. Their extensive use dates from the later 13th century.

diaeresis: two dots placed over the second of two vowels to show that it must be pronounced, e.g. coöperate (co-operate).

Dibdin, Thomas Frognall, 1776-1847: a famous English bibliographer who, when librarian to Lord Spencer, did much to improve the Althorp collection. Of his numerous writings 'Bibliomania', 1809, an edition of Ames's and Herbert's 'The Typographical antiquities of Great Britain', 1810–19, and 'The Bibliographical Decameron', 1817, deserve mention.

It was after the sale in 1812 of a copy of Boccaccio's 'Il Decamerone', printed by Valdarfer, Venice, 1474, for the sum of £2260 (at the Roxburghe sale) that Dibdin proposed an association of bibliophiles to be known as the *Roxburghe Club*, q.v.

diced: the tooled cover of a book on which the decoration consists of cubes or squares.

dichromate process: see *chromate process*.

Dickinson, John, 1782–1869: the inventor of a *cylinder machine*, q.v., for making endless lengths of paper. His patent (No. 3191 of 1809) describes how the mould wire revolves in a trough of stuff. In the earlier model of Joseph Bramah the stuff had been allowed to drop on the mould wheel from a cistern.

See J. Evans, 'The Endless Web', Cape, 1955.

dictio probatoria: the first word or two on the second leaf of a medieval manuscript, used as a means of identification and help in establishing the date or place of origin.

See also *initia*.

dictionary: 1. a book explaining the words of a language, usually in the form of an alphabetically arranged sequence which includes the orthography, pronunciation, and meaning of each entry word.

The dictionary traces its beginnings to the *glossary*, q.v., and Joannes de Garlandia was one of the first writers to use the word 'Dictionarius'; this was for a collection of Latin vocables arranged by subjects, *c.* 1225. In the next century Peter Berchorius compiled a handbook to the chief words of the Vulgate 'Dictionarium morale utriusque Testamenti'.

Not until the 17th century were dictionaries compiled giving explanations in English of English words, and they were usually limited to difficult (hard) words. The first to appear was Robert Cawdrey's 'Table Alphabeticall', 1604, of some 3000 words. In 1623 Henry Cockeram's 'The English Dictionary' appeared —the first to have this title. Nathan Bailey's etymological dictionary, 1721; Samuel Johnson's dictionary of 1755; and John Walker's of 1791 are among the landmarks of English lexicography.

The most famous English dictionary, the 'Oxford English Dictionary' (O.E.D.), was conceived at a meeting of the Philological Society in 1858. The dictionary was to be on an historical basis so that the changes in form and meaning which any given word had undergone since its appearance in the English language could be known. In 1879 the Clarendon Press arranged to finance the editing of the work, the editor being J. A. H. Murray (thus the dictionary is sometimes called 'Murray's Dictionary'). The first edition appeared in ten volumes between 1884 and 1928.

See also *concordance*, *encyclopaedia*, *index*, *lexicon*, *vocabulary*.

2. a reference book on any subject where items are arranged in alphabetical order and are shorter than in an encyclopaedia. E.g. 'Dictionary of National Biography', O.U.P.; 'Short Dictionary of Furniture', Allen & Unwin, etc.

Didot: a French printing and publishing business founded in 1713 by François Didot (1689–1759), and still existing. Other members of the family interested themselves in improving printing methods, establishing a paper mill, designing type-faces, and standardizing type-sizes. See *Didot point*.

For a specimen of Didot roman see *letters—forms and styles*.

Didot point: the Continental unit of measurement for type established by the French typefounder François A. Didot in 1775. One Didot point equals 0·0148 in.; one English point equals 0·013837 in.

Other sizes are:

5-point	0·074 in.	10-point	0·148 in.
6-point	0·089 in.	12-point	0·178 in.
7-point	0·103 in.	14-point	0·207 in.
8-point	0·118 in.	18-point	0·267 in.
9-point	0·133 in.	24-point	0·356 in.

See also *cicero*.

die: an intaglio engraved stamp used for impressing a design.

die-case: another name for the matrix case of the *Monotype*, q.v.

Digby, Sir Kenelm, 1603–65: the donor, in 1634, to the Bodleian of a valuable collection of over 200 vellum manuscripts, mostly from English medieval scriptoria. Digby had also a fine library at his Paris house, part of it coming to London after his death, part passing to the Bibliothèque Nationale where it remains today.

digester: a vessel in which wood, esparto, or rags are boiled with chemicals in the first stages of paper-making. Digesters can be stationary, revolving, spherical, upright or horizontal. Cf. *boiler*.

digit: 1. any number between 0 and 9.

2. the printers' symbol ☛. Also known as *fist*, *hand*, or *index*.

Dijck, Christoffel van, 1601–*c.* 1669: a goldsmith of Amsterdam who in 1648 established what became the leading Dutch type-foundry of the 17th century. His types were used in England, Thomas Marshall buying several founts on behalf of Oxford University about 1670, while Richard Bentley bought van Dijck roman and italic types for Cambridge University where they were in use from 1697 onwards.

In 1673 his foundry was acquired by Daniel Elzevier whose widow issued a specimen sheet of the stock in 1681. Some of the punches were subsequently in the possession of Enschedé of Haarlem by whom, says Updike, the romans were melted down in 1808.

No original van Dijck specimen sheet is known to survive, but the Monotype Series 203, roman and italic, cut under the guidance of Jan van Krimpen in 1935, was inspired by types used in Holland by firms known to have possessed van Dijck's types.

Dioscorides: see *Vienna Dioscorides*.

diplomatic: the science of seeking to establish the authenticity of old writings, documents, charters, etc.

diptych: two tablets, generally of ebony or boxwood, adorned with carved ivory, gold or jewels, bearing writing upon their waxed inner surfaces, and hinged to open like a book. Their use dates from the Roman Empire where the Consuls gave them as New Year's Day presents; these were larger than normal and often bore an image of the donor or of the Caesar. The most lavishly embellished specimens belong to the Byzantine Era, A.D. 530–60.

direct half-tone: a half-tone for which the screen negative is made direct from the subject and not from a photograph of it.

direct printing: printing in which the inked impression is made directly from forme to paper, as in letterpress, and is not offset on to it.

direct rotary printing: lithographic printing in a rotary machine (sheet or reel fed) on the direct principle, i.e.:

not by offset. Although originally aluminium plates were used on a large scale, the use of zinc has predominated to such an extent that it has given the process its name. The first successful machine was built about 1899 by the Aluminium Rotary Press Co. in the U.S.A. Direct zinc rotary printing has lost its importance since the development of the offset method. It occurs in combination with offset printing in some perfecting machines, and in reel presses in which the web can be guided between different cylinders according to the way it is desired to utilize the capacity of the press to furnish printing alternatives. (G. U.)

direction line: the line on which *catchwords*, q.v., were formerly printed. It is now used if the abbreviated title of a book follows the signature mark to guide the binder when gathering. See also *designation marks*.

director: an alternative name for *guide letters*, q.v.

directory: 1. a book giving instructions or directions for the order of Divine Service.

2. a book which lists persons or business houses, either by trade, residence, or alphabetically by name. The oldest directory in Europe appeared in London in 1595.

dirty proofs: proofs containing numerous printing errors.

disc inker: an inking system found particularly in platen machines whereby inking is done on a round disc which revolves about a central axis. Sometimes the disc is divided into an outer ring and a central disc, moving in opposite directions. (G. U.)

display: printed matter, normally hand-set, to which prominence is given by size or position as distinct from continuous reading matter, e.g. prelims, part and chapter titles, headings, advertisements.

display type: larger type-faces designed for headings, advertisements, etc. Berry & Johnson, in their 'Encyclopaedia', list many faces specially designed for display. In normal book faces, sizes above 14-point, requiring to be hand-set, are regarded as display type.

distribute: the returning of individual letters and spaces into their correct places in the case, or for melting, after use in the forme. This is done after printing when type need not be kept standing for reprints. Usually abbreviated as *dis.*

distributing machine: a machine for distributing type. During the experimental days of type-composing machines there were also constructed several models of distributing machine. Each type unit had its special nick combination which, during distribution, guided the unit to its correct place. The best known of such machines were Green & Burr's built in 1880, and Dow's built in 1886: the former dispersed 12,000 types an hour, the latter is said to have reached a capacity of 40,000 an hour. (G. U.)

distribution imprint: a statement on the verso of a title-page or the last page of a book to indicate the branches or representatives through which the publisher's books are distributed.

distributor rollers: rollers on a printing press used to spread ink on the ink slab, roll it to the correct consistency, and transfer it to other rollers which ink the forme. They are made entirely of metal, or of rubber or composition on a metal core. (G. U.)

Ditchling Press: see *St Dominic's Press.*

Diurnal: 1. a book containing the day-hours (except matins).

2. a newspaper published daily.

divinity calf: bindings in plain dark brown calfskin, usually with bevelled boards, blind tooled with single lines which terminate in Oxford corners: the style is often a feature of theological works.

See also *Yapp.*

divinity circuit: see *circuit edges.*

division of words: the division of words at the end of a line of type is done according to generally accepted rules and recommendations set out in house-style manuals. The main principle is that a word should be divided after a vowel, turning over the consonant, unless two consonants occur together, when the break should come between them.

doctor blade: 1. a thin steel blade used to scrape superfluous ink from a photogravure cylinder during running. Plastic and bakelized cotton are modern alternatives to steel.

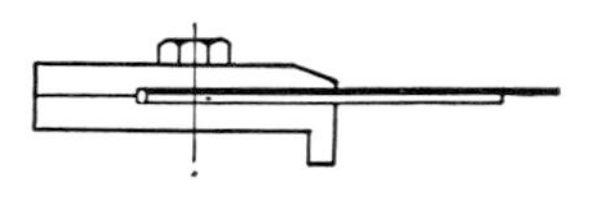

Doctor blade

2. a flexible steel blade used to keep clean the steam-heated rollers which smooth the damp web of paper when in the Fourdrinier. Similar blades are also fitted to calender and other rolls over which paper is passed during manufacture.

Dodsley, Robert, 1703–64: the leading 18th-century London publisher of belles-lettres. He published for Pope, Johnson, Goldsmith, Gray, and is also remembered as the founder of 'The Annual Register', 1759, which continues today.

Doesborgh, Jan van, fl. 1508–30: a printer of Antwerp, important as being one of the early Dutch printers to produce books specially for the English market; this branch of the Dutch trade having been first systematically developed by *Leeu*, q.v. Whereas Leeu had mostly used Caxton's editions for his reprints (a Jason, 'Chronicles of England', etc.) Doesborgh appears to have printed some fifteen original English works. Among them were a Robin Hood, 'Euryalus and Lucretia', 'Life of Virgilius', 'Tyll Howleglas', and 'The Wonderful Shape'.

dolphin: a fish used in Christian archaeology as a symbol of diligence, swiftness, and love. It was often entwined about an anchor, in which form Aldus Manutius used it for his device. It was revived in a similar way in the 19th century by William Pickering.

Domesday characters: special letters for the contractions used in the Domesday Book, charters, and other Anglo-Norman-Saxon records. They were cut in wood until *c.* 1712 when Robert Andrews cut them as types for Mrs. Elstob. A later, and better, version by Joseph Jackson under the supervision of Abraham Farley was used by George Nichols for his folio facsimile of the Domesday book, 2 vols., 1773–83. Vincent Figgins cut and cast founts in 1800 and 1805 for Eyre and Strahan, the King's Printers.

Such contractions as ꝑ (pro = for) may still be seen in contemporary legal works.

Donatus, Aelius: a Roman scholar of the 4th century, famous as the author of a Latin grammar, 'Ars grammatica'. His 'Ars minor', on the eight parts of speech, was used for generations as a manual of elementary instruction. It was often printed from wood blocks about the time of the invention of printing, and is frequently referred to in historical and bibliographical literature. (With M. L.)

See also *Costeriana, Cracow fragments.*

Donkin, Bryan, 1768–1855: an inventor, and employee of John Hall of Dartford, who was responsible for the practical development by 1803 of the *Fourdrinier machine*, q.v. He based his work on a machine devised in 1798 by Nicolas Louis Robert of the Didot paper-mill at Essonnes, France. A model of this had been brought to England by John Gamble, patented by him, and shown to the brothers Fourdrinier. It was they who engaged Donkin to experiment with the model. The first machine was built at Frogmore Mill, Herts, *c.* 1803. Donkin also invented a composition printing roller.

dorse: the back or verso of a manuscript or parchment sheet.

dos à dos: two books bound back to back, i.e. with a common back board in the middle and the fore-edges of one adjacent to the spine of the other.

dot-etching: see *retouching* (2).

dotting wheels: small hand-tools of varying design used by graphic artists when engraving metal plates.

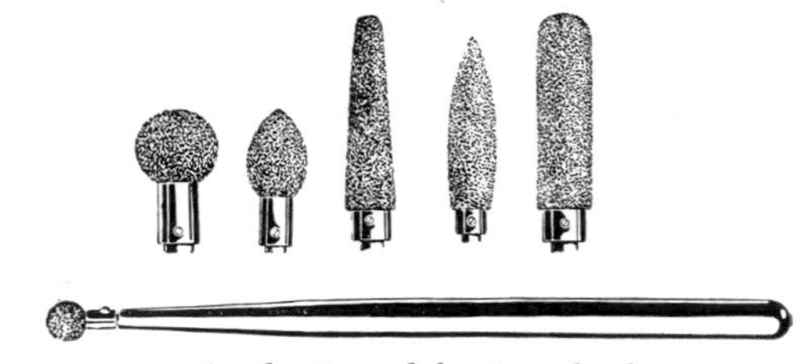

A selection of dotting wheels

double: 1. words or lines repeated in error when composing.

2. a prefix to standard paper-size names. The double of any paper size is ascertained by multiplying the lesser of the two dimensions by two, e.g. crown, 15 in. by 20 in.; double crown, 20 in. by 30 in.

See also *paper sizes.*

doublé: see *doublures.*

double case: see *case.*

double character: a double type; a diphthong or ligature of two letters on one type-body. (M. L.)

double column: matter set to half the width of a normal page line, with an em or more space or a rule between the columns, e.g. as in a dictionary having two columns per page. Sometimes referred to as *half-measure.*

Double Crown Club: a dining club, founded in 1924 by Hubert Foss, Holbrook Jackson, and Oliver Simon, among whose members were the most distinguished printers, typographers, book designers, and bibliophiles of the time. Dinners were held in various London restaurants where papers were read and discussed. As can be imagined the printed announcements and menus for these occasions were varied and elegant. The club is still active.

double dagger (or **double obelisk**): the printer's sign ‡.

See also *reference marks.*

double edition: 2500 copies of a book. The term is associated with a regulation of the *Stationers' Company*, q.v., dated 1587, which prescribed the number of copies which were to be printed from one setting of the type: an edition was usually 1250 to 1500 copies. Double editions were not usual.

double pica: the former name for a size of type, about 22-point; now superseded by 24-point.

double quotes: see *punctuation marks.*

double rule: brass rule, having two lines of different thickness of face, compared with a parallel rule, which has two lines of the same thickness. (M. L.)

double setting: the re-setting of part of a book after some of the type has been distributed. This is made necessary when more copies are needed than were originally planned. Cf. *reimposition.*

double sized: paper which has been well sized in the beater, and is then passed through a tub of animal size.

double-spread: two facing pages on which matter is continued directly across as if they were one page. When printing an illustration in this way two blocks must be used unless the spread comes in the middle of a signature. Cf. *conjugate leaves, opening.*

double title-page: a book having a left-hand and a right-hand title-page. One may be a series title-page, the other being particular to each title in the series.

double-tone ink: a combination of an oil-soluble dye with a stable body-pigment of different colour, and a medium. Such inks are used to print half-tones with a gravure effect. The half-tones are printed in the normal way, but some hours later overtones appear on the print; these are caused by the dye spreading as a halo round the dots which form the image. The finish and tone of the paper also affect the result. Cf. *duplex half-tone.*

doublures: decorative linings of leather or watered silk forming the inside face of book covers. Turkish examples date from the 14th century, but the earliest known European specimens are in an Italian binding of 1550 now in the Bibliothèque Nationale, Paris. Their use was revived in the reign of Louis XIV (1643–1715), and has continued to be a feature of French bindings.

Douce, Francis, 1757–1834: an antiquarian and bibliophile who bequeathed his important collection of books and illuminated manuscripts to the Bodleian.

Doves Press: a private press founded in 1900 by Thomas James Cobden-Sanderson (who had previously owned a bindery) and Sir Emery Walker. For their special use a type of Jenson (1476) was redrawn by an employee of Walker under Cobden-Sanderson's supervision, the punches being cut by E. P. Prince. The most important publication was the Doves Bible in five volumes which appeared in 1903–5. The press closed in 1917 when Cobden-Sanderson (who had worked alone since 1908) threw type, matrices and punches from Hammersmith Bridge into the Thames.

Dow, Alexander: the Bostonian inventor of an ingenious type-setting machine, 1885–86. It had an automatic spacing mechanism which in the course of setting registered the width of types set, and at the end of the line divided the remaining empty space by the number of inter-word spaces, registering the correct spacing between the words. Another feature was a machine attached to it for quick distribution. (G. U.)

Dow-Birmetals etching machine: an adaptation of the American Dow machine for etching photoengraved magnesium alloy plates, made under licence by Birmetals Ltd., Birmingham.

Briefly, a series of paddles revolving in a large enclosed tank project nitric acid vertically over the plate to be etched (plate size up to 26 in. by 24 in.), while the latter is rotated and also moved laterally. The time taken to reach an etch depth of 0·02 in. is from 5 to 12 minutes, depending on the freshness of the etchant. Problems of undercutting, which are usual in line work, are ingeniously obviated by adding certain chemicals to the nitric acid: the effect of these is to deposit a film or coating on the metal. Explaining this principle, the Dow Chemical Company states: 'When the etching fluid strikes the non-image areas, it does so at an angle of nearly 90°, with enough force to break the film, and etching takes place. When the fluid strikes the plate parallel to the sides of the image, there is insufficient force to break the film, and no etching occurs. The gelatine, a component of the etchant, has a controlling effect on the film, causing a greater depth of etch in small non-printing areas. The chemical additives have the effect of powdering the plate continuously, giving a nearly perfect sidewall etch.'

Modifications of this process for newspaper half-tone work have been made by the American Newspaper Publishers Association (ANPA).

A satisfactory method of producing Dow-etched line and tone combination plates was announced in Britain in 1957. The new technique is based on the substitution of sodium sulphate for gelatine. In the Dow-Birmetals method two solutions are used. The first is nitric acid, a wetting agent, diethylbenzine, sodium sulphate, and water to a total of thirty-five gallons. The bath is conditioned by dissolving in it a predetermined quantity of magnesium. The printed line and tone image plate, retouched where necessary, is immersed in a de-scumming bath to prepare the non-image areas for etching. It is rinsed and put in the Dow machine. Etching time is nine minutes. The plate is then rinsed, wiped, dried, and tested for depth of etch (0·005 in. for the highlights of a 65-line screen half-tone, open line from 0·014 to 0·016 in.).

After pumping the first solution into a storage

Dressing the forme

tank, a deepening solution is flowed in. This is the same as is used for normal line work in the Dow machine but without gelatine. The plates are etched for five minutes, by which time the open areas will be about 0·035 in. deep. Research continues on the production of combination plates with fine screen dots (up to 120 screen) for normal working conditions.

Dowty Award: an annual award, established in 1956, of a travelling scholarship of £350 given to a writer, under thirty-five, for a published work in the field of imaginative writing. The money is provided by Sir George Dowty, President of the Cheltenham Literary Festival, at which the award is made. The first winner was Charles Whiting, author of 'Lest I Fall', Cape, 1956.

drag: when the end of a sheet printed on a cylinder press does not print clear and sharp, because of not being held close to the cylinder, it is said to drag. (M. L.)

dragon's blood: a dark-red powdered resin which is dusted against the sides of etched lines in line-block-making. After heating the plate, this powder becomes acid resisting and prevents undercutting of the lines when the plates are re-dipped in the etching bath to deepen those lines of the design which require it.

draw out: a printing fault caused when the roller pulls out a loose type.

draw sheet: the sheet which is drawn over the make-ready on a letterpress printing machine cylinder.
See also *dressing the cylinder.*

drawn on: a paper book cover which is attached by gluing it to the back. If the end-papers are pasted down it is said to be *drawn on solid.*

dressed forme: see *forme.*

dressers: various tools used for the trimming, cutting, and planing of cast types, stereos, blocks, etc., it being important that these should all have true and precise surfaces and dimensions. Also known as *trimmers.* (G. U.)

dressing: 1. the fitting of furniture between and around the pages in a chase prior to locking up the forme.
2. to fit an illustration block into type set up for text so that they can be printed together.

dressing the cylinder: the fitting of several sheets of paper to a printing cylinder, which is the first stage in preparing it for use. A ground sheet is pasted and fitted so that it dries smooth and tight. Further sheets and a final manila draw-sheet are then fitted; each must lie flat and be free from bulges, the whole operation requiring great care.
See also *make-ready.*

driers: compounds of cobalt, lead, or manganese, usually dispersed in an oil or resinous medium, which are added to printing inks to shorten the drying time, and often to modify the printed impression in some way.

drill: a coarse cotton cloth used by bookbinders.

drive: another name for *strike*, q.v.

drive out: 1. said of type which occupies much lateral space.
2. an instruction to the compositor that wide spaces are to be inserted between words. Cf. *keep in.*

drolleries: small humorous drawings used to enliven the margins of illuminated manuscripts. They were popular in 13th-century France, whence they spread elsewhere, especially to Italy.

drop: to unlock a forme and remove the chase and furniture after printing, the type being either distributed or tied up and stored.

drop fingers: metal strips which assist the sheet of paper in its passage from the feedboard to the impression cylinder.

drop folios: page numbers when printed at the foot of each page.

drop guides: the *feed-guides*, q.v., on a cylinder press. (M. L.)

drop initial: the initial capital letter at the beginning of a chapter, approximately aligned at the top with the cap line of the first line of text and ranging at the foot over two or more lines.

drop roller: a roller used to convey ink in the inking device of a printing press (or moisture in the damping device of a lithographic press) from the slowly revolving ductor roller to the rapidly moving distributor rollers. The drop roller, which is on free bearings, comes into alternate contact with both revolving systems, adapting itself to the speed of each. (G. U.)

Dropmore Press: a private press in London, founded in 1945 by Lord Kemsley, with the aim of producing, by experiment and new ways of production, fine books of uncommon literary merit. Some of the equipment of the former Corvinus Press was taken over. The press was disbanded *c.* 1956.

Many of the books were designed by Robert Harling. Most were set by Monotype, the galleys being adjusted or even re-set by hand when necessary: this reduced costs, but not at the expense of quality. Editions were usually of from 300 to 500 copies; they rarely exceeded 1000.

The most important and splendid works issued were 'The Royal Philatelic Collection' by Sir John Wilson, Bart., edited by C. Winchester, 1952, and 'The Holkham Bible Picture Book' with commentary by W. O. Hassall, 1954.

dropped head: the heading or title of a chapter which is set lower than the first line of text on a full page of text. Chapter headings and the headings of each separate item of prelims should be dropped to a uniform height throughout the book. In pamphlets published without a title-page the title may appear as a dropped head on the first page of text.

drum cylinder press: a printing machine in which the sheet of paper is carried to the impression on a large cylinder. Early cylinder presses were, in general, of this large-cylinder type, but they have been mostly superseded by the two-revolution small-cylinder machines. (M. L.)

dry-coated paper: a variety of coated paper developed in 1955 at the Battelle Memorial Institute, Columbus, Ohio. Briefly, an electrically charged dust-cloud of coating material is deposited on a web of paper by strong electrostatic fields. The coating material has a particle size of from 5 to 10 microns, and the cloud is charged by unipolar corona discharge.

dry colour: any dry colouring matter suitable for grinding or mixing in oil, water, or other medium, for printing. (M. L.)

dry end: that section of a paper-making machine where the paper is dried by winding it in a figure-eight fashion over a series of steam-heated drying cylinders, and subsequently finished by the calender rolls at the end of the machine for reeling on to a shell or spindle. The craftsman responsible for this stage of paper-making, and thus for the moisture content of the paper, is known as the *drierman*. Cf. *wet end.*

dry mounting: the mounting of carbon tissue in photogravure work by means of an apparatus so equipped that the damping, and the period of damping before the paper is pressed to the metal plate, can be reduced to a minimum. Also used in conjunction with heat-sensitive adhesives. (G. U.)

dry offset: letterpress printing in which the impression of type and blocks is taken by a rubber roller and offset on to paper. This avoids extensive *make-ready*, q.v.

dry paper: a term used at the Oxford University Press 'to distinguish machine-finished printing papers from India papers' (Batey). 'Such paper is not wetted before being printed, because damping would take the gloss off; nor do the sheets require glazing or rolling after printing. . . .' (Hart).

dry plate: a photographic negative (and transparent positive) material consisting of a silver bromide gelatine emulsion, poured on a glass base-plate. As distinct from the 'wet plate', a dry plate can be kept in a dry state without losing its sensitivity which, in addition, is greater than that of the former. The whole development of modern photography is based on the dry plate, or on film produced on this principle. It was discovered in 1871 by *Maddox*, q.v. (G. U.)

dry-point: 1. an engraving process in which a design is hand-cut directly on to a burnished copper plate (more rarely zinc) with a steel or diamond point, no acid being used. A ground is used when first tracing the design with a needle, and then washed off. Ink is applied, and after removing the surplus, the lines are deepened as required; their main characteristic is a softened edge due to the burr raised by the point as it is drawn through the metal. After rolling ink over the plate the surplus is wiped off with a rag and the palm of the hand; the ink retained by the burr softens the printed image. Dry-point, which can be combined with *aquatint*, q.v., is not suitable for long runs as the burr wears down. When dry-point is used for retouching etched plates the burr must be removed so that the lines have a greater likeness to the etched ones.

2. a print taken from such a plate. (With G.U.)

dry pressing: to press out indentations made by type when printing, so that the printed sheet is perfectly smooth on the back. (M.L.)

dry (relief) offset: a printing process in which photoengraved plates are printed by the offset transfer principle. Dry offset can reproduce anything reproducible by offset lithography or letterpress, but is not yet in extensive use for bookwork.

The photoengraver prepares from the assembled copy a relief-etched magnesium plate. This is fitted to the plate cylinder of an indirect rotary press. The inked impression is printed on to a rubber blanket cylinder, and is finally offset via this on to the paper as the sheet is carried round the impression cylinder.

In America, in 1951, photocomposition and etched magnesium plates were successfully combined for indirect rotary printing. The body matter was set on the Intertype Fotosetter, and the plates were made direct from the negatives.

drying cylinder: a steam-heated cylinder over which the damp web of paper is passed to dry it before calendering and reeling.

dryworker: an employee of a hand-made paper-making establishment who takes *packs* of paper, q.v., to the pressing room. About twelve packs will have been loaded on a truck by the layerman prior to this. The packs are pressed, opened, pressed, opened again, and pressed a third time. They are then taken away for loft drying, and the dryworkers lay the sheets on canvas (which is now preferred to the former practice of hanging the sheets on hessian ropes).

Ducali bindings: 16th-century Venetian bindings used for the decrees of the Doges. They were a combination of Western and Oriental styles. The board was covered with a paper composition, the centre and corners being recessed; thinly pared leather was then pasted on and a coating of coloured lacquer was applied to complete the background. Gold-painted arabesques formed the final decoration. Variations of the style were practised for other patrons.

duck: a strong linen or cotton cloth used in binding.

duck-foot quotes: a form of inverted commas used on the Continent, viz. « ». Also known as *guillemets*. They were first used in 1546 by Guillaume Le Bé of Paris.

While French printers use the form of quotes shown above, Swiss and German practice is » «.

duct: the ink reservoir on a printing machine.

ductor: a roller which conveys the ink from the duct to the *distributor rollers*, q.v.

due book: the book in which a publishing office enters orders for titles which are binding, reprinting, or temporarily out of stock.

Dufay, Louis: the inventor of the colour processes known as *diopticolour* and *dioptichrome* (1908), which in collaboration with Spicers Ltd. and Ilford Ltd. were developed into the *Dufaycolor* method, a process depending on regular colour screens for the production of coloured pictures by the additive principle. The colour screen is produced by taking a purple-coloured film and printing it over with a network of fine lines (20 per mm.), after which the colour is bleached from the parts of the film not protected by the network. These are now coloured green in another colour bath, the print is removed, and a new network of lines is printed on it at an angle of 90° to the first. Bleaching is then done again, and the uncoloured lines are reddened in a third bath. In this way a colour screen with a regular pattern of blue and green rectangles and red lines is obtained. The width of the different networks of lines has been chosen so that in the final result the different colours appear in approximately equal total surfaces. The light-sensitive emulsion is placed above the colour screen, and exposure takes place with the base of the film, not the emulsion, turned to the objective. (G.U.)

See also *colour photography*, *three-colour analysis*.

Duff, Edward Gordon, 1863–1924: an English bibliographer, many of whose important researches into early printing and the book trade were published by the Bibliographical Society. He also wrote 'Early Printed Books', Kegan Paul, 1893, and 'Fifteenth-Century English Books', 1917.

dummy: a prototype of a proposed book, either bound or not, made up of the same weight of paper and number of leaves which the book is expected to need. The purpose of the dummy is to show the bulk

(*Double-tone ink*)

see page 109

Half-tone printed in duplex ink on coated stock, 150-*line screen*

The same block printed in ordinary ink

(Photo by Lennart of Petersens.)

(*Duplex half-tone*)

DUPLEX HALF-TONE

Printed on coated stock with a 175-line screen. By combining a black plate with a tint block a monochrome effect is obtained, but it is much richer and better toned than that obtainable by single-colour half-tone

Enlargement of the screen dots on which the above picture is based

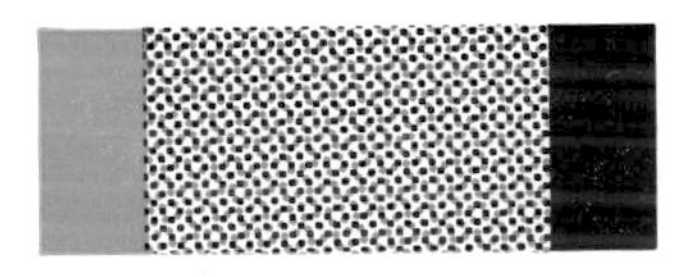

as well as the page size of the book. From the dummy, the size of the binder's brasses can be ascertained and it is also of assistance in planning the layout of the jacket. In general, a dummy helps the designer and publisher to form a picture of the book and to consider the relation between size, bulk and price. Also known as *mock-up* or *size copy*.

Dun Emer Press: the name by which the *Cuala Press*, q.v., was first known. It was founded in 1902 by Elizabeth C. Yeats, sister of the poet, at Dundrum in Ireland. She was at first advised and instructed by Sir Emery Walker.

Eleven books were issued under the imprint Dun Emer Press, the first being 'In the Seven Woods', 1903.

See 'The Dun Emer and the Cuala Press, 1903–[1930]', Edinburgh, 1932.

duodecimo: see *twelvemo*.

Duodo bindings: Parisian bindings made for Pietro Duodo, Venetian ambassador to Henry IV of France, 1594–97. They were characterized by delicate leaf and floral motifs, with an armorial panel on the upper cover and the motto 'Expectata non eludet' on the lower. These bindings were long thought to have been made by the Eves for Marguerite de Valois.

duotone: an illustration process in which the image is printed in two colours, e.g. black and dark green or dark blue. Two negatives are made from a monochrome original, one for the darker shade with the greater detail, the other for the lighter flat tint.

duotype: two half-tone plates made from a single half-tone negative of a black and white original, but differently etched to give two colour-values. When superimposed during printing they give the desired colour combination. (Not used in Britain.)

duplex half-tone: screen reproduction in two printings, generally black and a colour tone, intended to give the impression of a mellow one-colour picture. The method is used in both letterpress and offset work.

See also *double-tone ink*. (G.U.)

duplex paper: see *twin-wire paper*.

duplex press: said of a printing machine which prints both sides of the paper, the sheet going from one printing forme to another at one feeding. (M.L.)

duplicate negative: a duplicate made from an original negative. This may be done by double copying, i.e. a transparency is made from the negative (a diapositive) and from this a new negative, or by direct copying and reverse developing, or by direct copying on a duplicate film. (G.U.)

Du Pré, Jean, fl. 1486–95: an important printer of Lyons, and, for a time, of Avignon. He printed grammars and works in Latin and French. The first roman founts used in Lyons were cut by him for an edition of Juvenal's 'Satires', 1490. His most important work was 'La mer des hystoires', 1491. On books signed by him his name appears as 'de prato'.

Dupré, Jean, fl. 1481–1504: an important Parisian printer whose first great work was the Paris Missal of 1481; it was the first printed Missal and probably the earliest book illustrated with woodcuts to appear in that city. He specialized in the printing of Books of Hours, Breviaries, and Missals, illustrated with cuts from wood or copper blocks, and also experimented in colour printing.

In 1483 he issued a translation of Boccaccio's 'De casibus virorum illustrium' with the title 'De la ruine des nobles hommes et femmes'; this was the first illustrated book written in French to be published in Paris. The identical blocks were used by Pynson for Lydgate's translation into English of the same work, 'Falle of princis', 1494.

Dupré's true surname was Larcher, and although he is thought to have known his contemporary, Jean Du Pré of Lyons, the two were not related.

Dürer, Albrecht, 1471–1528: the Nuremberg artist-draughtsman whose designs for woodcuts illustrate many famous books, e.g. Apocalypse, 1498; the 'Passio Christi', 1511; and 'Divae Parthenices Mariae historia' printed in 1511 by Hieronymus Hölzel. After his apprenticeship to Wolgemut, 1486–90, he visited Basle and Strasbourg, both important centres of book production, and worked in both places. The cutting of the blocks was done for him. Dürer's copper engravings and woodcuts were known throughout Europe, and were widely copied and even forged. See also *bookplates, woodcut*.

Durham Cassiodorus: a mid-8th-century English manuscript, less carefully illuminated than many of its contemporaries. This version of the 'Commentary on the Psalms' (Cassiodorus) was written by several scribes. The book is now in Durham Cathedral.

Durrow, Book of: a Latin text of the Gospels, written in the late 7th century, of either Irish or Northumbrian origin, most probably the latter. It is decorated in a then new and vigorously native style. The figures of saints are little more than barbaric symbols, but the intricate geometric patterns, based on a cross, panels and borders, the work of skilled artists, derive in all probability from late Roman art in Britain as seen in mosaics, and in part from contemporary Anglo-Saxon and Irish metalwork and enamelwork, with traces of Coptic influence. Yellow, green, and red were the only colours used.

The work is now in Trinity College, Dublin.

dust: a fault in printing which occurs when loose paper fibres or other particles collect during the running of the press on the type-faces and inking system; dust-spreading papers are also troublesome on the rubber blanket of an offset press. (G. U.)

dust cover, dust jacket, dust wrapper: see *jacket.*

duster: in the paper-making industry, a dusting machine; an equipment of huge, hollow-meshed wire drums, with revolving blades for stirring up rags and sifting out the dirt. (M. L.)

dutch leaf: an alloy of copper and zinc which, after being beaten into leaf form, is used in tooling as an imitation of gold leaf. It quickly discolours and is seldom used. Also known as *dutch gold.*

dutch mordant: an etching fluid made up of potassium chlorate (2%) and hydrochloric acid (10%)—or double these quantities—for use in aquatint and hard- or soft-ground etching.

dutch paper: at one time limited to Van Gelder's hand-made paper, but now descriptive of any deckle-edged paper produced in Holland, however made.

dwell: the brief moment of contact between paper and type during which an impression is made. The term is particular to a hand- or platen-press.

Dwiggins, William Addison, 1880–1956: a distinguished American calligrapher, typographer, book illustrator, and designer, who was at one time associated with the Harvard and Yale University Presses. He will be remembered for his book jackets, end-papers, hand-drawn lettering for title-pages, and original bindings. Of his type designs cut for Linotype and Machinery Ltd., Electra, 1935, Caledonia, 1939 (in U.S.A.), and Metro, late 1920's, are used in Britain.

E

Eadwine Psalter: a copy of the 9th-century Carolingian *Utrecht Psalter*, q.v. This example of Canterbury Romanesque illumination was written at Christ Church about 1147 (suggests Dodwell) by the scribe Eadwine. Three or more artists added the illuminations, being influenced in their style by the Hildesheim Psalter of the St Albans school.

The slender figures are elongated, with craning necks and solemn mien, but without the lightness and animation of the Utrecht original. Other differences include the use of bright colours, the painting of large decorative initials in the text, and the addition of illustrations to the commentary on four of the psalms: there is also a full-page portrait of Eadwine, which marks a new development in 12th-century art.

The manuscript is now in Trinity College Library, Cambridge.

Early English Text Society: a society founded in 1864 by F. J. Furnivall, with the aim of making widely available to subscribing members printed and reprinted editions of surviving literature written in Early and Middle English. Some 350 volumes have been issued to date, distribution being effected by the Oxford University Press.

early impression: said of a print from an engraving; it is considered more valuable than a later impression when the plate has become worn. (M. L.)

easer: a substance added to printing ink to modify it for some purpose. This may be to make it more fluid, or affect its speed of drying, colour, paper penetrating properties, or liability to set-off. Varnishes or oils can be used as easers for ink reduction.

East, Thomas, fl. 1565–1607: a London printer, noteworthy for several important books he printed. Between *c.* 1567 and *c.* 1572 he was in partnership with Henry Middleton. East issued several books of voyages and travels, including an edition of John Mandeville, 1568, and also a popular nautical handbook, Bourne's 'A Regiment for the sea', 1580.

He also printed one or two medical works including one each on the waters of Bath and Buxton written by John Jones, 1572. In 1579 he printed for Gabriel Cawood John Lyly's famous 'Euphues', and in 1581 the second edition of Spenser's 'Shepheards Calendar' for John Harrison II. His edition of 'De proprietatibus rerum' (Bartholomeus) of 1582 was one of the more carefully printed books of this time.

In 1588 he printed William Byrd's 'Psalmes, Sonets and songs of sadnes and pietie' being assigned the latter's patent. This was followed by other musical works.

East Anglian School: the leading late 13th- and early 14th-century school of illumination in England flourished at its best in the monasteries of Ely, Peterborough, Bury, Norwich, and Gorleston during the years 1300–25. The art here achieved its greatest technical perfection and final development before the secularizing influence of lay work for lay patrons presaged the decline of the early 15th century.

The most important survivals are Psalters. The basic decorative feature of their pages was a large, irregular band of gold, blue, or lake, often framing the text. Armorial shields and portrait medallions were set along the band which was elsewhere embellished with leaves of several kinds (not all in natural colours), wild flowers (usually correctly coloured), grotesques, drolleries, and small allegorical scenes. There was an increased use of gold and purple.

Briefly, emphasis was more on profusely ornamented borders than narrative miniatures. The Beatus page of the Psalters was often filled with Biblical scenes and the Jesse Tree, becoming the most important single page.

The influence of this school spread, via Belgium, to 14th-century Cologne.

See also *Arundel*, *Gorleston*, *Luttrell*, and *Ormesby Psalters*.

Echternach MSS.: the name given to a series of Northumbrian manuscripts, written in the 8th century, of which the most famous is the *Willibrord Gospels*, now in the Bibliothèque Nationale, Paris. This work, probably done by the artists of the *Book of Durrow*, q.v., was formerly at Echternach in Luxembourg where it was taken by St Willibrord.

The figures are largely symbols, usually separated by areas of blank space from the enclosing border of geometrical patterns.

écrasé leather: crushed leather, i.e. leather which has been mechanically crushed to give it a grained effect.

edge-rolled: said of the board edges of a leather-bound book which have been tooled with a fillet.

edge trimmer: a machine for trimming the edges of blocks, stereotypes, etc. The machine illustrated has a strong, rapidly revolving plate carrying three cutters. Simple hand-tools (trimmers) can be used as an alternative. Also called a *Bowler*. (G.U.)

The Hunter–Penrose edge trimmer

edges: see *bleed, burnished, circuit, cropped, cut edges, edge-rolled, foot, fore-edge, gilt edges, gilt top, goffered, gutters* (1), *marbling, opened, tail* (1 and 2), *thumb index, top edge gilt, trimmed, uncut, unopened, witness* (2), *Yapp*.

Edinburgh Bibliographical Society: founded in 1890. Its objects are the discussion and elucidation of questions connected with books, printed or manuscript, especially Scottish; the promotion and encouragement of bibliographical studies; the exhibition of rare or remarkable books; and the printing of bibliographical works, in particular in a series of transactions.

editio princeps: the first printed edition of a work which previously existed only in manuscript form. The term is confined to books printed in the 15th and 16th centuries.

edition: the whole number of copies of a work printed from the same set of type (or from stereos and electros of that type) and issued at any time. An edition may consist of a number of impressions if the matter is not altered to any appreciable extent. See also *abridged edition, authorized edition, collected edition, definitive edition, de luxe edition, editio princeps, facsimile, facsimile reprint, fine paper copy, first edition, impression, issue, large paper edition, library edition, limited edition, new edition, pirated edition, plant-free reprint, re-issue, reprint, revised edition, school edition, special edition, state, trade edition, unauthorized edition, variorum edition.*

edition binding: the machine binding in cased form in substantial quantities of a title for supply by a publisher to the trade. Synonymous with *publisher's binding*.

See also *bookbinding styles and binding features*.

editor: one who arranges for publication the writings of another or others. His work may be the preparation of a manuscript for the printer, the annotating of a text, or merely the selecting of material. Cf. *compiler*.

Edwards of Halifax: a distinguished Yorkshire family of binders and booksellers. *William Edwards* (1723–1808) founded the Halifax firm by 1755. He was noted for *fore-edge paintings* and *Etruscan bindings*, qq.v. He also used vellum to cover books, and he decorated these with paintings of portraits or scenes. To make them durable he conceived the idea of using pearl ash to make the vellum transparent; thus the painting could be done underneath. A patent (No. 1462) was taken out by his son *James Edwards* in 1785, for 'my said new invention of Embellishing books bound in vellum, by making drawings on the vellum which are not liable to be defaced but by destroying the vellum itself. . . . Copper plates may also be impressed so as to have a similar effect.' Evidence of his career suggests that James was a business-man rather than a craftsman, and as books so made were produced in Halifax at a time when James was elsewhere, it is not unlikely that his father invented the process.

In 1783 William Edwards bought the libraries of several deceased bibliophiles. Realizing that the handsomely bound books would sell better in London, he opened a bookshop in Pall Mall in 1785 with his sons *James* (1756–1816) and *John* (1758–*c*. 91) as managers. The shop flourished, rapidly becoming 'the resort of the gay morning loungers of both sexes'.

James achieved a certain notoriety among bibliophiles by his purchase of the Bedford Missal in 1786, for 203 guineas; he kept it until 1815. He travelled widely, buying books and libraries in Germany, France, and Italy, to be sold, apparently at great profit, in Pall Mall. At the same time he made his father's binding styles known abroad, thus the French bibliophile Antoine Renouard (1765–1853) owned several volumes with Edwards's fore-edge paintings, and Pierre Didot (1761–1853) printed in Paris the 'Book of Common Prayer', 1791, to be 'sold by W. Edwards & Sons, Halifax'. Between 1788 and 1797 the name of Edwards appears as a publisher's imprint, thus in 1791 Bodoni printed at Parma an edition of 'Castle of Otranto', by Walpole, for 'J. Edwards, Bookseller, of London'. Copies of both these works were bound in Etruscan calf with fore-edge paintings. James retired in 1804, and sold his famous library in 1815: curiously enough, no fore-edge painted bindings were listed in the sale catalogue.

The search of John Edwards for fine volumes for sale in the Pall Mall shop led him principally to Paris (where he died). In their catalogue of French books, 1791, the brothers listed books formerly owned by Diane de Poitiers 'who availed herself of the devotion of two Kings of France to enrich her own library with the choicest treasures of theirs'.

Another son, *Thomas Edwards* (1762–1834), succeeded to his father's business in 1808, acquiring also the vellum patent from James, and a valuable collection of books. It is probable that Thomas and his father were the only practising binders in the family. He remained in Halifax. After trying without success to dispose of his stock of finely bound books in 1820 and 1821, he auctioned much of it in Manchester, and retired in 1826.

William's youngest son was *Richard Edwards* (1768–1827) who opened a bookshop in Bond Street, London. He specialized in the sale of the then popular illustrated book, and published in his own name. In 1797 he commissioned an edition of Young's 'Night thoughts', illustrated by William Blake. Of the 537 designs Blake prepared forty-three were used. After closing his shop, Richard lived in Malta, later moving to France where he died at St Omer.

e.g.: an abbreviation for the Latin 'exempli gratia', i.e. for example.

Egerton, Francis Henry, eighth Earl of Bridgewater, 1756–1829: a wealthy bibliophile who bequeathed to the British Museum a collection of about sixty-seven volumes of manuscripts and ninety-six charters, together with a fund for the purchase of more. (The collection is still known by the family name; the fund by the title.) As a result of this financial provision the Egerton MSS. number more than 2000.

Egerton, Sir Thomas (later Viscount Brackley), 1540–1617: the founder of one of the oldest private libraries in Britain. This was begun in 1600 and much enlarged by his son, the first Earl of Bridgewater, after whom the library was ultimately known. In 1917 a large portion of the archives, manuscripts, and family papers was bought by *Henry E. Huntington*, q.v., for his library in San Marino, California.

eggshell finish: a relatively rough finish imparted to drawing and notepaper by omitting calendering. It is very similar to antique finish. When made by hand such paper is glazed between glazed boards or thick paper instead of zinc.

egyptian: a group of display types having heavy slab-serifs and little contrast in the thickness of strokes. They were much used in 19th-century England by jobbing printers, and were introduced to the trade (by Vincent Figgins?) about 1815, being then known as *antique*. Early sanserif types were also known as egyptians and only gradually was the name limited to slab-serif faces and the name *grotesque* given to sanserifs. Modern egyptians are Beton, Cairo, Karnak, Luxor, Playbill, Rockwell, etc.

Ehmcke, Fritz Helmut, 1878– : a German graphic artist and type-designer who founded the Steglitzer Werkstatt in Berlin in 1900. He was partnered by *F. W. Kleukens*, q.v., and G. Belwe. They planned to print beautiful books in the spirit of Morris and his followers, but the only book they issued was an edition of Elizabeth Browning's 'Sonnets', 1903. Ehmcke designed several types for various foundries, including D. Stempel. Many of them were used for the publications of the *Rupprecht-Presse*, q.v., which Ehmcke founded at Mainz in 1914.

eighteenmo: a book made up from printed sheets which have been folded to form sections of eighteen leaves, thus having thirty-six pages per section. Written 18mo. Also called *octodecimo*.

ejector: in the Linotype and Intertype casting machines the device for ejecting cast lines formerly consisted of an iron plate of a particular size for each length and body of line. This was inserted into a slide-valve behind the mould wheel when the latter was drawn forward. The modern universal ejector consists, in the Linotype, of a line of metal blades inserted one above the other in a holder behind the mould wheel. During operation a movable vertical rail in the holder locks as many of the blades as are required for the length of line. On the Intertype the ejector consists of a holder containing ten blades for particular lengths of line. Here the blade required is caught by moving a pointer in accordance with a marked scale. For illustration see *Intertype*. (G.U.)

electric etching: a method of etching copper blocks electrically to disintegrate the metal on those parts of the plate not protected to resist it. This is an alternative to using acid or other chemicals.

electricity in paper: see *static electricity*.

electro: see *electrotype*.

Electrofax: the trade name of an electrostatic printing process, somewhat similar to *xerography*, q.v.

electronic colour scanners: machines employing the scanning technique to effect the correction of colour plates to suit the printing inks. Some work from the colour original, as the Hunter–Penrose Autoscan, and the Springfield scanner; others work from monochrome colour separation negatives or positives,

The Finella Klischograph

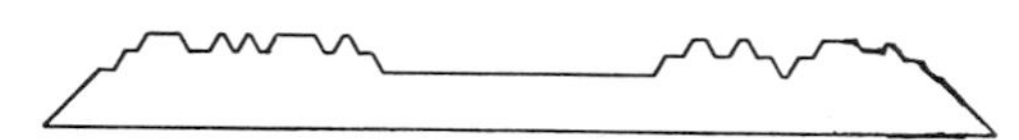

Section of a Klischograph block. The engraving depth varies in relation to the brightness of the original

The Elgrama machine produces single-line screen blocks

The Elgrama. Right, cylinder bearing the original. Left, engraving head

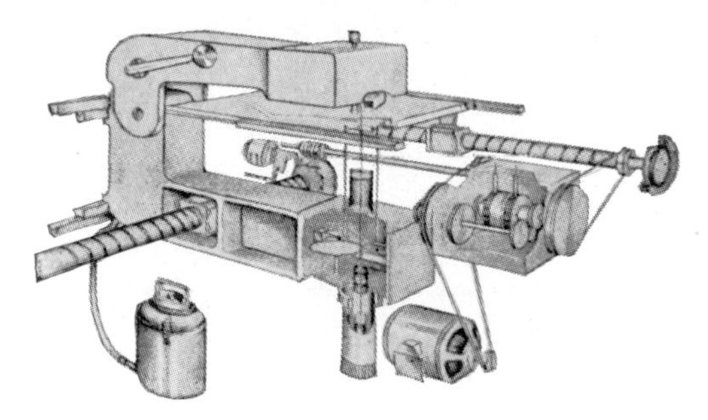

*Section of Klischograph Model K*150. *Top, engraving head; below, plate bearing the original (face down) with the blank printing plate (face up) to be engraved, above it*

The Finella Klischograph has a device for obviating moiré

The Fairchild Scan-a-Sizer for enlarging or reducing copy. The original (left) lies flat and gives optically a picture to the desired scale. This is transferred directly by scanning to the engraving cylinder (right)

as the Acme, and the R.C.A. colour correctors, but the colour Klischograph works from a flat colour drawing, makes the colour correction, and engraves a printing plate in one operation.

electronic guillotine: see *guillotine*.

electronic photoengraving machine: a machine for the automatic production of half-tone printing plates, using the principle that rapidly varying light intensities can be converted into positively related movements of a cutting or burning stylus. These machines produce a metal or plastic plate from which printing is done. Examples are the American Fairchild *Scan-a-Graver*, the Swiss *Elgrama*, the French *Luxographe*, and the German *Klischograph*, qq.v.

electrotint: a printing block produced by drawing with varnish on a metal plate and electrically depositing metal on to the parts not covered by the varnish.

electrotype: a duplicate printing forme made in a galvanic bath by precipitating copper on a matrix. The matrix is a cast in plastic material of an original printing forme (block, wood engraving, type matter, etc.). The matrix material is often wax which, when mixed with resin and a little turpentine, is moulded into a slab, half a centimetre thick, on a metal base. Graphite is brushed into the wax surface, and the printing forme, similarly treated with graphite, is pressed against it. The wax forme so obtained is again treated with graphite, whereupon those areas on which no copper is to be deposited are passed over with a hot iron which removes the graphite from them. By this graphite treatment the wax matrix is made electrically conductive and can be immersed as a cathode in a galvanic bath. When making 'Albert Fischer' galvanos the matrix is stamped in lead. Great pressure is used, but no heat. A sheet of lead is laid on the printing forme, covered with sheets of waste-paper, and finally a steel plate. In the stamping press it may be necessary (to obtain sufficient pressure) to fasten a narrow blade in the upper press head, by means of which the maximum pressure can be exerted on one strip of the forme at a time, the forme being moved gradually and subjected to fresh stamping. Various other metals are used for making matrices, e.g. aluminium Tenaplate, made by Tenak Products Inc., Chicago. Plastic resin, e.g. Vinylite, covered with silver after stamping, is also used.

In the British Patramould process grease is first removed from the forme with a solvent. A piece of ebonite material is cut, about 1 in. larger than the surface to be moulded, laid on the forme, and covered with a felt. The whole is put in a hot box or oven, or put on a hot plate, and heated to 175° F. It is then pressed in an electro moulding press at about $\frac{1}{4}$ ton per sq. in., and allowed to cool under pressure to 86° F. The resulting mould is sprayed or brushed with a sensitizing solution so that it will receive the copper deposit. It is then sprayed simultaneously with two fluids, one of silver solution, the other of formaldehyde reducing solution, by using a special spray gun. The resulting silvered surface is next washed with water. The mould is then put in an ordinary copper depositing bath where a copper shell is 'grown' on. The shell can be removed from the mould by flexing the latter: subsequent treatment of the shell is the same as in other methods of mould production.

Electroplating can be done in a bath of potassium cyanide or neutral-acid solutions of copper sulphate. For the former a 3% potassium cuprous cyanide solution with additions of potassium cyanide, sodium sulphate, and sodium bisulphate, can be used. In such a bath the current density should not exceed 0·3 amp/dm^2. In a bath of 20% copper sulphate solution with an admixture of 3% sulphuric acid, 1·3–10 amp/dm^2 can be used. The fluid is circulated by injecting air. Pure copper is always used as the anode. When sufficient thickness has been obtained in the copper layer (up to $\frac{1}{2}$ mm.) the deposit is freed from the matrix, tin-plated on the back, and cast with type metal. It is levelled, planed to the required thickness, trimmed, etc., and mounted as a block. Sometimes the 'printing side' of the deposit is filled in with a gypsum pulp which should solidify before the metal is cast on the back.

In depositing copper on smooth metal surfaces baths are often used with a higher temperature and with admixtures (phenosulphonic acid, etc.) in which case a current density of 15–20 amp/dm^2 can be used. (G.U.)

Cabinet with built-in sprayer for coating plastic matrices with a conductive metal layer. The matrix is obtained by hot stamping. Monomelt Co., Minneapolis

electrotypograph: an electrically operated type-setting machine.

elephant folio: a large folio, 14 in. by 23 in. approx.
See also *book sizes*.

Elgrama: an electronic engraving machine, made by Elgrama A. G., Zürich, for making half-tone, colour process blocks, line blocks, and combined line and half-tone blocks; its versatility is at present (1955) unique. The block may be of copper, zinc, brass, or plastic, with a maximum size of 30 cm. by 42 cm. The original is not interpreted into dots, as in normal half-tone, but in parallel lines. For this a single-line screen is used with rulings from 45 to 200 lines per inch. A revolving shaft carries the original to be scanned and the plate to be engraved, engraving being done by a V-shaped cutter.

Multi-colour blocks are made from separation prints (previously obtained from four colour-corrected negatives) by scanning from different angles. This obviates moiré.

Elrod caster: a mould machine for casting leads and rule borders in lengths from 1- to 36-point thick. Larger sizes are cored to reduce weight and save metal. The moulds consist of rectangular steel units with a duct in the shape of the lead or rule. Molten metal is pressed through the mould by means of a pump which at each piston-stroke feeds in a standard amount of metal. Before this has had time to cool a second pump-stroke impels fresh metal forward so as to fuse with the first. Before leaving the mould the cast line passes a cooler; it then moves to a cutter which can be set to cut lengths of from 6 to 144 ems of 12-point. The machine is made by the Ludlow Typograph Co. of Chicago. (G. U.)

Elzevir (or **Elsevier**): a famous Dutch family of booksellers and printers, in business from 1583–1791. Lodewijck (Louis) Elzevir (1542–1617), who was publisher to Leyden University, established the firm in that city in 1583. He commissioned others to print for him. Presses were bought in 1618. From 1625 Bonaventura Elzevir and his nephew Abraham led the business, initiating in 1629 their famed 32mo editions with engraved title-pages, narrow margins, and solid-looking text; of these, their Caesar of 1635 is one of the best. (Books published elsewhere in this size were often known as 'Elzevirs'.)

The distinctive type-face they used, cut by Christoffel van Dijck, had a great influence, and a derivation of both the face and format was revived with great effect in mid-19th-century France, particularly by Perrin, Lemerre, and Beaudoire.

Before closing in 1791 the firm had issued over 2000 works.

em: 1. the square of the body of any size of type.

2. the standard of typographic measurement, for which a 12-point em is the basis. This equals 0·166 in. and there are approximately six 12-point ems in one inch. This unit is used for computing the area of a printed page no matter what size of type is used for setting the text; thus if the area is twenty ems wide and thirty ems deep the width is 240-point and the depth 360-point. Synonymous with *pica* (2).

See also *em quad, en*.

em quad: the unit of spacing material, being a type body cast less than type height. It is always the square of the size of type it accompanies, e.g. an em quad of 10-point type is 10 by 10 points. Em quads are used to indent paragraphs and may follow a full stop. They are also cast in units of two or three. The popular name for an em quad is *mutton*.

emblem books: illustrated books popular in the 16th and 17th centuries. The emblem was a woodcut or engraving used as a pictorial device and interpreted by a motto, epigram, or brief sentence. The first anthology of emblems, printed at Augsburg in 1531 by Heinrich Steiner, was the 'Emblemata libellus' which the Italian Andrea Alciati partly compiled from translations of Greek epigrams and Francesco Colonna's 'Hypnerotomachia Poliphili', Venice, 1499; the illustrations were by Jörg Breu who worked for many Augsburg printers.

The first to be published in England was 'A choice of emblemes' by Geoffrey Whitney, 1586. As the idea spread north the Jesuits adapted it to religious instruction.

embossing: relief printing or stamping in which dies are used to raise letters or a design above the surface of paper, cloth, or leather. Braille is an example of this but dots instead of letters are raised.

embossing plate: a plate cut or etched below its surface for producing a raised design on the surface of a sheet. (M. L.)

embossing press: a machine used largely in bookbinderies for impressing book-cover designs. (M. L.)

embroidered bindings: bindings in which decoration in gold and silver thread was done on velvet-covered boards. These were particularly popular in Elizabethan England, many examples being made by Court ladies. (G. U.)

emerald: a size of type common in England, larger than nonpareil and smaller than minion, about 6½-point. Formerly known as *minionette*. (M. L.)

emptying the stick: lifting the lines of type from the composing stick to the galley. (M. L.)

emulsion: a viscous fluid comprising finely distributed insoluble substances in a liquid of a consistency which keeps them in suspension. In reproduction work the term usually implies bromide collodion emulsion. (G. U.)

en: half the printer's unit of square measure, i.e. half an em.

See also *cast-up*, *en quad*.

en quad: half an *em quad*, q.v. The popular name for an en quad is *nut*.

enamel paper: synonymous with *coated paper*, q.v.

enamel process: copying on a fish-glue layer containing dichromate. The method (also known as the *hot top enamel process*) is used for making copper half-tone blocks and for a number of other reproduction processes. Fish-glue is made in qualities suitable for this purpose, and the American fish-glue made by Le Page was at one time used all over the world. Its dry substance content was about 50%. One part of such glue is stirred with two parts of water to which is added one part of 20% ammonium dichromate solution and a few drops of ammonia: this solution is suitable for preparing a copperplate. The mixture must be allowed to stand for two hours and filtered before use. The solution is twice poured over the cleaned copperplate which is then dried in a whirler. After printing, the plate is developed in cold water, rinsed, and immersed in a colour bath consisting of a 1% methyl violet solution. The plate is again rinsed and dried prior to burning in. A hardening of the colour layer may be effected in a solution containing 5% ammonium dichromate and $\frac{1}{2}$% chrome alum.

enamelled bindings: see *champlevé*, *cloisonné*.

enchiridion: a manual or handbook of devotions. The most famous work to include the word in the title is perhaps 'Enchiridion Der kleine Catechismus für die gemeine Pfarher vnd Prediger, Gemehrt vnd gebessert, durch Mart. Luther', Wittenberg, 1529.

encyclopaedia: a work of reference containing a summary of human knowledge arranged, usually alphabetically, according to some plan. Such works trace their origins at least as far as Pliny, A.D. 23–79.

See S. H. Steinberg's article 'Encyclopaedias' in 'Signature', No. 12, 1951, pp. 3–22.

end a break: an instruction to the compositor that the last line of a take of copy is to be filled with quad spacing after setting the last word. Cf. *end even*.

See also *break-line*, *run on*.

end even: an instruction to the compositor that the last word of a take of copy is to end a line, in other words, there will not be any space after it. Cf. *end a break*.

See also *break-line*, *run on*.

end-matter: an alternative name for *subsidiaries*, q.v.

end-papers: the leaves of paper at the front and end of a book which cover the inner sides of the boards and serve together with the linings to secure the book to its case or binding. The simplest form, and as used in publishers' binding, is a four-page sheet of cartridge paper tipped to the first sheet of the text and a similar sheet tipped at the end of the book. The outer leaf of each end-paper is known as the *paste-down* and the inner leaf as the *fly leaf*. The paper should be strong and suitable for pasting. An off-white shade tones in well with the average run of book papers. It is essential that the grain direction should be from head to tail otherwise severe warping of the boards is likely to occur.

Coloured end-papers are frequently used but with some risk of discoloration. End-papers are sometimes printed with reference matter or with a decorative design. Fancy papers with figured or marbled designs lend a finish to the book but may require lining with a suitable paper, especially if the reverse side of the paper is unsightly.

Elaborations are to mount the end-paper to a folded four-page of blank paper similar to the text, the additional leaves thereby created also being known as *fly leaves*; to add a strip of coloured cloth to the joints known as *cloth joints*, q.v.; to add a guard at the back which wraps round the first section and thus the end-paper becomes sewn in but without the sewing appearing in the joints. End-papers which are mounted in any way are known as *made end-papers*. (L. K.)

See also *doublures*, *marbling*, *scratted paper*.

engine-sized: paper which has been hardened, or sized, by the addition of such moisture-resistant substances as casein, starch, and rosin to the pulp, either in the beater or at a later stage prior to the stuff actually flowing on to the machine wire. (This idea was conceived in 1807 by a German chemist.) Engine-sized paper is weaker than *tub-sized*, q.v., and less resistant to penetration by the oil of printing ink or atmospheric action. Abbreviated as *E.S.*

See also *animal-sized*.

Engleheart, Francis, 1775–1849: a London engraver who achieved fame as a book illustrator. He engraved for this purpose works by Cook, Stothard, Smirke, and other artists. Examples of his skill are to be seen in the edition of 'Don Quixote' published by Cadell and Davies.

English (or **english**): 1. the former name for a size of type, now standardized as 14-point.

2. prior to 1800, all black-letter type-faces used in England. It was thus possible to write 'English English' for a 14-point black-letter face.

The English Catalogue of Books: the annual cumulative edition of the year's books as listed weekly in '*The Publishers' Circular*', q.v.

English finish: a calendered paper with a smooth, matt surface. The term is an Americanism meaning 'smoother than antique'.

English Historical Society: a society founded in 1836 'for the printing of chronicles from the earliest period to the accession of Henry VIII'. It ceased its activities in 1856.

English red: a mineral colouring substance, chiefly consisting of ferric oxides. It is noted for its covering properties, and is used for this purpose in certain photographic reproduction work. (G.U.)

English Stock: the name given to the group of publications of which the *Stationers' Company*, q.v., held the sole rights of printing and distribution. Included were almanacs and prognostications, A B C primers, catechisms, psalters, and psalms in metre. The rights were secured in perpetuity in a patent granted in 1603 by James I to the Master, Wardens, and Assistants of the Company, an arrangement which extended benefit to more than a hundred members.

This was the formal establishment, in one patent, of corporate activity which had developed in the previous twenty years, and embodied patents previously granted to individual printers, namely to William Seres, in 1553, for primers containing the psalter, and the catechism in English; to John Day, in 1560, for A B C primers with the little catechism and the psalms in metre; and to Richard Watkins and James Roberts, in 1571, for almanacs and prognostications. The according of such profitable monopolies to a handful of men caused dissatisfaction among less fortunate printers, and in the 1580's the principal patentees spread a measure of their interests among named assigns within the Company.

By 1594 a partnership was formed to manage the Day and Seres privileges, and Stock-keepers were elected. In 1603 members of the Company put up £9000 (suggests Blagden) to finance the English Stock. The turnover on these popular books was considerable, in some years exceeding £5000, while dividends of up to 12½ per cent were paid, and the sum of £200 was distributed annually among the poor of the Company. Six Stock-keepers were elected to serve for one year. They managed the Stock under the supervision of the Master, Wardens, and Court, an arrangement which continues to the present. A Liveryman may still be invited to invest money in the Stock: dividends are small.

engraver's proof: a careful impression of an engraving, made on fine paper with good ink, furnished by the engraver to show the excellence of his work; usually better than later impressions by the printer. (M.L.)

engraving: 1. any metal plate or wooden block on the surface of which a design or lettering has been cut with a graver or etched.

2. a print taken from such a plate.

See also *copperplate, photoengraving, stipple engraving, wood engraving.*

enlarged edition: see *revised edition.*

enlumine: an obsolete term for 'to illuminate'.

See also *illumination.*

enlumineur: an illuminator of manuscripts. (M.L.)

Enschedé: the most famous Dutch type-founding and printing concern. Established in Haarlem, 1703, by Izaac Enschedé (1681–1761), it has, since 1771, traded under the name Johannes Enschedé en Zonen. The present director is Frans Enschedé, born 1893.

The punch-cutter Johann Michael Fleischman (1701–68) cut music types for the firm in 1760, in addition to much other work of note. Their Lutetia type, cut 1923–27, and Romulus, 1931–35, are well known in Britain; they were designed by *Jan van Krimpen*, q.v.

Harry Carter has written a detailed history of the firm in 'Signature', No. 4, 1947, pp. 29–50.

entrelac initials: decorated initials, used at the beginning of chapters, in which the letter forms part of an interlaced design or tracery.

The 16th-century French printer Geofroy Tory was noted for his examples.

entrelacs: border decorations of curving garlands and leaves. These derive from Mohammedan arabesques, and early printed specimens decorate the 'Historia Romana' of Appianus as printed by Erhard Ratdolt of Augsburg in 1477.

As a feature of book covers they have embellished the work of most great French binders since the 16th century.

ephemeris (pl. **ephemerides**): 1. an almanac or calendar.

2. an obsolete term for a diary; its origin in this sense going back at least to the 4th century B.C.

3. a title-word of many 17th- and 18th-century periodicals.

4. an astronomical almanac giving the daily positions of stars and other heavenly bodies.

epigraph: a short sentence or quotation placed at the beginning of each chapter of a book to indicate the main theme or idea in it.

epitome: a condensed version or summary of a work in which only the essential matter of the original is retained.

Eragny Press: a private press founded in 1894 by Lucien Pissarro (eldest son of Camille Pissarro) who settled at Hammersmith, London, from the Normandy village of Eragny. His first book was 'The Queen of the Fishes', 1894. The first sixteen books were printed for him by the *Vale Press*, q.v., Vale type being used.

In 1904 he employed E. P. Prince to cut a type of his own design: to this Pissarro gave the name 'Brook'. For his illustrations he effectively developed the art of wood engraving in colours. In all stages of book production, from printing to binding, he was assisted only by his wife, Esther, in making the octavo volumes he issued. The press closed in 1914, having issued thirty-two books. Pissarro also designed typefaces for the Kunera Press and Silver Thistle Press in Holland.

Erkensator: a centrifugal strainer designed to prevent minute impurities entering the paper-making machine. The prototype was named after its inventor; there are now other models.

erotica: works treating of sexual passion.

erratum (pl. **errata**): an author's or printer's error, only discovered after the book has been printed. If noticed in time the erratum can be set up and worked off with the prelims; it must otherwise be separately printed, cut, and pasted in. Also known as *corrigendum*.

Erwin screen: a half-tone screen which may be used when printing on uncoated stock. It is formed in irregular particles, as distinct from the ruled lines of the standard screen, these giving the print a fine stone-like texture. See also *screen*.

E.S.: an abbreviation for *engine-sized*, q.v.

esparto: a long, rough grass with fine, soft fibres. It grows in southern Spain and North Africa and is used for paper-making (mostly in Britain). Its suitability for this purpose was discovered by Thomas Routledge of Eynsham Mills, Oxford, who exhibited sheets made from it in the 1851 Exhibition; commercial production came ten years later when he patented his process. Esparto papers bulk well and are used as body papers for certain grades of coated stock.

Essex House Press: a private press founded in London in 1898 by Charles Robert Ashbee, and later moved to Chipping Campden, Glos. He sought to perpetuate the traditions established by the *Kelmscott Press*, q.v., and bought printing presses from the latter. In 1901 Ashbee designed the Endeavour type, cut by E. P. Prince, and in the same year added a bindery to his premises for individual orders.

Some ninety books were issued before the press closed in 1910, many having coloured title-pages and initials, but none being outstanding typographically.

Essling, François-Victor, Prince d', 1799–1863: a Parisian bibliophile who collected early printed books and Livres d'Heures. His library was sold in 1847.

His son, *Victor Masséna* (1836–1910), is remembered for his studies on the early Venetian woodcut published as 'Les livres à figures vénitiens de la fin du XVe siècle et du commencement du XVIe', 3 vols., Florence, 1907–14. This, and his work on the printed Missals of Venice, are used by present-day bibliographers and rare-book cataloguers.

Estienne: a firm of Parisian scholar-printers, founded in 1501 by Henry Estienne. On his death in 1520 his widow married *Simon de Colines*, q.v. Her son Robert (1503–59) founded his own business in 1524 and later married the daughter of *Jodocus Badius Ascensius*, q.v. The careful editing of the classical texts, dictionaries, and translations issued by Robert Estienne was matched by fine presswork. He occasionally used a roman face modelled on that of Manutius and probably cut by Garamond, also ornaments designed by Tory. For his Greek New Testament, 3rd ed., 1550, fifteen manuscript versions were compared.

From 1550 until his death he worked in Geneva, embracing Calvinism. He was succeeded by his son who maintained the scholastic traditions.

See E. Armstrong, 'Robert Estienne, Royal Printer', C.U.P., 1954.

estimating: to printers, estimating means to calculate or compute the value or work of a printing order; an important part of a printer's work, involving knowledge and judgement.

See also *cast-off*. (M. L.)

etch proof: see *reproduction proof*.

etching: 1. the treatment of surfaces with substances which have a chemical effect on them, either by dissolving the material as in block etching, photogravure etching, art graphic etching (see below), glass etching, etc., or by setting up reacting products which give the surface different properties as in lithographic etching on zinc and aluminium.

See also *block*, *lithography*, *photogravure*.

2. *Art graphic etching*. The basis of all etching methods properly so named is the treatment with acid of a metal plate on which certain parts of the surface are protected by the application of a *ground*. According to the manner of applying the ground and the artist's method of carrying out the etching, the processes have been given different names. The chief methods in use are *hard ground etching*, *soft ground etching* and *aquatint*.

As with certain other art graphic processes hard ground etching is ascribed to the Augsburg artist and armourer Daniel Hopfer (*c.* 1470–1536); his most famous work appears in the 'Sachsenspiegel', 1516, but about 1510 he had made prints from etched iron plates as a cheaper alternative to copper. The earliest dated etching is a single leaf by Urs Graf, 1513, now in Basle Museum: from 1515–18 Albrecht Dürer furthered the new art, but it was Rembrandt (1606–69) who worked with the greatest mastery.

A cleaned and polished plate of copper or zinc is warmed. A quantity of ground (a mixture of wax, asphalt, and hartshorn) is evenly distributed with a dabber or roller until it forms a thin film over the whole surface. While still hot it is smoked over a wax taper or something similar. On the grounded plate a tracing of the drawing to be reproduced is laid and the two are lightly rolled through a press; the result is an image of the drawing in grey lines on a black ground. Going over these lines with a round polished needle exposes the metal at the point of contact. Before etching commences the back and edges of the plate must be given a protecting coat of varnish. Repeated dippings of the plate in an acid bath, with a trial pull after each immersion, are needed to etch the lines to the required depth. The finest lines are etched first, and after removing the plate from the bath and drying it, these lines are varnished over. This etching by stages continues until the darkest lines have been etched sufficiently. Nitric acid is the usual mordant, a bath of 20% acid being usual for zinc, and a somewhat stronger solution for copper. A ferric chloride bath is also used for copper, and another mordant, the *dutch mordant*, contains 10% hydrochloric acid and 2% potassium chlorate: the latter mixture is more powerful than nitric acid, resulting in greater blackening in the lines. By using the two mordants alternately, special effects can be obtained. A variant of the hard ground etching method just described is to incise and partly etch the deepest lines first, after which the finer lines are drawn and etched without varnishing the previously etched lines. The lines drawn first are thus etched most. The lines can be incised with the plate immersed in the mordant the whole time, whereby the most delicate shading can be obtained.

Soft ground etching was introduced in the later 18th century to facilitate the reproduction of pencil or crayon textures; etchings by Cotman are, perhaps, the best known in this medium. The copper plate is heated and given a thin coating of soft ground consisting of ordinary hard ground mixed with axle grease or tallow. As this remains soft after cooling a hand support or bridge must be used when drawing. A sheet of tissue or other slightly grained paper is carefully stretched across the soft ground; on this the drawing is made with a pencil, chalk, or a small stick. Tones can be produced by pressing the thumb on the paper, or alternatively a piece of gauze or other fabric can be used. The ground adheres firmly to those parts of the tissue-paper pressed on to it by the pencil, so that on removal of the paper the metal under the ground is exposed. Etching is usually done in one immersion. Such etchings have heavier lines than hard ground etchings, and, of course, are characterized by their soft tones. For *aquatint* see separate entry.

3. a print taken from the plates described in (2) above. (G. U.)

Etching needle

Etching Club: a printing society, instituted in London in 1838. Editions of Goldsmith's 'Deserted Village', 1841, and 'Songs of Shakespeare', 1843, were published with illustrations by the Club. (M. L.)

etching machine: an apparatus for the etching of blocks (see *blockmaking*) by means of an etching fluid kept in continuous motion. The etching machine was invented by Louis Edward Levy, of Philadelphia, about 1900. In his machine the block is suspended underneath the lid of a trough from the bottom of which acid is air-sprayed against the image surface.

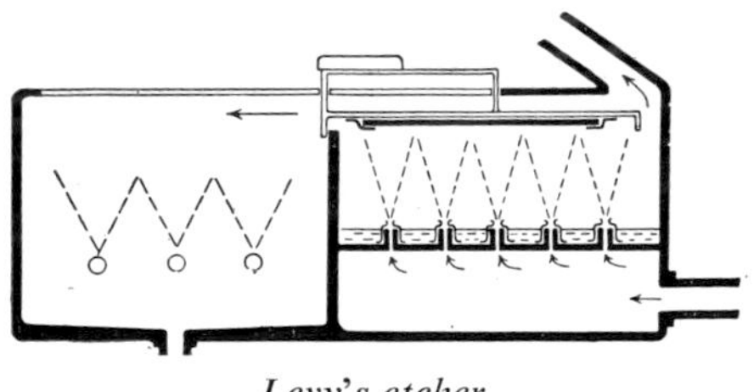

Levy's etcher

The lid with the block can then be moved over to an adjacent trough where it is washed with water in a similar manner.

Among other well-known makes is the Sirius etcher devised by the Swede Axel Holström (see diagram). (G. U.)

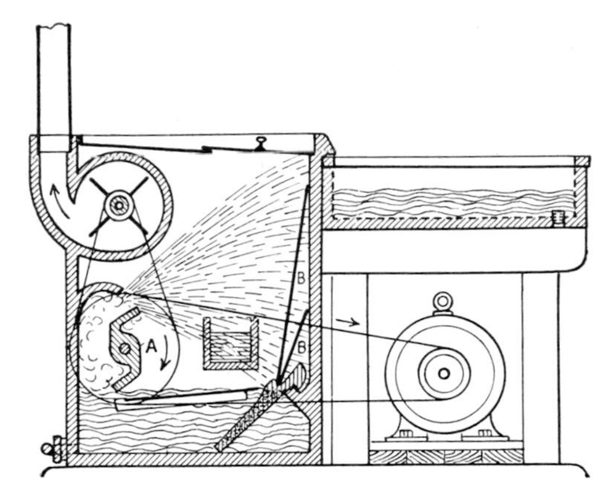

The Holström etcher, 1911. *The whirler (A) throws acid against the block (inclined at B). On the right is a water trough for washing*

Etruscan bindings: bindings of calfskin, decorated with patterns adapted from Etruscan vases and other classical ornaments. The style was used (and may have been originated) by William Edwards of Halifax in the 18th century. His method was to brush acid on the calf, thus burning the pattern into the skin. Tree-calf panels were occasionally surrounded with Etruscan borders.

See also *Edwards of Halifax.*

eutectic: see *type metal.*

Eve bindings: books bound in the workshops of the Frenchmen Nicolas Eve, fl. 1578–82, and his son or nephew Clovis, fl. 1584–1635. (They were Court binders and booksellers to successive Kings of France during these years.) Typical designs had a field powdered with fleurs-de-lis, and, occasionally, a centre-piece of the Crucifixion or the Royal Arms; some examples were in the *fanfare style*, q.v. The Eves were among the first binders to conceive the pattern on the two covers and the spine as a unit.

Only three extant bindings are positively known to be their work; they are powdered with fleurs-de-lis.

See also *Marguerite de Valois.*

even folio: the page number of the left-hand pages, 2, 4, etc. The odd folio is the number on the right-hand page. (M. L.)

even s. caps.: an abbreviation for 'even small capitals', indicating to the printer that a large capital is not to be used as in *caps and smalls*, q.v., but that words are to be set in small capitals on the type size body. Further abbreviated as *even s.c.*

Everdamp paper: see *transfer paper.*

ex libris: 1. a Latin phrase meaning 'out of the books', used on a bookplate before the name of the owner.

2. the Continental term for a bookplate.

excelsior: a size of type, one-half the size of brevier, or about 4-point. (M. L.)

excerpts: quotations or passages selected from books: they may not be reprinted without permission from the publishers of the originals.

exotic types: non-roman faces, i.e. arabic, hebrew, etc.

expandable cloth: a variety of cloth, notably that made under the trade name of *Bookflex*, woven with a crinkled cross-thread especially for lining up the backs of books. The cloth will expand with the book during *rounding* and *backing*, qq.v. (L. K.)

See also *Steamset binding.*

expanded type: type with a flattened, oblong appearance. A modern example is the Chisel Expanded series of Stephenson Blake Ltd., Sheffield.

'Expectata non eludet': see *Duodo bindings.*

explicit: the last words of the text of an early printed book which sometimes stated the title, but more often the place and date of a book's publication and the printer's name. The word is contracted from the Latin 'Explicitus est liber', i.e. 'it is unrolled to the end', a phrase which originated when the form of a manuscript was a roll or *volumen*, q.v. The word *colophon* (1), q.v., is an alternative.

See also *incipit.*

expurgated edition: an edition of a book from which parts which might be thought objectionable, usually on moral grounds, have been omitted.

extended: synonymous with *expanded type*, q.v.

extended delivery: see *delivery flies.*

extender: a transparent or semi-opaque chemical which is added in powder form to printing ink, either to vary the colour strength or improve the working properties. Alumina hydrate is an example.

extension cover: a paper cover which extends beyond the outer edges of the pages of a booklet or pamphlet, compared with a cover which is *trimmed flush.* (M. L.)

extra bound: a book bound by hand, with all plates guarded, the boards laced on by five cords, a tight or hollow back, a morocco cover, all edges gilt, and special attention given to the end-papers, headbands, and finishing details, especially an abundance of gold tooling.

extra calf: said of an extra-bound book covered in specially selected high-grade calf instead of morocco.

extra cloth: used for bookbindings, in plain finish and a variety of patterns; the cloth is well covered with colour, concealing the weave and giving a solid colour effect. (M. L.)

extra illustrated: see *Grangerized.*

extracts: lengthy quotations set within the main text of a work. They are sometimes set in smaller type and/or indented one em on the left or indented both left and right. Alternatively, extracts may be set in the same size as the text and full out, but preceded and followed by extra space and within quotes.

extruders: the collective term for *ascenders* and *descenders,* qq.v.

Exultet roll: an illuminated manuscript roll on which was written the hymn sung at the benediction of the paschal candle at Easter. Fine examples were made in southern Italy during the Middle Ages. (After O.E.D.)

Eyre & Spottiswoode Literary Fellowship: an award made by the publishing house of this name for a biographical study, a novel, or an historical study which may be the author's first or second book. The award consists of a payment of £250 and an advance on royalties of £250.

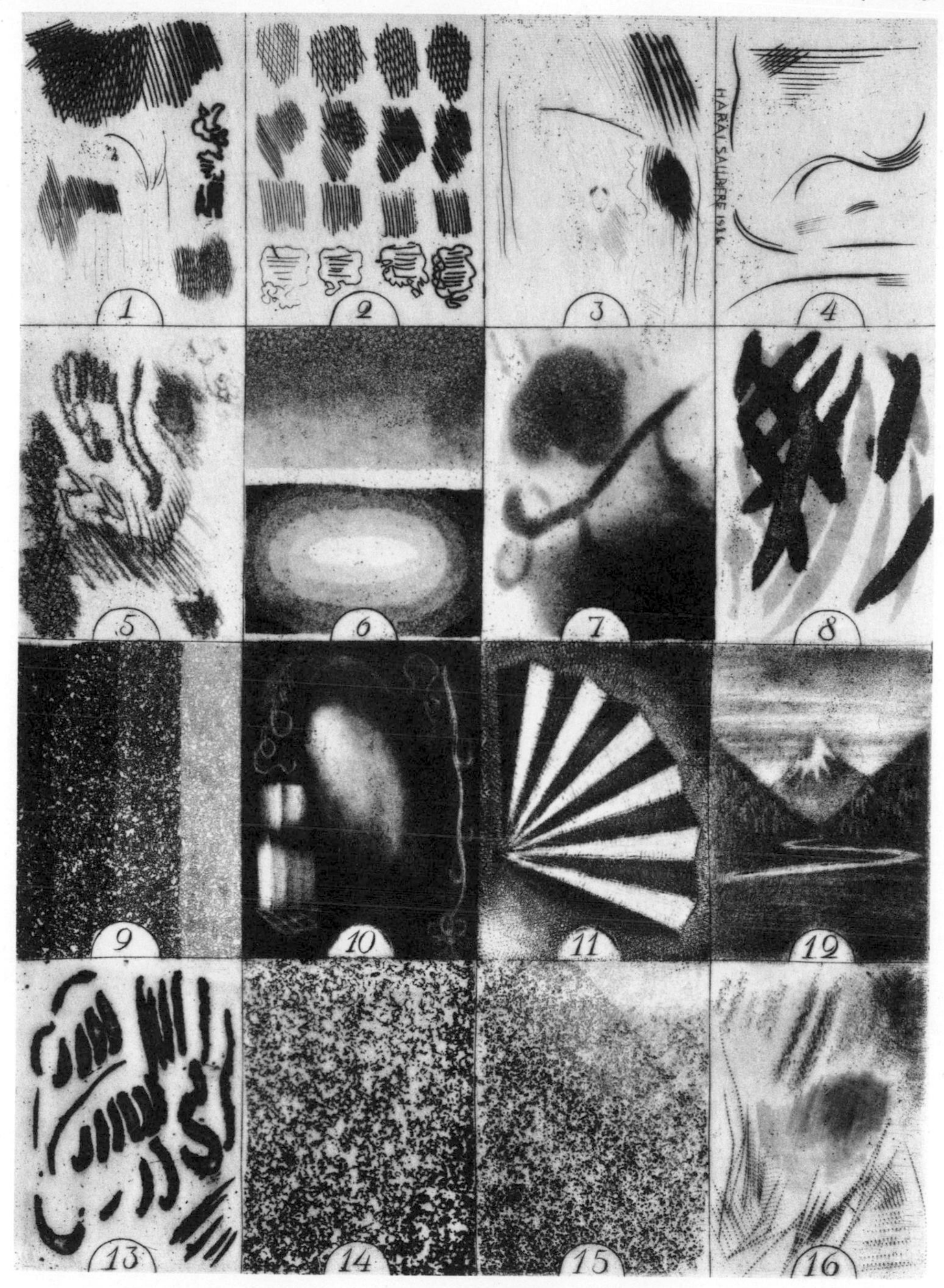

ETCHING METHODS USED IN GRAPHIC ART

1. *Lines etched with nitric acid.* 2. *Lines etched with Dutch mordant.* 3. *Dry-point.* 4. *Lines engraved with a burin.* 5. *Soft ground.* 6. *Aquatint.* 7. *Diluted aquatint.* 8. *Sugar (reverse) aquatint.* 9. *Aquatint on a mastic base.* 10. *Mezzotint.* 11. *Mezzotint on a surface roughened with a dotting wheel.* 12. *Mezzotint on a surface roughened with sandpaper.* 13. *Pen method (reverse aquatint).* 14. *Positive sprayed ground (aquatint).* 15. *Negative sprayed ground (aquatint).* 16. *Dotting wheel method.*

The above examples of etching methods were made by Harald Sallberg and reproduced in collotype from a copperplate printing press impression.

F

Fabriano: an Italian hand-made paper. It was in Fabriano that Italy's first paper-mill was established prior to 1283.

Fabroleen: a cheaper variety of *linson*, q.v.

fac initial: an initial letter surrounded by a panel made up of small type-borders of florets; common in typography of the 17th and 18th centuries. (M.L.)

face: 1. the printing surface of any type character.
2. the group or family to which any particular type design belongs.

facet: the obliquely bevelled edge on a block or other printing plate. A facet *hook* or *clip* is a device for holding the block to an iron base. (G.U.)

Clip for holding blocks to their base

facet edge: the impression left on paper by the edge of a printing plate when copperplate printing.

facetiae: a collection of humorous writings or witticisms, especially popular in the 15th–16th centuries, although of earlier origin. Their revival dates from 1471 when Poggio of Florence issued his 'Libri IV facetiarum'.

facsimile edition: in its modern sense, an exact copy of a book made either photographically or by an offset process. Used to avoid setting up new type when republishing an out-of-print book.

In an earlier sense a facsimile edition was published to make widely available copies of a work which existed only as a rare manuscript or incunabulum. One of the earliest facsimile editions was Plantin's reproduction in 1626 of the 6th-century 'Martyrologium Hieronymianum' which he engraved on copper plates. Cf. *period printing*.

facsimile half-tones: highlight half-tones, when the half-tone screen is eliminated from the highlights. They are used to reproduce pencil, crayon, or charcoal drawings. (M.L.)

facsimile reprint: a re-set of an old book in which the identical face and size of type are used.

factotum: a printer's ornament having a space in the centre of which any letter of the alphabet may be inserted. It is then used for printing an initial capital letter at the beginning of a chapter. Especially applied to early printed books.
See also *guide letters*.

fair calf: an alternative name for *law calf*, q.v.

fair dealing: see *Copyright Act*.

Fairchild Scan-a-Graver: see *Scan-a-Graver*.

false bands: bands of thin leather, thin card, or board, which are glued on to a hollow-backed book before the leather cover is fitted on. The appearance of a flexibly sewn book is thus simulated. Cf. *raised bands*.

family: a group of printing types in *series*, q.v., with common characteristics in design but of different weights. Thus the Times family of the Monotype Corporation includes Times Bold, Times New Roman, Times Titling, Times Extended Titling, and others.

fancy dash: brass rules, such as —◆—◆—◆— (M.L.)

fanfare: a late 16th- to early 17th-century French style of decorating book covers, based on earlier Italian examples, but in its later and more stylized form attributed to Nicolas and Clovis Eve. Designs varied, later examples having geometrical compartments filled with branches of foliage, small tools, and arabesques. The name *fanfare* derives from a copy of 'Les Fanfares et Corvées Abbadesques des Roules-Bontemps', 1613, bound in this manner, which was used as a model in 1829 by Thouvenin when binding a book for the collector Charles Nodier.

fantasie, lettres de: lavishly ornamented letters often

used in the 19th century for initials and display work. Their popularity has somewhat waned.

A 19th-century lettre de fantasie

fascicule: a single number of a work published in instalments. Also called *fascicle* or *fasciculus*.

fashion boards: simple body boards lined on one side with a good rag cartridge paper, and with a thin paper on the other to prevent warping. They are used by artists when preparing originals for blocks.
See also *not*.

fat-face type: display types having letters with vertical strokes nearly half as thick as the letters are high, vertical shading, and unbracketed or only slightly bracketed serifs. Fat-face types as fully developed date from 1809 and were probably the design of Robert Thorne; their origin is often disputed, it being claimed that certain display letters of William Cottrell, *c.* 1766, were prototypes. Modern versions are many and include Corvinus and Ultra Bodoni.
See also *letters—forms and styles*.

fat matter: printing copy which can be set easily since it includes much space, e.g. in a novel which is mostly dialogue. This is distinct from difficult copy, which is known as *lean matter*. (Relates to piecework.)

faults in printing: see *printing faults*.

Favil Press: a private press founded in London by P. A. L. C. Sainsbury in 1920, whose partner, C. A. Birnstingl, bought it in 1922. In addition to jobbing work the press issued books, mostly of poetry, including works by Osbert, Edith, and Sacheverell Sitwell. It ceased publishing about 1948.
See also *Cayme Press*.

Fawcett, Samuel: a Lancashire engraver who, in 1890, worked with Karl Klíč on the *photogravure process*, q.v. Fawcett and Klíč first introduced the use of the cross-line screen for photogravure, thus simplifying the problem of mechanical wiping.

feathering: 1. a fault in printing caused by using an ink containing too much solvent, or an unsuitable paper. The feathered effect is visible when ink spreads beyond the printed impression via the fibres of the paper.

2. the thinning down of the overlapping edges of a join in two pieces of paper. This is done by a bookbinder when restoring a volume: he is careful to choose paper of similar texture to the original, and may need to tone down the colour of the new piece.

featherweight paper: a light bulky paper (75% air space), preferably with a high esparto content, made with little or no calendering. It is slightly porous and does not handle well. Paper giving a standard bulk and above is termed featherweight, the same grade giving under the standard bulk is termed *antique*, q.v.

fecit: a Latin word meaning 'he has made it', frequently added to an artist's name on a drawing or engraving. (M. L.)

Federation Costing System: a system of costing recommended and applied by the British Federation of Master Printers.

The first British Cost Congress met in London in February 1913 to hear the report of a committee formed by printers in 1911 to consider rising costs and the ways of increasing prices. A universal costing system has still not been adopted by every printer in Britain, but the Federation Costing System is now widely accepted.

See also *chargeable time*, *Standard Cost-finding System*.

Fedorov, Ivan, fl. 1563–83: the first-known printer in Russia. With Petr Timofeev Msitlavec he set up a press in Moscow where he printed the 'Apostol' (Acts and Epistles of the Apostles) in 1564, using Cyrillic type. Some time later his press was burnt, so he went to Lithuania and also the Ukraine, printing the Russian Bible at Ostrog in 1581.

Russian bibliographers have not yet established whether or not six unsigned and undated liturgical books were printed by a Moscow press between 1556 and 1563. They have been tentatively assigned to Marusha Nefediev, who would thus be Russia's first printer.

feed board: the platform on a printing machine on to which single sheets of paper are passed from the stock pile and from which they pass to the impression cylinder.

feed-guides: any one, or a pair, of several kinds of appliance for holding the paper sheets in a uniformly straight position while the impression is made. (M. L.)

feeder: an apparatus for feeding and positioning paper sheets in printing presses, and in paper processing machines of various kinds. Feeding was formerly done entirely by hand, but gradually technical means were devised, at first for moving the sheet forward and adjusting it, while the sheets in the pile were still separated by hand. From this 'semi-automatic' feeding, which still exists in some machines, the modern entirely automatic feeders have developed. One of the first practicable feeders for cylinder presses was built in 1896 by the Swede Lagerman, who also built a platen press in 1902 with wholly automatic feeding and delivery (Lagerman press). Modern machines are often constructed with built-in feeders of various kinds, but large presses are usually supplied without feeders which are manufactured and fitted as separate units. There are many such feeders differing mainly in

An older model of the Swedish Dux feeder with a spreading wheel

the manner of separating the sheets from the feeding pile. Some of them have purely mechanical frictional spreading arrangements which spread out the uppermost sheets, so that they are released singly at the

Continuous feeder

edge and can be gripped by devices with reels and transporting bands for conveying them to the press. Others employ a combination of friction, suction, or blowing.

In continuous feeders (see illustration) the sheets can be fed continuously to the apparatus. This is an American invention.

The widely used British equivalent, supplied by the Cross Feeder Co., will operate at speeds in excess of 4000 sheets per hour. The sheets are slightly fanned and laid by hand on an upper table from which they are conveyed mechanically, as laid, to a lower table. At each feeding cycle the uppermost sheet on the lower table is urged forward by friction wheels (known as combers) until its leading edge lifts light metal triggers. The movement of the triggers serves to put mechanism in motion which lifts the combers, hence movement of the sheet is arrested. At that point the sheet is taken over by the printing (or folding) machine and the cycle is repeated.

Separating mechanism in the Dexter pile feeder. A revolving plate (1) *lifts the corners of the sheet, and the separating wheel* (2) *releases the top sheet from the pile. This is then lifted by the suction mouthpiece* (3), *while the mouthpiece* (4) *drops and blows air under it. Lateral adjustment is by the supporting plate* (5). *The feeder has two such separators*

The latest American Dexter pile feeder has separating devices in the rear corners of the sheet (see illustration). When revolving discs or combers have loosened the pile, the top sheet is lifted by the vacuum, blown from below, and conveyed by suction pipes to the feeding table. The American Harris feeder and the British H.T.B. automatic stream feeder work on a similar principle. Almost all modern feeders adopt a method of separating sheets by suction mouthpieces which lift an edge of the paper with a loosening motion, so that the paper becomes accessible to the conveying apparatus.

On the H.T.B. pile feeder sheets are fed into the machine by a separator which travels down the stationary pile. Actual feeding is by gripper chains.

The Universal, Dux, Reinhart, Simplex, and König

feeders, and some of the Spiess models, work with suction pipes provided with a number of fixed or spring-actuated mouthpieces along the front edge of the sheets; the Swedish Elless apparatus (see below) has suction devices at the back edge of the sheet.

When the sheet has been released from the pile it has to be conveyed to the actual machine (printing, folding, die-cutting, etc.). Wholly automatic platen and other small presses often have special devices for conveying and adjusting the sheets (Heidelberg, Lagerman), but usually sheets are carried over a sloping feeding table equipped with endless conveying belts and rollers on which the paper is kept pressed by reels or 'smoothers' of various kinds. The lower part of the feeding table serves as a register table on which devices for positioning the sheet are installed (see *feeding*). The conveying devices of the feeding table are often constructed with a slowing arrangement so that the sheet reaches the feeding guides smoothly and gently. In order to gain as much time as possible for the work of adjustment, the next sheet should be as close to the feeding guides as can be managed as soon as the adjusted sheet leaves them free. Stream feeders have been devised as a step in this direction.

Stream feeders. Instead of allowing the sheets to be fed one by one they are allowed to slide forward in a continuous stream, partly overlapping. Advantages are that sheets lying one above the other have a more even and steady passage over the feeding table, and each sheet is quite close to the front guides when the previous sheet leaves the table. Although the idea of stream feeding was known in the 1870's, practical constructions did not appear until the late 1920's. H.T.B., L. & M., the Interflow, and the Elless are well-known makes.

The Elless stream feeder. Elless, Gothenburg

The Elless feeder with stream feeding has been manufactured in Sweden since 1929. It works on the back edge of the sheet and by this means the speed of working has been increased in a simple manner, the back edge of the succeeding sheets being accessible as soon as the top sheet has moved slightly forward. The sheets are separated at the back edge of the pile by a vacuum and blower, and when the top sheet is raised from the pile by suction, it is released entirely by a current of air which passes under it. The sheet is then gripped by forwarding suckers which carry it to the drop wheels and tape roller, and as soon as it has been pushed forward so much that the back edge of the sheet beneath it is released for the operating devices, the latter sheet is dealt with in the same way and is pushed in under the previous one, by which means stream feeding is achieved.

Modern feeders are usually equipped with automatic stopping arrangements consisting partly of driving and partly of releasing devices. The former are of various kinds; mechanical detectors, electrical rubbing contacts, photoelectric cells, or micro-circuit breakers. In the event of sheets failing to reach

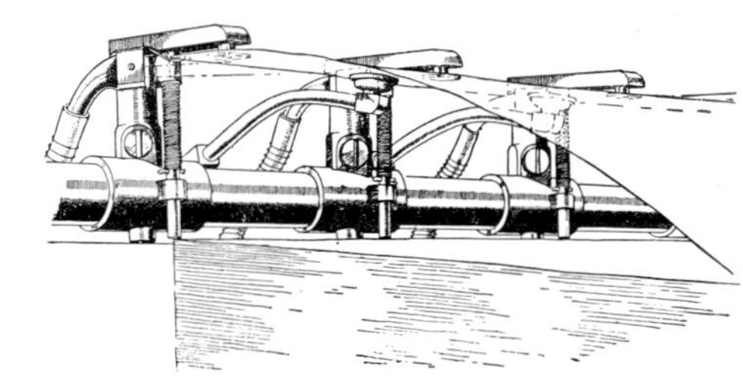

The Dux stream feeder. The mouthpieces on a suction pipe grip the front edge of the sheet and lift it, whereupon another suction pipe with suction plugs turned upwards grips the sheet and carries it away while the first set of grippers seize the next sheet

the lays, reaching them in a crooked position, or of several coming forward together, these devices stop the feeder and release the pressure in the printing press, or in some way affect the machine which is being fed. The diagram shows a detector device which operates in such a way that if sheets fail to come for-

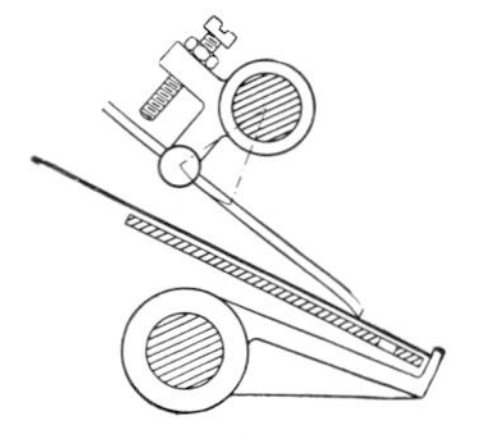

Detector (see text)

ward correctly a pin drops in the plate of the table and the machine is stopped. If the sheet lies correctly against the front lays it covers the hole, so that the pin passes by. The double-sheet detector of the Elless feeder is shown in the illustration.

In large machines the feeder is installed as a separate pile feeder standing on the floor, with automatic

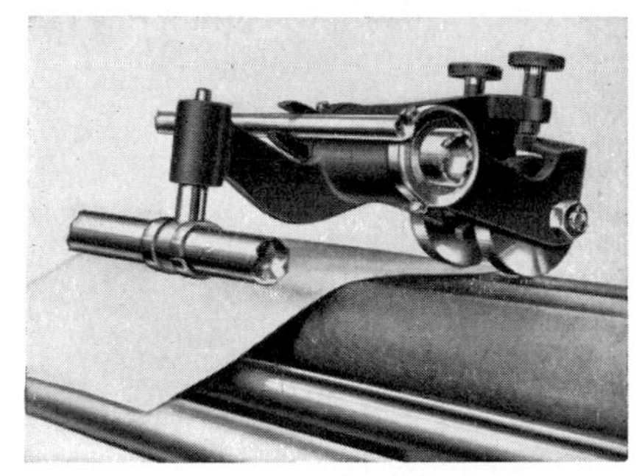

The Elless feeder has a caliper detector

Elless feeder with reloading device

hoisting devices which enable high piles of paper to be stacked up by the machine so that they can be quickly introduced into the feeder when the previous pile has been consumed. Sometimes the apparatus is equipped with a reloading device for changing piles without stopping the press. For some purposes the feeder is equipped with double separators or double lifts which enable two sheets to be conveyed side by side, even with paper of different thicknesses. (G. U.)

See also *Miehle, Nivetron sheet control.*

feeding: the insertion of a sheet of paper into the printing press. This was formerly done entirely by hand, and pinning devices were used to obtain register. Hand-feeding still survives, but pinning or pointing devices have largely been replaced by feed guides or *lays* along which the front edge and one side edge of the sheet are placed. Three-guide adjustment is most usual, i.e. to two front lays and one side lay. The two front lays are usually placed slightly inside the outer edges, about $\frac{1}{4}$ of the length of the sheet, while the side lay (of hammer or finger type) should be placed about $\frac{1}{3}$ of the depth of the sheet, reckoned from the front edge.

Side-register device on the register table of the Dux feeder. A rail let into the plate forms the lower arm of a pair of tongs, movable sideways, the upper arm of which remains open when moved from left to right (as shown here). When moved in the opposite direction, the upper arm drops towards the lower, and pulls the sheet held between them to the lay edge. The whole device is movable along the three rails which run across the feeding table

In the platen press paper is fed by hand or machine directly on to the platen; the lays supporting the front edge are adjusted and the sheet grippers fixed rigid. The side lay consists as a rule of a gauge pin fixed to the tympan.

In cylinder and other presses feeding usually proceeds automatically from a feeding table, the lower edge of which is flush with the cylinder. In stop-cylinder presses the adjustment can be made by lays placed on the stationary cylinder (see illustration under *stop-cylinder press*), but in such machines it sometimes happens (and in two-revolution presses and others with constantly revolving cylinders it is essential) that the front lays should be so fixed on the lower edge of the table that they either move upwards or are lowered at the moment when the sheet is to be seized by the passing cylinder grippers. High-speed machines are often equipped with pre-grippers which turn or revolve between the feeding table and the cylinder, and can accelerate the sheet in a short time from its motionless state to the speed of the cylinder. The side adjustment is done by guiding the sheet which rests against the front lays to the side lay. In automatic feeders this lateral movement is mechanized.

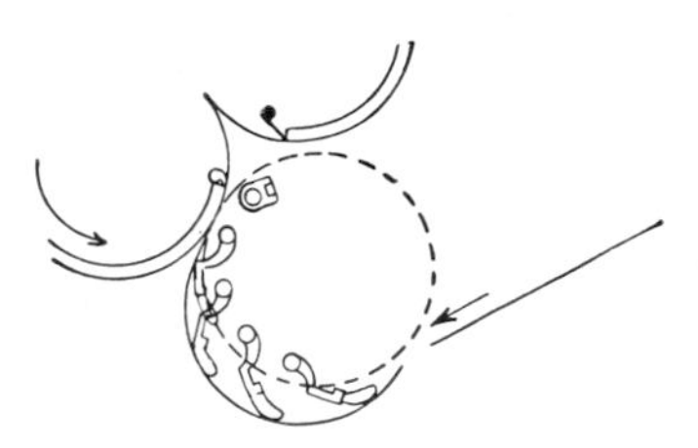

The Planeta system for conveying paper to the impression cylinder

In American offset machines a system of feeding is used in which the front edge of the sheet rests against a number of non-adjustable front lays and, after being adjusted to the side lay, is gripped by crown wheels which revolve on an underlying axle and led in towards the cylinder grippers at a speed slightly greater than the periphery speed of the cylinder. There the edge of the paper strikes against guides

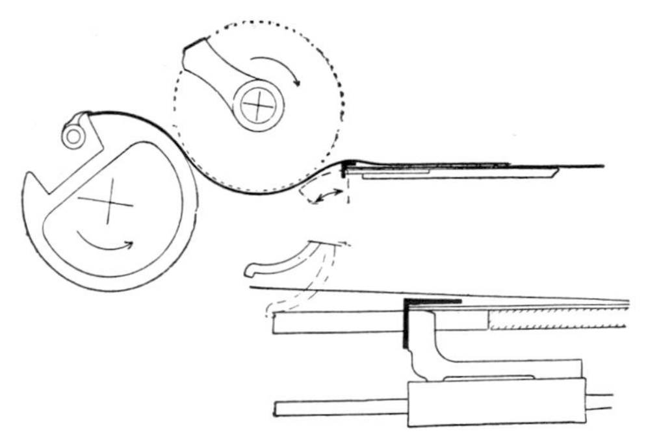

Feeding device in the Roland-Ultra, with pre-adjustment of the sheet and turning and revolving pre-grippers. Below, diagram of the register fingers which steer the sheet to the actual front feed lays

before the grippers close. The sheet is adjusted in this direction solely by adjusting the position of the printing plate.

In high-speed sheet-fed rotary presses the diameter of the cylinder is so small that almost the whole of its circumference is filled by the printing surface; for this reason a sheet must be ready to be gripped by the grippers almost as soon as the previous sheet has left the feeding table. This is facilitated by modern stream-feeding devices, but in addition there are special arrangements in many printing presses. The Planeta-Super offset machines have an additional cylinder for transporting paper, provided with eccentrically moving flaps which increase the diameter of the cylinder and consequently the speed of the paper, so that the latter leaves the table more rapidly (see illustration). The Roland-Ultra presses have a special pre-adjustment of the sheets, so that they reach the front feeding guides almost exactly adjusted (see illustration). Cf. *delivery*. (G. U.)

feeding edge: see *gripper edge*.

feet: the base on which a type stands, being formed by a separating groove cut in it. Type not standing squarely is said to be 'off its feet'.

Felicia Hemans Prize: an annual award of a bronze medal and a small sum of money (*c.* £2) for a lyrical poem written by past and present members of University College or of the University of Liverpool. Verse submitted may be published or unpublished.

Fell types: the type-face purchased by Doctor John Fell for the Oxford University Press, *c.* 1672. They were cut by Dirck and Bartholomew Voskens of Amsterdam and were a source of inspiration to English type-designers of the time. They are in use today at the Clarendon Press, having been revived in 1876 by C. H. O. Daniel.

felt finish: a variety of finish given to sheets of paper by drying them with felt webs having a surface differing from that usually employed.

felt side: the upper side of a sheet as it is formed on the wire of a paper-making machine. It is smoother than the under, or wire, side.

See also *twin-wire paper*.

felting: the binding together of fibres in the wet pulp when making paper.

fere-humanistica: a 14th-century Italian book script which was developed by Petrarch and Salutati from earlier Latin hands.

From 1460–85 it was cut and cast as a type-face, being used in Germany and elsewhere (in England at Oxford) for printing classical texts. It was without the serifs of roman or the hair-lines of gothic. The Gutenberg (?) edition of 'Catholicon', Mainz, 1460, is an example.

In 'Old English Letter Foundries' T. B. Reed suggests, p. 49, that contemporary French printers possibly called this hand *lettre de somme*.

See also *letters—forms and styles*.

Ferrar, Nicholas, 1592–1637: see *Little Gidding bindings.*

ferrotype: a method used in the mid-19th century for making photographic positives by direct exposure in a camera on black-lacquered iron plates coated with iodized silver collodion, or by the eventual transfer to such plates of a collodion film which had been exposed on some other base.

Ferrotype plates were later produced on a factory scale, prepared with silver bromide emulsion, which after developing was treated with sublimate, the silver image being thereby bleached to whiteness. Thus a distinct positive was obtained, but could not, however, be copied.

Unprepared ferrotype plates have more recently been used as glazing plates for obtaining a high gloss on photographic prints. (G. U.)

festoon: a garland of flowers and foliage suspended between two points. A form of decoration used to embellish the head of a printed page.

festoon drying: a method of drying paper in a uniformly warm room. The sheets are hung and conveyed by means of a series of hoops. (M. L.)

fettling: the lubrication and cleaning of objects requiring surface treatment. Stereotypes, for example, are electrolytically fettled before being nickel-plated by suspending them as cathodes in a bath of sodium hydroxide, soda, and cyanide compounds of copper; the copper coating is a sign that the stereotypes are clean. (G. U.)

fibre: a plant cell, largely composed of cellulose; the basic element of paper-making material. (M. L.)

fiction series: cheap reprints of fiction issued in uniform cloth covers, a style belonging to the years 1830–90.

See also *three-decker novel, yellow-backs.*

Field, Richard, d. 1624: the printer of Shakespeare's first published work 'Venus and Adonis', 1593. He was also a Master of the Stationers' Company.

Figgins, Vincent, 1776–1844: a London type-founder who had been apprenticed to Joseph Jackson before establishing his own business *c.* 1792. One of his first commissions was the cutting of a two-line english roman for *Thomas Bensley*, q.v., and a double-pica greek for Oxford University. He continued to cut and cast new types, particularly important being his Oriental founts. His specimen book of 1815 showed an early example of *egyptian*, q.v.

He was succeeded by two sons and other direct descendants until 1907 when the firm was reconstituted by R. H. Stevens. It now trades as Stevens, Shanks & Sons.

figure: 1. an illustration forming part of a page of text with which it is printed from a block imposed together with the type. Cf. *plate* (3).

2. see *numerals.*

fillers: an alternative name for *loading*, q.v.

fillet: 1. a narrow line, plain, or of a repeated ornament, impressed on the cover of a book. It is usually gilded.

2. the wheel tool, having a single-notched edge, used for cornering when impressing 1. above.

filling in: a faulty impression in printing caused when the type characters or the spaces between the dots of a half-tone block fill with ink. This may be due to using an unsuitable ink or too much of it; the forme being too high or the rollers incorrectly set; or a paper which fluffs.

Clogging or *choking* are alternative names for filling in.

filling-in guards: see *compensation guards.*

film (photographic): one or several light-sensitive layers which are cast on a transparent base of celluloid, cellulose acetate, or something similar. The film may be in sheet or roll form, and in various sizes. The celluloid film base is highly inflammable and is no longer used in Britain; much less combustible is the so-called 'safety film' made on a cellulose acetate or similar base.

A two-layer negative film came into use in the thirties of the present century. By casting two layers of emulsion of different sensitivity one over the other, greater exposure latitude is possible. For example, in the event of over-exposure, the more sensitive layer becomes dense and an even grey when developed, but the less sensitive layer is still in a position to give a detailed image.

As a protection from halation a coloured gelatine layer is frequently coated on the back of the film base. (G. U.)

filmsetting: the process of using photographic film and a *photo-composing machine*, q.v., for letterpress composition.

filter: 1. an apparatus for separating a liquid or gas from any fine insoluble substances in its contents. Filter paper or glass wool are among filters for liquids.

2. *Colour filter.* A glass plate or gelatine film (coloured), or a tank containing a coloured liquid which allows certain kinds of light to pass through but absorbs light of a different colour. The colour

density of the filter is, as a rule, indicated in grammes of dye-stuff per square metre of filter surface. Colour filters are important in photographic reproduction processes. According to their intended use they may be classed under the following main types: *protective filters* for dark-room lamps, which enable sensitized films to be handled with safety; *corrective filters* which are used when exposing to correct the colour of the lighting according to the spectral sensitivity of the plate so as to obtain correct tone values; *contrast filters* (detail filters) used to accentuate the contrasts between details of a subject which, while of different colour, have practically the same luminous effect, and would be difficult to distinguish in the final picture; *separation filters* for three-colour analysis; *monochromatic filters* which allow only a small colour area to pass through and are chiefly used in scientific work; special filters of various kinds, e.g. the *Davis–Gibson filter* used for determining the degree of sensitivity of material sensitive to light.

3. *Heat filter*, e.g. a solution of alum used in projectors to absorb dark heat radiation. (G.U.)

filter factor: a number denoting by how many times the period of exposure of a film is to be prolonged due to the light absorption properties of a coloured filter, as compared with exposure without a filter. This factor is determined from the colour density of the filter, and also from the colour sensitivity of the negative material employed and the colour of the light used for the exposure. Any given filter factor for a certain filter thus applies only to a definite light source and to a definite kind of plate or film. (G.U.)

fine etching: the giving of correct emphasis to the middle tones and high lights of a half-tone plate, after its first dipping in an acid bath, by staging out the darker tones so that only those parts of the plate which require it are affected by the acid.

See also *staging out*.

fine paper copy: a copy of a book printed on better paper than the ordinary edition, usually hand-made paper.

fine rule: a rule of hair-line thickness.

fingers: the grippers on a press which hold the sheet when printing. (M.L.)

finis: the Latin for 'end', at one time used at the end of a book. It now rarely appears. (M.L.)

finish: the surface given to paper during manufacture. Factors affecting this are ingredients, sizing, and calendering.

See also *paper finishes and varieties*.

finishing: the polishing of the leather, lettering, and embellishing of a hand-bound book, done by the finisher. He uses brass tools in wooden handles (often designing his own); a burnisher, gouges (for curves), fillets and pallets (for lines), rolls, flowers, and letters. The term finishing is not applied to *cased books*, q.v.

See also *bookbinding tools, cap*. Cf. *forwarding*.

first edition: all copies of a book as first printed and published. Repeated printings from the same type, plates, or stereos, without major textual alterations, are still part of the first edition. A second edition implies re-set type, or changes of format or text.

See also *edition, first impression*.

First Edition Club: a club founded in 1922 by A. J. A. Symons and Max Judge with the objects of promoting the study of book-collecting and bibliography, maintaining club premises for members, inspiring by example an improvement in the standard of book production, issuing books unlikely to be sponsored by ordinary trade publishers, and arranging exhibitions of books and manuscripts. In 1928 the club moved to Bedford Square.

Several important exhibitions have been held (e.g. fine bindings and type specimen books), and among publications of note are 'Bibliography of the Principal Modern Presses' by G. S. Tomkinson, and 'Book Clubs and Printing Societies of Great Britain and Ireland' by H. Williams, 1929. These productions show care and taste: for this the Curwen Press has been largely responsible.

first gluing: see *gluing-up*.

first impression: all copies of a book resulting from the first printing of type or plates. Minor corrections may be made for a second or subsequent impression.

See also *issue*.

first lining: see *lining*.

First Novel Award: an annual house dinner in honour of the author of what is considered to be the most promising first novel of the year. It was instituted in 1954 by the Authors' Club, Whitehall Court, London. Under the club's rules only male authors are eligible, and a panel of members makes a preliminary selection from novels submitted by publishers; the final choice is then made by a distinguished author. The first award was to David Unwin for his 'The Governor's Wife'.

fish-glue enamel: a dichromated colloid used as a photoengraving resist for half-tone blockmaking.

Fishenden, Richard Bertram, 1880–1956: for many years Britain's leading authority on printing and the graphic arts as interpreted by printing processes. As a youth he studied process engraving technique, then in its infancy, and in 1902 he began lecturing in the Manchester College of Technology, remaining as head of the printing department until 1921. In this year he joined Stephenson Blake, the letter founders, leaving in 1931 to join Lorilleux and Bolton, ink-makers. In 1942 he was appointed technical editor of the 'King Penguin' books, and a year later was adviser to Spicers, the paper-makers. These two posts were held concurrently.

It was, however, as the editor of 'Penrose Annual' from 1935 to 1956 that he was known throughout Europe and America. Under his direction this volume, recording all aspects of printing, developed into a work of considerable authority.

fitting: the degree of proximity between adjacent type characters.

fixing: the post-developing treatment of photographic material involves the neutralizing of its sensitivity to light by releasing any substances sensitive to light which remain uninfluenced. Should these consist of silver chloride or silver bromide, sodium thiosulphate is generally used, while the fixing medium frequently employed in the case of silver iodide is potassium cyanide. 100 grammes of 20% sodium thiosulphate solution will dissolve 5·8 grammes of silver bromide or 0·6 grammes of silver iodide; 100 grammes of 5% potassium cyanide solution will dissolve 6·5 grammes of silver bromide or 8·2 grammes of silver iodide. In the case of silver bromide gelatine material an acid fixing bath containing about 20% sodium thiosulphate and 2% sodium metabisulphate is mostly used.

Fixing time may be about ten minutes or, as a rule, twice the time needed for the layer to become clear. After fixing, the fixing salt must be completely rinsed off the layer, which takes some time since the fixing salt adheres to the gelatine layer. Rinse for half an hour, preferably in running water, or in repeated rinsing baths, adding, with advantage, 1% of soda to the first of these. Any fixing salt remaining will lead to the formation of silver sulphide and a gradual deterioration of the image. Delicate gelatine layers are often fixed in hardening fixing baths made by an addition of 1% alum. (G. U.)

fl.: see *floreat dates.*

flare the balls: to hold *ink balls,* q.v., over a piece of burning paper to make them tacky.

flat: a flat printing plate.

flat backs: a binding style in which the rounding of the back is omitted. The *spine,* q.v., is thus flat and narrower than it would be if rounded.

flat bed: said of a press having the printing forme on a plane surface, as distinct from one having a curved printing surface. (M. L.)

flat-bed cylinder press: a printing machine having a flat bed on which the forme is placed and moved to and fro under the cylinder.

See also *letterpress machine, Wharfedale machine.*

flat-bed web press: a machine for printing from a flat forme on to an endless roll of paper. The flat-bed web press, the duplex press, was introduced in 1891, being intended for small newspapers. The original duplex press was built by the Duplex Printing Press Co., Mich., U.S.A., and had two beds, one above the

The Cox-o-type, a flat-bed web press made by Goss

other, against which pressure was exercised by two cylinders fitted on a stand common to both and moving to and fro. The paper course was fed between the lower bed and cylinder and then perfected between the upper bed and its cylinder. At the

A flat-bed web press for newspaper placards

moment of printing the paper course remained motionless, but on the cylinders leaving the forme the paper was pulled forward into position for the following printing. The paper course ran on to the folding section for cutting, folding, and pasting. (G. U.)

flat proofs: prints made from the separate plates used in colour printing.

flat pull: see *rough pull.*

flat stitching: the stitching of a pamphlet or book by means of wire or linen thread in such a way that this passes from the side right through the whole book (which must have a flat back). (G.U.)

flat tint plate: a piece of zinc plate, shaped as required, for printing a flat tint.

Fleischhack overlay: a method of mechanical overlay. An impression (without ink) is taken from the forme on a coloured foil. Where this is exposed to a greater pressure it becomes more transparent than where the pressure has been less. The foil is then copied on a chromate gelatine layer which, according to the illumination, is treated with water in approximately the same way as a collotype plate. A gelatine relief is thus obtained which serves the purpose of an overlay sheet on the tympan of the press. (G.U.)

Fleischman, Johann Michael, 1701–68: a Nuremberg punch-cutter. The fount of roman and italic he cut for Heinrich Wetstein, a type-founder of Amsterdam, passed with the latter's stock to the Enschedé family in 1743. The precision and clarity of the Fleischman types made them popular and led to the long association of Fleischman with Enschedé en Zonen. Of particular importance was the music type he completed in 1760.

Fleuron Society: a printing society formed in 1922 by Francis Meynell, Stanley Morison, Holbrook Jackson, Bernard Newdigate, and Oliver Simon. It stimulated typographical activities, including the production by Morison and Simon of 'The Fleuron—a journal of typography', in 1923. It was set in the new Monotype Garamond type. After 1924 it was transferred to the C.U.P., and ceased publication in 1930. (M.L.)

fleurons: see *flowers.*

Flexiback: the trade name of a *thermoplastic binder,* q.v., made by the Book Machinery Co. of London.

Briefly, folded and collated sections are fed into the machine which, in one operation, produces a completely lined book, thus avoiding the usual separate stages of sewing, nipping, back gluing, and lining. The adhesive used is a polyvinyl cold emulsion synthetic glue.

flexible binding: a binding style in which boards are omitted. Such volumes are usually covered in real or imitation leather, on to which the end-papers are pasted direct. The leather may be slightly stiffened by first pasting on to it a stout paper or very thin card. Cf. *flexible sewing.*

flexible glue: a bookbinding glue which contains a hygroscopic additive to prevent it from drying out completely. It is used for gluing-up the back of a book after sewing.

flexible sewing: the oldest and strongest method of sewing the sections of a book on to raised bands or cords. The stitching thread passes around each cord: greater strength results, and the book can be opened flat at any page. See also *sunken flexible.*

Flexographic process: an American development of aniline printing, introduced by the Mosstype Corporation, New York. Printing is done from flexible rubber stereos made from line or half-tone blocks.

flimsy: the sheets of thin, tough, and semi-transparent bond paper used for planning in the layout department.

floating accents: see *accents.*

floating fleurons: decorative panels in which small ornaments are used to build up a design for printing as an embellishment to a chapter heading, etc.

floating the forme: the filling with plaster of any spaces below the level of type shoulders or hollow quads. This is done before pouring melted wax on to a forme of type to make a mould for electrotyping.

flong: the material used for moulds in *stereotyping,* q.v. There are two kinds—wet and dry. *Wet flong* consists of alternate layers of blotting paper and tissue paper pasted and rolled together into a unit with a blotting-paper base and a tissue face. The flong is placed tissue side down on to the forme and beaten into it. The flong-bearing forme is next dried in a hot press. *Dry flong* is made in the same way but dried before use. Sheets of it are placed on the forme, which is passed under a heavy roller or through a hydraulic moulding press to force it into the type. When preparing stereos for use on a rotary machine the flong is bent to a semicircular shape and placed, impression side inwards, on a moulding cylinder known as an autoplate machine; molten metal is poured between the mould and the cylindrical core to form the stereo.

floreat dates: the approximate dates when a person was alive or flourished in the capacity for which he was famous; used when exact dates are uncertain. Abbreviated as fl.

Florence Press: a press founded at Letchworth in 1908, with the aim of producing cheaply fine books in large editions. In 1909 E. P. Prince cut the Florence type designed by H. P. Horne for the press. Messrs. Chatto & Windus were the trade publishers.

Florentine woodcuts: a group of artists and craftsmen, working in Florence between 1492 and 1508, produced what are often considered the finest of early book illustrations. The five hundred or so cuts appeared on chap-books, sermons, and ephemeral texts, written in Italian, and mostly badly printed on poor paper. Their unique quality was a finely executed combination, on the same cut, of black on white and white on black technique. Examples survive in the Tracts of Savonarola, printed by Antonio Miscomini, 1496.

Their prototype was contained in an edition of 'Fior di Virtù', 1491.

floret: a binder's tool used to impress a flower or leaf design.

See also *flowers.*

floriated: said of a border, initial, or book cover which is decorated with small flower or leaf ornaments. Initials floriated with acanthus leaves date from the late 12th century, and these developed, in the following century, into *historiated letters,* q.v.

flourishes: curved lines and ornaments for use with lines of type, made of brass or cast metal. (M.L.)

flowers: type ornaments used to embellish page-borders, chapter headings, tail-pieces, title-pages, and generally to enliven printed matter.

Probably the earliest use of the decorative printing types known as flowers was in Dominico Capranica's 'Arte de ben morire', printed by Giovanni and Alberto Aluise at Verona in 1478 (Hain 4398). In addition to forming a page-border they were set up with lines of display type.

Basic designs, popular since the early 16th century, have been the acorn, vine leaf, and arabesque. They may be traced to the Venetian pattern-books of arabesques and other decorative material, deriving from the Near East, used by metal-workers, engravers, weavers, painters, and bookbinders. Venetian binders (notably Aldus) used small stamps, known as *piccoli ferri,* bearing motifs adapted from the pattern-books, and it seems that early punch-cutters copied these for casting on type-bodies. With the simple leaf, tendril, acorn, or arabesque as a unit, printers either set them singly or built up elaborate patterns to fill as much of a page as they wished. Of early printers Aldus, Ratdolt, Giolito, de Tournes, Tory, and Granjon made extensive use of flowers, while later, P-S. Fournier was an inspired cutter of new designs.

Flowers have been particularly popular in the present century, and the number of flower matrices available from Monotype and Linotype together with the decorative units of the major European foundries must total several thousands, and new designs continue to be made. Notable examples have been commissioned by the Curwen Press and the Fanfare Press, among others, for their exclusive use.

Flowers are variously known as *fleurons, florets, printers' flowers,* and, in Germany, as *Röslein.*

For much of my information I am indebted to John Ryder's 'A Suite of Fleurons', Phoenix House, 1956.

See also *Aldine leaves, floating fleurons.*

Monotype Borders

Vine leaf ornament of 1512. Mono. 224

A Venetian arabesque of 1552. Mono. 280

An arrangement of Granjon's arabesque (*c.* 1565). Mono. 310, 311, 312

Arrangements of an arabesque which appeared on Plantin's 1567 specimen sheet. Mono. 1294, 1295

Lyonaise flower of 1570. Mono. 219

Sunray 1740. Fournier, after Louis Luce. Mono. 675

Fournier flowers 1736–67. Mono. 475, 476

Mono. 468, 469

Mono. 467

Mono. 274, 275

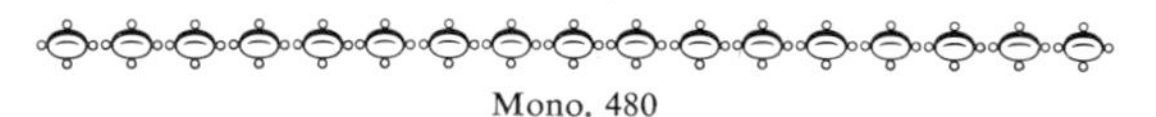

Mono. 480

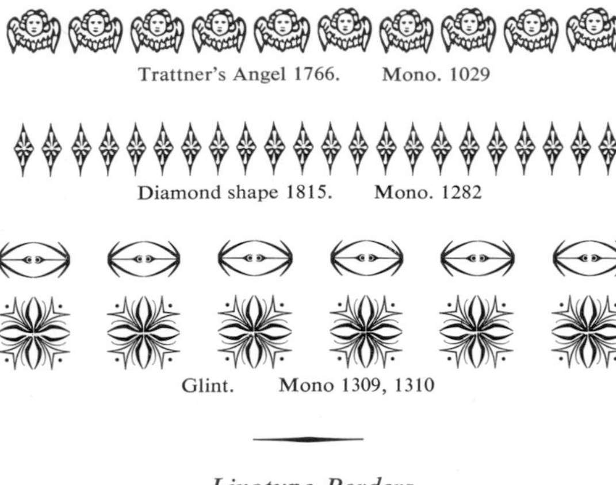

Trattner's Angel 1766. Mono. 1029

Diamond shape 1815. Mono. 1282

Glint. Mono 1309, 1310

Linotype Borders

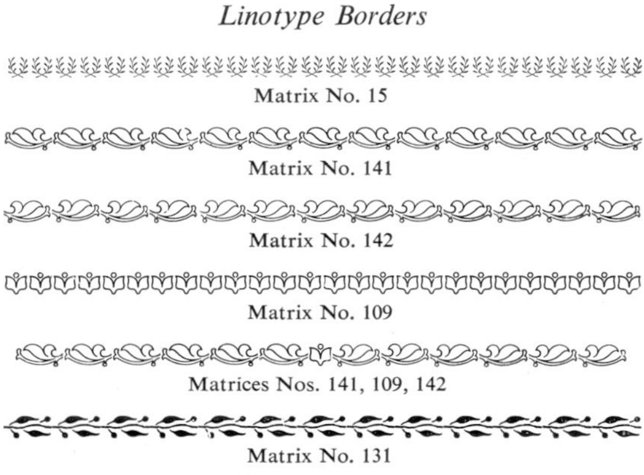

Matrix No. 15

Matrix No. 141

Matrix No. 142

Matrix No. 109

Matrices Nos. 141, 109, 142

Matrix No. 131

Matrix No. 124

Matrix No. 200

Matrices Nos. 146, 148, 147

Matrices Nos. 125, 127, 126

Matrix No. 197

Slide No. 1267A

Slide No. 1283A

Slide No. 1312A

Matrix No. 317

Matrices Nos. 280, 281

Bauer

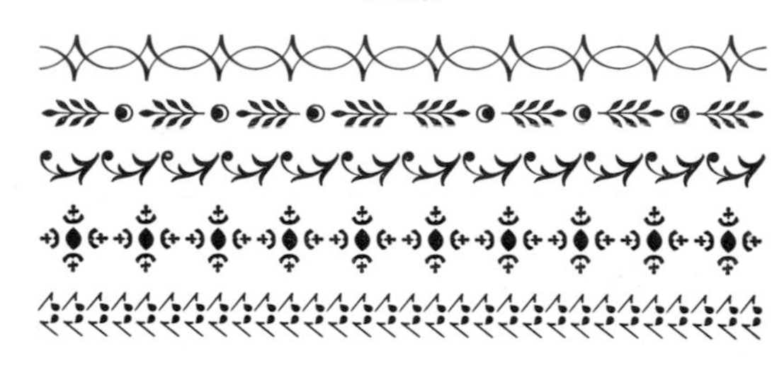

Curwen Press Borders

Edward Bawden Harry Carter

Edward Bawden Edward Bawden

Reiner Borders (Simson Shand)

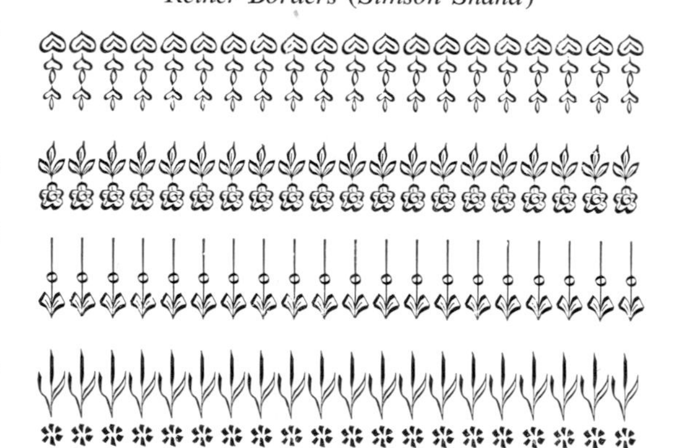

Type-foundry Amsterdam

Stephenson Blake

Stempel

Fluorescence process: a Kodak process designed to reproduce water-colour sketches, painted with special pigments, as half-tones. Differently sensitized plates and special filters are used, exposures being made with ultraviolet and white lights.

flush boards: a method of binding in which boards are glued to the paste-downs and the book then receives a paper cover which in turn is glued to the boards. The book, boards, and cover are *cut flush.* An alternative name is *stiffened cut flush.* (L. K.)

flush paragraphs: paragraphs in which the first word is not indented but set flush with the vertical line of the text.

flush work: binding styles in which the cover is applied before cutting and cut with the book. Thus in the finished book the edges of the cover are level with the edges of the book. (L. K.)

fly: see *delivery flies.*

fly leaf: see *end-papers.*

fly-title: 1. a leaf indicating the beginning of a distinct portion of a book. An anthology of plays will usually have a fly-title for each.

2. an alternative name in England for *bastard title, half-title.*

Flying Fame Press: a private press founded in 1912 by Claud Lovat Fraser, Holbrook Jackson, and Ralph Hodgson, with the aim of publishing in chap-book and broadside form original prose and verse, with illustrations. The press continued until the First World War.

flyswing: a very thin skiver leather widely used for title labels on cloth- and leather-bound books: after mounting the leather label the normal procedure is to letter in gold. (L. K.)

foil: see *blocking foils.*

Folchart Psalter: a 9th-century Carolingian manuscript, notable for the finely decorated initials which embellish its pages, made for Folchardus, a monk of St Gall.

fold to paper: an instruction to the folding department that the printed sheets are to be folded so that the edges of the leaves and the *bolts* are all level in the folded sheets. Cf. *fold to print.* (L. K.)

fold to print: an instruction to the folding department that sheets are to be folded in register, i.e. the edges of the printed areas are to be placed exactly over one another before the fold is made.

folded and collated copies: the usually folded and collated copies of a work sent to the publisher for approval of printing before binding commences. Also known as *advance sheets.* Books are often sold in bulk in this form, e.g. to American publishers for casing in U.S.A.

folding: the folding of flat printed sheets to book size. The number of pages in the folded sheet is always a multiple of four (i.e. two leaves) hence, when the sheet is subsequently opened and sewn through the last fold, all leaves are secured. The thickness of the paper is the principal element in determining the number of pages in a folded sheet as sheets which are too thick or too thin do not make a satisfactory section for binding. Printer's formes and binder's folding machines are largely standardized and as a result folded sheets are usually of 8, 16 or 32 pages, 12- or 24-page sheets being exceptional. The flat printed sheet may contain as many as 128 pages but folding machines convert such sheets into either eight individual 16-page folded sections or four sections each of 32 pages. Printed sheets of 64 pages or 32 pages are much used and slit and folded into lesser sheets by folding machines.

The printing size will be determined by the size of paper available and the machines on which the work will be printed and folded, the larger sizes being economic only for long runs. The various folding machines show great diversity in the pattern of the folds they produce hence it is essential that the sheets should be printed to the precise imposition demanded by the machine on which they will be folded. The procedure is made simple in trade practice by the use of *Book Impositions 1956*, q.v.

In general terms, anything which can be folded by machine can be folded by hand, but work which is being printed for hand-folding is normally printed in small-size sheets or alternatively cut by guillotine into its component sections before folding. (L. K.)

See also *folding machines.*

folding chases: a pair of chases used to lock up large many-page formes.

folding in gangs: folding in a machine which takes a large sheet and folds several sections at one operation. As it passes through the machine, the sheet is folded, cut into sections, the heads are slit, and the sections are delivered singly or inset.

folding machine: a machine for folding printed sheets for bookbinding. The first is thought to have been invented by the Englishman Blake about 1850. He built a machine for hand-feeding based upon the knife and roller method of making the fold. Present-day machines are based on one of two principles, viz. knife-folding or buckle-folding, and the two methods may be combined in a single machine.

In the knife-folder a blunt-edged knife is set

parallel with and above the slot formed by two rollers. The rollers are continuously revolving so that when a sheet of paper is placed over the rollers and the knife descends the paper is caught between the rollers and carried away by them, a fold being made where the knife made contact.

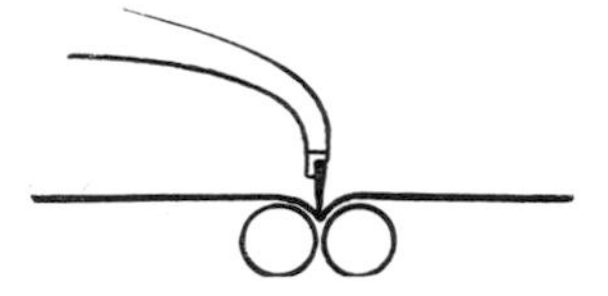

Principle of knife-folding

In practice the sheets are fed, one at a time, to stops either by hand or by mechanical feeders (see *feeders*) and carried by moving tapes beneath the knife where they are mechanically precisely positioned for folding. The knife having descended, the sheet, now with one fold in it, is carried by the rollers and tapes to a second unit of knife and rollers where a second fold is made and so on for the third and maybe fourth fold, the folded sheets being delivered into a stacker from which they are removed by hand. If any knife unit is at right-angles to the previous knife unit a fold at right-angles to the previous fold is made, but if the machine is constructed with the folding units parallel to preceding folds then parallel folds are made. If it is desired to slit the sheet into individual sections during folding, the sheet, when passing from one folding unit to the next, will travel through rotary slitters and the individual parts of the sheets will be conveyed to individual folding units. Thus a sheet printed with 64 pages can be slit into four parts producing four individual 16-page folded sections. Machines are normally provided with perforators which will perforate the bolts, thus avoiding creasing.

Buckle-folders work on an entirely different principle. The sheet is fed end on between a pair of continuously revolving rollers and the leading edge is guided between two closely spaced plates, the plane of the plates being at 45° to the plane of feeding. The plates are fitted with internal adjustable stops and when the leading edge of the sheet comes in contact with these stops further forward movement is arrested. The latter half of the sheet, however, is still being propelled forward by the rollers and, the sheet being already bent at 45°, buckles at the point of entry to the plates. The buckle is gripped between the lower of the aforementioned rollers and a third roller in contact with it and the buckle passes between these rollers, thus forming a fold. The portion of the sheet between the plates is by this action immediately withdrawn, leaving the mechanism clear for the next sheet. The sheet continues to be propelled by rollers and the folded edge may be deflected into a second and following that a third

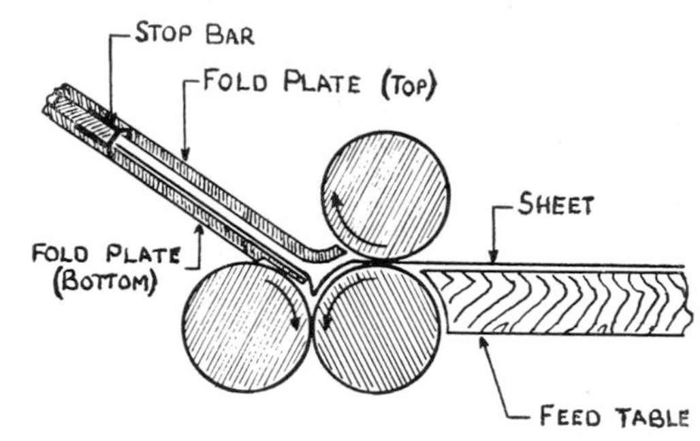

Principle of plate- or buckle-folding

plate and additional folds parallel to the first thus made.

Such machines frequently incorporate knife-folding units, the knives being used to make folds at right-angles to the parallel buckle-folds. As with knife-folding machines, perforators and slitters are incorporated for use at varying stages of folding.

In general it may be said that buckle-folders may be run at a rather higher speed than knife-folders, but knife-folders are usually favoured by book-binders as they are better adapted for dealing with a great diversity of papers. The simplest form of folding machine is one constructed to make one fold only but the largest knife-machines will fold a flat sheet of 128 pages and from it produce four 32-page folded sections, each of four folds. Buckle-folders, by means of the use of or the by-passing of a large number of plates and knives, in their most complex forms will produce almost any series of folds, but in general such machines are more used for the production of publicity matter than book work.

Camco knife-machine folding quad sheets and producing four 16-page sheets, as shown, or two 32-page folded sheets

Notable British manufacturers are Camco (Machinery) Limited of Letchworth and Cundall Folding Machine Company Limited of Luton, while the Dexter Folder Company is prominent in the U.S. (L.K.)

folding plate: an illustration printed on a page larger than those of the text it is to accompany, so that it must be given one or more folds before insertion.

folds: see *folding.*

Folger, Henry Clay, 1857–1930: a New York bibliophile who spent some forty years assembling a library of 20,000 volumes of Shakespeariana, early Elizabethan English literature, and various editions of Shakespeare's works including fifty first folios. He bequeathed his collection to the nation, and it is now kept in a special building in Washington, D.C.

foliation: the forerunner of pagination; only the recto sides of manuscripts or early printed books being numbered, usually in roman numerals. Leaf numerals were printed as early as 1470, Johannes da Spira of Venice being the first printer to do this.
See also *pagination.*

folio: 1. the book size resulting from folding a sheet with one fold, thus giving pages half the size of the sheet. To define fully the size the paper size also must be stated, e.g. *Crown folio.* In practice double-size paper folded twice, or quad-size paper folded three times would be used, thus producing the requisite folio size but in sections convenient for binding. Abbreviated as *Fo.,* or *fo.*
2. a leaf of paper or parchment numbered only on the front.
3. the number of a page (this is a loose usage of the term).
See also *blind folio, drop folio.*

follow copy: an instruction to the compositor indicating that the spelling and punctuation of a manuscript are to be followed, even if unorthodox, in preference to the *style of the house,* q.v. A well-known saying of Horace Greenley may be recalled: 'Follow copy even if it goes out of the window.'

Fomm, August: see *guillotine.*

font: a corruption of *fount,* q.v.

foolscap: a standard size of printing paper, $13\frac{1}{2} \times$ 17 in.

foot: 1. the margin at the bottom of a page; also the bottom edge of a book.
2. the undersurface of type.

footline: the last line of a page, particularly that containing folio or signature mark.

footnotes: short notes, printed at the foot of a page, to which the attention of the reader is drawn by textual reference marks. Footnotes should be set in type two sizes smaller than that used for the text.

footstick: a wedge of wood or metal placed along the foot of pages when locking them up, and secured in the chase by quoins.
See also *sidestick.*

fore-edge (pronounced *forage*): the outer edge of a book parallel to the back. Synonymous with *foredge.*

fore-edge margin: the outer margin of a page, parallel to the *backs,* q.v.

fore-edge painting: a water colour painted on the fanned out fore-edge of a book. When the painting is dry the edges are gilded or marbled in the normal way, so that the closed book shows no trace of the painting.
The decorating of the fore-edge with a painting may date back to 1530 when Thomas Berthelet bound for Henry VIII. At this time the fore-edge was treated as a solid panel for a heraldic or other motif in gold and colours. The originator of the idea of painting a design on the fanned out leaves, so that it was invisible when the book was shut, is unknown, though Samuel Mearne, binder to Charles II from 1660 to 1683, is thought to have employed one or more artists and binders who made such paintings. The first known *dated* disappearing fore-edge painting is on a Bible of 1651, where the painting of the Leigh arms is signed 'Lewis fecit, Anno Dom. 1653' (the Bible is in New York Public Library). The binding is in Mearne's cottage style, but the connection between Lewis and Mearne is only conjectural. Of important, but rare, examples of early 18th-century books decorated with fore-edge paintings is an edition of Horace in two volumes, published (1733–37) by John Pine. One of the subscribers to the work was the Spanish Prince of Asturia whose set bears his arms and scrolls painted under the fore-edge (since 1881 these volumes have been in Columbia University Library).
It was William Edwards of Halifax, however, who, about 1750, pioneered the art of painting landscapes on fore-edges; hitherto, floral scrolls and armorial bearings had been the subjects. He at first worked in monochrome—brown or grey—but later in a full range of colours. Portraits were also included, often flanking a landscape. Subjects depicted included the countryside, buildings, sports, and scenes based on the theme of the book decorated (e.g. Cowper's 'Poems' carrying a scene from John Gilpin's ride). The types of book most frequently embellished in

this way were Bibles and prayer-books, the classics, travel books, and poetry.

There are also double paintings, one scene made with the leaves fanned over to the right, and a second scene painted with them fanned to the left. This idea may have been originated by William Edwards since no example painted before 1785 is known, and most of the books with such fore-edges appear to have been done between that date and 1835 (i.e. the Edwards era).

Among the many other 19th-century London binders and publishers who made or commissioned fore-edge paintings should be mentioned Kalthoeber, J. Bohn, Walther, Thos. Gosden, Taylor & Hessey, John Whittaker, R. & J. Faulder, and Miss B. Currie, an employee of Rivière.

Although fore-edge paintings have been made for nearly 300 years, the delicacy and skill of the Edwards has only rarely been equalled and never excelled.

See also *Edwards of Halifax, Etruscan bindings.*

fore-stay: the frontal wooden support for the carriage of a hand-printing press. The rear of the carriage was secured to the *cheeks*, q.v.

forel bindings: early English bindings in which oak boards were covered with roughly dressed deerskins. They were made by monks in the 8th and 9th centuries.

foreword: introductory and often laudatory remarks to a work or about its author written by someone other than the author. The foreword will not normally be changed for successive editions. Cf. *preface* and *introduction.*

Forman Scholarship: see *Thomas Forman Scholarship.*

Formapex: the trade name of a paper-based resin-bonded laminate used for mounting blocks. It is claimed to be incompressible, flat, light, and stable, and is sold in heights suitable for Scan, original, and duplicate plates. Special cutters are needed for planing and cutting Formapex. Plates are adhered to the mounts with double-coated tissue tape. Used mounts can be cut up for furniture and spacing material.

format: 1. a loose indication of the size of a book, being based on the number of times the printed sheets have been folded.

See also *folio, quarto, octavo.*

2. the general appearance or style of a book, i.e. size, shape, quality of paper, type-face, binding. (This is a loose usage.)

forme: type matter and blocks assembled into pages and locked up in a chase ready for printing. The impression taken from it is a signature. A 'naked forme' consists of pages of type secured by page-cord; a 'dressed forme' is one of pages of type with furniture between and around them and the page-cord removed.

A special trolley used to move a complete forme

former: the enlarged model of a letter or other character used for making a steel punch.

Formschneider: the German term for a block-cutter. Before printing from movable type was invented the craft of block-cutting was well established in Germany, notably in such towns as Ulm and Augsburg where the cutters were organized into guilds. Due to a dispute between the new printers of the mid-15th century and the older cutters over the right to publish illustrations in books it was decided that while printers might publish illustrated works the actual cutting of the blocks they used must be done by an approved Formschneider. This may account for the technical superiority of the cuts in German incunabula over many of those printed elsewhere.

One of the most accomplished of these craftsmen was Jost de Negker (*c.* 1485–1544) who in 1508 was invited by Maximilian I to leave his native Antwerp and settle in Augsburg. Here he cut blocks of illustrations by Hans Burgkmair and Hans Schäufelein for the 'Theuerdank', 1517.

See also *Florentine woodcuts.*

forwarding: properly, the processes involved in the binding by hand of a book subsequent to cutting and up to the point of fitting on its cover or case: loosely, the stages (including covering) prior to decoration, lettering, and other finishing work. Cf. *finishing.*

forwarding sucker: a rubber suction device which assists in passing sheets of paper singly on to the feed board of a printing machine.

Fotomat: the matrix used in the *Intertype Fotosetter*, q.v. Each matrix has a transparent negative character fitted in its side.

Fotosetter: see *Intertype Fotosetter.*

foul case: a compositor's case in which types have been distributed into wrong compartments.

foul proof: a proof having many faults marked in it.

Foulis, Robert, 1707–76: one of Scotland's best known printers of the 18th century. He opened a bookselling business in Glasgow in 1741, and began printing in the same year. In 1743 he was appointed University Printer. His brother Andrew (1712–75) joined him in 1744. Mostly they published reprints of standard authors, plainly printed with no extraneous ornament, and soon established a reputation for their carefully edited editions of Greek and Latin classics. For these they used the types of Alexander Wilson. Their edition of Horace, 1744, and Homer, 1756–58, are considered among the finest ever printed.

After 1776 the firm was continued by Robert's son Andrew, who interested himself in *stereotype*, q.v.

founder's type: type cast by a typefounder for hand composition as distinct from that cast on Linotype, Monotype, Intertype, or Ludlow machines (the last two have square ems).

See also *fount scheme*.

foundry clump: lengths of type-high metal used at the sides and ends of a forme when a stereotype or electrotype is being made.

foundry proof: a proof pulled before the forme is sent to the foundry to be stereotyped or electrotyped. It accompanies the forme.

fount: a complete set of type characters of the same design and size, i.e. upper and lower case, numerals, punctuation marks, accents, ligatures, etc. A type family includes founts of roman, sloped roman, chancery italic, semi-bold, semi-bold condensed, sanserif, and greek.

fount case: a case used for extra sorts when there is no room in the ordinary case.

fount scheme: the assembly of mixed type-faces as sold by the typefounder to the printer. (Also known as *bill of type, bill of fount.*) These are made up into pages about 8 in. by 4 in., weighing about 9 lb. In his 'Typographia' J. Johnson states that letter founders call 3000 lower-case m's a bill.

The following table gives the proportions generally adopted by British foundries for supplying 1000 lb. of any fount of body letter. It corresponds to a fount of 12-point containing 4200 m's, with other letters in proportion.

Capitals	lb.	oz.	Lower Case	lb.	oz.
A	6	0	a	48	0
B	3	8	b	10	0
C	4	8	c	16	0
D	5	0	d	25	0
E	5	8	e	65	0
F	3	8	f	10	0
G	4	0	g	11	0
H	4	6	h	40	0
I	4	8	i	28	0
J	2	4	j	1	8
K	3	0	k	5	0
L	4	12	l	14	0
M	4	12	m	28	0
N	4	0	n	52	0
O	3	12	o	46	0
P	3	10	p	11	0
Q	2	0	q	3	0
R	4	0	r	30	0
S	4	0	s	36	0
T	5	8	t	38	0
U	3	4	u	23	0
V	3	0	v	8	0
W	5	8	w	18	0
X	2	0	x	2	8
Y	3	0	y	13	8
Z	0	14	z	1	0
Æ	0	12	æ	0	12
Œ	0	10	œ	0	9

Small Capitals

	lb.	oz.		lb.	oz.
A	2	0	O	1	4
B	1	3	P	1	3
C	1	8	Q	0	11
D	1	11	R	1	5
E	1	13	S	1	5
F	1	3	T	1	13
G	1	5	U	1	1
H	1	7	V	1	0
I	1	8	W	1	13
J	0	12	X	0	11
K	1	0	Y	1	0
L	1	9	Z	0	5
M	1	10	Æ	0	4
N	1	5	Œ	0	3½

fountain: see *ink fountain.*

four-colour process: see *colour separation.*

four-colour press: four-colour printing presses are now usual for much large quantity magazine printing. A four-colour flat-bed letterpress machine would be too cumbersome to be practical, but four-colour sheet-fed offset machines are coming increasingly into use. Four-colour rotary letterpress machines are widely used in America and a number of sheet-fed four-colour gravure machines are in use in Germany.

four-magazine mixer: a slug-casting machine equipped with four matrix magazines from which mixed setting can be done. (G.U.)

See also *Linotype.*

Fourdrinier machine: the standard paper-making machine, invented in France by *Nicolas Louis Robert* before 1798, and subsequently developed in England by *Bryan Donkin*, qq.v., on behalf of Henry and Sealy Fourdrinier after whom it is named. It was not perfected until 1806. During the years of experiment Didot (the first sponsor of Robert) came to England to supervise the work of Donkin. Most of the British patents, at first held by Didot's English relative, John Gamble, were bought by the Fourdriniers in 1804. In 1806 they patented an improved wire cloth (Pat. No. 1951). Due to defects in their patent rights, however, the Fourdriniers and Gamble went bankrupt in 1810. Later they continued activity, patenting various improvements, but never enjoyed the financial rewards their inventions merited. Sealy died in 1847, Henry in 1854.

The Fourdrinier machine was the first on which it was possible to make a continuous roll of paper, and its principles are used today. The fluid pulp is kept in a tank from which it flows on to a moving mesh belt. In moving, the pulp is strained, and by agitation the fibres are shaken into a web. This passes under the dandy roll, various suction boxes, steam-heated drying rollers, through the calender, to be wound on a reel, re-wound and cut as required. The speed of the machine varies from 200–1000 feet per minute. Cf. *cylinder machine.*

See also *dandy roll, dry end, wet end, wire.*

Fournier, Pierre-Simon, 1712–68: a distinguished French engraver and typefounder who, in 1745, designed an early *transitional* face, q.v. He was the author of an important treatise on type-design 'Manuel typographique', 2 vols, 1764–66, and is further remembered for the *Fournier point*, a unit of type measurement he established in 1737, one point being 0·0137 in. This was superseded in France by the *Didot point*, q.v.

See also *flowers.*

The modern Fournier type of the Monotype Corporation appeared in 1925 as Series 185; Barbou, a second Fournier type re-cut by Monotype, and only available in one size at C.U.P., was the face Stanley Morison had intended to be cut. This appeared in 1926 as Series 178. (See 'Tally of Types', C.U.P., 1953.)

foxed: said of book pages discoloured by damp which has affected impurities in the paper.

See also *bleaching paper.*

Foyle Prize for Poetry: an annual award of £250 made by W. A. Foyle for the best volume of poetry published in the United Kingdom. Inaugurated in 1949.

fractions: see *split fractions.*

Fraktur: 1. the German name for *black letter*, q.v.

2. a German black-letter type-face believed to have originated in Augsburg, *c.* 1510, from designs by Leonhard Wagner, based on the 15th-century lettre bâtarde. The first book to be printed in this type was the Prayer-Book of Maximilian I, dated 1513.

Fraktur types rapidly replaced roman in Germany where, in the late 16th century, foreign words set in roman appeared in pages of black-letter text, much as italic is used today to distinguish an occasional foreign word in an English text. Several attempts were made to popularize roman, unsuccessfully in the 18th century, for scientific literature in the 19th, and finally, by decree, in 1941.

See also *letters—forms and styles.*

frame: the cabinet containing cases of type, galley units, drawers, cupboards, bins for spacing, and a place for the compositor to work at.

See also *hand composition.*

A typical frame

Frankfurt Fair: a trade fair held at Frankfurt-am-Main each Lent and Michaelmas during the 16th and 17th centuries. Writing of it in 1574 Henri Estienne II said that here a prince could equip an army. Its interest within the scope of this work lies in the important book market which was part of the fair. Booksellers, bibliophiles' agents, and other buyers came from all parts of Europe. Until 1564, when the Augsburg bookseller Georg Willer issued a catalogue of new books on sale at the Frankfurt Fair, booksellers' catalogues were unknown and the only reliable means of knowing what was being published in Europe was to journey to Frankfurt. The first catalogue issued by the fair authorities was printed by Peter Schmidt in 1590. John Bill, buyer for Sir Thomas Bodley, issued an edition of the Frankfurt catalogue for the English public, the first appearing about 1618.

We also learn (from James Allestrye in 1653) that 'it is a very usual thing for the booksellers of Germany to send the titles of their books to be put in the catalogue before they are printed, so that at present they are not to be had' (a practice not unknown 300 years later).

In 1579 Kaiser Rudolf III established a censorship of books exhibited. Between 1661 and 1685 the unpopular bailiff Georg Friedrich Sperling pursued his duties as censor with such zeal and dishonesty that the Frankfurt book market lost popularity. Another factor which marked its decay from the mid-17th century was the growth of a public which preferred to read in the vernacular, and the barter system by which Latin books had been freely traded at Frankfurt could no longer flourish. The market for purely German books centred on Leipzig.

The Frankfurt book market has taken on a new lease of life in post-war Germany. It opened in 1949 under the auspices of the publishers and booksellers of Hesse, and since 1950 has been organized by the West German Publishers and Booksellers Associations (Börsenverein Deutscher Verleger- und Buchhändler-Verbände e.V.).

See also *Leipzig Fair*.

Franklin, Benjamin, 1706–90: one of the most eminent Americans who was printer, author, scientist, and statesman. After serving his apprenticeship in Boston, and also working in London with Samuel Palmer, he established himself as a master-printer in Philadelphia, 1728; his office developed into one of the leading printing offices of his day. He also gave active assistance in setting up printing offices in other cities. His interest in printing was lifelong, and even his Will began 'I, Benjamin Franklin, Printer....'

He instigated the building of the first copperplate printing press in America, and in 1785 erected a type-foundry in Philadelphia which operated for a few years.

Both the hand-press in use at that time and later platen presses were called *Franklin Press* after him. (G. U.)

Fraser, Alexander: the builder of a type-composing and distributing machine patented in 1872 in Edinburgh.

Frederick Niven Literary Award: an award of £100 made for the most outstanding contribution to some branch of literature by a Scottish author. It is awarded in memory of Frederick Niven, the novelist.

Fredericksen, C. W., 1823–97: an American businessman and book-collector who first assembled an important Shakespearian library, but later turned to early 19th-century poetry and especially Shelley, of whose letters he had no fewer than sixty.

free hand: the irregular and more quickly written form of *set hand* which was widely used in England from the 12th–16th centuries.

See also *set hand.*

french calf: calfskins used to cover the nap rollers of a lithographic printing machine.

French Cape Levant: a handsome morocco leather used for book covers, made from the skin of a large Cape goat. This is said to have a Levant grain which is larger than the small pin-head grain of ordinary morocco. It was extensively used by French master-binders, who produced beautiful results.

french fold: said of a sheet printed on one side only and then folded into a section with bolts uncut; the insides are blank.

See also *orihon.*

french folio, thin, smooth, sized paper, thicker than tissue, much used by pressmen for overlays and underlays in make-ready. (M. L.)

french furniture: large, hollow metal *quads*, q.v.

french headcaps: see *headcap.*

French illumination: in the 11th and 12th centuries illumination flourished in such centres as Chartres, Clairvaux, Limoges, Lyons, and Paris. Perhaps the most important single feature was the decorated initial, since the illustration of texts was restricted in extent and treatment.

Paris was the great centre of 13th-century French Gothic, much work being done in lay workshops, with more emphasis on fine craftsmanship than innovation. By the 14th century a secular iconography replaced the religious, largely due to the patronage of such wealthy noblemen as the *Duc de Berry*, q.v., and the growing popularity of fables, romances, and chronicles. The illuminators, freed from tradition, largely abandoned symbolism for poetic naturalism. The most beautiful Books of Hours of the Middle Ages were made in France for castles, not churches or monasteries; of these the 'Breviaire de Belleville' made in the atelier of Jean Pucelle (fl. 1320–50) was the first to depict the months with separate scenes, and with these the development of French landscape art may be said to have begun.

In the 15th century Italian and Flemish influences were important, the latter largely due to artists brought together by the Dukes of Burgundy.

See also *Channel School*.

french joints: in binding if the boards are set away from the joints a space is left into which the covering material is pressed, forming a gully. This is of particular advantage with heavy boards, and thick covering material such as buckram, which need this assistance to make a free-hinging joint. Synonymous with *grooved joints*, *sunk joints*. (L.K.)

French joint

french nick: an incision on the back of a type-body, i.e. on the lateral surface bordering the upper edge of the type-face. (G.U.)

french rule: a straight length of brass or type-metal rule which is divided in the middle by a diamond-shaped ornament.

french sewing: 1. the normal method of machine-sewing, i.e. without tapes.

2. in hand-sewing, a method of sewing a book without the usual frame, the sections being sewn at the edge of the binder's bench. The needle enters the first section at the kettle-stitch point and emerges at one or two points along the back. Loops are left for the needle to pass through when sewing the second section. The thread is now tightened and tied. As sewing proceeds the thread is connected to the previous section at these points.

french shell: a variety of marbled paper used in France in the 18th century.

See also *marbling*.

french three-line: a combination of lines used in the ornamentation of bindings in France, its feature being a fine double line accompanied by a single line. This linear motif was used, for example, in the *fanfare* style, q.v. (G.U.)

fret: a pattern made up of interlaced bands or fillets. Such patterns can be made up as type borders for page decoration, or tooled on a book cover.

friar: a white patch left on a forme due to imperfect inking. Cf. *monk*.

Friburger, Michael: see *Crantz, Martin*.

Friends of the National Libraries: a society formed in London, in 1931, to promote the acquisition by the National Libraries of printed books and manuscripts of historical, literary or archaeological importance, or photographic reproductions of these should they have left or be about to leave Britain. The British Museum and the National Libraries of Scotland and Wales are the primary beneficiaries, but university, municipal, or other libraries may also be assisted.

Over 100 libraries have received help since 1931, varying in extent from a contribution towards the purchase of the Holkham books for the British Museum, to a small grant towards the cost of family papers for the local collection of a provincial library.

A minimum subscription of one guinea is the membership fee, and more Friends are needed: enquiries should be sent to the British Museum.

frisket: a thin rectangular iron frame covered with brown paper and attached by a hinge to the upper part of the *tympan*, q.v. It is used to hold the sheet to the tympan and lift it off the forme after printing. The centre part of the brown paper is cut away over the printing area, the remainder preventing the chase and furniture soiling the sheet.

Froben, Johann, 1460–1527: a distinguished printer, pupil and successor of Johannes Amerbach (fl. 1477–1513), who worked in Basle. He employed scholars to edit the classical and humanistic texts he produced, notable among them being Erasmus of Rotterdam. He printed the first Greek New Testament. About 1518 he commissioned Hans Holbein for four years to design title-page borders and other decorations.

The business was continued by his son Hieronymus (1501–65) and grandson Ambrosius (1537–95).

front delivery: the delivery from a cylinder press of the printed sheet in such a way that it is brought forward in the direction of the cylinder motion with the impression side uppermost. This serves the dual purpose of facilitating constant supervision of the sheets and easy assembling of the pile. Front delivery is usual in two-revolution presses, but less so in stop-cylinder presses where the working of the machine presents certain construction difficulties if this is to be arranged. (G.U.)

front matter: an alternative name for the *preliminary matter*, q.v.

frontispiece: an illustration facing the title-page, either printed with the text or separately pasted or guarded into a book.

frothing: a possible trouble which may arise when coating paper. It results in minute unsurfaced dots on the finished sheet.

frotton printing: a method of taking an impression from type by rubbing the verso of a leaf laid upon it. This method was used before the invention of the press.

Fry, Joseph, 1728–87: a typefounder who, in 1764, established in Bristol a type-foundry which is in business today (*c.* 1768 it was moved to London). He was at first partnered by William Pine, a printer, but it was his son Dr. Edmund Fry (d. 1835) who from 1782 developed the business into one of the first rank.

Frye, Bartholomew: a bookbinder of Halifax, where contemporary records show him to have been working between 1809 (when he was a Freemason) and 1818. He may have been associated with William Edwards and was certainly skilled in the various Edwards styles. A copy of the Bible, printed in 1811 by C. Whittingham for Reeves, and now in Halifax Public Library, bears Frye's ticket and has an attractive fore-edge painting of a cathedral.

He also used transparent vellum painted panels inserted into morocco-covered boards. The combination of the two skins was probably done to counteract the tendency to warp of vellum used alone.

See also *Edwards of Halifax.*

Fugger, Raimund von, 1489–1535: a German merchant-prince and book collector of taste, whose 15,000 volumes are now in the Österreichische Nationalbibliothek, Vienna. His son *Johann Jakob* (1516–75) was also a bibliophile, and bought the library of Hartmann Schedel: the whole collection passed via Albert V of Bavaria to what is now the Bavarian State Library, Munich. Another son, *Ulrich* (1526–84), and also *Marcus von Fugger* (1529–97), were owners of important libraries. The family maintained a bindery at their Augsburg residence.

fugitive colours: colours or inks which are not permanent, and change or fade when exposed to light. (M.L.)

full bound: a book wholly covered in one material, usually leather; thus *full calf, full morocco,* etc. If in cloth, the term *full cloth* can be used. Cf. *half-bound.*

full colour: the rich black effect of a printed page which results when ample ink has been used on suitably chosen stock, as contrasted to the light grey effect produced when only little is used.

See also *tonal colour.*

full face: see *full on the body.*

full gilt: a book having all its edges gilded.

full on the body: a fount of capitals designed to cover the full size of the body.

See also *titling alphabet.*

full out: said of matter which begins flush with the margin. Cf. *indented.*

full point: a full stop.

full press: when printing was done in hand-presses, two men used to operate them, one to roll the ink, the other to put in the sheet and pull the impression: this was termed working on a full press. (M.L.)

furnish: the collective term for all the ingredients used together in any single variety of paper, i.e. esparto grass, chemical wood, rag, loading, etc. Percentages of each vary.

furniture: lengths of wood, plastic or metal used in a forme for making margins or filling large blank areas on a page. They are made to standard point widths and lengths and are less than type height. Duralumin is often used for lightness.

fusible: a relief (positive) image, cast in type metal in a hand-mould, made from a brass or phosphor-bronze matrix plate engraved with a letter or other character (in reverse).

This relief master letter is electroplated with nickel and copper to form the negative electro (character in reverse) which is trued up to provide the type matrix.

The foregoing is a stage in the preparation of a new type-face, or when making italic or script forms.

fusile types: an 18th-century expression for types made from molten lead poured into a mould.

Fust, Johann, fl. 1450–66: a merchant of Mainz who, between 1450 and 1455, advanced money to *Gutenberg,* q.v., to develop his invention of printing, for their mutual benefit. Fust later took over the business and entered into partnership with Peter Schöffer: together they issued in 1457 the famous and beautiful Psalter of which the red and blue initials were the first example of colour printing. It was also the first printed book to contain a colophon giving printer, place of printing, and date. The considerable time the printing of the Psalter must have taken, and the previous association of Fust with Gutenberg, justify the assumption that the latter must have worked on the preparatory stages.

The 48-line Bible they issued in 1462 was the first printed Bible to bear a date.

Fust died from the plague when on a visit to Paris in 1466.

See 'Der Prozess Fust gegen Gutenberg', Wiesbaden, 1954.

ADDENDA

Film-Klischee: a process devised by Film-Klischee GmbH, Munich, for the making of half-tone blocks by the swelled gelatine principle. It was introduced to the British trade in 1957.

The Film-Klischee base, which will become the printing block, is a gelatine film 10 thou. thick. A high-quality screened negative is exposed in contact with it. This is developed in normal developer, fixed in a hypo solution, and washed first in water and then formaldehyde. At this stage the film is in the form of a positive transparency, without relief. Immersion in a special solution causes the undeveloped (clear) areas of the transparency to swell. Washing in water follows. Finally, washing in methyl alcohol causes the swelled parts of the film to shrink and sink below the level of the developed (image) area. The film is now in positive relief. Adhesive is used to mount it to a supporting plate of metal or plastic, flat or curved. It can also be moulded into a stereo.

Fine etching, required for work of the highest quality, is not possible, nor is it suitable for line work. The film is stable, long lasting, and has good ink-transferring qualities. It is cleaned with normal solvents.

Friedenspreis des deutschen Buchhandels: established in 1950, being an annual award of ten thousand marks made to a writer of any nationality who is considered to have contributed by his work and way of life to peace and freedom amongst men. The award is sponsored by the West German book trade and is presented at the annual Frankfurt Fair. Past winners have included Schweitzer, Burchhardt, and Thornton Wilder. The 1958 winner was Karl Jaspers.

G

Gaco: the name of a proprietary polyvinyl photo-resist for the sensitization of magnesium plates. It was announced in 1950 by the Jones Graphic Products Co. of Albuquerque, New Mexico.

The plate is first scrubbed with a preparation of pumice and ammonium dichromate solution, and then flowed with Gaco solution. The coating is dried in a whirler. After exposure, the plate is developed in an aqueous solution of logwood extract, and sprayed with water. The image is fixed in a mixture of chromic acid and a wetting agent. It is then rinsed, dried, and burnt-in for five minutes at a temperature of 450–475° F. Prior to etching, the plate is freed from scum and rinsed. Gaco resist is recommended when preparing plates for the *Dow-Birmetals Process*, q.v.

Galetzka, Ambrosius, fl. ?: the inventor of an offset reproduction process reminiscent of the *Bassist process*, q.v. Screen transparencies are made by copying on material consisting of cellulose-gelatined and copper-coated glass treated with a sensitized preparation. After copying, the released copper is removed, and the remaining dots can be etched rather like a half-tone block. Galetzka also invented *ambrogal printing*, an offset process reminiscent of American aquatone printing. Celluloid sheets coated with a layer of cellulose derivate are sensitized by preparing them in a 3% solution of ammonium dichromate, and copied under screen or slot negatives. After developing, a sheet is obtained, suitable for lithographic printing, in which the dots of the image are sunk in a water-absorbent layer. (G.U.)

galley: 1. a long sheet bearing a proof of unpaged type composition. A subsequent intermediate stage between galley proofs and page proofs is *page on galley* for which the type has been broken up into pages but is still not imposed. This stage is not, however, customary unless the setting is difficult.

The earliest proof sheets of which fragments still exist were pulled about 1458, but galley proofs as now used were an early 19th-century innovation.

See also *proof.*

2. the steel tray, open at one end, on which set-up type-matter is placed and made up into pages. Type on the galley can be corrected more conveniently than elsewhere.

Galley Club: a London club, revived in 1955 from a former club of this name, for the study of all aspects of book production. It is open to persons employed or interested in the various relevant trades (printing, blockmaking, paper-making, and binding, as well as publishers, typographers, jacket designers, and artists), and exists to promote social contact between those engaged in book production.

galley press: a small press on which proofs are pulled in long strips or *galleys*, q.v.

galley proof: any proof taken of type-matter while it is still on the galley, before it is made up into pages. (M.L.)

Gally press: a platen machine built by an American, J. Merrit Gally, in 1869; it was the first large printing press to have a cylindrical inking device, and to have lateral motion of both the vertical bed and platen. It was imported into Europe about 1880 by Schelter & Gieseke of Leipzig, who gave it the name Phoenix. For the principle of construction see *platen press.*

See also *König, Friedrich.* (G.U.)

galvanic: the name of various processes based on the effect of a direct current in an electrolytic bath. The name derives from the Italian scientist Luigi Galvani (1737–98). Hence *galvanic etching*, the etching of a metal plate (block or photogravure forme) by inserting it as an anode in a galvanic bath. Copper is very suitable for etching in this way, as is steel, but the galvanic etching of zinc is difficult due to the disturbing effect of sludge. (G.U.)

See also *nickel plating.*

Gamble, John, fl. 1801: the man responsible for the introduction into England of Nicolas Louis Robert's paper-making machine, later to be known as the *Fourdrinier*, q.v.

See also *Robert, Nicolas Louis.*

Garamond, Claude, d. 1561: a 16th-century French typefounder who worked for, among others, Robert Estienne. He was the first to cut a face in which roman and italic types were treated as belonging to one fount. He was also the pioneer of italic capitals. For his fount of old-face letters, cut between 1530–40, he is now best known; these were modelled on the type cut by Griffo for Manutius. The modern version of Garamond, based on the roman of Jean Jannon of Sedan, 1621, is seen to best effect on antique papers.

See also *grecs du roi.*

garter: the band or ring which secured the *hose*, q.v., of a hand printing press.

gas black: a black pigment for printing ink, produced by burning gas without sufficient air for combustion. Thick soot is deposited on metal cylinders in very much the same way as lampblack from oil. Gas black is practically pure carbon. (M. L.)

Gascon: see *Le Gascon.*

gathering: 1. the process of assembling in their proper order the folded sections of a book. This can be done by hand (when a revolving table with the sections

Table for hand-gathering (*Krause, Leipzig*)

Mechanical gatherer (*Sheridan, New York*)

piled in sequence helps) or on a large mechanical gatherer, the latter being usual in big modern binderies.

2. an alternative name, used by bibliophiles, for a *section, signature*, or *quire*, qq.v. (With G. U.)

gauffered edges: see *goffered edges.*

gauge: a piece of wood or metal (reglet, slug, or brass rule) used to determine a measure of any kind, to preserve uniform length of pages, width of margin, etc. (M. L.)

gauge-pin: a flat pin or metal device for use on the platen of a press to hold the sheet in position. (M. L.)

Ged, William, 1690–1749: the goldsmith of Edinburgh who invented a form of *stereotype*, q.v.

gel: the gelation or drying of printing ink on paper; this is by oxidation, evaporation, and penetration.

gelatine printing: gelatine is a refined form of glue and is used for many purposes in printing. It is the basis of the process known as the hectograph, by which anything written with copying ink, after being transferred to a sheet of gelatine, may again be transferred from the gelatine to paper. Several processes of photo-gelatine printing, known as albertype, collotype, heliotype, etc., are much like lithography, a coating of gelatine upon a sheet of glass or metal being used instead of the lithographic stone. (M. L.)

gem: the name of a former size of type, approximately 4-point.

Gemini, Thomas, fl. 1545–60: a London printer who is remembered as a pioneer in England of copperplate engraving, his 'Compendiosa totius anatomiae', 1545, being illustrated in this way.

Genoud, Claude: see *stereotype.*

Gering, Ulrich, d. 1510: the associate of Crantz and Friburger in establishing the first press in France. He also worked alone, his most notable production being the Paris Missal of 1497.

Gertrude Page Fund: a fund established by the late Gertrude Page to assist authors and journalists in times of temporary need, particularly when this is due to illness. Grants, which never exceed £30, are made by the Society of Authors.

Gesamtkatalog der Wiegendrucke: an author catalogue of incunabula which gives the location of all copies of a work when fewer than ten are believed to exist. Publication of this German work began in Leipzig in 1925; it is not yet completed. Abbreviated as *GKDW* or *GKW.*

Gesellschaft der Bibliophilen: the principal bibliophilic society in Germany, founded in 1899 at the instigation of Fedor von Zobeltitz (1857–1934). It is the oldest of its kind in Germany. Zobeltitz was concerned at the lack of organized and informed interest in rare and beautiful books, and worked hard to remedy this. In 1897 he issued 'Zeitschrift für Bücherfreunde' as a means of stimulating a wider knowledge of books.

The society now publishes 'Imprimatur', an annual journal for bibliophiles and typophiles.

Gesner, Conrad, 1516–65: of Zürich, a professor of physics, naturalist, and doctor of medicine. In addition to numerous writings on natural history and medicine, he wrote a Greek dictionary (Basle, *c.* 1541), and compiled one of the first bibliographies, 'Bibliotheca universalis', 3 vols., Zürich, 1545–49 (with appendix, 1555), an immense biographical dictionary of Latin, Greek, and Hebrew writers and books.

Gesta Romanorum: an anthology of classical anecdotes of ancient Rome. The first collection, in Latin, appeared in the early 14th century. Until the 16th century the work was a popular source-book for preachers and writers. The first translation into English, by Wynkyn de Worde, appeared *c.* 1510.

get in: to set copy in less space than estimated. Also to set type very close, or to use thin spacing so that the matter will fit within required limits.

ghost: a printing fault seen on the printed sheet as the image of a line of type, or of a block in the forme, which shows on a solid block. This occurs when badly set rollers repeat on the solid block.

Ghotan, Bartholomaeus: a German printer who first worked in Magdeburg and Lübeck, moving to Stockholm in 1486, where he printed five works of which a Missal for Strängnäs, 1487, was the most important. In 1493 he went to Russia to establish a printing press, but is said to have been robbed there of all he possessed, and he finally drowned in Russia some time before 1496. (G.U.)

giggering: polishing a blind impression on a leather binding by rubbing a short tool in it.

gilder's tip: see *tip*.

gilding rolls: in bookbinding, brass rolls faced with ornamental designs, used for gold tooling. (M.L.)

Gill, Eric, 1882–1940: an English artist, engraver, typographer, type-designer, sculptor, and philosopher, whose influence on contemporary book production has been profound and world wide. His most famous type-face, Perpetua, which is in use throughout the world, was designed and cut in 1927–28. Perpetua became a family—light, medium, bold—as did his other equally well-known design commissioned by Monotype in 1927, Gill Sans. A less well-known book-face was Joanna, 1930, which he described as 'an attempt to design a book-face free from all fancy business'.

In 1934 Gill designed a special type for the printing of Sterne's 'Sentimental Journey' for the Limited Editions Club of New York. This alphabet became the basis of Linotype's Pilgrim face which appeared in 1953. See also *St Dominic's Press*.

See E. R. Gill, 'Bibliography of Eric Gill', Cassell, 1953.

gilt after rounding: synonymous with *gilt solid*, q.v.

gilt edges: book edges which have been covered with gold leaf. For this binding process the trimmed book is put in a simple screw press (see illustration) where the edges are shaved in order to obtain as smooth a surface as possible. The surface is then primed with paste and Armenian bole and polished with paper shavings or something similar. A diluted solution of albumen or gelatine is spread on as a medium, and then the gold leaf is applied (laying on). After a short period for drying glazing is done with a burnisher, if necessary at first through waxed paper and then directly on the edges. Different qualities of book paper call for slight variations of treatment. It is usual to dust the sheets with talcum to prevent them sticking together. Abbreviated as *g.e.*

For varieties of gilt edges see under *bookbinding styles and binding features.* (G.U.)

Edge gilding in a hand-press with extended support. On the table are burnishers, gold cushion, press lever, etc.

gilt solid: said of a fore-edge which has been gilded after the book has been rounded: special semicircular burnishers are required. The alternative is to gild it flat. Also known as *gilt after rounding.* (G.U.)

gilt top: a book having the top only gilded. Abbreviated as *g.t.*, *g.t.e.*, or *t.e.g.*

The burnishing of 'gilt solid' edges

Giolito, Gabriel, fl. 1539–78: the most influential of an important family of Venetian publisher-printers who was associated with the development and use of flowers, head-pieces, and decorated title-pages. Many of his books were printed in italics, and reprints of Ariosto, Boccaccio, Dante, and Petrarch, together with translated classics and works in Spanish, were among the *c.* 850 he issued.

Giornale della Libreria: the official bibliography of the Italian book trade, prepared by the Associazione Italiana degli Editori. It is based on publishers' announcements, and also gives domestic and foreign book-trade news.

girdle book: a book which had a leather cover almost like a bag, enabling monks and clergy to carry and protect their breviaries. The leather cover extended beyond the limits of the book itself, and could either be fixed to the girdle or gathered into a knot for carrying by hand. (Illustrated under *bookbinding*.)

girts: two leather straps encircling a barrel (or windlass) underneath the *plank*, q.v., of a hand printing press. The straps were attached to the *rounce*, q.v., the turning of which caused the forme to be moved under the platen for an impression to be made.

Giunta: a famous Italian family of printers and publishers who worked in Venice from 1489, and in Florence from 1497 until the middle of the 16th century; there were also branches in Lyons, Rome, London, Burgos, and Salamanca. The printer's mark of the Giunta family, a Florentine lily, is reproduced under *device*, q.v.

Lucantonio Giunta (1457–1538), noted for an Italian version of the Bible illustrated by nearly 400 woodcuts, was the most famous of the family and founder of the Venetian house. Numerous Venetian printers worked for him, notable among them being *Johannes da Spira*, q.v.

Philippus (1450–1517), a brother, established the Florentine premises from which he first issued Greek and Latin classics. The Lyons branch, founded in 1520 by Jacques Giunta (1486–1546), specialized in law, medicine, and theology.

GKDW or **GKW:** the abbreviation for '*Gesamtkatalog der Wiegendrucke*', q.v.

GL: a bibliographer's abbreviation, used in catalogues and lists, to indicate that a foreign book, not German, Scandinavian, or Dutch, is printed in *gothic letter*. Cf. *BL*.

glair: an adhesive mixture of egg white (albumen) and vinegar, a thin coating of which is applied to a book cover before blocking or finishing in gold leaf. It causes the gold to adhere permanently to the book when a heated tool or die stamp is impressed upon it.

glassine: a translucent glazed paper occasionally used for jackets.

glazed morocco: goatskin which has been polished and flattened by calendering.

glazed roller: a lithographic roller particularly suitable for short runs of colour work, as it may be quickly washed for re-use. A *nap roller*, q.v., is given several coats of hard-drying ink, each being allowed to dry before applying the next.

See also *composition roller*.

gloss: 1. a word of explanation inserted in the margin or text of a book in order to clarify a foreign or difficult passage, e.g. an edition of the Iliad set with an interlinear English translation may be referred to as 'with glosses'. In strict usage a gloss is not synonymous with a free translation; the former is a word by word rendering into a second language, preserving the order of the first.

2. the light reflectance of paper. The machine finishing of paper by pressure under rolls imparts a slight gloss. Gloss can be measured by various instruments. Cf. *smoothness*.

gloss ink: a printing ink consisting of a synthetic resin base and drying oils. Such inks dry quickly, without penetration, and are suitable for use on coated papers in both letterpress and lithographic printing.

glossary: an alphabetically arranged sequence of unfamiliar, little used, or technical terms together with explanations of them. It is thus to be distinguished from a *dictionary*, q.v., which embraces all the words of a language.

Glossographers or glossators, as compilers of glossaries are known, were active in Greece in the 4th century B.C. Somewhat later the law books of Justinian attracted writers of alphabetically arranged *glossae nomicae*. These were cumulated in the 12th century as the *Glossa ordinaria*.

Bilingual glossaries, e.g. of Greek explanations to Latin texts, date back to the 6th century A.D., as do interpretations into non-classical languages. Biblical and medico-botanical glossaries continued to be written until the 14th century.

In England, early manuscripts were glossed either in Latin or Anglo-Saxon, and the glossaries of several manuscripts in a monastic library would be brought together as a *glossarium*. Such a compilation is the 'Corpus Glossary', which was probably written about 725 and is now in Corpus Christi College, Cambridge. It contains an alphabetical sequence of over 2000 words or *lemmata*.

See also *concordance*, *encyclopaedia*, *index*, *lexicon*, *vocabulary*.

glue: see *adhesives*.

gluing-up: a stage in the binding of a book after sewing, nipping, and cutting, but prior to rounding and backing. The object is to cause glue to penetrate to a limited degree between the sections, thereby strengthening the effect of sewing. The hand method is now largely superseded by special gluing-up machines. It is important that gluing-up, rounding, and backing all be completed before the glue sets hard.

See also *pasting*.

glyphography: a process for making letterpress printing blocks with designs in relief. The design is engraved on to a waxed copper plate and dusted with powdered graphite. The surface is then used to make an electrotype.

Godfray, Thomas, fl. 1510–32: a London printer, considered the first in England to receive an exclusive patent for printing a book. This was for 'The History of King Boccus', printed 'at the coste and charge of Dan Robert Saltwode, monk of saynt Austens of Canterbury', 1510.

goffered edges: the gilt edges of a book which have been decorated by the finisher who uses heated tools to indent a small repeating pattern in them. The style was popular in the 16th and 17th centuries. Also called *chased edges* or *gauffered edges*.

gold: the traditional material for the decoration of books and manuscripts. From the 4th–11th centuries, when first used, powdered gold contained in an adhesive medium was painted on to the surface to be embellished; in the 12th century a method was found of affixing gold in leaf form to a prepared surface.

See also *Armenian bole*, *blocking foils*, *dutch leaf*, *gold blocking*, *gold leaf*, *illumination*, *oriental leaf*, *palladium*.

gold bindings: book bindings of which the boards were overlaid with panels of thinly beaten gold, richly chased and often inlaid with silver, enamel, or jewels. These superb examples of the medieval goldsmith's art (as distinct from the binder's) were made as early as the 7th century for wealthy monasteries or churches to enclose their more valuable manuscripts.

gold blocking: the stamping of a design on a book cover, using a heated die or block in a press, and gold leaf. Cf. *gold tooling*.

gold-blocking press: a bookbinding machine for press gilding and other cover decoration. In principle the press consists of two smooth plates which can be brought together. A die is fixed on the upper one and the book cover rests on the lower plate, in most cases on a matrix (counter punch) built up of millboard.

Hand-operated gold-blocking press

The upper plate is heated by gas or electricity, the temperature being controlled by a thermostat. Both plates are exchangeable so that a die or matrix setting can be preserved for future use.

In the *hand-press* commonly used the lower plate moves towards the fixed upper plate, pressure being applied by a knee-joint construction.

There are *machine presses* of various design. In some cases the lower plate remains stationary while the upper one moves; in other makes the lower plate protrudes at first in front of the press for feeding, being then inserted and pressed upwards by the force of the machine.

Both hand and machine presses can be adapted for the automatic laying of foil on reels. There are machine presses with built in inking devices, and also entirely automatic presses which feed the covers independently from a magazine and perform the printing.

The Victoria Hercules mechanically operated gold-blocking press

Device for feeding and laying on gold foil in a blocking press

The first die-stamping and gilding press for bookbinding purposes was built in 1832 by Thomas de la Rue in London. An improved model was built in 1857 by Karl Krause of Leipzig. (G.U.)

gold knife: a flat blade, sharpened on both sides, used by bookbinders for cutting gold leaf. (M.L.)

gold leaf: the traditional material used on books for spinal lettering, edge gilding, and gold tooling. For beauty and durability of impression it has not been superseded by any of the cheaper substitutes found today. The thickness of leaf used by binders is four millionths of an inch, and its preparation is a highly skilled craft. Pure gold is melted with small amounts of silver and copper and cast into bars of $\frac{3}{4}$-carat silver and copper with 23$\frac{1}{4}$-carat gold. The bars are rolled into ribbons which are cut into 2-in. squares. These are interleaved with 4-in. squares of Montgolfier paper. A pile of about two hundred layers is made and encased with two bands of parchment, the whole being known as a *cutch.* The pile is hand-beaten until the gold pieces are extended to 4-in. squares. The gold is quartered and placed between vellum squares, a pile of eight hundred skins and leaves being formed. A second beating is given in a *shoder*. After another quartering of the gold the pieces are interleaved with gold-beater's skin to form a *mould* and beaten for four hours. The resulting gold leaves are made up into rouged tissue-paper books, twenty-five pieces per book. One ounce of gold will make about 250 sq. ft. of leaf.

The gold-beater's skins used for the mould are made from ox intestines, Frederick Puckridge and Nephew being the only firm in Britain to prepare them. A mould contains eleven hundred skins.

While much leaf is made in the traditional way described, a mechanical hammer has been devised to eliminate hand-beating, and a method has been found to produce gold in roll form with the same consistency as the leaf but without beating.

The British firm of G. M. Whiley Ltd., using hand and mechanical methods, produces most of the gold leaf used by bookbinders.

See also *skewings.*

gold size: see *bronzing size.*

gold tooling: the pressing of a design, with heated tools applied by hand, upon gold leaf which is laid on the cover of a book. The cover is first marked up with the main lines of the design, coated with glair, then the gold leaf is laid on, and finally the impression is made. In some cases a blind impression is first made before coating with glair to achieve a clearer result when executing intricate patterns. In recent times imitation gold leaf (80% copper with 20% zinc) or foil is often used: this carries its own adhesive for which heat is also required, but glair is not necessary; while primarily used for machine blocking, its disadvantages are a lack of sharpness and a tendency to tarnish quickly, so that it is best avoided for hand tooling.

Gold tooling was introduced into Europe in the late 15th century, being probably of Moorish origin, and coming via Spain to Italy. Gilders from Persia and Turkey were working in Venice at that time, but in their technique the design was first blind-stamped before applying liquid gold paint with a brush. Thomas Berthelet may have introduced the art into England; from 1530 he was printer to Henry VIII and later to Edward VI. Workmen in his employ used white leather, deerskin or vellum, copying their designs from Italian examples, and using doublures.

See also *tooling*, *Whittinton*.

Golden Cockerel Press: a famous private press founded in 1920 at Waltham St Lawrence, Berks, by Harold M. Taylor, and continued in 1924 by Robert Gibbings. They aimed at making finely produced books available to a wide public at reasonable prices. Such eminent artists as Eric Gill, Robert Gibbings, Osbert Lancaster, the Nash brothers, and Blair Hughes-Stanton were commissioned to illustrate them. The press was acquired in 1933 by Christopher Sandford of the Boar's Head Press, who at varying times was assisted by Owen Rutter, Francis Newberry and Michael Samuelson.

The press continues to publish, but its books are no longer printed by hand.

Golden Legend: see *Legenda aurea.*

Goldschmidt, Ernst Philip, 1887–1954: a scholarly antiquarian bookseller, born in Vienna, who from 1924 had his business in Bond Street, London.

He will be remembered for his great work on (and financial support of) the '*Gesamtkatalog der Wiegendrucke*', q.v., also for his writings on the Renaissance book.

good: said of composed type which, after printing off, may be required for further use and is not to be distributed.

See also *blocked up*, *dead matter*, *kill*, *live matter*.

goose: an abbreviation of *waygoose*, q.v.

Gordon press: a popular platen press invented by George P. Gordon about 1858. (M. L.)

Gorleston Psalter: an early 14th-century English Psalter, probably written by or for Augustinian friars of Norfolk. This example of East Anglian illumination is notable for the finely drawn grotesque creatures and agricultural scenes which fill the margins, for its delicacy, and light colours. It is also an early manuscript to be decorated with heraldic devices. The work includes a whole-page Crucifixion scene added later.

The Psalter is now in the British Museum.

Gospel: a book containing the four versions of the life and teachings of Christ as written by the four evangelists.

gothic: 1. a book hand evolved in northern Europe in the 12th century; letters had a strong vertical stress with angular extremities.

2. formerly a name for black-letter or Old English type-faces, but now sometimes loosely used to include all sanserif faces. Among varieties of gothic in use in 15th-century Europe were *bastarda*, *lettre de forme*, and *lettre de somme*, qq.v.

See also *letters—forms and styles*.

Gothic illumination: the Gothic era of manuscript painting in England, particularly in East Anglia during the 13th and 14th centuries, was characterized by a softening of the 12th-century Romanesque style. Basically, the latter was the art of draughtsmen, 13th-century Gothic that of painters. Thus pattern and flow of line were superseded in importance by modelling of form, greater naturalism and range of colour. French Gothic influenced English art, and their interdependence caused the name Channel School to be given to work done in southern England and northern France.

Complete Bibles and Apocalypses were the favourite works, and the Jesse Tree with the Virgin and Child, or Christ alone, was often depicted. Characteristic features were the use of gold, lake, and blue as main colours, historiated initials and diapered backgrounds. Gold-edged bands of colour led from historiated initials up or down the margin, and along the top or bottom of the page. Scrolls and dragons enlivened earlier borders; leaves, grotesques, birds, drolleries, and heraldic shields being introduced later. Centres were Canterbury, Rochester, Peterborough, Salisbury, York, and St Albans.

In later Gothic art much attention was paid to small-scale background detail, and in the early 15th century lightly drawn borders of buds, leaves, and flowers are typical. By the end of this century the delicate tinted grisaille drawings popular in France began to appear in England. In general, continental work now influenced English illumination until the 16th century, when the printed book eclipsed the written and painted manuscript.

gótico-mudéjar: a style of bookbinding done in Catalonia from the 13th to 15th centuries. The lines of the design were drawn on dampened leather with a blunt tool and formed compartments for the main decoration which was made by impressing small stamps of real or imaginary birds, flowers, fishes, or other emblems. No gold was used. Cf. *mudéjar bindings*.

gouache: opaque water-colour for which the pigments are mixed with white lead, bone ash, or chalk.

Gouache colours were used for the illumination of manuscripts, particularly in the 14th and 15th centuries.

Goudy, Frederic W., 1865–1947: the foremost of recent American type-designers, and founder in 1903 of the Village Press, Park Ridge, Illinois, which later moved to Marlborough, New York. He also established the journal 'Ars Typographica'. Among the more important of the hundred or so types he designed are Village, 1903, Forum, 1911, Kennerly, 1911, and the old-face Goudy family, 1921. The reader is referred to 'A Half-century of Type Design and Typography, 1895–1945', 2 vols., New York, 1947.

gouge: a brass finishing tool for impressing curved lines on book covers.

Gough, Richard, 1735–1809: an antiquarian, author, and collector who bequeathed to the Bodleian his important library of topographical works.

Grabhorn Press: an American private press founded in 1919 by Robert and Edwin Grabhorn of San Francisco. Much of their hand-done work was for other publishers and book clubs in California.

Gradual: a book containing the Song of Ascents, i.e. the antiphon between the Epistle and the Gospel sung at the foot of the altar steps in services of the Roman Catholic Church.

Graesse, Johann Georg Theodor, 1814–85: a German librarian and bibliographer. In 1843 he was appointed librarian to the Elector of Saxony. He is remembered for his history of world literature, 1837–59, and more widely for his bibliography 'Trésor de livres rares et précieux', 7 vols., Dresden, 1859–69.

Grafton, Richard, d. 1572: a London printer who, in association with Edward Whitchurch, supervised the printing in Antwerp by Jacob van Meteren of the Matthews Bible. This had been prepared from the versions of Tyndale and Coverdale by the Royal Patentee, Thomas Matthews (pseudonym for John Rogers) in 1537. They also completed during 1538–39 the printing in London of the first Great Bible which had been begun in Paris in 1537 by François Regnault, who worked under the supervision of Coverdale.

Grafton was King's Printer of Acts and Statutes to Henry VIII and Edward VI, and held, with Whitchurch, licences for service books and Latin primers.

grain direction: the direction in which the majority of fibres lie in a sheet of paper. After the pulp flows on to the moving web of a paper-making machine the fibres tend to lie parallel with one another in the direction of movement. On damping with adhesives, paper swells to a greater degree across the grain than in the grain direction, and it is of importance in bookbinding for this and other reasons that the paper used for the text should be made so that the grain direction runs from head to tail in the finished book. The terms *grain direction* and *machine direction* are synonymous.

grained leather: tanned skin on which the natural grain has been worked up to raise and accentuate it. The grain side is that on which the hair grows. Graining is also artificially produced by stamping the skin with engraved metal plates.

graining: the giving of a moisture-retaining surface to a lithographic plate by abrasion. A smooth plate is placed in a trough and covered with a double layer of glass or steel marbles (the latter are better since they last longer and give a finer grain). An abrasive is added. Mechanical agitation produces the required surface. Such plates may be used many times; after each, the ink is cleaned off and the old image destroyed by immersion in a chemical bath: it is then grained as above.

Among abrasives used are carborundum, aluminium oxide, crushed garnet, or crushed quartz.

graining boards: boards or metal plates used by the binder to produce a diced effect on covers. The boards have a pattern in relief of parallel lines running diagonally.

grammes per square metre: see *paper substance*.

Grandjean, Philippe, 1666–1714: the famous Parisian type-engraver who in 1691 refurbished the *grecs du roi* cut by Garamond in 1544. In 1693 he began the famous series of roman and italic types known as *romain du roi*, q.v. These were continued by his pupil Alexandre, and completed by Louis Luce in 1745. The Grandjean romain du roi was the first face to which a lateral trait was added to the stem of the lower-case l, a distinctive mark of all subsequent types cut for the Imprimerie Royale as a deterrent to piracy.

Grange Press: a private printing press established near Darlington about 1768 by George Allan who issued numerous books and pamphlets on the history and antiquities of Durham.

Grangerized: any book in which blank leaves are left for the addition by the purchaser of illustrations to his taste. The term derives from James Granger, (1723–76), copies of whose 'Biographical History of England', 5 vols., 1769–74, were bound up with blank leaves in this way, although the idea had been used in the 17th century, notably by Ferrar.

Plate-graining machine

Sand-blaster for graining offset plates

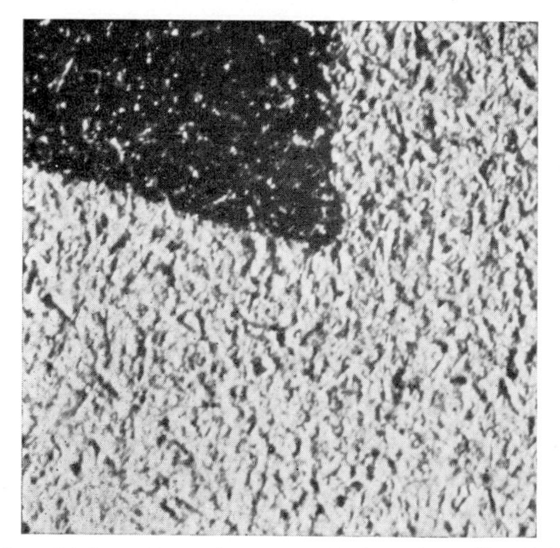

Magnified section of a grained plate for offset lithography

Granjon, Robert, fl. 1545–88: a type-designer, punch-cutter, and printer who was probably the son of Jean Granjon. He worked in Paris, Lyons (1557–62), Antwerp, and Rome. He is remembered for his French italic known as *civilité*, q.v., for his flowers, and for his long association with Plantin.

graphite: a crystalline, allotropic form of carbon made up of hexagonal laminas. It occurs in a natural state and is mined in Siberia, Germany, Austria, the U.S.A., Ceylon, and elsewhere. It is also produced by heating anthracite in an electric furnace (Acheson graphite).

In galvanoplastics graphite is used for making matrices electrically conductive, being brushed on by hand or machine. Colloidal graphite solutions (extra finely proportioned mixtures) are used as lubricants. (G. U.)

graver: a steel tool used for incising designs in wood blocks or metal plates, or for adding detail to etched plates.

For illustration see *burin.*

gravure: see *photogravure.*

gravure à la poupée: see *colour printing.*

great primer: the name for a former size of type, now standardized as 18-point. Early printers often referred to this size as *Bible Text* from its use in Bibles.

Great Totham Press: a private press established *c.* 1831 near Malden, Essex, by Charles Clarke, 1806–80, from which he issued reprints of tracts and extracts from rare books in addition to numerous broadsides.

grecs du roi: the cursive greek face cut and cast at the instigation of Francis I of France by Claude Garamond, *c.* 1542, after the script of Angelos Vergetios of Crete. It featured a large number of ligatured letters and contractions. Robert Estienne printed in 1543 his 'Alphabetum Graecum' as a specimen of the new type. Revised versions followed in 1546, 1550, and 1691.

Greek fret: a style of ornament much used in Greek art, characterized by angular alternations and interlocking lines in various patterns. It is a common motif for typographic borders. (M. L.)

green: immature paper.

Greenaway Medal: see *Kate Greenaway Medal.*

Gregynog Press: a private press founded in 1922 by the late Gwendolyn and Margaret Davies of Newtown, Montgomeryshire. The ladies took little part in the practical management; they commissioned a succession of controllers who included Robert Maynard, William MacCance, Loyd Haberley, and James Wardrop. The first book was issued in 1923; the last in 1940, when the press closed. The bindery continued until 1945.

The aim of the press was to 'introduce and encourage fine printing in Wales'. The use of wood engravings was a tradition soon established, work being commissioned from such artists as Reynolds Stone, Agnes Miller Parker, and Blair Hughes-Stanton whose illustrations for an edition of 'Comus', 1931, are well known.

Grenville, Sir Thomas, 1755–1846: a notable English book collector whose library of some 20,000 volumes included a 42-line Bible, a Mainz Psalter of 1457, the Aldus Manutius Virgil of 1501 and 1505, letters of Columbus and Vespucci, and an important collection of Italian and Spanish romance poems. He is said to have spent about £54,000 on acquiring his library, for which he sought the most perfect copies, and a further £56,000 to have them bound.

He bequeathed his collection to the British Museum (1847), and the library is housed there in a room named after him.

grey veil: a defect found on photographic negatives due to faulty dark-room lighting, over-developing, too long storage of negatives, defective dark slides, or exhalations from wooden dark slides. The veil can sometimes be removed with Farmer's reducer. It shows itself as a more or less close grey silver layer over the whole picture or large parts of it. (G. U.)

griffin: a fabulous creature, part eagle and part lion, which often appears in German woodcuts of printing shops where the griffin segreant is depicted holding a pair of ink balls. An example, by Abraham von Werdt, is reproduced in the 'Oxford Junior Encyclopaedia', Vol. IV. (See also the cover of this book.)

Whether the link between the griffin and printing is coincidental or symbolic is obscured by conjecture and legend. There is a popular tradition that the Emperor Frederick III (reigned 1440–93) granted a coat of arms to the German Guild of Book Printers. No proof of this has been found. (It is known, however, that Frederick granted arms to Johann Mentelin of Strasbourg in 1466, but these included a lion, not a griffin.) The legend is stated as fact by T. C. Hansard in 'Typographia', 1825—'The Emperor permitted printers to wear gold and silver, and granted coat-armour to the *Typothetae* and *Typographi.* This armorial bearing is still claimed by the professors of the art in Germany.' The arms, which form an engraved frontispiece to their 'Printer's Manual' show a griffin holding two ink balls over a closed and crowned helmet, and a double-headed Imperial eagle on a gold field, bearing in its claws a copyholder and a composing stick.

The griffin as adopted by the Swedish Book Printers' Association in 1926

The eagle, lion, and griffin were among the most popular beasts in heraldry, and this may have led to their use in the arms referred to above. Discussing this use H. W. Davies in 'Devices of the Early Printers, 1457–1560', 1935, says '. . . Centaurs are from ancient legend; Griffins from Assyria. . . . The printers seem to have chosen these various creatures rather as emblems or symbols of pride, self-confidence, not to say boastfulness, as watchers over their owners' interests, as protection against the envious. . . .' The inclusion of the eagle may also be due partly to its being the national emblem of Germany, and partly to its being the emblem of St John, patron of the scriveners. Other writers suggest the two creatures were first used in the arms described in 1640, the year of the Jubilee of the Book Printers in Germany.

The griffin has often been used in printers' marks; the printer Jakob Bellaert of Haarlem used the griffin as his device from 1483 onwards. This is to be seen in his edition of 'De proprietatibus rerum' of Bartholomaeus Anglicus, 1485. Writing of Bellaert, Davies (op. cit.) states that this was 'the first device of the press, the first at Haarlem, the earliest book with it being dated 10 Dec. 1483. . . . The griffin or gryphon is the first to appear in a device.' Karl Faulmann suggests a reason for this when writing in 'Illustrierte Geschichte der Buchdruckerkunst,' Vienna, 1882: 'In der Geschichte der Buchdruckerkunst kommt der Greif zuerst in Haarlem vor, wo Jakob Bellaert im Hause zum Greif druckte. . . .' which implies that Bellaert chose the griffin as his device because the house where he worked had one cut in stone as a house sign. This has not been confirmed, and the house no longer stands.

Among other printers to adopt a griffin were the Gryphius family and the Viennese brothers Alantsee (fl. 1505–51) who used two griffins segreant. (The Viennese printer Johann Singriener (1510–46) used two lions rampant, each with one ink ball.) Writing of William Gryffyth, who printed in the later 16th century, R. B. McKerrow in 'Printers' and Publishers' Devices, etc.' states 'It is doubtful whether his use of the griffin as a device refers to his early sign or to his name'.

I am indebted to Dr. Josef Stummvoll, Director of the Österreichische Nationalbibliothek, Vienna; Professor Aloys Ruppel of the Gutenberg Museum, Mainz; and J. D. A. Barnicot, Director of the British Council Books Department, London, for many of the above details.

Griffo, Francesco, fl. 1499: of Bologna, where he was one of the first independent punch-cutters in Italy. He cut the earliest italic type which was used by *Aldus Manutius*, q.v. The fount was of lower-case letters only. No less important was the first roman type he cut for Aldus which the latter used for Cardinal Bembo's 'De Aetna' in 1495. This face was the inspiration for types designed during the next three centuries by *Garamond*, *Granjon*, *Van Dijck*, *Jannon*, and *Caslon*, qq.v. In 1929 it was revived by the Monotype Corporation as Bembo, Series 270.

grinding: see *stone grinding*.

gripper edge: the edge which is caught by the grippers as a sheet of paper is fed into a cylinder press.

grippers: on job presses, the iron fingers attached to the platen to keep the sheet in place and take it off the type after the impression; on cylinders, the short curved metal fingers attached to an operating rod which grip the sheet and carry it around the impression.

In sheet machines of high speed there are pre-grippers for carrying the sheet lying on the feeding table to the revolving cylinder. (M.L. & G.U.)

grisaille: a grey monochrome stain used as a background on 15th-century manuscripts for the gold, white, and touches of red which were the only colours used on it. See also *illumination*.

Grolier bindings: books bound for the Frenchman Jean Grolier, Vicomte d'Aguisy (1479–1565). The varying styles used may be classed in three main groups: 1. with simple interlaced strapwork, small flowers, and tools cut solid; 2. plain or coloured ground with an intricate interlaced fillet; 3. without a fillet, decorated with azured stamps. The books were bound in morocco, and on many, two compartments formed part of the cover design, one for the title and one for the words 'IO GROLIERII ET AMICORVM'. The bindings with this inscription are of French workmanship and were made after *c.* 1535, but there is a small group made by Italian craftsmen, probably from Milan. The main decorative feature of these is a painted plaquette—an impression in relief on gesso showing a classical scene—inserted on the front board, and no inscription.

Grolier was one of the first collectors to have the title lettered on the spine of his books.

Grolier Club: a New York club for bibliophiles, founded in 1884 by, among others, *Theodore de Vinne*, q.v., and Robert Hoe. In addition to various club activities for promoting the graphic arts, a number of bibliographical works have been published, perhaps the most famous of these being 'One hundred Books famous in English Literature', 1902.

groove: the channel which runs set-wise across the bottom surface of a shank of type, i.e. between the feet.

grooved joints: see *french joints*.

grotesque: a name given to 19th-century sanserif display types. In the present century they tended to pass into obscurity in the inter-war years, being superseded by such modern sanserif faces as Futura, Gill, Granby, and Vogue: these were more rigid and geometric.

Since 1947 revivals of hand-cut 19th-century grotesques have come into favour for display work. Stephenson Blake's 'Grotesque No. 9' and Monotype's Series 383 are examples. Also known as *grots*.

ground: the combination of beeswax, asphaltum, gum-mastic, and pitch which, in the form of a thin coating, protects the non-image-bearing parts of an etching plate from the action of acid.

ground wood: a paper pulp made by mechanically grinding wood against a grindstone, in distinction from pulp made by cooking or digesting wood chips in a solution of soda or other chemicals. Ground wood paper is of low grade. (M.L.)

Gryphius, Sebastian, *c.* 1524–56: one of the leading printers and publishers of Lyons, who was also a skilled punch-cutter at a time when printers had begun to leave this craft to others. He issued cheap 12mo and 16mo editions of Greek and Latin classics, printed in italic types. Among his more important publications was the 'Commentaria linguae latinae', 1536–38, with a fellow scholar-printer Etienne Dolet (burnt alive in 1544). Jean de Tournes was an apprentice of Gryphius.

After his death the business was continued by his heirs until 1564: in 1566 it passed to his son, Antoine, who was active until 1593.

g.s.m.: the abbreviation for *grammes per square metre.* See also *paper substance.*

guarding: the inserting into a book of two separate plates which have been first glued to a narrow strip of paper or linen. The four-page unit they thus become is either wrapped around or inserted within a section when gathering. Single plates can be similarly guarded. Cf. *hooked.*

guards: narrow strips of linen or paper to which the inner margins of single plates are pasted prior to sewing them with the sections of a book. Four-page plate units are also strengthened in this way before sewing. A pair of leaves to be positioned around a section is guarded on its inner side; an inner pair of leaves is guarded on the outside, the sewing thread passing through the centre of the guard. The operation is known as *guarding* or *guarding-in.*

See also *compensation guards, continuous guard, hooked, inserted, meeting guards, plating, thrown out.*

guide book: a book or booklet containing information for travellers, tourists, sight-seers, exhibition visitors, etc.

Of world renown is the extensive series begun in 1832 by Karl Baedeker of Coblenz. The first was for the Rhine journey from Mainz to Coblenz. These authoritative guide books are still issued and are continually revised.

guide letters: small letters inserted in the otherwise blank space left for an illuminated, historiated, or rubricated capital to be executed by hand after a work had been printed: a feature of early printed books and still earlier manuscripts.

See also *factotum, illumination, initial letters, versals.*

Guild of Contemporary Bookbinders: founded in 1951 as 'The Hampstead Guild of Scribes and Bookbinders'. In spirit it succeeded the Hampstead Bindery which, about 1900, operated with the *Guild of Women Binders,* q.v. While originally centred in Hampstead, London, the present Guild arrived at a stage when no member lived there, and as the calligraphic element also dwindled the present title was adopted. Edgar Mansfield, a well-known British binder, is the president, and Arthur Johnson is secretary.

The aims of the Guild are simply '. . . to foster a high standard of craftsmanship and design in bookbinding'. Membership is open, by election, to any amateur or professional bookbinder. Candidates submit two bindings on which a vote is taken, and there is a bias in favour of those who seem likely to continue binding in years to come, for the Guild's policy is to hold frequent exhibitions.

Guild of Women Binders: an association of women bookbinders formed in 1898 by Frank Kerslake. The women worked in their own homes or in local ateliers. The Guild was closely associated with the Hampstead Bindery, and the two were awarded a silver medal for work they submitted to the Paris Exhibition of 1900. Shortly after this the Guild was dissolved. See G. E. Anstruther, 'The Bindings of Tomorrow. . . .'. 1902.

guillemets: see *duck-foot quotes.*

guillotine: a machine for the simultaneous cutting of a large number of sheets, either flat or folded and stitched. The usual paper guillotine is a *single-edge cutter,* in which a heavy blade slides between vertical runners, and is intended for comparatively large edge lengths, while for trimming books there are special *three-edge cutters.*

Guillotines came into use in the 1830's when Thirault built a model with a fixed blade in 1837. In 1844 and 1852 Guillaume Massiquot patented machines very similar to those in use today. Since the middle of the 19th century considerable improvements were made by August Fomm and Karl Krause of Leipzig, and Furnival in England. The Americans Oswego and Seybold should be noted.

The main parts of a single-edge cutter are a *table* on which the material to be cut is piled; a movable *back gauge,* perpendicular to the table, against which

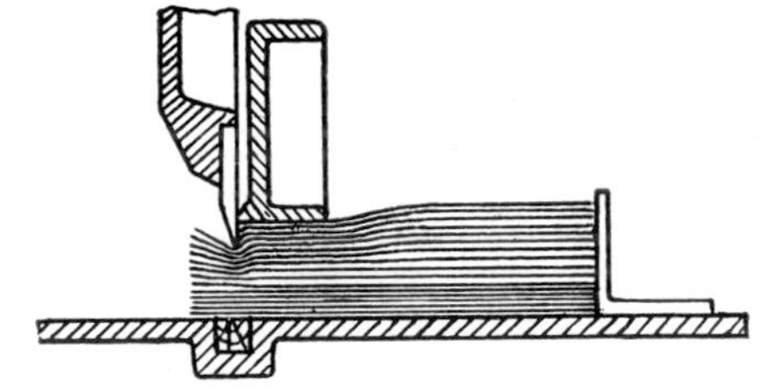

Diagram of a guillotine showing knife in the cutting beam in front of the press beam, cutting stick let into the table, and back gauge

the back edge of the pile rests; a *clamp* or *press beam* which compresses and secures the front edge of the pile (i.e. the edge to be cut); a *cutter* fixed in a cutting beam which descends immediately in front of the press beam, while the cutter cuts through the paper and finally stops at a *cutting stick* let into the table. (See illustration.)

Pressure can be applied by hand with a screw spindle; cutting, too, can be done by hand-operated levers, but electric power is now usual on both large and small machines.

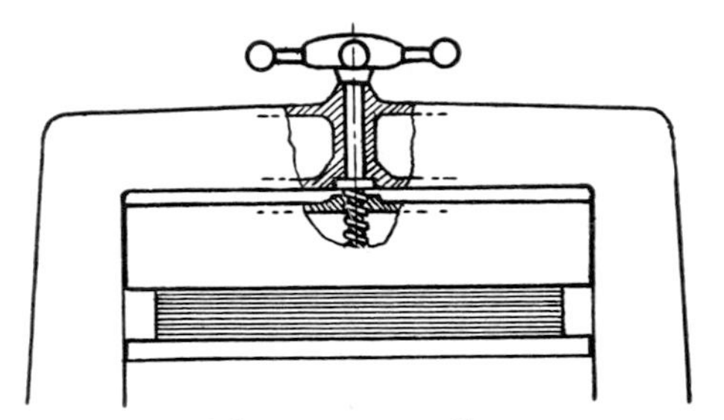

Hand-press in a guillotine

Seybold guillotine, model 60

Three-edge cutters, designed for cutting the three edges of a book, are of two types: three-edge machines and three-cutter machines. The three-edge machine, which is the older, is built like a single-edge cutter, but the table revolves and the press beam is replaced by a pressing plate, the size of the book. The table can be turned into three fixed positions in which the book is cut in turn at the fore-edge, tail, and head.

The three-cutter machine, built by August Fomm, Leipzig, in 1908, operates with a stationary table and three cutters, the book being cut simultaneously at the head and tail by two parallel cutters, and immediately after at the fore-edge by a third cutter (see illustration).

Modern *electronic guillotines* are those in which movements are actuated by a series of relays and contactors brought into operation through the medium of a number of thyratrons, tubes, and a photoelectric eye unit. All operations are mechanical,

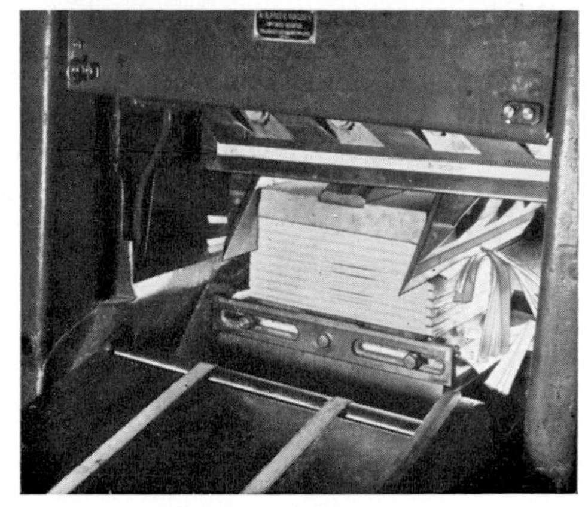

Three-cutter machine

being set in motion by push-buttons or the tripping of micro-switches which control the electronic circuit and thus the cutter.

A guide rail at the front of the machine carries the photoelectric cell and its lens. Interruption of the light beam between the two sends an electrical impulse to various tubes and thence to various

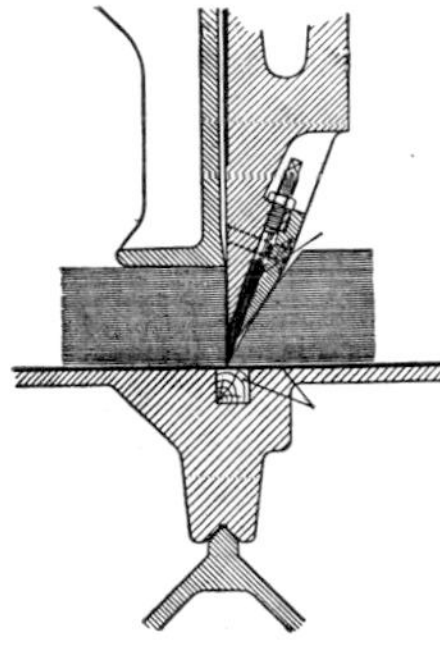

A device introduced by Karl Krause, Leipzig, for fixing the blade in the cutting beam so that material is saved

circuits. One of these leads to the electro-magnetic clutch which activates the knife and clamp. Another circuit operates the back-fence motor.

Ease of operation, with greater accuracy and safety, are among advantages claimed for electronic guillotines. Makes now in use in Britain are Furnival, Krause, Polar, and Soag.

guinea edge: the pattern tooled on a book edge by a fillet which impresses a design like the grooved edge of a guinea.

Guinness Poetry Award: an award announced in 1956 by Arthur Guinness, Son & Co., for the three best poems, in English, published in print for the first time in Great Britain and Ireland during the period of twelve months beginning on July 1st, 1956. The amounts are £300, £200, and £100. The award will be made annually if the judges can find suitable poems. No submissions should be made as the company will collect poems as they are published. There are no restrictions as to length or subject.

Günther, Albert: a firm of craftsmen bookbinders established in Vienna early in the 19th century and still producing work done with the same attention to forwarding and finishing. Examples are to be found in the Vatican, Royal Households, and the national libraries of many countries.

The Treaties of the Congress of Vienna, 1815, and the Austrian State Treaty, 1955, were bound by this firm. The present craftsman-director is Kurt Kierger.

Gutenberg, Johann, *c.* 1394–1468: the reputed inventor of printing from movable types, who was born in Mainz as Johann Gensfleisch zum Gutenberg. As a result of disputes between the craftsman and wealthier citizens he left Mainz, probably in 1428, and lived at any rate between 1434 and 1444 in Strasbourg where he worked as a goldsmith with the help of Hans Dünne. In 1438 he was working with Hans Riff, Andreas Dritzehn, and Andreas Heilmann on a secret project. He was then in possession of a press built for him by Konrad Saspach, and is known to have bought quantities of lead. In 1439 he was involved in a lawsuit there, and the documents of the case (still extant in the 1880's) indicate that he was interested in printing, and had invented a press for taking multiple impressions from blocks. It is uncertain, however, whether his invention of separately cast letters had already been made.

In 1450 he was again in Mainz where he came into contact with a rich merchant, Johann Fust, who lent him 800 rhein. Gulden for completing his work. For this loan Gutenberg had to mortgage his tools and equipment. Two years later Fust advanced more funds and undertook to pay the cost of rent, assistants' wages, and materials, on the understanding that Gutenberg's work should be 'for the benefit of both'. The work referred to was probably the 42-line Bible which appeared not later than 1456, and possibly, too, the Mainz Psalter of 1457, published from the offices of Fust and Schöffer.

In 1455 Fust sought the return of his loan (which, with interest at 6%, now amounted to 2026 Gulden), and as Gutenberg was unable to repay it, legal proceedings were instituted. Some of the documents in this lawsuit, the Helmasperger notarial instrument, have been preserved (in Göttingen University Library) and constitute one of our principal sources for Gutenberg's biography. The verdict of the case is not on record, but it is evident that all Gutenberg's books and equipment were taken over by Fust who continued to carry on the business with the help of Peter Schöffer. Nothing is known of Gutenberg's subsequent life until 1465 when he secured an appointment at the court of Adolf of Nassau, Archbishop of Mainz; here he is believed to have acquired further printing equipment with the financial help of Dr.

Extract from the '*Sibyllenbuch*', *c.* 1455 (*Reduced*)

The first page of the 'Turkish Calendar', 1455 (*Reduced*)

Konrad Humery. According to an old record Gutenberg died in February 1468, the Archbishop handing over his printing press to Humery.

No printed work extant bears Gutenberg's name, but in addition to the 42-line Bible some smaller works, which must for various reasons be dated prior to August 1456 (when his equipment passed to Fust) are often ascribed to him *without, however, final proof.* These include the 'Sibyllenbuch' of 1455 and some Donatus grammars in the same gothic text type; at least one of three astrological calendars for 1448, 1456, and 1457; a printed explanation of the Papal bull concerning the crusade against the Turks which cannot have been printed later than 1456; a call in verse for war on the Turks (the 'Turkish Calendar', 1455); and some forms for letters of indulgence. The 'Catholicon' of Johannes Balbus de Janua, dated Mainz 1460, was once ascribed to Gutenberg but is now attributed by German bibliophiles to Peter Schöffer. The Psalter of 1457, printed, according to the colophon, by Fust and Schöffer, must be held to include Gutenberg's work.

See also *Bible printing*, *Cracow fragments*, *printing—historical survey*. (With G.U.)

Guthlac Roll: a roll on which were drawn a series of roundels depicting the life of St Guthlac of Crowland. They were probably intended as designs for stained glass or enamels. The roll may have been made at Crowland *c.* 1196, or a little later. It was formerly in the Harley collection, and is now in the British Museum.

gutter: 1. the spacing material in a forme between two outer or fore-edge margins of two adjacent pages. Gutters are so called because, in former times, the pieces of wooden furniture used for these places had a gutter or rounded channel cut in the top surface to prevent it from receiving ink from the roller when the forme was inked. See also *margins.*

2. in a unit of two facing pages the space comprising the two facing back margins is sometimes called the *gutter.*

3. see *grooves.*

gutting: 1. the practice of reviewing a book, not by critically appraising it, but by disclosing the main lines of the book and its plot, i.e. by 'tearing the guts' out of it. Publishers naturally deplore this practice.

2. a colloquialism for the judicious selection by a publisher of such felicitous phrases from reviews of a book as are likely, when printed on the jacket or in advertisements, to further the sale of it. An inspired copywriter's skilled substitution of 'leaders' for rude or offensive words can transform even the unkindest of notices into fulsome and useful praise.

ADDENDUM

Glindura: the trade name of a British non-woven bookbinding fabric. Like the similar material *linson*, q.v., it is widely used for cased and limp books. Cheaper forms of Glindura are sold under the names *Durabak* and *Glintene.*

H

Haas: a family of printers and typefounders in Basle, where Johann Wilhelm Haas inherited Genath's typefoundry in 1740. His son, Wilhelm Haas (der Vater) (1741–1800) took over the business in 1764, and incorporated with it the office of Jean Pistorius about 1770. Early in the 1770's he experimented with typecasting methods, and in 1772 he built an improved all-iron hand-press. In collaboration with Preuschen in Karlsruhe methods were worked out for producing maps typographically (1790). He retired in 1791, being succeeded by his son Wilhelm (der Sohn), (1766–1835) who further improved the hand-press in 1789. (Illustrated on page 172.)

The firm continues as Haas'sche Schriftgiesserei A.G. (G. U.)

Hadego: see *photo-composing machine*.

Haebler, Konrad, 1857–1946: a prominent German bibliographer remembered for his research work and writings on the incunabula and type history of Spain, Italy, and Portugal, also for his pioneer work for the '*Gesamtkatalog der Wiegendrucke*', q.v.

Among his studies were 'Typenrepertorium der Wiegendrucke', 6 vols., Halle and Leipzig, 1905–24, and 'Handbuch der Inkunabelkunde', 1925, in addition to writings on bookbinding.

Hafod Press: a private printing press established in 1803 at Hafod (Wales) by Thomas Johnes. The first work issued was the 'Chronicles' of Froissart in four volumes, 1803–5. Of similar importance was an edition of Monstrelet's 'Chronicles' in five volumes, dated 1809, published 1810. No books were published after 1810 and Mr. Johnes died in 1816.

Johnes employed James Henderson to work his press, but while books were carefully printed they were not in any way remarkable.

Hain, Ludwig, 1781–1836: the compiler of '*Repertorium bibliographicum ad annum* 1500', q.v.

hair-lines: the thin strokes of a type-face.

hair-spaces: the thinnest spacing material, cast less than type height, and used between letters. Hair-spaces vary in thickness, according to body size, from eight to twelve to the em.

hair-line rule: the thinnest of printers' *brass rules*, q.v.

Hakluyt Society: a society founded in London in 1846 for the printing of 'rare and valuable voyages, travels, naval expeditions, and other valuable records'. It is named after the geographer and traveller Richard Hakluyt, 1553–1616. Publication began in 1847 with 'Observations on his voyage into the South Sea in 1593' by Sir John Hawkins.

Since 1955, the Cambridge University Press has handled publication and sales.

half-bound: a book having the back and corners bound in one material, the sides in another. It is customary for only the top edge to be gilded.

See also *siding*.

half-cloth: a half-bound book with cloth-covered spine and corners, and paper-covered boards. The title on the spine is usually on a printed label.

half-diamond indention: a manner of setting type when successive lines are indented at both ends, each one being shorter than the preceding line. Also known as *in pendentive*.

half-leather: a half-bound book having leather as the covering material for the spine and corners with cloth or paper sides.

half-line drawing: a block made by exposing a line drawing through a half-line screen. The printed result is lighter in tone than the original.

half-measure: see *double column*.

half see safe: an expression used by a bookseller when ordering copies of a book from a publisher to indicate that, while all copies will be paid for, the publisher may be asked to take back half the quantity and offer the bookseller another title in lieu. Cf. *see safe*.

See also *terms*.

half sheet: literally, a sheet half the size of the normal. For example, a book is being printed in 32-page sheets but there is a 16-page oddment to complete; then the latter will constitute a *half sheet*. The same term would be used for an 8-page oddment when printing sheets of 16 pages. In both cases it would be convenient for the printer to use the full-size paper but impose the sheet for *work and turn*, q.v., and subsequently cut in half. (L. K.)

half-stuff: the wet pulp to which the raw materials of paper are reduced in the potcher before being mixed with other ingredients and beaten.

See also *stuff*.

half-title: the title of a book as printed on the leaf preceding the title-page. The use of such a page dates from the latter half of the 17th century, though a blank leaf had been included in books to protect their title-pages from earlier times. Also known as *bastard title* or *fly-title*.

half-tone block: a zinc or copper printing plate prepared by the *half-tone process*, q.v., and mounted to type height on wood or metal for use in letterpress printing.

See also *blockmaking*, *Collobloc*.

half-tone intaglio: see *intaglio half-tone*.

half-tone paper: any coated, high machine finished, or super-calendered stock, of good colour, and with a smooth surface which is suitable for printing half-tone blocks.

half-tone process: the preparation of zinc or copper plates for reproducing illustrations (black and white or coloured) from continuous tone. The image to be reproduced is photographed through a ruled glass screen on to a sensitized plate. The screen breaks up the different tones of the original picture into dots of varying size, their number per square inch being determined by the fineness of the ruled lines on the screen. The image on the sensitized plate is etched into relief on a copper plate for letterpress printing.

Since the mid-19th century Fox Talbot and others experimented with screens with a view to producing printing blocks. Properly said, screen process work is held to have been first carried out by F. von Egloffstein in 1865, or perhaps by Bullock, and somewhat later (1879) by J. W. Swan, but Georg Meisenbach of Munich, who made the method practicable in every way, is generally considered to have been its inventor. In 1881 he produced his first half-tones, some of which still exist, and in 1882 he and von Schmädel patented a half-tone method the procedure of which was as follows. From a negative was produced a transparent positive which was put in contact with a line screen and photographed. After half the required exposure time the screen was turned 90° and exposure completed. The negative was transferred to zinc, developed, and etched with acid. News of the method spread, and reproduction technicians in various places made improvements. Angerer in Vienna produced in 1883 a screen negative direct from

Meisenbach's first half-tone, patent dated May 9th, 1882

the original picture, but still employed single-line screens which required turning during exposure. Among American experimenters were S. H. Horgan, F. E. Ives, and von Nemethy of Chicago; to the last named is accredited the invention (1888) of the squared screen now in general use, which was brought to perfection by Max Levy. A variety of line screen had also been invented in 1871 by Carl Carleman of Sweden. (G.U.)

See also *bumping up*, *contact screen*, *direct half-tone*, *fine etching*, *screen*, *screen process work*, *staging out*.

half-tone screen: a sheet of glass bearing a meshwork of lines ruled at right-angles. (It is made from two separate sheets of plate glass cemented into a unit with the ruled lines inside.) This is used to translate the subject of a half-tone illustration into dots. Screens are classified and referred to by the number of lines per inch. In making the separate exposures of three- and four-colour work (see *subtractive process*) the screen is moved 30° between each.

See also *contact screen*, *Erwin screen*, *moiré*, *single-line half-tone*.

half-uncial: the alphabet of mixed uncial and cursive letters used in Europe as a book hand from the 6th–12th centuries. The original Roman half-uncial formed the basis of several national book hands, e.g. Irish, Merovingian, Lombardic. The Irish half-uncial was introduced to England at Lindisfarne in 634 where it developed independently and later influenced Carolingian minuscule letters.

See also *letters—forms and styles*.

Halkett, Samuel, 1814–71: librarian of the Faculty of Advocates, Edinburgh. For many years he collected material for a dictionary of anonymous English

Letterpress half-tone, 200-*line screen*
Photo: *Stora Kopparberg*

works; on his death the manuscript was continued and more than doubled by John Laing (1809–80), librarian of New College, Edinburgh. His daughter, Catherine Laing, finally edited the work which was published as 'A Dictionary of the Anonymous and Pseudonymous Literature of Great Britain', 4 vols., Paterson, 1882–88. It quickly became a standard work. A revised edition by James Kennedy, W. A. Smith, and A. F. Johnson was published in 7 volumes by Oliver & Boyd, 1926–32; with a continuation as volume 8, 1956.

Hammersmith Workshops: see *St Dominic's Press.*

Hampstead Bindery: see *Guild of Contemporary Bookbinders.*

Han, Ulrich, fl. 1467–78: a German printer working in Rome, from whose press came what is held to be the first Italian book illustrated by woodcuts, the 'Meditationes vitae Christi' by Cardinal Johannes de Turrecremata, 1467. (It is claimed, but not proved, that prior to moving to Rome Han was the first printer in Vienna.) With the advice of Johannes Campanus he issued classical and humanistic works. Two Roman Missals from Han appeared in 1475 and 1476.

Hand and Flower Press: a small post-war private press founded at Aldington, Kent, by Erica Marx. Printing is done by such firms as the Chiswick, Curwen, and Ditchling presses.

hand-binding: successive stages in the hand-binding of books, after sewing, are grouped under two heads:— *forwarding*, which includes gluing the sections, rounding and backing, and covering with leather; finally, *finishing*, which includes lettering the title in gold, and embellishing.

See also *bookbinding methods and processes.*

hand-coloured illustrations: the hand-colouring of copper engravings dates from the early 18th century. The work was mostly done in workshops where women and even children, engaged by the artist of the original, produced between two and three hundred plates a week.

In the 19th century coloured lithographs of botanical, zoological, landscape, and costume subjects were made in the same way.

Hand-colouring today, as distinct from the retouching by hand of machine-printed colour work, is mostly limited to small, costly editions, particularly in France, though in Britain the Curwen Press and the Folio Society, to name but two, have issued fairly large editions so illustrated and at modest prices.

See also *illumination, pochoir.*

hand composition: type-setting by hand proceeds today as in the early days of printing. The compositor's tools are a composing stick, a composing rule, a steel scale, a galley, a bodkin, and tweezers. His material consists of types, rules, ornaments, quads, leads, quoins, furniture, and a chase.

Types are removed by hand from a case in which each character has its own compartment. Cases are kept in wood or metal cabinets which also serve as work-tables for the compositor, and are mostly set up in rows to form an alley in which he works; he usually stands. Cases were formerly used in pairs, an upper and a lower, and those containing the particular type required were put in position on the cabinet, being supported there by a frame and bracket. As hand composition is now mainly used only for display work a single double-case, the California job case (see illustration), is usual. The *lay of the case* (arrangement of the characters in it) is not standardized in Britain, but the size is, i.e. 32½ by 14½ by 1½ or 1¾ in. (in U.S.A. 32 by 16 by 1½ in.).

The manuscript to be set is held in a copyholder; it should be near but above the case for ease of access to the latter. The letters selected are put in a composing stick (clearly shown in the illustration) which is made of steel, in various lengths; some are calibrated in 12-point ems and ens. The stick has a fixed side and a sliding one by means of which the stick is adjusted and secured to the proper measure. If uncalibrated, a steel type-scale can be used: this is marked in various point ems (1, 5, 6, 8, 10, and 12) and inches. The final stage in preparing the stick for use is the fitting to it of a brass setting rule. These pieces of brass vary in length, are type high, and about three points thick: at one end is a projecting lip. The composing stick is held in the left hand, and the types are picked singly out of the case with the right and placed next to each other in the stick, word by word and line by line. Thick spaces, i.e. a blank type equal to a third of the body in width, are placed between words as they are set. In order that the type should slide easily and not catch in previous lines, the setting rule acts as a partition, and by its protruding lip can easily be lifted when the line is completed, and be placed in front of it for the setting of a fresh line.

It is very seldom that a line is filled by a word. If there is no room for one or two letters in the last word, space is made for them by removing the thick spaces and inserting thinner ones; the compositor begins this at the right-hand edge. Alternatively, he may decide to remove the partly completed last word and spread out the remainder in order to fill the measure; he then starts on the left and increases the intervals with one or more thin spaces. A further solution is the division by hyphen of the last word. His craftsmanship is revealed by the apparent evenness of the setting, resulting from well-positioned spacing; quick decisions and an eye for the shape of letters are

A compositor at work.
He stands before the case (1) *with the copyholder* (2) *on his left. The composing stick* (3) *is in his left hand. On the bench to the right of the case are a galley* (4) *with furniture* (5) *and tweezers and bodkin* (6). *Also visible are a roll of page cord and a sponge for damping* (7). *In the background are cases in their cabinet* (8), *quoin shelves* (9), *and slip galleys* (10)

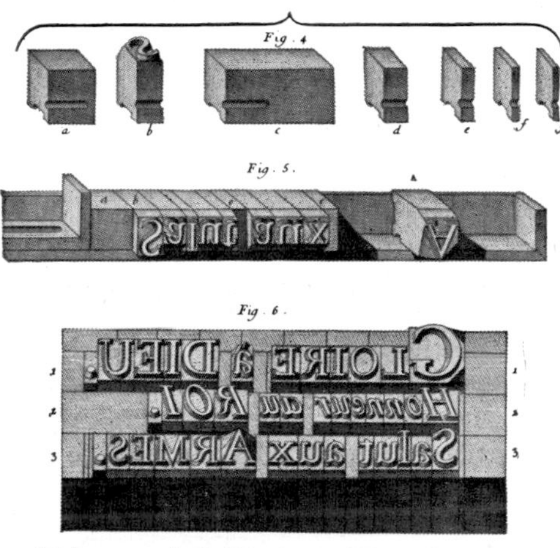

From Diderot and d'Alembert, 'Encyclopédie', Paris, 1751–80

also required of him. Each line should be read and corrected as soon as composed. When the composing stick is full (which means a varying number of completed lines, according to the body) the matter is lifted out of it and placed on the galley where the number of lines required for a page is made up and checked by a page gauge. The completed page is tied up with page-cord and can now be moved as a firm unit (unsuccessful attempts have been made to tie and untie a page by machine). Before making up the matter into pages it is usual to set it up in long slips and pull *galley proofs* for reading and correcting (see *proof, proof corrections*). Any blocks are inserted during the making up. A headline and footline are placed above and below the matter, and in one of these the page number is placed.

On the iron imposing surface the pages are imposed in the order proper for their correct sequence on the printed and folded sheet. A metal chase is now fitted round the pages, furniture and quoins are put between them and the chase (*dressing the forme*), and the whole is tightened by locking the quoins: it is now known as a *forme*.

When printing is completed, the matter which is

not to be left standing or used for making stereos should be cleaned and distributed, i.e. the types, furniture, leads, and spaces returned to the case or bins. (See also *washing up*.)

From an aesthetic point of view hand composition is preferable to mechanical, and even the latter must be finished off by hand; but most people, including many printers, would have difficulty in determining which of two well-printed pages had been hand-set and which by machine. (With G.U.)

hand-folding: the folding of sheets into sections by hand instead of by machine.

See also *folding*.

hand-gravure: a method of copperplate printing. After inking, and before each impression is taken, the surface of the plate is wiped by hand. (M.L.)

hand-letters: brass letters, mounted in wooden handles, which are used by the finisher for lettering the title, etc., on the cover of a hand-bound book.

See also *binder's brass*, *pallet*.

hand-made paper: fine-quality grain-free paper made by dipping a mould into rag pulp and skilfully shaking it until a sheet is formed. Wet sheets are pressed between felts (see *post*). On removal from the post they are further dried in a *pack*, q.v. At this stage the paper is known as waterleaf. Loft drying, tub-sizing, and further drying follow. Plate-finishing is the last stage in the manufacture of this relatively expensive paper.

See also *coucher*, *dryworker*, *layerman*, *paper-making*, *pilcher*, *rag paper*, *slice boy*, *upper end boy*, *Whatman paper*.

hand-matrix: a matrix intended for slug-casting machines (accents, fractions, etc.) which is not given a place in the matrix magazine, but is kept in a special hand-matrix case from which the compositor takes the matrices required and places them by hand in the assembler box. On being distributed, these matrices slide through a groove to the hand-matrix assembler, and are removed by the compositor to the hand-matrix case. (G.U.)

hand-press: 1. a printing press in which the forme is inked, the paper is fed and removed, and the pressure is applied by hand. There are various transitional stages from the hand-press to the printing machine in which one or more of these actions are performed automatically or partly mechanically. (*a*) *The hand-press for printing books* dates back to Gutenberg's day, but the presses used at that time for printing books differed very little from the wine- or cheese-presses of old. Gutenberg's first press was built in accordance with his instructions by Konrad Saspach, a turner, but no description of it survives. The oldest known illustration of a printing press is reproduced here from 'Dance of Death', printed in Lyons about 1499. The interior of the Jodocus Badius printing shop, *c.* 1520, is more realistic.

Pressure was applied by means of a screw which was

From 'Dance of Death', Lyons, c. 1499

turned by a lever and pressed a platen against the forme lying on the bed. The bed rested on a fore-stay in such a way that it could be pushed in and out under the platen. When the bed was pulled out, the printer could lay the forme on it, and then do the inking with

The Badius printing press, from a 16*th-century woodcut*

two ink balls. The sheet of paper was laid on the tympan, the frisket was closed, and then the tympan with the frisket and paper was laid over the forme (see illustration). The bed was drawn in under the platen and the impression made. The object of the tympan was to distribute the pressure of the platen evenly over the forme, that of the frisket to protect the margin of the paper from coming in contact with the forme and possibly being soiled. The oldest hand-presses were built entirely of wood (hence the name *joiner's press*) and the pressure obtainable was so small that large formes had to be printed in stages by

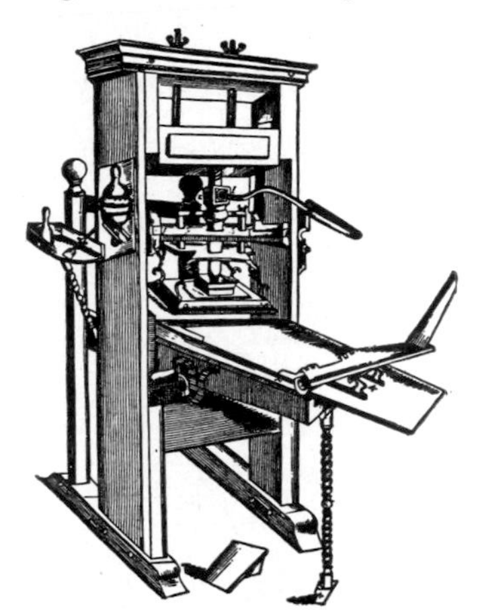

A wooden printing press. From 'Mechanick Exercises' by Joseph Moxon, 1683

drawing the bed gradually under the platen, which often had a surface only one-half or one-third the size of the surface of the bed. Usually half a quire of paper (a 'layer') was placed in the tympan at a time, and as the impressions were taken, the top sheet was removed. Wooden presses were retained, with some minor improvements, until far into the 19th century. Wilhelm Blaeu of Amsterdam introduced a spring-actuated connection between the screw and the platen *c*. 1620, and in 1772 Wilhelm Haas of Basle built a hand-press with a platen and bed of iron.

The press of Wilhelm Haas, sen., Basle, 1772

The 'Scottish table press' built in 1813 by John Ruthven of Edinburgh had a platen which moved sideways, while the bed remained stationary, and was lifted against the platen in printing. About 1810 a hand-press without a screw, the Columbian press,

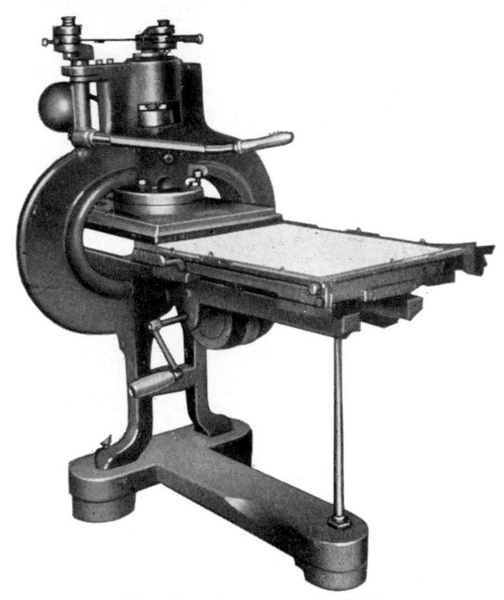

The Stanhope press, 1800

was invented in Philadelphia by George Clymer; pressure was obtained by a set of levers connected with a counterweight (in the form of the American eagle). This was copied in various parts of Europe. In England the *Albion press* was devised in 1823 by R. W. Cope; the pressure in it was applied by a toggle

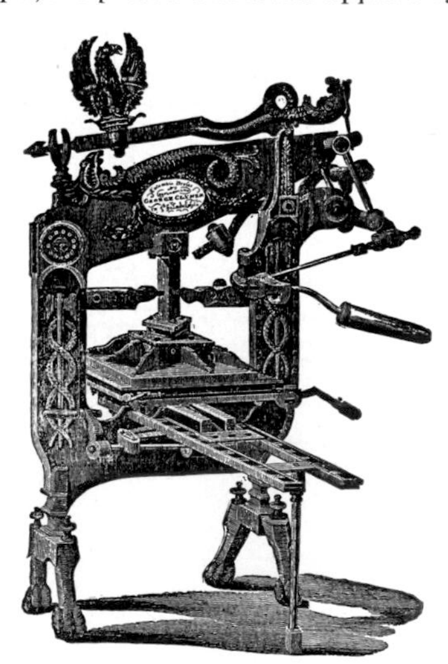

George Clymer's Columbian press, 1817

joint. This principle was first used in New York in 1822, and in the following decades it was embodied in many well-known presses (Washington press, Hagar press, Dingler press). The two halves of the toggle, the chill and the wedge, form an elbow or

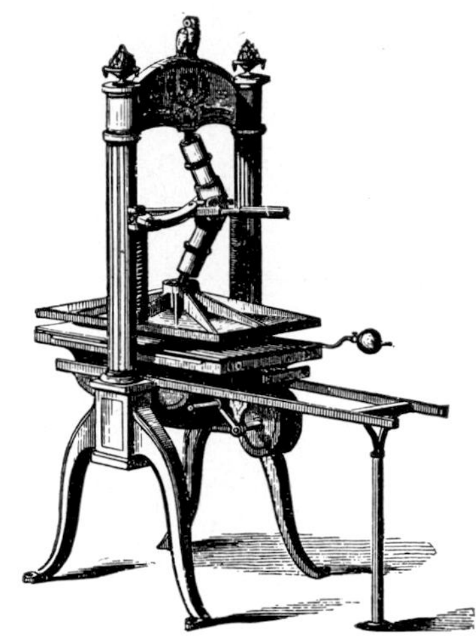

The Hagar press, showing the toggle joint

knee joint; when they are forced into a straight line (on turning a lever) considerable pressure is obtained. Hand-presses of this type are still used for proofing, and work satisfactorily when care is given to the

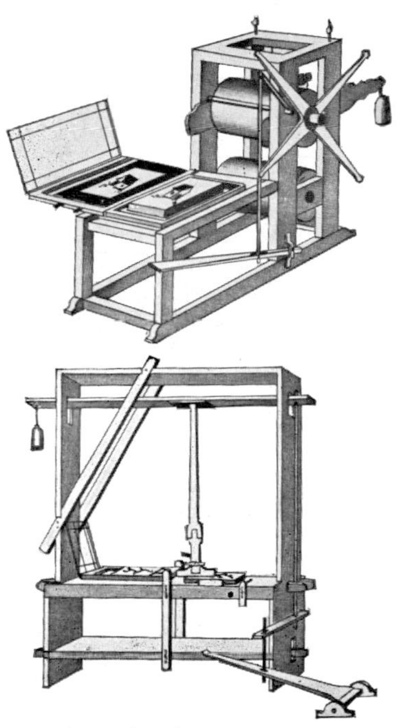

Senefelder's first hand-presses. Top, a primitive copperplate press. Below, a gallows press

condition of the tympan and adjustment of the impression.

See also *Albion press, Blaeu press, cheeks, coffin, fore-stay, frisket, garter, girts, hose, ink ball, joiner's press, letterpress machines, plank, platen press, rounce, Stanhope press, tympan, winter.*

(*b*) *The hand-press for lithographic printing* has been equipped with rubbers for applying pressure from the days of Senefelder. As the lithographic forme has a practically level surface without differences in height, the available force must be distributed over the whole surface and the pressure per unit of surface would be insufficient, if an attempt were made, as in the platen press, to print a large surface at one time. Instead pressure is applied only to one narrow strip at a time; this is done by means of a blade placed on edge under

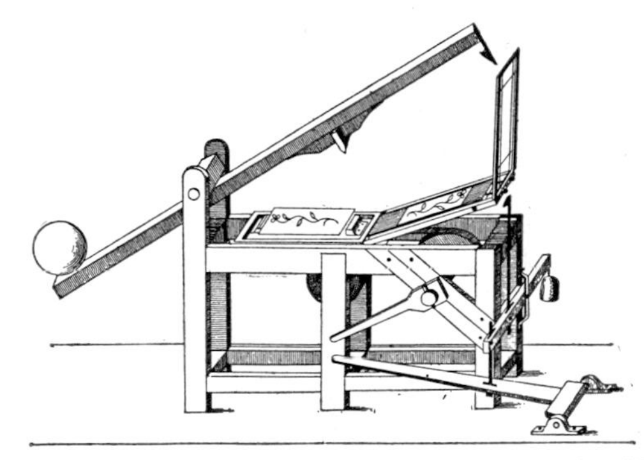

Rubber press, from Senefelder's handbook of 1818

which the printing stone or plate is moved forward. The rubber press illustrated in Senefelder's 'Lehrbuch des Steindrucks' is reproduced here. For more modern rubber presses see *transfer press.*

(*c*) *The hand-press for copperplate printing* (engraving) is described under *copperplate printing press,* q.v.

2. a bookbinding press used for edge gilding. It consists of a wooden block with two protruding screw-spindles of wood or iron running loosely through a second wooden block which can be pressed by means of butterfly nuts against the book or books laid between the blocks. For tightening or loosening the nuts a wooden spanner is used, and as a support under the hand-press a press jack is fitted. For an illustration see *gilt edges.* (G. U.)

hand-roller: a roller used in a hand-press for inking type.

See also *ink ball.*

hand-set: type matter which has been composed letter by letter in a stick.

hand-sewing: the sewing of books by hand. The work is done in a sewing frame, which is a simple device consisting of a board with two vertical screws and the

Hand-sewing; the sewing heart is seen by the girl's left hand

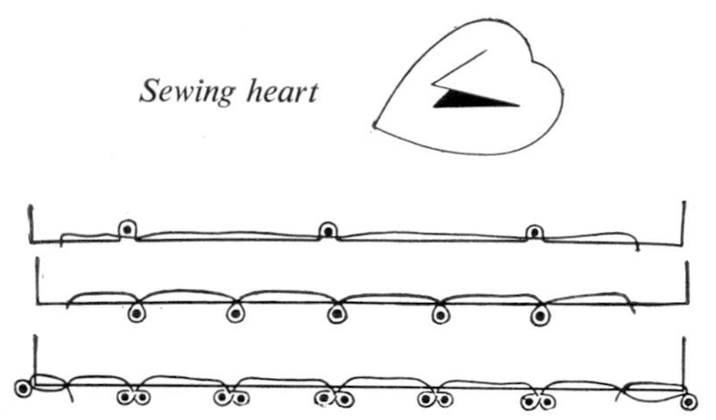

Sewing heart

Top to bottom, Sunk cords; Raised bands; Double raised bands

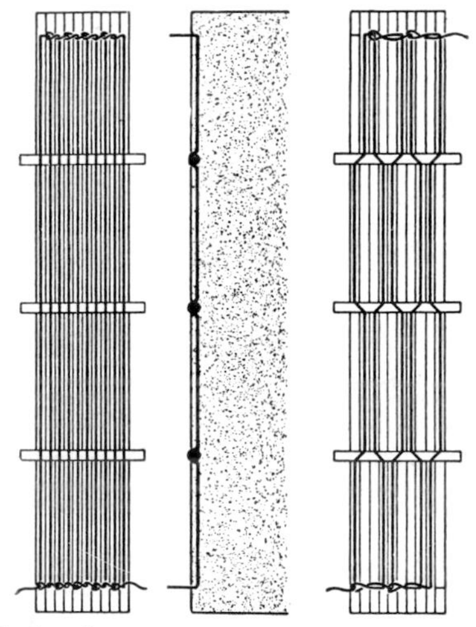

'All along' sewing *'Two sheets on'*

nuts for them: a crossbar rests on the nuts. Between the bar and the front edge of the base-board hemp or flax cords (or tape) are fitted, fastened by sewing hooks, and stretched by raising the bar. (See illustration.)

The book to be sewn, made up of folded sections, lies on the left of the sewing frame, the last section of the book being on top. One section at a time is laid with its back to the cords and sewn through the back fold in such a way that the threads lie like stitches, a few cm. in length, in the middle double page of the sheet, going out and round for each stitch. Formerly the cords lay entirely outside the back of the book (see *raised bands*), but now sawing-in is usual, which means that before being sewn the book is given grooves ($\frac{1}{32}$ in. deep) to make room for the cords. Cutting is done in a small press. If sewing is done on three cords, five cuts are made, the outer two being for the knotted sewing threads which link one section to the next (kettle-stitches). In addition, the three middle cuts are usually filed with a three-edge file. The first and last sections of a book are sewn 'all along' to give strength, i.e. the threads run from one kettle-stitch through the middle spread to the nearest cord, out and round the latter, and back into the same section, and so on to the second kettle-stitch, where the thread is fastened into a knot before being led into the next section. In heavy books with thick sections each is sewn all along; for books with thin sections *two sheets on*, q.v., may be used, which means that two sections are sewn simultaneously with stitches entering alternately the first and the second. By this means the sewing threads in the sections run alternately to the right and the left from each stitch, and the back of the book will not be unduly thick.

To find easily the middle spread of a section when sewing, a 'sewing heart' is sometimes used to mark it; this is a piece of cardboard cut with a flap (see diagram). Linen thread is usually used for sewing, and the needle is like a large-eyed darning needle. Several books of the same size, and with the same arrangement of stitches, can be sewn one above the other in the same frame. They then form a rack which is divided into separate books by 'cutting off', care being taken to allow two inches of tape or cord to project from the sides of each book. (G.U.)

See also *bookbinding methods and processes.*

handbook: a reference book, manual, or treatise of convenient size; a handy guide book. (M.L.)

hanging figures: the numerals of certain type-designs which range within the limits of the extruders. E.g. the Caslon figures 3, 4, 5, 6, 7, 8, 9, as distinct from the 1, 2, and 0 of the same face. Old-face types usually have hanging figures, though in some faces alternative *ranging figures*, q.v., are available (e.g. Plantin).

hanging paragraph: a paragraph with the first line set to full width, the remaining lines in it being indented one or more ems from the left margin.
See also *in pendentive.*

Hans Christian Andersen Medal: an award made by the International Board on Books for Young People, in a contest open to the world. The Board was set up at a conference of publishers, booksellers, authors, and others interested in children's books, held in 1951 at Munich. The result of the first competition was announced in 1956, when Eleanor Farjeon and Edward Ardizzone were jointly awarded the medal for 'The Little Bookroom', O.U.P., 1955.

Hanserd Knollys Society: a printing society instituted in London, 1845-51, for the publication of the works of early English and other Baptist writers. (M.L.)

hard-grain morocco: goatskin finished with a deep pin-head grain by hand-boarding. The leather is very supple.

hard-ground etching: see *etching.*

hard packing: thin card or stiff paper used to cover the cylinder of a printing machine so as to obtain a sharp impression, with little indentation, when printing on to smooth, hard paper.

hard sized: paper which contains the maximum of size. Cf. *double sized.*

Hargrave, Francis, *c.* 1741–1821: a legal author and antiquary whose important collection of books and manuscripts was in 1813 purchased by the nation for the British Museum.

Harleian Society: a society founded in 1869 for the printing of 'heraldic visitations of counties, and any manuscripts relating to genealogy, family history and heraldry'.

Harley, Sir Robert, 1579–1656: the first member of the Harley family to assemble (at Brampton Bryan) 'an extraordinary library of manuscript and printed books, which had been collected from one descent to another'. In 1644 the castle was besieged and burned, the library of books valued at £200 being destroyed with it. The family library was re-developed by his grandson, the first Earl of Oxford.
See next entry.

Harley, Robert, first Earl of Oxford, 1661–1724: the founder, in 1705, of the famous Harleian collection. Within twenty years he had assembled over 40,000 books and 6000 manuscript volumes, many finely illuminated. Subjects were English history, early theology (especially the Eastern Church), and the classics.

His son Edward (1689–1741) added to the collection. At his death it numbered 50,000 printed books, 14,236 charters and rolls, and 7639 manuscripts. Large sums were spent on binding, for which Thomas Elliott and Christopher Chapman were employed; they mostly used red morocco supplied by the Earl, on which an ornate centre-piece and a broad border, or a narrow roll border were tooled.

That the library was developed so skilfully was largely due to Humphrey Wanley, who from 1708–26 was the Harleian librarian-collector. It is from his diary we learn that Elliott and Chapman were rival binders, not partners as was long supposed.

The manuscripts were purchased for the British Museum in 1753. The printed books were sold.

Harmsworth Award: an annual award of £100 offered by the Irish Academy of Letters, Dublin, for the best work of imaginative writing by an Irish author.
This has now lapsed.

Harrild, Robert: see *inkers.*

Harris press: an American automatic platen press constructed and manufactured by the brothers Alfred and Charles Harris, 1890–91, for producing and selling which the Harris Automatic Press Co. was established in 1895. Alfred Harris also built a lithographic offset press, the first fully satisfactory one being supplied to the currency printing works in Pittsburgh, 1906. In 1909 the Harris offset press was given a pile feeder. The Premier and Potter Press Manuf. Co. and other undertakings were incorporated in the company, and in 1927 the name was changed to the Harris–Seybold–Potter Co., now the Harris–Seybold Co., with works in Cleveland and Dayton, Ohio, U.S.A. (G.U.)

Harrison, Thomas: see *Thomas Harrison Memorial Award.*

Harrison Vertical press: a stop-cylinder printing press in which the forme is moved vertically. The impression cylinder is fixed, and revolves during the downward movement of the bed only. In this it differs from other *vertical presses,* q.v., where bed and cylinder reciprocate in opposite directions. Speeds are from 2500 to 4500 impressions an hour.

Hattersley, Robert: the inventor of a composing machine which was used by several provincial newspaper offices in England. It appeared in 1859. The depression of keys released types, stacked in grooves, into a short line for justification. Distribution was by hand.

Hausleiter process: see *offset reproduction.*

Hawthornden Prize: the prize established in 1919 by Alice Warrender as an annual award of £100 and a medal to an English writer under 41 years of age for the best work of imaginative literature.

Hayday, James, 1796–1872: a London bookbinder. A feature of his work was all-along sewing with silk thread and tight backs made of *Turkey morocco*, q.v.

Haye MS: three medieval treatises, 'L'Arbre des Batailles', 'L'Ordre de Chevalerie', and 'Le Governement des Princes', translated into Scots by Gilbert of the Haye for the Earl of Orkney. The considerable importance of the manuscript derives principally from the binding, of which it is the earliest surviving Scottish example. It was the work of Patrick Lowes, whose stamped inscription on the cover 'Patricius Lowes me ligavit', makes the book doubly unique as the first-known British binding made before 1500 to bear the binder's full name.

Lowes used no fewer than thirty-three stamps, apparently made in Cologne, arranging them in a pattern deriving from Cologne or Erfurt. The principal stamps bear the Tudor rose, rosettes, and the twelve Apostles with their emblems, mostly within frames made by a four-line fillet.

The translation is dated 1456, but the binding was not made before 1480; it 'may well be ten or fifteen years later' (G. D. Hobson).

The book is now in the National Library of Scotland.

head: the margin at the top of a page. See also *margins*.

head margin: the margin above the first line of text or the headline on each page. Ideally its width is half the tail or bottom margin.

head-piece: a decorative device occasionally printed in the blank space above the beginning of a chapter or other division of a book. It may be specially drawn or built up from *flowers*, q.v. Cf. *tail-piece*.

headband: a narrow band made up of coloured silk threads wound about a short length of hemp, catgut, cane, or leather, and sewn (in poorer work glued) to the sections of a book by passing the silk round the *kettle-stitch*, q.v., at every fifth turn. Sometimes the headband is also sewn to the cover for greater strength, but nowadays only in very high-class work is the headband hand-made and sewn round the kettle-stitch. Manufactured headbands, plain or multi-coloured, are supplied generally in quantities of gross yards for attaching by hand or machine.

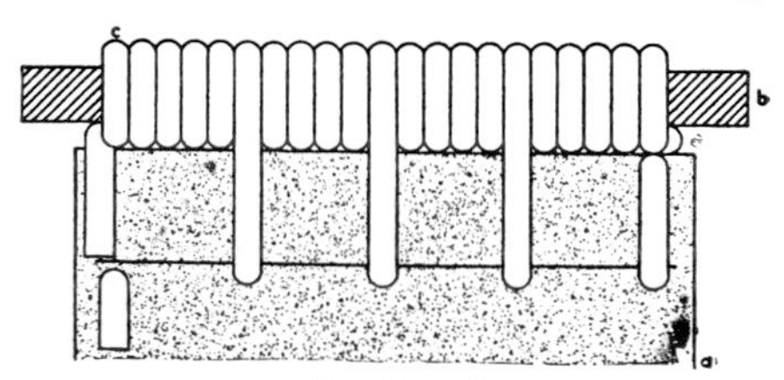

Headband
a = body of book; b = catgut, hemp, or leather; c = silk thread

Most Continental binders favour headbanding, which is not generally practised in cased books in Britain. Headbands were in use in 15th-century England.

headcap: the shaped fold of leather at the head and tail of the spine. When the glued leather cover of a book is fitted to the body, a piece of sized Italian hemp is put inside the turn-in at the head and tail of the spine. This is done whether *headbands*, q.v., are used or not; if they are, they are left visible.

heading: see *chapter heading*, *cross-heads*, *shoulder-heads*, *side-heads*.

headline: the title of a book as printed at the top of every page of text: also known as a *page head*. Variants of this are title on the verso pages, chapter title on the recto; or chapter title on the verso pages and a brief indication of page subject on the recto: such headlines are also referred to as *running heads*.

heat-set inks: printing inks designed to dry quickly and facilitate faster printing. Ingredients vary but usually contain a concentrated pigment, synthetic resins and a volatile petroleum oil. These are combined to form a thermoplastic fluid. The printed web of paper is heated to vaporize the oil and then quickly cooled to harden the plastic residue on the sheet.

Heath, Charles: the reputed inventor, *c*. 1818, of *steel engraving*, q.v.

Heber, Richard, 1773–1833: a wealthy bibliophile and founder of the Athenaeum Club. His library of about 146,800 volumes was stored in his eight houses in England and on the Continent. Of special importance were the works on English poetry and the classics. He bought at all auctions and even purchased whole libraries.

His collection was sold from 1834–37, the British Museum and the Bodleian Library acquiring some items.

Heidelberg: the name of automatic printing presses made by the Schnellpressenfabrik A.G., Heidelberg. The first machine was built in 1914; this was a platen machine in which paper was fed by revolving wings. By 1932 this design had developed into the present Super-Heidelberg with paper dimensions 26 cm. by 36 cm. (inside chase size 26 cm. by 34 cm.) and a catalogued speed of 4000 copies an hour.

The Large Heidelberg constructed on the same principle uses paper of 34 cm. by 46 cm. The Cylinder

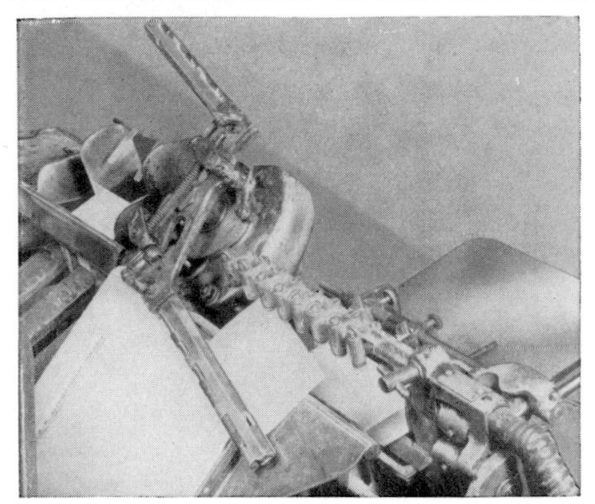

The Heidelberg feeder. The sheet is first lifted by a suction device, and is then gripped by a swinging arm which carries it into position for printing, and subsequently conveys it to the delivery table

The Cylinder Heidelberg

Heidelberg, first marketed in 1936, is a single-revolution machine in which the cylinder, with a constant speed, makes one revolution for each impression, while the speed of the bed in returning (running without load) is almost twice as great as when the forme is under pressure. The size of the paper is 50 cm. by 65 cm., the printing surface 44 cm. by 65 cm. Catalogued speed 3600 impressions an hour.

The latest model (1954) of the Original Heidelberg Cylinder Press will take sheets up to 54 cm. by 72 cm., and has four forme rollers. (G. U.)

See also *letterpress machines*.

height to paper: the overall height of printing plates and type in letterpress printing. This is standardized in Great Britain as 0·918 in. from feet to face. (An exception is the Oxford University Press which works to its own type height of 0·9395 in.)

Heinemann Foundation for Literature: an award made for a work in any branch of literature, originally written in English, judged by the Royal Society of Literature to be of real literary worth. Works may be submitted by publishers, not authors.

heliogravure: 1. a means for the reproduction by process work of line drawings. The original is exposed in a camera, so that a negative is obtained which is printed on carbon tissue, and sensitized by immersion in a solution of 3 to 4% potassium dichromate solution. The printed paper is softened in cold water and smoothed out with the layer on a silver-plated copper plate. After developing in water at 105° F (40° C), a gelatine relief is obtained which is made electrically conductive (after drying) by black-leading. The copper plate is suspended as a cathode in a galvanic copper-plating bath, and in this a copper film is precipitated on to the relief image which can be removed from the base, due to the silver-plating, when it has become thick enough. This precipitate can be used as a printing plate. The method originated from experiments by Paul Pretsch, *c.* 1854.

It can be used for developing the original plates of maps by a method devised by Emil Mariot of Graz, Austria, in 1867.

2. the terms heliogravure and photogravure are occasionally loosely used without discrimination to describe the latter process. (G. U.)

See also *photogravure*.

hell-box: a receptacle for broken or discarded type.

Hemans Prize: see *Felicia Hemans Prize*.

Hempel quoin: a patent steel quoin used for locking up type in the chase. It was invented by Henry A. Hempel about 1878. Two wedge-shaped units, with toothed inner sides, are operated by a key which pushes the wedges outwards, thereby creating pressure between type and chase. For an illustration see *quoins*.

heraldic colours: the standard colours (or tinctures) used in heraldry are occasionally printed in monochrome when the expense of colour reproduction is not warranted. Hatching is used to distinguish the various colours, and a standard system is in use throughout most of the world: this is said to have been first employed for Langrius's armorial chart of the Duchy of Brabant, 1600, and popularized by the Jesuit Silvester de Petra Sancta for the book 'Tesserae gentilitiae', Rome, 1638. (With G. U.)

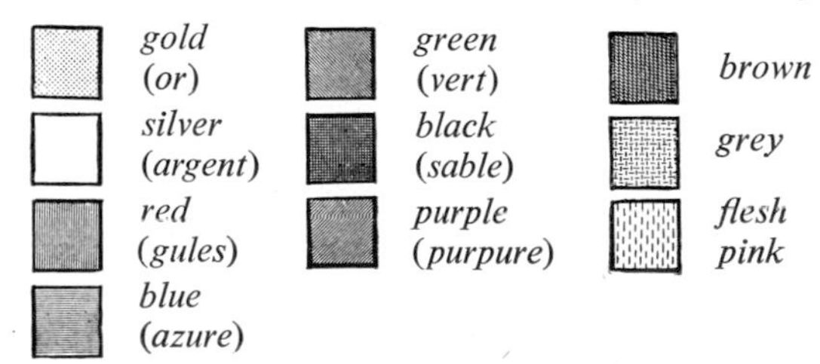

Heraldic tinctures and metals

herbal: a book giving the names and descriptions of plants in general. Herbals are believed to date from the 4th century B.C. (Theophrastus); and a noteworthy early example is the *Vienna Dioscorides*, q.v.

An early printed herbal was the 'Herbarius' printed by Johannes Philippus de Lignamine, Rome, *c.* 1483, of unknown origin but probably based on a 2nd-century A.D. work of Apuleius Platonicus. The first printed illustrated herbal was 'Herbarius Moguntinus' which Peter Schöffer issued in 1484; his 'Hortus sanitatis', probably compiled by Johann Wonnecke von Cube, appearing in 1485. In England Rycharde Banckes's 'Here begynnyth a new mater, the whiche sheweth and treateth of ye vertues & proprytes of herbes, the whiche is called an Herball' was printed in London in 1525.

Herbert, William, third Earl of Pembroke, 1580–1630: an English statesman deserving mention here for his purchase in 1629 of the 242 Greek manuscripts from the Venetian Barocci library. At this time Pembroke was Chancellor of Oxford University and it was to the Bodleian Library there that he gave most of the collection. The twenty-four items he retained were later bought by Oliver Cromwell who gave them to the Bodleian in 1654.

Hermann, Caspar: a German-American printer who introduced *offset printing*, q.v., into Europe in 1907. In 1908 he patented the first practical offset press for perfecting the paper. He subsequently made several inventions used in lithographic printing, e.g. *homogeneous printing*, q.v. (G.U.)

Herringman, Henry: an enterprising publisher of Restoration London. He acquired the copyrights of works by many poets and dramatists including Dryden, Davenant, Cowley, Waller, and also of the scientist John Boyle.

heures, livre d': see *Book of Hours*.

heuristic: the search for and location of manuscripts.

Heynlin von Stein, Johann: the Rector, in 1469, of the Sorbonne. With Guillaume Fichet he was responsible for bringing together in Paris the first printers of that city, *Crantz*, *Friburger*, and *Gering*, qq.v. Heynlin also advised what works they should print, and himself edited the first book to appear, 'Epistolae' of Gasparino Barzizi, 1470.

Hibbert, George, 1757–1837: a London business-man who assembled a valuable collection of books of early English poetry. He was a member of the Roxburghe Club, and printed in 1819 as his contribution to their series of publications 'Six Bookes of Metamorphoses by Ovyde' from a manuscript preserved in the Pepysian Library.

Hibbert Press: a private printing press established at Kentish Town, London, by Julian Hibbert (d. 1834). He is remembered for two books he issued, 'Orpheus Umnoi', 1827 (extracted from Hermann's edition of the Orphica), which he printed in uncial letters as an experiment, and 'Peri deicidaimoniac', 1828 (Plutarch and Theophrastus on Superstition).

Hiberno-Saxon illumination: the origins of Celtic illumination are obscure since examples survive only in such fully mature works as the *Book of Durrow*, *Book of Kells*, and *Lindisfarne Gospels*, qq.v. These 7th- and 8th-century manuscripts of the Gospels were made in Christian monasteries of northern Ireland or Northumbria whence the art of illuminating was brought by Irish monks. There was usually a whole-page representation of the Evangelists, one before each Gospel. The initial and first few words of the text were illuminated, and there were some full pages based on cruciform patterns. Gold and silver were rarely used, and never extensively. Drawings were not in perspective; typical designs had an all-over effect of continuous pattern, mostly strapwork, with convoluting lacertine animals.

The influence in Europe of Celtic and Anglo-Saxon illumination was wide and profound; monks emigrated and established monasteries which became important centres of learning (e.g. at Bobbio in Italy, 613; at St Gall in Switzerland, *c.* 612; Salzburg in 739; Echternach in 698).

With the arrival in England of the Danish hordes little illuminating was done in the 9th century. In 954 Aethelwold founded a monastery at Abingdon, later moving to Winchester where his patronage of painting led to the *Winchester School*, q.v., and a new flowering of art.

From 970–1070 there was a noteworthy series of manuscripts illustrated by lively outline drawings or sketches, done in brown ink, and positioned on the page close to the text they depicted: colour washes were sometimes added. In style and treatment the hunchbacked figures with curiously protuding necks and tapering legs derive from the *Utrecht Psalter*, q.v. An example of this style is the Malmesbury Prudentius, *c.* 1040, now in Cambridge University Library.

For some of the important manuscripts and other schools in pre-Conquest England see references under *illumination*.

hic nullus est defectus: Latin words, meaning that 'nothing is omitted here', sometimes found in early printed books where a blank page occurs, to inform the reader of this fact. Before the days of galley proofs, later to be paged, it was customary to divide the manuscript of a lengthy book between several presses (not necessarily within one workshop) and the exact calculation of how much matter would make up a page was not always achieved. Hence the occasional need for a page cramped with contractions, the insertion of an extra leaf within a quire, or the inscription noted above.

hieratic: a cursive form of hieroglyphics used principally by religious scribes in ancient Egypt for the writing of texts on papyrus. It was originally written in vertical columns but later in horizontal lines from right to left and continued in use until the 3rd century A.D.

See also *letters—forms and styles.*

hieratica: 1. the finest quality of papyrus used in Rome at the time of Pliny, A.D. 23–79. Under Augustus Caesar its name was changed to 'Augusta'.

2. the trade name for a certain quality of paper.

hieroglyphics: literally, 'holy stone-writing,' being the form of communicating thought by pictorial symbols used in Egypt from 3000 B.C. The meaning of the symbols was discovered by Champollion in 1799 when he deciphered the Rosetta Stone on which was a parallel text in hieroglyphics, *demotic* script, q.v., and Greek.

See also *letters—forms and styles.*

High House Press: a hand-press started by J. E. Masters of Shaftesbury in 1924. He issued reprints of lesser-known poetry of the 15th and 17th centuries, and also modern poetry. (M. L.)

See S. Matthewman, 'The High House Press: a short history and appreciations', 1930.

high mill finish: calendered paper with a surface intermediate between M.F. and super-calendered paper.

high quads: spaces cast nearly type high. Used in plaster stereotyping.

Higonnet–Moyroud photo-composing machine: see *Photon.*

Hildesheim Psalter: a 12th-century manuscript from the Abbey of St Albans. Notable are the numerous figures, often ugly, and complicated initials in which the animals seem to derive from bestiaries of the period.

hinged: plates, or other separate sheets to be inserted in a book, which have been given a narrow fold on their inner edges; they will thus lie flat and turn easily when bound.

hinges: the channels lying between the two halves of the end-papers where the body of the book is fixed to the covers. See also *joints.*

historiated letters: initial capital letters embellished with detailed drawings illustrating an incident in the text they introduce. English examples are found in 11th–13th-century manuscripts.

See also *illumination, rubricator.*

Hoe: an important American firm of printing machine manufacturers which traces its origins to the arrival there in 1805 of Robert Hoe (1784–1833) from Leicestershire. With Peter and Matthew Smith as partners he built platen and flat-bed presses. The firm developed considerably after 1830, when cylinder presses of the Napier type were built in an improved form.

It was Richard March Hoe (1812–86) who built the first rotary printing press. In his 'Type Revolving Machine', 1846, ordinary matter was used with wedge-shaped leads, etc., directly justified on a cylinder of large diameter. Paper was sheet-fed by boys, being taken from the feed-board by automatic grippers, and pressed on to the large forme cylinder by from four to ten impression cylinders, each having its own feeder (see illustration under *letterpress machines*). This rotary sheet press became very popular for newspaper work, and R. Hoe & Co., New York (founded 1823), have ever since been specialists for newspaper printing presses. Type-revolving presses were made until 1876 when they were superseded by the Hoe web-perfecting press of 1871.

The firm later took up the manufacture of tin printing and offset machines, among which a 4- to 6-colour offset sheet press 125 cm. by 180 cm. should be mentioned (see illustration under *offset press*). (With G.U.)

Hoerner plates: plastic plates for the printing of halftones, devised by a Herr Hoerner (W. Germany), in 1954.

The original to be reproduced is photographed through a screen with a standard process camera. The negative is contact-printed on to a sheet of Perlon (trade name of a synthetic material) which has been sensitized on both sides. As the sheet is transparent both sides are exposed. Upon immersion in a developing bath the unexposed areas of the contact side are removed, leaving a screened printing surface of conical-shaped dots.

If the reverse of the plate is developed a dot-for-dot make-ready results.

Holbein, Hans, 1497–1543: worked for a time at Basle where he designed small woodcut decorations and title-page borders for Froben and other publishers. He employed a craftsman cutter for the blocks (Ger. Formschneider).

Probably his best-known book illustrations appear in 'Les Simulachres et Historiées Faces de la Mort', a series of forty-one small cuts, one per page, with a Bible verse above and a French poem under each.

This was printed by Gaspar and Melchior Treschel, Lyons, 1538.

Holbein's work was widely copied and imitated by other printers of the day.

Hole, Henry F. P. W., fl. 1800: a wood engraver and pupil of *Thomas Bewick*, q.v.; he was one of the engravers who cut Thurston's designs for Ackermann's 'Religious Emblems', 1809.

Hole, Robert, fl. 1600: one of the earliest English engravers of music on copper. An example of his work is 'Parthenia in-violata or mayden-musicke for the virginals and bass-viol' which he engraved and published *c.* 1611.

holiday: said of any area on a paste-covered surface which is unintentionally left uncoated, e.g. on a lining paper.

holing out: the punching of holes through the boards of a book which is being hand-bound; this is done prior to lacing.

Holkham Bible Picture Book: a manuscript containing 'a pictorial representation of the Creation and Fall, . . . the story of Christ, interspersed with apocryphal incidents, and finally the signs of the end of the world and the Last Judgement' (Hassall). The work had no contemporary title, the present one being suggested by M. R. James in 1922. It consists of 231 pictures on forty-two leaves, all but two leaves being illustrated, and was probably made in London for a Dominican patron between 1326 and 1331.

It appears that the draughtsman was the first to work on the book. Using a fine quill, his strokes are vigorous, accurate, and observant, ranging from gross caricature to sublime beauty. The work of the colourist was less successful, on occasion masking the delicacy of the drawing or even misinterpreting the meaning. No gold was used. After the colourist came the scribe who added an explanatory text in Anglo-Norman (the language of the upper-class laity), using a large 14th-century hand. A rubrisher added occasional initials in red, and also patterns to some of the robes. Dr. Hassall suggests the scribe was one of no great literary ability who probably had no written text from which to copy, resulting in mistakes.

The book is now in the British Museum, but students should see 'The Holkham Bible Picture Book', with introduction and commentary by W. O. Hassall, Dropmore Press, 1954, on which the above note is based.

Hollander: the standard beating machine, of which there are several varieties, for reducing half-stuff to pulp. This means the separation and reduction in length of the fibres and the gelatinization of their surfaces (which imparts bonding property and subsequent strength to the paper). The machine was invented in Holland in the 17th century (inventor unknown), hence the name. Before this, beating was done by a battery of hammers or stampers rising and falling on rags contained with water in an oblong tank. Basically, the Hollander is an oblong vat of cast iron or cement, lined with tiles, and having a central wall, called a mid-feather, around which the stuff is circulated.

In the U.S.A. it is usually called a *beater*.

Hollar, Wenzel, 1607–77: a Bohemian engraver who was the most prolific etcher and copperplate engraver of the 17th century. He worked in Frankfurt, Strasbourg, and Cologne until 1637 when, after meeting the Earl of Arundel, he came to London and introduced the art of etching. He did title-pages and illustrations for several publishers, but his collections of women's fashions are perhaps best known today.

Holle, Lienhart, fl. 1482: a wooden-block cutter of Ulm who began printing in 1482. In this year he printed Ptolemy's 'Cosmographia', edited by Nicolaus Germanus, with thirty-two woodcut maps. The type was a clear text. He printed 'Das Buch der Weisheit' in 1483. A year later he was forced to flee from creditors and his press was acquired by Johann Reger, who also issued 'Cosmographia' (1486).

hollow back: the type of back in a book which when the book is open leaves a hollow space between the (decorated) spine and the sewn back of the book. Cf. *tight back*. (L.K.)

hollow quads: large quads are sometimes cast with hollow parts to make them lighter and save metal.

hollows: strips of heavy paper, which, one per case, are glued between the boards of a book, across the back, as a support for the spine and as a basis for the spinal blocking.

See also *lining up*, *Oxford hollow*.

Folded hollow

holograph: written wholly in the author's handwriting.

homogeneous printing: a lithographic process devised by Caspar Hermann for obtaining seemingly genuine half-tones in autolithography. It was not, however, of any practical importance. (G.U.)

hook in: to set words, for which there is no room when setting a line of type to a given measure, within a square bracket on the line below or above.

hooked: said of single-leaf illustrations printed on slightly wider paper than the text they are to accompany. This allows for an inner marginal fold, or hinge, which fits round the back of the section to which the plate belongs. Alternatively, the plate can be folded round an inner pair of pages, nearer the appropriate text.
See also *guards*.

hooks: an obsolete term for printers' brackets or parentheses.

Hopfer, Daniel, *c.* 1470–1536: a German armorial engraver who is regarded as the originator of several methods of graphic etching. He worked in Augsburg where he probably became interested in the graphic arts through his attempts to reproduce his armorial engravings. His title-pages and borders are important; for these he achieved an effect of white against a black background. Notable is his work for an edition of the 'Sachsenspiegel', 1516. (With G.U.)

Horae: see *Book of Hours*.

horn book: a form of child's primer in use in England from the 15th–18th centuries. The earliest examples were made from 'wainscot' (thin panels of oak) and had a label bearing the alphabet, simple spelling, numbers, and the Lord's Prayer pasted on the wood and covered with a thin transparent veneer of cattle horn. A wooden handle was fixed to the frame. In later examples the back of the panel was covered with morocco or roan stamped with an ornamental device. Other, but rare, examples were made entirely of cowhide with a window cut in the upper portion.
See also *battledore*.

hose: the wooden sleeve enclosing the screw (spindle) which raises and lowers the platen of a hand printing press. The hose, which enables the spindle to be turned without turning the platen, is secured to the spindle by a ring or *garter*. It probably originated in Blaeu's press of *c.* 1620.
See also *hand-press*.

hot plate: an iron plate, several mm. thick, resting on a wooden frame and heated from below by gas, a spirit lamp, or electric elements. It is used in etching and copperplate printing. (G.U.)

hot-pressed: paper glazed by heated metal plates; limited to the finest qualities. Abbreviated as *H.P.*

hot-rolled: paper glazed by steam-heated calenders.

hot-top enamel: see *enamel process*.

Hours: see *Book of Hours*.

house corrections: alterations made to proofs or script by the publisher or printer, as distinct from those made by the author.

house organ: a publication, issued regularly or irregularly, devoted to the affairs of a business concern, and of particular interest to its staff, clients, and friends. It is not normally sold. (M.L.)

house style: see *style of the house*.

Howard, Thomas, second Earl of Arundel, 1585–1646: the assembler of an important collection of State Papers, charters, registers, and early literary works, as well as Latin, Greek, and French manuscripts. Notable additions were the *Arundel Psalter*, q.v., and the library of the Nuremberg bibliophile, Bilibald Pirckheimer (1470–1530), which Howard acquired in 1636.
In 1666 Henry Howard, grandson of Thomas, disposed of the library. Half the manuscripts he gave to the College of Arms; the books and the other half were given to the Royal Society which was accommodated in Arundel House. The printed books were ultimately sold, partly by Quaritch in 1870, and partly by Sotheby in 1925.

H.P.: see *hot-pressed.*

Hubbard, Elbert, 1856–1915: the founder of the *Roycroft Press*, q.v.

Huber press: several styles of this cylinder press were made—a single-cylinder, a two-colour, and a perfecting press—all built upon the two-revolution principle, and designed by the Huber–Hodgman Press Company of America. (M.L.)

Huebner, William C.: an American inventor and builder of several machines used in the graphic art industry. He directs the Huebner Laboratories which collaborate with the Lanston Monotype Machine Co., Philadelphia. (G.U.)
See also *dark-room camera, step-and-repeat machine.*

Huebner photo-setter: see *photo-composing machine.*

Huguenot Society: a society founded in London in 1885 for the printing of information on the French Huguenots and their settlements in Great Britain.

humanistic: the term given to the revived Carolingian script used by the Italian renaissance scholars on which the earliest roman or venetian type-designs were based, the first being cut by Adolf Rusch of Strasbourg in 1464.
See also *letters—forms and styles.*

humidified: said of paper which has been artificially matured to influence its working properties.

humidifier: see *conditioning.*

Humphrey, Duke of Gloucester, 1391–1447: an English statesman who, between 1439 and 1446, donated about 600 manuscripts to Oxford University. Subjects included medicine, science, and theology, also Latin and Italian poetry.

Only three works now remain in the Bodleian as most of them were destroyed or scattered in 1550 when Edward VI ordered the reformation of the University; a few are in the British Museum, the Bibliothèque Nationale, Paris, and in three Oxford colleges.

Hungarian leather: see *tawing.*

Hunter, Dard, 1883: born in Steubenville, Ohio. He studied in Vienna where he designed several books for a Viennese publisher before going to London in 1911. There he acquired a considerable knowledge of paper-making in addition to working as a commercial artist. He subsequently returned to America to become the leading authority on paper-making and a writer on the subject.

See Dard Hunter, 'My Life with Paper', New York, Knopf, 1958.

Huntington, Henry E., 1850–1927: one of the wealthiest of American bibliophiles of whose library in California it is claimed there are as many books printed before 1640 as are in the British Museum. He bought extensively in Europe. Included in his library are 5400 incunabula, 20,000 English first editions, twenty-five Caxtons, Shakespeare folios, some 55,000 Americana, etc.

Huntington, Robert, 1637–1701: an orientalist from whom the Bodleian acquired some 680 Oriental manuscripts, including Coptic Gospels, which he had brought back from the Nitrian Convents of Egypt in 1678.

Hupp, Otto, 1859–1949: a German craftsman, engraver, and type-cutter. He made some beautiful typefaces for Genzsch & Heyse, e.g. Neudeutsch, 1899; Gebr. Klingspor, e.g. Liturgisch, 1906, and others. He was greatly interested in a revival of German printing, and did important research into Gutenberg's history and that of other early printers. (With G.U.)

Husník, Jakob, 1837–1916: a Prague professor who was an outstanding technician in reproduction work. He made important contributions to the development of *collotype,* q.v., and other chromate processes. He also indicated the theoretical conditions for *mercurography,* a quicksilver process which was brought out later under the name of pantone printing. (G.U.)

Huss, Martinus, fl. 1478–80: the printer of Lyons who, in 1478, issued the first illustrated book in France, 'Miroir de la rédemption de l'umain lynage' in which he used 256 woodcuts taken from an edition of 'Speculum humanae salvationis' by Bernard Richel of Basle, 1476. Huss, who had learned the craft of printing in Basle, worked for a time with Johann Siber.

Huth, Henry, 1815–78: a banker and bibliophile who from 1855 began to develop his library. By the time of his death he had such rarities as a Mazarin Bible, block books, a Coverdale Bible, 1535, Caxtons, Aldines, etc.

The library was increased in importance by his son, Alfred Henry Huth (1850–1910), who bequeathed fifty items from the collection to the British Museum: among those chosen were twelve illuminated manuscripts, first-edition quartos of some Shakespeare plays, and important early printed German and Spanish works. Much of the library was auctioned in 1911 and 1912, realizing about £300,000. The majority of the treasures went to American collections.

hydraulic press: a powerful standing press the platen of which is operated by water at very high pressure. Such presses are used both in printing works and binderies wherever great pressure is needed. In *edition binding* they have been superseded by the *pneumatic press,* q.v. (L.K.)

Hypnerotomachia Poliphili: see *Colonna, Francesco.*

I

Ibarra, Joaquim, 1725–85: a distinguished printer of Madrid, and Court printer to Carlos III, who had a great influence on raising the standards of printing, not only in Spain, but in Europe generally. His edition of Sallust, with parallel Latin and Spanish texts, 1772, and his 'Don Quixote', 4 vols., 1780, are considered his finest works.

ibid.: an abbreviation for the Latin 'ibidem', i.e. in the same place.

Ibotson, Richard: a paper-maker of Poyle, Middlesex, who was one of the first to buy a Fourdrinier machine. In 1830 he invented the slotted strainer, or screen plate, a great advance on previous methods of straining paper pulp. (M. L.)

I.C.B.A.: see *International Community of Booksellers Associations.*

Idotron: an electronic device fitted to a printing press for colour density control, enabling the printer to maintain uniform colour throughout a run. It is made by J. F. Crosfield Ltd., London.

A scanning head, mounted on the press after the last colour-printing cylinder, scans marks printed in each colour, and at the same time actuates measuring instruments which indicate the density of each colour. When the printer is satisfied with the colours he sets a meter for each. Should any colour-change occur during the run the particular meter dial will show it.

i.e.: an abbreviation for the Latin 'id est' (that is).

ILAB: the initials of the *International League of Antiquarian Booksellers*, q.v.

Illig, Moritz Friedrich: the reputed discoverer of the suitability of resin as an ingredient to make paper non-absorbent.

See also *size.*

illuminated: 1. said of books or manuscripts having letters, initial words, or borders painted in gold, silver, or colours. Illuminated initials were a development of *versals*, q.v.

See also *rubricated.*

2. a slang term for the glosses in a Greek or Latin text having an interlinear translation.

illumination: the decoration of a manuscript or incunabulum with gold or silver and colours, the result being a compound of illustration and ornament.

Until the 14th century illuminating was mostly done by monks for religious houses, and while the exchanging or giving of books between monasteries influenced work done in various centres, a continuity of tradition in the choice and treatment of subject was inevitable. From this time, however, groups of artists travelling the country or established in city workshops were commissioned by wealthy nobles and other lay patrons. Several artists worked on one manuscript and were paid on piece-rates, the patron specifying the number of initials and scenes he required.

A design was first drawn and sized with a mixture of clay, gypsum or lime, to be followed by an adhesive such as egg-white; gold or silver was laid on and burnished, finally colours were applied, their traditional association with certain subjects being a guide to the artist. The eight colours mostly employed (yellow, red, blue, green, white, black, rose, purple) were made from mineral earths or plants, e.g. yellow from turmeric roots, white from burnt bones, purple from turnsole or shellfish (murex), red from minium, black from sloe berries, green from copper, etc. Precise directions for making colours were written by the 12th-century monk Theophilus Presbyter in his 'Schedula diversarum artium', where he warns that ingredients must be varied according to the quality of the parchment, and that a good craftsman must devise his own recipes.

Earliest surviving examples of the art are fragments of papyrus rolls, and notable is an 'Iliad' on vellum, now in Milan, dating from the 3rd–5th centuries, of which about sixty pictures remain.

From the 6th–11th centuries the purpose of illumination was to tell a story or compose a pattern, thus backgrounds carefully drawn from nature had no place, and we see figures with green or blue hair and red skies. Symbols often interpreted a subject; thus an angel was associated with St Matthew, a lion with Mark, an ox with Luke, and an eagle with John, walls for the heavenly city, and a gaping-mouthed whale for the entrance of hell, etc.

In the mid-11th and 12th centuries, in Western Europe, outline figure drawings within a system of frames, owing something to the art of glass staining, became important. Gold or purely ornamental backgrounds were usual.

By the 13th century Byzantine influence spread to such German scriptoria as Echternach, Fulda, Salzburg, Regensburg, Cologne, and Hildesheim. In France, however, Gothic art developed in historiated initials, a greater realism in ornament, architectural details, and costume. In this great change the scriptoria of Paris led the way.

In Europe generally, from the 14th century onwards, great attention was paid to faces, which were almost portraits. Actual buildings and nature scenes were painted with great fidelity, and backgrounds were often crowded with happenings not connected with the subject of the work being illustrated.

For notes on national schools and periods see *Byzantine illumination, Canterbury School, Carolingian illumination, Channel School, French-, Gothic-, Hiberno-Saxon-, Italian illumination, Northumbrian School, Ottonian-, Romanesque illumination, St Albans-, Salisbury-, Salzburg School, Spanish illumination, Winchester School.*

For short notes on individual manuscripts see *Anglo-Saxon Chronicle, Arundel Psalter, Ashburnham Pentateuch, Athelstan Psalter, Augustine Gospels, Bedford Missal, Benedictional of St Aethelwold, Berry, Carmelite Missal, Cathach Psalter, Cerne, Book of, Codex Alexandrinus, -Amiatinus, -Argenteus, -Bezae, -Laudianus, -Rescriptus Aphraëmi, -Rossanensis, -Sinaiticus, Cura Pastoralis, Durham Cassiodorus, Durrow, Book of, Echternach MSS., Folchart Psalter, Gorleston Psalter, Guthlac Roll, Haye MS., Hildesheim Psalter, Holkham Bible Picture Book, Kells, Book of, Laurentian Codex, Lindisfarne Gospels, Luttrel Psalter, Minnesängerhandschriften, Missale speciale Constantiense, Ormesby Psalter, Psalter of Alphonso, Queen Mary's Psalter, Sacramentary of Robert of Jumièges, St Chad Gospels, St Gall Gospels, St Omer Psalter, Sherborne Missal, Stonyhurst Gospel, Tickhill Psalter, Utrecht Psalter, Vienna Dioscorides, Vienna Genesis, Winchester Bible.*

See also *acanthus, armarian, babery, bestiary, calligraphy, chrysographer, codex aureus, cumdach, diapered* (3), *drolleries, factotum, floriated, gold, gouache, grisaille, guide letters, historiated letters, inhabited scroll, initial letters, lacertine animals, limner, murex, phylactery, putti, rubricator, scriptorium, untouched, versals.*

illustration of books: from the days of the Egyptian papyrus to the invention of printing the written word has been supplemented or made clearer by some form of picture. (See *illumination.*) Illustrations in the first printed books were made from wooden blocks (see *block book, woodcut*). Towards the end of the 15th century the art of printing from engraved metal plates developed, and by the late 16th had superseded the importance of the woodcut. *Etching* and *copperplate engraving*, qq.v., were all important in the 18th century.

Lithography, q.v., was invented in 1798 as a new medium for the book illustrator, and one which has never been superseded: it is particularly suitable for coloured reproduction work. The somewhat inflexible and impersonal nature of the photographic reproduction processes which dominated the 19th century was followed in the early present century by a revival of craftsmanship in which wood engravers and autolithographers created their designs directly on the printing medium.

In the 20th century, too, the purpose of illustration has occasionally been deflected from its original aim of furthering the message of the writer, notably by Ambroise Vollard who commissioned artists and then added text to their designs.

No useful purpose would be served by cataloguing here the numerous book illustrators of all ages and countries, but among skilled and original artists whose work has appeared in British books published in this century should be mentioned Edward Ardizzone, Edward Bawden, John Buckland-Wright, John Farleigh, Barnett Freedman, Robert Gibbings, Eric Gill, Blair Hughes-Stanton, Lynton Lamb, Clare Leighton, Mervyn Peake, John Piper, Eric Ravilious, Reynolds Stone, and Rex Whistler.

In America Rockwell Kent, W. A. Dwiggins, and E. McKnight Kauffer are of note.

See also *aquatint, collotype, dry-point, half-tone, line engraving, mezzotint, photogravure, wood engraving.*

image: the subject to be reproduced as an illustration by a printing process.

image area: the part of a printing plate or cylinder which bears the design to be printed.

imbrication: a style of book-cover decoration in which the pattern is one of overlapping leaves or scales.

imitation art paper: a cheaper form of art paper. Loading is added to the pulp in the beater, and the sheet, when formed, is sprayed with water to bring the clay to the surface before calendering. Cheaper qualities often have an uneven surface and duller finish. As with art paper, such heavier faces as Bodoni, Plantin, or Times New Roman should be used for printing text.

See also *water finish.*

imitation leather: paper or cloth finished and embossed to give the impression of leather.

See also *leather varieties.*

imitation morocco: any imitation of morocco leather. (L.K.)

imitation parchment: a variety of tough paper, devised in 1857 to imitate the natural skin, by W. E. Gaine.

imitation russia: see *American russia.*

impensis: a Latin word meaning 'at the expense of'. It occasionally appears in early printed works followed by the name of the patron, publisher, or other person who financed publication.

imperfections: 1. a bookbinding term used (anomalously) for good sheets required to complete an order for binding. Faulty or damaged sheets are known as *bad sheets.*

2. copies of books which contain printing or binding faults. The publisher usually exchanges or perfects such books when returned by a bookseller or member of the public, and pays all expenses including postage. Copies are not returned for the insertion of corrigenda or errata slips since these are not connected with defective make-up.

Imperial press: a platen jobbing press which had a moving platen and a stationary perpendicular bed. Its distinctive feature was a second ink fountain with distributing rollers below the bed, from which the forme rollers received a fresh supply of ink before their start back on the upward motion. Now obsolete.

imposing surface: the iron surface on which a forme is *imposed,* q.v. It was formerly made of stone.

imposing to quire: the arranging of pages in the chase so that when printed the work can be made up by insetting one folded sheet inside another.

imposition: the arranging of pages of type in a chase in a particular sequence (known as the *imposing scheme*) so that when folded the printed pages will be in consecutive order. Furniture is added and the whole is locked up into a forme. Imposition is done in close liaison with the folding department, where it must suit the particular folding machine used by the binder.

See also *book impositions, folding, tack marks.*

Imposition also refers to the appearance of the margins on a pair of facing pages. Normally the printer submits for approval a margin or imposition sheet before completing page proofs.

impressed watermark: the design left on sheets of paper by a rubber stereo placed against paper at the press rolls. This is an alternative to the genuine watermark. Also called *press mark.*

impression: 1. all copies of a book printed at one time from the same type or plates. An edition may be printed unaltered in several impressions. Often referred to as a *printing.* Cf. *issue.*

2. the pressure applied to a forme of type by the cylinder or platen.

See also *make-ready.*

impression cylinder: the cylinder around which the paper is carried during its contact with type, plates, or a rubber offset roller.

impressor regius: the Latin equivalent of *Imprimeur du roi* or *Queen's Printer,* qq.v.

imprimatur: the Latin for 'let it be printed'. Originally a statement appearing in early printed books to show that permission to print the work had been granted by some authority empowered to do so, but now confined to works officially approved by a Bishop of the Roman Catholic Church as being free of doctrinal or moral error.

See also *cum licentia, licence leaf, nihil obstat, privilege.*

Imprimerie Royale du Louvre: the French royal printing house established (1638) at the instigation of Cardinal Richelieu for Louis XIII. Its finest production during the 17th century was the eight-volume Vulgate Bible, 1642.

After the Revolution, *c.* 1795, it was renamed Imprimerie Nationale. One of the most historic collections of types in the world is to be seen here; this is the 'Cabinet des Poinçons'.

See also *romain du roi Louis XIV.*

Imprimeur du roi: the former French equivalent for our present *Queen's Printer,* q.v. The office was created by Charles VIII who bestowed the title on Pierre Le Rouge, printer of 'La Mer des Histoires', 1488–89: last to receive the title was A. F. Didot, in 1829.

'The Imprint': a periodical established in January 1913 by Gerard Meynell, Edward Johnston (who designed the sanserif type used throughout London Transport), and J. H. Mason. Its aim was to raise the standard of printing.

Meynell and Mason designed a new type-face for this journal, Monotype series 101, which is widely used today. The ninth and last issue of 'The Imprint' appeared in 1913.

imprint: 1. printer's. The name of the printer and place of printing which the law requires shall identify every printed paper or book which, at the time it is printed, is meant to be published (*vide* 'Newspapers, Printers, and Reading Rooms Repeal Act, 1869'). This usually appears on the reverse of the title-page, or on the last printed page of a book. The first book to have imprint and title together on the title-page was the 'Calendario' of Johannes Regiomontanus, printed at Venice in 1476 by Erhard Ratdolt and his associates.

2. publisher's. The name of the publisher which, with place and date of publication, is usually printed at the foot of the title-page.

imprint date: the publication date as stated on the title-page or its verso.

in boards: said of a book which is cut after the boards have been attached. The book is taken from the sewer, end-papered, glued up, rounded and backed, and the boards are laced on. It is pressed and cut with a plough.

in boards extra: an 'in boards' binding with edges gilt solid.

in pendentive: a manner of setting in which successive lines are set in decreasing width. The first line (or two) is set to the full measure, subsequent lines are indented left and right of a central axis so that the last line of a page or paragraph is occupied by a single word. The effect is of a triangle resting on its apex. Examples are to be found in 16th-century French books.

See also *hanging paragraph.*

in print: a trade phrase referring to books obtainable from the publisher as distinct from *reprinting* or *out of print*, qq.v.

in quires: unbound printed sheets, especially in the flat. The term is also loosely used of sheets which have been processed up to the point of folding and gathering. It is gradually losing ground in favour of the term *in sheets* with which it is synonymous.

See also *sheet stock*, *quire*. (L.K.)

in sheets: see *in quires.*

in slip: said of matter in galleys before making up into pages.

incipit: the Latin for 'it begins'. The words 'hic incipit' and the first words of the text are the means of entitling and identifying manuscripts, and also incunabula, published without a title-page. For these introductory words majuscule letters or a distinguishing colour were used. An alternative is the *initia*, q.v.

See also *explicit*, *label title*, *title-page*.

incunabulum (pl. **incunabula**): a book printed before 1500, i.e. in the infancy of printing. The word derives from the Latin 'cunae' = cradle, it being said that Philippe Labbé (1607–67), a Parisian bibliographer, was the first to apply the term 'incunabula' to the early art of printing, not to the books themselves, which were not so described until the late 18th century.

The German term 'Der Wiegendruck' came into use towards the end of the 19th century, largely because the word 'Inkunabel' had acquired a wider connotation, e.g. 'Inkunabel der Lithographie', 'Inkunabel des Kupferstichs', etc.

Early printers were often scholars and authors who brought to their new craft such traditions of manuscript writing as the absence of a title-page, separately inserted initials drawn by hand, and the script writer's contractions for many words. Their aim was an imitation of fine manuscripts, and it was not until the turn of the century that printers discarded these standards.

Venice developed as a centre of printing, attracting Wendelin de Spira, Erhard Ratdolt, Nicolas Jenson, Aldus Manutius, and others. The types they used were derivations of *humanistic scripts*, q.v., later to become known as roman types. Editions were small, rarely exceeding 300 copies until *c.* 1500 when 500 copies became a standard.

As incunabula were usually simply bound in leather-covered boards with blind stamped decoration, their collectors in later years often had them rebound in finely tooled covers; thus original bindings are now comparatively rare.

incut notes: see *side notes.*

indented: a line of type set in from the margin, e.g. the first line of a paragraph.

See also *hanging paragraph*, *in pendentive*, *run out and indented.*

indention: the setting of a line of type to a narrower measure, e.g. the first line of a paragraph, or a list of items. An em quad indention is normal for the average 24 em line. Subdivisions are indented as follows: 1, 2, 3, a, b, c, i, ii, iii, e.g.

1. Useful Arts
   (*a*) Engineering
      (i) Steam
      (ii) Electrical
      (iii) Hydraulic
   (*b*) Agriculture
      (i) Farming
      (ii) Gardening
      (iii) Forestry
      (iv) Animal Husbandry
2. Fine Arts
   (*a*) Music
      (i) Orchestral
      (ii) Operatic etc.

See also *in pendentive.*

independents: separately published pamphlets which are subsequently bound together.

index: 1. a standard size of board, 25½ in. by 30½ in.
2. an alphabetical list, appearing at the beginning or end of a book, giving names of persons, places, subjects, etc., mentioned in the text, and the numbers of the pages or sections where they appear (pl. *indexes* or *indices*—the latter for scientific works only).
3. See *digit* (2).

Index librorum prohibitorum: the official list, published by the Roman Catholic Church, of books which may not be read or possessed by Roman Catholics without authorization, or which may only be read in approved expurgated editions (the passages to be deleted being listed in the 'Index expurgatorius'). The first list to be issued under this title was in 1564, and included the rules of the Council of Trent. It is still issued in revised form.

The practice of prohibiting the reading of books inimical to the views of the prohibiting authority dates back at least to the time of St Paul, when the Christian settlement at Ephesus (near Smyrna, Turkey) collected and publicly burnt all the superstitious books they could find.

Pope Gelasius issued in 496 a decree in which the reading of a number of apocryphal and heretical books was proscribed. In England, Henry VIII forbade the reading of certain books in 1526.

The first Roman Index was published under Paul IV in 1559, its severity being mitigated, however, by a decree of the Holy Office published in the same year ('Moderatio Indicis librorum prohibitorum'). The 1564 list of forbidden books, drawn up by a commission appointed by the Council of Trent, was revised in 1897 at the instigation of Pope Leo XIII; about 1000 titles were dropped, and the rules were somewhat modified.

india paper: originally (1768) a soft absorbent paper, cream or buff in colour, imported from China for use in the proofs of engravings. Later (1875), a thin opaque paper made from hemp or rag. Cheaper varieties can be made from chemically treated wood pulp. Sometimes known as *Bible paper*, q.v.

See also *Cambridge india paper*, *Oxford india paper*.

india tint: paper of a faintly buff colour, sometimes used in book work.

inedited: 1. a work published without editorial changes; such a work may contain indelicate passages.
2. unpublished works, especially letters, memoirs, etc.

inferior figures: small letters or figures printed at the foot of ordinary letters, e.g. as in chemical formulae, H_2SO_4, etc., and cast partly below the base line.

See also *superior figures*.

infra-red drying: the drying by means of infra-red rays of a printed paper web running on a high-speed press. This alternative to drying by heated cylinders uses the principle that the maximum evaporation of ink solvent from the surface of a paper web can be achieved by molecular agitation within the solvent. Such agitation can be induced by infra-red rays of predetermined wavelength. Factors affecting the process are the colour of the ink, and whether its base is alcohol or water. As further radiation is impeded if the layer of evaporated ink is not quickly removed, a strong jet of cold air is used to blow it away.

In 1954 a Norwegian, Odd Hultgreen, devised an infra-red drying unit known as the *LIICA*; it is made in America and Europe. The dryer has several ceramic elements which emit the rays, and a jet through which air from a pressure chamber is fed at a velocity of 9000 ft. per minute. It is fitted to a printing press, occupying an area 7 in. long and any machine width. The number of units required depends on the machine, its speed, and the type of ink solvent to be evaporated. For a web-fed gravure press, using alcohol-based ink, one dryer is needed for every 100 ft. per minute of web speed. Using water-based ink at the same speed, three would be needed.

The speed at which a rotary press will print may be limited by the speed at which the printed web can be dried, and this alternative to heat-drying offers an opportunity to run the press at a higher speed.

inhabited scroll: an arabesque pattern of foliage in which figures appear. This was an early feature of illuminated manuscripts. In pre-Conquest England the Anglo-Saxon artist drew birds or beasts on a scroll formed from an acanthus leaf: the inclusion of human figures was a later addition.

initia: literally, beginnings. A name given to the first words or sentence of the first and last pages of a manuscript; used as an alternative to the *incipit*, q.v., to identify works written or printed before the title-page was introduced.

As the first and last pages of a manuscript were liable to damage the initia of the second and penultimate, or of all four (i.e. *dictio probatoria* or *initia foliorum*), were used, a custom said to have originated in Paris.

initial letters: 1. manuscript. The use of decorated initials in manuscripts dates from the earliest times. Developing from *versals*, q.v., initials of the 10th century were embellished with drawings of animals; colours, gold and silver were in use by the 8th century. Interlaced foliage, which often extended the length and foot of a page, was also a feature of 10th–11th-century initials.

2. incunabula. Initials were at first entered by a rubrisher after the sheets were printed. Decorative coloured initials were used by Schöffer in 1457. Zainer and Ratdolt were pioneers of woodcut initials. The Holbein–Froben alphabets, the entrelacs of Tory, and the later copper engravings of France were other developments of the printed initial.

3. modern printed. Large capital letters, often decorated, are used at the beginning of a work or chapter. Ideally an initial should range with the top and bottom of so many lines of type, it should 'fit'; there being no extra space above or beneath. Alternatively an initial may 'stand' on the first line of type and extend above. A variation of either of the foregoing is the initial which extends slightly into the margin.

See also *guide letters*, *illumination*, *versals*, *vignette* (2).

ink: see *printing ink*.

ink ball: a sheepskin- or buckskin-covered pad, stuffed with horsehair and cotton, affixed to a wooden handle. These heavy and ponderous pads, used in pairs, were the means of inking set-up type from the 15th century until about 1800 when they were gradually superseded by the hand *ink roller*, q.v.

Alternative names are *dabber*, *ink pelt*, *pelt ball*. See also *flare the balls*, *griffin*.

Ink balls

ink blocking: the blocking of titles, etc., on book covers in black or coloured inks. An unheated press and quick-drying binder's inks are used.

ink consumption: the quantity of ink consumed in printing a work. This depends on the nature of the printed matter, the properties of the paper and ink, and the size of the work and number of copies run off. As a guide for calculating the consumption of ink the following approximate figures can be given, representing the consumption in kilogrammes per 1,000 impressions for one square metre (10,000 sq. cm.) of printing surface. The figures in the table (except those for four-colour work) refer to black ink in letterpress. For example, if 3000 copies of an illustrated catalogue are to be printed on glazed stock, with 320 pages each having a type area of 11 × 18 cm., the type area will be 320 × 11 × 18 cm. = 6·3 sq. m. The consumption of ink will be 3 × 6·3 × the figure in the table for glazed stock, i.e 0·9. The consumption of ink will thus be 17 kg.

For coloured ink in general the figures should be increased by about 25%, for chrome yellow by about 45%, and for opaque white by 65%. Double-tone ink should be calculated at a 15% higher consumption; metallic colours (gold and silver) at 100–125%. In superimposing several colours a smaller quantity is required for those printed last. In mixed work which can be classified under different headings in the table each kind is calculated separately. The figures can also be used for offset printing but should be reduced by 25%.

Paper quality (*see notes*)	1	2	3	4
Spaced matter	0·7	0·5	0·4	0·35
Ordinary letterpress	1·1	0·7	0·6	0·5
Illustrated catalogues	1·8	1·3	0·9	0·8
Heavy tabular work and forms	2·7	2·0	1·4	1·2
White-faced letters	5·5	4·0	2·8	2·5
Whole plates	9·3	6·7	4·6	4·2
Four-colour reproduction:				
yellow			2·8	1·7
black			1·8	1·1
red			2·2	1·3
blue			2·2	1·3

Notes

1. Thick unsized paper, blotting paper, unglazed soft pamphlet covers, antique paper, engraving paper, etc.
2. Dull printing paper, bond paper, sulphite (MG), pamphlet covers, etc.
3. Glazed printing paper, manila, rag paper, Bristol and higher quality boards.
4. Coated stock (matt or glazed), label chromo paper, highly glazed Bristol, millboard, etc. (G. U.)

ink coverage: the area which can be satisfactorily printed with a known amount of printing ink. By custom of the trade ink is sold by weight, not volume. As ingredients vary, so will the same weight of different inks vary in volume and cover different areas of paper. The surface of the paper to be printed also affects the amount of ink needed, rough-surfaced or heavily coated papers requiring more ink to print a given area than smooth stock.

See also *full colour*.

ink fly: a problem when operating high-speed presses. At high speeds the ink tends to fly off the rollers in the form of a mist.

ink fountain: the receptacle in which ink is placed on a press, and from which distributing rollers take the ink automatically and spread it over the printing forme. (M. L.)

ink grinding: mixing and distributing the pigment in the vehicle in order to obtain ink of a consistency suitable for printing. Grinding is done both in ink factories and in many printing works, in each case by means of similarly constructed ink-grinding mills. In the printing press a final grinding of the ink is done between the grinding rollers of the inking device. (G. U.)

ink-grinding mill: a machine for grinding ink for printing. The quantity of ink is forced between rollers of steel or porphyry, and in more complicated mills through a whole series of rollers in pairs. The rollers

Ink-grinding mill

are often equipped with a cooling device as so much heat is generated in grinding the ink that the temperature may be raised to a degree which would damage it. A type of ink-grinding mill used in a printing works is illustrated. (G. U.)

ink roller: a device for the inking up of type by hand. Early attempts to replace the clumsy ink balls which had been in use since the 15th century were made by William Nicholson and Earl Stanhope about 1800. They were not successful; and the actual inventor of the new roller which came into use about 1813 is unknown. This roller had a canvas-covered stock coated with a mixture of glue and treacle.

There are now many kinds of plastic roller available, but experiments continue.

See also *inkers, roller*.

ink slice: a spatulate tool for use in grinding, mixing, and transferring ink to the duct and rollers. (G. U.)

Ink slice

ink spread: a feature of offset printing which occurs during the transfer of ink from plate to paper via the rubber blanket. Thus, for example, printed half-tone dots occupy a larger area than the dots of the plate. The amount of spread varies, the highlights being less affected than the dark tones.

ink table: the flat surface across which an ink roller is moved until it bears an evenly distributed film of ink. The roller is then ready for inking up type on a hand-press. The table may be of iron or plate glass.

inkers: the rollers on a printing press which apply ink to the type and block surfaces. An inking roller was invented in 1810 by Robert Harrild for the Lewes printer, John Baxter, but there were other experimenters.

See also *disc inker, distributor rollers, drop roller, ink ball, ink slice, roller*.

inking device: the arrangement in printing machines for the automatic inking up of printing formes. Friedrich König, the inventor of the modern letterpress machine, also indicated the basic principles of most inking systems now in use in letterpress and lithographic machines. Only intaglio machines have any major difference.

The inking device of a letterpress machine must perform three functions: feeding the ink, distributing it, and inking up the forme. Feeding can be done from an open ink box with a fountain roller, or by means of a pump in which the ink is pressed out over

Fountain roller inker

the distributor rollers (note the difference from an inking device in which the ink is pumped from a bigger container into an ordinary fountain roller device), or by spraying. Distribution is done by rollers which either operate against a round disc which turns slightly between each inking (*disc inker*), or against a table moving to and fro (*table ink distribution*), or against a cylinder with a diameter

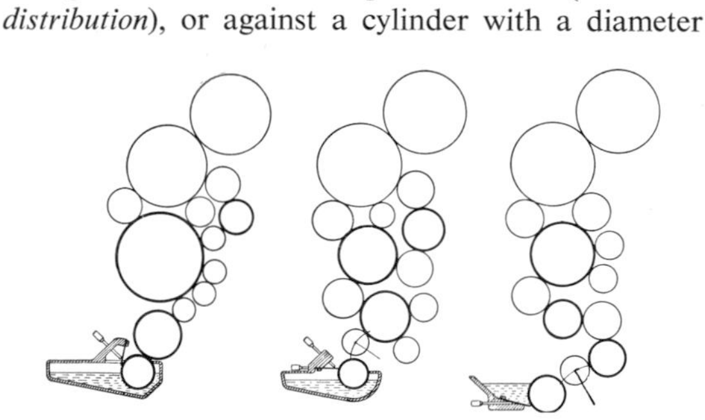

Diagram of inking devices for rotary presses. Left, English-American type with bathing fountain roller and continuous feeding by transfer roller (film inking device). Right, Swiss-German types with drop roller and, in one case, bathing fountain roller

larger than that of the rollers (*cylinder inking arrangement*). From these the ink is conveyed to a varying number of *forme rollers* which ink up the forme.

In König's first press (1803) a pumping device was used for supplying the ink, a piston driven by the machine squeezing ink out of a container through a narrow slot in its base, whence the stream of ink was carried via a steel roller to a leather-covered distri-

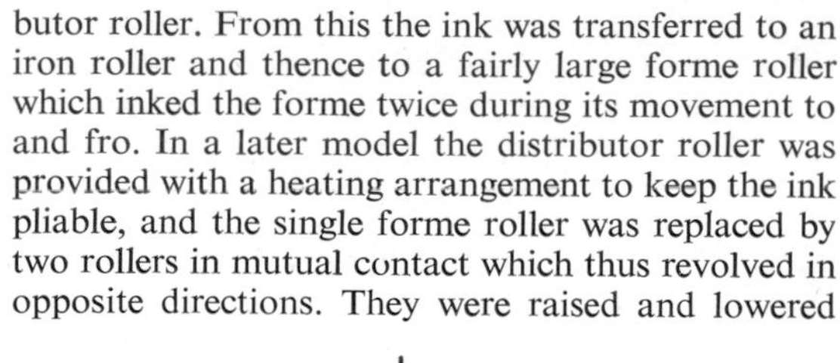

butor roller. From this the ink was transferred to an iron roller and thence to a fairly large forme roller which inked the forme twice during its movement to and fro. In a later model the distributor roller was provided with a heating arrangement to keep the ink pliable, and the single forme roller was replaced by two rollers in mutual contact which thus revolved in opposite directions. They were raised and lowered

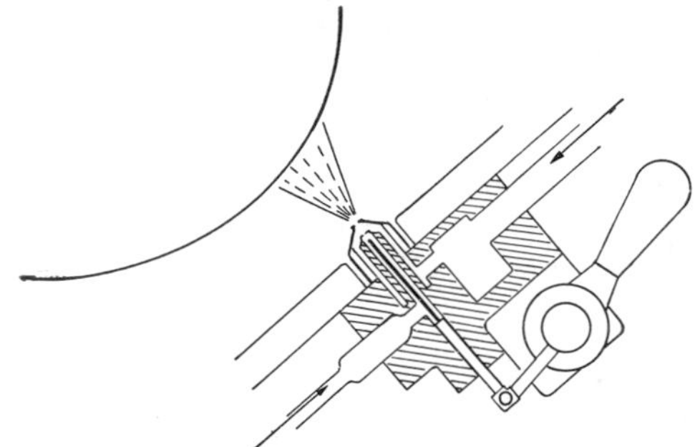

Frankenthal spray inker

alternately, so that the forme was inked up by one when moving forward and by the other when returning. In 1825 König built the first *fountain roller device*: an open ink container has a fountain blade and a cylindrical fountain roller at the bottom which, in revolving, draws the ink through an adjustable slit between the roller and the blade. This allows the quantity of ink to be varied both for the inking device as a whole and from one edge of the forme to

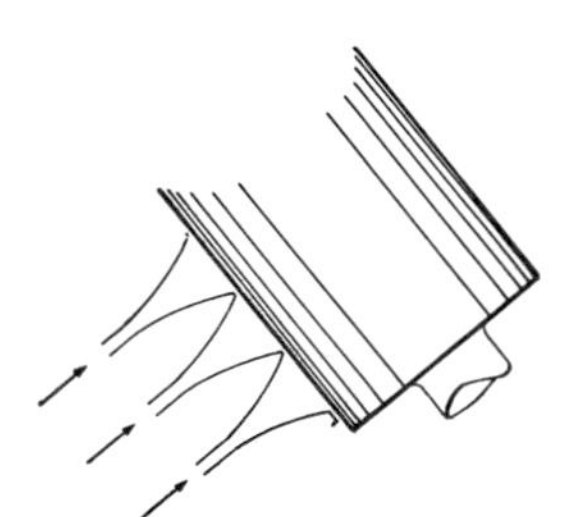

Hoe's pumping inker

the other. The fountain roller makes only part of a revolution for each inking up. The ink is transferred from the fountain roller to the distributor rollers by means of a *drop roller* (*ductor*). The use of the drop roller, which is brought into alternate contact with the fountain roller and the first distributor roller (being moved by friction with whichever roller it is in contact at any moment), solved the problem of transferring ink from the slowly revolving fountain roller to the rapidly revolving distributor rollers, the peripheral speed of which must adapt itself to the movement of the printing forme in accordance with the rule that all surfaces which are in contact must have the same speed. In some later models, especially on rapid rotary presses, the fountain feeding principle is carried out differently, i.e. the drop roller is replaced by a screw spindle which feeds the ink to the distributors.

H. A. Wise Wood (U.S.A.) has patented a construction for a *film inking device* in which the surplus ink

Disc inker on a Craftsman platen press

is scraped off the fountain roller by an adjustable blade. A rapidly revolving *transfer roller* lies at a minimum distance from the slowly moving fountain roller, and the distance between them is so adjusted that the ink film, but not the fountain roller itself, comes in contact with the transfer roller. There is

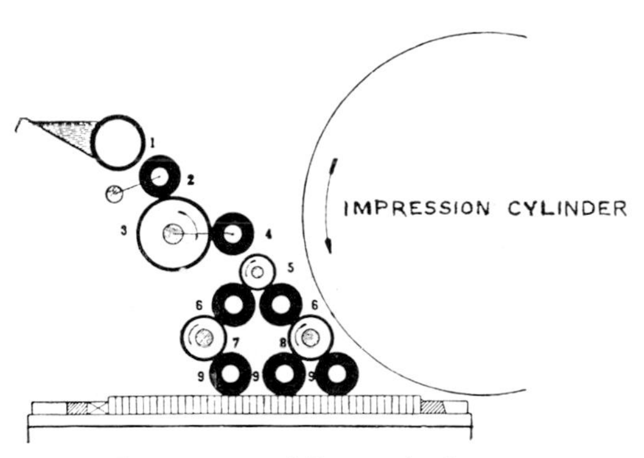

Inker on a Heidelberg cylinder press

1. *fountain roller*, 2. *drop roller*, 3. *ink cylinder*, 4. *transfer roller*, 5–8. *distributor rollers*, 9. *forme rollers*

also a *ductor blade* on the fountain roller which collects remains of ink, paper fluff, etc., that would otherwise accumulate in the ink duct. In several modern rotary machines König's original principle of feeding ink by a pump has been reverted to. Hoe & Co. were the first to build a pump inking device consisting of several pumps which force the ink out through individual mouthpieces quite close to the first distributor roller. The width of the mouthpieces is adjusted to the column width of the printing forme. Hoe also experimented with *spraying inking devices* in which, on the injector principle, outflowing air pressure carries the ink with it, very finely distributed, to the distributor rollers. The Frankenthalfabriken have a similar model. (See diagrams.) If the narrow

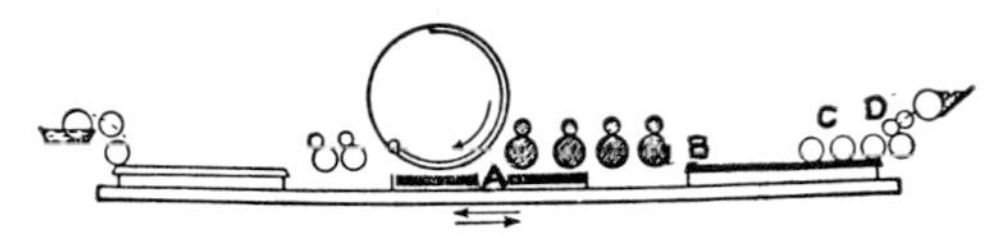

A = Stone
B = Inking (printing) rollers
C = Distributing rollers
D = Vibrator

The stone printing press has table ink distribution and a similarly constructed damping unit

mouthpiece becomes clogged by dry ink when the inker has been standing idle, a pin can be pushed through the opening by the handle seen in the diagram.

Disc inking arrangements are only used on small platen presses. On most modern machines there are cylinder inking devices; on two-revolution letterpress machines mostly table ink distributors. In letterpress

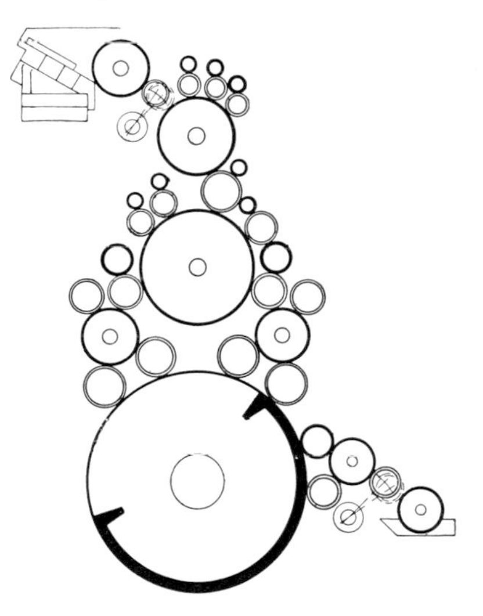

The inking device of an offset press is characterized by its large number of distributor rollers. The damping unit (lower right) is much simpler

machines both the distributor and forme rollers are made of composition or rubber, while distributing cylinders are generally made of steel. In older machines the rollers revolved only by friction with the surfaces with which they were in contact, ultimately with the printing forme. In modern machines the distributor rollers and sometimes the forme rollers also are mechanically operated, with the exception of a few heavy rollers and riders. In addition, one or more of the distributor rollers moves laterally.

Lithographic presses, i.e. stone printing and offset machines, have inking systems similar in basic principle to letterpress machines. Stone printing machines are usually stop-cylinder presses with table ink distribution, while offset machines are purely rotary presses with cylinder inkers. Lithographic machines also have a damping unit designed on the same basis. The rollers in these presses must be of waterproof material, special composition, rubber, or leather. The distributors are mostly rubber or glazed rollers, while the forme rollers are nap or rubber. (See *composition, glazed, nap rollers.*)

Collotype presses are built in all essential respects like stone printing presses, but composition or leather nap rollers are also generally used as forme rollers.

Intaglio presses are inked up on a totally different principle, and the hardest problem is not the inking up of the forme but the removal of superfluous ink from the blank areas. The construction of the inking system is very closely connected with the construction and working of the rest of the machine.

See also *copperplate printing press, photogravure printing press.* (G. U.)

inking up: the provision on lithographic stones or printing plates of a suitable layer of ink for further treatment of the surface. For example, transferred or copied plates must be provided by means of washing and renewed rolling with a layer of ink to protect the image when the plate is etched. A plate which is to be stored after printing has been completed must have the drying printing ink replaced by transfer ink; this is done by inking up or rolling. (G. U.)

inkstone: the name given to the duct cylinder belonging to the usual inking system of lithographic and letterpress machines. The term derives from the stone slab used by hand-press printers as a base for grinding the ink and inking up the hand-roller. Machine printers also use such stones for preparing ink. (G. U.)

inlaid bindings: see *inlaying.*

inlaying: 1. the manner of decorating a book cover by affixing to it strips or panels of leather differing in texture or colour from the rest of the cover. Inlaid bindings were extensively produced in 17th- and 18th-century France, in particular by Le Monnier; still later, examples were made by the Frenchmen Trautz and Bauzonnet Also known as *mosaic bindings.* Cf. *onlaying.*

2. the setting of a leaf or plate into a larger page by cutting out a portion of the latter and pasting the leaf over the gap.

inline letters: display and jobbing work letters in which hand-tooling of the main strokes results in a white line forming their central part when printed. The effect is one of blackness relieved by white, and thus distinguishable from *outline letters,* q.v.

inner forme: see *sheet work.*

inner margin: see *backs.*

insert: 1. essentially, a folded section placed into another folded section so that the subsequent sewing passes through the back folds of both sections. The insert may be of four pages only or multiples of four pages and may be placed in the centre of the host sections, on the outside, or, more rarely, in an intermediate position. The method is of considerable value in binding for the incorporation of plates as an alternative to tipping in the plates with paste. A systematic use of inserting is in the folding of 32-page sections, many folding machines achieving this by slitting the printed sheet into 16-page units and then inserting one unit into another if desired, thus producing 16-page sections or 32-page sections at will. In such 32-page work the outer 16 pages bear the signature mark, e.g. B, and the inner 16 pages will then bear the signature B*.

Where inserted plates are on the outside of the host section they are sometimes termed *outserts* or *wrap rounds.*

More than one insert can be added to a folded section but, to produce a satisfactory binding, sections must not be too thick.

2. attempts have been made to reserve the term *inset* for the above and use *insert* to indicate slips, bookmarks, and the like (usually bearing advertisement matter) thrown between the leaves after binding. These, however, are generally referred to as *loose inserts* or *throw ins* to avoid ambiguity.

The term *inset* is synonymous with *insert.*

3. a small map or diagram, enclosed within rules, and printed inside the border of a large one is termed an inset. (L. K.)

inserted after binding: bulky maps, plans, and the like which have many folds have to be tipped into a book after binding as they interfere with edge cutting. *Compensation guards,* q.v., may be required to prevent the book from gaping. (L. K.)

See also *nibbed.*

insides: the eighteen quires inside a ream of paper, the top and bottom quires being known as *outsides.* Insides are all 'good' sheets and a full ream is charged extra.

Insular hand: the name given to the Hiberno-Saxon script widely used in England until the Norman Conquest for non-Latin texts. Its origins may be traced to 6th-century Ireland. An example is the first London Charter, 1066, which may be seen in the Guildhall Library.

intaglio: printing from a metal plate, usually copper, on which the image areas of the printing surface are incised by gravers or etched by acid. The whole plate is inked and wiped, leaving ink only in the engraved parts; it is then placed with a damp sheet of printing paper on the bed of the press, layers of felt are added, and all pass through the press. The thickness of the layer of ink transferred to the paper is proportionate to the depth of the incised or etched hollow. As distinct from planographic and letterpress printing intaglio plates leave a layer of ink on the paper which can often be felt. Intaglio is the principle of *etching, line engraving, dry-point, mezzotint, aquatint,* and *photogravure,* qq.v. The first book to have illustrations produced by an intaglio process was 'Il monte santo di Dio', Florence, 1477.

intaglio half-tone: a printing process in which dots of varying size but uniform depth are etched into a hard-wearing copper plate or cylinder. When preparing the plate or cylinder the necessary division of the picture surface is effected by means of screen process work in a camera just as when making half-tone blocks. In 1891 Adolf Brandweiner of Vienna produced printing cylinders by copying a screen positive on carbon tissue and transferring this to a copper cylinder for etching and printing by means of a doctor-blade device. At the same time Rolffs and Mertens were working with screen positives which were copied direct on the cylinder prepared with chromate glue. Karl Klíč's process with picture positives, without a screen, and separate copying of a screen mesh, due to Nefgen's initiative in the Deutsche Photogravur A.G. founded by him in association with Rolffs and Mertens in 1906, spread rapidly, and superseded the intaglio half-tone method, which has, however, been revived in recent years in modified form.

In America, a combined process invented by A. Dultgen, involving double copying on pigment paper of a continuous tone positive and a half-tone screen positive, is in use. (G. U.)

integral cover: a cover of the same paper as the inside of a booklet. Such a publication is also called self-covered or self-contained. (M. L.)

intensification: the adding of either more metal (silver, mercury) or a colouring substance to an original silver image. Intensification of the silver image in photographic negatives is often done in order to increase the contrast, and in reproduction photography especially to obtain density. A *mercury intensifier* (sublimate intensifier) has long been in use. An aqueous solution of 2% mercuric chloride plus 2% potassium bromide can be used; in this the plate is immersed until the image becomes pure white (of silver bromide and mercuric bromide), after which it is re-developed in a sulphite bath, in dilute ammonia, or in an ordinary developing solution. The sublimate intensifier is used for preference when reproducing fine line drawings, e.g. maps, on a wet plate, as it is easier to keep the finest lines in the negative open than with the silver intensifiers mentioned below which are otherwise most in use.

A *copper-silver-iodine intensifier* is much used in reproduction work, particularly for 'wet plate' negatives. The negative is freed from fog by previous reduction and is then intensified. In doing this the plate is first bathed in a 10% solution of copper sulphate with the addition of 4% potassium bromide. In this bath the plate is bleached to whiteness (when a mixture of copper bromide and silver bromide occurs). After rinsing, the plate is re-developed with a 5% solution of silver nitrate. It is usual in 'wet plate' treatment to combine the copper-silver intensification with cyanide iodide reduction.

See also *iodized collodion process.*

Lead intensification is done by bathing the negative in a solution of 5% lead nitrate plus 5% potassium ferricyanide whereby the silver image becomes light (formation of lead ferrocyanide and silver ferrocyanide). The negative is cleared in diluted hydrochloric acid in which the image becomes white, and is then re-developed in a bath of 5% sodium sulphide plus 5% ammonium sulphide. (Or it may be coloured yellow with potassium dichromate.)

In some cases intensification before fixing the negative is done. For this purpose solutions of organic developers are used (e.g. metol) with the addition of some citric acid, mixed with a solution of silver nitrate. The effect is similar in the case of so-called physical developing. (G. U.)

Cf. *reduction.*

interlaying: the placing of a sheet or sheets of paper between a printing plate and its block or mount. This varies from below the pressure on different parts of the plate.

See also *make-ready.*

interleaved: 1. a book having blank leaves between the printed pages for the entering by hand of notes.

2. a book having thin tissues inserted to prevent the illustrations and text from rubbing. These protecting leaves may be pasted to the inner margins

of the plates or be left loose. They are known as *tissued plates*.

3. a plate to the inner margin of which is pasted a thin leaf bearing a descriptive caption. A leaf of Cellophane is a modern variation of this. Known as *interleaved plates*.

interlinear matter: explanatory notes, or translation, set in small type between the lines of text they accompany.

intermediate channel: the part of a Linotype in which matrices are transferred to the second elevator.

International Bureau of the Federations of Master Printers: an international body, founded in 1929, to further the economic and technical interests of the the employers' organizations affiliated to it. These aims are achieved in such ways as the collation of wages and working conditions agreements; the dissemination of information about the industry; the investigation of new methods and materials; and the international exchange of sons of master printers with a view to broadening their experience. Triennial congresses are held, and a council of administration under the directorship of Eddie Kopley conducts the regular business of the Bureau.

Members represent organizations in Europe, India, New Zealand, South Africa, and the U.S.A.

International Community of Booksellers Associations: an organization founded in 1956 to improve and extend the book trade on an international basis. The educational training of young assistants, the examination of book distribution costs, underselling, and related matters were among topics planned for co-operative discussion. Representatives of the following countries joined the Association as founder members: Belgium, Denmark, Great Britain, France, Italy, Austria, Sweden, Switzerland, West Germany and West Berlin.

The name is abbreviated as *ICBA*

International Graphical Federation: inaugurated in 1949 as an international federation of printing trade unions, and established on a free trade-union basis to protect and further the occupational, economic, and idealistic interests of print workers. Membership is open to trade unions of workers in three groups: letterpress; bookbinding and paper and board conversion; and lithography, offset, photogravure, process engraving, and photography. Present members are from Europe, Asia, Africa, and Australia, but Communist countries and the Americas are not represented. Periodic conferences are held, and special importance is attached to the exchange of information and experience on health and welfare problems of the printing-trade worker. Headquarters are in Berne.

International League of Antiquarian Booksellers: founded in 1942, a trade association of booksellers in thirteen countries whose members deal principally in books which are no longer in print.

The League has published a directory giving the specialities of each of the 2500 (in 1953) members, and other reference works are published. An annual conference is held, usually in some European capital.

The name is abbreviated as *ILAB*.

International Publishers Association: an association founded in Paris in 1896 to consider problems common to the publishing and bookselling trades. Papers are read and discussed at congresses held periodically in various cities, while a permanent office is maintained in Zürich.

International Typographical Union: an international body proposed in 1956 at a meeting in Paris of a group of type-founders, type-designers, and composing machine manufacturers from Denmark, France, Germany, Great Britain, Holland, Italy, and Switzerland. It is intended to unite professional typographers and protect the basic principles of typography against the development of new techniques which may threaten them. More specifically, it is intended to deal with such matters as the establishment of a code of author rights in typographical material and the protection of type-designs, standardization of type-widths and weights, problems arising from filmsetting, and arbitration in disputes between members.

British members of the working committee are John Dreyfus, Stanley Morison, and Walter Tracy. Headquarters are in Geneva where an international centre of typographical documentation and an information service for co-ordinating activities are expected to develop. In addition to the trades concerned with the manufacture of type and composing equipment members will be drawn from printing schools, publishers, printers, and graphic artists.

In 1957 the name was changed to *Association Typographique Internationale*.

Intertype: as in the case of other leading composing machine manufacturers, Intertype originated in America. In the latter part of 1911, Mr. Herman Ridder, who at that time was the Executive Officer of the Associated Press and the American Publishers' Association, resolved that the time was appropriate to undertake the development of a new line composing and casting machine. This resolution was

Intertype ejector, showing a blade in operation

followed by a search of existing patents on the subject and by the distribution of a prospectus, which was issued under the name of the International Typesetting Machine Company, of New York, for the purpose of interesting capital in this venture. A new factory building was completed in Brooklyn, New York, in October of 1912, and the first model was completed and demonstrated to interested parties in November 1912. In March of the following year the first tool-made Intertype was installed in the New York *Journal of Commerce*, and that machine was converted in 1917 into a three-magazine Intertype machine.

Intertype model with side magazine unit

The inventor of the Monoline machine, Scudder, who had been Mergenthaler's assistant and works manager at the Linotype works in Brooklyn; Homans from the Paige and Unitype typesetting machine makers; and Bertram from the Monotype works were engaged as technicians and managers. In 1914 the Intertype appeared on the market and

Adjusting the quadder

Blank slug device

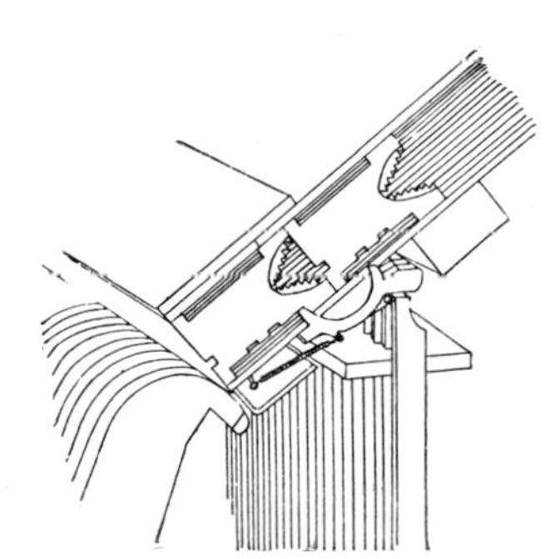

Matrix escapement mechanism

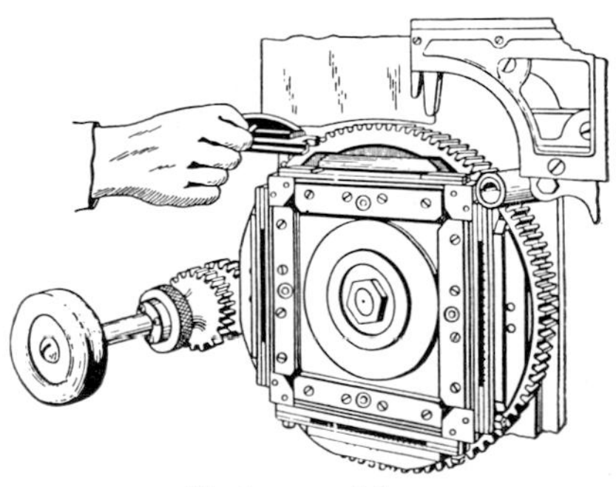

Fitting mould cap

had rapid sales both in the U.S.A. and Europe, to which a number of machines were exported in the first year.

The principle is essentially the same as that of the Linotype, and matrices of the same appearance are used; the end-product, too, is a single-line slug (with a measure from 4 to 30 ems; or up to 42 ems on a special long-measure machine). Various details, however, differ, being frequently simplified. The matrix release mechanism in the magazine consists of only two parts: an escapement pawl, the lugs of which control the release of matrices, and a return spring. The direct-action keyrods, which are interchangeable, all have over-motion which protects actuating mechanism from undue wear and tear. Matrix magazines, moulds and other equipment also are interchangeable. Change of measure, type-face and body size are simplified. For ejecting, twelve one-piece blades of different sizes are assembled in a magazine, and the one required is engaged by moving an indicator along a graduated scale. An air cooler for cooling moulds, automatic metal feeder, etc., are available as extra equipment.

Interchangeable matrix magazines are removed and replaced at the rear of earlier models. The four light-weight magazines of later models (C4, F4, G4) are removed and replaced on sliding carriages at the front of the machine. Ninety-channel main magazines are interchangeable for use on all models. The first Intertype model (A) was built for one magazine with ninety matrix channels. It was followed by models B and C with two and three magazines respectively in which the different magazines were brought into position by means of a lever. The matrices from different main magazines cannot be mixed in the same line in these early models. Headings and display can be set up in the line by

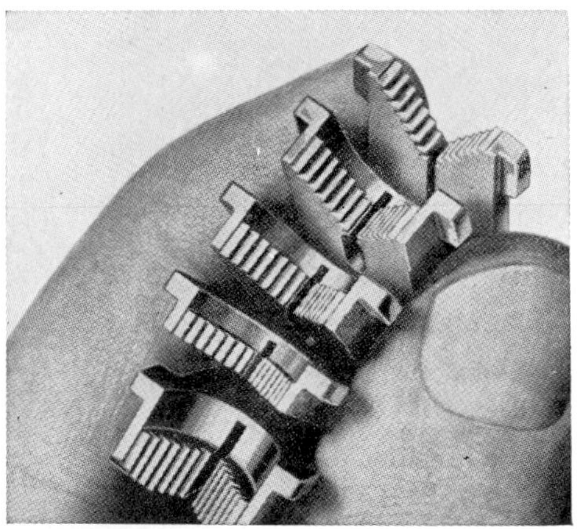

Intertype matrices have teeth of 'full' width; a system now used in the Linotype

means of side magazines with thirty-four channels, by using the 124 combinations afforded by the seven-toothed matrices. Both text and display headings are available from main magazines on the G 72/90 machine.

Mixed composition was done in model E which had two magazines and a special distributor for each, to which an oscillating mechanism released the matrices from the matrix line after casting. Model E has been further developed in models F and G with four magazines, of which two at a time can be used for mixed or straight setting and display. Among later improvements the automatic quadding and centering device should be mentioned, by which the work of completing the line from the keyboard with quad matrices is rendered unnecessary. The compositor need only strike the letter matrices included in the line, move an indicator, and the machine does the quadding or centering automatically.

Hand-matrices for display can be used for the Intertype machine; they are hand set in a special composing stick and the line is then inserted in the first elevator jaws for casting. This insertion is facilitated by means of a special articulated first elevator head.

Intertype matrices and moulds are made for bodies of 5 to 60 points. With the rapid growth of Intertype, to meet world-wide demands, factories were built at Slough, England, and Berlin, Germany.

See also *Intertype Fotosetter*, *teletypesetting*.

Intertype Fotosetter: a photographic composing machine constructed by Intertype which works mainly on the same principle of circulating matrices as their slug-casting machine. Briefly, keyboard operation releases matrices from the magazines in which they are stored. The Fotosetter matrix, known as a *Fotomat*, carries a photographic negative character embedded in its side; it is in other respects like an ordinary toothed Intertype matrix in appearance. The thickness of the body controls setwise spacing of the character images.

The lines are made up of separately photographed characters (see diagram) in measures from 4 to 42 ems. Justification is pre-arranged and automatic; interlinear spacing is obtained by adjusting as required the micrometer film feed dial. Exposed film for developing is removed in a light-proof receiver. Any errors discovered at this stage can be corrected by cutting out the line(s) from the original film and inserting a corrected strip on special precision Intertype Fotosetter correction devices. The corrected film (negative or positive), or paper positive, is then ready for the plate-maker.

Four magazines can be mounted on the machine at the same time, each with 114 characters; eight lenses enable the camera to set eight different sizes of type from one fount of matrices, so that with four founts a total of 3648 characters is available direct from the keyboard. The pie system provides an unlimited range of other special characters. Enlargements of Fotosetter typesetting can be made on a standard photographic enlarger, with great fidelity.

The first machine has been in use since 1947.

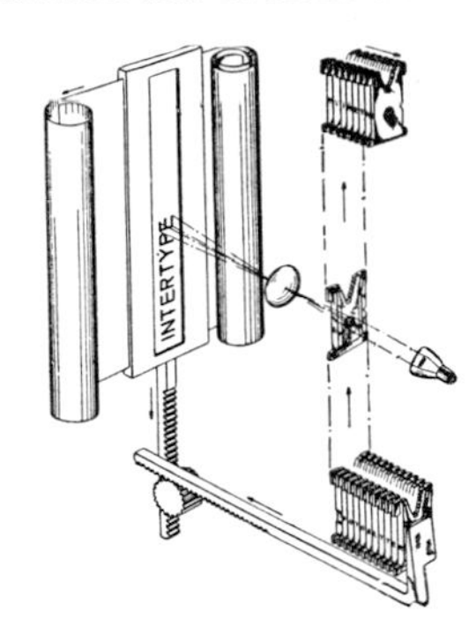

Diagram showing how the individual matrix characters are photographed separately on to a roll of film or paper while held absolutely stationary

introduction: a declaration by the author of his viewpoint, or an outline of his subject matter. While normally part of the prelims it is not uncommon to find the introduction forming the first chapter. In either case it is part of the work and is not always changed for successive editions (as the preface may be). While some authorities claim synonymity for the terms *foreword* and *introduction* the two are demonstrably different in purpose.

See *foreword, preface.*

inverted commas: “ ”, in Britain. In Germany and Austria they are set thus: „ “.

See also *duck-foot quotes.*

iodized collodion process: a process invented by Scott Archer in 1851 and still much used in photographic reproduction; it is now known as the *wet-plate process.* It is based on the sensitivity to light of iodized silver when nitrate of silver is present. A 2% solution of collodion, with the addition of iodized salts soluble in spirits of ether (e.g. ammonium iodide, cadmium iodide, or bromide and chloride salts), is poured on a glass plate. The salts can be added by dissolving them separately in anhydrous alcohol, after which they are mixed with the solution of collodion. The admixture of salts is usually within 1½ to 2% of the weight of the collodion. The bromide content produces ‘half-tone’ iodizing, the chloride content ‘full-tone’ iodizing, i.e. material suitable for line drawings. When the collodion layer solidifies, the plate is put in a bath of 10% silver nitrate, acidified with some nitric acid and saturated beforehand with iodized silver. This causes a deposit of iodized silver on the layer. The plate is taken from the bath and placed wet in the dark slide, after which it is immediately exposed in the camera. Developing is done straight away with a solution of ferrous sulphate and acetic acid, the metallic silver attached to the plate being reduced out of the silver bath. This precipitation of silver occurs in the form of a deposit on the exposed grains of iodized silver, and is in proportion to the quantity of light which has struck them. Such a developing process is called *physical developing* and implies that the sensitized substance (the iodized silver) apparently remains chemically unchanged. After developing, the negative is fixed with fixing soda or potassium cyanide which dissolves the iodized silver. This negative material is particularly suitable for line drawings owing to the sharpness of the image, and for large sizes owing to the comparative cheapness of the materials.

However, the silver picture obtained by developing the wet plate has so little density that in most cases it has to be intensified in order to be fit for printing. At the same time the reproduction negative must show completely clear dots and lines, and this can be done by reducing. Reducing can be done first and be followed by intensifying, or vice versa. In the former case Farmer’s reducer or a cyanide iodide reducer is used (see *reducing*), the negative being treated with a mixture of a potassium cyanide solution, after which it is intensified.

In intensifying before reducing the procedure is usually as follows. The fixed and washed negative is bleached by means of a solution of copper sulphate (12%) and potassium bromide (4%), after which it is washed for about a minute and re-developed in a 5% silver nitrate solution. In an iodine-potassium iodide solution the silver of the image is converted to yellowish-white silver iodide, and then the negative is cleared (reduced) by pouring a potassium cyanide solution of about 4% over it, and finally rinsed in running water and densified with a 5% sodium sulphide solution. The procedure can be repeated. In reproducing fine-line drawings (e.g. maps) intensification by mercury is usual. The wet-plate layer can be stripped off the glass and transferred to a new base. This is sometimes used to turn negatives laterally and sometimes to combine several negatives as one composite negative. For this purpose the layer can be strengthened by first pouring a rubber solution over it, and then a solution of collodion or gelatine. (G. U.)

i.p.h.: impressions per hour.

iridescent printing: rainbow printing, colour printing done so that different strips of the sheet are printed in different colours with soft, toning transitions between each. Iridescent printing is also used in press blocking, many colours being inked in simultaneously on the dies where they run into each other, a method fashionable at the beginning of this century. (G. U.)

Irish bindings: the important era for bookbinding in Ireland was the 18th century; before 1700 little elaborate work had been done. Books were mostly bound for institutions or for presentation rather than for bibliophiles, and the Parliamentary Journals bound from about 1740 for the Parliament House in Dublin represent the finest examples of Irish binding. The crimson morocco volumes had as their main features a cottage-roof pattern, and a central inlaid panel or a lozenge of fawn leather, ornamented with natural forms extending over the whole cover. The treatment of these features varied, as did the tooling, from year to year, no two volumes being alike (unless one year's records exceeded one volume).

The 149 volumes of Journals were burned during the political disturbances of 1922, but a series of rubbings taken by Sir Edward Sullivan is kept in the National Library, Dublin.

See M. Craig, 'Irish Bookbindings, 1600–1800', Cassell, 1954.

Irish half-uncial: a book hand developed in Ireland about A.D. 600. It was derived from Roman cursive and uncial letters, differing from the latter by having new forms of b, d, g, m, r, and s. The *Book of Kells*, q.v., is the finest manuscript in this script, which indirectly became the basis for our lower-case roman letters.

See also *Carolingian script*.

iron mount: an iron base for blocks. The block base is made up of small units, the dimensions of which correspond to standard type-unit dimensions. The blocks can be fastened by brads (spikes) or by other means. (G. U.)

See also *block*, *mount*, *plate-dog*.

ironing: the making of a smooth panel or square by the heavy impression of a heated block. Similar to hot-pressing. (M. L.)

isagoge: introduction. The name derives from the Greek 'eisagoge'.

issue: part of an edition; being copies of a book made up from sheets run off for the first printing but with a new title-page and matter added as an appendix or correction, or with rearranged existing matter. Before the term 'issue' can first be applied, copies of the work without any of the changes now involved must have already been published. Bibliographers then speak of a 'first issue' and a 'second issue' of the 'first edition'. The term is less precisely used in the book trade. Cf. *new edition*.

See also *impression*, *state*.

Italian illumination: the pilgrimage to Rome brought to Italian scriptoria influences from France and Byzantium. In the 8th century there were centres at Bobbio and Monte Cassino. In the 11th century *Exultet Rolls*, q.v., decorated with line drawings were widely circulated. In the 14th century choir-books with large historiated initials are characteristic, to be followed in the 15th by a fully developed national art which flourished in Venice, Milan, Florence, and Naples. Latin and Greek classics were extensively produced, and such styles as marble backgrounds and jewelled thrones were copied in 15th-century France, probably by emigrant artists.

See Mario Salmi, 'Italian Manuscript Miniatures', Collins, 1957.

italic: a type-face designed about 1500 by Francesco Griffo for Aldus Manutius of Venice. Letters slope to the right and are founded on humanistic cursive script. A Virgil, 1501, was the first book to be printed in the new face. A feature of early specimens was the large number of ligatures. Manutius had only lower-case letters cut, using them with small roman capitals: Garamond was the first to cut italic capitals, and an early printer to use them was Gryphius of Lyons, 1538. When preparing a manuscript a straight line is ruled under all words to be set in italic type; if bold-face italic is to be used a wavy line is drawn under the straight one.

See also *letters—forms and styles*.

Italtype: a slug-composing machine, made in Milan, and announced in 1952. It basically resembles other slug-casting machines, but is said to be quieter, due to its direct-coupling transmission and fibre gears. Models with from one to four magazines are available, and the magazine-changing mechanism is electrically operated from its own motor.

In addition to the maker's Italtype matrices those of Intertype and Linotype can also be used.

Ives, Frederic E., 1856–1937: an American technician whose inventions and theoretical research work in the half-tone process have proved of great importance to graphic technology. Among his contributions to colour photography mention should be made of the perfecting of the chromoscope, and the working out of various methods of reproducing in colour. In Philadelphia July 28th is called 'Ives' Day'. (G. U.)

ivory boards: see *boards*.

ADDENDA

incunabulum (see also page 188): the limit of 1500 for the term incunabulum may derive from the earliest known catalogue of them: this was an appendix to Johann Saubert's 'Historia bibliothecae Noribergensis . . . catalogus librorum proximis ab inventione annis usque ad a. Chr. 1500 editorum', 1643. In 1653 Labbé issued a list of incunabula in the Royal Library, Paris. The first attempt to make a list of all known incunabula was by Cornelius à Beughem, a bookseller of Emmerich-am-Rhein, in his 'Incunabula typographiae', 1688. The last of these early attempts to catalogue known incunabula was Michel Maittaire's chronological list 'Annales typographici', 5 vols., 1719–41.

See also *Brunet*, *Graesse*, *Haebler*, *Hain*, *Panzer*, *Proctor*, and *Gesamtkatalog der Wiegendrucke*.

Index Translationum: an international bibliography of translations which since 1949 has been published annually by Unesco. It continues the work of the same name published from 1932 to 1940 by the League of Nations. About fifty countries are represented and the translations are set out by country of publication. Subdivision within each country is by alphabetical arrangement within the ten main sections of the Universal Decimal Classification. An author index lists all writers whose works have been translated during the period covered by any particular Index.

a

b

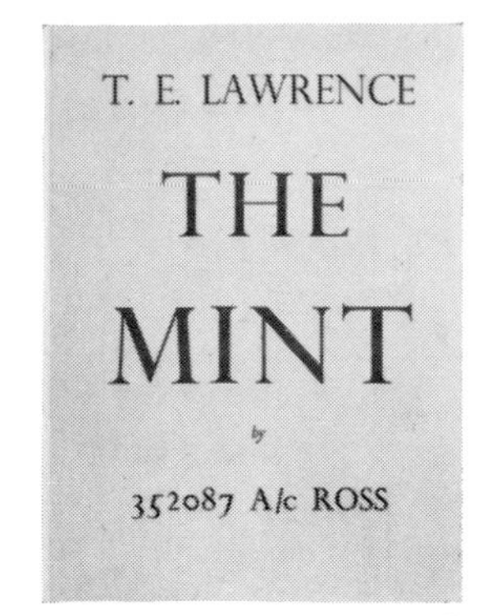

c

d

e

f

g

h

i

j

k

l

a. *Aubrey Beardsley* (1909) (*Dent*)
b. *Typography in one colour* (*Faber*)
c. *Typography in two colours* (*Cape*)
d. *Typography in two colours by Stanley Morison, one of the yellow paper series* (*Gollancz*)
e. *Artist lettering by Hans Tisdall* (*Cape*)
f. *Artist design by Barnett Freedman in three-colour lithography from artist's own separations* (*Faber*)
g. *Artist lettering by Sexauer-Effert* (*German*)
h. *Reverse block in one colour* (*Allen & Unwin*)
i. *Artist design by Salter in four-colour photo-lithography* (*U.S.A.*)
j. *Photographic* (*N. Kaye*)
k. *Artist design by Charles Mozley in three-colour photo-lithography* (*Bodley Head*)
l. *Artist lettering by Miriam Woods* (*U.S.A.*)

J

jacket: the coloured paper protecting cover in which a bound book is usually sold in the U.K. and the U.S.A. Copies of Heath's 'Keepsake', 1833, are held to be the first book for which a paper protecting wrapper was provided. It was not until the end of the century that they were widely adopted, and even later that jackets were used for blurbs relative to the book they enclosed. Jacket designing and printing has now become a highly skilful and costly part of book production involving frequently a graphic artist and lithography. It is regarded as an important factor in promoting book sales. Also known as *book jacket*, *dust cover*, *dust jacket*, or *wrapper*.

See C. Rosner, 'The Growth of the Book Jacket', Sylvan Press, 1954.

jaconet: a cotton fabric, glazed on one side, used as a lining for the spines of books.

Jaggard, William and Isaac: the London printers of the First Folio of William Shakespeare, 1621–23. Isaac was a pioneer in England of italic types.

James Tait Black Memorial Prizes: the prizes founded in 1918 by Mrs. J. C. Black, widow of a partner of Messrs. A. & C. Black of London. They are awarded each spring for the best biography and best work of fiction of the previous year. The judge is the Professor of English Literature at Edinburgh University.

Jänecke: a famous Hanover firm of ink-makers whose ink was used by the Ashendene, Essex House, and Kelmscott presses.

Janinet, Jean François, 1752–1814: a French graphic artist notable for his copperplate engravings in colour. These were done in aquatint, for which he used as many as seven plates, and were chiefly reproductions of the work of contemporary painters. (G. U.)

Jannon, Jean, 1580–1658: born in Geneva. He worked as a punch-cutter in Sedan, France. In his specimen of 1621 appeared the fount Caractères de l'Université, based on Claude Garamond's roman of *c.* 1540. Some matrices of Jannon's fount survive in the Imprimerie Nationale, Paris, where they were thought by French authorities to have been cut by Garamond. Thus when the Monotype Corporation revived the Caractères de l'Université in 1922 they reasonably enough gave the name Garamond to the series. It was in 1926 that Mrs. Beatrice Warde discovered the Jannon specimen sheet of 1621 and made the correct attribution of the design to him.

Jansenist bindings: late 17th-century French bindings of austere design with no ornamentation on the outside of the cover but with richly tooled doublures.

Janson, Anton, 1620–87: a Dutch type-founder. trained in Amsterdam by *Christoffel van Dijck*, q.v. He later worked in Frankfurt-am-Main and from 1656 in Leipzig, where he established the first independent type-foundry in 1659. Janson's roman, with a strong Dutch influence, was popular in Germany.

Punches believed to be the work of Janson were acquired by the Ehrhardt foundry of Leipzig about 1710, and passed later to the Stempel foundry of Frankfurt. Linotype's revival of Janson appeared in 1934 in America.

Jansson, Johannes, *c.* 1596–1664: a Dutch printer and publisher noted for his finely printed atlases. About 1616 he took over sole control of the business founded by Gerard Mercator, whose plates had passed to Jodocus Hondius and his son Hendrik in 1604. Jansson entered into partnership with Hendrik.

Janus-Presse: the first German private press devoted to the production of finely made books. It was established in 1907 at Leipzig by Carl Ernst Poeschel and Walter Tiemann who together issued fine books, printed by hand in black and red. It closed in 1923.

Japanese paper: a thin, tough, and highly absorbent paper of silky texture used for artists' proofs. It is made from the inner bark of various plants cultivated in Japan, particularly the mulberry.

See also *china paper*.

Japanese vellum: a thick, hand-made paper which is tough and usually cream in colour.

Jean Berte process: a printing process in which non-metallic blocks (i.e. rubber, linoleum, or composition) are used for printing flat water-colours on matt paper.

Jenson, Nicolas, 1420–81: a distinguished printer of his day whose work inspired generations of printers, especially in the 19th-century English revival of fine printing. He was born near Troyes in France, probably studied his craft at Mainz, and in 1470 established himself at Venice where he perfected the roman typeface. He cut twenty-three majuscules (no J, U, and W) and a similar set of minuscules (with u for v) and two diphthongs (ae and oe). After his death his punches, matrices and types passed to Manutius.

See also *venetian types.*

For a specimen see *letters—forms and styles.*

jest-book: a book of amusing stories or jests, popular in the 18th century.

jetté en moule: a phrase held by some to refer to a process of casting letters, for printing, from a mould of sand, clay, or metal, originating in Flanders *c.* 1445. Proof of this has not been finally established, but is based on a passage written in the diary of the Abbot of St Aubert in Cambrai in which he records the acquiring in Bruges of a Doctrinal 'jetté en molle'.

See also *Costeriana, metallography* (2).

job inks: inks used for most book work and general printing; black pigment forms 25% of the weight, gums and oil forming the balance.

jobbing printing: display and commercial printing other than book or newspaper work.

jobbing types: types used for *jobbing printing,* q.v.

Jochen Klepper Award: a silver memorial plaque commemorating the German poet who died under the Nazis in 1942. It is awarded annually by the Vaganten Theatre in Berlin to the author whose play has been the most successful of the season. In 1955 it was presented to Christopher Fry for his 'A Sleep of Prisoners'.

jogger: a machine for *knocking up* paper, q.v. In 1954 Ilya Scheinker of New York announced a new silent electro-mechanical jogging table for use when collating printed sheets. The machine is built in four sizes and operates flat, vertically, or tilted as desired. Since each side of the table is separately adjustable the simultaneous knocking up of different stocks can be effected.

John Llewelyn Rhys Memorial Prize: a prize established in 1921 by J. L. Rhys as an annual award to a British man or woman under 30 for a memorable work, either 'in achievement or promise', published for the first time in the previous year.

John of Westphalia: an early printer of the Low Countries, who came with his types from Italy to establish, with Thierry Martens, the first press at Alost in 1473. He was also known as *John of Paderborn.*

His second press was at Louvain, 1474–96, where there was a flourishing university. He printed editions of Virgil, Juvenal, Barzizza, etc.

Johnston, Edward, 1872–1944: a teacher of calligraphy (Royal College of Art, 1920–35) whose influence on calligraphers and typographers was profound and widespread (particularly in Britain and Germany). This was partly due to his awareness of the fundamental principle that writing and printing are interdependent parts of a whole, and his ability to demonstrate and teach this. No less influential were his pupils Eric Gill and William Graily Hewitt, while Jan Tschichold admits to having studied Johnston's teachings as outlined in his 'Writing and Illuminating, and Lettering' (1906), Pitman, 1945.

The original broadsheet examples of Johnston's writing, published in 1916 by Douglas Pepler at Hammersmith, are now collectors' items.

joiner's press: the name given to the early printing presses which were made entirely of wood.

joint author: one who collaborates in the writing of a book with one or more associates. The part for which each is responsible is not always indicated.

joints: the parts on either side of a book about which the boards hinge; the abutments formed for the boards in *rounding* and *backing,* q.v. (L.K.)

See also *cloth joints, french joints.*

Jordan: a pulp-beating and refining machine used in making certain grades of paper; a cone fitted with blades revolves in an outer casing similarly fitted. It was invented in 1859 by Jordan of Hartford, Conn., U.S.A.

journey terms: terms given by a publisher to a bookseller who has placed a re-order for a stock title with the publisher's traveller. Journey terms should not be confused with *subscription terms,* q.v., which are given on orders for a book before first publication.

See also *terms* (1).

journeyman: one who has completed his apprenticeship.

Jugge, Richard, *c.* 1531–77: an Elizabethan printer who alone, or with John Cawood, held for a time the sole right to print the Bible. He printed the first edition of the Bishop's Bible in 1568.

justification: 1. the spacing of words to a given width of line, done by the compositor when setting up type, or by machine as on the Monotype; the words will thus align at the right-hand margin. In the early days of printing a compositor would often contract or modify the spelling of words to simplify justification, a practice of the still earlier times when books were hand-written.

See also *spacebands*.

2. the levelling and squaring-up by the type-founder of a *strike*, q.v. He also ensures that the face of a type character is at the proper depth.

Justowriter: the trade name of an American machine for typewriter type composition. Two electrically-driven units are used, each having a typewriter keyboard. As words are typed on paper on the first, or trial machine, a moving tape is punched with a code for each letter and the spacing needed to justify each line. When this tape is run through the second machine automatic interpretation of the punched code produces automatically typed and justified lines. The type is 12-point and can be any one of several typefaces fitted by the manufacturer. The finished and corrected page is suitable for reproduction by photo offset or photogravure. This process is classed as *near-print*.

jute board: a strong, light binding board.

K

Kaláb, Method: a distinguished contemporary Czech typographer and book designer of the Průmyslová tiskárna, Prague, skilled in the use of ornamental borders and the disposition of matter on the printed page.

Kalthoeber, Christian Samuel, fl. 1780–1809: a German bookbinder working in London. He used *fore-edge paintings*, q.v., on his finest work, and in general copied rather than initiated binding styles.

kaolin: a substance produced by the weathering of felspathic rocks, and consisting of silicate of alumina. Used as a loading for paper. (M. L.)

Kastenbein, Karl: the inventor, in 1869, of the first mechanical composing machine to be used by a London newspaper. This was in 1872 when 'The Times' bought his machine. The depression of keys released appropriate characters from a reservoir of sorts into a composing stick where a second operative justified them. Average speed was 3500 ens an hour. The machine included a hand-operated distributor which returned sorts to the reservoir after plates had been cast. From 1875, a caster, invented by Frederick Wicks (1840–1910), supplied daily freshly cast type, obviating the use of worn type.

Kate Greenaway Medal: an annual award, established in 1955, made by the Library Association to the illustrator of an outstanding picture book for children. The recipient must be a British subject and domiciled in the U.K.

Katherine Mansfield Prize: an award of £100 a year, made in alternate years, first to a French and then to a British novelist. The award, which was announced in 1957, is made by the French Riviera town of Menton where the famous short-story writer frequently stayed.

keep down: an instruction to the compositor to use capitals sparingly. Cf. *keep up*.

keep in: 1. said of type which does not take up much lateral space.

2. an instruction to the compositor that narrow spaces are to be inserted between words. Cf. *drive out*.

keep out: to use unnecessarily wide inter-word spacing so that matter makes as many lines as possible.

See also *fat matter*, *lean matter*.

keep standing: an instruction given to the printer to hold the type after running off for a possible reprinting. After an agreed period the printer may charge a rental for holding.

See also *dead matter*, *distribute*.

keep up: in setting up type, to use more capital letters than grammatical usage requires.

keepsake: a book of poetry, elaborate in format, popular in early Victorian England.

Kefer (or **Keffer**), **Heinrich,** fl. 1455–73: an associate of Gutenberg in Mainz. It is suggested in the 'Gutenberg Jahrbuch', 1950, that Kefer may have settled in Bamberg about 1459 and there printed the 36-line Bible, previously attributed to *Pfister*, q.v.

He later went to Nuremberg where Johann Sensenschmidt established the first press in 1470. Together they issued in 1473 the 'Pantheologia' of Rainerius de Pisis.

Kells, Book of: an important example of Hiberno-Saxon art, illuminated either at the Columbian monastery of Iona or at the Abbey of Kells in Ireland, and probably in the late 8th or early 9th century. The 339 surviving leaves contain an incomplete Latin text of the Gospels, written in a combination of uncial and round half-uncial scripts, the version being the Irish recension of the Vulgate.

The ornamentation includes leaf and plant forms, zoomorphic forms, interlaced geometrical patterns, and curious figures. The use of lapis lazuli blue, the unusual square punctuation marks, and the introduction of vine foliage as a new decorative element in Celtic art all suggest a later date for its composition than the 7th–8th century once assigned. No gold was used. Since 1661 the work has been in Trinity College, Dublin.

See 'Book of Kells', described by Sir Edward Sullivan. 5th ed., Studio, 1952.

Kelmscott Press: the private press founded at Hammersmith, London, in 1891, by William Morris in close association with Emery Walker. They turned for their inspiration to the roman types of the 15th century and the use of woodcut title-pages. Work was based on the double page as a unit. The fifty or so books to leave the press during the eight years of its existence had a great influence, and while not being slavishly copied, gave impetus to a revival of good book production. The special types cut for Morris by E. P. Prince were the Golden, 1890, based on types of Jenson and Rubens; the gothic Troy, 1891; and the Chaucer, 1892.

Ker, John, third Duke of Roxburghe, 1740–1804: *see Roxburghe, John Ker*, third Duke of.

kerfs: two shallow grooves sawn into the back of the gathered sections, between ¼ in. and ½ in. from the top and bottom of the book. When positioning the sections for this in the marking-up press allowance for trimming is made. The loops of the *kettle-stitches*, q.v., fit in these grooves.

kerned letters: type-faces in which part of the letter projects beyond the body, e.g. an italic '*f*' which is kerned on both sides.

Kerned type

kettle-stitch: a knot made at the head and tail of each sewn section when fastening them together.
See also *hand-sewing*, *kerfs*.

key: 1. a binder's tool for securing the bands when sewing.
2. the block in letterpress printing, or the plate in lithographic printing, which is used to fix the position and register in colour work.

keyboard: the rows of keys for composing in type-setting machines. In the Intertype, Linograph, and Linotype machines the keyboard has six horizontal and fifteen vertical rows with lower-case letters on the left and upper-case on the right. The keyboard of the type-setting machine is similar in its layout to that on a Remington typewriter. The 277 keys of the Monotype machine are arranged in sections of lower-case and upper-case types of two complete alphabets and small caps. The mutual position of the keys in each alphabet is about the same as on an ordinary type-writer. (G.U.)

keying: the keyboard operation in mechanical type-setting to produce either a perforated spool of paper from which individual types are cast (as in Monotype), or to release matrices from which a single line is cast (as in Linotype).

kill: to distribute a job when no longer required.
See also *dead matter*, *live matter*.

King Athelstan's Psalter: see *Athelstan Psalter*.

King's Gold Medal for Poetry: see *Queen's Gold Medal for Poetry*.

King's Printer: see *Queen's Printer*.

kipskin: a skin midway between calf and cowhide, sometimes used for bookbinding.

kiss impression: one in which the ink is deposited on the paper by the lightest possible surface contact and is not impressed into it. This technique is required when printing on coated papers.
See also *dwell*.

Klepper Award: see *Jochen Klepper Award*.

Kleukens, Friedrich Wilhelm, 1878–1956: a German graphic arts teacher and type-designer who directed the Ernst Ludwig-Presse at Darmstadt from 1907–14. He designed four special types for the press (obtainable from Bauersche Giesserei and D. Stempel). From 1914 his brother *Christian Heinrich Kleukens* (1880–1954) directed the press before founding the Kleukens-Presse in 1919, and the Mainzer-Presse in 1929. The latter also wrote several books on printing and typography.

Klíč, Karl, 1841–1926: the inventor of modern doctor-blade photogravure. From 1875–78 he evolved an etching process with the transfer of carbon tissue, Klíčotype, intended for producing letterpress blocks; but from this there developed what we now call *photogravure*, q.v. The first photogravure reproductions were printed by Pisani, a Viennese copperplate printer, but Klíč kept the process secret until it was made public in 1886 without his permission. In 1890 he made a thorough study of calico printing at Neunkirchen (Austria) and of the *doctor blade* already used for such work. By 1894, by the introduction of the cross-line screen and using carbon tissue, invented by Sir Joseph Swan, he succeeded in combining photogravure and doctor-blade printing in the process now known by the name *intaglio* *printing*. By that time he had removed to England where the Rembrandt Intaglio Printing Co. was established at Lancaster under his direction. Even then he preserved the secret of producing these 'Rembrandt Prints' which were first issued in 1895. Colour printing of great technical perfection was also produced. In 1906 Klíč returned to Vienna. His name is also spelled *Klietsch*. (G. U.)

Klingspor, Karl, 1869–1950: the best known of a 19th- and 20th-century German family of typefounders, Gebr. Klingspor, Offenbach-am-Main. The firm traces its origins to the Rudhardschen Foundry founded in 1842, the present name being adopted in 1906.

Karl Klingspor issued several types designed by Peter Behrens, *Otto Hupp*, *Rudolph Koch*, and *Walter Tiemann*, qq.v., which have been acclaimed throughout Europe.

Klischograph: a German electronic photoengraving machine which produces a plastic, zinc, copper, or magnesium half-tone plate. The original to be reproduced is placed face down on a glass plate, a blank plastic printing plate (face up) is fitted above it, and the two are clamped. An optical device (or scanner) under the table is used to scan the original, light reflected from the picture being picked up by two photoelectric cells. These transmit impulses through amplifiers to the engraving head above the plastic plate, and hence to the V-shaped engraving needle which digs dots of a size and depth varying in relation to the brightness of the original. The engraving head is stationary and the plastic plate and original are reciprocated under it, scanning being done diagonally. As each line is completed the scanner returns into position for the next line. The machine will also engrave the back of the plate for removing highlight areas. The Klischograph, also known in Britain as the *Clichograph*, was devised by Dr. Rudolph Hell of Kiel.

There is a Klischograph Model K160 for making separate colour blocks for three- and four-colour printing. Scanning and engraving are done as on the standard model, but colour filters are used to separate the image into primary colours. The fine point of light which scans the original image is picked up by two photoelectric cells. The first of these transmits, via an amplifier, information about the primary colour: the second controls the electrical operation for colour correction. These impulses control the engraving needle fixed above the rotating engraving table. By 1957 blocks 6 in. by 8 in., with a 120-line screen equivalent, could be made. This model is known in Britain as the *Finella Klischograph*.

The *Multi-Vario Klischograph*, an enlarging and reducing machine, was announced in 1957. This permits a maximum block size of approximately 12 in. by 16 in., and a continuous size variation four times enlargement to one-third reduction. Engraving speed has been increased. The machine will produce half-tone blocks on plastic or metal in screen rulings of 60, 75, 100, and 133 lines, as well as line and combination blocks. Fully corrected three- and four-colour blocks can be produced in the same size variations.

knife folding: see *folding machine*.

Knight, Charles, 1743–1827: a pioneer in London of *stipple engraving*, it being claimed that he was a pupil of *Bartolozzi*, q.v.

knocking up: the adjustment on one or two edges of a pile of printed or unprinted sheets so that they can be cut squarely, or used for some purpose requiring squared-up sheets. Thin paper is often knocked up in a jogger, particularly between printing and cutting. The machine consists of a sloping rectangular plate on which several sheets are laid at a time. By agitation, the sheets are made to lie along two supporting edges on both the lower sides of the plate. The shaking of the plate, suspended on springs, is done by revolving eccentric plates. Sometimes an auxiliary table is placed next to the machine on which the pile is laid and is exposed to a current of air; this separates the sheets before they are laid on the shaking plate. (G. U.)

The Soag Jogger

Koberger, Anton, 1440–1513: an eminent early printer of Nuremberg who issued more than 200 works. He is especially noted for his Bibles and theological books in Latin, also for Hartmann Schedel and Georg Alt's 'Liber chronicarum' (Nuremberg

Chronicle), 1493. This outline of geography and history was illustrated by the woodcuts of Wilhelm Pleydenwurff and Michael Wolgemut; the presswork was not of high standard, and many of the 1809 blocks were repeated.

Koch, Rudolph, 1876–1934: a prominent German type-designer and teacher noted for his display types. Among his faces known in England, where he worked for a time, are Maximilian, 1913; Locarno; Neuland, 1923; and Kabel (Cable sanserif), 1927. In 1906 he joined the Klingspor Foundry, remaining there until his death.

Kodachrome: see *colour photography*.

Kodak Lithofoil: thin aluminium sheeting with one side satinized and coated with a stable sensitized layer, devised by Kodak for the small offset-litho printer. Its use is simple. Exposure is done in a vacuum frame under any source rich in blue and ultra-violet light. After exposure the plate is swabbed with diluted Lithofoil developer. This removes any unexposed coating. It is then swabbed with a Kodak stabilizer which makes the exposed areas hard and water-resistant, and also converts the unexposed areas to a non-oxidizing water-attracting surface. The plate is then inked, and rinsed with water prior to gumming. It can then be dried and stored, or put on the press. Special damping solutions are unnecessary, any non-alkaline water being adequate. The fine grain of the satinized surface and the minimum damping needed enable fine screen images to be printed with high ink density.

Kodak screen products: see *contact screen*.

Kodak short run colour system: a recently developed system of three-colour offset-litho printing, devised in America by the Eastman Kodak Co. for runs of up to 5000 impressions. This alternative to the normal high cost of camera work, plate-making, and colour correction is made possible by standardizing procedures so that many operations are eliminated or reduced, by using punched film to give automatic register control at all stages from original to final reproduction, by using masking for colour correction instead of hand-work, and by using carefully selected inks for printing. The equipment at present in use produces a standard print from 35 mm. up to 9 × 6 cm. transparencies.

The stages of the process are 1. the preparation from the transparency, by contact exposure, of a single mask to reduce contrast and give some colour correction; 2. the making of direct half-tone separation negatives through neutral contact screens on to Kodalith pan film; 3. printing the negatives on to pre-sensitized lithographic plates; 4. printing with specially prepared inks and using a densitometer for balance control.

The special equipment for the process is being made in America.

Koebau: an abbreviation and trade-mark of Schnellpressenfabrik König & Bauer A.G., Würzburg. This world-famous printing-press factory was established in 1817 by *Friedrich König*, q.v., and Friedrich Andreas Bauer. The company pioneered many new models and improved others. Its present products include rotary reel machines for letterpress and photogravure, stereo machines of all kinds, the Sturmvogel two-revolution press and the Rex stop-cylinder machine for letterpress, and the Tiepolo sheet press for intaglio printing. (G.U.)

Their large sheet-fed letterpress rotary machine, the Pax, takes a maximum sheet of 52 in. by 76 in. at a speed of 5000 to 5500 impressions an hour.

Koelhoff, Johann, fl. 1472–93: an early printer of Cologne, remembered for having been the first to print *signatures*, q.v.

He was succeeded by his son, Johann, who worked in Cologne until 1502. His fame rests on the 'Cologne Chronicle' which he began in 1499.

See also *Ulrich Zell*.

Koenig: an alternative spelling of *König*, q.v.

König, Friedrich, 1774–1833: the inventor of the cylinder press. In 1803 König began construction of a printing press in Wolfgang Kummer's workshop in Suhl which may be called an automatic hand-press. It performed automatically the inking up, insertion of the bed, printing, and drawing out of the bed. The press was made of wood and wrought iron. In 1806, after a short visit to St Petersburg, König went to London and there he entered into partnership with Thomas Bensley. With the assistance of Bensley and others he patented (1810) an improved Suhl press, entirely of iron, which he completed in 1811. Both this and the earlier model had a cylinder inking device, ink being supplied from a box-like container with a slit in the base. Ink was pressed through this to the rollers by a piston.

In 1811 König patented a cylinder press which was completed in December 1812. This printed 800 sheets an hour, and Walter, the owner of 'The Times', ordered two twin machines (their construction was patented in 1813); they consisted of two single presses built symmetrically round a central inking device. The forme pressed against one cylinder while moving forward, and against the other on its return. By this means double production was achieved and the press printed 1100 sheets an hour. The issue of

'The Times' of November 29th, 1814, was the first to be printed on the new press.

In 1810 König began his collaboration with F. A. Bauer, a German mechanic also living in London. After taking out a further patent for the basic model of a two-revolution press (1814), and building his first perfecting machine on this system (1816), König entered into partnership with Bauer and the firm of König & Bauer was founded in 1817 (see *Koebau*). König then returned to Germany, while Bauer continued his work in London where he completed the first single-cylinder two-revolution press. In Würzburg work began under great difficulties, but was later successful. König constantly produced new models, being succeeded after his death by Bauer, and subsequently by his sons Friedrich and Wilhelm König.

The spelling *König* used here is that adopted by 'Schweizer Lexikon' and 'Lexikon des Buchwesens' (Kirchner), 1952; in other works ('Encyclopaedia Britannica') it is spelled *Koenig*. (G. U.)

Koran: the sacred book of Islam, being the word of God as made known to his Prophet, Mohammed, by the angel Gabriel. These revelations, which began in 610, cover a period of twenty years and constitute the foundation of the Islamic faith.

While probably written or dictated during Mohammed's lifetime the present arrangement of its 114 chapters is of later date. The first complete written version is believed to be the compilation of Mohammed's secretary, Zayid ibn Thābit. A later recension was made in 651 by Zayid and three others during the reign of 'Othman, and this is still the standard text. Copies were sent to the principal cities of the caliphate and the work of preparing them grew into an esteemed and important craft. Sumptuous examples illuminated in gold and colours were made, the finest being Persian. The earliest *dated* complete Koran (A.D. 784) is now in Cairo. Modern Oriental copies are usually handwritten and then lithographed. The first *official* printed version was issued by the Egyptian Government in 1925.

The first European translation (into Latin) was commissioned about 1143 by Petrus Venerabilis, Abbot of Cluny. It was the work of Robert of Retina and Herbert of Dalmatia. A printed version of this was published at Basle by Theodore Bibliander in 1543. Copies of an Arabic edition printed at Rome about 1520 by Paganini de Paganini no longer survive.

kraft paper: strong brown paper, made from sulphate pulp, used for packing books in addition to many other purposes.

Krause, Jacob, 1526–85: court bookbinder to the Elector August of Saxony from 1566, and the most renowned German bookbinder of his day. His technically perfect bindings were made in Venetian-Oriental styles, and many had painted fore-edges or goffered edges. (G. U.)

Krause, Karl: a German precision-instrument maker who in 1855 established a business in Leipzig which is still active. The firm has made several contributions to the development of machines for the graphic industries. In 1857 a new gilding press was introduced, in 1858 a new guillotine, and in 1877 a three-bladed *guillotine*, q.v. In the 1920's the firm brought out a *step-and-repeat machine*, q.v. (G. U.)

Krimpen, Jan van, 1892–1958: one of the most famous of recent type-designers who, in 1925, became artistic adviser to the Dutch printing firm Enschedé en Zonen. Types of his known in Britain are Lutetia, Romulus, Antigone, Romanée, and Cancelleresca: they were cut by P. H. Rädisch. Van Krimpen also designed a face for the Oxford University Press.

The most recent on the Monotype list is Spectrum (1955).

See J. Dreyfus, 'The Work of J. van Krimpen', Sylvan Press, 1952, and J. van Krimpen, 'On designing and devising type', Sylvan Press, 1957.

Kunera Press: the name to which J. F. van Royen changed his *Zilverdistel Press*, q.v.

L

label title: the name given to the first form of title-page in early printed books (1470–1550). Title and author's name were printed on an otherwise blank protecting leaf at the beginning of a book. The earliest extant example is a Papal Bull printed at Mainz in 1463, probably by Fust and Schöffer; a second is the 'Sermo ad populum' of Werner Rolewinck, printed in 1470 by Arnold ter Hoernen at Cologne.

The first decorated title-page proper was in the Calendar of Regiomontanus (Johannes Müller), Venice, 1476, printed by Ratdolt, Löslein, and Maler.

Label titles were sometimes printed from wooden blocks, thus the addition of an illustration was easy: an example is seen in the 'Testament' of Lydgate, printed in 1515 by Pynson.

The first English label title was printed by Machlinia for 'Treatise of the pestilence', *c.* 1489.

See also *incipit*.

labels: paper or other material separate from that used for binding a book, on which the author's name and title are printed or stamped and fixed to the spine or front board. The use of gold-lettered morocco labels dates from the 17th century; printed paper labels belong to the era 1760–1830, but their use has not entirely ceased.

See also *flyswing*, *lettering piece*, *panel*.

Laboratory Press: an American private press founded in 1923 at the Carnegie Institute of Technology in Pittsburgh by Porter Garnett. It published reprints of rare books, keepsakes, etc., great attention being paid to the faithful reproduction of the originals.

lace bindings: a style of book-cover decoration devised in the 18th century by Parisian craftsmen. Elaborate tooling of a broad lace-like border covered most of the cover, with a small space in the centre for an armorial shield. The finest examples were made by Pierre-Paul Dubuisson and the Deromes. Also known as *dentelle bindings*.

lace borders: lace-like paper borders which occasionally appear in 19th-century French books as a frame for a whole-page illustration. The paper is pierced as in a paper doily. Examples may be seen in the Victoria and Albert Museum.

laced on: said of boards which are held to the book by the cords on to which the sections have been sewn. The cords, with their ends splayed and moistened with paste, pass through holes pierced in the boards.

See also *holing out*.

lacertine animals: a name given to the elongated animal forms used from the 8th century as part of the ornamentation of illuminated manuscripts. The bodies of such animals formed involved spiral patterns and terminated in the head of a lion, dog, or lizard.

lacing in: the affixing of laced-on boards.

lacquered bindings: 16th–19th century Persian, Turkish, and Indian book bindings of which the principal decoration was a painted miniature covered with a protective film of transparent varnish, and without the usual fold-over flap. In Europe, lacquered strapwork decorated, among others, *Lyonnese* and *Grolier* bindings, qq.v.

laid paper: paper which, when held up to light, shows a series of ribbed lines, the vertical or chain lines being about 1 in. apart, and the horizontal or laid lines being close together. This effect is caused by the weave of the dandy roll. (Cf. *wove paper*.) To obtain the best impression when printing on laid papers care should be taken that the narrow lines run across the page, the wide lines down it.

See also *water lines*, *wire-mark*.

Laing, John, 1809–80: the Edinburgh librarian who compiled jointly with *Samuel Halkett*, q.v., 'A Dictionary of the Anonymous and Pseudonymous Literature of Great Britain', 1882–88.

Lair, John: the printer of Siegburg near Cologne who worked in England as *John Siberch*, q.v.

lambskin: a smooth-finished leather used for binding; it is similar to calf but less durable.

lampblack: pure carbon deposit, formerly the most important black pigment used in the manufacture of printing inks. (M.L.)

L & M: an abbreviation for Linotype & Machinery Ltd., London, with works in Altrincham, makers of the *Linotype* type-setting machine, q.v., and printing presses of many kinds, including two-revolution letterpress machines of the Miehle type, perfecting machines, multicolour presses, and sheet presses for intaglio printing from curved plates. The company was among the first to manufacture offset presses for printing on paper. (G. U.)

landscape: see *oblong*.

Lansdowne Collection: the important library of William Petty, first Marquess of Lansdowne (previously Lord Shelburne) (1737–1805). In addition to printed books on English Church history was a manuscript collection of Elizabethan and James I State Papers (including those of Lord Burghley). These were purchased for the British Museum in 1807.

Lanston, Tolbert, 1844–1913: the inventor of the *Monotype* type-setting and casting machine, q.v. Lanston was born in Troy, Ohio, U.S.A., and was originally a lawyer. He took out his first patent in 1885, being helped financially by J. M. Dove, and an early model was exhibited at the Columbian World's Fair, 1893. Production began a year later, in Philadelphia, where Sellers & Co. were contracted to build the machines. John S. Bancroft of this firm had charge of the work, and by 1899 he had considerably improved technical details and given the machine the basis of its present form.

To seek capital four early Monotype machines were shipped to London in 1897. While crossing the Atlantic the Earl of Dunraven learned of the machine and later formed a syndicate to purchase the British rights for £220,000. In the same year the Lanston Monotype Corporation was founded with a capital of £550,000. (The name was changed to The Monotype Corporation Limited in 1931.)

For detailed history see 'The Monotype Recorder', Vol. XXXIX, No. 1, Autumn 1949. (With G. U.)

lapidary type: a fount of capital letters designed to reproduce those on Roman monumental inscriptions. Erhard Ratdolt cut and cast examples at Augsburg in 1505.

lapis lazuli: the shade of blue favoured by illuminators of manuscripts. Made from the crushed stone.

large paper edition: a special or de luxe edition of a book, having large fore-edge and foot margins, but printed from the same type as the standard edition, sometimes numbered and autographed. In the 18th century the classics were often issued in this form; an alternative was to prepare two editions of a book, the type being specially set for the large paper edition, the cheap edition being somewhat cramped.

Latin abbreviations: the monks' tradition of abbreviating certain nouns and verbs when writing Latin and Greek texts was continued by printers of books in the 15th and 16th centuries. Usage varied, being dictated by custom and not rule, but the following list gives a selection of the commonest Latin non-legal abbreviations: it is reprinted from R. B. McKerrow's 'An Introduction to Bibliography for Literary Students', O.U.P., 1928, by courtesy of the Clarendon Press.

aliqñ—aliquando
ałr—aliter
añ—ante
apłice—apostolice
apłoꝝ—apostolorum
bñ—bene
cãm—causam
corꝑibus—corporibus
dc̃m—dictum
dño—domino
dñs—dominus
ds̃—Deus
ẽ—est
eẽ—esse
eẽt—esset
em̃—enim
ẽt—etiam
etem̃—etenim
fr̃em—fratrem
g̊—ergo
gr̃a—gratia
hẽant̃—habeantur
hẽat—habeat
.i.—id est
igr̃, ig̃r, ġ—igitur
ip̃ius—ipsius
ip̃oꝝ—ipsorum
ĩr (perhaps for ir̃)—ire
lrãs, lrĩs—litteras, litteris
mõ—modo
mr̃is—matris
.n.—enim
nr̃—noster
nr̃is—nostris
oẽs—omnes
oĩm—omnium
or̃o—oratio
orõnẽ—orationem
pñtes—praesentes
pꝑ—propter
pr̃—pater
pr̃is—patris
p̄t—potest
qđ—quod
qm̃—quoniam
rõ—ratio
r̃furr̃ctõem—resurrectionem
.ſ.—scilicet
ſc̃us—sanctus
ſñĩa—sententia
ſꝑ—semper
ſpm̃—spiritum
ſpũs—spiritus
ſt̃e—sancte
tm̃—tantum
tñ—tamen
tp̃a—tempora
tꝑe—tempore
tp̃s—tempus
uñ—unde
xp̃s—Christus

Laureate press: a platen press of the Universal style, with a rigid, upright bed. (M. L.)

Laurentian Codex: an 11th-century codex of the works of Sophocles, Apollonius Rhodius, and Aeschylus, found in the 15th century by Aurispa for his patron Niccolo de' Niccoli. It is now in the Biblioteca Mediceo-Laurenziana, Florence.

Laurentii, Nicolaus, fl. 1477–86: a printer of Breslau who went to Florence where he worked with Johannes Petri of Mainz, and also at the Dominican house of St Jacobum de Ripoli. He is remembered as having been the first printer to include illustrations from copperplates in a book: the work was Antonio Bettini's 'Monte santo di' Dio', 1477 (GKW 2204). Other examples were used in the first illustrated edition of Dante's 'La Divina Commedia', 1481 (GKW 7966), which had nineteen copperplate engravings by Baccio Baldini after the designs of Sandro Botticelli.

law calf: tanned, uncoloured calfskin, which in the 19th century was often used in England for the covers of law books. Also called *fair calf.*

law sheep: sheepskin used as in *law calf,* q.v.

lay edges: the two edges of a sheet which are placed flush with the side and front lay gauges (or marks) on a printing machine. This ensures the sheet will be removed properly by the grippers, and have uniform margins when printed. The front edge is the *gripper edge* and the side edge the *side lay.*
See also *feeding.*

lay of the case: the disposition of the letters and punctuation marks in a compositor's case. By custom, the usage of John Johnson, William Savage, and John Southward (all 19th-century printers) has influenced present-day standardization in Britain.

lay-sheet: the sheet of glass, or other transparent material, on which the negatives or positives of text and illustrations are assembled preparatory to printing down a photo-offset plate.

layerman: the craftsman who takes the still moist sheets of *leaf* (2) from the *post,* qq.v. He places them in piles of about 230 sheets on a felt-covered zinc plate, and lightly presses the pile under a second plate. The pile is opened and re-assembled several times, the process usually being continued over several days.
See also *slice boy.*

laying on: the placing of gold leaf on a surface when gilding. In gilding by hand or with a press the leaf is transferred from its cushion by means of a suitably shaped wad of cottonwool or a piece of felt. When the gold leaf is on reels, it is transferred directly from them. In edge-gilding leaf is transferred from the gold cushion by means of a gilder's tip, a simple wooden frame over which threads or a network of threads are stretched. (G.U.)
See also *gilt edges, gold leaf.*

laying press: see *lying press.*

laying the fount: putting type into the case when a new fount is laid.

layout: 1. the preparation of copy for setting up in type, indicating the type to be used, and the position of blocks, etc. The layout of the preliminary matter and of the jacket call for the skilled attention of a typographer.

2. a sketch or outline which gives the general appearance of a printed page. This is done on sheets of paper, usually 17 in. by 22 in., ruled in 12-point squares.

l.c.: see *lower case.*

lead moulding: a process of making electros of half-tone printing surfaces in which lead is used instead of wax. A sheet of soft lead is forced into the forme under great pressure and a mould obtained. A copper shell is deposited on this.

leaded: said of type which is set with leads between the lines. Cf. *set solid.*

leaders: a sequence of dots or hyphens used to direct the eye across a printed page, e.g. as in a table of contents. They are cast on 5- to 18-point bodies with one, two, or three dots to an em. In modern typography the use of leaders is avoided by setting contents pages to a narrower measure than text pages.

leading: the insertion of *leads,* q.v.

leads: thin strips of lead of varying thickness used to separate lines of type. Thicknesses are 1-point, 1½-point (thin), 2-point, and 3-point (thick). An alternative way to increase the space between lines without using leads is to employ type cast on bodies larger than normal, e.g. 10-point on 12-point, known as *long-bodied type.*
See also *reglets.*

leaf: 1. *gold leaf,* q.v.
2. newly formed sheets of paper before they are dried and finished.
3. each of the folios which result when a sheet of paper is folded. Each side of a leaf is a page. In the late 16th century the term leaf denoted a whole printed sheet; furthermore, a particular printer was occasionally accorded the right to print the first leaf of a book for which another printer held the right to print the remainder.

lean matter: see *fat matter.*

leather: skin from any of several animals prepared as a material for covering books: goat, calf, sheep, pig, and seal are mostly used.

leather joints: inner leather hinges made with the end-papers of a heavy, hand-bound book. These give additional strength. (G.U.)
See also *tooling.*

leather preservation: early leather bindings can be preserved by the following treatment. A weak soap solution should be used for gently washing the cover, a little methylated spirit being lightly dabbed on any

Morocco

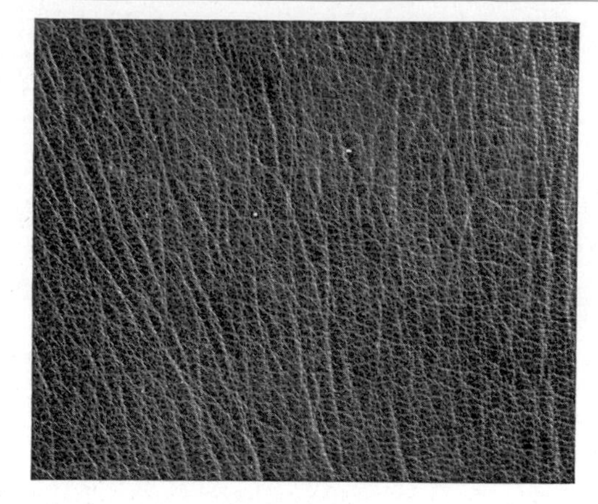

Oasis goat

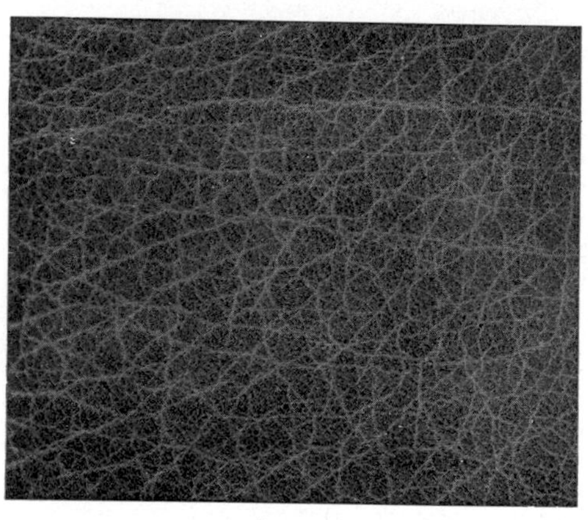

Écrasé

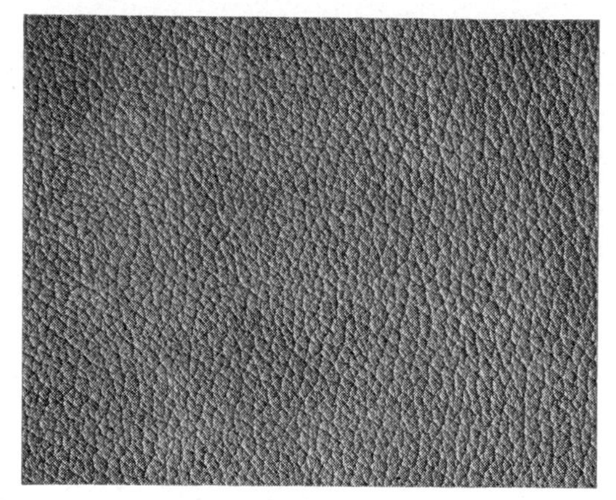

Calf

traces of varnish. With cottonwool a preservative solution is then applied. This is made up of hexane, lanolin, cedarwood oil, and beeswax (available commercially as Boots C1590). The preparation should soak in for a day, after which the book should be polished with a soft brush.

A method of protecting leather against deterioration through exposure to polluted atmosphere was evolved by R. Faraday Innes and published in 1933. It involves the introduction of certain chemicals in the course of manufacture, and leather made in this way may be stamped 'Guaranteed to Resist P.I.R.A. Test'. The British Museum Laboratory reports favourably on such leather, and it is commercially available. (L.K.)

leather varieties and finishes: see *Alaska seal, basil, buckskin, calf, cheveril, Cordovan, cowhide, cross-grained morocco, crushed Levant, deerskin, écrasé, fair calf, flyswing, French Cape Levant, glazed morocco, grained, hard-grain morocco, imitation leather, lambskin, law calf, law sheep, leatherette, levant, morocco, mottled calf, Niger morocco, oasis goat, ooze, parchment, paste-grain, peccary, Persian morocco, roan, russia cowhide, russia leather, Rutland, seal, sheepskin, skivers, smooth calf, Smyrna morocco, Spanish calf, sprinkled calf, stained calf, straight-grain morocco, tree-calf, Turkey leather, Turkey morocco, vellum.*

leatherette: a bookbinding fabric made of a strong base paper, M.G., which is coated and embossed, or printed and embossed, to resemble grained leather. Colours and finishes are many.

Le Blon, Jacques Christophe, 1667–1741: a painter and engraver of Frankfurt-am-Main, and the pioneer of modern three-colour reproduction. After his apprenticeship in Zürich and Rome he moved to Amsterdam where he experimented with the reproduction of paintings in colour print, being inspired by the publication of Newton's recent discoveries concerning the composition of light.

From 1720 he worked in London, and formed a company with some publishers for issuing coloured reproductions of famous paintings. The undertaking proved a financial failure and Le Blon moved to Paris about 1735. His licence for colour printing limited the work Gauthier d'Agoty, one of his imitators, was trying to do.

At first Le Blon used seven printing plates, one for each colour of Newton's spectrum. By degrees he reduced these to three, done in mezzotint, retouched with a graver, and printed in yellow, red, and blue, sometimes supplemented with a fourth plate for black. Only thirty-four of Le Blon's engravings have been preserved in one or more copies. They are artistic and technically skilful. His successor d'Agoty also made good reproductions, but had generally to use more colours, at least four or five. (G.U.)

See also *colour printing*, *subtractive colour synthesis*.

lectionary: a book containing lessons or Scriptural extracts to be read at Divine Service.

lectori: a note 'to the reader' in the form of a preface.

Lee Priory Press: an English private press, established in 1813 by Johnson and Warwick, under the patronage and editorship of Sir Samuel Egerton Brydges (1762–1837), who undertook to supply the copy. It issued limited editions of minor Elizabethan literature until it closed about December 1822.

Leeu, Gerard de, fl. 1477–93: a printer of Gouda in Holland where he issued 'Dialogus creaturarum moralisatus' in 1480. This was illustrated with 121 woodcuts, and due to its success was widely copied in Holland and elsewhere. He issued about 145 works.

In 1493 he was printing 'Cronycles of the londe of Englõd' (STC 9994) when, it is said, he was stabbed to death by one of his workmen.

Le Gascon, fl. 1620–30: a leading Parisian bookbinder whose identity has not been accurately established. He favoured a simplified style of fillet frames with large fleurons in the corners, usually tooled in red morocco of an exclusive colour. Some 350 bindings attributed to him are in the Bibliothèque Nationale, Paris. They bear the coat of arms of Loménie de Brienne. Le Gascon is also associated, perhaps inaccurately, with *pointillé* bindings, q.v., but there is no pointillé on the examples referred to above.

legend: correctly, the name for the descriptive matter printed below an illustration. The custom of printing and publishing establishments is to prefer the term *caption*, q.v.

Legenda: a book of sermons, lessons from the Bible, and hagiographies for use at Divine Service.

Legenda aurea: a collection of lives of the saints, written between 1263 and 1272 by Archbishop Jacobus de Voragine. The work was widely copied (and translated) in manuscript form, and later engaged the attention of many well-known early printers in England, France, Germany, Holland, and Spain.

In England, Caxton (1483) and Wynkyn de Worde (1493) printed editions, both using the same woodcuts (STC 24873–24880).

In France, Nicolaus Philippi and Marcus Reinhart issued the first printed edition at Lyons in 1478; another edition (in French) with similar woodcuts was printed in 1483 by Mathias Huss and Petrus Ungarius.

In Germany, Günther Zainer issued the editio princeps at Augsburg in 1471 ('Der Heyligen leben'). This was illustrated with 258 woodcuts.

legibility: the cumulative effect on the human eye of printed matter. This depends on the size, shape, and degree of density of letters, their distance from one another, the space between words, the length of lines, and the width of interlinear spacing. Colour, paper quality, and light also affect legibility, as do the sight, proficiency in reading, and intellectual level of the reader. Doctors, teachers, and psychologists have studied the problem since the end of the 19th century (in Germany and France). Important results have been achieved in America (Luckiesh, 'Reading as a Visual Task', New York, 1945) and Britain (Burt, 'A Psychological Study of Typography', London, 1959).

Scientists recommend not more than thirteen words to a line, with type varying between 9- and 12-point according to the measure and size of page, matt white paper, and ink of good density. Balanced margins, clear type without dazzle or eye-catching affectations in its design, are among other desiderata.

Leipzig Fair: from the late 16th century onwards the book fairs of Leipzig developed in importance just as the town became the centre of the German book trade. The first catalogue of books shown at the fair was published in 1594 by Henning Gross. By 1765 the rival Frankfurt Fair had lost much of its trade, and visitors came from all parts of Europe to Leipzig. By the 19th century the Cantate Fair was the main event of the publishing trade in Germany.

While somewhat restricted in scope at the present

time, the Leipzig book fairs have been held since 1945, forming part of a general trade fair at which British firms are represented.

See also *Frankfurt Fair*.

Le Monnier bindings: the style of bindings associated principally with the Frenchman Jean Charles Henri Le Monnier, who in 1757 was binder to the Duke of Orleans. Features of his work were mosaics of landscapes, allegorical scenes, etc. He also used yellow, red, and green morocco on a ground of coloured mastic. The Le Monnier family were binders from 1623–*c.* 1800.

Lenox, James, 1800–80: one of the most famous American book-collectors who appears to have acquired the major portion of his library between 1840 and 1880. He was the most active Bible collector of his age and bought the first 42-line Gutenberg Bible to be imported to America. His vast collection is now in New York Public Library.

Le Rouge, Pierre, fl. 1478–92: a printer of Chablis and Paris. His most important work was an edition of 'La Mer des Histoires', 2 vols., 1488, based on the editio princeps of the 'Rudimentum nouitiorum', Lucas Brandis, Lübeck, 1475. Woodcuts and border pieces made this one of the most beautiful of early French books.

He also printed for other Parisian publishers, notable being an edition of 'L'art de bien mourir' for Antoine Vérard. In the colophon of this and other books Le Rouge styles himself 'Imprimeur du Roy'.

Le Roy, Guillaume, fl. 1473–88: the first printer of Lyons where he worked until 1483 for Barthélemy Buyer. Of the forty titles he issued, many were in French, and often illustrated with woodcuts.

Le Suer, Vincent and Pierre, jun.: the best known of a French family of wood engravers who, in the early 18th century, were renowned for their head- and tail-pieces.

letra de Tortis: the Spanish name for *lettre de somme*, q.v. So called after the Venetian printer Battista de Tortis who used it in the 1490's for his law books.

letter: 1. a single type.

2. a group of type, e.g. roman letter, black letter, etc.

lettera antiqua tonda: a 16th-century script used by, among others, the great Italian writing masters Tagliente and Arrighi of Venice (fl. 1524). Each letter was carefully made, being considered and written as a unit rather than as part of a word. In appearance the writing was not unlike early venetian types. In the mid-16th century Cresci used this hand when writing Service books for the Sistine Chapel in Rome.

lettera rotunda: a round gothic script used in the scriptoria of 13th-century Italy.

See also *black letter*.

lettera Venetae: the name given by German printers (*c.* 1485–90) to the rotunda or round gothic types of Italian origin.

lettering on the spine: when the lettering on the spine or jacket of a book is not to be set across it, the direction of the lettering may be downward or upward. The Publishers Association and the Associated Booksellers of Great Britain recommended in 1948 that such lettering should be downward, so that the title can be easily read when the book lies flat, face upward. This contradicted their 1926 recommendation that 'when the volume stands on the shelf the lettering reads from bottom to top'.

lettering piece: a thin leather label, lettered in gold with the title and author's name, affixed to the spine (and sometimes to the front board) of a leather-bound book. A separate label in a contrasting colour may be affixed bearing the volume number.

See also *flyswing*, *labels*.

letterpress: 1. the text of a book, including the line illustrations, but not any 'plates'.

2. printing done from raised types or blocks as distinct from intaglio or lithographic plates. A feature of letterpress printing is its crispness due to pressure on the type tending to concentrate the ink at the edges of the letters.

See also *letterpress machines*.

letterpress machines: printing presses in which the impression is taken from raised types or blocks, i.e. relief printing. The earliest letterpress machines were *platen presses*, q.v., and their somewhat simple construction was not much changed until the 19th century. In 1803–4 König constructed an entirely automatic platen press known as the Suhler press (after the Thuringian town of Suhl, where it was made in Kummer's mechanical workshop). It was not successful, and only in 1850 did a practical working platen press, having automatic inking and printing, make its appearance. George Phineas Gordon of New York took out in 1862 a patent for a press of this kind which had ink table grinding. About this time, also in America, O. F. Degener's Franklin press appeared, later to be manufactured in Europe (in England under the name of 'Minerva'). The Franklin or Liberty press (patented in 1857) embodied a bed as well as a platen, which were swung together on one axis. About 1870 J. M. Gally constructed a platen press with cylinder inking (later incorporated in the Suhler), and his machine became the prototype of the widely used Victoria press built by the Rockstroh Werke.

Suhler press, 1803

Long before the platen press was perfected the *cylinder press* was invented; the first, constructed and patented in 1811 by König, was a *stop-cylinder press*. It was completed in December 1812. Here the forme moved to and fro on a flat bed underneath a cylinder which made a one-third revolution while printing from the forme in its forward movement. On the return of the forme the cylinder was stationary, without coming into contact with it, this interval being used for feeding the paper. The sheets were held tightly against the cylinder by a tape frame. The *inking device*, q.v., consisted of an ink pump, grinding rollers, and forme rollers. Capacity was 800 sheets an hour. Two years later a double press was ready, and it was first used for printing 'The Times' on November 29th, 1814. This press had two cylinders placed symmetrically round an inking device, the forme being printed during its forward movement against one of the cylinders, and during its receding movement against the other. Both cylinders had a feed and distribution table. Sheets were guided by tapes running on reels. Capacity was 1100 sheets an hour. In 1814 König patented a *two-revolution machine*, i.e. a press in which the cylinder was in continuous motion, but in which printing took place only during every second revolution. In 1815–16 König constructed the first *perfecting machine*, and in this the inking rollers were solid cast cylinders instead of the leather rollers used previously. To secure the sheets during printing David Napier & Son introduced grippers. In early cylinder presses the bed on which the forme rested was moved to and fro by a toothed

König's cylinder machine of 1812

wheel in gear with a journal bearing on one side of a frame under the bed (see diagram of Babcock's Optimus press). When the wheel reached the end of the journal bearing, it was made to turn round the end cog, so that, while continuing its motion, it was in gear with the journal bearing alternately from above and below, this giving the to and fro motion.

In 1845 the Maschinenfabrik of Augsburg introduced the *crank motion*. Here, on the under-side of the bed are two rails resting against two or more pairs of wheels which run on rails at the bottom of the press (see illustration). The bed is set in its forward and reverse motion by a connecting rod. In modern models the large wheel construction is replaced by a *gliding movement* in which the bed bottom rails glide against the supporting rails; in larger presses, however, steel reels are introduced between the rails to reduce friction. The reels are mounted in a sledge which follows the bed in its movement (the sledge thereby moving half the way completed by the bed). The connecting rod sets in motion a cog-wheel geared with transmissions on the bottom side of the bed, and does so at the same time as it runs against a fixed transmission gear in the bottom plate.

An alternative method for effecting the to and fro motion is the *circular movement*. In a fixed gear rim, toothed on the inside, runs a cog-wheel ('dancing master') of exactly half the diameter of the former. This is set in motion by other cog-wheels, and the movement is transmitted by means of a gear and shaft to the bed. (See diagram.) This principle is now chiefly used on small machines.

The original idea of driving the bed may be said to have been revived in the modern two-motion press. Babcock's Optimus press has a pronounced 'mangle' motion, while the Century and Miehle machines have an upper and lower gear on the bottom side of the bed, and these are worked by a cog-wheel. (See diagram.)

Letterpress machines

Press with crank motion, about 1900

Circular movement mechanism

In the Century drive the two gears are immediately above one another with an intervening space not exceeding the cog-wheel diameter (see diagram), whereas Miehle's *double shuttle motion* is characterized by the transmission gears being shifted sideways a distance equal to their width, while the vertical distance between them is equal to the cog-wheel diameter. The cog-wheel or *shuttle* is shifted sideways at the turning points and a crank connected with it and having a double pulley intercepts the bed with the aid of grooves, forcing the cog-wheel to turn at the moment when the bed is running free.

To act as brakes to the movements of the bed, and to give a smooth motion, *buffers* are usually fitted in cylinder presses. These consist of air-pumps the pistons of which are connected with the bed; they can be adjusted according to the speed of the press.

In relation to the movement of the cylinder and its size in proportion to the forme, we generally distinguish in modern printing presses between *stop-cylinder presses*, q.v., in which the cylinder completes one revolution during the forward movement of the bed, remaining motionless during the return, and *two-revolution presses*, q.v., with a continuously rotating cylinder which at every second revolution makes an empty movement, the cylinder being raised above

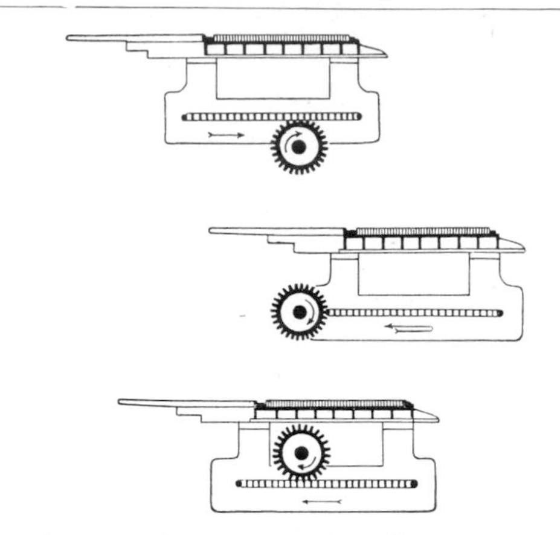

Modern mangle motion. Babcock's Optimus press

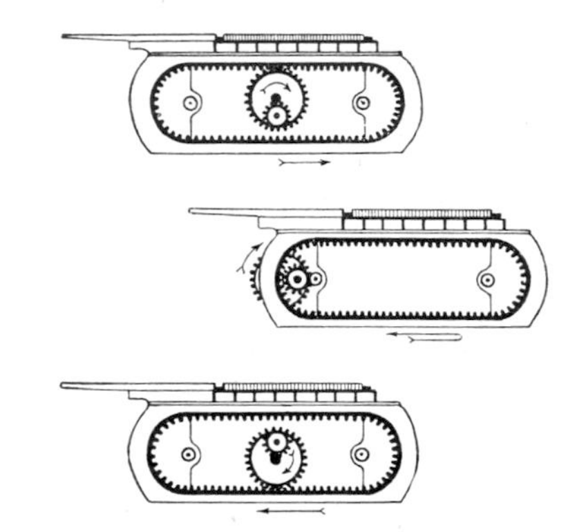

Principle of Century machine drive

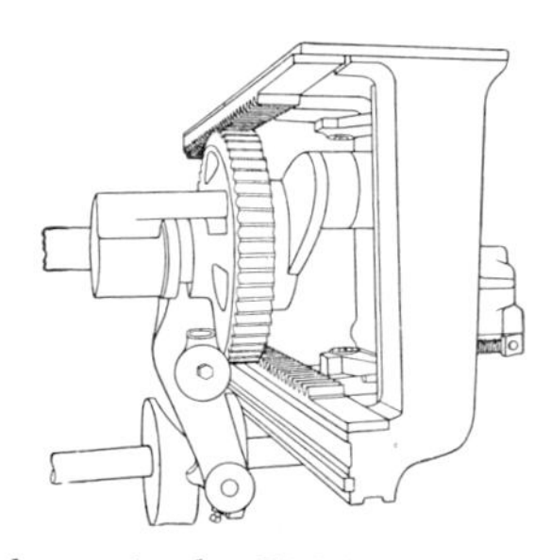

Shuttle and gate in the GMA two-revolution press

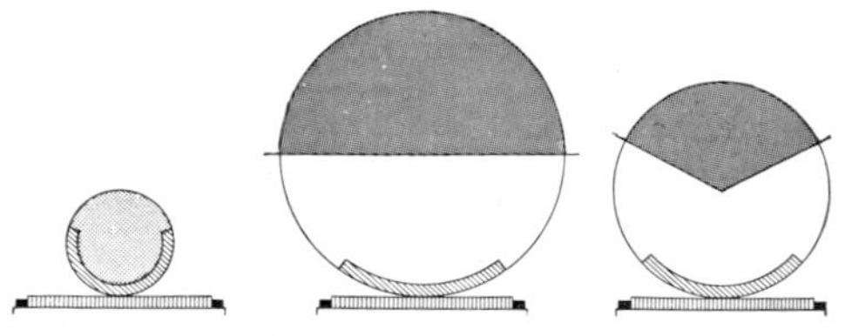

Cylinder periphery in two-revolution press (*left*), *single-revolution press* (*centre*), *and Heidelberg press* (*right*)

the forme. In addition, there are *single-revolution presses*, also having a continuously running cylinder, but with a diameter twice that of the two-revolution press. Printing is done during the first half of the revolution, the bed returning to its original position during the second half. In the Heidelberg press the bed is given greater speed during its return movement, thus permitting the utilization of a correspondingly larger part of the cylinder capacity for the printing, and by maintaining the same peripheral speed the time required to complete a revolution is reduced.

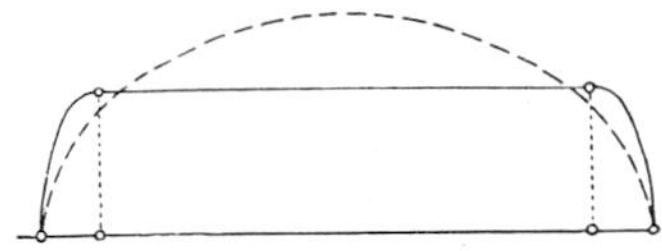

Variations in the speed of the bed in an ordinary stop-cylinder press (*broken line*) *and in a modern two-revolution press with shuttle movement* (*unbroken line*)

Rocking-cylinder machines have a cylinder which either accompanies the bed in its forward movement, being then raised and swung back to its original position, or else it accompanies the bed all the time, effecting printing in both directions.

There were early experiments to substitute a rotary motion for the to and fro motion of the bed. In 1846 Richard M. Hoe of New York patented a *rotary sheet press* which had ordinary types on large forme cylinders. Two years later Applegath & Cowper of London built a similar press with a vertical cylinder. Both were used for newspaper printing.

Rotary printing from curved formes was made possible by the development of *stereotyping*, q.v., and the first to adapt it for printing on a continuous roll of paper was William Bullock who, in 1863, patented a rotary press which in its final workable form was completed in 1865.

Presses for the simultaneous printing of both sides of the paper, known as *perfecting machines*, were, as stated previously, first constructed by König: their most extensive use is in rotary press printing on roll paper, thus enabling folding and cutting to be combined direct with the printing press.

Multi-colour presses are designed for the simultaneous printing of the several colours of a colour print. Among early models may be mentioned the Congreve press. Modern multi-colour letterpress machines, having separate formes for each colour, are usually built as two or more single-colour presses coupled together. Illustrated is a Miehle two-colour two-revolution machine having two printing cylinders and an intermediate ferry cylinder to carry the sheet from one to the other. By combining a two-revolution press with a rotary feed, two-colour printing is facilitated. This method, known in America as the Upham system, and in Germany as the Beckmann system, assumes that one is able to fit together the flat forme

Hoe's rotary sheet press of 1846

blocks with the corresponding blocks or stereotypes of the rotary forme. (G.U.)

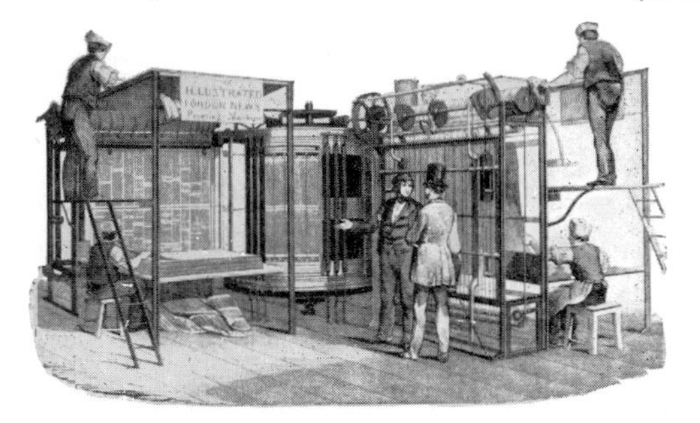

Applegath & Cowper's rotary sheet press of 1848

Letterpress USA: a country of origin imprint adopted in 1955 by American letterpress firms as an approved variant of the legend 'Printed in USA' which was previously required by Federal law to identify printing done in America, and to distinguish it from imported documents or books. Litho firms use the form 'Lithographed in USA'.

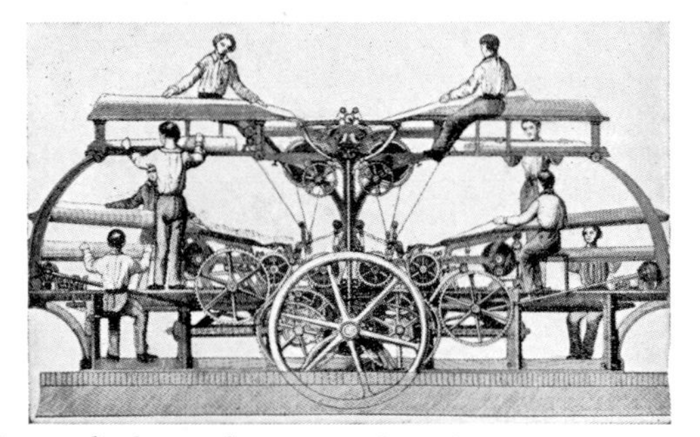

Four-cylinder perfecting machine for newspaper work, built by J. G. A. Eickhoff about 1875. *Capacity* 3000–4000 *copies an hour*

letters—forms and styles: in manuscripts the forms of letters greatly depend on technical factors, viz. the writing implement, the liquid, and the way the implement is held and moved forward when writing. The history of letters prevailing at different times may be divided into the era dominated by the manuscript, and the post-Gutenberg era of the printed letter. The development of the letter can be followed from the earliest stages of *picture writing* and *ideographic writing* to the *phonetic writing* of our time. An example of picture writing is the earlier form of the Egyptian hieroglyphs (Greek: hieros, sacred; glyphein, carve), which were conventional simplifications of pictures representing, at first, concrete ideas. Hieroglyphic writing is thought to have originated prior to 3000 B.C. From this developed two forms, viz. the *hieratic* of the priests, and the *demotic* of the people, qq.v. The hieroglyphs were usually written on papyrus which continued in use until A.D. 300 (and in the Papal Court still later) when parchment became more and more a substitute for it. Writing on papyrus was done on rolls from 8 in. to 16 in. wide and sometimes 10 or 20 yards long; such books were called *volumen* (= a roll). Among other writing tools a *calamus* (a reed) was used. Chinese writing is an example of ideographic writing; here several signs which separately have different meanings are combined to denote an idea. About 1500 B.C. Egyptian hieroglyphs developed a phonetic tendency in which each sign also represented a phonetic sound. Later,

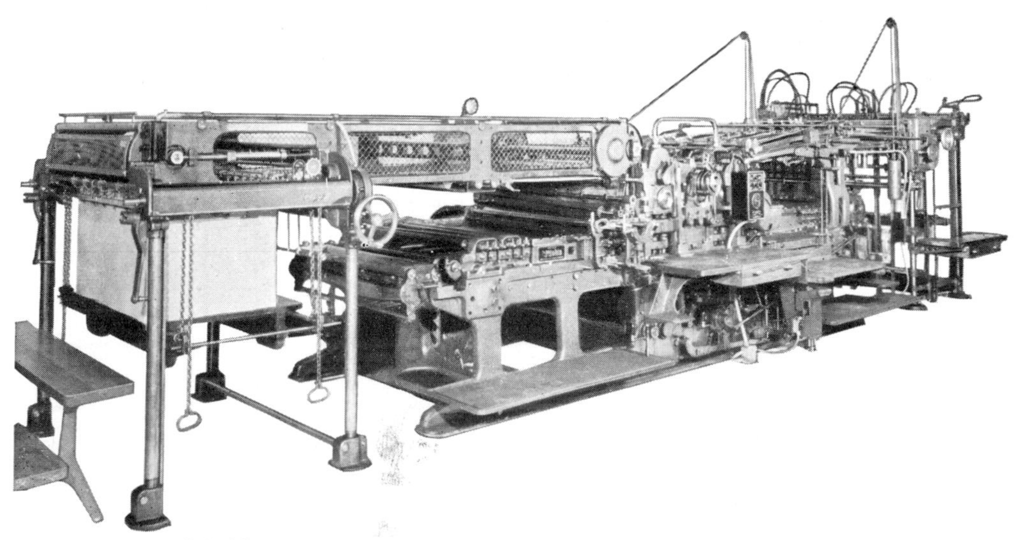

Miehle two-colour two-revolution press with pile delivery, 1946

the Phoenicians adopted the principle and applied it to their language. Through their medium the alphabet came to Greece about 900 B.C., where it was adapted to Greek linguistic usage. The Greeks introduced vowels, and later, the western habit of writing from left to right. The Greek alphabet quickly became useful alike in commerce and the spread of culture, being taken by colonists to the inhabitants of Italy. This led to the Greek alphabet becoming the prototype of the Roman. Later, it was borrowed via the Bulgarians to represent the sounds of the Slavonic group of languages, and thus it forms an essential part of Russian.

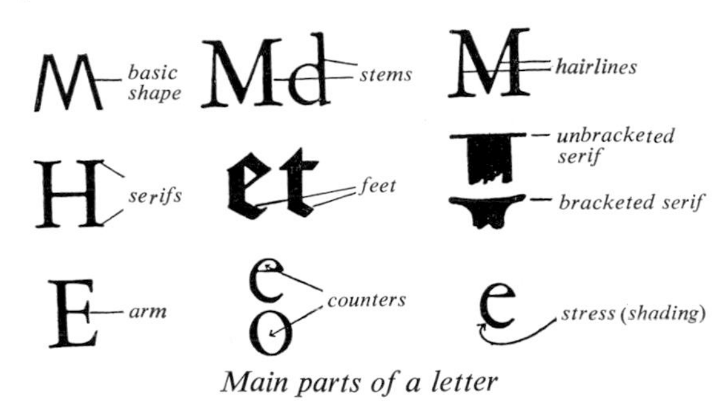

Main parts of a letter

Roman square capitals. About the time of Christ's birth the Roman or Latin alphabet had developed into one of capitals only, known as Roman square capitals, which were first used for inscriptions carved in stone. Letters were characterized by a severe

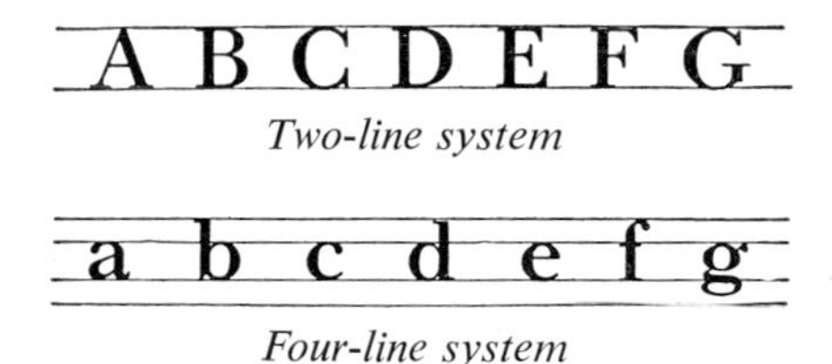

Two-line system

Four-line system

monumental beauty which has never been surpassed. The letters have been preserved in their original form up to the present, and served as a basis for later developed variants of scripts and printing types. The

Egyptian hieroglyphics

Romans adapted the Greek signs for their own phonetic requirements. Some of the letters which lacked corresponding Latin sound values were removed, and certain additions were made. An important form of square capitals was employed at Pompeii (destroyed in A.D. 79) where the letters were made with a flat brush—*Pompeian mural writing.* Here writing received the linear shapes character-

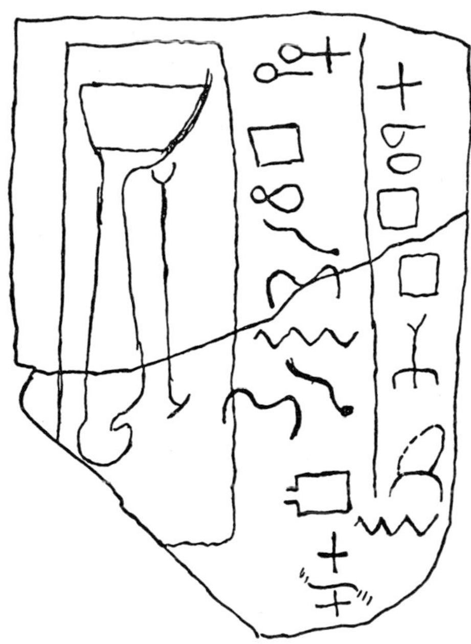

Sinaitic writing c. 1800 B.C.

Greek writing, 6th century B.C.

istic of broad nib or flat brush technique which remains one of the features of later development. When the writing tool is held at an angle of 45° to the line of writing some of the stems and curves become accentuated, while others become fine. This

ABCDEFG
HIKLMNOP
QRSTVXYZ

Roman square capitals

writing technique also influenced the cutting of letters on stone.

Rustic capitals. The writing which came into use for books from about the 2nd century A.D., and in

Broad pen strokes

which the writings of the classic authors were first recorded, is known as rustic capitals. The writing tool was a reed with its rather flat nib held parallel to the line, an unusual position for writing. The result was an alphabet with fine upward stems and bold

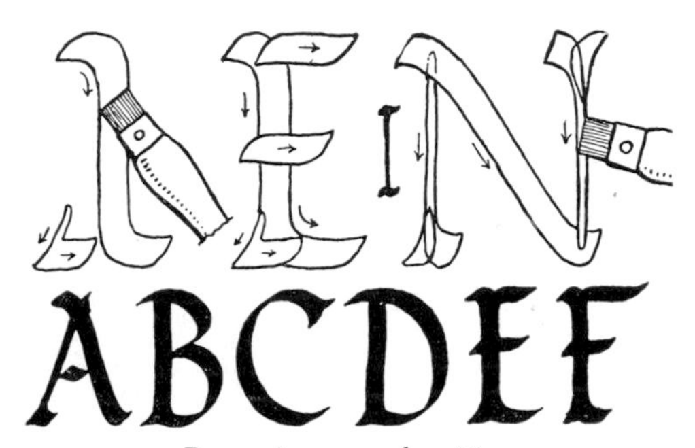

Pompeian mural writing

horizontal lines. Rustic capitals, named, it is suggested, from the rustic simplicity of their character, form a narrow, often exaggerated writing which is difficult to read. They continued in occasional use for titles or headings right up to the Middle Ages.

Rustic capitals, A.D. 200

Roman current writing. This was a running script developed in daily use from Roman capitals. When writing rapidly short-cuts were resorted to, and simplified forms adopted. The pointed stylus served as a writing tool, and the surface was a waxed tablet; both contributed to a delicate outline which in time became extremely difficult to decipher. Towards the Fall of the Roman Empire current writing developed into an easy, elegant hand, and in it were created the original forms of the small letters—minuscules on a 4-line basis, in contradistinction to the 2-line capitals, or majuscules.

Uncials. About the 4th century A.D. there arose a conventional script for books, especially those of the Christian Church, the so-called uncials. Uncials contain several of the minuscules formed in the current script, but these are here based on the 2-line principle. Attention is drawn to new forms of D, E, H, M, and Q. Factors contributing to the greater evenness and calligraphic quality of uncials were the introduction of parchment which had a better writing surface than papyrus, and the substitution of the quill for the reed. Uncials were influenced in their shape by Byzantine art.

Half-uncials. By the Fall of the Roman Empire a more extreme form of uncials had developed, the so-called half-uncials or semi-uncials, which consisted mostly of minuscule forms. The script is based on four-lines, and may be regarded as a transition stage to the later Roman minuscules. During the 6th–12th centuries the use of uncials spread throughout Europe, receiving certain national modifications in each country. Of importance is the Irish half-uncial in which the famous *Book of Kells*, q.v., is written.

Carolingian script. At the same time as the half-uncial there are national forms of writing used partly in official hands, and partly in everyday scripts. These national forms were to a certain extent developments of the Roman cursive, but owing to frequent peculiarities, writing became in time less legible. The first to bring about an effective reform in the art was the Emperor Charlemagne, who at the close of the 8th century called an English scholar, Alcuin of York, to his Court to improve the standard of writing in the

Development of Roman current script from capitals to small letters

Roman current script, c. A.D. 400

Uncials

Half-uncials

Irish half-uncials

Carolingian domains. From Tours, where Alcuin became Abbot in the Monastery of St Martin, influences spread for remodelling the art of writing, which turned out to be of essential significance for its later development.

Carolingian script, c. 1100

On the basis of the half-uncial and the national scripts was worked out the Carolingian minuscule, and this is the prototype of our common alphabet. The Carolingian script reached all the civilized West, and owing to its clarity and beauty became a noble means of expression for the writer. When the Gothic era began about the 11th century Carolingian script was somewhat adapted to harmonize with the new conceptions: Gothic scripts and later type-faces may therefore be regarded as converting Carolingian script into Gothic.

Gothic scripts. After a long period of development, during which several transitional forms were created, the Gothic style in France, Germany and England produced about the 14th century a conventional script, in France called *lettre de forme*, in Germany *Textur*, and in England *black letter*. Black letter is characterized by its intense blackness, acute angles, and the absence of curves. Instead of serifs the main strokes conclude in short 'feet' set at an angle. The script was made very cramped and narrow; the powerful colour and the stiff shapes forming a distinct surface ornament, a plaited pattern, which gave the name textus (= plaited). Although the unusually short vertical strokes allow the lines to be closely

Black letter

written, legibility tends to be reduced in consequence. An alphabet of initial letters, majuscules (in print: capitals), was introduced, based in the first place on uncials, the Gothic counterparts of which were often somewhat difficult to read. Black letter, as the earlier uncials, was the special script adopted by the Church. With the exception of Italy and Spain it was in general European use throughout the Middle Ages; it was moreover the basis of the type-faces of the mid-15th century. In Italy the Gothic style did not flourish: in the art of writing there, however, the form of letters received the impress of the Gothic spirit, but the strict angular forms of black letter were not popular. Instead was developed the *rotunda* or round Gothic script, which in its main features reflects the style of the period, yet in details preserves Romanesque features. Rotunda is characterized by the richness of its curves; it is broad and not cramped, and its forms retain the outlines of Carolingian script. Rotunda also spread to regions north of the Alps, and was

Rotunda

extensively used in the Middle Ages, and later adapted as a type for printing. Erhardt Ratdolt, for example, produced exquisite examples of type based on rotunda.

Several forms of Gothic script developed parallel with the conventional variants. In France the *lettre bâtarde* had a particular vogue. Whereas black letter and the various related scripts were firstly dedicated to Latin and the solemn writings of the Church, various forms of *Bastarda* were employed for vernacular texts. Bastarda is a current form of Gothic

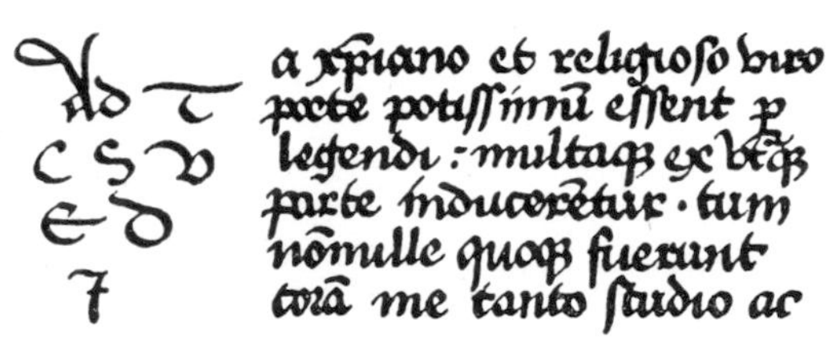

Lettre bâtarde

script written in a dashing, rapid fashion. Calligraphic details often present themselves (e.g. *d* in the lettre bâtarde); the elegant curves also give an easy flow to the outline, but Gothic blackness and heaviness are still noticeable.

A form of writing in Germany corresponding to the lettre bâtarde was the *Schwabacher* script, which

abcdefghijklmnopqrſ
stuvwxyzäáöö David
ABCDEFGHJKL
MNNOPQRST
UVWXYZ Markör.

Schwabacher

in spite of its rustic and less elegant appearance nevertheless points towards a transition to the characteristic *German type*. Schwabacher introduces curved strokes to the Gothic form; especially characteristic is the *g*, the upper part of which protrudes to the right. The German *Fraktur* (Latin fractus = broken) is a particularly Teutonic form of Gothic script, influenced by the Renaissance, which made its appearance at the beginning of the 16th century. The first printed version was in a Prayer Book issued by Martin Schönsperger in 1513 for the Kaiser Maximilian; another early example was cut by Hieronymus Andreae, Formschneider, after designs by Johann Neudörffer. Fraktur types were used extensively in the Scandinavian and Baltic

ABCDEFGHIJKLMNOP
QRSTUVWXYZabcdefghij
klmnopqrſstuvwxyz1234567890

J. F. Unger's Fraktur, 1793

countries until the end of the 19th century, and in Germany and Switzerland they have not been entirely superseded by roman. Characteristic of this type are the interchanging curves and angles, and the small flourishing ornaments to many of the vertical strokes (Ger. Schnörkel). During the German Baroque era Fraktur tended to develop an excessive turgidity and blackness. About 1800 a modified, more readable type was introduced by Unger, and this later influenced the Weiss-Fraktur. Walter Tiemann and Rudolf Koch have both designed modern Frakturs.

Roman type. The Renaissance humanists readopted the Carolingian script, believing this to be more in keeping with the classical spirit than Gothic. This script when cut as type was subsequently known as *roman*. The difference between the earlier Carolingian and the new roman was not great. Roman

mander ayde au peuple de Rome,&
iamais ne faire refus de ſe ſoubmettre
a lauctorite & empire des ſequa:
noys. ¶ Davantage Diuiciacus me cer:
tifia que entre tous les heduez/il eſtoit
ſeul, lequel iamais on nauoit ſceu in:
duyre a faire ſerment ou bailer ſes en:
fans en ouſtage, Et que pour ceſte
cauſe il eſtoit parti de ſa cite, & ſan
eſtoit alle a Rome pour demander
ayde au Senat, pource que luy ſeul ne:
ſtoit oblige ne par ſerment, ne par —

Roman type, 1520

capitals were accepted as initial letters, and thus we find in the 15th-century script the direct prototype of our present printing types. On the basis of the Italian cancellaresca corsiva used in government offices and the Papal chancery from the end of the 14th century, a roman cursive (*italic*) was formed. In 1500 it was cut as a type-face for Aldus Manutius of Venice. It was at first intended for the printing of complete books, and it was only during the 16th century that it was combined with vertical type to be used as an alternative with the latter. Roman cursive is also the basis of our present *handwriting*. Roman cursive was initially closely allied to the forms of Renaissance script then in vogue, but under the influ-

GEOR.

P hillyrides Chiron, Amythaoniusq; Melampus.
S æuit et in lucem ſtygiis emiſſa tenebris
P allida Tiſiphone, morbos agit ante, metumq;,
I nq; dies auidum ſurgens caput altius effert,
B alatu pecorum, et crebris mugitibus amnes,
A renteſq; ſonant ripæ, colleſq; ſupini.
I amq; cateruatim dat ſtragem, atq; aggerat ipſis
I n ſtabulis, turpi dilapſa cadauera tabo,
D onec humo tegere, ac foueis abſcondere diſcunt.
N am neq; erat coriis uſus, nec uiſcera quiſquam,
A ut undis abolere poteſt, aut uincere flamma.
N ec tondere quidem morbo, illuuieq; pereſa
V ellera, nec telas poſſunt attingere putres,
V erum etiam inuiſos ſi quis tentarat amictus,
A rdentes papulæ, atq; immundus olentia ſudor
M embra ſequebatur, nec longo deinde moranti
T empore, contactos artus ſacer ignis edebat.

Virgil, printed in italic by Aldus Manutius, 1501

ence of copperplate engraving and, later, lithography, it became more and more impersonal and artificial.

15*th-century roman*. The earliest form of roman printing types is regarded as a special group, known as *venetian*, and differs slightly from later groups. Type-faces of this group have a rustic and powerful

Cæsareæ extra Aulam modeſta tur/ter
poſt hac Vt et inuriys ffa Barali Quartier

quam eſse victoriæ Symbolum noſti. Hac ſi
potiri vis, & ex officina tua, Calligraphiæ

Inquiſizion F Theologia efectos
Reales D R S C R A L P

maligne ſolum ſterile ſuſtentat. &
P S G J f quidquid F M

Aufmerkſamkeit Reinlichkeit

bleibende Achtung und
k Bewunderung erregen

Leipziger Schulschrift ß h

The development of italic, 1500–1900

English copperplate writing, 18*th century*

form, clearly reflecting the calligraphic nature of their prototype. The first types, whether gothic or roman, represented an attempt to imitate the handwritten manuscripts they now replaced. Adolf Rusch of Strasbourg, Wendelin da Spira and Nicolas Jenson, both of Venice, are the pioneers of the 15th-century roman type-face. Many consider Jenson's types are still unsurpassed for beauty and legibility.

Q Ommodū ad te dederā lit
nane Dionyſius fuerit: eg
ſē: ſed totū remiſiſſē ſi ueniſſet
ſic in tuis litteris quas Arpini acc
uellē. Ego uolebā autē uel cupie
plane cū i formianum ueniſſ&
ſolebā: at ille perpauca locutus
ſcerē ſe rebus ſuis impeditū nob
accæpi dolorē. Intellexi fortunā
Fortaſſe miraberis in maxīs ho

From Cicero, 'Epistolae ad Brutum'. Jenson, 1470

Old face. Soon after the end of the 15th century roman type underwent a change in the direction of greater sharpness and easier, more elegant forms. The beginning of this development is noticeable in the types of Aldus Manutius, but it was brought to perfection by Claude Garamond. Old-face types preserved the alternating thick and fine strokes and the slanting distribution of the centres of gravity of the curves as occurring in the manuscript. Serifs are bracketed, but more flexible and finer than in the roman of the 15th century. During the 18th and 19th centuries, with certain interruptions, old face still retained its popularity, and is now the type form most used in western countries. Bembo, Garamond,

:~: Deo optimo & Immortali auspice :~

A abcdeefgghiklmnopqrsstuxx
xyxyzz&&

Cosi ua il stato human: Chi questa sera finisce
il corso suo, chi diman nasce. Sol
virtu doma Morte horrida
, e, altera.

Ludo. Vicentinus Rome in Parhione
scribebat.

· ANN · MDXXII ·

Deo, & Virtuti omnia debent,

From the writing book of Ludovico degli Arrighi, 1522

Serenissimo atq; Excell.mo: Venetiarum Principi Dno D. Leonardo Lau-
redano Antonius Borromeus
Cogitanti mihi a seculi primordio per tot s. caldeorum persarumq;
ac lacedemoniorum grecorum, ac demum christianorum imperatores
discurrenti complures ac fere omnes preter duos occurere: quos
fortuna potius q̄ uirtutes aut Dei nutus ad tale dignitatis culmen
euexit: Unum Moysem: ut populum eius in seruitutem egiptiorum
redactum ac pene nomine extinctum liberaret Alterum uero

Roman cursive as a book script, Venice, 1521

Granjon, and Weiss roman are among popular versions used.

Transitional faces. During the 18th century, roman type became more geometric in design, and the forms of the letters more severe and sharp. By way of transition to this stage are various type-faces which cannot easily be assigned to any particular group. William Caslon's types represent an art which most closely approaches the old face or medieval roman. These types, cut about 1720, were broad and had a marked difference between thick and thin strokes. A more geometric character is obvious in the types of John Baskerville, cut in the middle of the 18th century. His types are broad and give an impression of serenity and dignity. It would seem that these, rather than Caslon's, were to be regarded as the direct precursors of the new form of letter that made its appearance at the end of the century.

Modern faces. In 18th-century France, as in England, there was a tendency to a more geometric type with a pronounced vertical construction. Early examples were Philippe Grandjean's *romain du roi*, q.v., dating from 1702; some of Fournier's types cut towards the mid-century; and types cut in 1732 by J. M. Fleischman for the Dutch firm Enschedé.

Bei uns in Deutſchland beſteht n
bei jeder Gelegenheit in allem un
iſt auch der Grund dafür, daß De
dertelang das Exerzierfeld für fre

Fleischman's roman cut for Enschedé of Haarlem

A fully developed modern-face roman was cut in 1784 by F. A. Didot, but it was Giambattista Bodoni who, at the end of the 18th century, brought perfection to the face. Characteristics are contrasting thick and thin strokes, serifs at right-angles, and curves thickened in the centre. Modern face was popular throughout Europe during the 19th century.

ABCDEFGHIJKLMNOPQR
STUVWXYZabcdefghijklmno
pqrſtuvwxyzſtßäöü1234567890

Didot roman, about 1800

Contemporary faces. Revivals of classic old, transitional, and modern faces are used today. But since 1900 entirely new faces, showing mainly old-face influences, have been designed by typographers in Europe and America. Notable are *Times New Roman* designed by Stanley Morison; Eric Gill's *Perpetua*; Frederic Goudy's *Goudy Modern*; W. A. Dwiggins's *Electra*, a narrow elegant type designed for Linotype; and Jan van Krimpen's *Lutetia*, etc.

Jobbing and display types. Social changes during the 19th century brought about a demand for types with mass appeal, and it was in 1810 that Robert Thorne produced the first actual jobbing type, a *bold-face roman.* In 1815 appeared the first of several *egyptians*, a heavy type with thick strokes and slab-serifs. In the 1830's sanserif types had a vogue which never wholly died, and modern sanserifs include *Futura* by Paul Renner, *Kabel* by Rudolph Koch, and *Gill sans* by Eric Gill. Towards the end of the 19th century advertising and commercial printing saw employed in their service an astonishing collection of script types, fat-face types, and similar unhappy fantasies which are now much less used. (G.U.)

See Appendix A for type specimens.

See also *accents, bastarda, Beneventan, black letter, book hand, calligraphy, cancellaresca corsiva, Carolingian script, codex aureus, Court hand, cuneiform script, cursive, demotic, fere-humanistica, free hand, gothic, half-uncial, hieratic, humanistic, Insular hand, Irish half-uncial, lettera antiqua tonda, lettera rotunda, Merovingian, neo-caroline, rustic capitals, scrittura umanistica, set hand, square capitals, text hand, textus, uncials.*

letterspacing: the inserting of spaces between the letters of a word to improve the appearance of a line of type, or on either side of certain large caps to give balance. Lower-case words do not need to be letter-spaced, but occasionally are so spaced for emphasis, e.g. in German, and in those editions of Shaw's plays where he supervised the typography.

Lettou, John, fl. 1480–83: an early printer who in 1480 founded his press in London where he worked for a time with *William de Machlinia*, q.v. Of his small output five were law books.

lettre bâtarde: the form of *bastarda*, q.v., used by French printers up to 1500. The sloping, light, pointed characters were influenced by Italian chancery hands and the legal scripts used in northern France.

See also *Fraktur.*

lettre de forme: a formal northern pointed black letter being narrow, tall and almost without curves. It was used in the 42-line Bible and the Mainz Psalter, etc.

See also *letters—forms and styles.*

lettre de somme: see *fere-humanistica, rotunda.*

levant: a good-quality morocco with a coarse grain; it is given a high polish and used for book covers.

See also *French Cape Levant.*

lever press: any printing press in which the impression is made by the moving of a lever, but the term is mostly applied to the type of presses used for proofing, etc., in which the lever is pulled down. (M. L.)

levigator: a heavy steel disc which is rotated by hand over a lithographic stone when preparing the surface; sand and water are used as an abrasive.
See also *stone grinding*.

Lewis, Charles, 1786–1836: one of the leading London bookbinders of his day, noted for his fine craftsmanship. He was the son of Johann Ludwig, a German who settled in England. Books he bound for Thomas Grenville may be seen in the British Museum.

lexicon: a dictionary of Greek, Hebrew, Arabic, and certain other literary languages. In this sense the word was used by the Humanists, e.g. 'Lexicon graeco-latinum', 1532. The word was later used for subjects as distinct from languages, thus the Swiss encyclopaedia 'Schweizer Lexikon', 7 vols., 1945–48, and Kirchner's 'Lexikon des Buchwesens', 1952, etc.
See also *dictionary*, *encyclopaedia*, *glossary*, *vocabulary*.

Liberty press: a platen press built by Friedrich Otto Degener, of Hanover, patented in U.S.A. in 1857. In this press the platen and bed swing against each other.
For an illustration see *platen press*. (G. U.)

Library Association Carnegie Medal: see *Carnegie Medal*.

Library Association Kate Greenaway Medal: see *Kate Greenaway Medal*.

Library Associations: arranged in order of foundation are the principal Library Associations of Europe and elsewhere.

1876	America	American Library Association.
1877	Britain	Library Association.
1892	Japan	Library Association.
1897	Austria	Österreichische Verein für Bibliothekwesen (now Vereinigung Österreichischer Bibliothekare).
1897	Switzerland	Vereinigung Schweizer Bibliothekare.
1900	Germany	1. Verein deutscher Bibliothekare.
1905	Denmark	Danmarks Biblioteksforening.
1906	France	Association des Bibliothécaires Français.
1907	Belgium	Association des conservateurs d'Archives, de Bibliothèques, et des Musées de Belgique.
1908	Holland	1. Centrale Vereeniging voor Oopenbare Leeszalen en Bibliotheken. This working closely with
1912	Holland	2. Nederlandsche Vereeniging van Bibliothecarissen.
1913	Norway	Norsk Biblioteksforening.
1915	Sweden	Sveriges Allmänna Biblioteksförening.
1917	Poland	Zwiazek Bibljotekarzy Polskich.
1919	Finland	Suomen Kirjastoseura.
1922	Germany	2. Verein deutscher Volksbibliothekare.
1923	Philippines	Philippine Library Association.
1929	China	Chung Hua T'u Shu Kuan Hsich Huei.
1930	Italy	Associazione dei Bibliotecari italiani.
1930	S. Africa	Library Association.
1934	Spain	Asociación de Bibliotecários y Bibliográfos de España.

library buckram: a special heavy-weave cloth, made of cotton, suitable for letterpress books, dyed and covered with a light coat of colour. (M. L.)

library edition: 1. an edition of a book having strengthened joints and covers.
2. the binding, more elegant than that of the trade edition, in which a set of volumes is sometimes bound.

Library Licence Scheme: an agreement between the Publishers Association, the Booksellers Association, and the Library Association, reached in 1929. By its provisions public libraries and certain other libraries which do not 'unreasonably withhold' the free use of their books from the public, may, if they comply with the conditions of the agreement, receive discount of 10% on copies of new net books. The Licence issued to a library names the bookseller/s empowered to grant it discount. The bookseller, who receives a copy, may not allow discount to a library which has not a Licence bearing his name.
See also *terms* 2.

Library Science Abstracts: a quarterly abstracting service, initiated by R. and M. Lock, published by the Library Association of Great Britain, since 1950, covering all the book arts, bibliography, documentation, and librarianship.

licence leaf: a separate leaf at the beginning of a book on which the *imprimatur*, q.v., is printed.

Liédet, Loyset, fl. 1461–78: a Flemish illuminator of Bruges and Hesdin. His atelier was commissioned by such patrons as Philip, Duke of Burgundy to produce Books of Hours, romances, and similar works popular with the wealthy laity of the day. Liédet's attention and skill were devoted to landscapes, architectural details, and costumes.

Examples of his work may be seen in the Bibliothèque Nationale, Paris.

lifted matter: type matter already set which is taken out of one job for use in another. (M. L.)

ligator: the Latin word for 'bookbinder'.

ligature: two or more letters joined together and often cast on one body, e.g. fi, fl, ffl.
See also *logotype*.

light face: the opposite of *bold face*, q.v. Many type families are made in varying weights, light, medium, bold, extra bold; medium being the normal book weight.

lignin: in paper-pulp making, a name given to the impurities found mixed with cellulose in wood. (M. L.)

LIICA dryer: see *infra-red drying*.

Limbourg brothers, fl. 1400–16: three brothers, Pol, Jan, and Hermann, who illuminated manuscripts for various wealthy patrons. Their most famous work was the sumptuous 'Très riches heures', made for the Duc de Berry and now in the Musée Condé, Chantilly.

limitation notice: a statement appearing in limited editions indicating how many copies have been printed, and usually bearing a handwritten serial number in each.

limited edition: an edition confined to a specific number of copies, and one which will not be reprinted in the same form. Copies of a limited edition are usually numbered.
See also *limitation notice*, *out of series*, *overs* (2).

Limited Editions Club: a New York club for discriminating book collectors, formed in 1929 under the direction of George Macy with the aim of publishing fine books for exclusive supply to a maximum of 1500 members. The publishing programme called for a book a month, costing $108 a year (now $180). Macy (d. 1956) invited the world's leading artists, typographers and printers to produce editions of the classics notable for fine composition and fine presswork, presented in a tall format uncommon in Europe.

The British Museum has a collection of Club books designed, illustrated, or printed in Britain. They include work by Eric Gill, Arthur Rackham, Oliver Simon, Sir Francis Meynell, Barnett Freedman, Edward Ardizzone, Lynton Lamb, Hans Schmoller, the Curwen Press, and Oxford University Press.

limner: one who embellished manuscripts in gold or colours.

limp binding: a style of binding books with thin flexible covers made without boards.
See also *Yapp*.

Lindisfarne Gospels: a Latin text of the Gospels dating from about 700, with Anglo-Saxon glosses added in the 10th century, at which time a colophon was inserted stating that the original was written by Bishop Eadfrith of Lindisfarne who died in 721.

The detailed geometrical patterns on a cruciform axis are a development in style of the larger scale backgrounds seen in the *Book of Durrow*, q.v., but the curious interlacing which distorts the birds and animals is new to Northumbrian art. An innovation was the occasional use of gold.

The work is now in the British Museum.

line and half-tone: an illustration process in which a line and half-tone negative are combined, printed on to a plate and etched as a unit.

line block (or **line etching**): a letterpress printing block made by photographic reproduction without a screen. Cf. *half-tone*. The lines of the printing surface stand out in relief, the non-printing areas being etched or cut away. Line blocks are usually made of zinc, hence the popular name *zinco*, but for certain classes of work copper is sometimes preferable. Mechanical tints may be combined with line blocks to represent any number of colours. (See *Ben Day tints*, *Zip-a-tone*.)

As long ago as 1822 Eberhard demonstrated the possibility of making a lithographic transfer on zinc and then etching the metal for a high-relief image, an idea taken up in 1840 by Höfel in Vienna. In the 1830's efforts were also made to produce printing blocks by means of lithographic stones with a relief image. However, Firmin Gillot of Paris is held to be the real inventor of the line block. (See *blockmaking*.) About 1850 Morse in New York developed a similar process, and somewhat later a process of the same kind was worked out independently by the State Printing House of Vienna after the director Auer had tried in vain to buy for Austria the rights of Gillot's invention. During the following years Pretsch, Nègre (with Gillot), and others made attempts with photogalvanic methods. Carl Angerer of Vienna studied the line-block process with Gillot in 1869, and later worked out the so-called 'Vienna method'; he also introduced the direct albumen process on the zinc plate, thereby arriving at the methods still used for block manufacture today.

'Phototype' and similar expressions have been used in various languages and at different times to denote the production of printing formes by a photographic process, e.g. collotype. (G. U.)

line engraving: an intaglio printing process for reproducing drawings. The design is transferred on to a copper plate into which the lines are then cut with a scorper, or graver; no acid is used. Printing is direct from the inked plate, but if thousands of copies are required a transfer print is made for affixing to a zinc lithographic plate. Line engravings cannot be printed together with type.

line gauge: the printer's rule. This is calibrated in picas and is 72 picas long (11·952 in.).

linen-faced: paper or cardboard having one or both sides faced with linen, to strengthen it; for book covers, especially children's books. (M. L.)

linen finish: the embossing of paper or book cloth to resemble coarsely woven linen. (L. K.)

linen paper: originally, a variety of paper made from pure linen rags, but now applied to papers having a surface which imitates the original.

liners: pieces of thin, strong paper pasted to the boards of a book which is to be bound in full leather. A single-width piece of paper is glued and applied to one side of the board only. It is pressed on and dried. A double-width sheet of paper is now glued and pressed on both sides of the board. The double thickness will cause the first side to curve on drying, and this concave side forms the inner board. This will be pulled flat by the leather which covers the book. End-papers, added last, are part of this skilled balancing of materials. As a check to later warping the grain direction of the lining paper must be vertical.

lining, lining up: the giving of strength and firmness to the back of a book by gluing a strip of mull to it after sewing and nipping. The mull should extend to ¼ in. from the head and tail of the book and project 1¼ in. on either side for affixing to the end-papers, and this is known as *first lining*. It is then covered with a strip of brown paper the full size of the back, known as *second lining*. Flexible glue is used.

See also *one on and two off*, *Oxford hollow*.

lining figures: synonymous with *ranging figures*, q.v.

lining papers: see *end-papers*.

lining-up table: see *register table*.

Linmaster: the name under which *linson*, q.v., is sold in America.

linocut: a relief printing block in which the design is cut with a knife and gouges into a linoleum surface. The medium is best suited to bold designs with few isolated lines.

Linofilm: a photo-composing machine built by the Mergenthaler Linotype Company of New York, and demonstrated in its prototype form in 1954.

The machine is in two units, a keyboard unit and a photographic unit. The first has a standard typewriter keyboard with an auxiliary panel having keys for hair-spacing between characters, line erasing, quadding, and fount selection; a justifying unit and a perforator are also here. (See, however, page 244.)

The operator sets the perforator (for lines up to 30 pica), selects the type size, and types. The product of his action is a paper strip which is electro-mechanically punched with a code according to the keys depressed. He is able to punch specifications for roman, italic, or bold in upper or lower case and small capitals, as well as spaces and lines (blank).

Justification is by a mechanical computer, and is automatically punched into the strip.

The photographic unit fulfils electrically the specifications of the punched tape. It embodies a reader for de-coding the strip and an optical projection device. The type characters are carried on a number of small glass plates, a fount on each, which are fitted to a vertical turntable. This is automatically controlled by the punchings on the tape, and places the required fount before the projecting lens system.

The end product is a positive with black letters on a clear base.

Linograph: a slug-casting machine devised by the Dane Hans Petersen, built by the Linograph Corporation, Davenport, Iowa, U.S.A., and first marketed in 1913. The *Linotype*, q.v., was taken as a model since at this time the patent rights had partially lapsed.

Linograph machine, 1939 *model*

Some alterations were made, e.g. the eccentric rods, rubber rollers, and angle supports were done away with in the release mechanism. The rubber rollers are replaced by a rotating grooved steel roller, and the eccentrics of the frame by a grooved eccentric steel disc fastened to the release rod. The matrix magazine is vertical and the channels contain fourteen matrices, with double channels for seven of the most frequently used letters. The second elevator of the Linotype distributor is discarded. The simplicity of the earliest Linograph machines tempted buyers; in six months a hundred machines were exported to Europe. After a time it was found that the simplifications caused difficulties. Reconstructed models began to approach the Linotype more closely. In 1939 a model was built with five matrix magazines, and the steel disc of the distributor replaced by rubber rollers and eccentrics. Each channel has seventeen matrices, the mechanism is open and accessible, and a second elevator accelerates distribution.

In 1944 the Intertype Co. bought the Linograph works. (G. U.)

linoleum dry-point: an illustration printed from a linoleum block, the design thereon being worked with a pointed tool.

Linotype: a machine for setting and casting type in continuous lines known as slugs (thus differing fundamentally from the *Monotype*, q.v., which casts separate types). It was invented by Ottmar Mergenthaler, and first demonstrated in 1886 at the printing works of the 'New York Tribune' where the first book printed from type set and cast by it was 'The Tribune Book of Open Air Sport'. After further experimenting the machine was given the outward appearance it still has. Regular manufacture began in 1890; in 1894 the first Linotype appeared in Europe, and they are now used extensively all over the world. Linotypes are made in Brooklyn, U.S.A., in Frankfurt, Germany, and in Altrincham, England.

Linotype setting tends to be cheaper than Monotype, but correction is dearer. While used widely for newspapers, Linotypes are now increasingly used for book work, and since the War the makers have introduced several new type-faces for this purpose, e.g. Pilgrim, Caledonia, Jubilee, etc. (See Appendix A.)

The machine, which requires but one operator, consists of three main parts: the *composing mechanism*, in which matrices are assembled in lines; the *casting mechanism*, in which the matrix line is justified and a slug cast from it; and the *distributing mechanism*, which returns the matrices, after casting, to the

Linotype with side magazine, American model 31

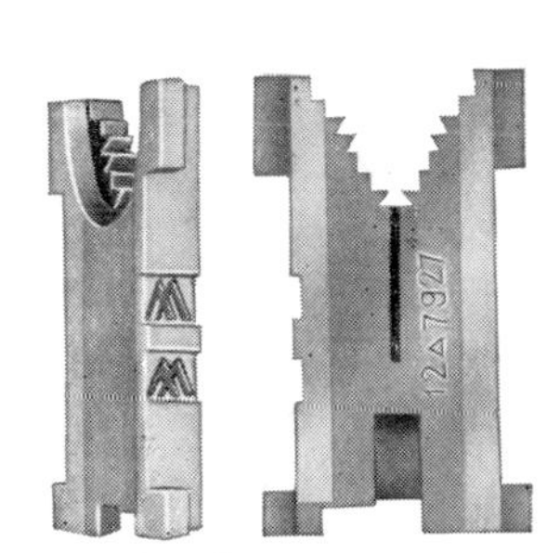

Duplex matrix

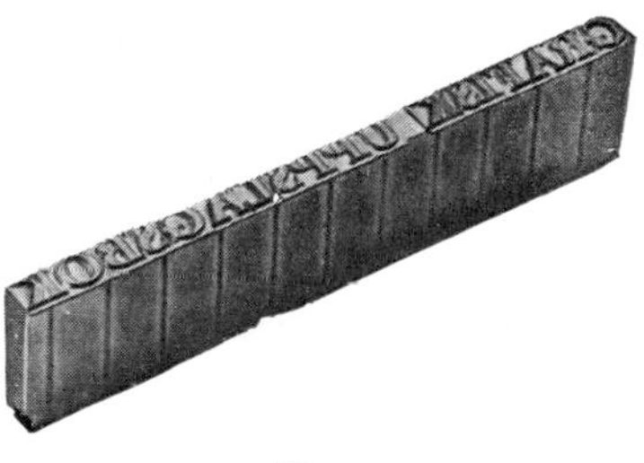

Slug

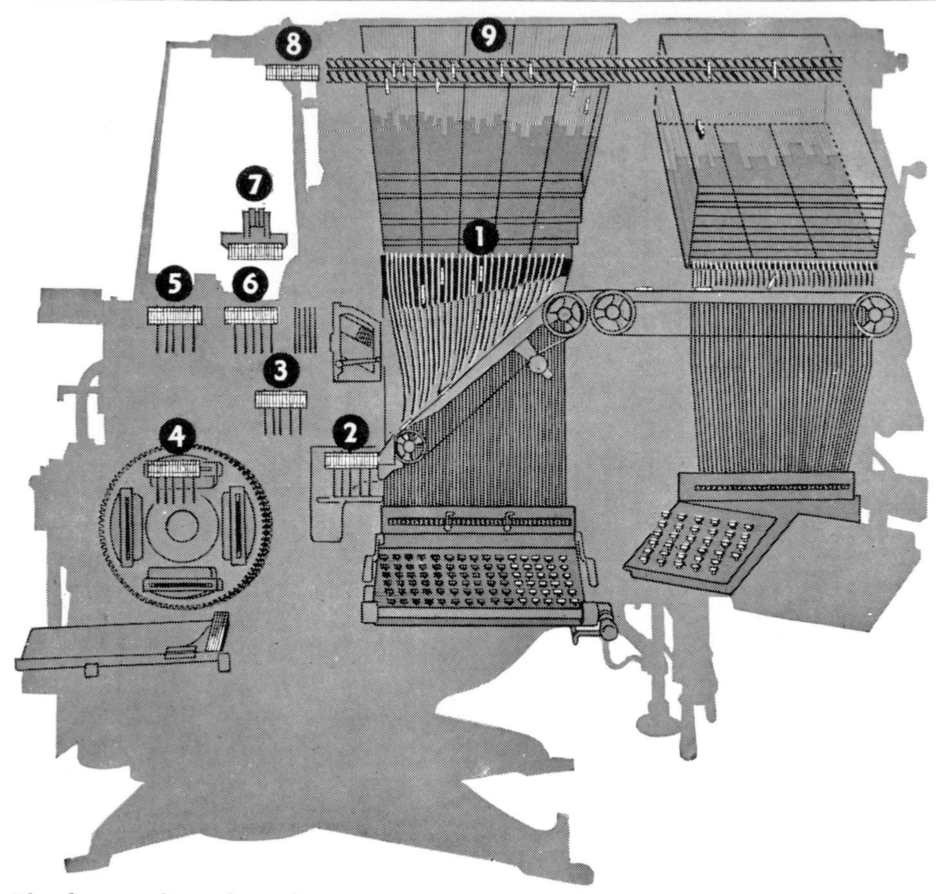

This diagram shows the path taken by the matrices as they circulate through the machine

1. *Matrices leaving the magazine in order required by the operator, having been released by the depression of keybuttons.* 2. *Matrices and spacebands in process of assembling in line formation.* 3. *Completely assembled matrices being transferred to the first elevator, after being released from the assembler by the operator (who now proceeds to set the line to follow).* 4. *Matrix line in front of the mould for justification and casting.* 5. *The matrix line after casting being carried upward for its transfer to the second elevator.* 6. *The matrix line is transferred to the second elevator ready for raising to the distributing mechanism. At this point the spacebands are separated from the matrix line and transferred to the spaceband box ready for use again.* 7. *The matrix line (now free of spacebands) being lifted to the level of the distributor bar suspended over the magazine.* 8. *Matrices being separated into single units again so as to be engaged by rotating screws, which propel them along the distributor bar.* 9. *Matrices passing along the distributor bar until released by their combination of teeth, which causes them to fall into their original channels ready for reassembling into new matrix lines.*

matrix magazine in the upper part of the machine. This has ninety channels in each of which twenty matrices of one kind can be stored.

The *composing mechanism* has a keyboard with ninety keys, each connected with its channel in the magazine. Matrices are made of brass, varying in thickness according to the type width, and with rectangular outer measurements of about 14 mm. by 32 mm. The top of the body ends in ears, between which, in an angular cut, are the toothed combinations required for distribution. At the base the matrices have a toe on either side; this guides the matrix into position in front of the mould. The ears and toes also serve to align the matrices and steer them in the magazine channels and during their transit from and to the magazine. The type character is stamped into the edge of the matrix body to a depth of 1·05 mm. In the two-letter (duplex)

The matrices slide towards a revolving belt which carries them into the assembler box

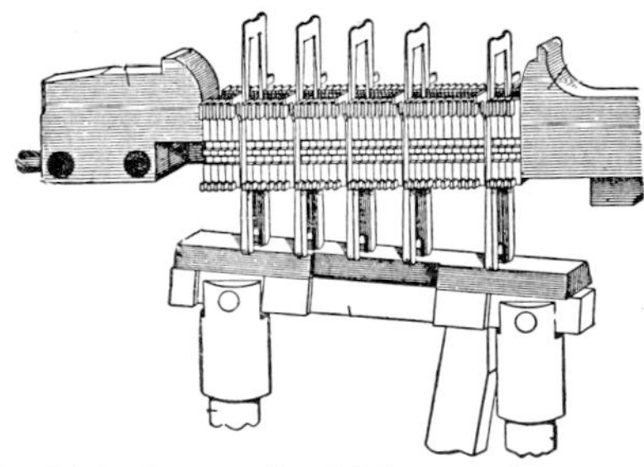

Block which thrusts the folding-wedge spacebands between words until the line fills the measure

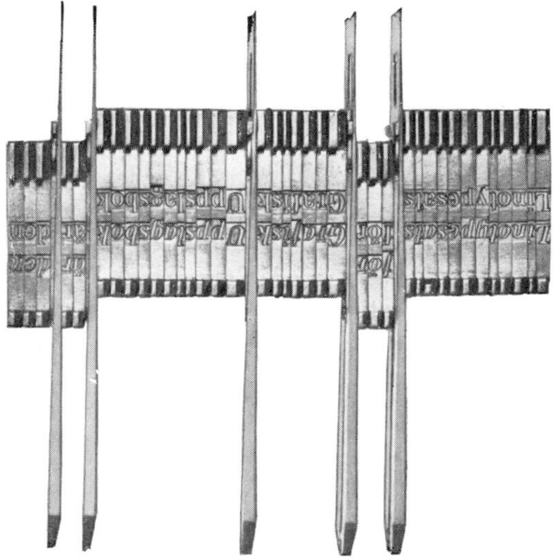

Line of duplex matrices ready for casting; some are in position for italics. Note the long spacebands. The slug will be cast from the dies forming a complete line

matrices the character is usually stamped in two different faces, e.g. roman and italic or bold face. The matrix magazines are inclined, so that the matrices would slide out of the channels were they not restrained by a pawl in front of the lowest matrix. Depressing a key on the keyboard pulls out the pawl's front tip of the appropriate channel, and releases the lowest matrix. To prevent the next matrix from following, there is an upper hole in the channel, in which the pawl's rear tip is pushed as the lower one is pulled out.

Released matrices slide from the magazine towards a revolving belt which conveys them into the assembly box: this is the composing stick of the Linotype, and is set to the required measure. Between each word the compositor strikes a spacing key at the side of the keyboard. This, in a way similar to the release of matrices, discharges from a separate magazine a steel spaceband. When the matrix line almost fills the assembler box the operator must judge whether the words already set will fill the measure, or how an over-long word must be divided. He then presses a lever on the right of the keyboard and the matrix line is raised. It meets two fingers, mounted on a carriage, ready to take charge of it and hold it securely on the way to the casting mechanism. The carriage with the matrix line is pushed by a spring and lever over to the casting mechanism on the left side of the machine.

The *casting mechanism* consists of the first elevator, which receives the matrix line from the transport carriage and immediately descends and places it between two vice jaws, separated by the width of the line measure; the air-cooled mould wheel which bears four moulds; the metal pot with a plunger (and the metal); the ejector; and the trimming knives which trim the slug to the exact body dimensions.

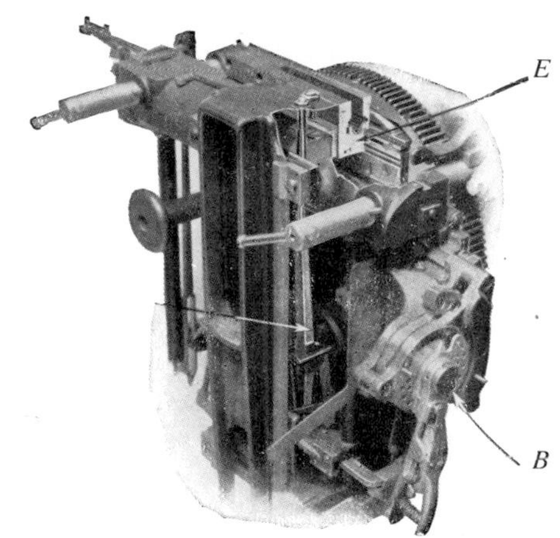

E *first elevator*. B *knife block which trims the cast line before ejecting it into the galley*

Second elevator which carries the matrix line from the casting mechanism

While the lift with the matrix line descends, the mould wheel makes a quarter of a revolution, bringing the mould to be used in casting opposite the matrix line. It is here that a horizontal iron block thrusts up against the spacebands, causing wedges to increase the inter-word spacing until the line is fully spaced within the vice. The mould wheel moves forward pressing the mould tightly against the matrix line; the plunger meanwhile descends into the cylinder of the metal pot and forces a stream of metal (at *c.* 550° F) into the mould where the line is cast. After

Screw rollers push the matrices over the opening of the magazine until they lose their support on the distributor bar and drop into their proper channels

casting, the mould wheel is pulled back, and makes three-quarters of a revolution, still bearing the cast slug from which the jet at the foot is planed off by a cutter. Simultaneously with the foregoing, the lift with the matrix line ascends and stops at the mouth of a transfer channel. An arm, the second elevator

Distributing mechanism in a Linotype double-decker (with two matrix magazines for mixed setting)

lever, descends and places its upper part, a grooved rail, into the mouth of the transfer channel. The matrix line is pushed from the first lift to the second, where the teeth of the matrices slide into grooves on the rail. The spacebands remain here, but while the

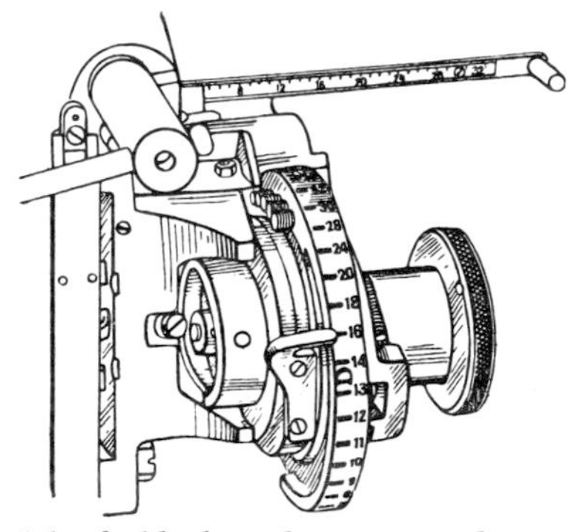

Universal knife block and measure adjustment on a modern Linotype

matrix line is raised again and placed at the mouth of the distributor, a hook slides along the transfer channel and sweeps them into their box ready for re-use.

An ejector blade now pushes the cast slug out of

the mould and between two parallel trimming knives; these reduce the slug to accurate body dimensions and it comes to rest in the galley.

The *distributing mechanism* consists of the distributing box, a seven-grooved distributor bar, and screw rollers. A pusher lever presses against the now raised matrix line and pushes it into the box, where a vertical finger at the bottom moves constantly up and down. The matrices are forced against this finger which, in its lowest position,

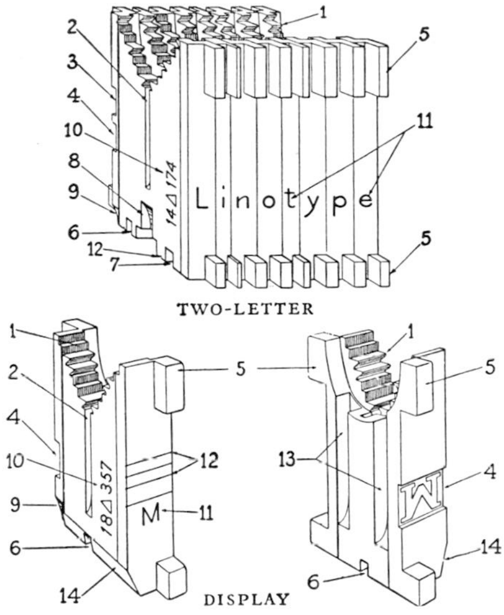

Parts of the Linotype matrix

1. *Tooth combination.* 2. *Separator slot.* 3. *Normal character position.* 4. *Italic position.* 5. *Lugs (ears).* 6. *Body distinguishing notch.* 7. *Bridge notch.* 8. *Channel cut out in matrices for certain models.* 9. *Safety bevelling.* 10. *Fount reference number. Point size indicated before diamond (not triangle), type-face identification number after.* 11. *Character stamped in the side of the matrix enabling the compositor to read the matrix line before sending it to be cast.* 12. *Lines incised in the base of duplex matrices or on the side of display matrices to indicate whether a matrix of another fount is unintentionally mixed in the magazine.* 13. *Channels cut in big matrices to make them lighter.* 14. *Chamfer on big matrices to facilitate distribution.*

grips the foremost matrix and carries it, in ascending, to a runner rail. Here the matrix is passed on to the seven-grooved distributor bar which has the same shape as the grooved rail in the second lift and the distributing box, though here the edges on the grooves are cut away at definite intervals according to a certain system. In the matrices the seven pairs of teeth are also cut off in particular combinations, so that when the matrices are forced by the spindles over the mouth of the matrix magazine, each matrix finds a place on the distributor bar where the edges supporting all the seven grooves of the matrix teeth are cut away; it therefore drops down into its right channel in the magazine. Extra sorts are cast from fully combinated matrices. These travel across the distributor bar and fall into the pie stacker.

During the last sixty-five years many new, improved and enlarged models of the Linotype have appeared. From the simple machine with one magazine, models with up to eight magazines have developed. At an early date machines were built to enable type from several magazines to be mixed. The first mixed composition machine of 1898 had two adjacent magazines and two keyboards. In 1906 this was reconstructed with one keyboard; in 1907 there followed a mixed composition machine with two magazines, one above the other, and two lines of

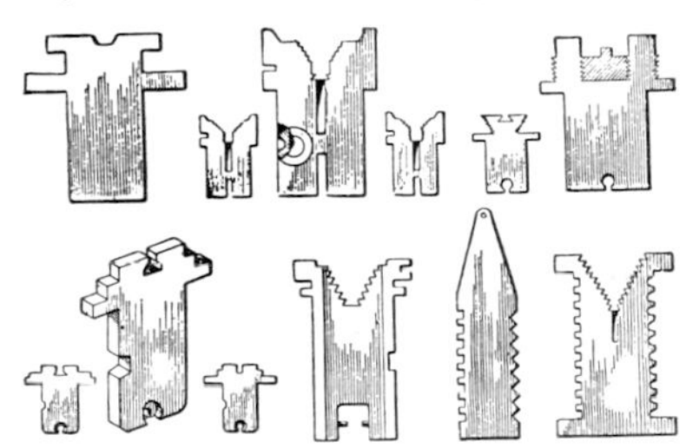

Development of the Linotype matrix

matrix releasing rods; in 1909 this was given only one line of releasing rods; and in 1914 the four-magazine machine for mixed composition was built. Since about 1920 models have been supplied, on request, with one or more additional side magazines, each with thirty-four matrix channels and special keyboards, while in 1924 the matrix release was transferred from the side magazine to the main keyboard. Special models have been built for setting type to 36-em measure. In standard machines the maximum measure is 30 ems. (With G.U.)

See also *All-purpose Linotype*, *Linograph*, *Monoline*, *teletypesetting*, *type metal.*

linson: the trade name for a British bookbinding fabric. It is a tough, fibrous paper which may be given an embossed surface to represent linen. It is available in a wide range of colours and finishes, is washable, extremely hard-wearing, and increasingly substitutes cloth, being much cheaper.

Lippmann process: see *colour photography.*

literal: a mistake in setting type which does not involve more than a letter-for-letter correction, such as a transposition, or a comma for a full point. It includes turned sorts, wrong founts, and battered letters.

literary agent: an agent, paid on a commission basis, who acts for an author by submitting his work to, and dealing with a publisher; and who may arrange the sale of translation or other rights.

This accepted feature of modern publishing was known in the 16th century when we learn, for example, that Francis Berkman of Cologne, who acted as agent for scholar-authors and their publishers in France and Germany, in 1513 gave the revised copy of 'Adagiorum Collectanea' (by Erasmus) not to Badius in Paris, as had been agreed, but to Froben in Basle.

literary news: notes about authors and their forthcoming works, sent by publishers to the literary editors of newspapers and periodicals.

Literary Prizes and Awards: see *Blackwell Prize, Café Royal Book Prize, Caldecott Medal, Carnegie Medal, Casement Award, Cromer Greek Prize, David Berry Prize, Dowty Award, Eyre & Spottiswoode Literary Fellowship, Felicia Hemans Prize, First Novel Award, Foyle Prize for Poetry, Frederick Niven Literary Award, Guinness Poetry Award, Hans Christian Andersen Medal, Harmsworth Award, Hawthornden Prize, Heinemann Foundation for Literature, James Tait Black Memorial Prizes, Jochen Klepper Award, John Llewelyn Rhys Memorial Prize, Kate Greenaway Medal, Katherine Mansfield Prize, Newdigate Prize Foundation, Nobel Prize for Literature, Prix Goncourt, Pulitzer Prizes, Queen's Gold Medal for Poetry, Robert Southey Literary Prize, Rogers Prize, Rose Mary Crawshay Prize, Rui Barbosa Prize, Saltire Award, Somerset Maugham Trust Fund, Swiney Prize, Tom-Gallon Trust.*

lithograph: an impression from a lithographic forme.

lithographer: the printing craftsman who prepares plates for lithographic printing, and controls the press while impressions are taken from them.

lithographic artist: a commercially employed craftsman who copies an original by direct drawing on to stone or grained plates for *autolithography*, q.v. He is thus distinguished from an *autolithographer*, who is an independent artist creating as he works an original drawing directly on the surface from which printing will be done.

See also *Plastocowell.*

lithographic paper: paper designed primarily for lithographic printing; the best quality is made from rag, the next from esparto, with a high machine finish or super-calendered surface. Any stretch must be the narrow way of the sheet. For offset lithography the foregoing specifications are not essential.

Lithography can be undertaken on other papers, and varieties as different as cartridge and art paper are often used.

lithographic press: a lithographic cylinder machine. Outwardly it does not differ much from a stop-cylinder press as used for bookwork. The feeding and delivery are done in the same way, and the movement of the bed with the printing stone is, on the whole, the same. In addition to the inking device (table inking rollers), however, the machine is fitted with a

The lithographic press of Georg Sigl, 1851

damping unit on the same principle. The inking rollers and damping unit are usually situated on either side of the cylinder. As it may be necessary to ink up the stone several times during printing the press is so equipped that the cylinder can be kept stationary while the stone moves to and fro under the inkers for ½ (as is usual in stop-cylinder printing), 1½, or 2½ revolutions. See also *Aqua-trol.*

The stone bed, on which the stone rests, can be raised or lowered according to the thickness of the stone, so that the printing surface is in the position required for correct peripheral speed relationship. Leather or rubber rollers are used for inking up, glazed rollers for ink mixing, and smooth or rough rollers against the stone. The damping rollers and damping table are covered with baize or a similar material. Litho machines can be used for printing from plates; in such cases the stone bed is replaced by one with stretching devices for the plates.

An English patent for a lithographic press was taken out in 1846. The first lithographic cylinder press was built by Sigl of Vienna in 1851 (see illustration). It had a reciprocating bed carrying the stone, a

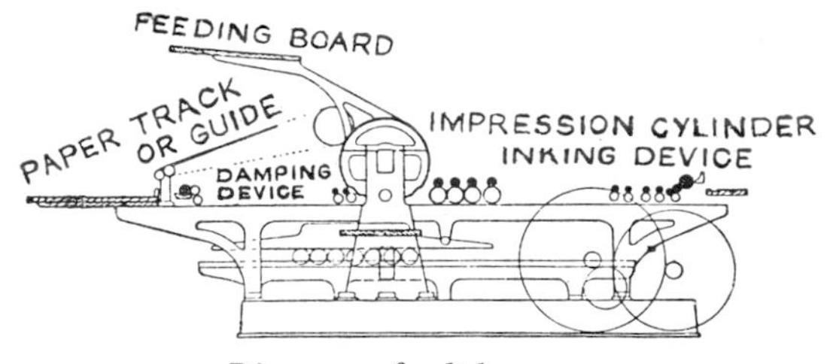

Diagram of a litho press

cylinder with grippers, a damping roller and an inking roller. A diagram of a litho machine designed by Hugo Koch is illustrated: many litho presses still look like it. (G.U.)

See, however, *offset press*.

lithographic printer: a *lithographer*, q.v.

lithographic retransfer: see *retransfer*.

lithographic roller: see *composition-*, *glazed-*, *nap roller*.

Lithographic Technical Foundation: an American organization, founded in 1924, 'for conducting research and education for better lithography'. This non-profit-making body is supported by contributions from lithographic firms and suppliers. A valuable service to members and others is the publication of the periodically issued 'Research Progress' as well as books on the subject.

lithographic transfer: see *transfer*.

lithography: originally, printing from a stone forme. The idea was conceived in Munich by Aloysius Senefelder in 1796, when he discovered the possibility of drawing on stone, and then relief-engraving it to a printing forme. By chance he made an inscription on limestone, and had the idea of treating the stone with acid to raise the script. He later found it was not necessary to raise the printing surface, but that the essential point was to make a greasy image surrounded with a water-attracting surface. Thus only the image would take up greasy ink and be transferred to paper. In this way he discovered the principle of 'chemical printing', i.e. actual lithography. (The term 'lithography' was first used in 1804.) In 1797 he built the first lithographic hand-press with grinders, in 1798 he experimented in stone engraving and lithographic transfers, in 1799 in crayon drawing, and during the first years of the 19th century his process spread to most European countries. In 1818 he published a 'Complete Handbook of Stone Printing' with a description of all his discoveries and inventions.

In 1805 Senefelder found that, in addition to stone, it was possible to lithograph on suitably prepared metal plates, and in 1818 he made an attempt to replace the expensive natural stone by artificial products. It was soon evident that the only entirely satisfactory stones were those obtained from Solnhofen in Bavaria, and the price of these increased as the demand for them grew.

About the year 1800 lithography was introduced into France by Nidermayer, a resident of Strasbourg, and in 1805 Andreas Dallarmi started a lithographic printing works in Rome. The method reached the U.S.A. in 1828 through Barnett and Doolittle. At an early date Senefelder came into association with distinguished artists who made drawings directly on his stones, e.g. Strixner and Piloty. (See *autolithography*.) In France the process was taken up with enthusiasm by artists, and since about 1815 France has been a home of artistic lithography. Lithography was used to a great extent by the political cartoonists who played so large a part in French society during that time. The most outstanding of them was probably Daumier (1808–79). Among German lithographers of the 19th century Adolf Menzel (1815–1905) is most important. The Spaniard Goya (1746–1828) was one of the first artists of considerable importance who also produced work in lithography.

Methods used for producing lithographic formes are described under *autolithography*, *stone engraving*, *stone printing*, *transfer*, qq.v.

See also *music printing*.

Chromolithography, or colour lithography, was probably practised successfully from the beginning. The term occurs for the first time in connection with a French patent taken out in 1837 by Gottfried Engelmann for stone engraving in colour with the individual colours of a crayon drawing. During the whole of the 19th century chromolithography remained the principal means of making coloured reproductions, and has survived with the same working methods until the present day, although here, as in all other spheres of graphic art, photographic process work predominates.

See also *photo-litho*, *offset reproduction*.

Lithographic printing was first done in a hand-press, with Senefelder's construction as a prototype, and it was not until 1851 that Georg Sigl built a cylinder machine for lithographic printing (see *stone printing*). For printing on tin a stone printing press on the offset principle was built by Barclay in 1875, but it was not until 1904 that Rubel perfected a method of offset lithography on paper. This is now the chief process used.

Modern lithographic offset printing is mostly done in rotary presses. This was facilitated by abandoning stone as the printing material and substituting zinc or aluminium plates, though other metals are also used. While stone has a surface in itself suitable for lithographic work, metal plates must undergo preparatory treatment to make them capable of holding the inked image and absorbing water. As the adhesion of ink or moisture is a phenomenon connected with surface, an increase of surface is achieved on a plate by *graining*, q.v., by which means the smooth metal surface is given a fine-grained structure. When the inked image has been transferred to the plate, the latter is desensitized with chemicals which cause deposits insoluble in water, and still finer grain on the empty spaces of the plate which thereby increase their capacity to absorb water. Before the plate is put in the printing press it is gummed with a solution of gum arabic and allowed to dry. The layer of gum held on the plate by the grained surface is not dissolved when moistened by water, but absorbs it, forming a swollen, grease-resisting layer. If corrections on the plate are necessary, both the layer of gum and the surface coating obtained by the 'etching' must be removed by 'counter-etching' for the surface to be receptive to thick ink. With reference to stainless steel and other materials for printing plates see *offset reproduction.*

See also *albumen process, bimetallic lithographic plates, deep-etch process, planographic printing.*

Lithotex-Dirats Etcher: an American machine for the quick, powderless etching of fast-etching photo-engraving zinc half-tone, line, or combination plates. It consists of a tank fitted with a series of paddles which throw the etchant with a vertical splash action. The plate, of an area of up to 24 in. by 24 in., is fixed to a plate holder supported by the lid of the machine. The holder is mounted on an electrically operated planetary gear system. By this means the plate is rotated at a uniform speed and is uniformly exposed to the etchant. Temperature, timing, and paddle-speed controls, and tap-water cooling are other features.

All three types of plate can be etched in the same fluid in one operation without stopping the machine. A zinc line or combination plate requires ten minutes to reach an etch depth of 0·020 in., and a half-tone requires two or three minutes for a depth of from 0·0025 in. to 0·006 in. according to the screen. The machine is suitable for magnesium plates.

The British agents are Pictorial Machinery Ltd.

lithotint: a picture printed from a lithographic stone to which a solution of crayon has been applied with a brush. The process was developed by Cattermole and Hullmandel.

lithotone: a one-way half-tone in which, by special photography, the printing surface is made up of lines instead of dots, the effect produced being that of a wood engraving. (M. L.)

Lithotype: see *typewriter composing machine.*

Little Britain: a London street between Aldersgate and Smithfield, associated in the late 17th and early 18th centuries with the publishing and selling of books in foreign languages. The street is named after the Dukes of Brittany who maintained a residence there.

Little Gidding bindings: a series of early 17th-century bindings done at Little Gidding in Huntingdonshire by Nicholas Ferrar and his family. The works bound were albums of Biblical texts cut from printed editions, to which the Ferrars added numerous illustrations, and gave the name 'Harmonies'. Early volumes were bound in gold-tooled morocco and had a separate velvet cover, also gold tooled. Later examples were bound in tooled velvet. Charles I was a great admirer of the Concordances made by this family.

It is probable that Katharine Moody, daughter of a Cambridge binder, taught the Ferrars how to bind.

live matter: a forme of type which awaits printing, stereotyping, or electrotyping.

Cf. *blocked up, dead matter.*

Livre d'Heures: see *Book of Hours.*

livres à vignettes: the name given to books having copperplate vignetted illustrations as their raison d'être. They had a great vogue in 18th-century France where an edition of Molière, in six volumes, 1734, led the fashion: François Joullain and Laurent Cars (1699–1771) etched and engraved the plates. Notable also was the work of the Cochin family and François Gravelot (1699–1773).

loading: clay, chalk, or similar minerals added to stuff when in the beater, or flowed into the stock as it goes through the sluice-gate of the Fourdrinier. Loading fills up spaces between the fibres, and increases the amount of paper which, when calendered, is given a smooth opaque finish resulting in a better printing surface.

See also *art paper, retention.*

loc. cit.: an abbreviation for the Latin 'loco citato', i.e. in the place cited.

lock-up table: any of several varieties of imposing surface specially equipped for the accurate imposition of formes for colour registration. A beam with sliding gauges, tee-squares, or a gridded visor, are among the fittings used to achieve precision.

Locking up a forme

The forme secured in its chase

locking up: the adjusting of quoins between the set-up type and the sides of the chase to secure the forme in position for printing.

loft dried: said of hand-made paper which has been dried by hanging the sheets on hessian ropes in a loft, the air temperature and moisture content being controlled.
See also *air dried, back mark* (1), *machine dried, relative humidity.*

logography: a method of casting several letters as a unit (or logotype) first patented by Henry Johnson of London in 1780. He had a fount of 3500 words and syllables, his view being that to cast such word-endings as -ing, -ity, -ment, -ton, etc., would save time. The idea was never fully developed due to opposition from compositors of the day.

logotype: a word or several letters cast as one unit.
See also *ligature, logography.*

Lombardic: see *Beneventan.*

long-bodied type: type cast on bodies larger than normal, e.g. 10-point on 12-point. This increases the space between lines without using *leads,* q.v.

long descenders: the letters g, j, p, q, and y made with descenders of extra length. They are obtainable as alternative characters on such proprietary faces as Linotype Caledonia and Times Roman, with their italics.

long primer: the former name for a size of type, about 10-point.

long ream: 500 or 516 sheets of paper.

long s: a lower-case s, printed ſ. It differs from a lower-case f in that the horizontal cross stroke projects only to the left. Until 1749 the long s was used by all English printers. In that year, exceptionally, Ames discarded it in his 'Typographical Antiquities', but it was not until John Bell's edition of Shakespeare in 1775 that the long s was generally discarded.

look through: an expression for appraising the quality of paper when a sheet is examined against light; being a means of determining whether the paper is laid or wove, and if the texture is marred by impurities.
See also *opacity, salle.*

lower case: the compositor's type-case in which small letters are kept, and also the letters themselves. The abbreviation *l.c.* is used as a proof correction mark to indicate that a capital letter is to be changed to a small. See also *case.*

Luce, Louis, 1695–1774: a distinguished French punch-cutter who worked for the Imprimerie Royale, Paris. His 'Essai d'une Nouvelle Typographie', Paris, 1771, displays specimens of his types and an extensive range of flowers. The book also gives an account of his principles of letter designing. On his death, the collection of flowers and borders was

Ludlow matrices for different sizes of type

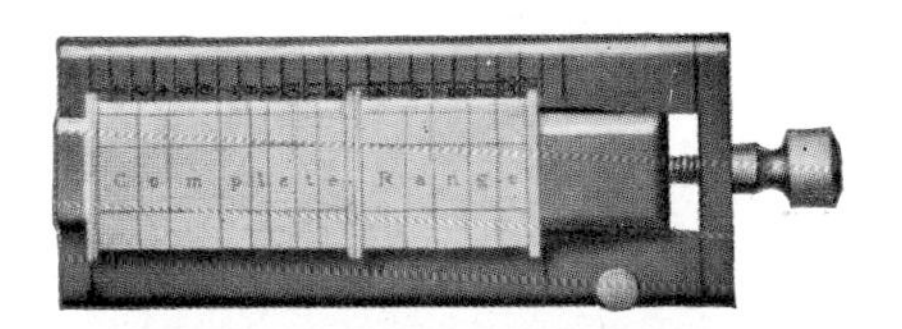

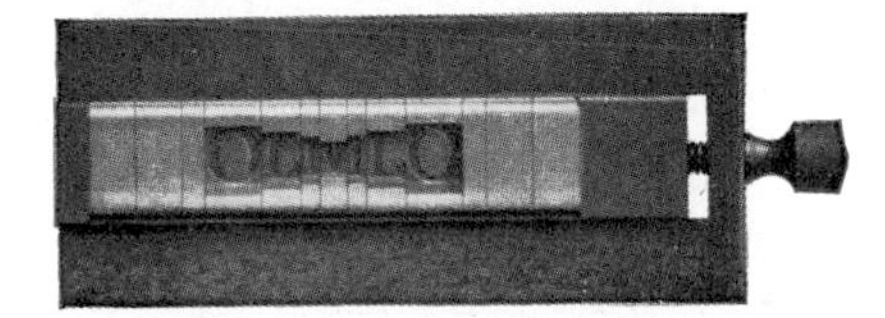

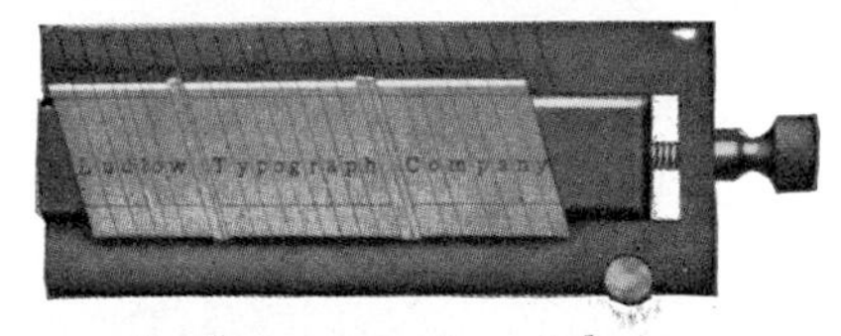

Ludlow composing sticks

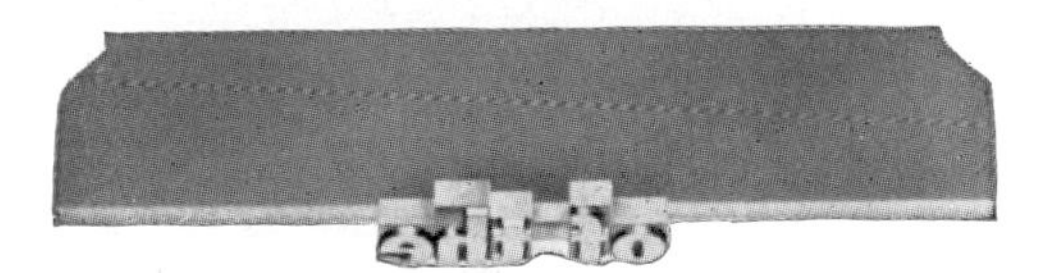

Ludlow slug

acquired by the Imprimerie Royale and is now in the *Cabinet des Poinçons*, q.v.

Ludlow caster: a semi-mechanical type-casting machine in which brass matrices are set by hand in a

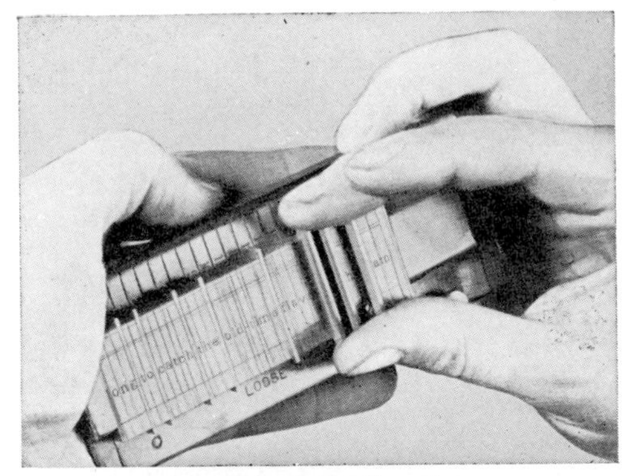

Justifying a Ludlow line

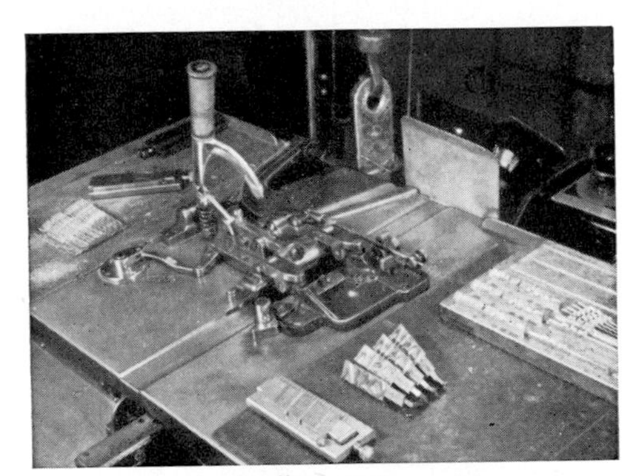

Ludlow caster

Cabinet for Ludlow matrices

stick, spaced, and cast in solid lines or slugs. It is most suitable for display work, jobbing printing, and the printing of forms, stationery, etc.

When the stick has been made up it is put in a groove on the top of the caster and locked in position; the machine automatically moves and places the mould against the line of matrices, casts, trims, and ejects the slug to the galley in about four seconds. The machine also has a repeat-casting arrangement that casts the same heading, rules, or set of rules, without interruption until stopped. The composing stick is taken out immediately after casting, and the matrices distributed.

The slugs, together with blank shoulder-high slugs to support overhanging portions, are assembled on the galley to make up the forme. For casting furniture, reglets, and rules on other than 6- or 12-point bodies, the Ludlow machine is supplemented by an Elrod caster.

The Ludlow Typograph Co. was founded in Chicago, 1906, to develop a type-casting machine devised by Washington I. Ludlow. This differed entirely from the present Ludlow system, which dates from 1911. The manufacture of Elrod casters was taken over by Ludlow in 1920. (G.U.)

lumbard: a paper size, $17\frac{1}{2}$ by $22\frac{1}{2}$ in. The term was used in 17th-century England but has been replaced by *demy*.

Luminotype: the first name for the *Uhertype*, q.v.

Luttrell, Narcissus, 1657–1732: the owner of an extensive library of which a special feature was a great collection of broadsides and other fugitive pieces. He purchased these day by day as issued. They included political tracts, ballads, elegies, and accounts of important happenings. Some of the Luttrell broadsides are now in the British Museum.

Luttrell Psalter: an English Psalter of the East Anglian School, written about 1340 for Sir Geoffrey Louterell of Lincolnshire. As usual in manuscripts illuminated at this time grotesque beasts and monkeys (babewyns) are the main decorative feature, with agricultural scenes, games and sports, also incidents from lives of the saints.

The work is in the British Museum.

Luxographe: an electronic photoengraving machine, introduced by Jean Mincel et Cie, Paris, for making plastic half-tone plates. The original, up to 8 in. by 12 in., is mounted on a cylinder and scanned electronically. Correlated with the movement of the scanner is a thermo-needle which burns half-tone screen dots into a plastic foil. Cut-out half-tones can also be made. The screen range is from 55 to 200.

It is very similar to the Fairchild *Scan-a-Graver*, q.v., with which it is now incorporated (1955).

lye: an alkaline preparation used for cleaning type after use.

See also *washing up*.

lying press: a movable horizontal press which lies on the binder's bench, or on trestles, and is used for holding or clamping books to aid a variety of binding operations. 'Usually ungrammatically called a *laying press*' (Cockerell).

Lyonnese: a style of book decoration practised in the 16th century in Lyons and elsewhere. Features were coloured varnishes applied on the cover to bring out selected parts of the design in slight relief, broad strapwork, and gold tooling.

In the 15th and 16th centuries Lyons was a major centre for the book arts; early experiments in woodcuts were made there, and one of the greatest early French printers, Jean de Tournes, worked in the city.

ADDENDA

lamination: the fusing to a paper base of a transparent material, e.g. cellulose acetate, to impart to the surface a high gloss or protective covering. Laminated jackets and laminated covers for paper-backed books are used extensively.

See also *boards* (2).

Linofilm (see also page 232): at its first European demonstration, in 1958, the Linofilm system of photo-composition comprised four units. In addition to the electric typewriter keyboard with its associated controls, and the photographic unit described on page 232, a *corrector* and a *composer* now complete the installation.

When using the corrector a strip of film requiring correction is placed in one galley and the film containing the corrected lines in an adjacent one. The type of correction desired is set on a dial, e.g. line for line, the replacing of one line by three or four, the substitution of a complete paragraph, etc. Point size is also set on a dial. When the machine is started it automatically removes the incorrect lines and butt-welds the corrected ones in place. Butt-welding eliminates thickening the film which would show up in plate-making.

The composer performs two basic functions: make-up and enlarging or reducing. It produces positive type on film or paper in sizes from 3- to 108-point to a maximum width of 96 picas in any depth. With a working surface about the size of a full-size newspaper page, it re-photographs the galley line by line, altering its position to suit a layout, and enlarging or reducing its size within certain limits. The operator is enabled by dials and controls to make into a single photographic positive any type-film material fed into the composer. This, with the addition of art work, is ready for plate-making operations.

M

machine-binding processes: briefly, and each by a separate machine, these are:—folding, up to 3000 sections per hour; bundling; affixing of end-papers to the first and last sections; gathering; sewing, about 3000 sections an hour; nipping; trimming; gluing; rounding and backing, about 1000 books an hour; lining; casing-in; and pressing the finished books. Cases are machine made, about 500 an hour.

machine clothing: the collective term for the wire, press felts and drier felts on a paper-making machine.

machine coated art: see *imitation art paper.*

machine direction: synonymous with *grain direction,* q.v.

machine dried: paper which has been dried by passing it over heated cylinders which form part of the Fourdrinier.

See also *air dried, loft dried, relative humidity.*

machine finish: paper made smooth, but not glossy, by receiving the normal finish of a Fourdrinier paper-making machine which completes its process by passing the paper over heated drums and through steel calendering rolls. These smooth the surface to the required degree. Abbreviated to *M.F.*

machine lay edges: see *lay edges.*

machine-made paper: the continuous web of paper made on the *Fourdrinier* or *cylinder machines,* qq.v.

machine proof: a proof taken when corrections marked on the galley proof and page proof have been made, and the forme is on the printing machine. The machine proof affords the last opportunity to correct mistakes before printing the book.

Also known as *press revise.*

machine-sewing: sewing the sections of a book by mechanical means; a necessary feature of modern commercial publishing. The bookbinding machine sews the sections of a book together, and at the same time the inner leaves of each folded sheet are sewn to the outer ones through the back fold.

The origin of the sewing machine is attributed to Philip Watt of London, 1832, but the first practicable thread-sewing machine was invented by David

Part of a Brehmer sewing machine

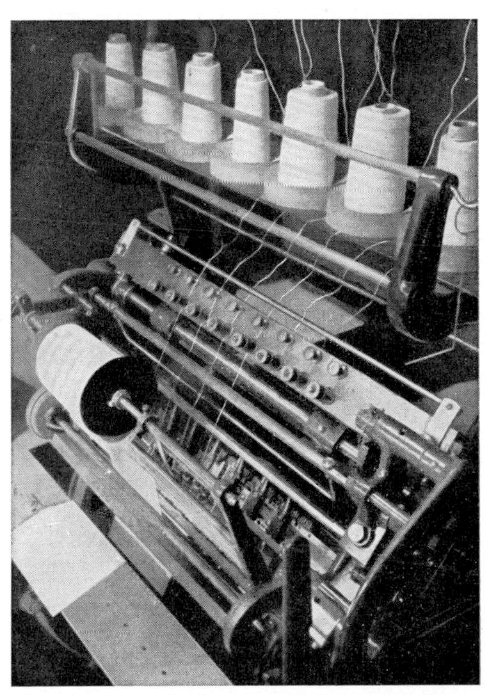

Sewing on a web of gauze which is carried over the backs of books and sewn to them by the movements of the sewing needles

This Brehmer machine is equipped for the semi-automatic cutting of the individual books in the rack

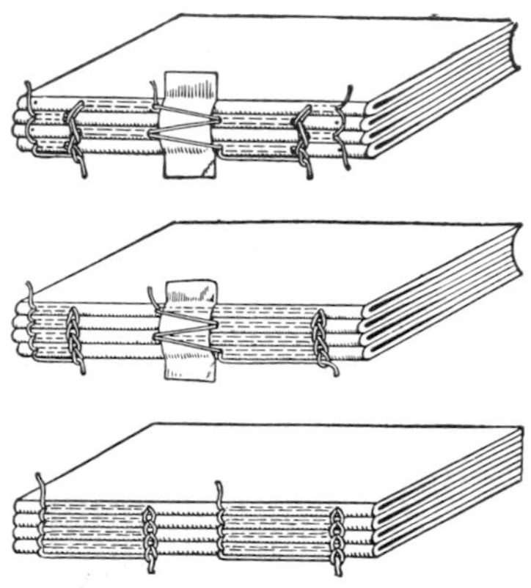

Top, off-and-on stitch on tapes
Middle, ordinary stitch on tapes
Bottom, ordinary french stitch

Smyth, U.S.A. (patented 1871), and his machine inspired the brothers Brehmer of Leipzig. Prior to 1928 the Smyth machine worked with a curved needle, the size of which determined the length of the stitches; modern high-speed machines (from sixty to ninety sections a minute) all work with straight needles. The Brehmer and Smyth semi-automatic machines appeared at the end of the 1920's, and in 1945 the latter was equipped with an automatic feeder.

The basic principle of machine-sewing is that one needle does not go along the section, taking its thread with it, but a series of needles operate, each with its kettle-stitches. Linen thread should be used, but cotton often is.

In the most usual type of machine one section after another is laid by hand on a feeding arm which brings the fresh section to the part of the book already sewn. As the illustration shows, the feeding arm forms a saddle with a pronounced ridge over which the half-open section is so placed that the back fold is just above the edge of the saddle. This has a row of holes through which piercers rise to enter the section. Immediately after, needles descend from above the machine, each with thread attached, and pass through the holes already pierced. The thread is now gripped by the side-needles of the feeding beam (arm) and drawn double for a few centimetres along the back fold to the hook-needles coming from above. The hook-needle grips the loop of the thread, and draws it up through the paper and also through the corresponding loop in the preceding section. (The Swiss factory Martini has introduced a screw-shaped hook-needle with a view to simplifying the construction of the sewing machine.) Then the feeding arm

Rear view of a sewing machine, showing the splits inserted between the books. Note the groove for cutting
(Gutberlet, Leipzig)

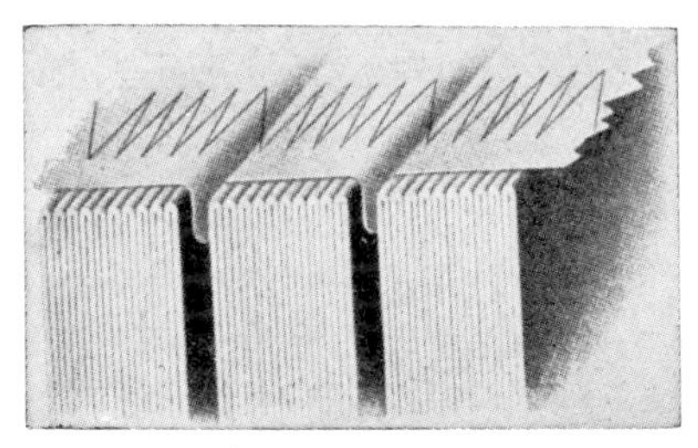

Sewing on a strip of gauze with the cloth dropped in a fold between books. After cutting apart, the extra strip of cloth is ready for securing the body of the book to the boards

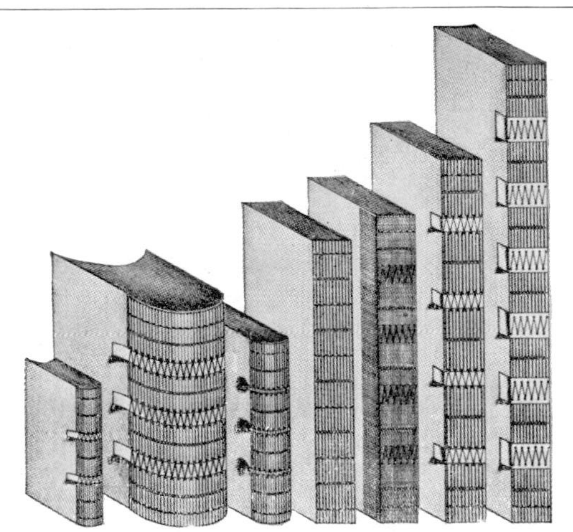

Different styles of machine-sewing: through and over tapes, on cloth (gauze), with thread only, with thread on tapes

goes out to bring in the next section, and so the work proceeds.

Sewing with thread alone is called *ordinary french stitch*. In most machines sewing can be done on gauze or tape fed from reels right across the back of the book. The sewing is done in the same way, but the thread passes through the cloth and through or over the tape. Some machines work with an *off-and-on stitch* which is suitable for books on thin paper, and corresponds to the 'two sheets on' method of hand-sewing. Whereas ordinary sewing is done by two needles for each stitch, the off-and-on stitch requires three working in combination, the threads being drawn alternately to one or other of the outer needles (see illustration). In the *staggered stitch* method the needle changes its position for each section, so that the threads form a zig-zag pattern across the tapes and are thus better secured to the back of the book. Thread can also be sewn over or under the material in other ways.

The operator at the sewing machine

In ordinary french stitch the books are sewn to each other until the machine is filled, when the books forming a span are taken out and separated by cutting, a process carried out automatically on some models or by a second operator on others. In sewing on gauze or tapes the width of the cloth for each book must be greater than the width of the back. This can be effected by inserting a split after each book, i.e. a wooden strip of a suitable width, usually with a metal gutter to facilitate cutting. In order to allow the sewn book to be moved forward with the necessary thread corresponding to the width of the split, a free stroke is made after each book. In another process the spare tape or gauze is dropped in a fold between the books. Various methods of machine-sewing are illustrated here.

In semi-automatic machines the sections are fed by hand on a carrying device in a prolongation of the feeding arm, whence they are automatically inserted on the latter. In one model of the Smyth Co. the feeding arm is replaced by four arms which swing inwards in turn.

In Britain, sewing through gauze is seldom practised, and the use of tapes is dying out due to improvements in back-lining techniques which make them superfluous. (G. U.)

See also *bookbinding methods and processes.*

machining: the actual process of printing; running the forme through the machine so that the paper receives the impression from it.

See also *presswork.*

Machlinia, William de, fl. 1482–90: an early printer of London who was in sometime partnership with *John Lettou*, q.v. Independently he is credited with about twenty books, some only extant in fragments, and also with having printed the first English *title-page*, q.v.

mackle: a printing fault seen as a blurred or double impression. This is caused by a shifting of the paper while the impression is being made. (M. L.)

Maddox, Richard Leach, 1816–1902: an Englishman who discovered the use of the *dry plate*, q.v., in 1871.

made end-paper: see *end-papers.*

made-up proof: synonymous with *page proof*, q.v.

magazine: the part of a Linotype machine in which the letters or the matrices are stored ready to be assembled into words and lines.

magenta ink: the name for the shade of red established as one of the British Standard four-colour letterpress printing inks. (See B.S. 1480: 1949 and B.S. 3020: 1959.)

magenta masking method: a Kodak process used for colour reproduction. Two magenta-dyed colour-correcting masks are placed in the screen holder of the camera to modify the light reflected from the original, or transmitted by the transparency, while colour-separation negatives are made.

See also *masking*.

Maggs Bros.: a leading London firm of antiquarian booksellers, specializing in manuscripts, incunabula, early illustrated books, and first editions.

It was about 1850 when Uriah Maggs and his father left the village of Midsomer Norton, in Somerset, for London. After the failure of several ventures Uriah Maggs decided in 1853 to take up bookselling, with his own library as the nucleus of his stock. After trading from his home he opened a shop in Paddington in 1855. In 1894 Uriah retired, leaving the business in the hands of his sons Benjamin and Henry. In 1901 the firm, now known as Maggs Bros., moved to the Strand. Catalogues were a regular feature. When Henry died in 1906 two other sons of the founder became partners in the firm, Charles and Ernest. In 1918 new premises were taken in Conduit Street, to be vacated in 1938 for the present Berkeley Square home. Ernest Maggs died in 1955.

The most important transaction of the firm was the negotiation in 1933 of the purchase from the Russian Government of the *Codex Sinaiticus*, q.v.

Mainz Psalter: a famous incunabulum printed in 1457 by Johann Fust and Peter Schöffer. It was the first book to have a full *colophon*, q.v. The Psalter, which is also known as the 'Psalter Moguntinum', is also remarkable for the initials which were the first successful attempt at two-colour printing.

See Sir Irvine Masson 'The Mainz Psalters and Canon Missae, 1457–1459', Bibliographical Society, 1954.

Maioli bindings: the styles of binding done by Parisian craftsmen for the French book-collector Thomas Mahieu, secretary to Catherine de Medici. (His name is latinized as Maiolus.) They belong to the period 1550–65. Styles varied, some having punched and gilded backgrounds for designs of curved strapwork and arabesques; ornaments were in outline or azured. They were often lavishly decorated with coloured inlays on a gilded ground, and showed a strong Venetian influence. A central panel on the cover bore the words 'THO MAIOLI ET AMICORVM'.

Maitland Club: a club founded in Glasgow in 1828 with the object of publishing books on the local history and literature of western Scotland. It ceased activity in 1859.

majuscule: an upper-case or capital letter. The earliest form of writing in Latin was in this style, but after a time the scribes found it easier to make small letters (*minuscule*, q.v.) and capitals were used only for emphasis and ornamental purposes. (M. L.)

make even: to make copy come out even at the end of a line. (M. L.)

make-ready: the skilled treatment of a forme of type, by which a trained machine-minder obtains the best results from type and blocks by patching up with paper, or cutting away on the impression cylinder or the platen bed; also by underlaying or interlaying the blocks. The amount and position of make-ready is determined by a trial pull.

See also *chalk overlay*, *dressing the cylinder*,

Make-ready on a cylinder press

Make-ready on a platen press

Fleischhack overlay, interlaying, mechanical overlay, overlaying, pre-press work, Primaton overlay, underlaying.

make-up: 1. the arranging by the compositor of type matter (including running heads, footnotes, and blocks) into pages and securing them with page-cord. They are then ready for locking in the chase.

See also *dressing* (1).

2. a list of the contents of a book in edition binding supplied by the publisher to instruct the binder, but only necessary where many plates, plans, etc., and other complications are involved. Hence *make-up copy*, i.e., a set of folded sheets and plates put in the correct order as a pattern. (L.K.)

Malin, Charles, 1883–1956: the Parisian punch-cutter who in 1926 cut the punches for Eric Gill's Perpetua type. They were cut in upper- and lower-case 12-point Didot, and were later brought to England for the Monotype Corporation. Malin subsequently cut some sizes of capitals for use as titling founts (Monotype Series 258).

He was commissioned by Stanley Morison to re-cut the italic of Arrighi's 'La Operina', 1522. The work was supervised by Frederic Warde, and the types (for hand composition) were first used in 1926. The Monotype fount for machine composition appeared in 1929 under the name 'Arrighi'. More recently he engraved the Dante type of *Giovanni Mardersteig*, q.v., which was first used in 1954 at the *Officina Bodoni*, q.v., and is now available in Britain from the Monotype Corporation.

Malone Society: a society founded in 1907 to publish 'faithful reprints of old plays, mostly Tudor, and of documents illustrative of the drama and the stage'.

Manchester Society of Book Collectors: a society founded in 1954 by a group of Lancashire bibliophiles to stimulate an interest in books and book collecting. Meetings are held to discuss their interests, to make known the bibliographical resources of the area, and to arrange book exhibitions.

manière anglaise: see *colour printing.*

manière criblée: an early method of engraving, using dots. An example may be seen in 'Horologium devotionis', printed by Ulrich Zell at Cologne, *c.* 1490.

See also *criblé initials.*

manila: a very strong vegetable fibre paper made from hemp, rope, jute, sulphite, sulphate, or mechanical wood pulp. It is sometimes used for covering brochures or similar publications.

See also *boards.*

Mansion, Colard, fl. 1450–84: a calligrapher of Bruges who, while establishing a printing press there about 1475, continued to copy manuscripts. His first signed and dated book was Boccaccio's 'Du dechiet des nobles hommes et femmes', 1476. This had separately printed copper engravings pasted in.

Writing of Mansion in 'Signature', N.S.15, 1952, q.v., L. A. Sheppard suggests he was probably the pupil of William Caxton who had come to Bruges from Cologne.

Manuale: a small book containing the forms used when administering the sacraments.

Manul process: see *reflex printing.*

manuscript: a work written by hand; the term derives from the Latin expression for this, viz.: 'codex manu scriptus', and denotes either a book written before the invention of printing or the written or typed work which an author submits for publication.

Manutius: see *Aldus Manutius.*

Manx Society: a printing society instituted at Douglas, Isle of Man, in 1858, for the publication of national documents of the Isle. (M.L.)

map printing: the earliest engraved maps in the world were in the edition of Ptolemy's 'Geographia' printed from copper plates at Bologna in 1477 (authorities disagree about the date). The first important maps printed in Germany were from woodcuts in an edition

Pinning down sections of a map when preparing a transfer

of Ptolemy issued at Ulm in 1482 by Leonardus Holle.

The earliest and most important maps to be printed in England from engraved copper plates were those of Christopher Saxton, the first of whose county maps was issued in 1574, the last in 1579. The cartographer rarely made his own plates, and those of Saxton were engraved partly by Augustine Ryther, and partly by Flemish refugees. In the 18th century, the engraved maps of Aaron Arrowsmith should be mentioned.

In the late 16th and 17th centuries the Dutch mapmakers were supreme, such names as Mercator, Ortelius, Blaeu, and Danckerts being renowned. In Antwerp, Christopher Plantin was an important printer of maps.

Sheets were issued either plain or hand-coloured.

All reproduction processes can now be used for the printing of maps, but lithography is the most popular. This is sometimes done in combination with stone or copperplate engraving, photo-litho or autolitho. Letterpress map printing from line blocks in black and colours is often used.

The transferring from copperplate or stone engravings to a lithographic printing forme is done by photography, by direct copying, or by *transfer*, q.v. Reproductions of maps are also made from originals drawn on paper or transparent material (Astrafoil, Kodatrace, etc.). The names, formerly drawn in by hand, are now often type-set and embodied in the original map as a tracing impression or patched in from type proofs. Letterpress can be photographed on to the sensitized original. (In 'The Oxford Atlas', 1951, however, the original maps were drawn and lettered by hand.)

When making printing plates for maps with rougher details (school walls) the map is drawn directly on the (offset) plate. (With G. U.)

See also *Astrascribe*.

mappamondae: maps made by medieval scholars to depict the world. They date from the 8th–15th centuries, and were often drawn to illustrate religious works. Many, too, were in the form of symbolic diagrams.

The 13th-century historian *Matthew Paris*, q.v., included examples in his writings.

marbled calf: calfskins made to resemble marble by chemical treatment. Used for bookbinding. (M. L.)

See also *marbling*, *tree-calf*.

marbles: glass, hardwood, porcelain, or steel marbles used for *graining*, q.v. They vary in size from ½ in. to 1¼ in. diameter. Other conditions being constant, small marbles give finer grain, and ½ in. steel marbles give the finest deep grain.

marbling: decorating book edges or sheets of paper by transferring floating colours from the surface of a gum solution. This solution is a size, preferably made from carragheen moss or gum tragacanth boiled in water. Strained size is poured in a shallow flat trough. Specially prepared water-colours mixed with ox-gall are floated on the surface and combed or twisted into patterns. Meanwhile the book edges or sheets are sponged with concentrated alum water as a mordant for the colours. After drying for ten minutes the books are held tightly closed while the edges are touched down on to the surface of the size, or if it be a sheet of paper this is gently laid down. Colours transfer at once, any dirty size being washed off with water.

Oil-colours can be used for marbling, but do not allow for such fine control or produce the clean sharp lines of water-colours. There are also imitations of marbled papers reproduced by lithography, but results are poor when compared with the genuine product.

Sydney M. Cockerell of Letchworth supplied the specimens of marbled papers in this book. They were made with water-colour marbling inks on a carragheen size base.

Historical note. The art of marbling is of obscure origin; it was practised in Japan *c.* A.D. 800, while for its later adoption in Europe artists in Holland, Germany, or Turkey have been suggested as initiators. Writing of this in his 'Sylva Sylvarum', 1627, Francis Bacon states: 'The Turks have a pretty art of chambletting paper which is not in use with us. They take divers oyled colours and put them severally upon water and stir the water lightly and then wet their paper (being of some thickness) with it and the

Touching the edges. The bath is prepared for making a 'splash' pattern

paper will be waved and veined like chamblett or marble.'

The Parisian bookbinder Macé Ruette (fl. 1598–1644) introduced marbled paper into France about 1610. According to Bacon it was first known in England about 1625. Marbled edges of books were introduced by the Dutch about 1675, at which time the best marbled papers were made in Holland.

An early manual to describe the process was 'Ars vitraria experimentalis' by the German Johannes Kunckel, 1674, while a well-known description of the principles involved was written by Josef Halfer, a bookbinder of Budapest, whose 'The Process of the Marbling Art' was published in 1884.

British marbled papers are currently used by craftsmen binders in many parts of the world.

Marchant, Guy, fl. 1483–1510: a distinguished early French printer working in Paris, particularly noted for his woodcuts to several editions of 'Danse macabre'.

Mardersteig, Giovanni: the inspired leader of the *Officina Bodoni*, q.v. He is known in Britain for the Fontana type he designed in 1936 for William Collins Ltd., based on a type cut about 1760 by Alexander Wilson of the Glasgow Letter Foundry; and his Dante type, 1954, which is available from Monotype.

margins: the blank areas on a printed page surrounding the matter. The four margins on a page are widely known as head, tail, fore-edge (outer) and back (inner); while two adjacent back margins are sometimes referred to as gutters. To most printers, however, the fore-edge margin is known as the gutter margin since it is between two adjacent fore-edges lying in the chase that the printer puts a gutter-stick. Confusion would be avoided if the word *gutter*, q.v., was only used in a printing works.

Margins vary in size according to the dimensions and 'colour' of two facing panels of type on two pages. A typical proportion, based on two facing pages, might be: head 1½ units, fore-edge 2 units, gutter (i.e. measurement across both backs) 2 units, tail 3 or more units.

See also *gutter*.

marginal notes: notes printed in the side margin of a page opposite the portion of text to which they refer. They are set in a distinguishing type.

See also *cut-in side notes, shoulder-notes*.

Marguerite de Valois, 1553–1615: the wife of Henry IV, King of France, and a great bibliophile. Her collection included items from the Duc de Berry's library. She employed Nicolas and Clovis Eve to bind for her, and it was at one time believed that books they lettered with the inscription 'Expectata non eludet' were made for her. It is more probable, however, that they were done for Pietro Duodo, Venetian ambassador to France about 1600.

Marion Press: one of the earliest private presses concerned with fine printing to be established in America. It was started at Jamaica, Long Island, in 1896 by Frank Hopkins (b. 1863) who had learned his craft at the De Vinne Press.

marked proof: the proof, usually on galleys, supplied to the author for correction. It bears on it the corrections and queries of the printer's reader.

marking up: a binder's term to describe the dividing of the back into equal parts, and indicating the position of the cords.

Marmion, Simon, *c.* 1425–89: a Flemish painter, much of whose work was done for churches. In addition he was commissioned to illuminate manuscripts. Among his patrons was Philip, Duke of Burgundy, for whom he worked from 1466–70 on one book alone. In his lifetime he was called 'prince d'enluminure'. The 'Grandes Chroniques' he made for the Abbot of St Bertin is his best work: it is now in Leningrad.

Marprelate Press: see *Waldegrave, Robert.*

Martens, Thierry, 1446/7–1534: an important humanist printer, who began printing at his native Alost in 1473 before moving to Louvain in 1498. Here he devoted himself to Greek and Latin studies, notably works by Erasmus, Rudolphus Agricola, and the first edition of More's 'Utopia', 1516. His small Greek quarto textbooks included Homer, Euripides, Plutarch, Demosthenes, and Plato. He was assisted by the scholar-printer Rutger Rescius, who in 1529 took over Martens' business. Between 1519 and 1545 Rutger was professor of Greek in the Collegium Trilingue, Louvain.

Martin, William, d. 1815: a London typefounder who, between 1790 and 1815, cut type for the 'Shakspeare Press' of John Boydell and George Nicol. He based his designs on the faces of Didot, Bodoni, and Baskerville.

masking: the correction of a separation negative by combining a negative obtained by the separation of colours with a transparent positive obtained from one of the other negatives. When necessary, a positive is corrected by a negative mask. The process is based on the following principle: a negative exposed, for example, through a green filter, a magenta printer, produces, in copying, a picture that contains too much of the green and blue portions of the subject. If a transparent positive is made from the blue-green printer negative and placed in register over the magenta printer negative, the result should be that the defect is partly corrected. For the process to be successful it is essential that both negative and positive are produced with the exact density previously calculated by experiment.

The corrected positive and negative are joined together in register, either by pasting or by placing the positive as a screen in front of the negative in a holder, when the positive intended for final reproduction is exposed from the latter. Detailed instructions for correcting masking have been drawn up by Kodak Ltd. who also make a densitometer for the purpose. The Kodak *magenta masking method*, q.v., embodies the use of a mask produced by exposing a plate placed in the screen-holder of a camera.

(G. U.)

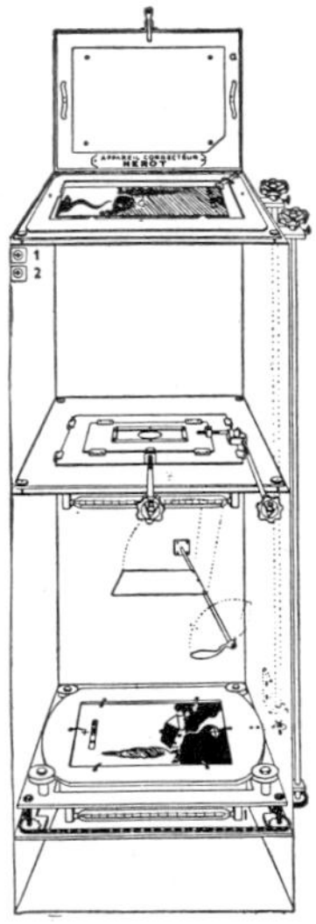

Auxiliary apparatus for correcting negatives by masking. Bottom, lighting; immediately above, corrected positive (mask). Centre, lens, with below it a movable white screen. Top, uncorrected negative and (opened upwards) frame for holding the sensitized positive material to be exposed. (Nérot-Bouzard)

Massiquot, Guillaume: see *guillotine*.

Master Bookbinders Alliance of London: the trade association of master bookbinders within the London district.

The Master Bookbinders Association really started as the Bookbinding Section of the London Chamber of Commerce. A meeting was held in 1891 with Sir Albert K. Rollitt, M.P. (chairman of the Council of the Chamber) as chairman. Those present who were members of the Chamber were asked to act as the Committee. George Simpson was elected chairman, and John Diprose deputy chairman. In 1910 it was decided to form a Master Bookbinders Association, but the Section still continued and for some time dealt with labour matters. Gradually the Association undertook all the work of the Section. In 1939 the Association became an Alliance of the *B.F.M.P.*, q.v., and is now known as the Master Bookbinders Alliance of London.

The aims of the Alliance are to organize the master bookbinders within the London district in order that they may deal collectively with all matters affecting them; to support and maintain the Standard Trade Conditions of the Alliance; and to do all things which may conduce to the protection and prosperity of members. Membership is confined to master bookbinders, whether individuals carrying on business alone, partnership firms, or limited companies in the London district. It is a condition of membership that an applicant shall be paying the prevailing London conditions, but in a particular instance and if recommended by the Executive Committee, the Alliance in general meeting may waive this condition.

mathematical setting: the setting up in type of the signs, symbols, letters, and figures which mathematical notation comprises. Mathematics is usually set on a Monotype keyboard, cast, and made up by hand.

An author must pay special attention to the presentation of formulae in his copy. Typed copy may lead to errors because the ordinary typewriter is not equipped to produce figures and signs in a sufficient variety of sizes or positions. Carefully written copy allows more flexibility for expressing notation. Whichever method is used, the manuscript should be read by a copy-preparer who will mark up the size, position, and spacing of the notation. This helps the compositor but he, too, needs to understand something of mathematical conventions if errors are to be avoided.

Since many special sorts are required for advanced mathematical formulae, setting is normally done in one of half a dozen type-faces of which Monotype Modern Series 7 is the most used. It is provided with over six hundred special sorts. Special matrix-case arrangements are used, and additional Monotype equipment will be needed by the book printer who wishes to undertake such work.

The printer who has only occasional demands for mathematical setting may find the production of type-set formulae very costly. This has led to the development of *pro-printing*, q.v.

See T. W. Chaundy and others, 'The Printing of Mathematics', O.U.P., 1954; and A. Phillips, 'Setting Mathematics', in 'The Monotype Recorder', Vol. XL, No. 4, Autumn 1956.

matrix: 1. a metal die from which a single type is cast, either as a unit or as part of a solid slug. In the 15th century matrices were made of lead, struck with copper punches (wooden punches may also have been used). As the need for a more durable metal was perceived, copper was used for the matrix and brass or steel for the punch.

See also *justification* (2), *punch*, *strike*.

2. the impression in papier mâché taken from a page of type for stereotyping.

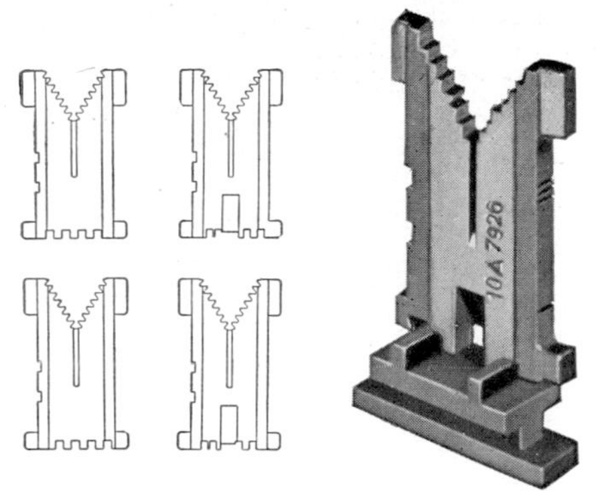

Linotype matrices showing the combination teeth which facilitate distribution

matt art: a clay-coated printing paper with a dull finish.
See also *art paper*.

matter: type, either set up for use or standing. Also copy to be set is sometimes called 'matter'.
See also *dead matter, open matter, solid matter, standing type*.

Maugham Trust Fund: see *Somerset Maugham Trust Fund*.

Mazarin Bible: a name occasionally given to the version of the Bible printed by Johann Gutenberg. A copy was found in 1760 in the Parisian library of Cardinal Mazarin (1602–61) who was a well-known bibliophile. This discovery focused bibliographical attention on the edition.
The library of Cardinal Mazarin is now in the Collège Mazarin, Paris.

mean line: the imaginary line running along the top of those lower-case letters which are without ascenders, i.e. a, c, e, i, m, n, o, r, s, u, v, w, x, z. Cf. *base line, cap line*.

Mearne bindings: bindings done in the workshop of Samuel Mearne, who from 1660–83 was binder, bookseller, and stationer to King Charles II of England. Many were based on French styles and included panels in coloured leathers applied as an overlay, also pointillé-filled compartments after the manner of the Le Gascon bindings. Yet other examples were in the *cottage* style, q.v. Suckerman was the head finisher of his bindery.
One of Mearne's duties was to seek out illicit presses on behalf of the Stationers' Company.
See also *fore-edge painting*.

measure: the width to which separate type-matter is set or a Linotype slug is cast; counted in ems.

mechanical overlay: a method of overlaying, in which an impression is taken on paper bearing a thin coating of chalk. The coating on the non-inked parts is then washed off with diluted acid leaving the inked design in relief. The resulting outline is fitted as an overlay on the cylinder or platen to increase or decrease the pressure. There are other patent overlay methods, and one increasingly used in Britain is the *Primaton*, q.v. See also *Fleischhack overlay*.

mechanical tints: see *Ben Day tints, Zip-a-tone*.

mechanical wood (or **mechanical furnish**): soft wood logs ground to pulp by a large grinding stone, all the impurities contained in the logs remaining in the pulp. It is strengthened with 25 to 35% of sulphite pulp and used in the manufacture of cheaper-quality printings such as newsprint. Cf. *chemical wood*.

Mediaan: the Belgian unit of type measurement in which 12-point equals 0·1649 in. or 4·18 mm.

medical and pharmaceutical symbols:

ʒ	dram	℥	ounce
♏	drop	O	pint
C	gallon	℞	recipe
gr.	grain	℈	scruple
♏	minim	fs	semi-
aa	of each	S	signa

Medici, Cosimo de, 1389–1464: an Italian nobleman, scholar, bibliophile, and patron of libraries. In 1433 he founded the San Giorgio Maggiore Library, Venice, and in 1441 he gave 400 of the classical manuscripts he had inherited from Niccolo de' Niccoli to the newly built library of San Marco Convent, Florence. He employed *Bisticci*, q.v., to copy books for Fiesole Abbey Library. A second 400 Niccoli manuscripts were added to his personal library. The Fiesole, Medici, and San Marco collections are now in the Biblioteca Mediceo-Laurenziana, Florence.

medium: 1. a standard size of printing paper, 18 in. by 23 in.
2. the liquid, usually linseed oil, in which the pigment of a printing ink is dispersed and via which it leaves an impression on paper.
3. an alternative name for a *Ben Day tint*, q.v.
4. the weight of type-face midway between light and bold. Normally used for the body of a book.

medium finish: a finish given to paper that is neither highly calendered nor antique, but intermediate between the two extremes. (M. L.)

meeting guards: V-shaped guards of paper to which folds of sections are sewn when it is desired that a book of narrow-margined pages shall open quite flat. The open side of each guard is then folded, the pile of sections pressed, marked up, sawn in, and sewn by the *all along* method, q.v.

Meisenbach, Georg, 1841–1912: the inventor of *half-tone* reproduction, q.v. From 1873 he worked in Munich, first as a copperplate engraver, and later on experiments for making printing blocks by means of photography. In 1881 he produced his first serviceable half-tone blocks in the printing house he had established with J. von Schmädel in 1878, and in 1882 he was granted British and German patents for his method. In 1884 The Meisenbach Co. Ltd. was formed in London, the management including J. W. Swan, who had also experimented with this process. The Munich business passed into the hands of Meisenbach's son August, and was amalgamated in 1892 with a Berlin firm under the name of Meisenbach, Riffarth & Co., now in Berlin only, but formerly also in Munich and Leipzig. (G. U.)

melting-pot: see *remelting pot.*

membrane: a skin parchment.

mending: inserting a corrected piece in a printing plate.

menologium: a calendar of saints' days of the Greek Church. Biographies of the saints are included. One of the most famous of Byzantine illuminated examples was commissioned by Basileios II (976–1025): it is now in the Vatican Library (Gr. 1613).

Mentelin, Johann, fl. 1460–78: the first printer of Strasbourg where he issued the 49-line Latin Bible in 1460 (GKW 4203), and the first Bible printed in German, 1466. He was a pioneer in Germany of the roman letter, and one of the earliest printers known to have issued advertisements of his books.

Menzel, Adolf von, 1815–1905: a German painter, designer, and lithographer, who became one of the most outstanding illustrators of books in 19th-century Europe. He earned his living from his drawings and lithographs when only nineteen. He lived in Berlin where his most important work was done for Kugler's 'Geschichte Friedrichs der Grosse', 1840, which included 400 illustrations. (With G. U.)

Mergenthaler, Ottmar, 1854–99: a German-American who invented the first Linotype type-setting machine in 1884, and the basis of its present form in 1886. He was born near Stuttgart, going to Washington, D.C., when eighteen. Later he went to Baltimore where he met the inventor of a 'Typewriter', Charles T. Moore, in 1876, and his partner Clephane.

Mergenthaler interested himself in the problem of mechanical type-setting, and his earliest satisfactory model was used on July 3rd, 1886, in the office of the 'New York Tribune'. Clephane financed Mergenthaler's inventions for many years.

Machines are made in America by Mergenthaler Linotype Co., Brooklyn, 1891; in Germany by Linotype G.m.b.H., Berlin and Frankfurt; and in Britain by Linotype & Machinery Ltd., London and Altrincham.

See also *Lintoype.*

Merovingian: a cursive script developed in Gaul as the national form of the Roman half-uncial, and used for manuscripts from the 5th–8th centuries. The compressed letters are not easy to read.

Merrymount Press: an American press founded in 1893 by *D. B. Updike*, q.v.

metal: see *type metal.*

metal feeder: a mechanical device for supplying fresh metal to the pot of a type-casting machine as the metal is used up. (G. U.)

See also *type metal.*

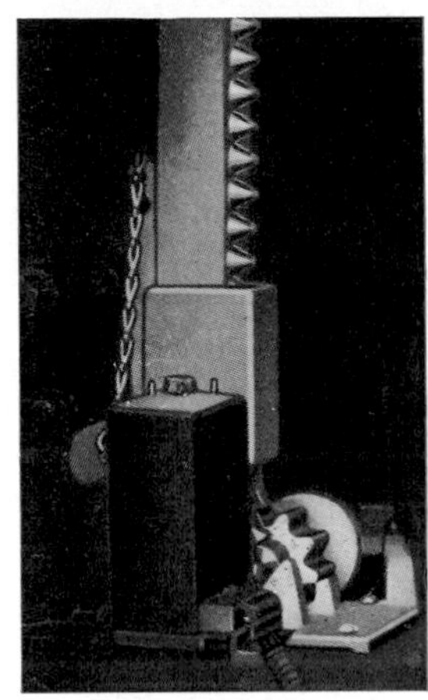

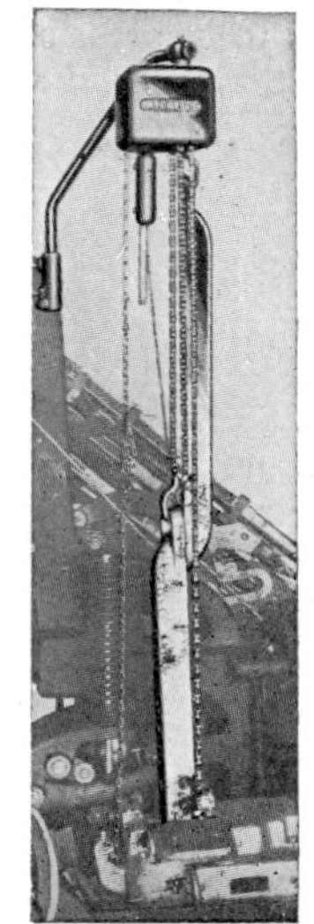

Left, Monobar metal feeder on a Linotype
Right, metal feeder for ingots on an Intertype

metal-pot: a heated container from which molten metal inside it is conveyed to the mould or casting-box in stereotyping, type-casting, etc. In type-casting machines the inner part of the metal pot is equipped with a cylinder rising from the bottom in which a pump piston works. The cylinder is open at the top and at the base has an upward neck which ends in the mouthpiece (see illustration). When a line is to be cast, the piston forces metal through the neck against the mouthpiece; as the piston rises again fresh metal pours from the pot through an influx hole into the cylinder.

For the large pots used in automatic casting machines for curved stereos see *casting box.* (G. U.)

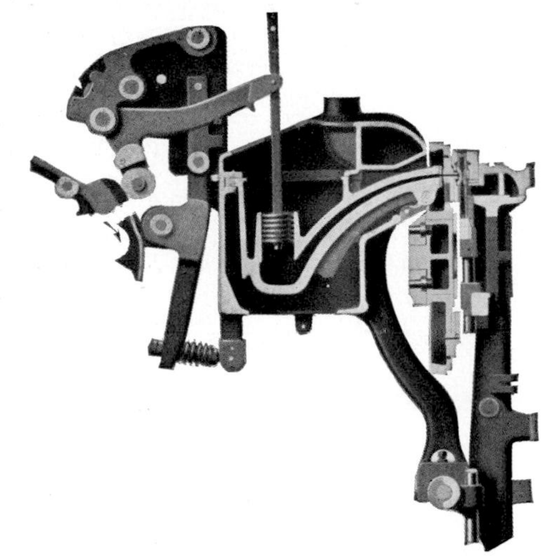

Metal-pot on a type-casting machine

metal printing: see *photo-lithographic plate.*

metallic inks: printing inks which produce an effect of gold, silver, copper, or bronze. For good results they must be used on coated stock, otherwise an underprinting in a coloured ink is first made from the same block to act as a size for the metal.

metallography: 1. metal-lithography, a printing process similar to lithography in which metal plates are used instead of stone. (O.E.D.). See also *lithography.*

2. the name given to the process of making a cast metal plate from a mould. Such plates are held to have been used in Holland as relief plates for printing in the early 15th century; they thus preceded the invention of printing from movable type. (After 'Library Association Record', 1931, pp. 153–62.)

Also known as *jetté en moule.*

meteorological symbols: the following symbols for recording weather were approved by the International Meteorological Organization at Warsaw, 1935.

- air, pure (abnormal visibility)
- aurora borealis
- dew
- drizzle
- duststorm
- fog
- fog, frost
- fog, ground
- fog, shallow
- frost, glazed
- frost, hoar
- gale
- ▲ hail
- △ hail, small
- hail, soft
- ∞ haze
- ice, grains of
- ice needles and crystals
- lightning, distant (i.e. thunder inaudible)
- lightning, sheet
- lunar corona
- lunar halo
- mirage
- mist
- • rain
- rain, shower of
- rainbow
- rime, hard
- rime, soft
- sandstorm
- sleet
- sleet shower
- snow
- snow, drifting (high up)
- snow, drifting (near ground)
- snow shower
- snowstorm
- solar corona
- ⊕ solar halo
- ⊙ sunshine
- thunder; also thunder and lightning
- 0 (after symbol) light*
- 2 (after symbol) heavy*

( ) enclose symbols when phenomena pass near but not over observing station.

* Used as superior figures, thus ▲² means heavy hail.

Meynell, Sir Francis, 1891– : one of Britain's leading book designers. In 1923 he founded the *Nonesuch Press,* q.v., having previously managed the Pelican Press, an establishment noted for a limited output of fine printing between 1916 and 1923. It was under this imprint that Francis Meynell issued 'Typography', 1923, which was both a notable type-specimen book and an essay on book production.

In 1954 the Limited Editions Club of New York awarded him their Aldus Statuette; the citation for this, written by Bruce Rogers, described Meynell as 'the father of fine book making in England'.

See also *Romney Street Press.*

Meynell, Gerard: a partner and director of the Westminster Press which in the first years of the present century was noted for fine printing. In 1913 he established '*The Imprint*', q.v.

mezzograph screen: a little-used screen with a fine grained surface made by melting bitumen dust on to a glass plate; it is employed in process engraving as an alternative to the normal ruled glass screen. Another screen, similar in scope, is the *Erwin,* q.v.

See also *screen.*

mezzotint: 1. an intaglio illustration process for reproducing tones as distinct from lines. A copper plate is given a pitted surface by passing a steel-toothed rocking tool (see *cradle*) over the whole of it. (If used in this state the whole printed sheet would be black.) The surface is now scraped with a knife and a scraping iron to remove all recesses save those required to print. Those areas which are to appear white are scraped quite smooth and burnished. Printing is done on dampened paper in a copperplate press.

The invention of mezzotint is ascribed to Ludwig von Siegen in 1642, but it was the influence of his friend, Prince Rupert of Bavaria, that made it better known, especially to the Dutchmen Wallerant Vaillant (1623–77) and Abraham Blooteling (1640–90) who developed it.

It was Prince Rupert who introduced mezzotint into England where William Sherwin produced the first-known dated print from a mezzotint plate in 1669. The process had its greatest vogue from 1670–1750. In England the finest work was done by such craftsmen as John Smith (1652–1742); James MacArdell (1729–65); John Raphael Smith (1752–1812); and Valentine Green (1739–1813): they reproduced paintings by Gainsborough, Rembrandt, Reynolds, and Romney. (With G.U.)

2. the print taken from a mezzotint plate.

M.F.: the abbreviation for *machine finish*, q.v.

M.G.: the abbreviation for *machine-glazed* paper. This is also known as *machine finish*, q.v.

Michel, Marius: the name used by Jean Michel (1821–90) and his son Henri François (1846–1925), who were distinguished Parisian binders and gilders. The father's work, while technically perfect, was largely traditional, but the son was more enterprising: he used curved stamps instead of small dies and fillets to work exotic flower and leaf forms, also attempting to relate the decoration on a book cover to its contents.

They both wrote works on bookbinding, notable being 'Essai sur la décoration extérieure des livres', 1878, and 'L'ornement des reliures modernes', 1889.

microfilm: a 16 or 35 mm. film-strip on which pages of books, newspapers, or documents are photographed. This saves both space and the handling of valuable originals. For viewing, the filmed records are projected through an enlarger on to a ground glass screen, or via a mirror on to a sheet of paper near the person who is reading.

mid-feather: the central partition in a Hollander around which the half-stuff circulates.

Middle Hill Press: a private printing press established about 1822 by the great Victorian collector of MSS., Sir Thomas Phillipps (1792–1872), of Broadway in Worcestershire. Publications included catalogues of manuscript collections, works of antiquarian interest, and genealogies. A vignette of Broadway Tower characterizes some of the title-pages. The collection of manuscripts and printed books has been dispersed by sales since 1886. (With M.L.)

Miehle: the name given to printing presses from the Miehle Printing Press & Mfg. Co., Chicago; the firm now has a London representation where the machines are British-built.

Robert Miehle (d. 1932) is regarded as the originator of the modern *two-revolution press*, q.v., although the principle was known and applied before his improved version appeared.

Among various models are the *Standard Miehle*, a two-revolution press with a printing surface of from 61 cm. by 94 cm. to 115·5 cm. by 177·5 cm. Miehle 1 has a printing surface of 87·5 cm. by 124·5 cm.; Miehle 2 of 77·5 cm. by 116·5 cm. Modern rapid two-revolution presses are made for the following formats of paper: Miehle 41 = 71 cm. by 104 cm., Miehle 46 = 84 cm. by 115·5 cm., Miehle 56 = 106·7 cm. by 142·2 cm. *Miehle two-colour press No.* 3 is suitable for four-colour process work.

The *Miehle Vertical* (see illustration) is an entirely automatic stop-cylinder press with vertically placed printing forme. During impression the cylinder and bed move in opposite directions, by which means the track bed is shortened. The cylinder revolves on the printing stroke only, a gap in the cylinder clearing the forme when the cylinder is tripped. The printing surface is 31·5 cm. by 48·3 cm. ($12\frac{1}{4}$ in. by 19 in.).

The Miehle Vertical, V 50. *The feeding apparatus and inking system are swung outwards for easy attention*

Paper format is 35·5 cm. by 50·8 cm. (14 in. by 20 in.), with a speed of from 3000 to 5000 copies an hour. Feed is by air separation and suction; delivery is made printed side up. (G.U.)

In 1955, the high-speed Miehle, made in Britain by L & M, was equipped with non-stop feeding and chain delivery. The Model 3 feeder used is an independent unit which can be moved away from the press to permit working on the forme; until it is returned the press cannot be started. When loading, the pile rests on steel laths placed on the feedboard,

see page 250

Small Scale Combed Pattern on Handmade Paper

Large Scale Combed Pattern on Handmade Paper

see page 250

Small Scale Combed Pattern on Kraft paper

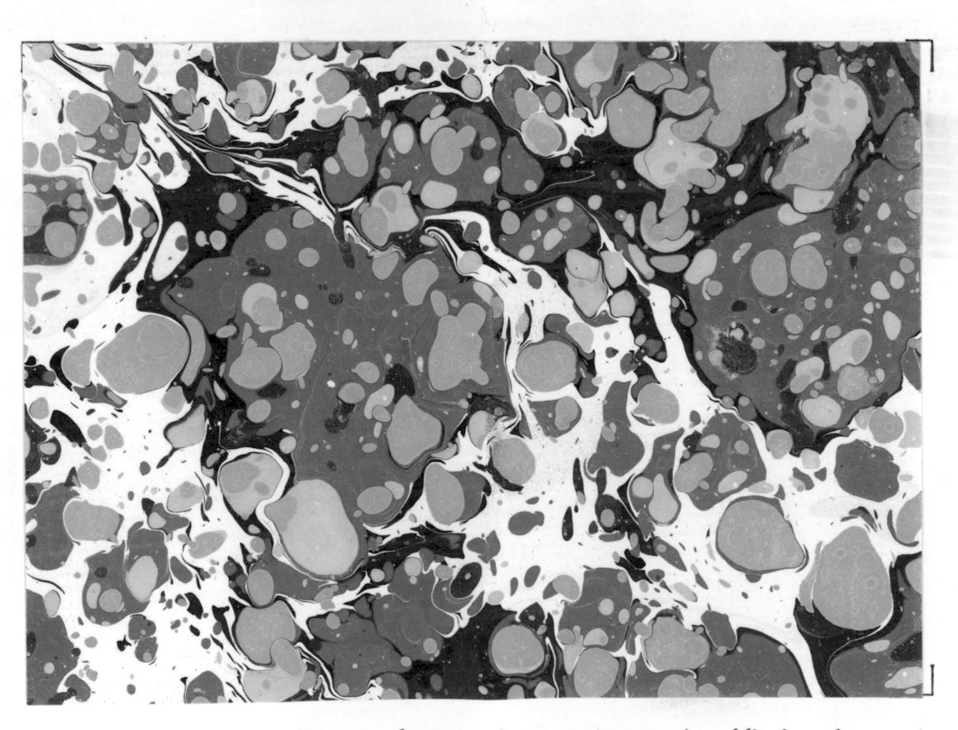

Uncombed Pattern. It is this type of pattern that gave the name 'marbling' to the process
These specimens are the work of Douglas Cockerell & Sons

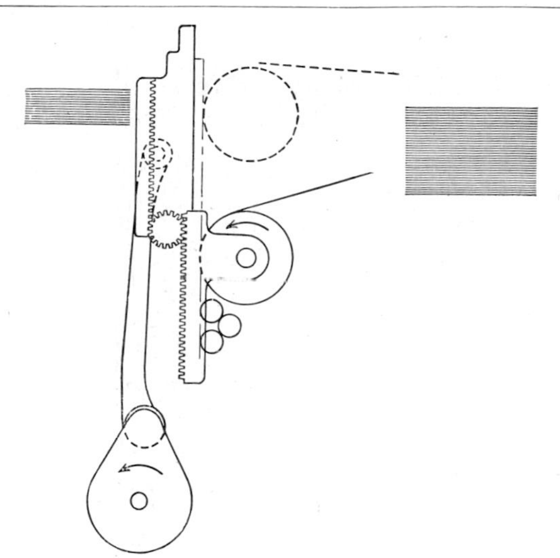

Diagram showing construction of the Miehle Vertical. The bed and cylinder move up and down but in opposite directions. When the latter returns to its starting point the printed sheet is seized by a swinging gripper rod and carried out between the cylinder and feeding table

and is built up to normal height. As running proceeds, a second feed board with laths is loaded. When the first pile is reduced to 3 in. a white light indicates that the feed board can be removed, leaving the pile on the laths (supported now by lifter bars). A red light warns the operator that the second pile should be positioned and wound up by hand until it contacts the first set of laths. These and the lifter bars are then removed. Feeding, using the system of combers and blowers on earlier Miehles, may be by stream or single sheets. Swinging grippers improve register.

In the chain-delivery mechanism the pile builds up on a standard stack board. When full, a sheet-catcher board is inserted to collect sheets until a fresh stack board can be positioned; the former then drops on to the latter and delivery continues without interruption.

mildew: a growth, caused by micro-organisms, whose spores, in a moist, warm atmosphere, become moulds, deriving their food from the material on which they form, e.g. the pages of books. During their growth they produce citric, gluconic, oxalic, or other organic acids damaging to the paper. Every part of an affected book must be treated with the inhibitor most suited to it. The best preventives are thorough cleanliness, sunlight, dry circulating air, temperatures below 65° F. Cedar wood and clove oil, or saddle soap, applied with a clean linen pad are recommended for leather bindings. (M. L.)

See also *leather preservation.*

Miliani, Pietro, 1744–1817: the founder of a famous Italian firm of hand-made paper makers of Fabriano. He was the first paper-maker in Italy to use a *Hollander*, q.v. Successive members of the family directed the business until the present century.

mill brand: in the paper trade, the trade-mark and brand name belonging to the manufacturer and so identified, as distinguished from a private jobber's brand, where the goods bear the jobber's identification but not the manufacturer's. (M. L.)

mill-finished: see *machine finish.*

mill ream: 472 sheets of hand-made or mould-made paper, good or retree; i.e. 18 'inside' quires of 24 sheets, and 2 'outside' quires of 20 sheets.

See also *mille, perfect, printer's ream, quire, ream.*

millboards: strong grey or black boards of good quality used for the covers of books. Ingredients include rope, fibre refuse, and wood pulp.

mille: the unit of 1000 sheets in which form British paper-makers and printers have agreed paper shall be sold. Packing is in parcels of 1000, 500, 250, or 100 sheets.

See also *mill ream, outsides, printer's ream, quire, ream, retree.*

Miller: the trade name for printing presses, automatic die-cutting machines, and other equipment from the Miller Printing Machinery Co., Pittsburgh, U.S.A. The name became known throughout the world by a trimmer first marketed about 1905. In 1915 an automatic feeder for platen presses was constructed, and in 1927 an entirely automatic cylinder press. Other models are a two-revolution machine for one and two colours, and entirely automatic die-cutting machines of cylinder machine construction. (G. U.)

Miller, William Henry, 1789–1848: a wealthy book collector who founded a library at Britwell Court, his Buckinghamshire home. Subjects were early English and Scottish literature, especially poetry; Miller bought many ballads and broadsides from the Heber library.

The Britwell collection remained in the family until 1917 when 346 items of Americana were sold to Henry E. Huntington. From this and subsequent sales the sum of nearly £250,000 has been realized.

minion: the name for a former size of type, now standardized as 7-point. The name may have originated in France where it was used first in the 17th century.

minium: red lead (ground cinnabar), mixed with water and egg-white, and used for rubrics in Egyptian papyri and when illuminating manuscripts.

Minnesängerhandschriften: the name for collections of 12th- and 13th-century German lyrics, originally written on single leaves, or on a few leaves, and brought together in the 13th and 14th centuries, probably for some patron as an act of preservation. About twenty such collections survive, some only in fragments, but the largest, best-known, and most beautiful is the 'Grosse Heidelberger Liederhandschrift', also known as the 'Manessische Liederhandschrift' after Rüdeger Manesse (*c.* 1252–1304) and his son Johann, both of Zürich.

Lyrics by 140 poets, written in Middle-High-German, survive on some 430 parchment leaves. There are 138 full-page illustrations, believed to be the work of four limners. They mostly depict knights (the poets) and ladies in stylized scenes of chivalry, often of considerable tenderness. Some show interesting details of games and sports (e.g. chess, falconry, fishing), while others show musical instruments. Clear shades of blue, red, and mauve are mostly used for the clothing; gold is used on armorial shields, and also in a very natural way to suggest the metal of weapons, jewellery, and the collars and cuffs of clothing.

The whole-page illustrations are bounded by simple narrow bands of gold and colours, with the name of the knight added in red at the head of the page.

The manuscript was in Zürich in the 14th century; it subsequently belonged to Ulrich von Fugger, and in 1584 it passed to the Bibliotheca Palatina. In 1657 it was sold to the Royal Library in Paris where it remained until 1888 when the German Government sponsored the purchase by a Strasbourg bookseller of 166 French manuscripts from the Ashburnham Library (they had been stolen from French libraries by Barrois and Libri). Twenty-three of these manuscripts were exchanged for the Manessische Liederhandschrift, which was restored to Heidelberg University Library.

mint: a term used in the second-hand book trade to describe the immaculate condition of a book which has not been used; as new.

minuscule: a lower-case or small letter. Cf. *majuscule.*

mirror: in photographic process work a reflecting surface is often used for reversing an image from right to left. A mirror or *prism,* q.v., is placed immediately in front of or behind the reproduction lens. It consists of a very carefully flat-ground and finely polished metal plate, fitted in a mirror casing in such a way that when it has been fastened to the lens the reflecting surface is at an angle of 45° to the main optical axis of the lens. In vertical cameras with a constant mirror position 'roof ridge mirrors' with two reflecting surfaces are used: here the image is reversed twice.

Mirror behind lens

An image is said to be 'reversed' when it is reversed from right to left. This can be achieved in process work by photographing through a mirror or prism, or by turning in connection with printing or transferring. In direct printing processes, the image must be turned sideways on the printing forme; in offset printing, face upwards. (G.U.)

miscellaneous binder: a binder of single books to the individual customer's order.

See also *craft bookbinding.*

misprint: a typographical error, made either through oversight, careless reading of copy, or an accident. (M.L.)

Missal: a book containing the Mass services for the whole year. Early examples were hand-written and illuminated. The term is also used for any illuminated prayer-book or Book of Hours.

missal caps: decorative capitals used in conjunction with black-letter type.

Missale plenarium: a term used in the 13th century to designate a full or complete Roman Missal. Prior to this no single manuscript had contained the whole Missal. From the end of the 7th century the name Missal had been given to the *Sacramentary* which included the Collects, Secrets, Prefaces, Canons, and Post-communions. Other volumes contained the Lessons, Epistles, Gospels, and the choral portions of the Mass. As the practice of incorporating the separate parts in one volume became general the adjective 'plenarium' fell into disuse.

Every diocese had its own Missal, and many churches in a diocese had uses of their own. A local usage would often be added in the form of marginal notes or at the end of the volume.

Missals were usually large and costly and it became customary, particularly in Germany and Switzerland, to have shortened versions containing the text of the Masses for Sundays and the principal feast days. Such abridgements were called *Missale speciale.*

Missale speciale Constantiense: an early printed Missal, of which three copies are known; they are at Munich, in the Bavarian State Library; New York, in the Pierpont Morgan Library: and Zürich, where the only perfect copy is in the Zentralbibliothek.

The Zürich copy has 192 leaves, printed in the smaller of the two types used for the Fust and Schöffer Psalter of 1457. The place of printing, printer and date have all been matters for conjecture, and thus controversy, since 1898 when Otto Hupp (1859–1949) published his conclusion that the Missal was printed by Gutenberg, and pre-dated the 42-line Bible. Experts have latterly suggested that the book was printed in or near Basle (where Gutenberg is not known to have worked), probably by a former employee of Gutenberg or Fust and Schöffer who had obtained matrices or type of the 1457 Psalter. In 1955, Victor Scholderer wrote in 'The Book Collector', Vol. 4, No. 1, 'an approximate dating in 1465 would not be at all inconsistent with what little is otherwise known of the beginnings of printing at Basle. Such a date would also square tolerably well with the period assigned to the canon cut in the "Missale abbreviatum".' This last is the work of the same press, shows the same type, and, in the only known copy, at the Benedictine Abbey of St Paul in Carinthia, Austria, has a cut to which experts assign the date 1450–65.

mitred: 1. the leather corners of a bound book when folded so that the inside line of joint is at an angle of 45° from the top and side edges of the book.

2. the ends of rules which are bevelled so that in forming right-angle joints of frames they will fit flush.

See also *Oxford corners*.

mixed composition: said of matter which in its setting calls for various type-founts, e.g. a single paragraph with words in bold-face or italic type among the main portion which is set in roman.

See also *fat matter*.

mock-up: see *dummy*.

modern face: type having contrasting thick and thin strokes, serifs at right-angles, and curves thickened in the centre, e.g. Modern Face and Bodoni. The style originated in France in the late 17th century for the type *romain du roi Louis XIV*, q.v. Types based on this were designed by Fournier in 1745, by F. A. Didot in 1784, and notably by Bodoni of Parma in 1790. In England, the Didot types were the basis of those cut in 1788 by Richard Austin for John Bell of the British Letter Foundry. Most modern-face types print well on smooth paper.

See also *letters—forms and styles*.

moiré: an imperfection, noticed when printing coloured half-tones, which is seen as a mechanical pattern of dots. This can be minimized by photographing each colour at a separate angle, or by using screens ruled at varying angles for each exposure.

See also *half-tone screen*.

moisture content: see *relative humidity*.

monastic bindings: the name now given to the diapered leather covers of manuscript volumes which were common in most North European monasteries up to the 15th century. Each square or diamond was filled with a small stamped design. No gold was used. An alternative name is *antique*.

monk: an ink blot or splash on a printed sheet. The term originated in the days when *ink balls*, q.v., were used to ink the formes. Cf. *black*, *friar*.

monograph: a treatise on a single subject.

Monoline: a type-setting machine constructed in 1893 by Wilbur Stephen Scudder. It worked on similar principles to the Linotype. Type matrices were in the shape of suspended bars, each provided with twelve type characters. By striking the keys in the machine the corresponding matrix was released and dropped perpendicularly into an assembler box where its position was regulated by a stopping mechanism. There were eight series of such matrix bars, each representing its width of type. Spacing, casting, and distribution of matrices and spacebars were done on approximately the same principle as in the Linotype.

The Monoline machine was simple and relatively cheap, yet it failed to establish a market. Manufacture ceased in 1910. Macnamara built an improved Monoline in 1906, but its manufacture was prevented by patent rights. (G. U.)

Monophoto: the registered trade-mark of the photocomposing machines manufactured by the Monotype Corporation Ltd. (M. L.)

See *photo-composing machine*.

Monotype: the registered trade-mark of the Monotype Corporation Ltd. under which all its products are manufactured, including the machine for setting and casting separate types, invented by *Tolbert Lanston*, q.v. Its main features were resolved by 1893, and by 1899 Lanston's colleague Bancroft had given the keyboard and caster the basic form they still have. Monotype composing and casting machines are made in the U.S.A. by Lanston Industries Incorporated, Philadelphia, and in England by the Monotype Corporation Ltd., Salfords, Redhill, Surrey. Representation is world wide.

Above Monotype keybanks is a drum with a justifying scale indicator. To facilitate reading the numbers on the scale a lighting and magnifying attachment can be supplied

A Monotype machine comprises two units: the *keyboard* and the *caster*, each with its own operator. The principle on which these work may be compared to that of a pianola, for in both systems a paper ribbon perforated by means of compressed air forms the link between the producing and the reproducing machine.

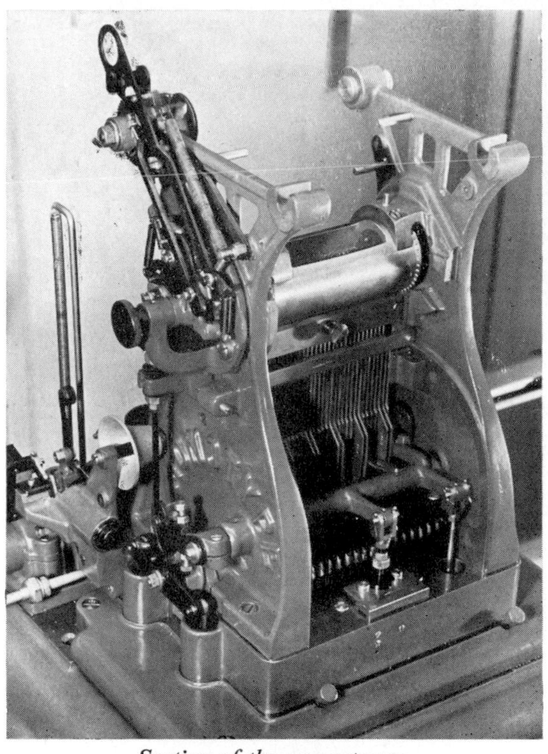

Section of the paper tower

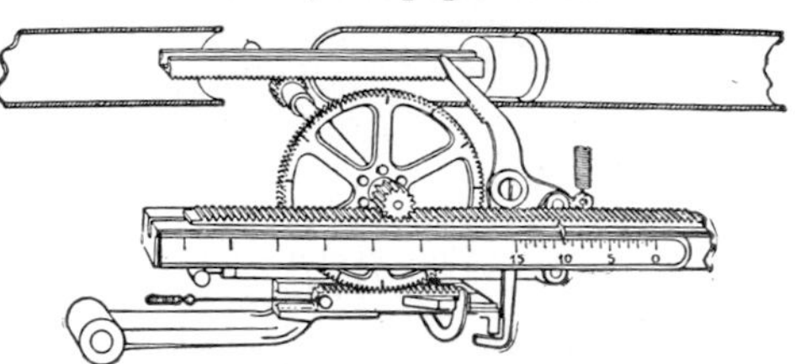

Unit wheel, unit rack, and em scale

Removing the paper reel after composing

Justifying drum with scale for 10¼ Set

The type-faces in the range of Monotype matrices are marked according to a special system; e.g. in the mark 135–11 (10D) 10¼ Set, Line 0·1302, the first number denotes the type series instead of its name (in this example Bodoni), the second number is the body of the type expressed in points, the figure in parentheses denotes on what Didot point body this type can be cast, the word Set preceded by a figure indicates the type width (in the same body a narrow type-face has a smaller set than a broad type), while the number following the word 'Line' indicates the measurement in fractions of an inch from the top edge of a matrix down to the foot of a letter.

Monotype Standard Keyboard. The first model in this range appeared in 1908. The keyboard consists of two keybanks with keys for letters, figures, and signs. The layout of the keys is based on the standard typewriter arrangement. On recent models the buttons are coloured as follows:

Roman caps and l.c.	Black characters on white body
Italic caps	White on blue
Italic l.c.	White on black
Small caps	Black on blue
Bold face	White on green
Justifying keys	Red

When a key is depressed a bar in the intermediate frames under the keyboard is given an upward movement, carrying with it two transverse bars. These in turn operate the two bars which open the plunger valves for directing compressed air to beneath two pistons which drive the dies on their extensions through the paper ribbon already mentioned. This ribbon has perforated transport holes on both edges in which toothed wheels engage and move it ⅛ in. forward at every stroke of the key. Thus the matter moves along the length of the ribbon.

As a rule every character has a combination of two holes, one on either side of an imaginary middle line on the 4$\frac{5}{16}$ in. wide ribbon. There is room for 31 holes, 3 of which are reserved for justifying. From the middle to the left edge the holes are denoted by the letters A to O, and to the right edge with the figures 1 to 15. For example, a marking such as D4 for a combination of holes indicates the exact position of a particular matrix in the matrix frame of the caster, on the same principle as the position of a figure on a chessboard. At the same time as the holes for a letter are punched, the thickness of the letter is registered. The letters of the alphabet have been divided into units of width (the 18th part of the widest characters) in such a way that the widest letters (with the same thickness as the em quad) are said to contain 18/18 (W, Æ, etc.); m, K, and others of the same thickness are 15/18; all numerals and most lower-case letters are 9/18 (en quad); i, l, etc., are 5/18. In both narrow and wide type-faces the em quad and types of the same thickness contain 18/18. (See *Monotype unit system.*)

Mounted at the centre of the keyboard unit, just above the keybanks, is the unit wheel (which has a tooth for each unit); below this is the unit rack which rises at every stroke of a key and engages the wheel. As each character key is struck, a pawl releases the unit wheel, which is rotated by compressed air driving a piston and rack. As the unit wheel turns, the distance covered by the unit rack corresponds to the width of the letter struck. When a job is given to the keyboard compositor, the type (e.g. 135–11, 10¼ Set) and measure must be stated. He adjusts the measure indicator and during operation the total of units for all characters struck is computed automatically. The key for interword spacing (variable key) registers 4 units for every stroke of the space key. When a line is filled to within 4 em quads, a bell rings to warn the compositor that the line will soon be ready for justifying. This is indicated on the justifying drum, an aluminium cylinder (on this occasion 10¼ Set) placed immediately above the unit wheel, which automatically divides the balance of the line equally among the spaces in the line. At each stroke of the

A Monotype Caster

A matrix case with matrices lies on the galley

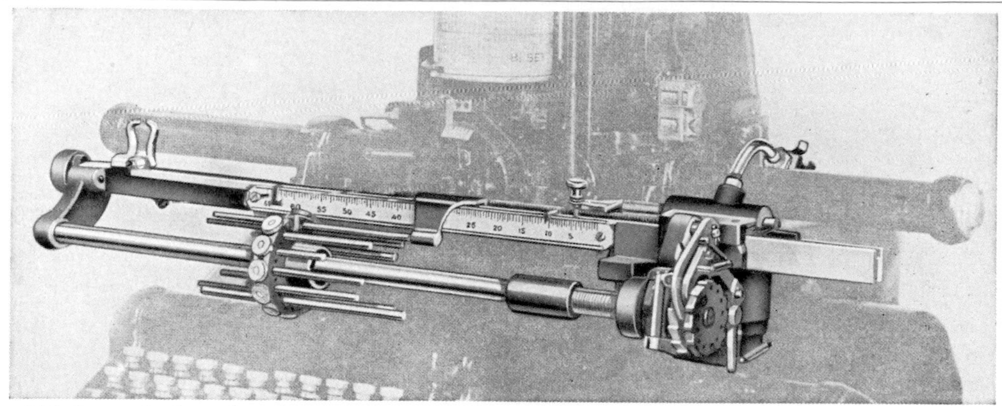

Tabulator. Rods under the em scale allow adjustments to be made for 12 different widths of column. The plate supporting the rods turns automatically when spacing is signalled. The tabulator is not part of the standard machine

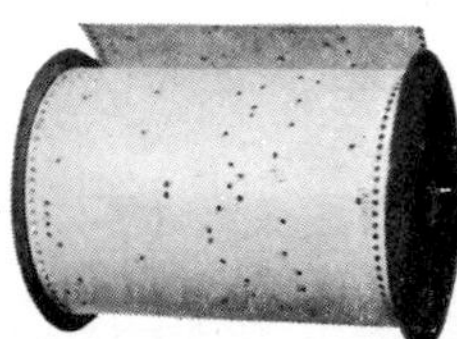

The finished paper reel

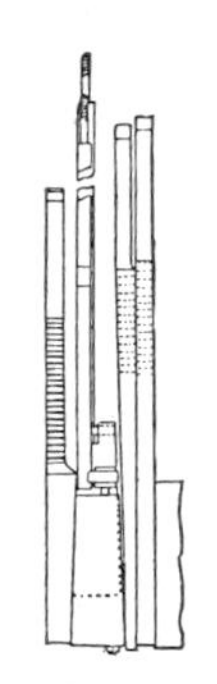

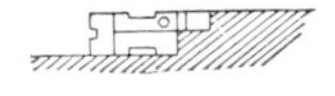

Set-wedge, transfer wedge (there are two, one over the other, one in use when casting characters, the other when casting spaces), and two interword spacing wedges

Below (left) is a set of stop-pins (one of which has just risen) which control the forward movement of the matrix case (slightly higher in the picture). The lateral movement of the matrix case is controlled by another set of pins (not shown here). Each pin corresponds to one of a combination of holes in the perforated strip (above, right)

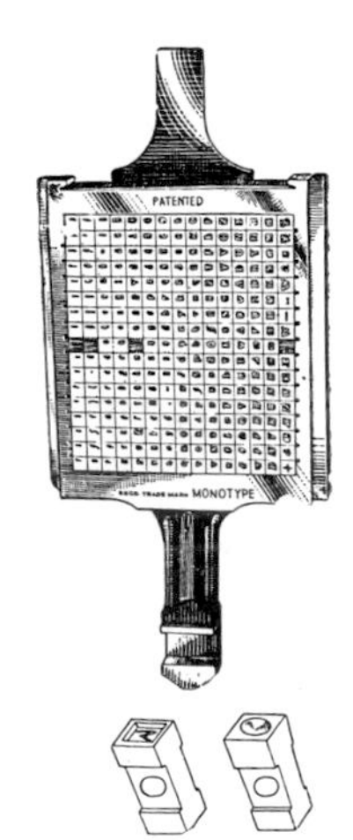

Matrix case and matrices

	NI	NL	A	B	C	D	E	F	G	H	I	J	K	L	M	N	O	
5	,	i	l	t	’	;	:	i	□	l	.	,	!	i	l	.	,	1
6	;	:	f	j	»	/	(	f	□	j	)	-	t	f	j	:	;	2
7	»	!	è	é	z	c	s	r	e	r	s	t	r	s	I	-	!	3
8	?	q	g	ö	v	b	o	c	e	I	z	é	è	?	e	c	z	4
9	t	å	a	7	4	1	å	g	a	1	4	7	a	p	ä	y	à	5
9	y	k	d	8	5	2	ä	o	.	2	5	8	d	g	ö	v	x	6
9	ä	h	0	9	6	3	à	ö	□	3	6	9	0	o	b	å	q	7
10	à	ü	I	n	ü	q	ﬂ	k	p	n	d	S	*	h	u	k	S	8
10	ﬁ	ﬂ	p	u	†	ﬁ	v	y	h	u	b	J	x	n	J	C	?	9
11	Q	Z	J	S	ﬀ	Q	w	Z	C	ﬀ	T	P	L	F	Y	Z	Q	10
12	w	C	Ö	G	L	O	æ	F	L	T	P	E	G	O	Ö	B	V	11
13	B	E	F	P	T	V	Ö	G	A	E	O	B	Ä	Å	R	U	N	12
14	Å	Ä	V	R	A	m	œ	Y	R	U	N	D	A	Ä	Å	w	X	13
15	X	Y	K	D	H	N	U	M	m	H	D	K	X	m	M	H	K	14
18	W	M	Æ	Œ	&	%	=	—	□	W	+	×	½	⅓	¼	¾	W	15
	NI	NL	A	B	C	D	E	F	G	H	I	J	K	L	M	N	O	

Specimen layout for a case with 255 matrices

Automatic leading attachment

variable space key, a pointer rises one section higher in front of the drum scale, which has 20 horizontal and 72 vertical sections. Two rows on the keyboard consist of 15 red keys numbered from 1 to 15 in each row. These are the justifying keys corresponding to the numbers on the drum, thus permitting the combinations from 1/1 to 15/15. If the pointer on the drum stops in a section with the figures 5/8 the compositor strikes upper red key 5 and lower red key 8; the whole line will then be properly justified when produced on the casting machine.

The perforated ribbon on the keyboard can be removed when desired, and be included with the same details to be sent to the caster operator as first sent to the keyboard operator (in this case 135–11, 10¼ Set). The keyboard functions by means of compressed air. The caster is motor-driven as are the perforated strip control, matrix frame positioning, mould dimensioning galley action and other operations of the machine. Should a change of type size and face be required, the caster operator must change the mould, matrix case and normal wedges, and be guided by complete details as supplied by the keyboard operator. The matrix frame contains 15 rows of 17 matrices made of hard bronze. Four of the matrices are for spaces or blank type and the other 251 are provided with a character cavity on the lower end and a conical hole at the upper end into which the centring pin of the caster enters so that the matrix is centred on the mould during casting. The set-wedge which limits the opening of the dimensioning blade of the mould for each casting must be stamped with the same Set as the type fount. It is made of steel and is graded from 5 to 18 units.

After securing the mould and the bridge (in which the matrix frame is carried) and putting in a 10¼ set-wedge, the operator connects the metal pump and casts a few em quads. The dimensions of these are checked most carefully. Considerable variations in thickness are rectified by adjusting a screw at the rear end of the dimensioning blade of the mould. For minute adjustment, a micrometer screw is used; this is behind the bridge. The measure of the trial em quad (18 units) in 10¼ Set is ascertained from a table (0·1418 in.).

The ribbon is fed into the caster to the point where the keyboard operator finished, so that the two perforations for justifying the line are presented first. The ribbon is fitted over a cylinder equipped on both sides with spur wheels which engage the transport holes of the ribbon and move it one perforation forward at every revolution of the caster. In a straight line from left to right the cylinder has 31 perforations above 31 air-pipes corresponding to the 31 holes which may be punched in the ribbon by the keyboard operator. When a combination of two perforations comes exactly over their openings in the cylinder, compressed air passes through the perforations into copper pipes which have their outlet under stop-pins located in two blocks lying at right-angles to each other. The air-pin block to the rear of the mould has 17 stop-pins (marked A to O, NI, NL) and the air-pin block to the left of the mould has 15 stop-pins (marked 1 to 15). Thus if the paper is perforated with the combination D4, compressed air will raise the stop-pin 4 in one block and D in the other. (A glance at the matrix frame illustrated here will show this to be an italic *b*.) A pair of tongs contacts each stop-pin and simultaneously adjusts the respective stop-racks which are then locked in this position. Each rack is moved by one set of matrix jaws which, by means of rods constituting extensions of the matrix frame, so adjust the latter that the matrix with the letter *b* is above the centre of the opening of the mould. The matrix frame then descends towards the mould, the coned centring pin holds the matrix in position, and the metal is pumped from below the mould. The cast letter is immediately water-cooled and the matrix case moves away from the mould. Types are ejected singly and assembled in a channel until a line is completed. The holes at the end of each line in the ribbon made when the compositor struck the justifying keys on the keyboard now give the line mechanism a signal and justifying wedges are adjusted and the cast line is ejected on to the galley. In the same point-size the lines are absolutely equal in length irrespective of whether they contain 40 or 80 characters. All the units (18th parts) occurring in the line plus the spacing must naturally constitute the full measure. Correction is of the letter or letters affected, not a whole line as in slug-casting machines.

The Monotype Corporation recommend the following running speeds for casters operating with the 15 by 17 extended matrix case:

5, 6, 7 point	180 r.p.m.	10,800 per hour
8, 9, 10 point	160 r.p.m.	9,600 per hour
11, 12 point	150 r.p.m.	6,000 per hour
14 point	100 r.p.m.	6,000 per hour
18 point	60 to 80 r.p.m.	4,200 per hour average
24 point	50 to 60 r.p.m.	3,300 per hour average

(These are maximum speeds for reliability)

A Monotype Super Caster

Mould for casting furniture in predetermined lengths in the Super Caster

The metal capacity of a standard medium electric melting-pot is 55 lb. The metal must be particularly pure, the best alloy for casting type being from 6 to 10% tin, and 15 to 19% antimony, the balance of lead. For spacing material a lower tin content can be used but the antimony content should be kept high to maintain sharpness of design and resistance to wear and tear (3% tin with 18% antimony). The former proportions are, however, often used for all work. The melting-pot has an automatic ingot feeder which lowers 16 lb. ingots as the level of the metal in the pot falls from its pre-determined height and automatically stops when the metal reaches its correct level.

Important improvements: Pre-War standard models had a 225 matrix case. Post-War models have 255. This has necessitated the addition of 28 keys to the keyboard (one full row left to right). In the caster the block A to O (15 stop-pins) is exchanged for a block with 17 stop-pins. Characters with matrices in the new matrix lines are represented by three holes on the perforated strip. Machines equipped with 255 matrices can also operate with 225.

Furniture mould core pieces and caps

A leading apparatus can be fitted on the caster which can automatically insert leads from 1- to 6-point between completed lines. This can be done without any special perforations in the strip, but if different combinations of leading are required under headings or between paragraphs, the keyboard operator must strike special keys to produce the necessary perforations in the strip for this alteration.

A tabulator can also be fitted to all Monotype keyboards. In newer models an attachment holding nine pointed metal markers can be fitted in front of the em scale; the pointers can be moved to indicate any required sub-measure in tabular composition.

Monotype Duplex Keyboards. These machines have keybanks similar to the standard models but have two paper towers and two unit-registering mechanisms. The same matter can thus be produced on two paper strips in one operation, though the body and size of the type may differ, as is often the case in a work published simultaneously in, say, an expensive and cheap edition. Composition is done as on the standard machine; in the two key-strokes necessary for spacing a finished line the air to the mechanism of the second tower is shut off by a valve. A work with many footnotes may be set on the Duplex machine as the manuscript passes only once through the compositor's hands.

By setting half the measure in each tower and combining the product from the caster, it is possible to compose lines from 60 to 120 ems of 12-point.

The second tower is often used for calculating lines in tables of figures. The tower not in use is shut off by the valve referred to and the composition on this tower remains a blank, i.e. without perforations.

Monotype Super Casters. These machines are specially designed for casting type for case and spacing material (quotations) from 5- to 72-point, rules and leads from 1- to 18-point cut automatically into various lengths, and foundry furniture (type high) in grades from 24- to 72-point. The machines have three interchangeable heads, one for moulds for text type, one for display type, and a third for rules and furniture. For casting type and spacing from 5- to 12-point, the moulds of the standard machine are used. Only one matrix at a time is used in a super caster. For display there are two moulds, one with insets or sub-moulds, from 14- to 36-point, the other with insets from 42- to 72-point. The bodies of the 42- to 72-point types are recessed for lightness. The metal used should have a tin content equal to half the antimony content; for larger sizes the proportion of antimony may be 22 or 24%. (With G. U.)

Monotype unit system: one-eighteenth of one point (0·0007685 in.) is the base unit of width to multiples of which all letters and spaces are cast on the Monotype.

montage: the assembling of portions of several photographs or drawings to form an original. The separate parts are cut out and assembled like a jig-saw puzzle, care being taken to avoid overlapping edges which would cause shadows.

Montague Press: an American private press founded in 1911 by Carl P. Rollins (b. 1880). In 1918 he was appointed printer to Yale University Press which he completely reorganized.

Moon: an embossed type-face invented by Dr. William Moon of Brighton, about 1850, for the printing of books to be read by blind persons whose affliction comes in later life. It is based on the Roman alphabet and employs simple lines and curves. Cf. *Braille.*

Moore, John, Bishop of Ely, 1646–1714: an eminent bibliophile whose collection of 29,000 books and some 1800 manuscripts was bought by George I who gave it to Cambridge University in 1715. Dibdin described Moore as 'the father of black-letter collectors in this country'.

mordant: 1. an adhesive for fixing gold leaf.
2. any fluid used to etch lines on a printing plate.

Mores, Edward Rowe, *c.* 1729–78: a scholar and antiquarian, remembered for his 'Dissertation on typographical founders and founderies'. He bought, in 1772, 'all the curious parts of that immense collection of punches, matrices, and types which had been accumulating from the days of Wynkyn de Worde to those of John James', a London type-founder. The collection was dispersed by sale in 1782.

Moretus, Jan, 1543–1610: an Antwerp printer who succeeded to the Plantin press in 1589, without, however, maintaining its standards. Of his sons, Jan (1576–1618) and Balthasar (1571–1641) who succeeded him, the latter produced the firm's finest work. He commissioned Rubens to prepare designs for many of his title-pages.

Descendants of the founder carried on the business until 1871, it being acquired in 1876 by the City of Antwerp for preservation as the 'Museum Plantin-Moretus'.

Morgan, John Pierpont, 1837–1913: an American financier, important here for the magnificent library of books and illuminated MSS. he assembled in New York. His son, J. P. Morgan, jun. (1867–1943), added to the collection and dedicated it to the public.

Morison, Stanley, 1889– : probably the most distinguished type-designer and typographer of the 20th century. He has been severally associated with the Pelican Press, the Monotype Corporation, Cambridge University Press, Victor Gollancz Ltd., 'The Times' (for which he designed Times New Roman), and the Fleuron.

See 'Signature' No. 3, March 1947, pp. 3–27; also 'A handlist of the writings of Stanley Morison', compiled by John Carter. (Privately published.) C.U.P., 1950.

morisques: typographical ornaments used to decorate the printed page, especially by Jean de Tournes of France in the 16th century.

moroccos: tanned goatskins, finished by glazing or polishing, and used for bookbinding. The use of morocco in France and Italy dates from the 16th century; in England it came into favour in the 17th century. Of all varieties Persian is the finest.

See also *cross-grain, French Cape Levant, glazed, hard-grain, Niger, Persian, straight-grain, Turkey morocco*. Cf. *calf.*

Morris, William, 1834–96: English poet, craftsman, socialist. In 1891 he started the *Kelmscott Press*, q.v., at Hammersmith, London, seeking to return to the style of the earliest printers and to break away from Victorian commercialism. The basic concepts of printing which he proclaimed were that the unit of book design should be the opening (two facing pages), and that type, imposition, paper, ink, and impression were interdependent. Morris had a tremendous influence on book design and production in England, Germany, and America. His principles inspired work done in the many private presses which were started as a result, and stimulated the improvement of standards in the wider field of commercial publishing; but his own books were costly and limited in number, while the richly inked gothic type and wooden blocks made their pages too heavy for easy reading.

To make Morris, his friends, their work and ideals better known the *William Morris Society* was established in London in 1955. Lectures, visits, and exhibitions are arranged, and a further function of the Society is to keep readily available to the public his literary works as well as his wall-papers and textiles.

mortise: 1. a space cut out of a printing plate in order to insert type or another plate.

2. the cutting away of metal from the non-printing area at the sides of a type to permit closer setting.

mosaic binding: see *inlaying*.

Moseley, Humphrey, fl. 1627–61: a celebrated London stationer and publisher of belles lettres and poetry, including works by Milton, Crashaw, Beaumont and Fletcher, Webster, Sir John Suckling, and the works of many other Elizabethan and Jacobean dramatists whose copyrights he acquired.

Motet Society: a society instituted in London in 1841, for the publication of ancient Church music. (M. L.)

mother set: a set of printing plates, e.g. of a standard reference work, kept solely for the purpose of electrotyping further sets from them.

mottled calf: calfskin, used for book covers, bearing an irregular pattern made by dabbing it with sponges dipped in acid or coloured dyes.

mottling: a fault in printing seen as an uneven impression and caused, especially in flat solid areas, by using too much pressure, an unsuitable paper, or an unsuitable ink.

mould: 1. the wire cloth and its surrounding frame on which pulp is shaken into a sheet of paper.

See also *paper-making*.

2. generally, any container in which molten metal is allowed to solidify into a required shape. In *type-casting*, q.v., the mould consists of a casting box with a matrix inside it. In *stereotyping*, q.v., an impression of a forme is taken in plaster or papier mâché; this, after drying, becomes the mould.

3. see *mildew*.

4. the special casting moulds on Linotype and Intertype machines are let into a mould wheel. Each mould consists of a base, screwed to the wheel and having surface rails for the matrix line, and a mould cap which is screwed to the base. Between the two measure and body liners are inserted, the length and thickness of which determine the opening and thus the size of the slug to be cast, and also an ejector blade. The Monotype mould is between the matrix case and the metal-pot; approximately in the middle

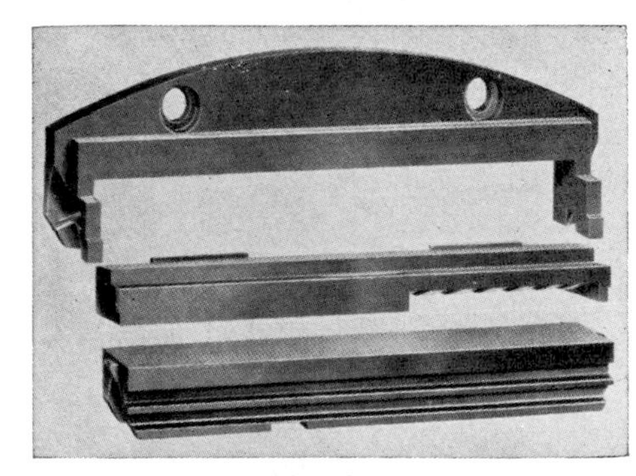

Intertype mould with liner and cover

it has a rectangular aperture of fixed size (body) in one direction and variable size in the other. The latter is determined by a movable wedge which alters the width according to the type being cast. The single matrix being cast at any given moment is positioned under a centring pin. (G. U.)

mould cleaners: felt wipers used on the Intertype and Linotype machines for cleaning the moulds as the mould wheel revolves. (G. U.)

mould machine: a cylinder machine used for the making of duplicator papers, liners, or *mould-made paper*, q.v.

mould-made paper: a manufactured imitation of hand-made paper. A machine for this purpose was invented by John Dickinson of Abbots Langley in 1808.

mould wheel: a wheel with a geared rim which has openings for the moulds used on the *Linotype* and *Intertype* casting machines, qq.v. When the wheel revolves the movement is controlled by a mould wheel brake fixed to the driving axle; a revolving brush behind the wheel serves as a cleaner. (G. U.)

Mould wheel for six moulds: four-mould wheels are usual

mount: pieces of wood or metal for mounting blocks, stereos, and electros.

Such block bases are made to standard point dimensions and can be assembled as needed for blocks of different sizes. To secure the block there are bases with inlet strips of wood to which the block is nailed. (G. U.)

Iron block bases with strips of wood inlet to take the nails

See also *blockmaking*, *facet*, *iron mount*, *plate-dog*.

mouthpiece: the orifice of a type-casting machine through which molten metal passes into the mould. In Intertype and Linotype machines this mouthpiece is in the form of a baffle plate with a row of holes about 2 mm. diameter and 6 mm. to 8 mm. from each other. (G. U.)

movable type: type cast as single-letter units. The term is usually limited to foundry type, set up by hand in a composing stick.

See also *printing—historical survey*, *type-casting*.

Moxon, Joseph, 1627–91: an hydrographer, instrument maker, author, and printer, who added a type-foundry to his London business in 1659. He may previously have worked in Holland for a time. In 1669 he issued his 'Prooves of the Several Sorts of Letters cast by Joseph Moxon'. This folio sheet shows eleven founts and is the first type-founder's full *specimen sheet*, q.v., known in England. In another work, 'Regulae Trium Ordinum . . . ', 1676, he outlined his rules for the geometrical proportion of letters and figures, but his fame rests on 'Mechanick Exercises', begun in 1677 as a series of monthly parts. Volume II of this work, 1683–84, was devoted to all aspects of printing and letter-founding, being the first English manual on the subject.

MS.: manuscript. **MSS.:** manuscripts.

mudéjar bindings: Spanish bindings of Cordovan leather done from the 13th–15th centuries. The main design was a blind-tooled pattern of double outline interlacings, or strapwork, with stamped strips of cords or knots, dots, curves, and rings as part of the subsidiary or background design. The Moorish inhabitants of 13th-century Christian Spain were known as mudéjares. They were allowed religious freedom and to practise their crafts, of which bookbinding was one.

See also *gótico mudéjar*.

mull: a coarse variety of muslin which forms the first lining of a case-bound book. It is glued to the back of the book, and in the course of binding adheres to the case in which it is largely responsible for holding the book. Abbreviated from the Hindi *mulmull*; it is also known as *scrim*.

Mullen, John W.: the inventor, in 1887, of an instrument designed to indicate the bursting strength of paper.

See also *paper testing*.

muller: the stone used as a levigator when grinding lithographic plates by hand.

Müller, Johann: see *stereotype*.

Müller, Johannes, 1436–76: see *Regiomontanus, Johannes*.

Muller stone: a stone or thick lump of glass, forming a kind of pestle, flat at the bottom, used for grinding pigments upon a slab of similar material. (M. L.)

Multifont type tray: the trade name for a British adaptation, by the Pitman Press, Bath, of the type-storage system invented in America by Robert H. Roy: it is there known as the *Rob Roy type tray*.

The unit is a steel tray 9 in. by 25½ in. on which are set out 108 small plastic boxes variously coloured. Type from the mechanical caster is laid in each box, the boxes are labelled with the character designation of each, and the loaded tray is then removed to the composing room. Different colour-combinations distinguish the various ranges of type in use at one time, and as any boxes not required for a particular job can be quickly removed, time is saved when laying a case with the special sorts required in scientific, mathematical, or mixed setting.

The Multifont Frame holds ninety-six trays in a quarter of the floor space needed for normal steel frames of the same capacity.

Multigraph: a machine for the cheap reproduction of brief matter by hand-set type on a light, quick-running press.

multiple rule: a rule in which two or more strips of brass or type metal are mounted on the same body.

muniments: the title-deeds or charters recording privileges belonging to a family, society, or corporation.

Munsell colour system: a system of colour measurement and notation devised by A. H. Munsell, of Massachusetts. It defines all colours in the psychological terms of hue, value, and chroma. (M. L.)

murex: a purple stain made from shellfish and used in the Middle Ages for the embellishment of manuscripts.

See also *illumination*.

music engraving: for engraving music, metal plates are used, formerly of pewter, but now a cheaper alloy of tin and lead. The plates are planed and the staves are made with a five-pointed scorer. The scoring must be repeated until the lines are sufficiently deep. After laying out the manuscript, the notes and any words are drawn on the plate with a needle and, guided by this work (which is in reverse), the letters and signs are punched in. The depth of punching may vary and any unevenness thus caused

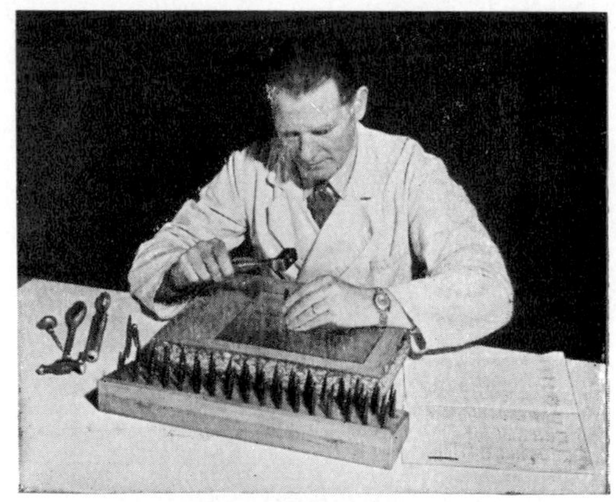

A music engraver at work

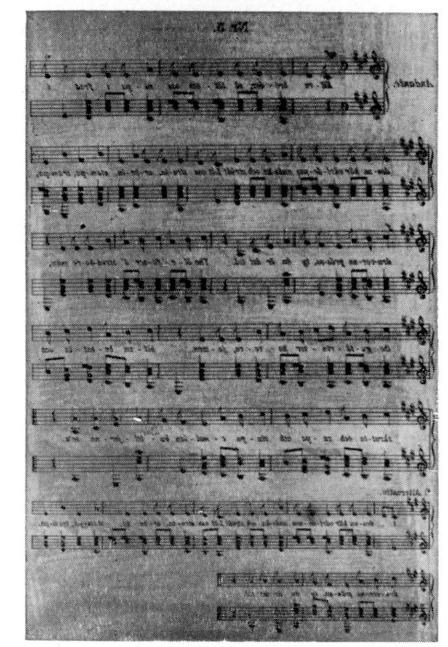

A finished plate

Music case and tools

on the back of the plate is removed by lightly hammering. Key signs, brackets, rests, etc., are on punches, but bars, slurs, and crescendos are usually hand-cut. The music engraver's case contains about 150 punches. Burrs on the front of the plates are removed with a scraper and a smoothing plane.

When engraving has been completed, an impression is taken for proof reading by colouring the plate (usually grey), and printing it in a small hand press. This gives a white script on a coloured ground. Corrections to the plates are made by flattening from the back the places where errors occur, and then engraving the correct notes. In order to identify on the back these places, the music engraver uses a pair of proof-reading marking callipers, with which he measures and scores the distance from the edge of the plate. When the plate is ready, positive impressions can be obtained by making prints on the intaglio principle, i.e. by inking the entire surface, wiping off the surplus, and allowing ink to remain only in the engraved depressions.

However, a plate of soft metal is not suitable for printing a large edition, and for this the music must be transferred to printing surfaces of other kinds. There are various methods. By a transfer, when using suitable ink and paper, lithographic printing plates for offset printing can be made. Impressions can also be taken for copying directly on prepared printing plates, or reproducing photographically.

See also *Hole, Robert, music printing.*

music printing: there are three main methods now in use for reproducing music script in print. The music can be set up in type with special sorts and printed by letterpress, it can be drawn on paper and reproduced photographically, or it can be produced by *music engraving*, q.v., in which case the actual printing is usually done by lithography.

Early printers left spaces in the text for the insertion by hand of the lines and musical notation; this was done in the Mainz Psalter of Fust and Schöffer: another method was to print the lines and insert the notes by hand. Alternatively, wooden or metal blocks were used at this time, an example being 'Musices opusculum' by Nicolaus Burtius, printed at Bologna by Ugo de Rugeriis in 1487.

Notes printed from movable types on hand-drawn stave-lines occur in 'Collectorium super Magnificat' of Jehan Charlier de Gerson, printed at Esslingen in 1473 by Conrad Fyner; the notation was in roman style with square symbols printed from quads.

A 'Graduale', probably printed at Ausgburg in 1473, of which a copy is in the British Museum, has gothic-style notation with symbols like four-pointed stars and the vertical strokes of gothic letters; the stave-lines are here printed.

Music printed by Ottaviano Petrucci, Venice, 1504. *He printed from movable types on previously printed staves*

Musical notation was first printed in Italy in Ulrich Han's 'Missale Romanum', 1476; Han first printed the staves in red, and with a second impression, the notes in black. In England, R. Higden's 'Polychronicon', printed in 1495 by Wynkyn de Worde, contained the earliest example of music printing: this took the form of eight notes built up from quads and rules.

The Venetian printer Ottaviano Petrucci invented in 1498 the printing from movable type of figured or measured music: this first appeared in his 'Harmonice musices odhecaton A', 1501. He carefully made several impressions in register to complete the music. Music printing in a single operation was probably first accomplished in 1525 by Pierre Haultin of Paris. His music types included parts of the staves on either side of the note in addition to the note itself. Between 1530 and 1640 printing from movable type was the general practice.

Music printed from engraved copper plates appeared first in Italy, about 1586, printed by S. Verovio, although it has been suggested that Petrus Sambonettus of Siena used such plates in 1515. In England, a set of nine 'Fantazies of III. Parts'

(Orlando Gibbons), *c.* 1606–10, may have been the first work so printed. By the end of this century music printing from engraved or punched metal plates was usual. The leading music engraver of the time was Thomas Cross (fl. 1683–1733) who stressed the superiority of engraved over punched plates with the words 'Beware of ye nonsensical puncht ones'. The engraved copper plates of Verovio were improved upon in 1724 when W. Croft used pewter plates on which notation was struck with punches.

Modern musical notation

Improved type-units were devised by Immanuel Breitkopf of Leipzig in 1754, and by Jean François Rosart, a contemporary. Breitkopf's improvement consisted of each type taking up only part of a single music line, with or without a note, so that the most complicated score could be type-set.

In the 19th century lithography became the leading method of printing music. Its inventor, Senefelder, was associated with Philipp H. André in the setting up of a lithographic works in London. The successor of André was Georg Johann Vollweiler who printed some music from stone at the Polyautographic Press (*c.* 1806). The first British firm to use lithography in a really large way was Augener & Co., 1853.

Later attempts were made to improve the method of printing from type, including the use of continuous steel rules for the staves and divided heads of notes. Notable was the progress made in this direction by William Clowes, jun. (1807–83). The music publisher Joseph Alfred Novello established a printing business in 1847 in which movable types were used, but by the turn of the century the firm was increasingly using the cheaper method of engraving.

In 1913 Linotype brought out a method of type-setting music script in vertical lines on a type-setting machine. Photographic type-setting machines for music printing have also been constructed, e.g. by B. Karlquist in 1949. (Partly G.U.)

Musical Antiquarian Society: a society instituted in London in 1840, for 'the reprinting of works of rarity, carefully edited'. (M.L.)

mutton: see *em quad.*

Mychell, John, fl. 1549–56: the first printer of Canterbury. His small output consisted of a Psalter and other religious works.

Myllar, Androw: a citizen of Edinburgh who held, jointly with *Walter Chepman,* q.v., the first licence to print in Scotland. Myllar had learned the craft of printing at Rouen, and brought French workmen with him to Edinburgh.

The granting of the licence in 1507 was probably a result of James IV's desire to have the newly compiled Aberdeen Breviary adopted throughout Scottish churches instead of the *Sarum use,* q.v. As Myllar's name does not appear in the Breviary, and Chepman is not known to have issued any works subsequently, it is probable that Myllar, the manager of the press, died while the Breviary was being printed.

ADDENDUM

Motif: a journal of the visual arts edited by Ruari McLean and James Shand, and published three times a year by the Shenval Press, London. It was established in 1958.

N

naked forme: see *forme*.

nap roller: the best quality lithographic roller consisting of a cylindrical wooden stock with two handles, covered with two or three layers of flannel to form a resilient packing for the outer cover of french calf. The latter is carefully sewn with the flesh or nap side outermost: the completed roller is then ready for oiling with tallow, vaseline or olive oil to make it waterproof and supple. Rolling in varnish is the subsequent stage to give a smooth velvet-like texture to the skin; this is alternated with careful scraping to remove loose fibres or dirt. When ready for use the surface should be soft with an even grain. During use the roller should be scraped daily to keep it in condition.

See also *composition roller, glazed roller*.

N.A.P.M.: see *National Association of Paper Merchants*.

narrow copy: a book with a board width less than two-thirds of its height.

National Association of Paper Merchants: the organization covering the British paper and board merchanting trade.

Until 1803 there was no permanent organization of the trade, though in the 18th century regional groups of paper-makers had met to discuss common problems. Thus in 1799 William Balston was chairman of the Master Paper Makers of Kent and also of the Master Paper Makers of England, who met in London. The Kent group represented more than thirty-seven manufacturers, the national group represented eighty. Their meetings were usually to deal with wage demands. The first union of paper-workers was established in 1800, though clubs and combinations of journeymen were active prior to this. The paper-makers had petitioned for an Act against workmen's combinations. It proved ineffectual, so in 1801 the Society of Master Paper Makers of the Counties of Kent and Surrey was formed to resist the workers' demands. June 1803 saw the formation of the United Society of Master Paper Makers of Great Britain, representing 120 firms, with Balston as chairman.

All through the 19th century co-ordinated activity among paper-makers was limited to combating taxation and resisting wage demands. It was not until the turn of the century that the need was felt to establish trade customs and organization. In 1903 the Association of Wholesale Stationers and Paper Merchants was formed for this purpose, and in 1906, in conjunction with the Paper Makers' Association, the first set of trade customs governing the sale of British paper was issued. In the next decade several local Associations were formed or developed, e.g. in Birmingham, Bradford, Leeds, Manchester, and Scotland. After 1918, when the Paper Makers' Association had been renamed the British Paper and Board Makers' Association, it was decided to form a national association of merchants to regulate the buying and selling of paper: this resulted in 1920 in the National Association of Wholesale Stationers and Paper Merchants. The scope of the Association was increased to include all merchants of paper and board, and the name National Association of Paper Merchants (N.A.P.M.) was adopted in 1930.

The objects of the N.A.P.M. are to take all possible action to safeguard and promote the interests of the paper-distributing trade, to negotiate with the Government and also other trade associations, and to deal with wage and labour matters. For the purposes of organization the United Kingdom is divided into eight areas, each under a committee; and each area is subdivided into trade sections for the various types of paper product (boards; corrugated; fancy; flint and enamels; featherweights; printings and writings; and wrappings).

Membership is open to firms, persons, and companies carrying on the business of paper or board merchants.

National Book Committee: a body formed in New York, in 1954, to further public interest in books. Its initial aims were the increasing of personal reading so that it develops into a lifetime habit, the extension of public library service, and the stimulation of an adequate flow oversea of those American books which will contribute to a clearer understanding of American policies, life, and thought.

National Book League: an independent and non-profit-making organization, developed in 1944 out of the National Book Council which was founded in 1925 on the initiative of Sir Stanley Unwin. Membership is open to all. It exists to stimulate a wider interest in reading and literature, and to further these aims holds excellent book exhibitions and issues authoritative bibliographies.

The League's address is 7 Albemarle Street, London, W.1.

National Book Trade Provident Society: an association existing to help members of the bookselling and publishing trades, also their dependants, by making grants of financial assistance when needed. In addition to donations from firms and individuals funds derive from members' dues (6/– a year, or £5 for life membership).

The society also operates a pension scheme to assist employers who could not independently provide pensions for their staff. Details can be obtained from the Secretary at 215 Watford Way, London, N.W.4.

See also *Book Trade Benevolent Committee.*

natural tint: a description for paper of a light cream colour.

nature printing: the process of pressing such objects as leaves or ferns on to a soft metal plate so as to impress their outlines in it. The idea of nature printing originated in the 15th century at which time the dried leaf or plant was uniformly blackened over a flame, placed under paper, and lightly rubbed, thus leaving an impression of the plant on the paper. The most successful of subsequent methods was devised in Vienna in 1852 by Louis Auer and Andrew Worring, two employees of the State Printing House. The plants were pressed into a plate of soft lead and an electrotype was made of the result. This was a quicker method and gave a permanent print of astonishing fidelity.

near-print: a general term for substitute printing processes. Typewriter-composition and offset printing form the basis of such techniques. The *Justowriter*, q.v., is an example.

neck: the part of a type character which is between the shoulder and the face; commonly called *bevel.*

negative: in photographing with a camera a negative image is normally obtained upon developing, from which positive pictures can be produced by contact printing or enlarging. (By reversal developing, positive pictures can be obtained direct, a principle used in colour photography.)

Transparent positives, properly diapositives, which are held up to light when viewing are often erroneously called negatives. (G. U.)

neo-caroline: another name for the humanistic script of the 15th century.

Neocol: a process invented by Murray C. Beebe for producing screen transparent positives which can be retouched for offset reproduction. A special base resembling asphalt on glass can be developed and etched after copying by using a mixture of benzine and paraffin. A copying medium for block copying is also given this name. (G. U.)

Nesbit, Charlton, 1775–1838: a distinguished wood engraver and one time apprentice of *Thomas Bewick*, q.v. He achieved considerable fame as a book illustrator, some of his best work appearing, with that of others, in Ackermann's 'Religious Emblems', 1809.

net: said of the price of any book which is not subject to a retail discount or reduction.

See also *Net Book Agreement*, 1957.

Net Book Agreement, 1957: an agreement between publishers that the net prices they fix for their books shall be the prices at which those books are sold to the public, and that they will not permit them to be sold at less than the net price. The 1901 Net Book Agreement, now replaced, was based on the right of the Publishers Association to act on behalf of its publisher members in ensuring that the conditions of supply of net books were observed.

The 1957 agreement was made necessary when the Restrictive Trading Practices Act of 1956 banned *collective* measures for the maintenance of resale prices. This meant that publishers, having stated their conditions of sale, could only take *individual* action against any offender selling their books at less than the net prices in breach of those conditions. A publisher can enforce the condition of sale right down the line of distribution, as, for example, in the case of books bought by a bookseller from a wholesaler.

The text of the 1957 Agreement is reproduced here by permission of the Publishers Association:

> We, the undersigned several firms of publishers, being desirous that in so far as we publish books at net prices (as to which each publisher is free to make his own decisions), those net prices shall normally be the prices at which such books are sold to the public as hereinafter defined, and in order to avoid disorganization in the book trade and to ensure that the public may be informed of and able uniformly to take advantage of the conditions under which net books may be sold at less than the net prices, hereby agree to adopt and each of us does hereby adopt the following standard sale conditions for the net books published by us within the United Kingdom:

Standard Conditions of Sale of Net Books

(i) Except as provided in clauses (ii) and (iv) hereof and except as we may otherwise direct net books shall not be sold or offered for sale or caused or permitted to be sold or offered for sale to the public at less than the net published prices.

(ii) A net book may be sold or offered for sale to the public at less than the net published price if

(*a*) it has been held in stock by the bookseller for a period of more than twelve months from the date of the latest purchase by him of any copy thereof and

(*b*) it has been offered to the publisher at cost price or at the proposed reduced price whichever shall be the lower and such offer has been refused by the publisher.

(iii) A net book may be sold or offered for sale to the public at less than the net published price if it is second hand and six months have elapsed since its date of publication.

(iv) A net book may be sold at a discount to such libraries, book agents (including Service Unit libraries), quantity buyers and institutions as are from time to time authorized by the Council of The Publishers Association of such amount and on such conditions as are laid down in the instrument of authorization. Such amount and conditions shall not initially be less or less favourable than those prevailing at the date of this Agreement.

(v) For the purposes of clause (i) hereof a book shall be considered as sold at less than the net published price if the bookseller

(*a*) offers or gives any consideration in cash to any purchaser except under licence from the Council of The Publishers Association or

(*b*) offers or gives any consideration in kind (e.g. card indexing, stamping, reinforced bindings, etc., at less that the actual cost thereof to the bookseller).

(vi) For the purposes of this Agreement and of these Standard Conditions:

Net book shall mean a book, pamphlet, map or other similar printed matter published at a net price. *Net price* and *net published price* shall mean the price fixed from time to time by the publisher below which the net book shall not be sold to the public.

Public shall be deemed to include schools, libraries, institutions and other non-trading bodies.

Person shall include any company, firm, corporation, club, institution, organization, association or other body.

(vii) The above conditions shall apply to all sales executed in the United Kingdom and the Republic of Ireland whether effected by wholesaler or retailer when the publisher's immediate trade customer, whether wholesaler or retailer, or the wholesaler's immediate trade customer, is in the United Kingdom or the Republic of Ireland.

We the undersigned several firms of publishers further agree to appoint and each of us does hereby appoint the Council of The Publishers Association to act as our agent in the collection of information concerning breaches of contract by persons selling or offering for sale net books, and in keeping each individual publisher informed of breaches in respect of such net books as are published by him and we further hereby undertake and agree that we will each enforce our contractual rights and our rights under the Restrictive Trade Practices Act 1956 if called upon to do so by the Council of The Publishers Association and provided that we shall be indemnified by The Publishers Association if so requested by us in respect of any costs of such action incurred by us or by the Council of The Publishers Association on our behalf.

(Here will follow the names and addresses of the signatory publishers.)

net net: an indication that a book so marked or described must be sold at the full published price, and that the publisher will not allow any discount to the book trade.

The use of this term is confined almost exclusively to reference works published at the lowest possible sum for the benefit of the trade, and not normally resold by its members.

Neumeister, Johann, fl. 1470–72: a German printer who, in 1470, established the first printing press at Foligno in Italy. He printed only three known works, but is remembered since one of these was the first edition of Dante's 'Divina commedia', 1472.

new edition: an edition of a book in which fresh material has been added and existing material revised. Also known as *revised edition*. Cf. *issue*.

New Sydenham Society: see *Sydenham Society*.

Newcastle on Tyne Typographical Society: a printing society instituted in 1818. Subjects published included poetry, angling, biography, history, coins and medals, and printing. (M. L.)

Newdigate Prize Foundation: a trust established by Sir Roger Newdigate (1719–1806) for the annual award of £21 for verse written by a member of Oxford University.

nib: the small projection on the end of a composing rule, by which the compositor takes the rule from between the lines after setting. (M. L.)

nibbed: a term used where folded maps and the like are trimmed to provide a wide tongue which is tipped to the text of a book. This permits free opening of the map. The tongue is termed a *nib*. (L.K.)

Nicholson, William: a London inventor of the 19th century for details of whose innovations see *ink roller, printing press, stereotype.*

nick: a groove on the body or shank of type cast as an aid to placing it the right way up in the composing stick and in identifying the fount. The single Monotype nick is simply to distinguish the front of the type from the back.

nickel-electro: when making electros of half-tones a lead mould is sometimes used. For long runs a nickel shell is deposited on this and then a final layer of copper. Cf. *nickel-faced electro.*

nickel-faced electro: the copper surface of an electro which is made more durable by coating it with nickel. Cf. *nickel-electro.*

nickel plating: the protective surface coating of nickel given to blocks, stereos, and other printing formes by nickel plating in a galvanic bath. The shining nickel surface resists both mechanical and chemical action. The plating bath usually consists of nickel sulphate or nickel ammonia sulphate in water; to this is added a conducting salt such as sal ammoniac, alkali citrate, etc., or boric acid, citric acid, or other weak acid. The degree of acid must be carefully checked and regulated during plating. A pH value of 5·5–5·8 is considered suitable. Cast or rolled nickel plates are used as anodes.

On many materials which have been nickel plated it is difficult or impossible to remove the coating. A not wholly successful coating can sometimes be improved by giving a coating of copper in a potassium cyanide copper bath (see *copper depositing*), and then re-nickelling. *Hard nickel plating* is the simultaneous depositing of nickel and cobalt. (G.U.)

Nicol, George, 1741–1829: bookseller to George III, and later, with *John Boydell,* q.v., founder of the 'Shakspeare Press'. His son William continued the press from 1819 until it closed in 1855.

Niepce, Joseph Nicéphore, 1765–1833: a French landowner and inventor who was a pioneer of photography. He used asphalt as a light-sensitive substance, and was the first to produce permanent photographs by means of a camera, 1822.

As the exposure time was too protracted, he combined with *L. J. M. Daguerre,* q.v., in improving the method. After the death of Niepce the latter discovered a quicker method of photography, using copper plates, 1837. (G.U.)

See also *daguerreotype.*

Niger morocco: a tough, but flexible, acid-free goatskin, dyed in various shades of red, or sometimes green, and used for fine bookbinding. A product of Nigeria.

nihil obstat: words meaning 'nothing hinders', which occasionally appear on the verso of the title-pages of Roman Catholic books as an indication that they are free of doctrinal or moral error, and have received a Catholic censor's approval.

See also *imprimatur.*

nipping: see *smashing.*

nipping up: a stage in hand-binding, prior to covering, in which nippers are used to give shape to the bands.

Nipping up the bands

After drawing the pasted cover over the book the leather is nipped up over the bands before being stretched and smoothed down on the boards.

Niven Literary Award: see *Frederick Niven Literary Award.*

Nivetron sheet control: an electromagnetic device, made by AB Inventing of Stockholm, for the control of sheet feed and delivery. It consists of front and side lay micro-switch controls, a micro-switch two-sheet caliper, detection fingers for the delivery strippers, a solenoid which operates the cylinder-trip and machine-braking mechanism, timing cams, and a control box. The controls are fitted to appropriate points on the press, and can be adjusted to detect crumpled sheets, sheets with folded corners, variations in the side lay or front lays, sheets fouling the front lays, etc. Visible and audible warnings attract the attention of the machine-man, and the press is automatically stopped. The control-panel light indicates where the fault is. In Britain the device is manufactured under licence by J. F. Crosfield Ltd., and can be fitted to most sheet-fed presses.

Nobel Prize for Literature: the prize founded by Alfred Bernhard Nobel in 1900, and awarded annually by the Swedish Academy, Stockholm, to 'the person who shall have produced in the field of literature the most distinguished work of an idealistic tendency'.

Nodis caster: a small type-casting machine in which Monotype, Linotype, or Intertype matrices may be used in addition to Nodis matrices.

nom-de-plume: a pen-name; assumed by an author who wishes to conceal his identity.

non-net books: copies of a work, usually a text-book sold in bulk to schools, on the sale of which a bookseller may, at his personal discretion, allow a discount. Copies may not, however, be sold at less than their cost to the bookseller.

See also *Net Book Agreement*, 1957, *terms*.

Non-Parliamentary papers: papers issued by Government Departments covering their activities.

Nonesuch Press: the publishing house established in 1923 by Miss Mendel, David Garnett, and Sir Francis Meynell, with the aim of adapting mechanical methods to the production of finely made books which were to be sold at modest cost through normal trade channels. Sir Francis prepared the designs and layout of each work.

After a period of inactivity during the war the Press re-started in 1953 with the production of the Nonesuch Shakespeare, in four volumes.

nonpareil: the name for a former size of type, now replaced by 6-point. The designation, used by Jean de Tournes of Lyons in 1547, and by his contemporaries, later spread throughout Europe. It is still used for a 6-point lead.

Norden, John, *c.* 1548–1625: an Elizabethan cartographer, remembered now for his uncompleted series of county maps and those of Tudor London, *c.* 1593. He was probably the first to enter the main roads of counties on maps.

Northumbrian School: a name given to the style of illumination characteristic of manuscripts originating in northern England during the era 650–850. It was here that monks from Ireland, England, and elsewhere gathered, their various influences being traceable in the development of manuscript painting.

Features are interlaced strapwork, at first largely geometric and probably deriving from Roman mosaics and sculpture, but later less disciplined and with the animal forms found in Anglo-Saxon jewellery of the period. A cruciform was often the basic design.

The finest surviving examples are the *Book of Durrow*, *Book of Kells*, *Echternach MSS.*, and *Lindisfarne Gospels*, qq.v.

Norton, Bonham, 1565–1635: a London publisher-printer, son of *William Norton*, q.v., and sometime Master of the Stationers' Company. He was also King's Printer for law books.

Norton, John, fl. 1590–1612: a nephew of *William Norton*, q.v., a London printer who was sometime Master of the Stationers' Company and Queen's Printer for Latin and Greek texts.

Norton, William, 1527–93: the first of a family of London printers. He was an original freeman of the Stationers' Company.

not: properly, *not glazed.* This is a finish in high-quality rag papers, and is midway between *rough*, which is without finish, and *hot pressed*, which is a smooth plate-glazed finish. Papers finished in all three ways are used in *fashion boards*, q.v.

Notary, Julian, fl. 1498–1520: a French binder-printer of London. Of his few surviving works a Sarum Missal printed for Wynkyn de Worde is the most important; in this he was partnered by Jean Barbier. While mostly a printer of service books he also issued 'The Golden Legend' in 1504, 'Chronicles of England' in 1515, and 'Kalender of Shepardes', *c.* 1518.

notes: references too long to be treated as *footnotes*, q.v. They may follow a chapter or appear at the end of a book, in a smaller size of type.

novel: 1. a fictitious prose narrative sufficiently long to fill one or more volumes.

See also *three-decker novel*, *yellow-backs*.

2. as *Novels*, constitutions or decrees of the Emperor Justinian, published *c.* 534 as supplements to his 'Corpus Juris Civilis'.

novela: a short prose narrative, usually dealing with one situation, generally of a surprising or unusual nature.

Novographic process: the trade name given by Messrs. Lowe & Brydone of London to the method of reproducing and printing books by photo offset lithography initiated by them in 1922. The first book produced by this method was E. A. Minchin's 'Introduction to the Study of Protozoa', London, Arnold. The process is now extensively used when reprinting out-of-print works.

Nu-chrome process: see *bimetallic lithographic plates.*

number books: books published serially. The term particularly relates to a method of publishing which in England developed in the 18th century whereby books were sold in consecutively numbered parts, or fascicules, issued monthly or weekly. Each part consisted of two or more sheets stitched together within blue-paper covers. The title-page for the whole book would either be issued and dated at the time of the first part, or with the last some weeks or months later. Publishing in fascicule form is still occasionally used for popular illustrated encyclopaedias, as for more scholarly works.

See R. M. Wiles, 'Serial publication in England before 1750', C.U.P., 1957.

numbered copy: a copy of a book issued in a *limited edition,* q.v., which has a notice, usually in the colophon, of the total number of copies of the work printed, and an individual copy number inserted by hand. The custom of numbering books in this way is said to have been originated by Bodoni.

The practice of numbering separately each copy of a work may also be used as a security measure for restricted official publications.

See also *out of series, overs.*

numerals: see *arabic numerals, hanging figures, ranging figures, roman numerals, split fractions.*

nut quad: see *en quad.*

ADDENDA

National Book Sale: a sale to the public of publishers' and booksellers' overstocks at bargain prices. The sale, which was proposed by Mr. Thomas Joy in an article 'Sales Weeks and the Bookseller' in 'The Publishers Circular' during 1936, was first held in 1955. A second sale was held in 1956 and a third in 1958. The sale is arranged by a joint committee appointed by the Publishers Association and the Booksellers Association under the chairmanship of Mr. Joy. This committee fixes the date of the sale period which is the same for the whole country.

A licence is issued to participating booksellers and publishers for which a fee is charged. The fees are used for sale publicity. Simple rules govern the sale: when the dates have been fixed no bookseller may sell in advance of or after the sale at reduced prices. Publishers agree that their overstocks may be sold at half-price or less. A bookseller may sell at any price but not higher than two-thirds of the published price.

In this way new books are available as genuine bargains and the public has quickly appreciated the good value offered. It is estimated that over a million books at bargain prices were sold in the ten-day period of the 1958 National Book Sale.

Nebitype: a machine for casting display matter in slugs from hand-set matrices, developed in Italy by an associate firm of the Società Nebiolo of Turin. The Nebitype will cast type in sizes from 18-point upwards in a line up to 42½ ems measure. Ludlow and Linotype matrices may be used in addition to the wide range offered by Nebiolo.

The machine was first shown in 1958.

O

oasis goat: 1. leather for book covers, obtained from goats found in the Cape of Good Hope region.

2. the trade name for a second-quality Niger morocco tanned in sumach and dyed.

obelisk: the printer's reference mark †, or *dagger*.

See also *reference marks*.

obituary roll: see *bead-roll*.

oblong: a book which is wider than it is high. Hence oblong quarto, oblong folio.

Synonymous with *landscape*.

obscene libel: any publication which tends to deprave and corrupt those whose minds are open to such immoral influences, and into whose hands the publication may fall. The issuing of such a work is a common law misdemeanour triable on indictment. In prosecutions the jury must read the publication said to be obscene and form their own opinions.

octateuch: a volume containing the first eight books of the Old Testament. They were extensively produced in Constantinople (843–1204) and were often illuminated.

octavo: written 8vo. The book size resulting from folding a sheet of paper with three right-angle folds, thus giving pages one-eighth the size of the sheet and forming a 16-page section. To define fully, the paper size must also be stated, e.g. Crown 8vo. If for binding purposes a 32-page section were required, paper of double size would be used and given four folds. (L. K.)

octodecimo: see *eighteenmo*.

odd: in paper-making, sheets that are not according to regular or standard sizes, weights, finishes, colours, etc. (M. L.)

odd folios: the page-numbers which come on the the first side of the leaf, 1, 3, 5, 7, 9, etc. (M. L.)

off: a forme is 'off' when all the sheets required have been printed, and it is ready to be taken off the press. (M. L.)

off-cut: waste portions of paper, boards, cloth, etc., resulting from trimming stock to the size required: if the off-cuts are of usable size they may serve for other jobs. (L. K.)

off its feet: said of type which does not stand squarely on its base. Type must stand exactly on its feet in order to give a good impression. (M. L.)

off-print: a separately printed copy of an article or paper which has appeared in a larger publication. It may or may not be enclosed in a cover. Also known as a *separate* or an *overprint*.

Officina Arbutucana: see *Strawberry Hill Press*.

Officina Bodoni: the famous Italian private press founded in 1923 at Montagnola di Lugano. It was granted an exclusive licence to use the punches of Bodoni, kept in the Museum of Parma. The leader of the press was *Giovanni Mardersteig*, q.v., who stated in 1929 'A book consists of five elements: the text, the type, the ink, the paper, and the binding. To create a unity from these five elements in such a way that the result is not a passing product of fashion, but assumes the validity of permanent value—that is our desire.'

The first work to appear was 'Orphei tragedia' of Angelo Poliziano, 1923, to be followed by editions of Shelley, Goethe, Shakespeare, Dante, Browning, Seneca, and Plato, all in their original languages. The books were printed on hand-made paper, either Fabriano or Du Marais.

In 1927 the press moved to Verona for its most ambitious project: this was an edition of Gabriele d'Annunzio in forty-nine volumes, sponsored by the Italian Government. It was completed in 1936.

Mardersteig later set up the Stamperia Valdonega in Verona where trade editions of machine-set and machine-printed books are produced in close collaboration with the Officina Bodoni.

See 'Officina Bodoni, Verona: catalogue of books printed on the hand-press, MCMXXIII–MCMLIV', British Museum, 1954.

Officina Serpentis: a private press founded in 1911 by E. W. Tieffenbach in Berlin, with the aim of reviving the former traditions of hand-printing, coloured initials, etc. The press issued many works by Martin Luther in addition to classics.

offset blanket: a series of layers of cotton, cemented into a unit with rubber solution, and given a final surface of rubber.

Blankets are made to standard thicknesses.

See also *offset printing*.

offset ink: ink for lithographic offset printing must be ground very fine, free from water-soluble particles, and must contain only lithographic varnish or certain lacquers as binding material. The ink must be insensitive to sulphur, since this is an ingredient of the rubber printing rollers. Great strength is demanded from offset ink, for the rubber has the disadvantage of not transferring all the ink to the paper which it takes up from the plate. The ink tends to emulsify, giving a weak impression or causing trouble on the machine. Modern offset inks, made from synthetic resin bases, are more stable. An example is 'Nuolith' ink by Coates Bros. (G. U.)

offset lithography: printing in which the inked impression from a lithographic plate is received upon a rubber surface (see *blanket*), from which it is transferred to the printing paper.

offset press: this usually means a machine for lithographic offset printing, although presses have been constructed for intaglio or letterpress work on the offset principle. The first offset presses were built for printing from stone on to tin, but about the time the idea was adapted for printing on paper metal plates for the printing surface came into common use, facilitating rotary printing. Offset presses for printing from stone fell into disuse, and attention was concentrated on presses to print from plates curved around cylinders. Where printing from flat lithographic plates or stones occurs now, in offset work, is for proof printing, or printing on glass or some special substance. In 1905 Rubel set up an offset machine at the Eastern Lithographic Co., New York, and imported a model into England in 1906. His machine was built according to the 'American' system by which three cylinders of equal size make a complete revolution for each impression. The model was built and sold all over the world by the Potter Printing Press Co.

In England the George Mann Co. patented in 1906 the offset machine shown in the diagram. It embodied the two-revolution system, the paper-carrying cylinder making two turns for each impression. In 1912 L & M brought out an offset press in which both the rubber and paper cylinders made two revolutions while the plate cylinder was making one. Machines based on the Potter system were made by Waite & Saville Ltd., in 1909, and by Furnival & Co. in 1912.

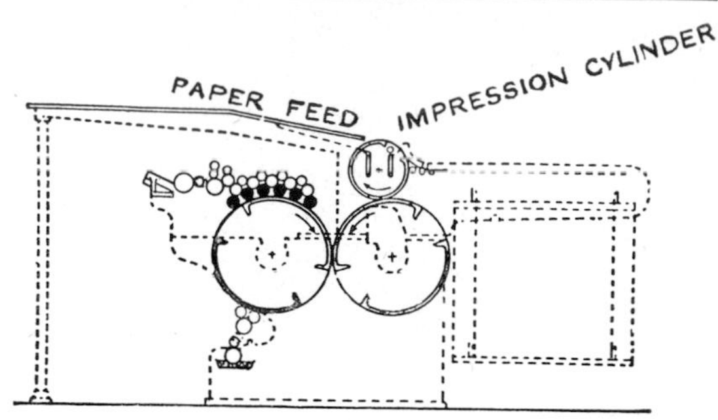

Offset press, George Mann, 1906

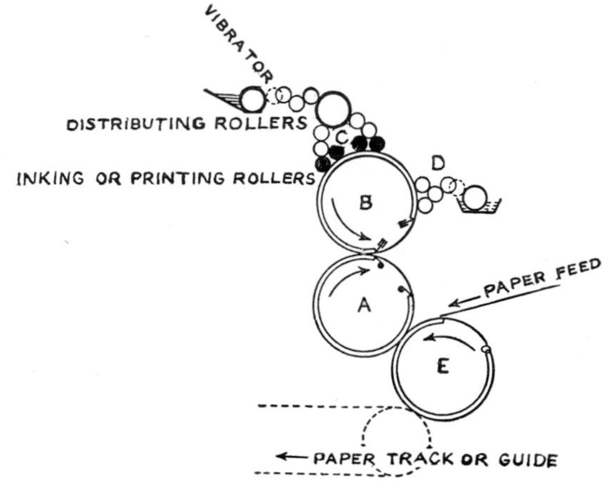

'Potter system' with three equal cylinders

Single-colour press on the two-cylinder system

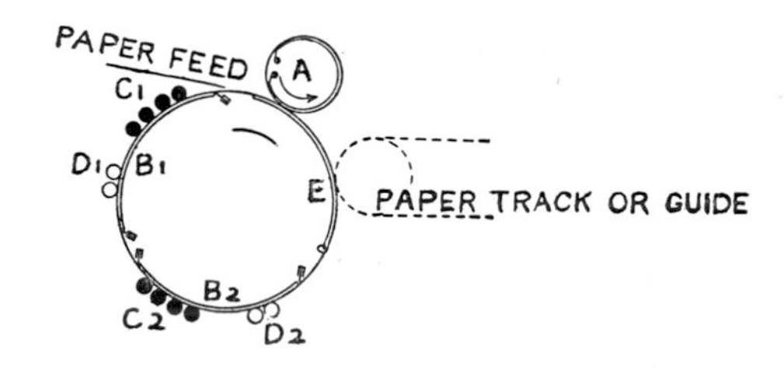

Two-colour machine on the two-cylinder system

A—rubber cylinder. B—forme cylinder. C—inkers (C and C, rise and fall alternately). D—damping device. E—portion of the cylinder bearing the paper which serves as an impression cylinder

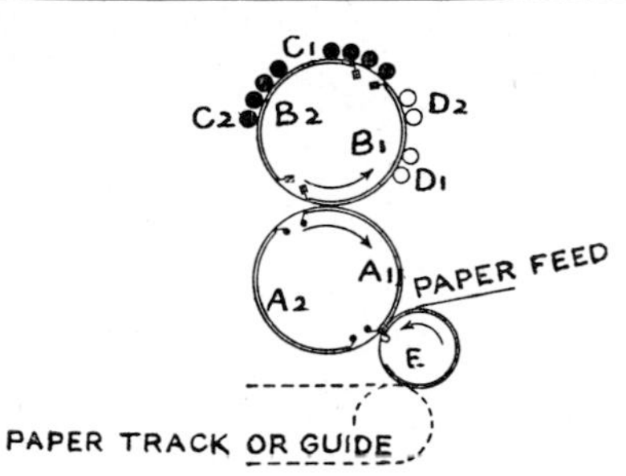

Two-colour press with a plate cylinder, and inkers which rise and fall alternately

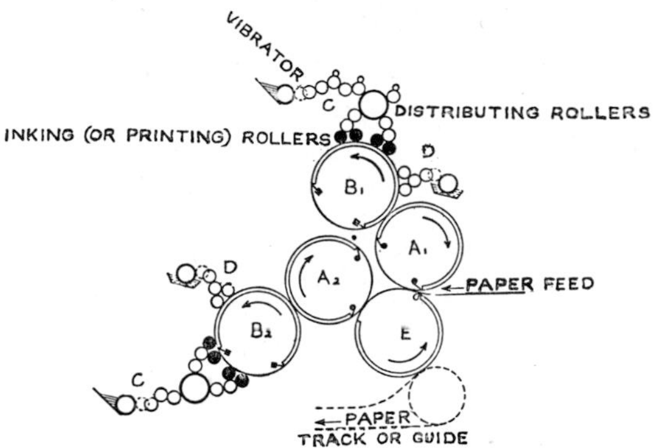

Modern two-colour machine (Roland)

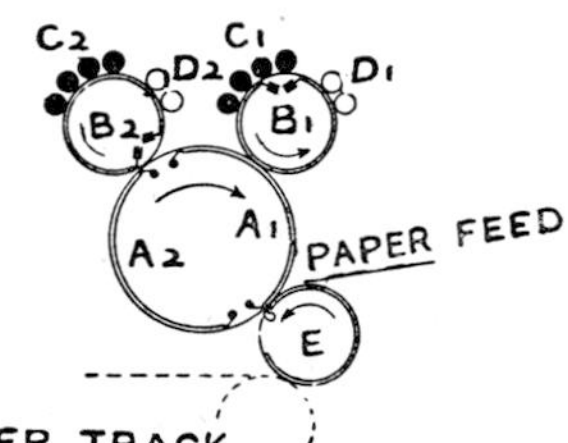

Two-colour machine with two plate cylinders, but only one rubber cylinder

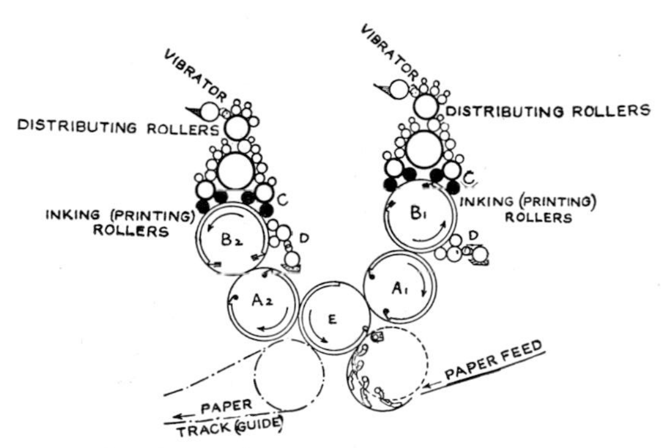

Modern two-colour machine (Planeta, Mann)

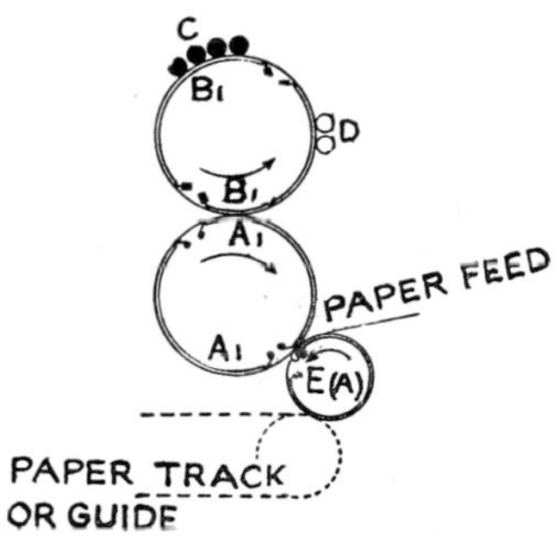

Sheet perfector with joint plate cylinder and joint rubber cylinder

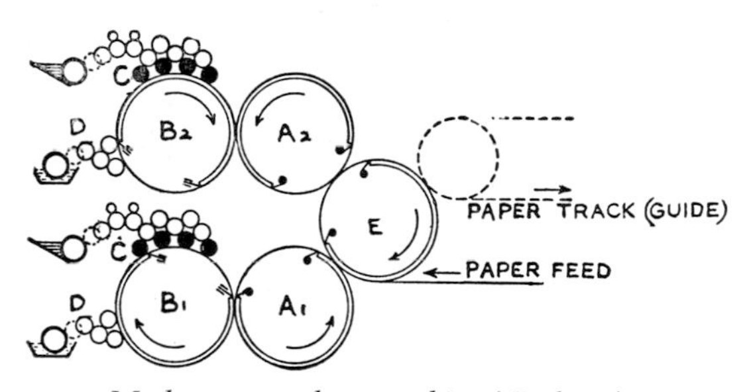

Modern two-colour machine (Crabtree)

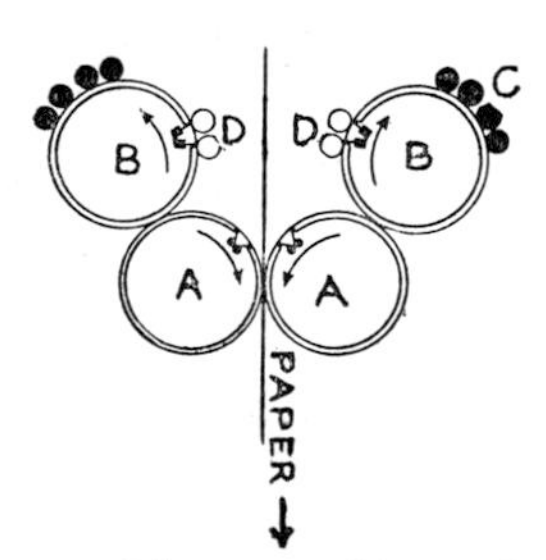

Reel-fed perfector. The two rubber cylinders serve as counter-pressure cylinders to one another

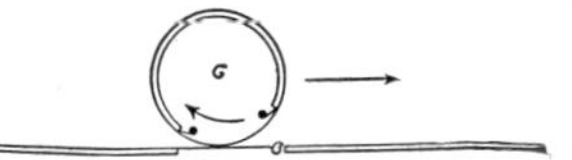

Usual construction of an offset proofing press. The cylinder rolls over a flat plate and sheet

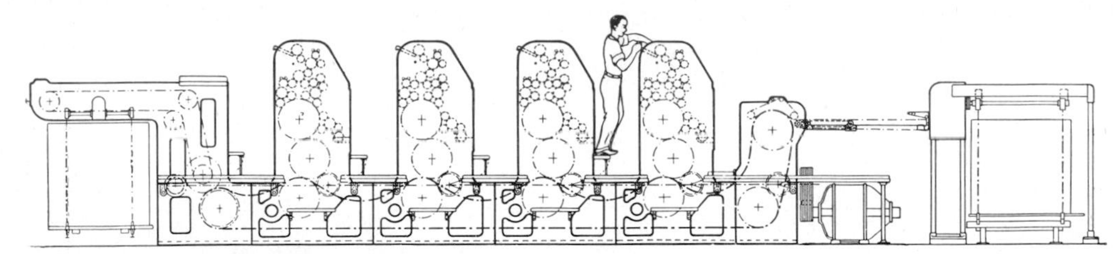

In Hoe's four-colour offset press the paper is guided through the machine by the same gripper rod

Roland two-colour offset press

Cylinder-adjusting arrangement in an offset press (Planeta, Mann)

Offset proofing press with inking and damping devices (Druckma, Leipzig)

Caspar Hermann introduced offset printing into Germany in 1907. He patented a two-cylinder offset press, and later an offset perfecting machine. The manufacture of offset machines was taken up by several German firms, but progress was interrupted by the 1914–18 war, and it was not until the late 1920's that German makers widely adopted the 'American' system which is now the main one used for modern machines. All modern offset presses have a chain delivery.

Different principles for the construction of two-colour or multicolour machines are shown in the accompanying diagrams. For such machines, too, the 'American' system predominates, but in combining two three-cylinder machines they can be given a joint paper cylinder, the result being a five-cylinder machine; or the two machines can be entirely separated which necessitates a transferring cylinder between them or seven cylinders in all. The Crabtree and Roland machines illustrated here are of the former type, as is the Planeta Super-Quinta, although the positioning of the cylinders and many other details vary.

Offset proof-printing machines (hand-presses) are usually constructed with a rubber cylinder which rolls over a flat printing plate (inked by hand or mechanically) and then over the paper. In addition to proof printing, such presses are used for direct transfers or for producing reversed proofs on transfer paper. (G. U.)

Inserting a printing plate into an offset press

offset printing: a planographic printing process in which the forme and sheet have no direct contact. The impression of printing plates is taken up by a rubber sheet or roller and from this transferred to the printing paper. Owing to the resilience of the rubber this indirect process gives sharp impressions even on unglazed paper. Generally the term offset is associated with lithography, though book printing can be done in this way, and attempts at intaglio-offset have been made.

Offset printing can be traced to a patent of Robert Barclay, 1875, who used a cylinder covered with card instead of a blanket, and in any case printed on tin. That it could be used for printing on paper was not discovered until 1904: this was by Rubel and Hermann in America; the latter introduced the process into Germany in 1907, and thus to Europe generally. (G. U.)

See also *offset press*, *photo-litho offset*.

offset reproduction: for reproducing text matter type is set, made up into pages, and a reading proof pulled. After correction, a perfect impression of the type is photographed and the negative placed with others, both of text and any accompanying illustrations, on a 'lay-sheet'. The assembled negatives are exposed to a sensitized grained metal plate. This is developed and placed on the cylinder of the offset press. The foregoing is for big printings: otherwise the text of an already printed copy is photographed.

For reproducing line drawings photo-litho paper which was copied and transferred was long in use, but for screen process work there was at first no better expedient than to produce ordinary printers' blocks and make transfers from them to the offset plates. By about 1920 it was realized that for first-class offset reproductions direct copying (without a transfer of the screen image to the printing plate) was necessary, and improved retouching methods (corresponding to tone etching in making half-tone blocks) were needed. The former was facilitated by the step-and-repeat machines then appearing in the U.S.A.; the latter has been done in many ways. An early practical method was that of Müller (about 1925) by which screen negatives exposed in a special way in the camera could be retouched with graphite, by painting, and scraping, prior to copying on the printing plate. The Chromorecta process invented by H. Schupp of Dresden in 1927 forms the basis of most modern methods of offset reproduction: it consists, briefly, in producing from a half-tone negative, by exposure in the camera, a screen transparency with cone-shaped dots in the bed which can be etched down by chemical means to the desired size without losing the covering power. The Hausleiter processes (F. H. Hausleiter, Munich, 1927) and Beka offset retouching methods (Bekk & Kaulen, Cologne) serve the same purpose, the latter also making it possible to strengthen the screen point. In all these methods the principal work is done on the screen transparency from which negatives are produced, if necessary, by contact copying or in an enlarging apparatus.

Offset plates were formerly made exclusively by copying negatives on chrome albumen (see *albumen process*); latterly, a partial change has occurred in favour of positive copying, especially in connection with the deep etching of the image in the printing plate. Such copying is generally done on chromate glue by various methods (Manultief, Bekatief), after which the image revealed on developing is etched to a certain depth before being inked in (see *deep-etch process*). Instead of the usual zinc or aluminium plates, bimetallic plates are used now for offset printing (for large editions), the copying and treatment of plates being done in such a way that an image is obtained in ink-attracting metal on a base of another metal to which the ink is less able to adhere. These methods include Alkuprint (copper surface and aluminium base) and the Pax method which also permits etching the copied screen point on the printing plate. Modern processes of this kind use a combination of copper and stainless steel (Aller), or of copper and chrome (Coates Bros.).

See also *Kodak Lithofoil*. (G. U.)

ola books: books in which are enshrined the Sinhalese literature of Ceylon. The books are made of olas or strips taken from the young leaves of the Talipot or Palmyra palm. After soaking in hot water the leaves are pressed smooth. They are cut into strips about 3 in. wide and from 1 to 3 feet long. Through a hole pierced at each end a cord is passed so as to secure the leaves between two lacquered wooden boards. They thus form a book.

Writing is done with an iron stylus and the incisions in the leaf are made more easily visible by rubbing in a mixture of charcoal and oil. It is probably due to the aromatic and preservative properties of the oil that the books have survived from pre-Christian days to the present. They are still made in the Buddhist monasteries of Ceylon.

Old English (or **English**): a black-letter type having angular emphasis, i.e. Old English.

old face: a roman type-face which is descended from a French modification (by Jenson) of the venetian letter. The prototype was cut in 1495 by Francesco Griffo for Aldus Manutius who used the first true form of it when printing Pietro Bembo's tract 'De Aetna ad Angelum Chabrielem liber', 1495. (This is now available in a revived Monotype version appropriately called Bembo.) Old-face types were based upon handwriting without being slavishly imitative, and the style was finally brought to maturity by Claude Garamond from 1530 40. It is distinguishable from the later *transitional* and *modern faces*, q.v., by its bracketed serifs, e.g.

Caslon Old Face

Contemporary taste is towards a revival of old faces, the most famous type of recent years, Gill's *Perpetua*, being an example. Nearly all old-face types print well on antique papers.

See also *letters—forms and styles*.

old style: 1. the somewhat lighter and more regularized versions of old face which, in the 19th century, were cut as modern adaptations of the latter. Extruders were shorter and letters narrower than old face, while having a more calligraphic quality than the generally cold, engraved modern face.

A famous example is that cut by Alexander Phemister for the Edinburgh foundry of Miller and Richard. Cast about 1860, it is still used extensively in Europe. (It must be stated that this is not a class of types as are old face, transitional, or modern.)

2. the American term for *old face*, q.v.

oleography: the reproducing of a painting by a lithographic colour process: after printing, the result is finished to resemble the surface of an oil painting on canvas.

omnibus book: a one-volume edition of books or papers previously published separately.

on sale or return: said of the terms offered by a publisher to a bookseller when a condition of supplying copies of a book is that the bookseller may return those unsold. Such books are not taken on the bookseller's stock-books, since nominally, at least, they remain the publisher's property.

See also *terms* (1).

one on and two off: said of a *hollow*, q.v., having one width of paper glued to the back of a book. The remainder of the piece forms a double fold (i.e. two layers) glued together as a support for the spine. For heavy books *two on and two off* may be necessary; for this a double layer of paper is glued to the back, and a double layer to the spine.

one-way half-tone: see *single-line half-tone*.

onlaying: a cheap variation of *inlaying*, q.v., in which decorative strips of leather are fixed with glue to the cover of a book.

ooze leather: calfskins or split sheepskins prepared to give them a suede or velvet finish on the flesh side; sometimes used for covering volumes of poetry, belles-lettres, etc.

o.p.: the abbreviation for *out of print*, q.v.

op. cit.: an abbreviation for the Latin 'opere citato', i.e. in the work quoted.

opacity: a term applied to printing papers to describe the degree of non-transparency. This is an important factor, especially in thin papers, as *show through*, q.v., may occur if paper is not sufficiently opaque.

open back: another name for *hollow back*, q.v.

open letters: display and jobbing type, usually known as *outline letters*, q.v.

open matter: type matter generously leaded. Cf. *set solid*.

opened: said of the edges of a book which have been hand-cut with a paper-knife, usually by the purchaser. Cf. *uncut*.

opening: any two facing pages. Cf. *conjugate leaves*, *double-spread*.

opisthograph: a manuscript or parchment bearing writing on both sides of the leaf. Also applied to early printed books bearing printing on both sides of the sheet. Cf. *anopisthographic printing*.

Oporinus, Johannes, 1507–68: a scholar-printer of Basle who issued a large output of classical works, the Koran, and also the Latin edition of Foxe's 'Book of Martyrs', 1559.

optic centre: the point on a page which appears central to the eye but which measurement will reveal is slightly higher than the geometric centre. This fact must be borne in mind when positioning display matter or illustrations. (G. U.)

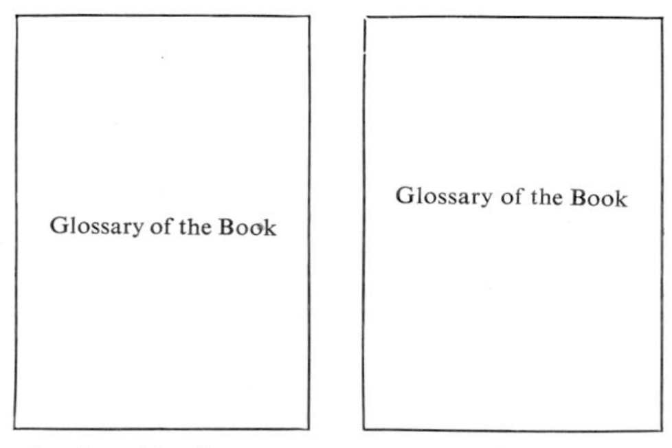

A title placed in the geometric centre of a page appears too low. The optic centre is higher (right)

ordinal: 1. a book of rules for a religious house or college.

2. a book giving the service to be used in ordaining priests.

oriental leaf: a mixture of bronze and brass which may be used as an alternative to gold foil in cheap bookwork.

oriental type: types used for the eastern languages, Arabic, Burmese, Tamil, Devanagari, Sinhalese, Thai, Syriac, etc., all of which are available on Monotype. (With M. L.)

original: the first engraving or plate, as distinguished from an electro or other duplicate; original copy. (M. L.)

orihon: a manuscript roll on which the writing was done in columns running the short way of the paper with margins between each. The roll was then folded, the margins having the effect of a closed fan. The term also describes a book made up of a continuous sheet, or of small single sheets, folded but uncut: such a book is held together by cords laced through holes pierced down one side. This form, still found in China and Japan, arises from the use there of extra thin paper which can only be printed on one side.

See also *french fold.*

Ormesby Psalter: one of the finest examples of the East Anglian School of manuscript illumination, begun in Norfolk or Suffolk during the later years of the 13th century. The work passed from owner to owner, each commissioning the decoration of a few pages; thus some pages show heraldic arms, others fabulous beasts and birds, while narrative border scenes are also found. The important Beatus page was completed about 1320 for the Foliot family. Some time later the still unfinished work passed to Robert of Ormesby who presented it to Norwich Cathedral.

The work is now in the Bodleian Library.

ornament: a generic term for the various kinds of decoration which compositors may use in conjunction with type, e.g. *borders, flowers, rules,* qq.v.

Orotype: a photo-composing machine in which raised letters (known as patrices) are assembled in lines by keyboard operation in a manner similar to the Linotype. The lines are justified, positioned, and printed line by line on to Cellophane film (or Baryta paper) for subsequent photographing. The printing unit, which has rollers for inking and a cylinder, is part of the machine and replaces the caster for metallic composition.

The Orotype, made by the Société de construction de locomotives

The Orotype patrix

orthochromatic: light-sensitive material (usually photographic film or plate) which has been sensitized to green and yellow rays in addition to the original sensitivity of the silver salts to blue, violet, and ultraviolet rays. (G. U.)

o.s.: the abbreviation for *out of stock,* q.v.

Ossianic Society: a printing society instituted at Dublin, in 1853, for the preservation and publication of manuscripts in the Irish language, with literal translations and notes. (M. L.)

ostrakon: a pottery sherd. Ostraka (or ostraca) were used in ancient Egypt for casual notes not intended for permanent preservation, being used for accounts and receipts in the Ptolemaic and Roman eras.

The largest collection in the world is in the Ashmolean Museum, Oxford; the ostraka there are written in Greek, Demotic, Coptic, and Arabic.

Ottonian illumination: in the 10th century German illuminators at the time of Otto I were particularly active, Reichenau, Echternach, Prüm, Fulda, and Cologne being the most important centres. Byzantine, Carolingian, and early Christian artistic influences are traceable in the work of the various scriptoria.

Whole pages were decorated in heavy, rich colours, with strongly drawn figures and formal symbolic scenes, showing little movement, set against a sombre gold or purple background. It was not unusual to include an illuminated dedication in which the patron of the work is shown receiving it from the scribe or artist.

out: copy which is accidentally omitted in composition.

out of print: said of a book which is not only unobtainable from the publisher but which is not likely to be reprinted. Abbreviated as OP. Cf. *out of stock*.

See also *publishers' abbreviated answers*.

out of register: see *register* (1).

out of series: a term applied to the un-numbered copies of a limited edition which have been printed and bound up as *overs*, q.v.

out of stock: said of a book of which the publisher is temporarily without copies, waiting for the binder to deliver. Abbreviated as OS. Cf. *out of print*.

outer forme: see *sheet work*.

outer margin: see *fore-edge*.

outline half-tone: an illustration (half-tone) in which the background and any unessential parts have been removed by routing or etching away the metal of the block. Also known as *deep-etch half-tone*. (G.U.)

See also *block*.

outline letters: letters, used for display and jobbing work, in which all the centre of the strokes is recessed (and thus beyond the reach of the inkers). The effect on the eye when such letters are printed is one of white areas rather than black. Cf. *inline letters*.

outright sale of copyright: a little used form of publishing contract whereby, for a single cash payment, an author cedes all rights in a book to the publisher of it.

See also *publishers' agreements*.

outsert, outset: see *insert*.

outsides: sheets of hand-made paper which are found, when sorting in the salle, to have torn edges, iron-mould, creases, or a broken surface. When reams of paper are made up outsides are marked XXX (cf. *retree*). When a mill ream consisted of 472 sheets there were eighteen quires of good paper plus a top and bottom quire of XXX to each.

over matter: set-up type which cannot be printed due to lack of space.

over-running: the re-adjusting of a paragraph of set-up type made necessary when corrections affecting the length of a line in it are made. Words from the end of one line of type are inserted at the beginning of the next; the remaining lines in the paragraph are adjusted until the matter fits.

overcasting: the manner of stitching employed in a book consisting of separate leaves or plates. (The same style of stitch is used for the edges of blankets.) While strength is given to a book sewn in this way it cannot be opened flat. Also called *oversewing* or *whipstitching*.

overlaying: a method of increasing pressure on the solids or dark tones of a printing plate, and decreasing it on the lighter tones or highlights, by placing appropriately shaped pieces of paper on the tympan.

See also *Fleischhack overlay*, *make-ready*, *mechanical overlay*, *Primaton overlay*.

overprint: see *off-print*.

overprinting: in blockmaking, the superimposing of one negative over another on the coated metal plate before developing.

See also addenda, p. 291.

overs: 1. extra sheets issued from the paper warehouse to the printing room to allow for make-ready, spoils, etc.

2. sheets or copies of a work printed in excess of a specified number. Bibliophiles also apply the term to limited editions, copies of which are numbered serially. Overs will be printed to make up spoiled copies, for reviewing purposes, or for presentation; they will not be numbered.

oversewing: see *overcasting*.

overstocks: quantities of titles held by booksellers and publishers for which a steady public demand has ceased. Booksellers may tend to order more copies of a particular title than they can hope to sell in order to obtain lower terms from the publisher; the latter may have over-estimated the sales potential

OFFSET REPRODUCTION

Reproduced photographically with a 150-line screen and printed in offset in six colours after Alexander Roslin's oil painting of Mme Marie Suzanne Roslin.

of a title. Possible solutions suggested by the 1948 Book Trade Committee included the controlled sale of overstocks by means of a National Sales Week; the easing of terms for minimum quantities; uniformity of terms offered by all publishers on books falling into the same classification, and their expression in terms of percentages.

Ovid Press: a private hand-press founded by J. Rodker in 1919. Before it closed in 1920 eight works were issued: authors and artists represented were T. S. Eliot, Ezra Pound, and E. Wadsworth.

Oxford Bibliographical Society: a society founded in 1922 with the general aim of furthering an interest in all matters pertaining to the book by holding lectures, exhibitions, and publishing papers.

Oxford corners: right-angles formed outside a printed frame (e.g. on a title-page) where the lines meet and project.

See also *mitred* (2).

Oxford corners

Oxford hollow: a flattened paper tube which is attached to the back of a book on one side and on the other is attached to the cover (spine), leaving a true hollow opening in between so that when the book is opened the back opens up independently of the spine. It is not suitable for machine methods, but many cased books have a hollow which is sometimes miscalled an Oxford hollow, and which gives the same effect as an Oxford hollow, although the linings on the back of the sections and the inner side of the spine are not joined at the shoulders as in true Oxford hollow style.

The O.U.P., who have supplied this note, state 'presumably the word Oxford was used to describe this kind of binding because undoubtedly the old Oxford bindery was the first to use it, particularly for leather-bound Bibles. It is properly applied only to a leather-bound book and is a style which is now used by most leather binders in place of what are known as flexible sewn books where the leather cover is attached directly to the back.'

Oxford imprints: 1. *Oxford: at the Clarendon Press.* This appears on books printed at Oxford for which the University, through the Delegates to the Press, assumes a particular responsibility. Profit is not a necessary factor when issuing such works, and they are never remaindered.

2. *London: Oxford University Press.* It was not until 1883 that the office of 'Publisher to the University of Oxford' was set up to publish in London books for which a less particular responsibility was assumed by the Oxford Delegates, and to publish books for other bodies, e.g. the British Museum, the Bibliographical Society, etc. Successive holders of the office have been Henry Frowde, 1883–1913; Sir Humphrey Milford, 1913–45; Geoffrey Cumberlege, 1945–56; J. G. N. Brown, 1956– . The name of the office holder no longer appears on the title-page or distribution imprints.

3. *Oxford Medical Publications.* This imprint first appeared in 1907 on popular medical works which until 1923 were published jointly with Hodder & Stoughton.

Oxford india paper: the thin tough opaque paper perfected in 1875 at the Wolvercote Mill of the Oxford University Press. Its formula remains a secret.

See also *Combe, Thomas.*

Oxford University Press: a learned press which traces its origins to 1478 when 'Expositio sancti Ieronimi in simbolum apostolorum' by T. Rufinus, Bishop of Aquileia, was printed in a type of Cologne origin. It is believed to be the work of Theodoric Rood (erroneously dated 1468). It was not until 1585 that the Press was properly established, and an official printer appointed. Charles Batey, Esq. has kindly supplied this list of holders of the office:

Oxford Printers

Theodoric Rood of Cologne	1478–85
Thomas Hunt	1485
John Scolar	1518*
Charles Kyrfoth	1519*

(*Writing in 'The First Cambridge Press', C.U.P., 1955, E. P. Goldschmidt doubts the ownership of presses in Oxford by these men. He says 'The few small quartos bearing the names and Oxford addresses of these two men are indubitably printed by Wynkyn de Worde in London. All the three types found in these books, as well as the woodcuts, are in Wynkyn de Worde's possession both before and after their publication.

'According to the rules we generally observe in making press attributions, it appears much more plausible to assume that these books were printed by de Worde on commission and for sale by Scolar or Kyrfoth from their Oxford premises, rather than a wandering to and fro of the printing equipment for such an insignificant purpose.')

Printers to the University

Joseph Barnes	1585–1617	Joshua Cooke	1775–1814
William Wrench	1617	Joseph Parker	1805–50
John Lichfield	1617–35	Samuel Collingwood	1792–1841
James Short	1618–24	Thomas Combe	1838–72
William Turner	1624–40	Edward Pickard Hall	1839–83
Leonard Lichfield I	1635–62	Horace Hart	1883–1915
Henry Hall	1642–81	Frederick Hall	1915–25
Leonard Lichfield II	1657–86	John Johnson	1925–46
Leonard Lichfield III	1689–1749	Charles Batey	1946–58
John Basket	1715–42	Vivian Ridler	1958–
Thomas Basket	1742–62		
William Jackson	1754–91		

See also *Clarendon, Delegates, Fell types, Oxford imprints.*

ADDENDA

Optak process: a reproduction process basically similar to *collotype*, q.v., but using fine-screen half-tone negatives printed down on to gelatine-coated metal plates. Printing is done on offset presses.

overprinting: 2. the adding of booksellers' addresses to prospectuses of books or other publicity material; space on the prospectus having been left blank at the time of the original printing.

P

pack: a pile of about 234 sheets of still-moist paper which is formed by the layerman on a felt-covered zinc plate. This stage of hand-made paper-making follows the pressing of a *post* of paper, q.v. If the paper is very thin the layerman will be assisted by a *slice boy*, q.v.

The pack will be pressed and parted and re-assembled, the process taking several days.

packing: the paper, rubber, or other material placed on the impression cylinder of a printing machine to give adequate overall pressure for printing. Known as *dressing the cylinder.*

padded sides: a term applied to leather binding in which cotton-wool has been inserted between the leather and the boards to give a padded effect. (L. K.)

Padeloup bindings: bindings done by the French family of Padeloup of which Antoine Michel (1685–1758) was the most distinguished. He was the French Court binder from 1733–44. Styles varied, but all were impeccably executed, especially his mosaics of coloured leathers with elaborate doublures. His name is associated with the development of *dentelle borders*, q.v.

page: either side of a leaf.

page-cord: waterproof cord used to secure type matter which has been made up into pages. The cord is removed prior to locking up the pages in the chase.

Page Fund: see *Gertrude Page Fund.*

page gauge: a measure to determine the length of the page of a work, commonly a piece of reglet, a lead, or rule notched to show the proper length, and used by the make-up hand to keep pages of a book of uniform length. (M. L.)

page head: see *headline.*

page papers: sheets of heavy paper or card upon which tied-up pages are placed for storage, instead of keeping them on galleys. (M. L.)

page proofs: proofs of type which has been paginated and locked up in a chase, the secondary stage in proofing. When galley proofs are returned to the printer, the corrections indicated by the reader and author are dealt with and then, normally, the type is made up into pages, and at this stage page proofs are pulled for further correction or approval. Also known as *made-up proofs.*

pagination: a sequence of numbers used to identify the pages of a book. Pagination was not in common use until the mid-16th century, prior to which only the recto of each leaf had been numbered, i.e. foliated.

In music published during the 18th century, especially by John Walsh, double, triple, and even quadruple pagination occurs, indicating the use in later editions of plates from former ones.

See also *foliation, preliminary matter.*

painted edges: see *fore-edge painting.*

paleography: the skilled study of ancient writing in which the date of a manuscript can be established by examining the manner in which the characters on it were made.

palimpsest: a parchment from which the original writing has been erased (but is still faintly visible) in order to write on it a second time. Also known as *codex rescriptus.*

palladium: a white metal which, when beaten into leaf form, is used for book decoration and edge gilding. It is very costly, and suitable either alone or with gold for the finest work as it does not tarnish quickly.

pallet: 1. a wooden storage device on which sheets of paper are stacked. It resembles a shallow box with open ends. The ends are used when, with a fork-lift truck, stacks of paper are to be lifted and moved from the warehouse to the machine-room. Cf. *stillage.*

2. finishing tools for impressing straight lines on covers. They are made of brass within a size range of $\frac{1}{16}$ in. to 2 in.

3. a small hand-tool in which letters are placed by the finisher prior to heating them and stamping

either the cover of a book, or a *panel*, q.v., for affixing to it.

See also *palleted.*

pallet knife: a thin, flat, flexible steel knife, used by the printer for mixing inks. (M. L.)

palleted: said of a binding which is signed, usually in gold letters, at the foot of the inside front board. A stamp, or pallet, bearing the complete name is used, e.g. *Bound by Sangorski & Sutcliffe, London.*

The term does not include gummed tickets, often used as an alternative.

Palmart, Lambert, fl. 1475: the printer of Flemish origin who worked at Valencia in Spain. The first work known to be his was 'Bellum Jugurthinium' of Sallustius Crispus, Valencia, 1475; though he may have printed a volume of Fenollar's poems 'Obres o trobes de labors de la Sacratissima Verge Maria' in 1474. (An Indulgence printed in 1473 by an unidentified printer was the first known piece of printing from movable types in Spain.)

Palmart used coarse roman types for the first five books he issued, gothic for the remaining ten. He died in 1490.

pamphlet: a short piece of polemical writing, intended for wide circulation, printed and issued as an unbound publication, with either stapled or sewn pages; it may or may not have a paper cover.

In 1712 the size of pamphlets was limited by Act of Parliament to two octavo sheets, i.e. 32 pages.

pandect: 1. a complete treatise or digest of a subject.

2. as *Pandects*, the digest or collection of legal opinions which Justinian ordered to be compiled, and to which he gave the force of law in 533.

panel: 1. the rectangular space, enclosed by a frame, on the spine of a book. In it the author's name or title may be blocked. A panel of one, two, or three lines or fillets may also form the decoration on the boards of a book, and be either gilt or plain.

See also *frame, labels, pallet*.

2. the list of books 'by the same author' facing the title-page. As this is included more for bibliographical than advertising purposes titles which are out of print or issued by other publishers may be given.

panel back: the spine of a hand-bound book on which decorated panels are tooled between raised bands.

panel stamp: a finisher's tool used in a blocking press to stamp a complete design on the sides of a book with one movement.

See also *blind-stamped panels.*

Panizzi, Sir Anthony, 1797–1879: born at Brescello, qualified for the law at Parma, fled to London in 1823, became Professor of Italian at London University in 1830, then Assistant Librarian at the British Museum. In 1837 he became Keeper of the Printed Books, finally, Principal Librarian in 1856. It was Panizzi's ideal to overcome the conception of the Museum as a private institution, and by his energy, administrative ability, exact scholarship, and single-mindedness, he was able to carry out huge reforms and create the great national institution which the British Museum is today. (M. L.)

Pannartz, Arnold: see *Sweynheym, Conrad.*

pantograph: an instrument for the copying of a design, either the same size, reduced, or enlarged. The pantograph is used extensively for drawing and engraving work in the graphic trades, and is usually constructed on the principle in the accompanying diagram, produced by Scheiner in the 17th century.

Pantograph reducing a drawing

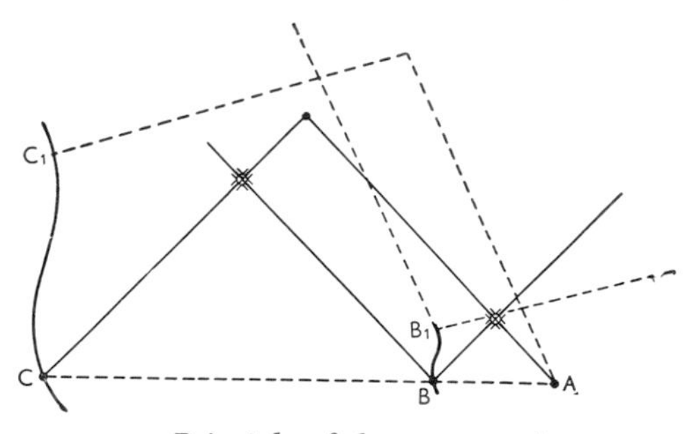

Principle of the pantograph

The continuous lines represent rods inclined towards each other. The pantograph is fixed at the pole A, the guiding pin at C is made to follow the outlines of the original picture (e.g. a map), and the drawing pin at B gives a reduced image of the same shape as the original. The rod B is movable, and is so adjusted that A, B, and C are in a straight line and that AB : AC = the reduction required. If the guiding pin is placed at B and the drawing pin at C, an enlargement is obtained in the same way.

Pantographs are also used when engraving type characters on copper or stone from drawings of letters. (G. U.)

See also *punch-cutting machine.*

Pantone: a little used planographic printing process in which plates in slight relief are used on letterpress machines to print fine screen work on rough-surfaced paper.

Panzer, Georg Wolfgang Franz, 1729–1805: a German theologian of Nuremberg, remembered for his bibliographical recording of early printing. Most important was the 'Annales typographici ad annum 1536', 11 vols., Nuremberg, 1793–1803, in which he grouped under place, date, and printer his descriptions of incunabula. He published a similar work, limited to books printed in German before 1526, entitled 'Annalen der älteren deutschen Litteratur', 1788–1805. His researches may be considered to have prepared the way for the compilers of the '*Gesamtkatalog der Wiegendrucke*', q.v.

Panzer's personal library is now part of the Landesbibliothek, Stuttgart.

paper: a substance consisting essentially of cellulose fibres interwoven into a compact web, made by chemical and mechanical processes from rags, straw, wood, bark, and other fibrous material, into thin sheets or strips. (After Funk & Wagnalls Dictionary.)

paper boards: a style of cased binding in which paper is used instead of cloth.

paper covers: a style of binding much used for cheap reprints, and, especially on the Continent, for original works in which no boards are used, and the stiff paper cover which encloses the book is adhered to the back. It may overlap by extending beyond the three edges, thus forming *squares*, q.v., or it may be trimmed or folded over so that the cover is flush with the edges.

The binding style with paper covers pasted down on to thin boards, cut flush head and tail, flaps turned over, is known as *stiffened paper covers.*

paper durability: the degree to which paper retains its original qualities when subjected to the strains of continuous use. Factors affecting this are the purity of the ingredients and the finish.

See also *paper-testing.*

paper finishes and varieties: see *air dried, animal-sized, antique, art, azure, Barber dried, Batchelor, B.P. chromo, calendered, cameo-coated, cartridge, charcoal, china, chromo-, clay-coated, Cobb's, cover, crash, cylinder dried, deckle edge, double sized, eggshell, engine-sized, English finish, featherweight, felt finish, french folio, gloss, ground wood, half-tone, hand-made, hard sized, high mill finish, hot-pressed, hot-rolled, imitation art, india, india tint, Japanese, parchment and vellum, laid, linen-faced, linen finish, linen paper, lithographic, loft dried, machine dried, machine finish, manila, matt art, mechanical wood, medium finish, mill brand, mould-made, not, odd, Oxford india paper, pebble finish, plate finish, plated, rag, repped, smoothness, soft paper, Spilman, sulphate pulp, sulphite pulp, super-calendered, text, tub-sized, twin-wire, Van Gelder, vat, water finish, waterleaf, wet strength, Whatman, wood free, wood pulp, wove.*

paper-making: the craft of making paper, excluding papyrus, was reputedly discovered about A.D. 104 by the eunuch Ts'ai Lun in China. It was made from mulberry and bamboo bark with probably other vegetable fibres. It is assumed that this paper was made by spreading the pulp on a woven or plaited cloth on which it was left to dry. Two centuries later a change had been made to trays consisting of closely laid bamboo laths joined into matting by hairs or silken threads woven into them at regular intervals. The matting was laid on a groundwork of stronger bamboo rods and was dipped in a vat of pulp. On removal, the water was allowed to run off and the layer of paper was laid out to dry, the flexible matting being rolled away from it.

The Moors introduced paper into Europe in the 11th century, and rag paper is said to have been made at Jativa in Spain in 1085. European paper was at first made as described above, but the material consisted almost exclusively of linen rags. These were converted into pulp after removing mechanical impurities, sorting, and washing, by steeping them in water, i.e. subjecting them to a process of fermentation which dissolved some of the particles and loosened the fibres. After steeping, the rags were disintegrated into a fibrous pulp by pounding them in mortars. The pulp was transferred to the paper vat (or trough) being here diluted with water to a thin gruel which was passed through strainers made of flat iron wires stretched as a foundation over a wooden frame. Here the sheet formed.

At the end of the 13th century paper manufacturing methods developed considerably, especially in Italy which then became the leading centre for paper. Pounding in mortars was replaced by a stamping machine, usually worked by a water-wheel, and the foundation of the moulding trays was made of drawn, round iron wires. (See *wove paper.*) Due to the altered methods of manufacture paper changed in character to some extent from this time. Prior to the 14th century paper was long-fibred, rough, and yellowish; subsequently it was pronouncedly short-fibred, thin, and flexible. The newly formed wet

The complete process of making paper by hand is shown in this copper engraving from Georg Böckler's 'Theatrum machinarum', Cologne, 1662

paper sheet was *couched* on a woollen felt, i.e. it was firmly pressed on to the cloth so that it adhered to it, thus the mould was freed for re-use. The couched sheet was covered by another felt, and this continued until a pile (or post) of alternating felt and paper was obtained. This was pressed in a screw press, by which means some of the water was removed. Then the sheets were taken out, laid in a fresh pile and pressed again, after which they were hung up to dry. In order to be sufficiently non-porous to writing ink, the dried sheets were next sized by steeping them in a solution of starch, replaced since the 14th century by animal glue, mostly made in the paper-mill's own sizing kitchen. After further pressing and drying the paper was glazed with a glazing stone. Glazing hammers worked by water-power were introduced about 1541, and glazing in a calender early in the 18th century in Holland.

It might be noted here that the first paper-mill established in Italy was at Fabriano prior to 1283, in France at Troyes in 1338, in Germany at Nuremberg in 1389, in Switzerland in 1411, and in Austria at Wiener-Neustadt in 1498. The first white printing paper to be made in England was by John Tate *c.* 1490. Paper was not made in Holland until the late 16th century, but by the mid-17th century the Dutch paper industry was of great importance in Europe. There, probably in the 1670's, one of the greatest aids to modern paper-making was invented, the *Hollander*. It may be described as an oval vat with a partition in the middle, though this does not extend to the ends of the vat. An enclosed channel is thus formed in which the pulp, diluted with water, is driven round by a rotating roller bearing knives which work against fixed knives in the channel bed. The distance between the roller and fixed knives can be adjusted.

Ingredients of present-day papers, which vary according to their intended use, include rags, esparto grass, wood pulp, china clay, chalk, size, dyes, and water. Paper is made by boiling, beating, pressing, and draining the materials. Originally laboriously made by hand, it is now made almost universally by machine.

The modern treatment of rags is largely mechanized. Rags are sorted and cut, and dust is removed before boiling. After *scouring* (boiling under pressure with alkali) various impurities dissolve and can be removed by washing. In a 'half-stuff Hollander' the rag pulp is ground into *half-stuff*, q.v., and is then bleached with chloride of lime in the same machine (in former times paper was bleached in the sun). After thorough washing the half-stuff is ready to be worked up into paper pulp; this is done in the same way whether the basic material is half-stuff of rags or pulp made from wood. The paper pulp is ground in a Hollander of the type already described, combined, if necessary, or at times entirely replaced by centrifugal-type machines and grinding mills. Fibrous material of different kinds is mixed in fixed proportions. Waste paper is often added, finely ground in crushing or grinding mills. In some cases the fibrous materials are separately broken and then put in a mixing Hollander. When treating paper pulp loading agents, size and colouring materials are also added. Treatment in the Hollander can be so controlled that 'long fibre' or 'short fibre' pulp results.

Properties of paper depend largely on the loading agents in addition to the fibre material and the degree of treatment. These agents consist of certain mineral substances (chiefly china clay) which affect the opacity of paper, its suitability for printing, etc. Sizing is mostly done in the pulp, i.e. in the paper pulp Hollander, by adding aluminium sulphate (alum) and resin soap. In the Delthirna method resin, dissolved in caustic soda, and aluminium sulphate are added to the pulp, when the sulphate precipitates the resin from the soda solution on to the paper fibres. In the Bewoid method (of Bruno Wieger, Brunswick) resin and water is run into the stuff chest with the alum and not in the beater. Other substances are also employed as sizing material.

Hand-made paper, q.v., is still made by the traditional method of dipping a mould into rag pulp and skilfully shaking it until a sheet is formed. The mould is a rectangular wooden frame over which is fastened a wire cloth (laid or wove); on this a loose wooden deckle rests, and it is this which determines the size and thickness of the sheet to be formed, and also gives the sheet its distinctive *deckle edge*, q.v. When the deckle has been removed the sheet is couched as previously described. Pressing is generally done in a hydraulic press at about two tons per sq. inch.

Machine-made paper. The standard paper-making machine was invented by a Frenchman, Nicolas Louis Robert, who took out his first patent for a long wire cloth machine in 1799. This was improved by the Englishman, *Bryan Donkin*, q.v., and the brothers Henry and Sealy Fourdrinier, after whom the machine was later called the *Fourdrinier*, q.v., In 1821 another Englishman, Crompton, added steam cylinders for drying the paper. In 1805 Joseph Bramah invented the *cylinder machine*, q.v., which was considerably improved upon in 1809 by John Dickinson and is now used chiefly for making boards.

Briefly, machine-made paper is manufactured as follows. From the Hollander, in which the pulp has been beaten, sized, and coloured at a pulp concentration of 3 to 6%, it is drawn off (further diluted in drawing off to a pulp content of 2 to 3%) into *mixing chests*. From these the pulp is pumped to the sand trap, a broad channel, the bottom of which is furnished with sloped baffles behind which heavy impurities collect and are removed. Centrifuges are also used for this purpose. The pulp is allowed to pass slowly through the sand trap, being diluted by recovered water from the machine to a concentration of about ½ to 1 %. The pulp next passes through the strainer, usually a slotted drum. The drum vibrates as it revolves, the clean pulp going through the slots, while clumps of fibre remain outside to be washed away. The pulp, now clear of impurities, is ready to enter the paper machine via the *flow box* (also called *breast box*). The diluted pulp flows out of the breast box over the breast board (of leather or rubber) on to the endless moving wire which is the main feature of the Fourdrinier. The pulp must be spread evenly on the wire. Moving rubber deckle straps at either side keep the pulp on the wire. In moving, the pulp is strained, and by lateral agitation the fibres are shaken into a web; water pours through the mesh in large quantities, along the numerous tube rolls which support the wire, into save-all trays. As this water contains valuable paper material it is led back and used for the diluting referred to above. After passing the tube rolls the wire is supported by a number of vacuum boxes, each connected with a suction pump. The object of these is to remove water which has not run off earlier. Between two such boxes a light *dandy roll*, q.v., of metal cloth revolves on a fixed axle over the wire. As the web of paper passes underneath, the dandy roll closes the surface of the web and impresses any watermark desired.

After the last suction box the wire with the paper is conveyed through the couching press, round the lower roller of which the returning empty wire is guided. The upper couching roller is covered with thick absorbent felt. After being couched in this press the web is sufficiently firm to move on independently to the first press. (Pressing by the couching press is often replaced by suction with a suction couch roll.) In the successive presses through which the web next passes it is guided by widely spaced woollen felts, between pairs of rollers, of which the upper roller is usually of granite, or granite composition, and the lower is usually covered with rubber. After leaving the third press the dryness of the paper is between 55 and 65%, and further drying is done by passing the web over a number of steam-heated cast-iron cylinders. The paper is guided round between ten and twenty such cylinders, pressed hard against them by thick felts. The web next passes through the finishing section, i.e. stacks of calender rolls, and finally round a water-cooled cylinder (to get rid of static electricity). It is now ready for winding on drums or reels.

It is still not ready for delivery, however. Even if it is to be used in reel form it has to be re-wound in order to obtain reels that are sufficiently even and firm. At the same time it is usually cut into narrower widths by revolving knives. Certain grades are *tub-sized* at this stage by passing the web through a solution of animal glue and then pressing and drying it. The *glazing* of the web is done by passing it through a calender separate from the Fourdrinier calender already referred to. This is a vertical stack of rolls, of alternately finely polished steel and compressed fibrous rolls, in which only one of the rolls is power-driven, the others rotating by friction with the paper which is thus polished. The web may be cut into sheets in machines so constructed that several webs are cut simultaneously. Paper cut into sheets is also glazed either in a calender or in a *plate glazer* in which the sheets, laid between metal plates or glazed boards, are pressed between steel rolls.

Special finishing is needed for the production of *art paper* (also known as *coated* or *enamelled paper*). The web is coated on one side (or both) with a composition of mineral salts (kaolin, gypsum, barium sulphate) and a binding material (casein, etc.). This is done on a machine which evenly coats the surface of the paper by brushing. Coated paper is dried in a drying chamber and glazed in a calender. A high degree of glazing can be obtained by polishing the surface. Some varieties of imitation coated papers are now made directly on the paper machine.

For offset paper in particular some mills give the paper a certain relative degree of moisture in a conditioning machine.

Paper that is cut to size is sorted, counted, and packed in wrappers; if necessary also between wooden boards. (G. U.)

See also *back-tenter, backwater, beating, bleaching, bowls, breaker, broke, calender, chemical wood, clearing the stuff, coating machine, conditioning, contraries, couch, coucher, counter-mark, crackle, cylinder machine, dandy roll, dead, digester, doctor blade* (2), *dry end, drying cylinder, duster, esparto, felt side, felting, festoon drying, fillers, finish, Fourdrinier, furnish, grain direction, half-stuff, Hollander, impressed watermark, Jordan, layerman, leaf* (2), *loading, look through, machine clothing, mid-feather, mould* (1), *opacity, pallet* (1), *pond, pope roll, post, potcher, pulp, rag cutter, relative humidity, retention, salle, size, slice, stillage, stock, stuff, substance, text* (2), *tranchefile, upper end boy, vatman, watermark, well closed, wet end, white water, wire, wire-mark.*

paper permanence: the degree of stability which paper can be expected to possess. This resistance to chemical change depends on the presence or absence of resin (which oxidizes in light and air), and the quality of the paper-making fibre.

Generally speaking, all-rag paper should retain its colour and quality indefinitely. Paper having an alpha-cellulose content of over 90% is similarly stable: bleached sulphite paper with an alpha-cellulose content of less than 85% will be less so.

A high residual acidity or excess of resin will increase the tendency of paper to discolour and become brittle as the years pass.

See also *paper-testing.*

paper sizes:

Foolscap	13½ in. by	17 in.
,, , Double	17	27
,, , Oblong Double	13½	34
,, , Quad	27	34
Pinched Post	14½	18½
Post	15¼	19
,, , Double	19	30½
Large Post	16½	21
,, , Double	21	33
Demy	17½	22½
,, , Double	22½	35
,, , Quad	35	45
Medium	18	23
,, , Double	23	36
Royal	20	25
,, , Double	25	40
Crown	15	20
,, , Double	20	30
,, , Quad	30	40
Imperial	22	30
,, , Double	30	44

(After B.S. 730: 1951.)

In America the prevailing practice is to specify the size of paper by inches and by its weight per ream rather than by name. The following are the ordinary sizes of book papers in the U.S.A.:

22 in. by	32 in.	33 in. by	44 in.
24	36	33	46
25	38	34	44
26	39	35	45
26	40	36	48
28	42	38	50
28	44	41	51
29	52	42	56
30½	41	44	56
32	44	44	64

For DIN sizes see addenda, page 335.

paper substance: leading British authorities express paper substance in pounds per ream of 500 sheets, or in grammes per square metre (g.s.m.). Although known for at least thirty years the g.s.m. is not extensively used by British printers despite its advantage of expressing paper weight (substance) in a basic figure which does not change whatever the size of paper or number of sheets. Thus if a ream of crown and one of quad demy are quoted as 85 g.s.m. it is apparent that their substance is the same, but from their respective weights of *c.* 18 lb. and *c.* 95 lb. the fact that the reams have the same substance is only revealed by consulting a table of equivalent weights.

The adoption of g.s.m. by the British trade would

follow the replacement of inches by centimetres for linear measurement.

Writing in 'Paper & Print' Vol. 27, No. 3, 1954, F. C. Avis suggests the oz. per sq. ft. as a British basic unit for paper substance so that the advantages claimed for the metric system would be available to the British printer in a familiar unit of measure.

paper substance conversions:

(i) lb. per ream into grammes per sq. metre:

$$\frac{\text{lb. per ream} \times 703{,}082}{\text{area of sheet in sq. in.} \times \text{number of sheets}} = \text{grammes per sq. metre (g.s.m.).}$$

(ii) grammes per sq. metre into lb. per ream:

$$\frac{\text{area of sheet in sq. in.} \times \text{number of sheets} \times \text{g.s.m.}}{703{,}082} = \text{lb. per ream.}$$

(iii) lb. per ream into oz. per sq. ft.:

$$\frac{\text{inches per sq. ft. } (12 \times 12) \times \text{oz. per lb. } (16) \times \text{weight of stock}}{\text{number of sheets} \times \text{area of sheet in sq. in.}} = \text{oz. per sq. ft.}$$

(iv) oz. per sq. ft. into lb. per ream:

$$\frac{\text{oz. per sq. ft.} \times \text{number of sheets} \times \text{area of sheet in sq. in.}}{\text{oz. per lb. } (16) \times \text{ins. per sq. ft. } (12 \times 12)} = \text{lb. per ream}$$

Note. (*a*) A decimalized figure for the oz. per sq. ft. is preferable to a fraction.

(*b*) The oz. per sq. ft. factor corresponding to the 703,082 figure of the g.s.m. method is 2304 (i.e. 12 × 12 × 16).

paper-testing: for the various purposes for which paper is used different properties are required, and many testing methods have been devised for ascertaining whether they are present or not. The development of methods for testing paper began in the latter half of the 19th century.

Methods of testing paper may be divided into three main groups: 1. testing the composition; 2. mechanical testing; 3. physical testing.

1. *Composition.* The first category consists mainly of *fibre analysis.* By de-fibring the paper the exposed fibres can be examined under a microscope. By adding various solutions different colour effects can be produced in fibres of different kinds, such as sulphite, sulphate, mechanical wood, straw, and rag. The proportion of different fibres can be established by comparison with standard samples, or by counting them. The *sizing content* can be ascertained by extracting the paper with a solvent, after which the solvent is evaporated and the residue weighed. The content of various *impregnating materials* can be established in a similar manner. The *ash content,* i.e. the proportion of incombustible inorganic matter, is determined by incineration and weighing the residue. The *copper number* is a measure of the content of reducing agents (oxycellulose and hydrocellulose).

2. *Mechanical testing.* In all mechanical and physical testing of paper it is very important that the tests should be carried out at a certain relative humidity and temperature, for paper is a hygroscopic substance which alters in its degree of moisture according to the relative humidity of the surrounding air. At the same time most of its mechanical and physical properties change. Since the end of the 19th century a relative humidity of 65% and a temperature of 69° F (20° C) have been accepted as a standard for paper-testing. Recently, in view of the fact that this humidity is higher than that at which paper is generally used, a relative atmospheric humidity of 50% has begun to be used in some tests, especially those relating to the printing properties of the paper. Mechanical testing includes, above all, the determination of *weight,* i.e. the weight of the paper per square metre, and *thickness.* The term 'bulk', which corresponds to the inverted value of the specific gravity, is often used as a mode of expressing the weight per unit of volume. For determining the *strength* of paper there are many methods and instruments. These tests have been standardized in most countries, but no international standard methods are as yet in existence. The most general tests are to determine *tensile strength.* This is usually expressed as the *breaking length* of the paper, and is defined as the length of the web of an arbitrary, but constant, width and weight which, when suspended from one end, breaks due to its own weight. In determining the tensile strength the *stretch* at the breaking point is also obtained, this being indicated in percentage and constituting a certain measure of the plasticity of the paper. The *bursting strength* is determined in a Schopper–Dalen apparatus, or a Mullen apparatus (with the paper clamped over a circular diaphragm of thin rubber and pressure applied from below until the paper bursts). This is indicated in lb. per sq. in. and known as a Mullen number. For some kinds of paper the determination of the *folding resistance* is of great

importance. The paper is folded many times in a special apparatus (e.g. Schopper) until it breaks at the fold, when the folding number can be read off by the counting device: different values will be obtained by folding with the grain direction or across it. Other mechanical tests determine the elasticity and tearing properties.

3. *Physical testing*. Physical tests of paper vary greatly according to the intended use of the paper. For printing paper there are many testing methods and only these will be dealt with here. The *moisture content* is found by weighing the paper before and after drying. It is important to determine the *stretch* and *shrinkage* of paper to be used in lithographic printing. The *degree of sizing*, of special interest in writing paper and many qualities of printing paper, is determined in innumerable ways. The *absorbent capacity* is important in view of the fact that paper must quickly absorb the oil in the ink. This is often expressed as the *castor oil number*, by which is meant the time required for the paper to absorb a thin film of castor oil.

The optical properties of paper are often of importance for its use in the graphic industry. *Opacity*, *transparency*, *whiteness*, *colour*, and *gloss* are determined by various instruments, latterly equipped with photoelectric cells. As yet there are no international testing methods. For all printing paper the *glazing* is important. This is determined by Bekk's or Bendtsen's apparatus, the latter being more modern. Both are based on the principle that the higher the glaze the less air can pass between the surface of the paper and a polished metal surface or edge.

It is often impossible to determine the suitability of paper for printing by employing the usual methods. In such cases a printing test must be made in unvarying external conditions. The result can be expressed in figures by using optical gauging methods. The tendency of paper to fluff often causes trouble in printing works, and attempts have been made to introduce methods for testing this, but none can be considered quite satisfactory. The sandy particles in paper are often a drawback owing to too rapid wear and tear of blocks and cylinders for intaglio printing. Their content can be easily and reliably determined by putting the paper under pressure on a polished glass plate in an apparatus constructed by Bekk, when the scratches made on the glass by the sandy particles can be examined and counted under a microscope. The determination of the durability and discoloration of paper also enters into the physical tests. (G. U.)

See also *smoothness*.

paper weight: see *paper substance*.

paper wrappered: said of a book enclosed in *paper covers*, q.v.

papier mâché: a greyish substance made from paper pulp which is used for taking moulds for stereotypes. These are taken in its soft state; when hard, the papier mâché moulds may be stored indefinitely prior to stereotyping, a precaution publishers frequently take when they authorize the distribution of a book's type.

Papillon, Jean Michel, 1698–1776: the most distinguished of a French family of wood engravers, who was renowned for the delicacy of his floral head- and tail-pieces.

papyrotype: a photo-lithographic method of printing illustrations devised in 1873 by a Captain Abney. The picture is first printed on a sensitized gelatine film and then transferred to a zinc plate or lithographic stone. (After O. E. D.)

papyrus: a giant rush from which the ancient Egyptians made sheets of writing material. Thin strips of

Greek papyrus roll

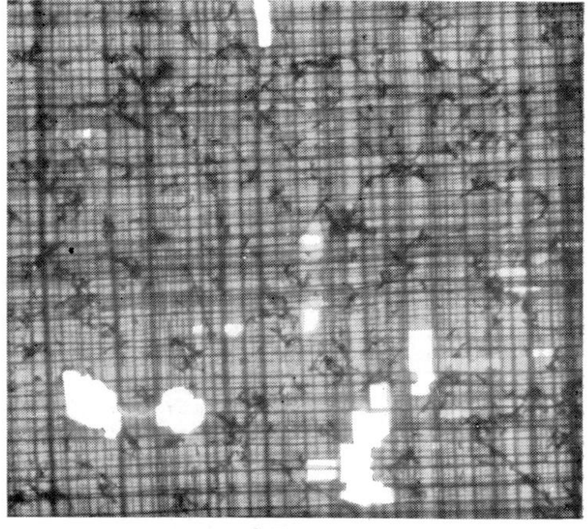

Fragment of Egyptian papyrus

stalk were placed side by side, and a second layer was added at right-angles to the first. After soaking in water, pressing, drying and polishing, the surface was ready for use. Papyrus was used in Greece and Rome from the 4th century B.C.; its last use in Europe was for Papal Bulls, *c.* 1051.

See also *capsa, hieratica.*

paragon: the name for a former size of type, about 20-point. The name, used in Holland as long ago as 1563, may have been an allusion to the beauty of the face rather than the size of the shank bearing it.

Also known as *two-line long primer.*

paragraph: the printer's sign ¶ used as a *reference mark*, q.v.

parallel: the printer's sign || used as a *reference mark*, q.v.

parallel folding: see *folding.*

parchment: the skin of a sheep or goat, and sometimes of other animals, which is scraped, dressed with lime and pumice, and prepared for writing upon.

Skin rolls were used in Egypt from *c.* 1500 B.C., and also by the Jews for synagogue rolls. Herodotus wrote that when papyrus was scarce the Ionians used the coarse skins of sheep and goats. It was, however, in the reign of Eumenes II (197–159 B.C.) at Pergamum that methods were found for the preparation of smoother close-textured skins. Pergamum became the main centre for the finest skins for writing, and by the 2nd or 3rd century A.D. 'pergamena' (whence 'parchment') was the accepted name for the material as now known.

Writing in 'The Alexandrian Library', 1952, E. A. Parsons comments that the distinction (in English) between *parchment* and *vellum* seems unsolvable, and suggests that usage favours the former as a general term, the latter for the refinements of the product. He quotes Horman's 'Vulgaria uiri doctissimi', Guil. Hormani, 1519: 'That stouffe that we wrythe vpon: and is made of beestis skynnes: is somtyme called parchement, somtyme velem, somtyme abortyue, somtyme membraan. Parchement: of the cyte where it was first made. Velem: bycause it is made of a caluys skynne. Abortyue: bycause the beest was scant parfecte. Membraan: bycause it was pulled of by hyldynge fro the beestis lymmes.'

parentheses: a punctuation mark or ornament ( ).

paring: thinning and chamfering the edges of leather to provide a neat turn-in over the boards in handbinding. (L.K.)

Paris, Matthew, fl. 1217–59: a monk of St Albans where he worked as a historian and illuminator. His great work was 'Chronica Majora' for which he revised the work of earlier scribes and wrote the years 1235–59. The first printed edition of this was published by Archbishop Parker in 1571.

See also *St Albans School.*

Parker, Matthew, 1501–75, Archbishop of Canterbury: a scholar and prelate whose important library of historical and ecclesiastical printed books and manuscripts is now at Corpus Christi College, Cambridge. Parker spent much money in efforts to secure for posterity manuscripts from former monastic libraries, and he employed agents at home and abroad.

At Lambeth Palace he installed 'limners, writers, and bookbinders' and he had many old books completed by inserting manuscript transcriptions from others. He also sponsored the publication of ancient chronicles and Saxon histories in addition to such works as the 'Bishop's' Bible.

He commissioned *John Day*, q.v., to print Aelfric's Saxon homily, edited as 'A testimonie of antiquitie' in 1567. This was the first book to be printed in Saxon characters: these were cut and cast by Day.

Parker Society: a society instituted at Cambridge in 1840, for the publication of ecclesiastical works.

Parliamentary papers: House of Lords and Commons Acts and Bills (e.g. Order Papers), also reports of Select Committees.

partial remainders: quantities of books offered at low prices by certain publishers to selected booksellers which they permit the latter to sell to the public at less than the published price, although the books, so far as other booksellers are concerned, are still net books. This practice is condemned by the Councils of the Publishers Association and the Booksellers Association.

parts of a book: in order of gathering within the covers these are half-title, frontispiece, title-page, printer's imprint and copyright note, dedication, preface, acknowledgements, table of contents, list of illustrations, introduction, errata, text pages, appendices, author's notes, glossary, bibliography, index, colophon. On examination it will be found that publishers vary the order slightly.

parts of type: type has the following main parts: *face, body, beard, shoulder, bowl, counter, pin-mark, nick, groove and feet, serif*, qq.v. The minutiae of a type-face are described in 'Type for Print' by D. Thomas, Whitaker, 1939, and in other manuals.

Parts of type

a *height to paper*
b *body, shank, or stem*
c *front*
d *feet*
e *groove*
f *nicks*
g *counter*
h *line to back*
i *face*
j *bevel or neck*
k *serif*
l *shoulder*
j + l *beard*

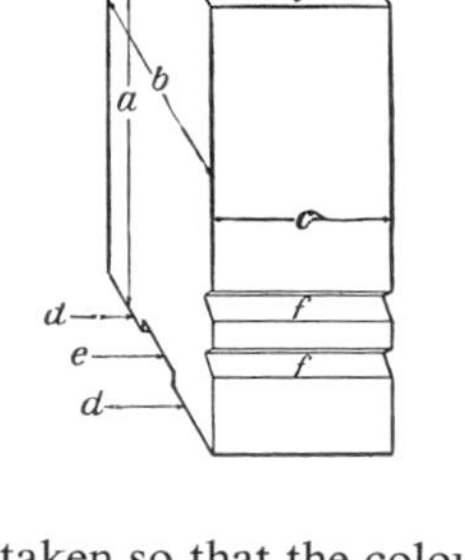

pass sheet: a specimen pull, taken so that the colour and general suitability of ink for the paper can be judged by the printer before running off an impression.

See also *proof.*

paste: a viscous substance made from starch (in flour). Wheat, potato, and rye flours become pasty at different temperatures, but when not made in a factory it is usual to stir the flour into boiling water. To prevent the paste from turning sour formalin, alum, or similar substances are added. When pure starch is treated with caustic soda (at room temperature) *paste starch* is formed which, when stirred in cold water, is suitable for mounting plates, maps, and similar work. Pastes are also made from synthetic resins, mostly under trade names.

See also *adhesives.* (G. U.)

paste-downs: the halves of end-papers which are pasted on to the boards of a book. (An alternative name is *board paper.*) The free halves form fly-leaves.

paste-grain: split sheepskin hardened by coating it with paste and given a highly polished surface.

paste in: see *tipped in.*

paste on: a plate or similar component of a book which is affixed by pasting all over. Cf. *tipped in.* (L.K.)

paste print: a process used by bookbinders in the 15th and 16th centuries for the decoration of bindings. A thin paste was spread on paper, allowed to dry, and treated with glue; on this was impressed a picture or text by means of brass stamps. The stamped picture was strewn all over with powdered velvet. Another method was to place a leaf of gold over the paste before stamping, and colouring certain parts of the stamp. The few surviving examples belong to the period 1458–1523. (G. U.)

paste-up: a layout of a number of pages, used to plan the positioning of blocks, legends, and text. This is made easier if a rubber gum is used to fix the proofs so that they can be moved.

pasteboard: see *boards.*

pasting: 1. the application of paste to a surface in bookbinding. This can be done by hand with a brush, or on a plate. *Plate pasting* is used when the object to be pasted is small or when it is inconvenient to use a brush. The paste is applied to a plate and the articles to be pasted are arranged in rows upon it. Bookbinders now use pasting machines which exist as independent units or built into other machines, e.g. casing-in machines. The pasting machine usually consists of a rotating cylinder to which the paste is carried from a container or through transfer cylinders, and against which the paper is fed.

2. a *pasting* is synonymous with a *tip in.*

Pasting by machine

pasting-up board: a smooth board, varnished to make it impervious to moisture, which is used for pasting up the transfer papers used in *lithography,* q.v.

PATRA: see *Printing, Packaging and Allied Trades Research Association.*

Patramould: see *electrotype.*

patron: a sponsor. From the early days of printing until the reign of George III (as in the still earlier times of hand-written works) a wealthy or titled patron often sponsored the printing of a work and, on occasion, commissioned the writing of it. The patron was the dedicatee, it being hoped that preferment or money would be the form of acknowledgement. English literature of the 16th and early 17th centuries could not have flourished without patronage, the authors' receipts from printer-publishers being modest.

See also *dedication, impensis, subscription works.*

Payne, David: see *Wharfedale machine.*

Payne, Roger, 1739–97: a distinguished English binder whose finest work was done between 1770–97. He used russia leather with a combination of blind and gold tooling, and cut his own tools for producing patterns of acorns, leaves, and vines. Typical designs were ornamental corners filled with stamped honeysuckle flowers and backgrounds of dots and circles, the whole effect being restrained rather than lavish.

Much of his work was done for Lord Spencer and the Rev. Clayton Cracherode, two bibliophiles whose collections are now in the John Rylands Library, Manchester (including the Aeschylus Payne bound in 1795), and the British Museum.

He took into partnership a Richard or David Weir whose wife worked for them as a restorer.

Pear Tree Press: a private printing press founded in Essex in 1899 by James Guthrie, and moved to Flansham in 1907. Mr. Guthrie specialized in the use of intaglio plates, doing the etching and printing (in two or more colours) by hand.

pearl: the name for a former size of type, approximately 5-point.

pebble finish: one of the many novel surfaces given to paper. It is produced by passing the sheets with strong pressure between steel rollers having a surface of the desired pattern. (M.L.)

peccary: the skin of a wild pig found in the Americas. It is occasionally used for fine book covers.

peculiars: type characters for the non-standard accent-bearing letters, e.g. those required when setting phonetics, or texts in Scandinavian, Slavic, Turkish, and certain other languages. (See *accents.*)

A selection of these is given here:

Å Ḃ Č Ḍ E̊ Ḟ Ğ Ḥ İ̊ Ķ Ł Ṁ Ṉ Ō Ṟ Ṣ Ť Ů V̌ Ŵ Ý Ż

Peerless press: an old style of platen jobbing press, using a toggle motion to give the impression. This press is no longer made, but there are still some of them in use. (M.L.)

Pelican Press: a small private press founded in 1916 as a department of the Victoria House Printing Co., London. It was at first under the supervision of Francis (now Sir Francis) Meynell.

An important collection of flowers and types was assembled and made known to the public in a specimen book 'Typography', 1923. Stanley Morison became typographical director in 1919, remaining there until 1921. Under this imprint he wrote 'The Craft of Printing', 1921, containing, he says, his initial effort to outline for his own satisfaction the nature of the tools he was using as 'layout artist' at the Pelican Press.

Pellechet, Marie, 1840–1900: a French bibliographer who devoted her whole life to the study and description of French incunabula. Her major work, 'Catalogue général des incunables des bibliothèques publiques de France', Paris, Picard, 1897–1909, was incomplete when she died. It was continued up to letter H by Marie L. Polain.

Pelletan, Édouard: a distinguished French publisher of the 20th century, much of whose work was printed by the Imprimerie Nationale.

pelt ball: see *ink ball.*

Penitential: a book of Church canons relating to penance.

Pentateuch: the first five books of the Old Testament, ascribed by tradition to Moses.

Percy Society: a society founded in London in 1840 for the printing of ballads. It also published medieval romances, interludes, and pamphlets. It closed in 1852.

perfect: in edition binding the printed sheets are said to be *perfect* as soon as some of all of the sheets (and plates) have been printed. At that point *perfect copies* are available for binding. (L.K.)

perfect binding: see *unsewn binding.*

perfect copy: 1. a complete set of folded sheets (and plates) ready for binding. The term is used in the sense that the printed matter is complete.

2. a bound book in saleable condition. (L.K.)

perfect ream: a ream of paper having 516 sheets. See also *mille, quire.*

perfecting: the printing of the second side of a sheet of paper. Also known as *backing-up.* This may be done in a machine using two cylinders to print both sides at one operation. For alternative methods see *sheet work, work and turn.*

period: a *punctuation mark,* q.v.

period printing: 1. the production of a book in a style associated with the historical period of its subject.

2. the reproduction of a book in the style of the original edition. Cf. *facsimile edition.*

peripheral speed relationship: when, in printing, a cylinder surface rolls on a flat surface (in a cylinder press) or against another cylinder surface (in a rotary press), both surfaces must have the same speed along the line of contact (periphery) for a good impression to be obtained. The packing, forme, offset rubber cloths with underlay, etc., must be adjusted with this in view, while ensuring that correct pressure is obtained between the surfaces and that the geared rails operate against each other in the intended line of division. An incorrect peripheral speed relationship may cause a lack of sharpness in the impression, and undue wear of the forme.

(G.U.)

periplus: a book giving an account of a voyage by sea, e.g. round a coastline.

See also *portolano*, *ruttier book*.

Persian morocco: a soft goatskin used for the finest book covers. Persian goat and Persian sheep are trade names for goat- and sheepskins tanned in India.

Petersen, Hans: the inventor, *c.* 1913, of the *Linograph*, q.v.

Petrucci, Ottaviano dei, 1466–1539: a printer of Fossombrone (1513–23) and Venice, who also established a paper-mill which operated until the 19th century. To Petrucci is attributed the invention of music printing from movable metal types. The first work in which they were used was 'Harmonice musices odhecaton', 1501, but the most important was his edition of 'Frottole', 1504–8.

See C. Sartori, 'Bibliografia delle opere musicale stampate da Ottaviano Petrucci', Florence, 1948.

pewter plates: see *music engraving*, *music printing*.

Pfister, Albrecht, fl. 1461–64: the printer of Bamberg, remembered for his use of the 36-line Bible type. Of the nine works he issued 'Der Edelstein' by Ulrich Boner, 1461, and the Biblia pauperum, *c.* 1462, are the best known, and the oldest books to contain woodcut illustrations. He first printed the text, then the cuts. (An example is shown under *woodcut*.)

Although the 36-line Bible has been attributed to Pfister it is more probably the work of Heinrich Kefer, formerly an associate of Gutenberg of Mainz, who came to Bamberg about 1459.

See 'Gutenberg Jahrbuch', 1950.

Pforzheimer, Carl H., 1879–1957: a New York banker and bibliophile whose library has, within the general framework of English and American literature, eight special collections. These are 1. the history of printing, beginning with a perfect copy of the Gutenberg Bible, and several German incunabula, the 'Recuyell of the Historyes of Troye' and other Caxtons, and—through succeeding centuries—examples of fine printing up to and including Bruce Rogers and other modern printers and designers; 2. English literature of the 15th to 18th centuries, as described in the catalogue 'English literature: 1475–1700', 3 vols., 1940 (150 sets printed). The early periods are well represented, being especially strong in Chapman, Gascoigne, Jonson and Spenser; letters of Queen Elizabeth I, John Locke, John Evelyn (including six holograph letters to Pepys); the Bulstrode Papers (over 1500 news-letters addressed to Sir Richard Bulstrode) and Marprelate Tracts. Also here is the octavo first edition of Bacon's 'Essayes', 1597, the only copy in a private collection; 3. first editions of outstanding works of English literature of the 18th century (also the manuscript of William Cowper's translations of the Iliad and Odyssey); 4. English literature of the 19th century, with numerous letters of the Brownings, note books of George Eliot, the complete manuscripts of Scott's 'Quentin Durward', 'Lord of the Isles', and 'The Betrothed', etc.; 5. a George Gissing collection, which includes the manuscript of 'The Private Papers of Henry Ryecroft'; 6. 17th- and 18th-century English chap-books; 7. American literature, particularly of the 19th century; 8. 'Shelley and his Circle'. This is the outstanding feature of the library, and one of the three major collections of Shelley in the world (the others being in the Bodleian and the British Museum). There is a large amount of manuscript material of Percy Bysshe Shelley and his wife, Byron, Hunt, Hogg, Peacock, Trelawny and Mary Wollstonecraft, and there are also first editions of the works, later editions, and studies. Mr. Pforzheimer stated that a series of five or six volumes of 'Shelley and his Circle' is in preparation: these volumes will include annotated full transcripts of letters and manuscripts, with bibliographical descriptions and commentary for the books.

pharmacopoeia: a book of medical recipes or prescriptions, and in precise usage, those to be employed by doctors with the approval of some state or national medical body. In the U.K. this is the General Medical Council, which, in Section 54 of its establishment Act of 1858, was instructed to compile a book of medicines and compounds, also the manner of their preparation, to be called 'British Pharmacopoeia': the exclusive rights to publish, print, and sell this were given by the Act of 1862. Other pharmacopoeias existing in the U.K. at that time were replaced. The first London pharmacopoeia, issued by the College of Physicians, appeared in 1618.

Origins of such books can be traced to the 1st century A.D., and Scribonius was an early collector of recipes. Among incunabula was the 'Nuovo receptario composito', Florence, 1498, or the still earlier 'Antidotarium' by Nicolas of Salerno which Jensen printed at Venice in 1471; but the 'Pharmacorum conficiendorum ratio, vulgo vocant dispensatorium' of Valerius Cordus, printed at Nuremberg in 1546 by J. Petreius was the first pharmacopoeia with official status to be published.

Philip the Good, Duke of Burgundy, 1396–1467: one of the greatest bibliophiles and patrons of learning of his day. He would admit only the finest manuscripts to his collection and employed such scribes and illuminators as Jehan Miélot, Jean Wauquelin, *Loyset Liédet*, and *Rogier van der Weyden*, qq.v., while *Colard Mansion*, q.v., was engaged as a supplier.

At the time of his death Philip left 3211 MSS. in Paris, Dijon, Ghent, Bruges, Antwerp and Brussels. His son Charles the Bold (1433–77) added to the collection, and it was later bequeathed to Philip's granddaughter. After her death in 1482 the manuscripts were partly dispersed, but about 540 volumes subsequently formed the basis of the Royal Library, Brussels. The Dijon group, after various wanderings, passed to the Bibliothèque Nationale, Paris.

Phillipps, Sir Thomas, 1792–1872: a wealthy bibliophile who devoted his whole life to the assembling of what was at one time the largest private collection of manuscripts in Europe (*c.* 60,000). His first aim was to preserve for posterity as many unpublished works as possible. He bought most of the manuscripts sold at the breaking up of the Gerard Meerman library (in 1887 these were in turn bought by the Prussian State Library).

Much of Phillipps's collection was dispersed at a series of sales which began in 1886 and ended in 1928.

See also *Middle Hill Press*.

The reader should consult 'Phillipps Studies', by A. N. L. Munby, C.U.P., 1951–56.

Philobiblon Society: a Victorian club founded in 1853 by Sylvain van der Weyer, Belgian Minister in London. The thirty-six members had social rather than literary prominence, and they met in each other's houses to examine rare books. Among Society presidents was Prince Albert, and among distinguished members Henry Huth. They intended from the outset to publish an annual volume of bibliographical miscellanies of special interest to bibliophiles. The last volume appeared in 1884, sponsored by Lord Houghton, and included some 'Unpublished Letters of S. T. Coleridge'.

In addition to the fifteen annual volumes other works were issued, among them 'Ancient Ballads and Broadsides in the Library of Henry Huth'. The books were all well produced, the Chiswick Press being commissioned to print them.

photo-composing machine: a machine for setting solid text by photographic means (as distinguished from metal-type composition), analogous in principle to Monotype, Linotype, or Intertype casting machines.

For the photo-mechanical reproduction of text in intaglio and lithographic offset printing the usual method is to compose the text as for letterpress. It was formerly necessary to take an impression from this on special paper, and then to photograph the sheets for subsequent treatment just as if they were picture originals to be reproduced. There now exist several machines for the direct photographic production of positives and negatives which can be copied. Among the earliest was the Hunter & August, built in England *c.* 1922.

The Monotype Corporation Ltd. have produced a photo-type composing machine, marketed under the registered trade-mark '*Monophoto*'. The sensitive film is mounted on a drum unit, which remains stationary during the letter by letter composition of a line of text, and is advanced line by line by micrometrically precise gear. At present these drums take a reel of film 10 in. wide and 24 in. long, with a line by line adjustment from 6-point to 24-point in half-point stages. The precise gear enables the drum to be accurately re-positioned for the insertion of dropped initial characters or other additional matter. It likewise enables double-column or multiple-column work to be produced on a single sensitive film.

Among other photo-composing machines are the *Photon*, *Linofilm*, *Uhertype*, *Orotype*, the *Fotosetter*, and the *Rotofoto*, qq.v. Popular on the Continent is the *Hadego* machine built by H. J. A. de Goeij in Holland. In this latter machine display-matrices of plastic with negative and positive types are composed by hand in a similar way to those on the Ludlow type-casting machine and then photographed. *Huebner's* photo-setting machine works with types photographed singly, a method used on the *Highton* machine where the characters placed on a disc are rotated past a lens system, a shutter opening at the moment when the desired image is in position for exposure.

See also *typewriter composing machine*.

photo-gelatine process: see *collotype*.

photo-litho offset: printing from photo-litho plates in which the image is first taken on a rubber blanket from which it passes to the paper. Such work has a softness which in the lighter tones given to line drawings is an advantage, but lacks the crispness and contrast obtained by impressing type and blocks as in letterpress.

photolitho-graphic: plate a fine-grained metal plate which is prepared for lithographic printing by either of two processes known as (1) the *albumen process*, or (2) the *deep-etch process*.

In (1) the plate is coated with a colloid solution of dichromate and egg albumen to make it light-sensitive. It is placed in contact with a photographic negative in a printing frame, and after exposure to light is covered with a waterproof developing ink and immersed in water to develop. The light-affected parts of the plate, i.e. the open or transparent parts of the negative, retain the ink and resist developing. The non-image areas are desensitized and, after gumming, the plate is ready for printing.

In (2) a photographic positive is used, as distinct from the negative of (1), and the surface of the plate is very slightly etched (in spite of the name deep-etch) to produce a more durable printing surface. The processes above described are known as *printing down* or *printing to metal*.

photo-lithography: in the widest sense of the term, planographic printing combining photography and lithography for the reproduction of illustrations or text. For line work a negative of the subject is made without a screen; for photographs or wash-drawings a screen is used; for reproducing complete books the pages are dismembered and photographed. In each case the negative is copied on to a *photo-lithographic plate* from which printing is done by *photo-litho offset*, qq.v.

In a narrower sense the term applies to photographic reproduction by line etching as distinct from a similar process by half-tone. The earliest history of photo-lithography is linked with that of making blocks, as the attempts at process work made in this field were based on the principle of copying on sensitized paper and transferring the picture obtained to stone or metal. In 1852 photo-lithos were made in various places, among others in Paris by Rose Joseph Lemercier. In 1855 Poitevin experimented with an albumen process on grained stone. In 1859 photo-lithos were made by J. W. Osborne who copied on albumen-dichromate paper with subsequent transfer. Though various methods were attempted to produce workable photo-lithos by copying direct on stone, photo-lithography at the end of the 19th century was dominated by Eugen Albert's photo-litho paper. A gelatined paper was sensitized by immersion in a bath of 4 to 6% dichromate solution, dried, and copied under a negative, blacked with greasy ink, developed in water, and finally transferred to a plate or stone. After the invention of half-tone, screen reproductions were also made for lithographic printing in the same way, but the result, especially in the case of the new method of offset printing (1904), was not satisfactory. Attempts were made to utilize zinc screen blocks which, after retouching, were transferred to the offset plate, but the trend was to invent methods for copying direct on the machine plate. With a view to this, for example, Albert's 'Drakorapid' process in combination with his polyeccentric lamp was used; this enabled retouching to be done on the copied offset plate.

Attempts were also made at colour reproduction methods where, from the separation negatives, intermediate copies were made on stone (Th. Kirsten) or paper, which, on being retouched, were photographed and copied. All these methods have been replaced by modern offset reproduction processes.

(G.U.)

photo-mechanical reproduction: see *photoengraving*.

photo-process engraving: the photographic printing of an acid resist on a metal plate and then etching the unprotected areas of it, causing the protected parts (the printing surface) to stand out in relief.

photo-setting machine: see *photo-composing machine*.

photo-typesetting: see *photo-composing machine*.

photo-zincography: the process of making a relief engraving on a zinc plate, somewhat in the same manner as photo-lithography; a photo-etching on zinc. (M.L.)

photoengraving: the preparation of a relief printing surface on a plate by one of several methods employing photographic, chemical, and mechanical means. The basic principle of engraving by photography on metal was discovered in 1824 by Niepce. Paul Pretsch of the Vienna State Printing House made printing formes with sensitive chromate colloids in the mid-19th century; by exposing such layers to light and developing them in water he was able to make both relief and intaglio formes.

Also known as *process engraving* or *photo-mechanical reproduction*. (G.U.)

See also *blockmaking Dow-Birmetals etching machine, dry (relief) offset, electronic photoengraving machine, Gaco*.

photogalvanic processes: methods for producing formes for letterpress and intaglio printing by galvanic means, the matrix or patrix being made by photographic expedients (bichromate gelatine relief, etc.). (G.U.)

photography: the production of pictures by means of the action of light on substances affected by it. The picture thus produced is called a photograph. Certain substances undergo a chemical change when acted upon by light, and at the same time there frequently occurs a change in the outward appearance of the

Impression taken from a block made by Paul Pretsch of Vienna. He used a photogalvanic method

substance, for instance in its colour. In a number of cases this sensitivity can be used for photographic purposes. This applies especially to the silver salts which are blackened by light during the formation of silver (C. V. Scheele in the 18th century), or which after exposure to light can be blackened by developing. The widest application is made of *silver bromide in gelatine* as a sensitive layer for developing purposes on plates, films, and paper. In reproduction photography silver bromide collodion and silver iodide collodion are used. Silver chloride (often mixed with silver bromide) in gelatine is used for developing paper, transparency plates, etc., and mixed with silver nitrate and organic silver salts in printing-out paper.

The sensitivity of *ferric salts* is utilized in various photographic printing processes which are based on the fact that light transforms ferric salts into ferrous salts, whereby both these associations are able to react in different ways with other substances, e.g. in blueprint processes.

The sensitivity of the *chromates* when mixed with such organic substances as gelatine, albumen, gum, etc., is largely used in photography in a narrower sense, and above all in reproduction processes.

See also *albumen process*, *blockmaking*, *chromate process*, *collotype*, *offset reproduction*, *photogravure*.

During recent years the sensitivity of *diazo compounds* has been used on a large scale, especially for photoprints. The sensitivity of certain other organic compounds has been used in colour photography.

The origins of the camera used in photography may be traced to an 11th-century instrument used in astronomy; and later, as the camera lucida, an apparatus for copying, reducing, or enlarging drawings (by Robert Hooke *c.* 1674, and W. H. Wollaston in 1807). There was also the camera obscura which was used in 1569 by Giovanni Battista della Porta, embodying a system of mirrors and lenses. This principle was adapted to photography *c.* 1794 by Thomas Wedgwood who made negative copies on paper from paintings on glass, and also micro-photographs, in 1802: he was assisted in some measure by Sir H. Davy. They used the action of light upon silver nitrate, but were not able to fix the images they obtained. The first permanent photographs were made in 1822 by the Frenchman J. N. Niepce who used a bituminous film. The exposure time of several hours was not practicable, and it was the method of *Daguerre*, q.v., made public in 1839, which was the first satisfactory process. He exposed a metal plate coated with silver iodide in a camera and treated it in a dark box with vaporized mercury. In the same year the Englishman Fox Talbot published a method for producing paper negatives by means of a camera and copying these on to silver chloride paper. The process was improved upon in 1841 (as Talbotype or Calotype) and became the basis of photography as we know it; the later substitution of glass plates for the original paper negative (by Niepce de St Victor in 1847, and Scott Archer in 1851) meant a great step forward. Further improvements were the *dry plate* introduced in 1871 by Dr. R. L. Maddox, and the discovery of sensitizing dyes in 1873 by H. W. Vogel, making it possible to render the negative material sensitive to yellow and green light (before this it had been sensitive to blue and violet only). Of great importance was Fox Talbot's discovery of the sensitivity to light of dichromated gelatine in 1852, followed by Poitevin's inventions fundamental to collotype, photo-lithography, and carbon print. Other inventors of the 1850's worked on methods for making intaglio plates photographically (Talbot, Pretsch, and others; see *photogravure*), and also letterpress printing blocks (Gillot, etc., see *line block*, *half-tone process*).

Photography is mostly done by exposing a negative in a camera and then developing and fixing it for the subsequent production of positives on sensitive paper; alternately, it may be used as the initial material for the production of a printing forme from which positive impressions can be made. In the latter case we speak of photo-mechanical reproduction. Photographic reproduction can, however, be done without the use of a camera by copying to full scale direct from the original (see *collotype*).

The production of photographs and photographic reproductions can be done in monochrome or colour; most colour processes, however, consist in part of processes similar in principle to the monochrome ones. (G. U.)

photogravure: making by the action of light an etched copper surface for printing from. Shortly after the appearance of photography attempts were made to produce printing plates for intaglio by photographic means. In Vienna J. Berres attempted to etch daguerreotypes, and elsewhere H. L. Fizeau used them in efforts to produce printing plates galvanically. After discovering the sensitivity of dichromate gelatine, Fox Talbot patented a process (1852) for producing printing plates with it, a method which may be considered the basis of all photogravure reproduction of modern times. Talbot prepared a copper plate by means of a mixture of dichromate and gelatine, and on this film a positive picture was copied. On developing, a relief was obtained through which the copper could be etched, preferably with ferric chloride. The speed with which the etching liquid penetrates the gelatine film varies according to the thickness, thus the contrasts of the image are interpreted by varying depths when etching. Talbot also found a way to improve the quality of etching by using successively several etching solutions of varying concentration, and he discovered the necessity of dividing the printing surface into a number of small ink containers which allowed the ink to be held by the plate. At first he impressed a gauze tissue on the gelatine layer before copying the picture, but later he adopted the method of covering the copper plate with fine bitumen powder which was then heated and fused (1859).

An asphaltum (bitumen) powder cupboard

In 1864 J. W. Swan patented a chromate gelatine process which consisted in preparing a gelatine film saturated with a pigment dye on a paper foundation, whereupon the carbon tissue was sensitized in a bath of dichromate solution. Karl Klíč later combined the work of Talbot and Swan in his photogravure process described below.

Apart from etching this copper plate by means of a gelatine relief, other methods have been devised for transforming a gelatine relief into a printing forme. In 1854 Paul Pretsch made such reliefs by a galvanic process, thereby laying the foundation for a reproduction method generally known as *heliogravure*. The use of the two names photogravure and heliogravure is not always consistent, the same term often being applied to both.

As long ago as 1783 a method was used for rotary intaglio printing on cloth and wallpaper where, to remove any surplus ink, a knife which moved across the forme was used: its inventor was Thomas Bell, and the knife developed into the modern *doctor blade*, q.v. A photogravure process had been invented in 1878 by Karl Klíč, a Bohemian living in Vienna,

Removal of the surplus ink by the doctor blade which glides across the forme

and in 1890 he combined with it his knowledge of the doctor-blade principle from the cloth print workshops. His methods embodied all the stages forming the modern process: copying an image and screens on a carbon tissue, transferring the carbon layer to a cylinder surface, etching the latter through the layer, rotary printing using a thinly flowing liquid, and removing the surplus with a knife (doctor blade). In 1895 Klíč founded The Rembrandt Intaglio Printing Co., in Lancaster, at the same time introducing etched cylinders instead of flat plates. Although he tried to keep his methods secret, about 1900 the inventors Ernst Rolffs of Siegburg and Eduard Mertens took out a patent, making their inventions and methods public. Under the guidance of Mertens the 1910 Easter isssue of the 'Freiburger Zeitung' was printed in a rotary letterpress machine for the text, combined with a gravure printing press, which worked at a speed of 8000 to 10,000 revs. an hour, for the illustrations. In 1906 Rolffs and Mertens together with August Nefgen and other inventors in this sphere formed a company, the Deutsche Photogravur A.G., which became the nucleus of the Tiefdrucksyndikat established in 1913, a world-wide association owning practically all the patents in gravure printing.

Summary of modern photogravure. The picture (image), which is a continuous tone positive, is transferred to a copper-surfaced cylinder by means of a pigmented gelatine-coated, sensitized carbon tissue on which the type or picture to be reproduced has been exposed. The assembling of the positives for this purpose is known as *planning*. After exposure the tissue is laid and mounted on the copper cylinder for developing by rotation in hot water. It is varnished in any areas which are not to be etched, fanned dry, and etched with ferric chloride.

Screen. Due to technical reasons fundamental to the printing process the picture etched into the copper is divided into a number of small cells which hold the ink. This is done by means of a screen imposed on the

The intaglio screen divides the surface of the cylinder into small cells which hold the ink

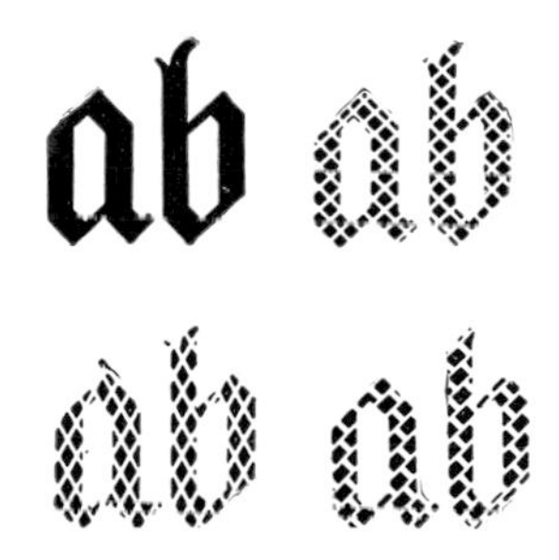

The text must also be screened. Top left, without a screen; top right, a normal square mesh screen; bottom left, a Schultz screen; bottom right, a Backstein screen

When etching is done properly the Backstein screen offers better support for the doctor blade than the square mesh screen (left)

carbon tissue which, unlike the half-tone screen, is not part of the design (cf. *autotype* and *screen reproduction*) but merely serves to divide the surface of the cylinder into etch-resisting walls for the cells which will hold the ink. There must be screen walls present over all the etched surface, i.e. illustrations, text, frames, etc. The screen was first used for photogravure by *Karl Klič* and his process manager *Samuel Fawcett*, qq.v., in Lancashire. Other types of screen are now in use, including irregular dotted screens. (See *screen.*) For practical reasons the screen is first copied on the carbon tissue, this being done in a *vacuum frame*, q.v., in which the screen is laid and fixed. After this the positive pictures and text, mounted on glass, are superimposed on the screened tissue. At one time it was common to copy, transfer, and etch the text first, and then to do so with the pictures. Later a method was devised for the simultaneous copying and transferring of illustration and text matter, but they were etched separately. In modern reproduction (especially magazine work where speed is essential) attempts have been made

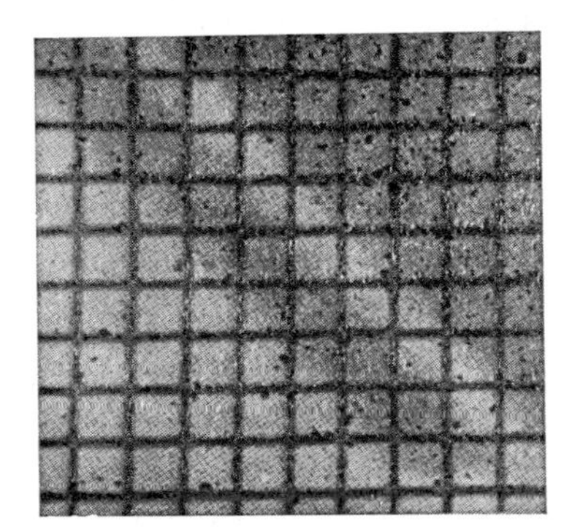

Micro-photograph of carbon tissue after screening

to do the etching as well in one operation. For this the transparencies (diapositives) must be made in a special way. The text transparencies present a sharp contrast of black and white. The time required for copying must be long enough to allow the gelatine film underneath this text surface to become hardened through. At the same time, during this protracted copying the highlights of the picture must not be excessively tanned, for which reason they must have a rather pronounced density in the transparency. The etching of the darkest tones in the picture must be about the same depth as that of the black text.

A way of solving the problem of a text-picture combination is offered by the *Rinco* process, by which the text is printed in white ink on glazed black paper and mounted, together with the picture negatives made on bromide paper, for photographing into a film positive. When this method is employed, it is necessary to maintain a very constant quality on the type pulls. For mass-produced publications, where speed is important, it is very valuable.

Planning. The positives which will be combined to make up a printed sheet are mounted on a polished glass plate. Under the plate is a carefully marked up plan of the layout to indicate its positioning. The margins outside the image area are covered with black strips which will ultimately make a 1 cm. or 2 cm. unexposed border on the carbon tissue (the unhardened gelatine under this border will then adhere more easily to the cylinder).

Exposure. The glass plate is put on the bed of a vacuum frame, the screened carbon tissue fitted to it, and an exposure made. Various light sources are used including arc lamps, mercury vapour lamps, and fluorescent tubes. Each kind has its special merits. The amount of exposure is controlled by a photometer.

Mounting. The carbon layer has to be transferred to the printing forme surface. This transfer must be done by damping the gelatine layer sufficiently for it to adhere, but damping must be restricted to the least possible amount in order to prevent any change in size of the tissue. Instead of by *wet* mounting, q.v., where the tissue is soaked in alcohol and water before mounting on the copper surface, rotary photogravure

Transferring the carbon tissue to a copper plate

work is usually by *dry* mounting. For this a dry-laying machine is used which enables damping to take place at the same time as transferring. The copper cylinder, or copper plate similarly fitted, is put in the machine and the margin of the carbon tissue is pasted to its surface. This may be done by means of adhesive tape or by careful damping of the unexposed marginal strip of the carbon tissue (see above). On revolving the cylinder a rubber roller presses the tissue against its surface, water being slowly fed in at the point where the paper comes into contact with the cylinder. The transfer being completed, the carbon tissue adhering to the cylinder is soaked in methylated spirit before development takes place in a bath of water at about 40° C (105° F). The backing paper may be removed in a little while, leaving the gelatine resist in relief on the copper surface: this must be treated continually with warm water until every trace of soluble gelatine is removed. The remaining gelatine relief is soaked first with diluted, and later with concentrated spirit, being then left to dry.

Etching. Before etching is begun any part of the surface of the cylinder which is not to be etched is covered with an asphalt (bituminous) varnish. Etching is then done with ferric chloride solution of varying strengths, commencing with a full strength and diluting as necessary. When etching is completed the copper surface is quickly washed with cold water, then with diluted acid, and finally the gelatine relief is rubbed off entirely with purified chalk and water. The asphalt coating can be

Etching a flat photogravure plate

washed off with benzol. The final stage, as a rule, is to wash the copper with a mixture of vinegar and common salt solution. For the printing of large editions, at least, it is usual to give the copper a chromium facing, after which the cylinder (or plate) is ready for the press from which printing will be done.

Copper cylinder. Formerly, doctor-blade gravure work was printed from thick copper plates or cylinders. The centre of such a cylinder was an iron core bearing a thick coating or galvanic deposit of copper. After printing, the surface of the cylinder was ground until any traces of etching were removed, then the copper surface was polished and used again. This continued until the reduction of the cylinder diameter caused inconvenience and it became necessary to give it its original size by re-plating. For this work gravure printing offices had special plants for plating, grinding, and polishing. The modern Ballard process considerably simplifies this by enabling the etched copper film to be stripped from the cylinder without difficulty, and another to be substituted galvanically

Machine for polishing and grinding photogravure cylinders. (Polimikra, Vomag)

and polished in one operation. In this way the cylinder always has the same diameter. Alternatively, under certain circumstances, detachable copper sleeves or thin copper plates covering the entire cylinder may be fitted to steel mandrels in the same way as the plate in an offset machine.

Experiments have been made for replacing the carbon tissue transfer by copying directly on a prepared plate or cylinder.

Photogravure has been known as 'copper gravure', and not without reason since practically no material other than copper is used for the formes. The carbon tissue transfer requires a scrupulously cleaned copper surface, which at the same time must be free from oxide stains. The surface is usually cleaned immediately before use with purified chalk and a little ammonia or potash solution as used for etching, all of which must be washed off afterwards. Sometimes the copper surface is treated with cyanide of potassium and silver nitrate solution, which gives a perfect surface for etching, but the cyanide is so poisonous that most firms avoid using it. The silver plating does not affect the etching procedure.

A means of identifying photogravure work is provided by the fine screen network which is faintly discernible in the finished reproduction; this is particularly so in the lack of sharpness it gives to accompanying type. (With G. U.)

See also *Colloplas, colour gravure.*

photogravure printing ink: thin, volatile ink which dries by evaporation of the solvent. It usually contains bitumen or resins, e.g. dammar, hartshorn, albertol or gilsonite asphalt in a solution of one or more volatile solvents such as zylol, toluol, and benzine with the addition of the pigment. At times benzol has also been used as a solvent, but its use is connected with a risk of poisoning. Water-based inks are in common use, particularly for security printing; an ink now used for food wrappers is made on an alcohol base, rendering it completely odourless after drying. (G. U.)

photogravure printing press: printing presses for gravure are constructed for work with sheets or reels of paper. Printing is mostly from a cylindrical forme.

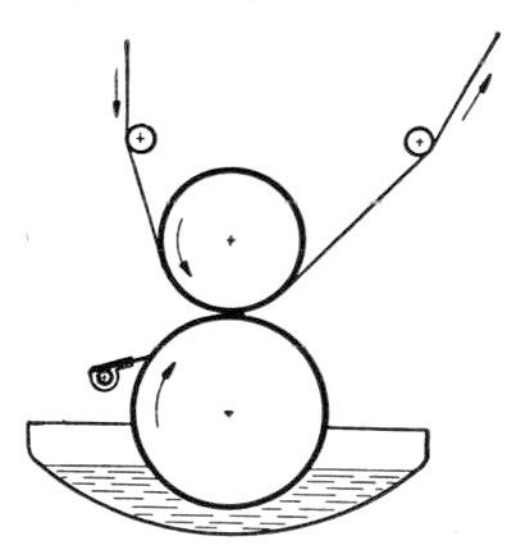

Reel-fed gravure press with the forme cylinder rotating in a trough of ink. The impression cylinder of rubber-covered steel is often water-cooled

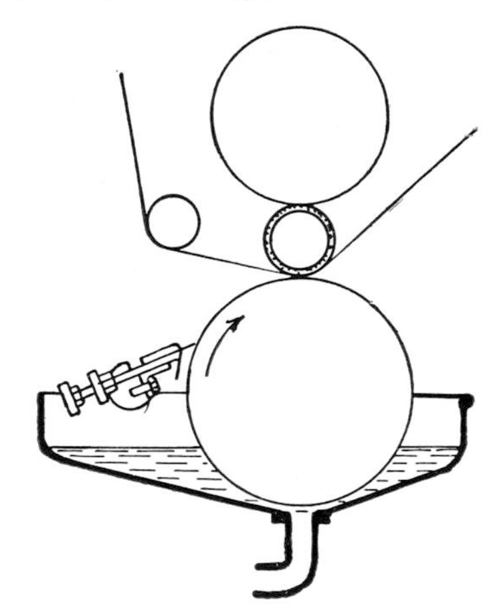

Reel-fed gravure press with a rubber impression cylinder (easily replaceable) pressed against the paper course by an uncovered steel cylinder

Arrangements for feeding the paper correspond largely to those for letterpress and offset printing (see *feeding*, *printing press*, *rotary press*). The printing mechanism, however, is built on a different principle. In photogravure the whole forme is coloured with thinly flowing ink, the surplus then being removed by the doctor blade (see diagrams). The inking arrange-

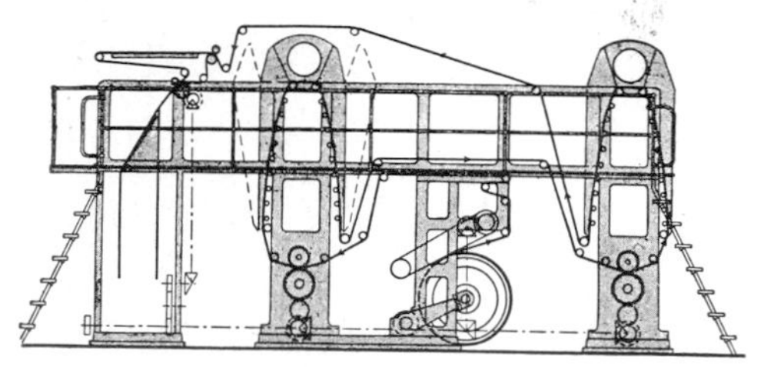

Vomag press with reel feeding and a Fuykers air dryer

ment can thus often be simplified by allowing the forme to revolve in a trough of ink. Above the trough is the doctor blade. As the cylinder must in most cases be removed for the transfer to it of the image and for etching, the bearings must be constructed with this in view. In reel-fed presses the paper course is pressed against the forme cylinder by another cylinder, known as the impression cylinder. Sometimes the impression is applied through an intermediate roller, but, in any case, the impression

In the Olympia gravure press drying is accelerated by conveying the paper vertically through a current of air on its way to the delivery table

cylinder is coated with a suitable rubber. In sheet presses, the printing cylinder supporting the sheet must have a circumference equal to or exactly double the size of the forme cylinder. The latter is more usual when working with entire copper cylinders, the forme cylinder then being inked and scraped with the blade twice for each impression. In presses for built-in copper plates forme cylinders double the size are used to avoid any excessive bending of the plate (see below).

In reel-fed presses it is desirable to increase the speed of printing as much as possible. Gravure ink dries by evaporation and ways have been tried to accelerate this so that the paper course can be introduced quickly into subsequent printing stages, or into folders or guillotines. It was formerly usual to conduct the paper across rotating steam-heated drying drums. Heating, however, was detrimental to the paper, due both to changes in size and dust from the dry paper fluffing the forme. There was the additional risk of static electricity arising in the paper with a danger of sparks igniting the inflammable vapours in the ink. Cool air drying, developed by Fuykers & Walber of Düsseldorf, was more successful, especially since 1934 when it was combined with a device for the recovery of the solvent from the ink. In Fuykers's air dryer fresh air is blown against the moving paper

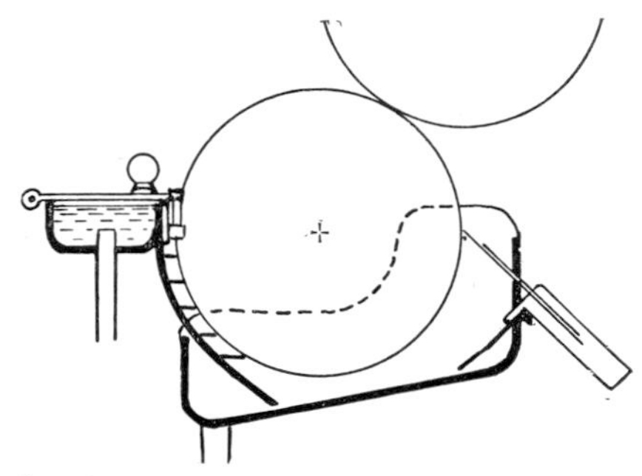

Cascade inker. The ink runs from the container down a series of ledges, washing the forme which rotates in the same direction. (*Vomag*)

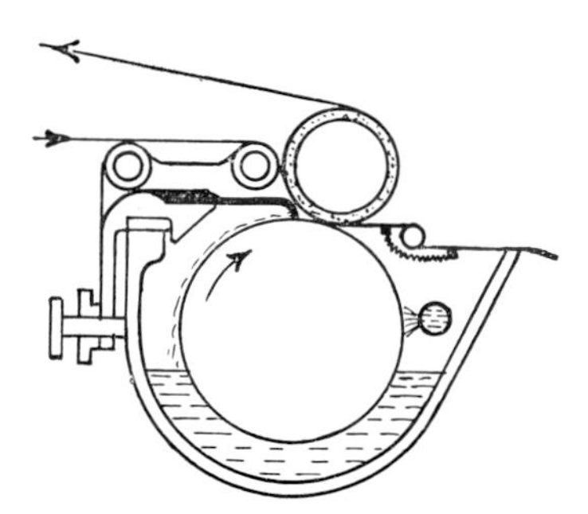

The Weiss enclosed inker (*see text*)

course from the mouthpieces of a drum arranged like a saddle over the printing mechanism. By entirely closing this, and then conducting the air current through a recovery apparatus, the evaporating solvent is recovered, and at the same time the often poisonous and inflammable vapours round the press are removed. In some modern high-speed presses working with extremely volatile solvents, practically the whole press is enclosed and the inking system

PHOTOGRAVURE
Photo: *Jaeger*.

forms an enclosed container limited above by the forme cylinder, on one side by the doctor blade, and on the other by a spring lid. Only the narrow strip of forme cylinder required for printing is to be found outside the enclosed container.

The doctor blade consists of a thin spring blade which rests at a certain pressure against the cylinder surface. In the knife-holder of the press the blade is strengthened by a thicker supporting blade. Many different types of doctor blade have been tried; one patent is an endless blade which wipes the cylinder, travels on, is cleaned, honed, lubricated, and comes round again to continue the operation. Different means of adjusting the blade to the cylinder have been tried, including hydraulic, but in every case the blade is set at an angle to the cylinder, the ink forming a lubricating film which is imperative if scratches on the forme cylinder are to be avoided. During printing the ink forms a lubricating film between blade and cylinder, it being important not to interfere with this. Modern rotary presses can be brought up to about 20,000 revs. an hour. When the printing formes consist of whole cylinders which by an earlier method are turned after each etching and occasionally given a new plating up to their original thickness, the varying diameter of the cylinder is apt to cause difficulties.

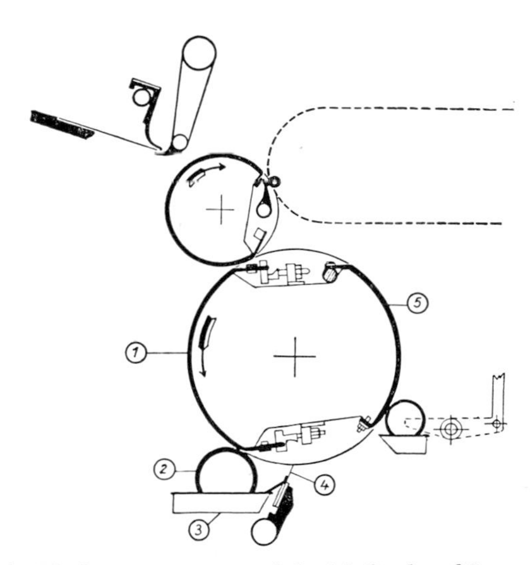

The Ideal gravure press made by Mailänder of Stuttgart. The paper is fed in sheets, and printing is done from a plate fitted to a large cylinder which has a cleaning device for the doctor blade. The plate is inked by a roller

1. *Printing plate.* 2. *Inking roller.* 3. *Ink trough.* 4. *Doctor blade.* 5. *Arrangement for removing remnants of colour from the blade, these being subsequently collected by a roller*

Attempts made to substitute copper plates for the cylinders are mostly confined to rotary sheet presses. Among these is the 'Ideal' gravure printing press made by the Schnellpressenfabrik J. G. Mailänder of Stuttgart, in which the plate cylinder is twice the size of the impression cylinder and has a knife-cleaning arrangement which frees the blade from remnants of colour after each impression. The 'Liti' Jonnisberg Press has a plate fitted round the whole circumference of the cylinder and the joint is filled with packing over which the blade glides without losing contact

On the Vomag Olympia press a copper sleeve forme can be fitted

with the cylinder surface. In other cases, it is usual in such presses to arrange for the blade to rise and descend when passing the joint. Vomag's 'Olympia' and Frankenthal-Albert's 'Palatia' have arrangements by which fitted copper plates as well as whole cylinders can be used. In the latter, when doing copperplate printing, a forme cylinder twice the size of the whole copper cylinder normally used is fitted. This is made possible by the bearing cases revolving to 180° and the distance between the cylinder axles being changed. The 'Olympia' press has a special cascade inking system and also a drying apparatus for the printed sheets. Rotary sheet presses for plates are also made by Linotype & Machinery Ltd. König & Bauer have built a rotary press (the 'Tiepolo')

The Tiepolo press has special bearings to facilitate the exchange of cylinders. (Koebau)

with a convenient arrangement for inserting the copper cylinder into the machine. The latter firm and Vomag are among well-known suppliers of reel-fed gravure printing presses. (G.U.)

Photon: a photo-composing machine invented by the Frenchmen René A. Higonnet and Louis M. Moyroud, after whom it was at first known. Its manufacture and technical development are sponsored by the Graphic Arts Research Foundation, of Cambridge, Mass., U.S.A., the machines being made by Photon Inc., their licensee.

The machine consists of three major components: a standard Underwood electric typewriter; a telephone relay system; and a photographing unit.

Operation. The family and size of type having been chosen, as well as the measure and leading, the operator types in the usual way on the keyboard. The keys, plus shift, allow eighty-eight character selections from each alphabet. As the operator depresses a key, an impulse is sent to what is called a memory or storage system. The operator continues typing until the line is within reasonable justification range of the predetermined measure. The memory unit records the amount of spacing required in incremental fashion. When the line is nearly full, the operator presses a line-release key. Now, in connection with a computer, the memory unit and computer automatically add whatever increased width is necessary to the spaces between the words to fill out the line. The typewriter produces a paper copy for proof purposes.

As a line is complete the decode and control unit automatically operates the photographic unit which exposes the letter characters and spaces one by one on a sensitized film.

Any individual character error may be corrected by returning the typewriter platen to the point of error, pressing a correction button, and over-striking the proper character. For more extensive correction within a line the whole line may be eliminated by pressing the appropriate control. Other controls permit selection of 1. point size, from 5- to 36-point; 2. point set or body width independent of size; 3. desired line width, up to 7 in.; 4. leading or space between lines, from ½-point up; 5. family or style of type.

Matrix. The machine has its types on a revolving glass matrix disc, about 8 in. diameter (cost, in 1955, about $500). On each disc there are eight rows of characters, arranged in concentric circles. There is only a single character of each family and style. Each circle contains two full founts, arranged in a semicircle. Thus one matrix disc contains sixteen founts, or some 1400 basic characters, plus border flowers. The disc rotates constantly, sweeping every character past the photographing position. A stroboscopic lamp passes light through the selected character on the disc into an optical system: this in turn projects the light in the form of a type character on the sensitized film. The type image is stopped on the film, since the duration of the stroboscopic light is of only a few microseconds' duration (eight characters can be photographed per second). Any character on the disc may be projected on to the film in twelve different point sizes. This means there are 192 normal founts under the control of the operator. Furthermore, any family, size, or style available at the keyboard may be placed in any single line being composed. Not only can type styles be mixed within a line, but point sizes and families may also be mixed without interfering with justification or alignment.

The Photon produces photographic negatives or positives which may be used for lithography, gravure, or to make letterpress blocks, e.g. Dow etched plates. In the U.S.A., the Dow Chemical Company and the American Newspaper Publishers Association combined in a programme to study high-speed etching techniques, and by 1954 Dow-ANPA magnesium plates for letterpress could be etched in 7 minutes. Using such plates an edition of the New Testament was produced by letterpress on Bible paper in 1954. Composition was done on the Photon, the type being Bodoni. Experts predicted in 1955 that the Photon may revolutionize the letterpress printing industry.

phototype: another name for *collotype*, q.v.

phototypography: the general name given to several processes in which printing surfaces are made by the aid of light; an engraving in relief is produced by photo-mechanical means.

phylactery: a narrow band or scroll on which was inscribed a name or a speech. They are occasionally seen in illuminated manuscripts or incunabula where they are drawn as if issuing from the mouths of characters, or they may be held in the hand.

Their use has not entirely died out and they now appear as 'balloons' coming from the mouths of characters in cartoons or comics.

phytoglyphy: the name given by Henry Bradbury to the process of *nature printing*, q.v., which he learned in Vienna and for which he took an English patent in 1853.

pica: 1. the name for a former size of type, now 12-point. The name may derive from the use in 15th-century England of types of this size for *Pye-books*

(1), q.v., or merely from the piebald effect of the printed page.

2. a unit of measure, e.g. for the width and depth of text on a page. A pica is 0·166 in. (Pica rhymes with Leica.) Synonymous with *em* (2).

pick brush: a brush used for cleaning formes of type. A 'pick' is a blob of ink adhering to type.

Pickering, William, 1796–1854: a London publisher who, in 1829, began a successful collaboration with *Charles Whittingham*, jun., q.v., of the Chiswick Press. His most notable publications were the Aldine edition of the English poets, and, in 1844, the reprints of various versions of the Book of Common Prayer. He also pioneered the introduction of cloth-covered boards. Pickering adapted to his use the anchor and dolphin device of Aldus Manutius, adding the words 'Aldi Discipulus Anglus'.

picking: an alternative name for *plucking*, q.v.

Pictograph bi-metal process: a British process for giving a copper image to grained or ungrained aluminium lithographic plates. After the aluminium plate has been deep-etched it is swabbed over the image areas with a patent solution. Copper is thereby deposited chemically in the form of a cell structure. After deposition, the plate is cleaned down and dried. It can then be filled in with a tough plastic 'strata base' which is grease receptive. The plastic base prevents the copper from becoming desensitized.

Such plates are durable and cheap, giving long runs with constant size of the smallest dot. They are made by Pictorial Machinery (Chemicals) Ltd.

pie: composed type which has been spilled and indiscriminately mixed.

piecework: a wage payment system whereby earnings are based on agreed rates for work done.

pierced: a block which has had a portion of its surface removed so that type may be inserted there.

pigskin: a strong leather, having a distinctive grain, used for covering heavy books. Decoration is most satisfactory when blind-stamped.

See also *blind-stamped panels*.

pilcher: a wad of three or four felts sewn together which is placed on top of a *post*, q.v., before pressing.

pile: a pile of paper placed on a transfer platform, feeder, or delivery table. *Pile feeder* and *pile delivery* are the names for apparatus which conveys sheets to the press from the pile of paper, or delivers them when printed from the press to a pile. *Pile reversers* are used for turning a whole pile of paper upside down, e.g. for perfecting. (G.U.)

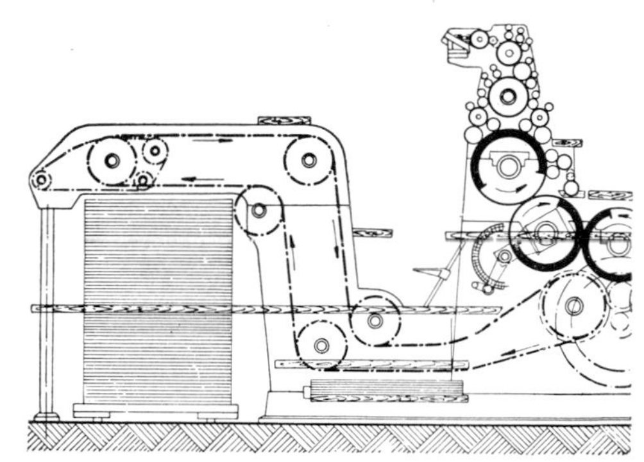

High pile delivery in a Planeta offset press

pillar: a good-quality paper made in Normandy between *c.* 1610 and 1680, and in only one size, 12½ in. by 16 in. A pillar was the watermark.

pin-mark: a round depression in the side of a shank of typefounder's type made by the pin which ejects the type from the mould.

pin seal: the fine-grained skin of the young seal used for costly bindings.

pinax (pl. **pinakes**): a Greek word (now rarely used) for a board or tablet on which was written a list, catalogue, or index. The term originated with Kallimachos, librarian of the Alexandrian Library, *c.* 260–240 B.C., who made an annotated catalogue in 120 volumes of the works in the library. How the entries were arranged is now a matter for conjecture since no evidence survives, but the *pinakes* laid the foundation for the first critical study of Greek literature.

Pinelli, Gian Vicenzio, 1538–1601: a famous Italian book-collector who established in Padua a library at which the bibliophiles of the day held meetings. After his death Pinelli's library suffered a curious fate. Nearly 300 manuscripts were confiscated for the St Mark's Library, Venice, while most of the remaining works were loaded in three ships bound for Naples (his birthplace). Pirates seized one ship, and the contents of the other two were bought by Cardinal Borromeo for his Ambrosiana Library in Milan. A small residue of the original collection had been kept in Padua by Pinelli's relatives. Successive generations developed this once more into an important library. On the death of Maffeo Pinelli the collection was brought to London and auctioned in 1789 and 1790 for £9356.

Pipe Roll Society: a society founded in 1883 for the printing of Pipe Rolls, charters and national manuscripts prior to 1200. (The Pipe, or Great, Roll was the document commenced in 1131 on which were entered in a large set hand the accounts due to the King from his lands and services.)

pirated edition: an edition of a work published without the permission of the copyright owner. Cf. *authorized edition.*

Pirckheimer, Bilibald: 1470–1530: a wealthy citizen and *Rat* of Nuremberg. He appears to have begun book-collecting when studying in Padua, 1490–97, and his books included much Latin and Italian literature. He returned to Nuremberg where his library came to be the most important in Germany and was made available to scholars. About 1501 he met *Albrecht Dürer*, q.v., and Conrad Celtes, while his house became a literary and artistic centre. Dürer designed at least two bookplates for Pirckheimer, one for quarto and one for folio volumes. Pirckheimer translated and published several Greek and Latin authors including Ptolemy's 'Geographia', Strasbourg, 1522.

His library survived him intact for about a hundred years but in 1636 was sold to Thomas Howard, Earl of Arundel. It passed in turn to his nephew, Henry Howard, Duke of Norfolk, who gave part of his uncle's library to the newly formed Royal Society and part to the College of Arms. The manuscripts in it were sold to the British Museum in 1830, while the non-scientific volumes (including the Pirckheimer books) were sold to Bernard Quaritch in 1870 and have since been dispersed.

Pissarro, Lucien, 1863–1944: see *Eragny Press.*

Pistorius, Cyriakus, *c.* 1629–*c.* 1690: a famous typefounder of Basle, whose business was taken over in 1692 by his son Johannes (1664–1730), and in 1707 by Wilhelm Haas.

Pitt Press: part of the Cambridge University Press, built in 1831 with the surplus subscriptions for the statue of the younger Pitt, a Cambridge student, erected in Hanover Square.

plagiarism: the copying of another person's writings and publishing the material copied as original matter.

plain rule: strips of brass or type metal which print an uninterrupted straight line. (M.L.)

planer: a slab of hard wood used to level the type in a chase by placing it on the surface and tapping it with a mallet.

Trumax planer

Bech planer

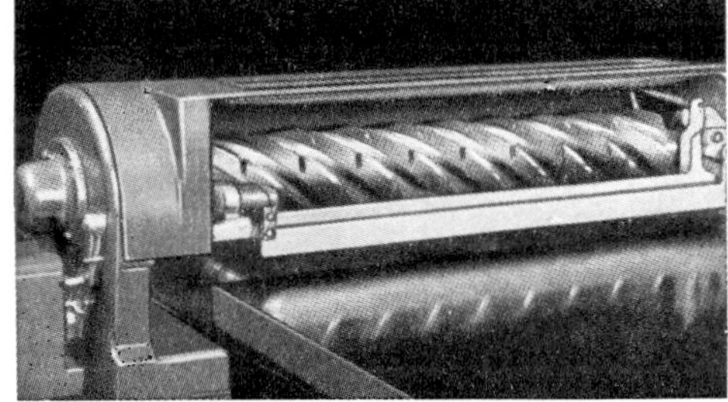

Plane-o-plate rotary helical cutter for flat plates (Monomelt Co. of Minneapolis)

planetary signs: see *astronomical symbols.*

planing machine: a machine for adjusting flat stereotype plates to an exact thickness. The Trumax planer illustrated has automatic feeding. In the hydraulically operated Bech model the cutter is fixed and the plate is carried under it on a movable table; the whole plate is finished with one motion. Rotary cutters may also be used for this purpose, and one is illustrated under *routing machine*, q.v. (G.U.)

plank: the heavy piece of hardwood (often mahogany) to which the *coffin* and *stone*, qq.v., of a hand-printing press were fixed. The plank rested on rails fitted to the carriage, the whole (i.e. forme, stone, coffin, and plank) being drawn under the platen by turning the *rounce*, q.v.

planographic printing: printing from level surfaces prepared so that the parts to be printed accept ink from the rollers while the non-image areas reject it. The image areas are greasy, the rest moist, utilizing the mutual repulsion of grease and water (the principle of lithography).

Printing is by the even pressure of a hand-roller or cylinder over the flat plate, or by offsetting the image from a curved plate on to a rubber roller and thence to the paper. Even colour is a characteristic of planographic printing. Also known as *surface printing.*

See also *lithography, photo-lithography.*

planography: now used as a substitute for zincography and aluminography. It refers to methods of printing from flat surfaces other than stone. (M.L.)

plant: 1. the fixtures, machinery, tools, apparatus, etc., necessary to carry out a mechanical operation.

2. a printing establishment. (M.L.)

plant-free reprint: an impression taken from standing type or plates after recovering initial costs. In explaining this term one of Britain's oldest publishing houses states 'we use the expression "plant" to cover all the initial costs of printing a book, i.e. composition, illustrations, making of blocks, making of moulds, casting of plates. Usually everything except the making of plates is charged to the first printing, which is run from type. We charge the casting of plates and the insertion therein of the blocks to the second printing. On the third printing there are none of these charges to be met, since they have all been paid and plates exist: this is what we call a "plant-free reprint".'

Plantin, Christopher, *c.* 1520–89: a Frenchman who in 1549 established a bindery at Antwerp, and about 1555 a printing and publishing business in the same city. He became one of the most noted printers of his era, developing the use of flowers, copperplate illustrations, and engraved title-pages. Among his punch-cutters were Granjon, Guyot, Haultin, Le Bé, and Van der Keere.

His best-known production was the Polyglot Bible (or Biblia regia) in eight volumes, 1568–72, commissioned and partly financed by King Philip II of Spain, for whom thirteen sets were printed on parchment; a general issue of twelve hundred sets was printed on paper. The languages were Hebrew, Greek, Aramaic, Latin, and Syriac; the editor was Benedictus Monatus.

The old-face type which bears his name was probably cut by Granjon or Garamond; in 1913 it was revived by Monotype in medium and light weights, being a somewhat heavy face with large x-height and thick serifs; it is, however, excellent for letterpress work on coated papers.

See also *Moretus, Jan.*

plaquette: a small tablet of metal bearing a design in relief cast from a wax mould. The principle was adopted in France during the 15th and 16th centuries as the central feature on the front covers of books. Fine, hand-painted examples were made for books in the library of *Jean Grolier*, q.v., the plaquettes being impressions in gesso, afterwards painted and inserted in the front board.

See also *Canevari Library.*

plaster-moulding process: the preparation of stereos by pressing a film of moist plaster on to a forme or block; a skilled operation which gives results of great detail. The mould of plaster is then prepared for casting.

plastic bindings: books in which the back edges of the leaves are united into a solid plastic unit to form the spine. Cf. *unsewn binding.*

plastic plates: printing stereos made from any of several plastic materials. They should be 12-point thick. Advantages are lightness and good resistance to chemical deterioration by inks and cleaning solvents. The printing image is less liable to damage by rough use and long runs than in metal plates.

See also *thermoplastic plates.*

Plastocowell: a reproduction process developed by W. S. Cowell Ltd., of Ipswich. The artist makes his drawing or painting in Photopake (a retouching paste) on a transparent grained plastic film. The paste contains fine opaque particles, and the concentration of these in any given area affects the strength of the tint. One sheet is made for each colour.

The plastic sheet is laid on a sensitized zinc plate, whereupon exposure to light prints the image on the metal which can be used for a lithographic forme or a letterpress line block in the usual way.

The absence of a photographic screen is a distinct advantage over normal photo-litho methods, and the elimination of hand-retouching is both more economical and, from the artist's viewpoint, more aesthetically satisfying. Various drawing techniques are employed and the possibilities are limited only by the artist's skill and understanding of the medium.

plate: 1. an electro or stereo of set-up type.

2. a sheet of wood or metal, bearing a design from which an impression is printed.

3. a full-page book illustration, printed separately from the text, and often on different paper. Cf. *figure*.

4. a photographic plate; whole, $8\frac{1}{2}$ in. by $6\frac{1}{2}$ in.; half, $6\frac{1}{2}$ in. by $4\frac{3}{4}$ in.

See also *interleaved* (2 and 3).

plate-boring machine: a machine for reducing curved stereotype plates to a required thickness. The boring machine may be intended solely for boring, or may comprise a complete finishing machine which also cools the plates (see illustration). Boring is done by pressing the plate against a water-cooled half-cylinder of large dimensions, and then a shaving is simultaneously removed from all the supporting ribs on the inner side of the plate by means of a steel cutter. By this treatment stereotype plates are corrected to a true cylindrical shape corresponding to the arch in the machine.

In cooling, water is sprayed on to the inner side of the plate only, and a considerable change occurs in its shape, though this disappears when the temperature over the whole plate evens. The machine can be fed by a stream of plates, so that three can be passing through at one time (boring, cooling, and brushing off the water). The output is three to four plates a minute. (G.U.)

See also *casting box*, *routing machine*.

Finishing machine for curved stereo plates. Boring is done under the central arch, cooling at the far end. The smaller machine is a cutter for edge trimming

Transporting finished plates

plate-dog: a device for holding blocks, stereos, etc., in position on a plate cylinder in a rotary press. (G.U.)

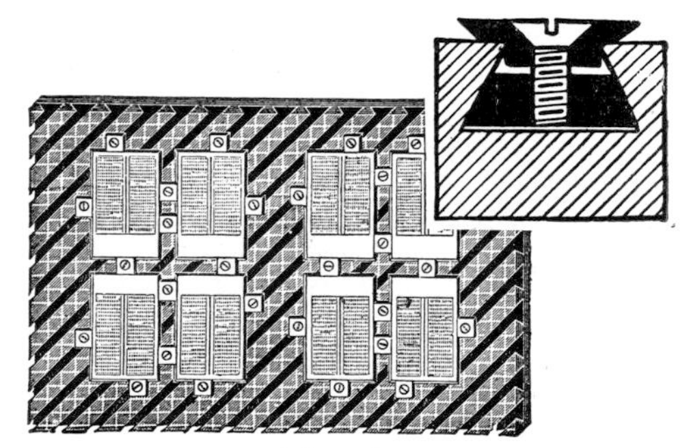

Plate-dog

plate finish (or **plate glazed**): the smooth surface given to sheets of paper by interleaving them with polished copper or zinc plates and then pressing them between chilled iron rollers.

plate folder: see *folding machine*.

plate mark: a line depressed into the paper by the edges of an intaglio engraved plate during printing.

plate pasting: see *pasting*.

plated paper: paper made of new and old rags, together with clay: has good printing qualities for copper engravings, etchings, and photogravures; not strong. It is usually unsized, and there is often a considerable difference between the two sides of the sheet. (M. L.)

platen press: the earliest hand-printing presses and their many improved successors were platen presses, since they had a heavy flat plate, or *platen*, which was lowered and pressed against a horizontal type forme. Modern platen presses are non-cylinder machines in which the forme of type is held on a flat bed (which may be sloping or standing vertically). They have inkers which, in small American presses, are in the form of rotating discs, while European models usually have cylindrical inkers, their movements being automatically connected with the motion of the platen. Printing is done on a platen which is a square steel slab covered with sheets of paper over which a final sheet is tightly stretched. This packing and its enclosing frame are known as the *tympan*,

Liberty press, 1857

which is used to adjust pressure. Sheets of paper to be printed are fed singly on to the tympan and held there by guide-pins or a *frisket*. Mechanical action then moves the flat surface of the paper-bearing platen into contact with the forme, and an impression is made.

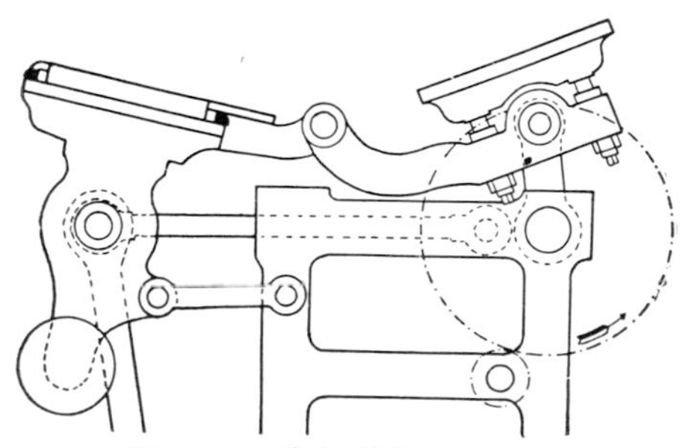

Diagram of the Liberty press

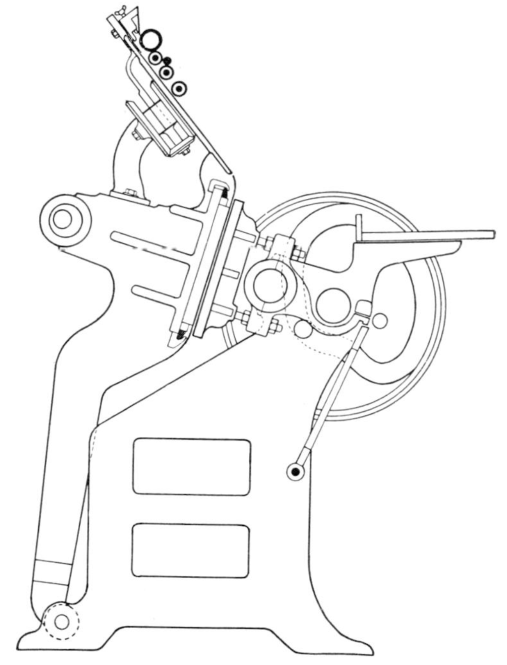

The principle of the Gordon press

The motion of small presses is actuated by a hand-lever (table presses) or a treadle (treadle presses), but this is no longer common. Some motor-driven platen machines have hand-feeding, which may be necessary for some of the multiple operations done in these presses, but the Thompson British Automatic Platen and similar machines have a completely automatic feed and delivery of the paper, locking register device, and geared inkers.

Platen presses may be classed under one or other of the following systems. The *Boston System* has a fixed bed against which a platen rotates. To this belong the Pearl, Golding, and a number of older models, and finally the modern Heidelberg. In the *Liberty press* bed and platen rotate towards each other round a joint axle, like a closing hinge. The *Gordon press* has a rotating platen and a bed which remains vertical but makes a slight rotating movement round a separate axle. This type includes the Craftsman Automaton. The *Gally press* and its modern successors (e.g. Victoria, Phoenix) have a stationary bed and a platen which rolls to a vertical position and then glides forward so that immediately before the impression the platen is parallel to the bed and moving perpendicularly towards it.

The movement of the platen and its pressure against the forme can be effected in various ways; the knee-lever motion of the Heidelberg is shown in the

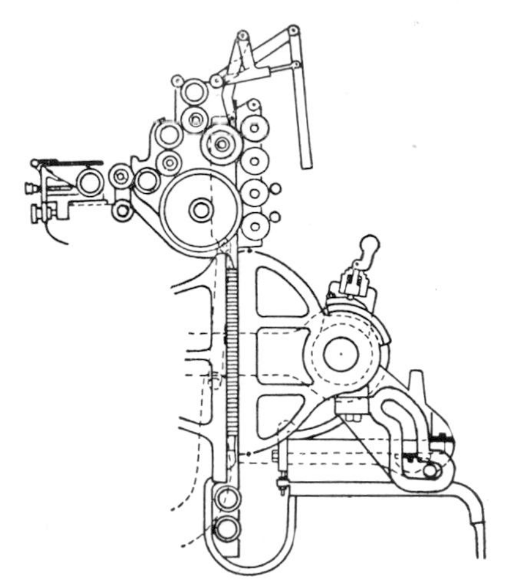

Modern Gally press (Victoria), with double inking rollers

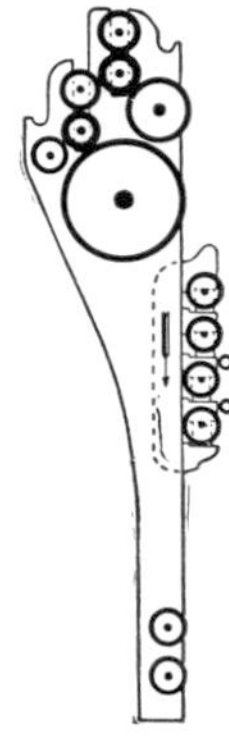

Standard inking arrangement on a Gally press. The four coupled rollers, inked from the cylinders above, move down to the forme and ink it with two rollers. At the lowest point these two rollers come into contact with both two ink-filled cylinders on the wagon, and with two rollers underneath the bed. In travelling upwards across the bed the forme is inked by all four forme rollers

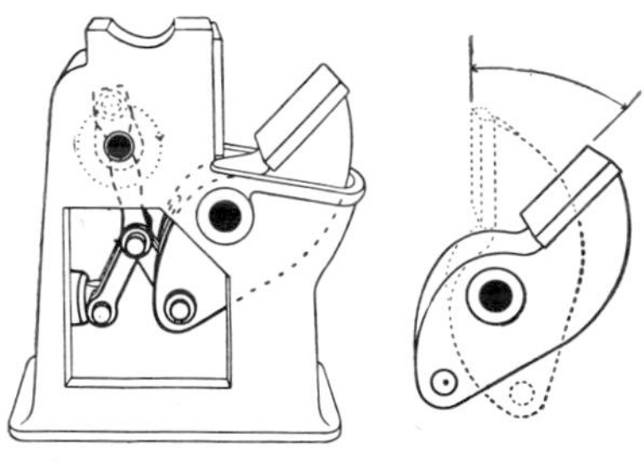

The knee-lever and platen motion of a Heidelberg

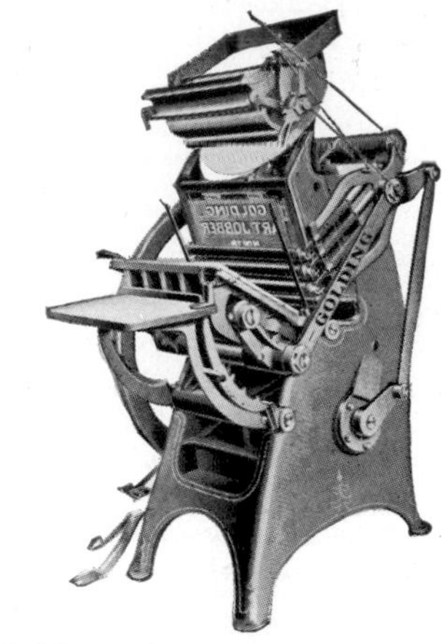

The Golding jobbing press has a disc inker

The Victoria platen press has a cylinder-inking system and a flywheel motion

diagram. It is common to utilize a crank movement in connection with a friction-coupled flywheel as in the Victoria (see diagram).

To secure an even motion free from vibration, and accurate impression, both platen and bed must be well proportioned: in large machines the latter is cast with the floor stand.

As an historical note it may be added that an early successful machine with a vertical platen was invented in America by George Phineas Gordon in 1862; this was introduced to the English trade under the name *Franklin*. The first machine in which vertical forme and platen moved laterally into contact was built by Merrit Gally in 1869, also in America. (With G.U.)

plating: 1. a printers' term for the preparation of stereotype or electrotype plates from set-up type.
2. see *guarding*.

Pleydenwurff, Wilhelm, fl. 1491–95: an artist of Nuremberg. He was the stepson of Michael Wolgemut with whom he was associated in designing the 1809 illustrations for Schedel's 'Die Weltchronik', 1493. The limits of Pleydenwurff's share in this important example of early German book illustration have not been precisely established.

Plomer, Henry Robert, 1856–1928: an official of the British Museum, who made valuable researches into the history of printing in England during the 16th century. Many of his writings were published by the Bibliographical Society in 'The Library', or as separate monographs.

Important was 'A Dictionary of Booksellers and Printers who were at work in England from 1641 to 1667', 1907 (supplement, 1668–1725, 1922); and 'Wynkyn de Worde and his Contemporaries', Grafton, 1925.

plough: a hand-machine used to cut the edges of a book. While still used for the edge-trimming of hand-bound books, elsewhere the quicker, but possibly less accurate *guillotine*, q.v., is used.

plucking: a printing fault which is caused by the ink plucking the surface of the paper and leaving irregular white patches in printed areas. The main causes of this are either too stiff an ink, or the surface of fibres on the paper being too loosely bonded.

pneumatic press: a press in which the pressure is applied through the medium of compressed air. Such presses are used for a variety of purposes in mechanized binderies. Except where extreme pressure is called for they have advantages of speed and cleanliness over *hydraulic presses*, q.v. (L.K.)

pochoir: the name for a hand-coloured illustration process occasionally used for contemporary French editions de luxe. The foundation is a monochrome print of the design. Stencils in celluloid or metal are made for various parts of the design, special brushes and pigments being used in colouring. The process was used in the 18th century.

pocket edition: a small octavo edition, usually not larger than foolscap octavo—6¾ in. by 4¼ in.

Poeschel, Carl Ernst, 1874–1944: a printer and, for a while, publisher of Leipzig. He entered his father's printing firm, Poeschel & Trepte, where he devoted himself to reviving in Germany the art of fine printing, much as did Morris and Cobden-Sanderson in England. He had various roman types of former days re-cut for his use, many by his friend Walter Tiemann.

In 1905 he took over, as a joint venture with Anton Kippenberg, the Insel-Verlag, which was noted for its fine typography and low-priced editions of high standard. In 1907 he founded the *Janus-Presse*, q.v.

Poet Laureate: a title and pension bestowed by the Sovereign upon an eminent poet who is expected to compose commemorative poems for national occasions. The first to receive a warrant from the King formally granting him the Office of Poet Laureate was John Dryden in 1668, though Ben Jonson, Sir William Davenant, and other former poets had styled themselves and been known by this title. The prototype for such an office is found in the *versificator regis* of the 13th century and the court minstrels of still earlier times. Holders of the office have been:

John Dryden	1668–88
Thomas Shadwell	1688–92
Nahum Tate	1692–1715
Nicholas Rowe	1715–18
Laurence Eusden	1718–30
Colley Cibber	1730–57
William Whitehead	1757–85
Thomas Wharton	1785–90
Henry James Pye	1790–1813
Robert Southey	1813–43
William Wordsworth	1843–50
Alfred Tennyson	1850–92
Alfred Austin	1896–1913
Robert Bridges	1913–30
John Masefield	1930–

Poetry Book Society: a body established in 1954, under the auspices of the Arts Council of Great Britain, to bring to the notice of its members 'the best English poetry being written today'. The annual subscription of two guineas is used as a deposit against which members receive four newly published volumes of poetry a year; titles are selected by a board appointed by a committee of management. Would-be members may subscribe at any bookseller's.

point: the unit of measurement for type, approximately seventy-two points equalling one linear inch. Former type names have been discarded and sizes previously known as nonpareil, brevier, pica, etc., have as their equivalents 6-point, 8-point, 12-point, etc. The point system was devised in 1737 by the Parisian typefounder, Pierre Fournier, to combat the confusion among European founders and printers. His unit was 0·0137 in. After subsequent changes a unit in which one point equals 0·0138 in. was adopted by American typefounders in 1871, and by British in 1898.

See also *body* (2), *cicero*, *Didot point*, *line gauge*, *long-bodied type*, *parts of type*, *type sizes*.

pointillé: a style of tooling dotted lines and curves on the covers of a book which, in the first half of the 17th century, was used by many French binders, notably Florimond Badier and Macé Ruette.

points: short pins in the sides of a tympan which pierce the sheets to ensure the pages will be in register when the reverse is printed.

Poitevin, Alphonse Louis, 1813–82: the French inventor, in 1855, of *carbon tissue*, q.v., the use of which, however, was developed by J. W. Swan between 1862–64.

See also *collotype*.

polaires: leather satchels used by 6th-century Irish ecclesiastics for carrying books. They were ordinarily made without decoration unless for a man of wealth in which case they bore a design stamped in relief.

Polidori Press: a private printing press established near Regent's Park, London, about 1840, by Gaetano Polidori, head of the London firm which in 1796 issued an Italian translation of 'Paradise Lost'. The first work issued was his translation into Italian of Milton's works, 3 vols., 1840. He also printed early verses written by his grandchildren Dante Gabriel and Christina Rossetti (1843 and 1847).

The press appears to have ceased activity about 1850, and Polidori died in 1854.

polished calf: calfskin which is given a high finish for use in fine bookwork.

Pollard, Alfred William, 1859–1944: an official of the British Museum who contributed important studies to our knowledge of early printed books. Many of his writings were published by the Bibliographical Society in 'The Library'; other studies appeared as 'Fine Books', Putnam, 1912, and 'Early Illustrated Books', Kegan Paul, 1917.

polyautography: the name by which *lithography*, q.v., was known in early 19th-century England.

polychromatic printing: the name given by William Savage to the *chiaroscuro* process, q.v., which he revived in the 19th century.

polyglot edition: a book, or series of books, giving versions of one text in different languages. The Bible is the text which has most frequently been selected for treatment in this way. The first printed polyglot Bible was the 'Biblia polyglotta Complutensis', printed 1514–17 by Arnao Guillen de Brocar at Alcalá de Henares (Complutum) for Cardinal Ximenes. Plantin's polyglot Bible had texts in Hebrew, Greek, Latin, Chaldaic, and Syriac; it appeared 1569–72: the Paris polyglot Bible, 1645, sponsored by Michel Le Jay, added Arabic and Samaritan to Plantin's text.

Notable among polyglot Bibles printed in England is Brian Walton's 'Biblia Sacra polyglotta', in nine languages, published in six volumes between 1653–57. The work interested Oliver Cromwell, and by his permission the paper on which it was printed was imported duty free. The Protector was therefore mentioned with peculiar respect on page 10 of the preface: at the Restoration the two-line passage was cancelled in the unsold copies, while words more appropriate to the times were substituted. From this has arisen the distinction of 'Republican' and 'Loyal' copies, the latter being more numerous.

polyptych: a codex consisting of more than three leaves.

polyvinyl alcohol enamel: a photoengraving resist used for coating zinc or copper half-tone plates.

pond: the box at the 'wet end' of a paper-making machine in which the pulp is contained until it is flowed on to the moving wire to be formed into paper.

Ponsonby, William, *c.* 1546–1604: a prominent Elizabethan bookseller-publisher who is best remembered for his association with Sir Philip Sidney and Spenser whose 'Faerie Queene' he published in 1590 and 1596.

Pontifical: a book containing the ceremonies and offices to be performed by bishops.

Ponton, Mungo, 1802–80: the Edinburgh scientist who invented a cheap and simple method of preparing paper for photographic drawing without the use of any silver salt. He made the discovery that the action of light renders potassium dichromate insoluble: this was fundamental to subsequent photo-mechanical reproduction processes.

pope roll: a moving roller at the 'dry end' of a Fourdrinier where the paper is reeled.

pornography: originally, a term restricted to descriptions of harlotry, but now extended to include all books having as their principal object the titillation of the sensualist. Such works are described as *obscene* when they have a tendency to corrupt and deprave people whose minds are open to such influences. The literary merits of many pornographic books are often only of the slightest; large private collections have been made, however, notably in France and Germany.

In Great Britain several acknowledged classics are still banned from the shelves of certain public libraries by the somewhat arbitrary and capricious censorship of their custodians. In 1954 the question of what was pornographic and obscene received one

of its periodical airings in the English law-courts. It was at Swindon that an edition of Boccaccio's 'Il Decamerone' was pronounced obscene, to the astonishment of the literary public of most of Europe.
See also *curiosa, erotica, facetiae, obscene libel.*

portas: see *portiforium.*

portiforium: the medieval Breviary, designed to be carried easily. Also known as a *portas.*

portolano: a sea chart giving plans of harbours, coastlines, and wind directions. Originating with Italian charts of the Mediterranean, they were later made for other areas and often issued in atlas form. The earliest dated example is that of Petrus Vesconte, 1311, and they continued to be made until the late 17th century. The earliest printed portolano was Bartolomeo's 'Isolario', published by Guglielmo de Piancerreto, Venice, *c.* 1486.
See also *atlas, mappamondae, periplus, ruttier book.*

post: a pile of wet sheets of paper, interleaved with felts, formed on the couch by the coucher who takes them from the hand-mould. He may be assisted by an *upper end boy,* q.v. The post, usually of six quires, about 18 in. high, is then covered with a final layer of felts (called a *pilcher*) and pressed at two tons per square inch.
For subsequent treatment see *pack.*

posthumous: said of a book which is first published after the author's death.

pot cassé: the line-drawing of a pierced urn (French 'toret') which, with the words NON PLVS, formed the distinguishing mark on the title-pages of books printed in the 16th century by *Geofroy Tory,* q.v. The broken urn was also part of his design for decorating book covers; from this emblem graceful arabesques flowed to fill the panel. (Tory did not bind books himself.)

potcher: a bleaching and washing machine which circulates the half-stuff as it comes from the breaker and separates the fibres. The half-stuff then passes to the *beater,* q.v.

Potter press: the first American offset press to embody the basic principle of all modern offset presses of three cylinders of equal size which make a complete revolution for each impression. It was manufactured by the Premier & Potter Printing Press Co., N.Y., now Harris-Seybold, Cleveland, Ohio. For diagram see *offset press.* (G.U.)

pouncing: the rubbing of tracing paper with pumice powder to roughen the surface slightly. This is done when the faintly greasy surface of the paper will not properly accept the ink of pen-drawings.

powdered: the effect obtained on a book cover when small flower ornaments are repeated regularly in rows over it. Early examples date from 1560 on books bound for Charles IX of France. Also known as *semis* or *semé.*

powdering: a printing fault in which the vehicle and pigment separate after printing, leaving the latter loosely on the surface of the paper. The cause may be an unduly mobile ink or an over-absorbent paper.

Powell, Roger: a former teacher of the Royal College of Art. He learned bookbinding with Douglas and Sydney Cockerell. A fine example of his work was done on the Oxford Lectern Bible, 1935. He was also commissioned to rebind the *Book of Kells,* q.v.

pre-press work: any of several techniques used in the modern composing room to prepare the forme with greater precision. This saves time on the press, reduces possible machine trouble, and leads to better printing.
Mechanical quoins, saw-trimmers for the accurate cutting of slugs and blocks, thickness gauges for type and slugs which are accurate to a thousandth of an inch, block levellers for planing wood and metal mounts, block and plate gauges, a make-up gauge for registering plates on their mounts, and a trolley for the careful moving of the forme, are among the many items of equipment used: but it is the pride and skill of the composing room staff which make these aids of value. Also called *pre-make-ready.*
See also *make-ready.*

preface: the author's personal remarks to the reader which often conclude with a paragraph of acknowledgements; it properly follows the bibliographical matter and dedication. It is usual to write a new preface to successive editions, outlining the extent of changes and additions. Cf. *foreword, introduction.*

preliminary matter: those pages of a book which precede the text. The order should be half-title, frontispiece, title-page, dedication, preface, acknowledgements, contents, list of illustrations, introduction. Minor variations of this order are found. Since preliminary matter (abbreviated to *prelims* or *preliminaries*) is normally set up after the text, it often has separate pagination in roman numerals. Also known as *front matter.*
See also *subsidiaries.*

Premier press: a two-revolution four-roller press covering in its product the whole range of letterpress printing; more especially good half-tone work in both black and colours. (M.L.)

preprint: the printing and publishing of a portion of a work prior to the publication of the whole. Cf. *off-print, separate.*

preserving leather bindings: see *leather preservation.*

press: the machine or apparatus used to press the paper on the type, engraving, etc. For printing, there are three distinct mechanical methods of imparting this impression: 1. by the *platen press*; 2. by the *flat-bed cylinder press*; 3. by the *rotary press*, qq.v.
See also *printing, printing press.* (M.L.)

press books: books published by *private presses*, q.v.

press-clipping bureau: an organization which, for a fee, collects reviews and notices of a book or its author from periodic literature.

press mark: see *impressed watermark.*

press number: a printer's mark placed at the foot of one or more pages in certain gatherings (but not all) of some 17th- and 18th-century books. While probably to indicate the presses on which a book was printed, the reasons for using these numbers have not yet been established beyond controversy.

press proofs: the final corrected proofs of a work. Usually a set of page proofs with the author's, publisher's, and printer's final corrections or approval.

press revise: an extra proof from the corrected type when ready for machining. The machine-man generally sends a press revise to the machine reviser (at the printer's) who finally passes for press. Also known as *machine revise.*

pressboards: see *millboards.*

pressman: the skilled operator of a printing machine. Also known as *machine-man* or *machine-minder.*
See also *presswork.*

presswork: the printing off on paper of matter set up in type, and in modern usage, the care and attention devoted to this as revealed by the quality of the result. Presswork includes the preparation of the impression cylinder for even printing and the control of ink-flow during the running of the press. An alternative name, inapplicable to work done on hand-presses, is *machining.*

Pretsch, Paul, 1808–73: a Viennese who, prior to 1853, was employed in the State Printing House. He later worked in London where he invented various methods of process work based on the sensitivity to light of a compound of dichromate and gelatine or glue, particularly photo-electric processes. (G.U.)
See also *heliogravure.*

Prideaux, Sarah Treverbian, fl. 1880–1910: a pupil of T. J. Cobden-Sanderson remembered for her works on bookbinding, 'Bibliography of Bookbinding', 1892, and 'Historical Sketch of Bookbinding', 1893.
Between 1884 and 1904 she bound for wealthy collectors.

prima: the page of printer's copy on which a new slip or galley proof begins. The first word of the slip proof is marked on the copy.

primary binding: the binding style used for a book when it is first published. Cf. *secondary binding.*

Primaton overlay: the trade name for a process of making mechanical overlays for letterpress half-tones by the use of plastic moulding powder. It was announced in 1954.
A thin M.F. paper, preferably with an esparto body, is used as the base. Coated stock and mechanical wood papers are unsuitable. To minimize shrinking, paper should be stored dry and be warmed before use.
After levelling-up the block, it is cleaned with petrol or spirit, and a proof is pulled. A special ink is supplied, but certain other linseed-oil-free inks can be used. The proof should be taken with full colour, but not enough to fill up the light and medium tones or spread ink on the half-tone dots. Two powders are used for the overlay; firstly, one of four grades of white, chosen according to the thickness of overlay needed, which is liberally dusted on the proof, any surplus being brushed off. The second powder is blue, and is dusted on as a filler and cleanser.
The layer of powder on the proof is fused into a solid film by heating it, preferably in a special regulated oven which automatically ejects the overlay when ready.
Where the overlay is placed directly under the top sheet on a cylinder press, this should be of waxed manila, as the coarser powders may wear unwaxed top sheets, especially on long runs.

Primer: a book for lay use containing the Hours of the Virgin, with the rubrics, and often prayers, written in English.

Prince, Edward P., 1847–1923: a London punch-cutter and typefounder. Types cut by him were used by the Ashendene, Doves, Eragny, Essex House, Florence, Kelmscott, and Riccardi Presses, as well as by many British foundries.

print: 1. to apply paper to inked blocks, type, or plates.
See also *printing.*
2. a picture or design taken from an inked block or plate.

printed edges: matter printed on the cut edges of books. When the printing is in aid of quick reference to the contents the fore-edge only is used, but advertising matter is printed on any of the cut edges. The printing is done from rubber type. (L.K.)

printer's devil: a humorous appellation for a printer's apprentice. It is said to date from 1561 on an occasion when a certain monk had to add fifteen pages to his book in order to correct an apprentice's errors; the work, the monk said, of 'the devil'.

Joseph Moxon wrote in 1683 that the boys who removed finished sheets from the tympan 'commonly black and Daub themselves; whence the Workmen do Jocosely call them *Devils*; and sometimes *Spirits* and sometimes *Flies*'.

printer's flowers: see *flowers*.

printer's mark: see *device*.

printer's ream: 516 sheets of paper.

See also *mill ream, mille, perfect, quire, ream*.

printing: 1. the taking of an impression on paper from inked type, plates, blocks, or cylinders. The different methods adopted for producing and inking the printing forme, and for transferring the image to paper, are primarily classified as *letterpress*, *intaglio*, and *planographic printing*, qq.v.

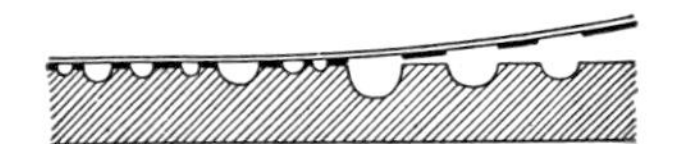

Letterpress printing, from raised elements

A forme made on the letterpress principle has all its printing elements at the same height in relation to the inking rollers and to the surface on which printing is done, while the non-printing areas of the forme are sunk below the plane of the printing elements (see diagram).

Intaglio printing works on the opposite principle, the forme in this case having its image areas sunk

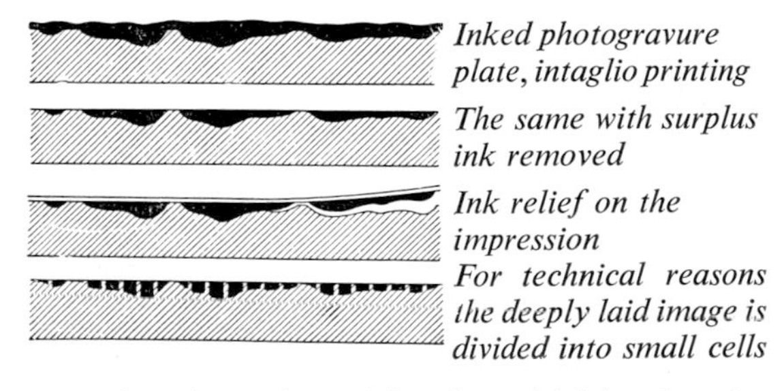

Inked photogravure plate, intaglio printing

The same with surplus ink removed

Ink relief on the impression

For technical reasons the deeply laid image is divided into small cells

lower than the surface of the plate which is otherwise smooth. Intaglio is the principle of etching, line-engraving, dry-point, mezzotint, aquatint, and photogravure.

The principle of planographic printing is based on the antipathy between grease and water, and on the differing degrees of adhesion of other substances to

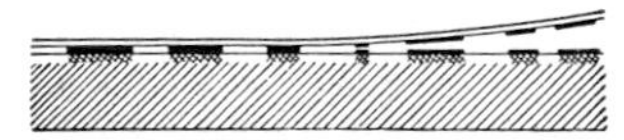

Planographic printing: full-faced image on an otherwise damp surface

greasy printing ink. It includes lithographic printing and collotype, though the latter may be said to occupy a special position.

2. see *impression* (1).

Enlargement of type when printed; top row, letterpress with thin ink on hard paper; middle, offset on matt paper; bottom, doctor-blade photogravure

printing down: the preparation of a photo-lithographic image for printing.

See *photo-lithographic plate*.

printing-down frame: a device for printing in process reproduction, consisting principally of a strong frame in which a sheet of plate-glass is inserted against which the negative (or positive) and the printing material are pressed, usually by extracting the air between them (see *vacuum frame*). In some cases, e.g. for printing on carbon tissue, the printing frame is fitted with a cooling device for the glass, necessitated by the long exposure periods. (G.U.)

printing faults: see *bad colour, black, chalking, clogged, creasing, crystallization, double, draw out, dust, feathering, filling in, friar, mackle, moiré, monk, mottling, plucking, powdering, rivers, set-off, show through, slur, squabble, sticking, wipe*.

printing—historical survey: printing by means of wooden blocks was done in China as long ago as the

8th century, the earliest known block-printing being the edition of a million copies of Chinese Buddhist texts ordered by the Empress Shotoku to be printed for distribution in Japan in A.D. 770, and we learn of printing in China with separate types from the 11th century. There are extant specimens of printing done in Korea by means of types, and some of the types themselves dating from the 15th century have been preserved. It has not, however, been possible to prove any connection between Asiatic and European printing at this time.

In Europe the art of printing began in the mid-15th century. Its invention is claimed, without proof, for Johann Gutenberg of Mainz, who apparently in the thirties of this century was occupied with the problem of printing by means of types. When judging the achievement ascribed to Gutenberg we must bear in mind that the joining of separate types into words is older, being used in the Middle Ages, for example, to punch legends on coins, seals, etc. There are also printed woodcuts dating from the early 15th century. Gutenberg's great achievement was to solve the problem of making a large number of uniform types through the invention of the mould (see *type-casting*), which he may have brought to its final form. It was an advantage for Gutenberg that he was a master goldsmith, and that he had been closely connected with the minting of coins. The methods and tools he used derived from metal working. The printing press used at the time of Gutenberg remained basically unchanged for centuries. Gutenberg, apparently, also invented a printing ink of a consistency differing from that used for the printing of woodcuts. In addition, there was a problem of a more artistic nature to be solved, namely the division of the current script into separate characters. Gutenberg endeavoured to imitate this as far as possible. He was thus obliged to use a larger number of types than are now employed, not only abbreviations and ligatures but also two variants of each type employed depending on what letter preceded it in the text. The number of types for the 42-line Bible was no less than 290. This complicated type system was soon abandoned, and its use is a criterion of the printing done by Gutenberg and his followers. In 1455 or 1456 his printing press was acquired by Johann Fust and Peter Schöffer, who continued working in Mainz. Printing spread next to Bamberg, where the 36-line Bible was printed about 1459. In 1461 a calendar was printed for the astronomical position of Vienna; whether actually in Vienna is uncertain, but it was not printed in Mainz. In Cologne, Strasbourg and Basle there were printing presses in operation in the mid-sixties of the century. Somewhat later important centres of printing developed in Nuremberg, Augsburg and Lübeck.

See also *Cracow fragments*.

The new art soon reached Italy: a recently found fragment of an Italian prayer-book shows that a printing press must have existed in northern Italy about 1462. The earliest dated book, an edition of Lactantius, 1465, was issued by the Germans Sweynheym and Pannartz at Subiaco near Rome. In Venice, the first press was established by Johannes da Spira in 1469. The city was the most important Italian centre for the new art, where such men as Nicolas Jenson, Erhard Ratdolt, and Aldus Manutius worked.

The date when printing began in Holland has not been established beyond doubt. There exists a small amount of printed matter of Dutch origin, mostly Latin grammars, the typography of which is most primitive. These so-called *Costeriana* are all undated, and attempts made to connect them with Laurens Coster of Haarlem, or at least to a very early period, have not proved convincing. The earliest Dutch printing datable with certainty is of the year 1470, in which year also the first printing press of France was established in Paris. From Spain there exists a printed letter of indulgence, the date of which must be given as 1473; the locality of its printing is unknown. In any case it could not have been Valencia, where the first press was set up in 1474.

England's first printer was William Caxton, whose earliest printing done in England was a letter of indulgence which must have been printed before the 13th December, 1476.

From Lübeck the art of printing was carried by Johann Snell to Denmark (1482) and Sweden (1483). Other dates (about which, as in the preceding, authorities differ) are 1468 Switzerland, 1473 Belgium and Austria-Hungary, 1487 Portugal, 1494 Bulgaria, 1508 Scotland and Roumania, 1551 Ireland, 1553 Russia, 1718 Wales (although the first book printed in Welsh, 'Yny Lhyvyr hwnny traethir', was dated 1546), 1885 Albania.

Books of the earliest period of printing, i.e. up to 1500, are called *incunabula*, q.v.

During the first half of the 16th century South Germany and Italy were the foremost European centres of the new art; in Augsburg and Nuremberg especially the art of book production was of very high standard. Such prominent artists as Dürer, Holbein, and Cranach developed the ornamentation of books, and decorated title-page borders and woodcut initials were characterisitic of the period. Great interest was also taken in type-design, and in the early 16th century the German Fraktur type came into use, to be extensively employed in all German-speaking countries. Basle also developed as a centre of fine printing. In Italy the achievements of Aldus Manutius impressed their stamp on the whole of the next century. Owing to Italian influence, the gothic character of the type hitherto prevailing in France and Spain was replaced by roman and italic, the latter created by Manutius. The first half of the 16th century is rightly called the golden age of printing, not only because of the high artistic quality of the work, but also considering the printers' social position in the community; many among them were learned and cultured men, and their offices became centres of scholarship. This applies to Manutius of Venice and Froben of Basle, with both of whom Erasmus worked for a number of years as editor and proof reader, and also to the Estienne family of Paris. In the later 16th century the Low Countries took the lead, especially through Christopher Plantin of Antwerp. He pioneered the extensive use of copperplate illustrations, a prototype for the 17th century. Printing in 17th-century Holland was led by the Elzevier family, who, owing to the scope of their bookselling organization, created greater demand for their products. Their elegant and cheap duodecimo volumes, printed in a distinct, if somewhat monotonous type, had a great vogue. In other respects the feature of 17th-century printing is its pomposity and heaviness, while the numerous copperplate illustrations and large-size format are unable to gloss over the rather mediocre typography.

In the 18th century France led in the art of printing as in culture generally. Illustrations and other decorative features took first place in book production. About the mid-century, the baroque style with its heaviness gave way to the easier elegance of the rococo. Vignettes, and head- and tail-pieces enjoyed a vogue. A reaction emphasizing the purely typographical side of the book began in the mid-century with John Baskerville of Birmingham, whose works were almost devoid of decorative elements. Instead, great attention was paid to the type forms, balance of the composition, presswork, and the quality of the paper. Baskerville's new roman type, later developed by Bodoni and Didot, was widely employed elsewhere, especially in France. A corresponding modernization of the Fraktur was attempted in Germany by Unger and Breitkopf. In Italy Giambattista Bodoni of Parma was one of the most skilled printers of the 18th century, if not of all time, and the most typical representative of a strict classicism in the art of printing.

The 19th century was characterized, firstly, by the great technical inventions, above all by the cylinder press of König, 1812. Graphic techniques were also revolutionized through lithography, steel engraving, wood engraving, and process work. Another feature was the number of new type-faces that made their appearance, particularly in England, during the early decades of the century, finding popularity also in other countries. Technical progress, however, had nothing to show in a corresponding general excellence of fine printing (Bulmer, Bentley, and Pickering excepted). Type-forms as well as typography were not, on the whole, based on any definite artistic rules. A reaction to this degeneration and lack of principle began in the nineties with the work of William Morris, and later in Germany with that of Karl Klingspor and his circle. Prototypes were sought from the golden age of printing, and this tendency, at first historical in scope, laid the foundation for the higher standard of printing now a feature of our century. (G. U.)

Printing Industry Research Association: the name by which the present *Printing, Packaging and Allied Trades Research Association*, q.v., was known when established in November 1930.

printing ink: this consists basically of finely ground pigment, which may be a plant dye, a mineral, or an earth, contained in a medium (or vehicle) to make it fluid. Its manufacture consists mainly of two processes, the production of the vehicle (e.g. boiling the oil) and the admixture and grinding of the pigment which is done in *ink-grinding mills*, q.v. As well as the pigment and vehicle printing ink contains other ingredients to give it special properties. Such ingredients include driers, resin, wax, oils, etc. Black ink is made from carbon black, and the medium is normally linseed oil.

Printing inks are divided into main categories according to the process for which they are intended. In each category a division can be made into *black* and *coloured* ink and into different classes according to the quality. Thus *letterpress inks*, black (ornamental printing ink, half-tone ink, jobbing ink, rotary printing ink) or coloured (trichromatic ink, rotary printing ink, special ink); *newspaper inks*; *lithographic printing inks* (offset ink, litho ink, collotype ink); *photogravure inks*, either actual photogravure ink or copperplate ink and die stamping ink; *aniline printing ink*; and special inks of various kinds, e.g. carbonizing ink.

Printing ink can also be divided according to the way in which it dries. Litho and ordinary letterpress inks dry by oxidation, and partly by penetration and evaporation; newspaper ink by absorption; aniline and photogravure printing inks by evaporation. Modern inks have been perfected which dry on contact with the paper, principally for use on rapid reel-fed rotary presses, but also for sheet work. There are *heat-set inks* which dry by passing the paper web through a heating chamber at a temperature of about 300° C (infra-red rays are also used for heating); *cold-set inks* which are solid at room temperatures and in using which the ink boxes, inkers, and forme cylinders must be heated, while the paper is conveyed after printing over a cooling cylinder; and *steam-set inks* which consist of artificial resin dissolved in a hygroscopic solvent, e.g. ethylene glucol, the web being passed through a steam chamber where the small quantity of water absorbed by the layer of ink causes the artificial resin to be deposited in a solid form. Another type of *quick-drying ink* is combined with a vehicle which would solidify at room temperature if this were not prevented by the admixture of certain substances. The admixtures are absorbed by the paper with the result that the impression dries quickly.

The consistency of ink is important. Ink is said to be *thin* when it is easily set in motion, and *stiff* when it offers comparatively strong resistance to changes in form. *Long* ink is viscous and can be drawn out into threads: the opposite is a *short* ink. With regard to printing varnishes a distinction is made between weak, medium, and strong or rigid varnish, the last being a varnish which is consistent, and at the same time often viscous. For printed matter which is to be glazed *varnishable ink* must be used, and for most purposes ink must be non-fading, i.e. fast colour. (G. U.)

See also *aniline-*, *collotype-*, *cyan-*, *double-tone-*, *gloss-*, *heat-set-*, *job-*, *magenta-*, *metallic-*, *offset-*, *wet printing process inks; easer*, *extender*, *ink coverage.*

printing-out paper: photographic copying paper on which the illustration appears direct when copying, and without undergoing any chemical treatment; this is in contrast to *developing paper*, q.v. In most cases the sensitized layer of the printing-out paper consists of silver chloride with silver nitrate and some organic silver salts (e.g. silver citrate) which adhere to the surface of the paper by means of some colloidal substance (i.e. gum-like substance). Before the colloidal layer is applied the surface of the rough paper is made smooth by a layer of baryta, generally composed of barium sulphate in gelatine.

Different types of printing-out paper were distinguished according to the properties of the colloid. The oldest was *salt paper*, introduced by Fox Talbot about 1840, in which either no colloid or else starch (arrowroot, etc.) was used. In *albumen paper*, the usual copying material in the later 19th century, the colloid consisted of white of egg. About 1890 *aristo paper* (with gelatine as the colloid) and *celloidin paper* (collodium) made their appearance, the latter being used extensively. By 1914 printing-out paper was to some extent superseded by developing paper. After a negative had been printed on to printing-out paper, which took from five to thirty minutes by daylight, it was *toned* and *fixed.* The former was done in a gold or platinum bath. Gold toning produced beautiful reddish-brown and, after longer treatment, blue tones; platinum toning shades ranged from brown to grey. There was also 'self-toning' printing-out paper which contained gold salts as a constituent, so that only fixing was necessary after copying.

Some special types of paper, e.g. pigmented paper, blue-print paper, etc., are sometimes classed as printing-out papers. (G. U.)

Printing, Packaging and Allied Trades Research Association: a body founded in 1930 to help its members by conducting research into problems which they submit, to issue reports of these researches and to circulate abstracts of technical information taken from some 250 journals published all over the world.

An elected Council represents all branches of the printing and allied trades. From members' subscriptions (varied according to the size of the firm and the facilities required) and an annual grant from the Department of Scientific and Industrial Research a laboratory staffed by qualified scientists is maintained at Leatherhead. There is a library, which includes an information service, where the monthly 'Printing Abstracts' (free to members) is prepared. Liaison visits between the Association and its members are a further valuable activity.

The name is usually abbreviated as PATRA.

printing press: a mechanical arrangement for taking impressions from an inked forme on paper or some other material. According to the principle of printing adopted, a distinction is made between presses for intaglio, lithographic, and letterpress printing. Printing presses may also be divided into the following main types according to the manner of applying the paper to the forme: *platen* presses, in which the paper is pressed by a flat surface on to the flat forme; the *rubber* press, in which the forme is also flat, but the pressure at any given moment is exerted only on a narrow strip of the paper by means of a rubber ruler which is moved over the paper as it rests on the forme; the *cylinder* press, in which the paper is pressed on the forme by a cylinder which rolls over it; and the *rotary* press, in which both the surfaces pressing on each other consist of cylinders between which the paper is conveyed in sheets or an endless web.

The earliest printing machines were hand-presses in which the inking of the forme, the feeding and extracting of the paper, and the application of pressure were done by hand. They were built of wood, and the first iron press, still embodying the screw principle of the former but here combined with a system of leverage, was made in England by the third Earl Stanhope towards the end of the 18th century. The lever principle proper appeared first on Dingler's Washington press of 1820. The idea of a mechanical

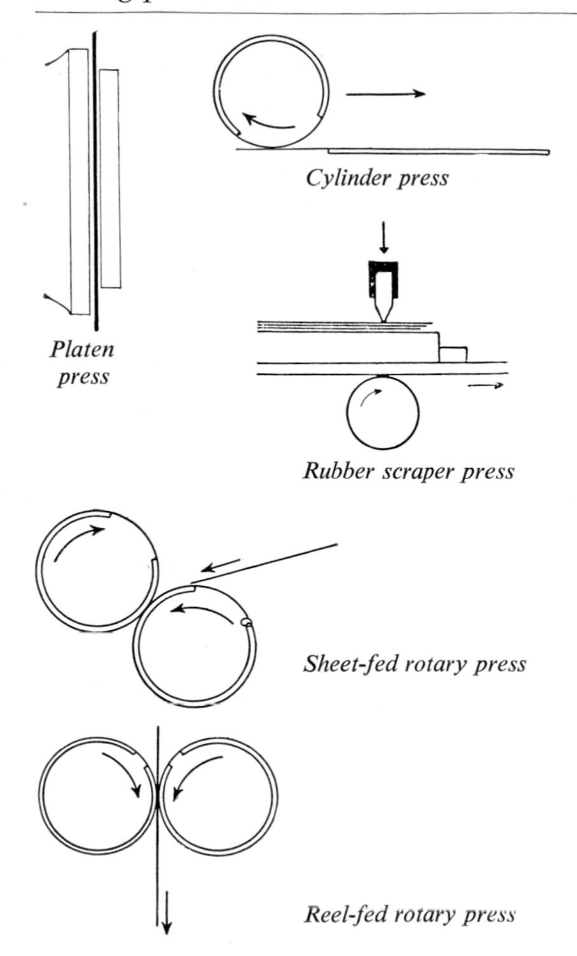

Cylinder press

Platen press

Rubber scraper press

Sheet-fed rotary press

Reel-fed rotary press

press (in which cylinder printing was also conceived) came from William Nicholson of London in 1790, but its successful development was not until 1810 when Friedrich König, with the financial backing of Bensley, built a mechanical platen press. König's cylinder machine was installed in 1812; with Andreas Bauer he experimented on a two-revolution machine in 1814–17, but the modern model was developed by Robert Miehle in 1883.

In the U.S.A. attempts have been made recently to employ a wholly different principle, it being unnecessary for the forme to have contact with the sheet. The ink is transferred by means of electrical fields of force, under the influence of which the ink can be made to jump to the paper. (See *Xerography.*)

See also *Albion-*, *Applegath-*, *Blaeu-*, *cylinder-*, *hand-*, *joiner's-*, *Miehle-*, *platen-*, *rotary-*, *Stanhope press.* (G. U.)

printing processes: for descriptions of the three basic processes see *intaglio, planographic, relief printing.*

printing societies: see *book clubs and printing societies.*

printing to metal: see *photo-lithographic plate.*

printing trade scholarship: see *Thomas Forman Scholarship.*

prism: in photographic reproduction a glass prism is used for refracting an image (see illustration). When light enters through a prism face it is totally reflected by the obliquely placed surface (the hypotenuse), and makes its exit through the other face practically undiminished in intensity. The prism is usually situated immediately in front of (sometimes behind) the lens of a process camera.

In recent times prism systems have been constructed for purposes of photographic reproduction, their object being to provide a reversed image without moving the camera to a so-called prism or mirror position, or, in the case of vertical cameras with a constant prism position, to give a directly reflected image. A prism construction patented by William C. Huebner was evolved for this purpose. With the lens it forms an 'image reversing lens'. (G. U.)

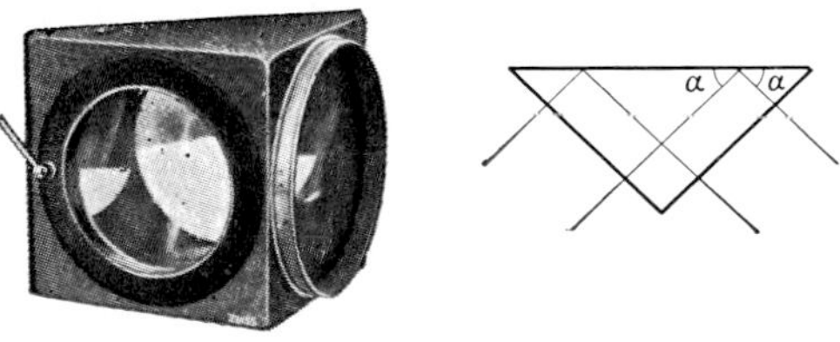

Prism for process camera

private press: usually, a small printing house which issues limited editions of carefully made books, or which prints books for societies or publishing clubs. Writing to the 'Monotype Recorder' in 1933, Eric Gill stated 'a "private" press prints solely what it chooses to print, whereas a "public" press prints what its customers demand of it. The distinction has nothing to do with the use of machinery or with questions of the artistic quality of the product.'

See Rae, T., and Handley-Taylor, G., 'Book of the Private Press', Signet Press, 1958.

Notes on the following private presses are given under their names: *Appledore*, *Arden*, *Ark*, *Ashendene*, *Asphodel*, *Auchinleck*, *Bampton*, *Beaumont*, *Beldornie*, *Blakeney*, *Boar's Head*, *Bremer-Presse*, *Candle*, *Caradoc*, *Cayme*, *Corvinus*, *Cranach*, *Cuala*, *Daniel*, *Darlington*, *Doves*, *Dropmore*, *Dun Emer*, *Eragny*, *Essex House*, *Favil*, *Florence*, *Flying Fame*, *Golden Cockerel*, *Grabhorn*, *Grange*, *Great Totham*, *Gregynog*, *Hafod*, *Hibbert*, *High House*, *Janus-Presse*, *Kelmscott*, *Laboratory*, *Lee Priory*, *Marion*, *Marprelate*, *Merrymount*, *Middle Hill*, *Montague*, *Nonesuch*, *Officina Bodoni*, *Officina Serpentis*, *Ovid*, *Pear*

Tree, Pelican, Polidori, Riccardi, Riverside, Rochester, Romney Street, Roycroft, St Dominic's, Sale Hill, Samurai, Strawberry Hill, Talbot, Temple Sheen, Trajanus-Presse, Trevecca, Unicorn, Vale, Village, Westminster, Zilverdistel.

See also *Appendix C, book clubs and printing societies.*

privately printed: said of books issued from a private press or for private distribution.

The first such book in England is said to be 'De antiquitate Britannicae ecclesiae Cantuariensis, cum Archiepiscopis eiusdem 70', printed at Lambeth in 1572 by John Day for Matthew Parker, Archbishop of Canterbury.

privately published: a work published at the expense of the author. It may, however, be offered for public sale, e.g. 'A World Bibliography of Bibliographies', by T. Besterman. Published by the author, 1947. Printed by the Oxford University Press.

privilege: a licence according the sole right to print and sell books, granted by Letters Patent from an authority. At the time of its origin, in 1469, a privilege was valid for a specified period and class of books, e.g. law-books, music, ballads, psalms; the title-pages of such works often bearing the words 'cum privilegio'. Of interest is the privilege granted in 1575 to William Byrd and Thomas Tallis who jointly held a monopoly for twenty-one years for the 'printinge of all musicke bookes'. Dissatisfaction, pirating and lawsuits resulted from these monopolies, and the only privileged presses today are Oxford University Press, Cambridge University Press, and Eyre & Spottiswoode (the Queen's Printer) who alone may print the Authorized Version of the Bible and the Book of Common Prayer. (See *Bible printing in England*, addenda, page 51.)

See also *Bible printing, imprimatur, nihil obstat, Queen's Printer, Star-chamber, Stationers' Company.*

Prix Goncourt: a French literary prize, awarded annually since 1903 by the Académie Goncourt, Paris, for the most remarkable imaginative work composed during the year by a young French writer.

The academy was founded by an endowment bequeathed by the novelist Edmond de Goncourt (1822–96).

Prizes: see *Literary Prizes and Awards.*

process block: the printing forme prepared by *process engraving*, q.v.

process embossing: see *embossing.*

process engraving: any of several photo-mechanical methods of producing relief blocks or plates for printing illustrations. Varieties of block are line and half-tone (and the duplicates of these—stereos, electros, rubber, or plastic casts), three- and four-colour blocks, and collotype. Also known as *photo-engraving* and *photo-mechanical reproduction.*

process work: a general term for the preparation of a printing forme by the use at some stage of photography. This thus includes *process engraving, photo-lithography*, and *photogravure*, qq.v.

Before photography in its proper sense had developed sufficiently to be of any practical value attempts had been made at process work, that is to say, transferring a picture to a forme with the aid of light. Thus Niepce made experiments with asphalt copying on a metal plate and then etching it, thereby obtaining an intaglio forme (1824). Shortly after the daguerreotype was made public in 1839 attempts were made to etch such photographic plates, and the French Academy made an award for such a method to J. Berres of Vienna. In the mid-century the Viennese Paul Pretsch made printing formes by various methods, some of which he patented, based largely on the sensitivity of chromate colloids. By exposing such layers to light and developing in warm or cold water he was able to make both relief and intaglio formes. He was more successful in the latter, and this dominated the early history of process work. Intaglio and photogravure printing after the work of Talbot, Swan, and Klíč reached practical perfection long before Meisenbach had perfected the half-tone process. Photo-lithography and collotype are based to a great extent on the work of Poitevin and J. Albert. (G.U.)

Processionale: a book containing the hymns, psalms, and litanies used during the processions in a church or cathedral.

Proctor, Robert George Collier, 1868–1903: the author of the 'Index to the early printed books in the British Museum . . . to 1500, with notes of those in the Bodleian Library', 1898–1903. This four-volume work lists some 10,000 items under country, town, and press. The numbers Proctor assigned to the books are still used to identify them. The work became the foundation of the British Museum 'Catalogue of books printed in the XVth century now in the British Museum', 1908, begun by A. W. Pollard. Proctor, who worked in the British Museum from 1893, made the study of incunabula his life-work, adding a great contribution to our knowledge of early printing in Augsburg, Venice, and in the Greek language.

profit-sharing agreement: a contract sometimes made between an author and a publisher whereby the latter recovers from receipts of sale all production and advertising costs for a book before the author receives any payment; subsequent profits from further sales are halved. It may thus be several years before either party benefits.

See also *publishers' agreements*.

prognostication: an almanac of astrological or other forecasts, usually compiled for one year.

progressive proofs: the proofs made in colour-printing as a guide to shade and registration. Each colour is shown separately and imposed on the preceding ones.

proof: an impression taken from type matter for checking and correction only, not as indicative of the appearance of the finished work. In bookwork, several proofs are taken, viz.: 1. *first proof*, a preliminary galley, corrected by the printer's reader and returned to the compositor; 2. *galley* or *slip proof*, the corrected galley, again checked by the reader, and sent to the author; 3. *page proof*, after making up the type into pages, and sometimes used instead of (2) for correction by the author, or submitted to an author after corrections he marked on (2) have been put right by the printer; 4. the returned author's proof—i.e. *marked proof*—is again read by the printer's reader to ensure the style of the house has been followed (if this is the desired style), to check illustrations, imprint, etc. The reader signs the proof; if he marks it *show revise*, a further proof must be submitted; *clean proof* means that a clean proof must be produced. The final instruction *press* is marked by the author or publisher.

See also *author's proof*, *flat pull*, *foundry proof*, *galley*, *pass sheet*, *press revise*, *prima*, *pull*, *reproduction proof*, *rough proof*.

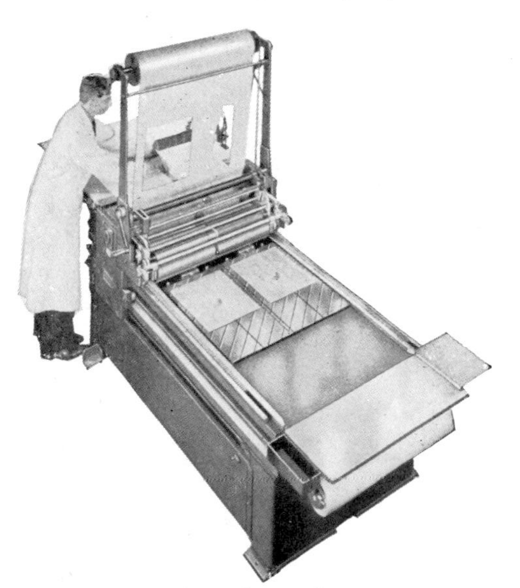

Vandercook proof press

proof corrections: additions or corrections to a proof made marginally in ink. Recognized symbols are used. (See B.S. 1219: 1958, reproduced as Appendix D.) A certain amount of correcting is allowed for in the printer's estimate to the publisher; corrections in excess of this are charged separately, the latter particularly referring to an author's alterations to his text after setting.

proof presses: small and medium-sized presses, operated either by hand or electrical power, for the making of proofs of type or other relief surfaces.

Automatic inking is now used to give an even film of ink. (M.L.)

proofing chromo: a superfine coated paper used by process engravers for block proofing. Also known as *B.P. chromo*.

pro-printing: the reproduction of printed matter without the use of letterpress type: duplicators or small office litho machines are used, litho plates being prepared by photography from typewritten copy, or stencils by direct typing.

prospectus: a publishers' sales device, being a descriptive leaflet outlining the plan of a work to be published. It usually contains a specimen page and illustration, and often a table of contents.

The first printed prospectus of a book was issued by Johann Mentelin at Strasbourg in 1469.

Protype: an American photo-lettering device for the production of display lettering, usually 18-point or larger, on paper or film. The result can be used for process engraving, litho, or gravure. Letters, words, lines, or complete layouts are composed on a proprietary sensitized paper or film 17 in. wide. From special negatives called Profonts the characters are contact printed on to the sensitized material. An ultra-violet lamp is used, and an advantage is that the material is insensitive to incandescent lighting or indirect sunlight, making a dark-room unnecessary. Line blocks for letterpress can be made from the positive, and magnesium plates can be prepared by the Dow-etch process.

Protype is distributed in Britain by Linotype & Machinery Ltd.

provenance: an indication of a book's previous ownership. A special binding, a bookplate, or an inscription of ownership may point to the collections, libraries, or sale-rooms through which a particular copy has passed.

Prudentius, Aurelius Clemens, 348–405: a poet of the early Latin Church whose 'Psychomachia' was a popular subject for 9th–12th-century scribes in England, Germany, and France. The Malmesbury Prudentius, now in Cambridge University Library, is the finest surviving English example of this poem about the struggle between the Virtues and Vices for possession of the soul. It was illustrated by lively outline sketches drawn in coloured inks, deriving in style from the *Utrecht Psalter*, q.v. (the latter was drawn in brown ink only).

Psalter: the Book of Psalms, either for devotional or liturgical use.

Psalter Moguntinum: see *Mainz Psalter*.

Psalter of Alphonso: an illuminated Psalter commissioned about 1284 by Edward I as a gift to his son, and completed, on the latter's death, by a second and inferior artist. Bands of colour fill up blanks after each verse, while narrow frame borders lead from some of the initials; the drolleries, birds, and animals which embellish the borders are most delicately drawn.

The work is sometimes known as the *Tenison Psalter*, being once owned by Archbishop Tenison (d. 1715); it is now in the British Museum.

pseudepigrapha: a collective term for writings or books falsely or erroneously ascribed to someone not the author.

pseudonymous: said of a book written and published under an assumed name.

publication date: 1. the date announced by a publisher before which no copies of a book may be sold.

2. the year of publication which, except in the case of juvenile and certain school books, should always be shown on a book. The date of first publication, where different from that of the current edition, should always be shown, and also, in the case of a technical book, whether it is a re-issue or a revised edition.

publisher: a person or a company in business to issue for sale to the public through booksellers books, music, periodicals, maps, etc. In the 16th century printers were usually publishers of the books they produced, but while all publishers were not printers many were booksellers. Publishing as a business separate from bookselling dates from the 19th century.

See 'Publishing and Bookselling', by F. A. Mumby, 4th ed., Cape, 1956.

publishers' abbreviated answers: the code of abbreviated answers, printed below, was approved by the Publishers Association in 1953: it supersedes earlier codes.

OP	Title discontinued.
TOP	No reprint at present in hand.
RP/6m	Reprint in hand: expected in (e.g.) about six months.
RP/Jan	Reprint in hand: expected in (e.g.) January.
NE/ND	New edition in preparation: no date can be given.
NE/6m	New edition in preparation: expected in about (e.g.) six months.
B/Jan.	Binding: expected in (e.g.) January.
B/12 Jan.	Binding: will be ready on (e.g.) January 12th.
B/ND	Binding: no date can be given.
NK	Not known, or not ours.
NP	Not yet published. (This replaces NO, which should not be used.)
OO/USA	Out of stock but on order from (e.g.) U.S.A.
OTO/USA	Only to order from (e.g.) U.S.A.

IMPORTANT

OS (out of stock), NO (not out), and an unqualified RP (reprinting) and B (binding) *should not be used.*

publishers' agreements: contracts between authors and publishers to establish the basis on which an author's writings shall be published and sold; while these vary in detail they are, in the main, usually within the framework of the following, qq.v.: *royalties*, a *profit-sharing agreement*, a *commission agreement*, or an *outright sale of copyright*. For fuller information see 'Truth about Publishing', by Sir Stanley Unwin. 7th ed. 1960. Chapter 4.

The Publishers Association: the representative body for the British book-publishing trade, founded in 1896. Membership is open to any publisher in the United Kingdom whose business or an appreciable part of whose business is the publication of books. The Association affords book-publishers the means of dealing collectively with the many problems that face them which are not otherwise susceptible of resolution. It regulates conditions of employment within the trade and supplies its members with information and advice on technical, legal, and economic aspects of publishing. The Association also represents publishers vis-à-vis the Government, local authorities, public and trade bodies.

Its original object was to maintain the prices of net books, and while this remains one of its activities, the Association is now largely engaged in assisting its members to secure a greater and more efficient distribution of their books. To this end Home and Export Market Research Departments are maintained. Both prepare statistical analyses of publishers' sales and markets, issue co-operative sales propaganda material, and initiate and encourage co-operative book exhibitions.

Contact is maintained with publishers oversea by direct relations with foreign publishers' associations, and through the Association's membership of the International Publishers Association.

An extensive classified addressing service is a modern development of the Association. This covers all home booksellers, oversea booksellers, and others known to be interested in British books. Members' advertising material can be issued for them, and, if necessary, be reproduced on their behalf.

The Association's address is 19 Bedford Square, London, W.C.1.

publisher's binding: the binding, usually cased, in which a publisher supplies books to the trade. Synonymous with *edition binding*, q.v.

See also *bookbinding*.

The Publishers' Circular and Booksellers' Record: a weekly book-trade paper which includes an author and title list of new British books; some Government publications are mentioned, but not musical scores. It was first issued fortnightly in 1837 by Sampson Low, who from 1845 also issued annual lists. From 1853 he gave these the title 'The British Catalogue of Books'. This title was merged with 'The London Catalogue' in 1860.

Since 1864 the two have appeared as 'The English Catalogue of Books': the first volume with the new name covered the years 1835–63 and included 'importations of original American works, and Continental English books'; American books are not mentioned after 1901.

In 1959 the title was changed to *British Books*.

publisher's cloth: the cloth casing which, since the late 1820's, has been the normal covering material for edition-bound books.

See also *edition binding*.

publisher's device: see *device*.

publisher's dummy: see *dummy*.

publisher's reader: one who reads, judges, criticizes and reports upon manuscripts submitted to a publisher.

publisher's series: reprints, often of the classics, which a publisher issues in uniform style of binding but which are not necessarily related by subject, e.g. 'World's Classics' of the O.U.P.

publisher's terms: see *terms*.

The Publishers' Weekly: a journal for the American book trade, founded in 1872 by Frederick Leypoldt. The weekly author list gives new U.S. non-Government publications, and there is a monthly title index. In addition to the main author list, which is partly annotated, there is a subsidiary list of paper-bound books, pamphlets, and minor pieces.

puddler: a printers' colloquialism for a compositor. The term was used in 19th-century London, if not elsewhere.

puff: exaggerated praise for a book, written by the author or a copy-writer, for use in advertisements or on book jackets. For pre-publication publicity a *preliminary puff* is supplied to travellers.

The term was used in the 17th century, and still is.

See also *blurb*, *gutting*.

pugillaria: the Roman table book. From two to eight wax-covered leaves of ivory, wood or metal, bearing on their waxed surfaces writing done with a stylus, were fastened together with leather thongs or rings. Covers were of parchment or skin, and later of wood.

Pulitzer Prizes: a series of literary prizes awarded annually since 1917, in the U.S.A., for the best drama, novel, and (since 1921) poetry written by American authors. Historical works, biographies, and journalistic work also qualify for special prizes.

Funds derive from an endowment provided by Joseph Pulitzer (1847–1911), a newspaper magnate and philanthropist.

pull: a proof of type. The term originates with the action in the early presses when, after an impression had been made, the bed was pulled out and the platen raised.

See also *proof*.

pulling: the removal of the cover, boards, end papers, tapes, and any lining material which, with the softening of old glue and cutting of sewing threads, are necessary stages in the preparation of a book for re-binding.

pulp: the wet mixture of various ingredients which flows on to the web of a paper-making machine, or is taken up in a hand-mould, to be formed into paper.

pulp board: see *boards*.

pulp water: an alternative name for *backwater*, q.v.

pumice stone: a light volcanic rock used for smoothing parchment prior to writing upon it, or when preparing it for re-use. This action is known as *pouncing*.
See also *palimpsest*.

punch: a piece of steel on which is engraved a type character. It is then hardened and used as a die to strike the matrices from which type is cast.
See also *justification* (2), *matrix* (1), *strike*.

punch-cutting machine: a machine which employs a *pantograph*, q.v., to cut in steel a reduction of an enlarged pattern of each letter or character. Without this machine, which was invented in 1884 by the American Linn Boyd Benton of Milwaukee, mechanical type-setting machines, with their need for profuse supplies of matrices, could not have developed. The first model was used by Ottmar Mergenthaler for the *Linotype*, q.v.

punctuation marks: listed alphabetically, and also under alternative names where applicable, are punctuation marks in common English use:

’	apostrophe
[ ]	brackets
:	colon
,	comma
—	dash
“ ”	double quotes
!	exclamation mark
.	full stop
-	hyphen
?	interrogation mark
“	inverted commas
( )	parentheses
.	period
.	point
?	question mark
“ ”	quotation marks (quotes)
;	semi-colon
‘ ’	single quotes
[ ]	square brackets

pure: see *wood free*.

put to bed: see *bed*.

putto: a small boy. The plural form *putti* describes the unclad boys and cherubs of whom drawings were an occasional feature of 15th- and 16th-century illuminated manuscripts made in Italy and elsewhere.

Pye, Sybil: a contemporary English bookbinder, important for her evolution of ‘a bold, personal style expressed chiefly in coloured inlays which form a mosaic of asymmetric shapes’. Sybil Pye was self-taught and began her activities about 1906, using tools given her by Charles Ricketts as well as others designed by herself. She has developed as a designer and craftswoman, making her somewhat unique in an age when modern English binderies have largely become workshops in which highly skilled copyists translate a design from paper to leather, a process in which the spirit of the original may be lost.

Pye-book: 1. briefly, the Directorium of the Roman Church which determines the appropriate office to be used when a movable holy day coincides with a fixed holy day.
2. a term used in 18th-century England for an alphabetical index to a collection of rolls or records.

Pynson, Richard, fl. 1490–1528: a printer of Norman birth who first published in association with Guillaume Le Talleur of Rouen, and later came to London, at first in association with John Russhe for whom he issued legal works. About 1490 he took over the business of *W. de Machlinia*, q.v. Pynson quickly became the most important printer of his day and was the second holder of the office of King’s Printer (1508). He introduced roman types into England in 1509, importing them from Paris: the first works in which he used roman were ‘Sermo Fratris Hieronymi de Ferraria’, and a speech by Petrus Gryphus of Pisa, both in 1509. The custom of enclosing the matter on title-pages with ornamental borders was popularized by him.
His most important works were John Lydgate’s translation of Boccaccio’s ‘Fall of princes’, 1494, in an edition of *c.* 600 copies, and a ‘Missale Sarum’, 1500, for Cardinal Morton.
On his retirement in 1528, Robert Redman acquired the business. Pynson died in 1530.

ADDENDA

paper sizes (see also page 298): the German DIN A series of paper sizes is widely used in many European countries. DIN stands for Deutsche Industrie Normen, a body comparable with the British Standards Institution. The A distinguishes this size from others known as B and C which apply to related envelope and poster sizes.

The main features of the DIN A series are that they apply to all types of paper, and that the proportions of a sheet remain constant when it is cut or folded in half across the long side. The letter A is always accompanied by a figure indicating the relation of a particular paper size to the basic size A0 which is 1 square metre. Thus half A0 is A1, half A1 is A2, and so on. For larger dimensions the A is preceded by a figure, thus 2A is twice the size of A0.

The following table shows seven trimmed sizes in the DIN A series which correspond most nearly to British sizes from 8-demy to demy 8vo.

	Millimetres	*Inches (approx.)*	*Demy sizes*
2A	1189 × 1682	$46\frac{13}{16} \times 66\frac{3}{16}$	45 × 70
A0	841 × 1189	$33\frac{1}{8} \times 46\frac{13}{16}$	35 × 45
A1	594 × 841	$23\frac{3}{8} \times 33\frac{1}{8}$	$22\frac{1}{2} \times 35$
A2	420 × 594	$16\frac{1}{2} \times 23\frac{3}{8}$	$17\frac{1}{2} \times 22\frac{1}{2}$
A3	297 × 420	$11\frac{11}{16} \times 16\frac{1}{2}$	$11\frac{1}{4} \times 17\frac{1}{2}$
A4	210 × 297	$8\frac{1}{4} \times 11\frac{11}{16}$	$8\frac{3}{4} \times 11\frac{1}{4}$
A5	148 × 210	$5\frac{13}{16} \times 8\frac{1}{4}$	$5\frac{5}{8} \times 8\frac{3}{4}$

(Continental practice is to state the smaller dimension first.)

Printing News: a weekly newspaper edited by James Moran and published by Printing News Ltd., London. It was established in 1955. The frequency of publication is particularly appropriate for the coverage of topical news of printing trade personalities, and business activities, in addition to reports on new equipment, and reviews of books and advertisement typography.

Q

qq.v.: see *q.v.*

quad: a prefix to standard paper-size names to denote a sheet four times the single and twice the double area, e.g. demy, 17½ in. by 22½ in.; double demy, 22½ in. by 35 in.; quad demy, 35 in. by 45 in.; double quad demy, 45 in. by 70 in.

quadrata: square capitals.

quads: blank types cast less than type height, in standard point sizes, and used as inter-word spacing material. Usual sizes are en, em, 2-em, 3-em, and 4-em quads. The word quad is shortened from *quadrat*, which term, however, is never used in full.

See also *spaces*.

Quantity Book-Buying Scheme: an arrangement jointly initiated in 1937 by the Publishers Association and the Booksellers Association whereby a bookseller was, as an exception to the *Net Book Agreement*, q.v., allowed to give a discount on the net price of a book where a large quantity of a specific net book was ordered.

This was simplified in 1951, and amended and extended in 1954 to cover large single orders for net books of an aggregate value of £250 or more, regardless of the number of copies of any one title contained in the order. The prime condition to be fulfilled before the Publishers Association will issue to the bookseller a licence for the granting of discount is that the books must be required for gift or presentation in connection with the purchaser's business, or for philanthropic or propaganda purposes. The provision of a library, whether recreational or educational, for use by the purchaser's own employees, free of charge, would qualify. Discount is never more than 10%, but may be less.

Quaritch, Bernard, 1819–99: one of the most famous antiquarian booksellers of Europe. He was born at Worbis in Saxony and in 1834 was apprenticed to a bookseller in Nordhausen, moving to Berlin in 1839. In 1842 he left Berlin for London, working there for Henry G. Bohn, at that time the leading secondhand bookseller. He became a British citizen. During 1844 he went for a time to Théophile Barrois, a noted French bookseller, but the next year found him back with Bohn.

It was in October 1847 that he founded his own business at 16 Castle Street, Leicester Square. His personality and developing reputation attracted the patronage of such famous people as W. E. Gladstone, Mr. Disraeli, Lord Dufferin, and Edward Fitzgerald (whose translation of the 'Rubáiyát' was first published by Quaritch in 1859). His first (broadsheet) catalogue appeared in 1847.

In 1858 his book-buying ventures started in earnest. He acquired his first Mazarin Bible for £596 and sold it to Lord Lindsay; he bought back this same copy in 1887 for £2650 and sold it to Lord Carysfort; in 1923 it went to America for £9500. No fewer than seven copies of this book passed through the hands of Bernard Quaritch or his son Alfred.

In 1860 the business was transferred to 15 Piccadilly. Patrons received here included the Earls of Kimberley, Northbrook, Derby, and Crawford; the Dukes of Devonshire and Somerset, Sir Henry Irving, Ellen Terry, Henry Huth, John Ruskin, and Sir Richard Burton. He continued to buy on a princely scale whenever a library was auctioned. At the Henry Perkins sale in 1873 Bernard Quaritch spent £10,775. His catalogue of 1874 listed most of the items acquired from the Perkins collection. No such catalogue of valuable books and manuscripts, classified and accompanied by a complete index, had ever before been attempted by any bookseller. It had 1889 pages and listed 23,000 items. At three sales between 1880 and 1884 Quaritch's purchases amounted to over £97,000, the £3900 he paid in 1884 for the Syston Park library copy of the Mazarin Bible was, up to that time, the highest price ever paid at a public auction for a printed book.

The acquisition of rare books and manuscripts in such quantities made Quaritch, in the last twenty years of the 19th century, the holder of the chief book treasures for sale in the European market. His last great catalogue, completed in 1888, listed 38,552 items, while its index, published in 1892, contained over 100,000 entries.

Quaritch was associated with William Morris for whom he published a series of translations of the Icelandic Sagas in 1891 ('The Saga Library'); he also published four of the Kelmscott Press books in 1892 and 1894.

In 1878 Quaritch founded the society known as '*Ye Sette of Odd Volumes*', q.v.

On the death of the founder the business was directed by his son Alfred, who had entered the firm in 1889. He was particularly active in America and assisted in the formation of a number of great collections there: he bought for J. P. Morgan, H. C. Folger, H. E. Huntington, and R. Hoe.

In 1907 the firm moved to its present address at 11 Grafton St., W.1. Alfred Quaritch died in 1913.

quarter-bound: a book bound with either leather spine and cloth sides, or cloth spine and paper sides. Cf. *half-bound.*

See also *siding.*

quarto: written 4to. The book size resulting from folding a sheet with two folds at right-angles, thus giving pages one-quarter the size of the sheet. To define fully the size, the paper size also must be stated, e.g. Crown 4to. In practice a double-size paper would be used to produce in three folds a 16-page section for binding, or a quad-size paper folded four times to produce 32-page sections for binding. (L.K.)

quarto galley: a galley about 8¾ in. by 12 in., or wide enough to hold quarto pages.

quaternion: a gathering made up from four sheets, folded once, in which form some bound manuscripts and early printed books were assembled; thus the 1st and 8th, 2nd and 7th, 3rd and 6th, 4th and 5th were conjugate leaves. Thus *ternion* (three sheets), *quinternion* (five sheets), and *sextern* (six sheets).

Queen Mary's Psalter: an early 14th-century English Psalter, probably written for Edward II. It is illustrated by miniatures of Christ's life and those of the saints, as well as drawings based on the Old Testament. Only light colouring is used. The fabulous beasts and birds which appear in contemporary Psalters are here absent. The decorations at the foot of each page are mostly scenes of people, and show traces of French influence.

The Psalter, now in the British Museum, is named after Queen Mary I who acquired it in 1553.

Queen's Gold Medal for Poetry: an award established in 1934 by King George V (when it was known as the King's Gold Medal for Poetry), and offered once in three years for a volume of poetry in English by a British subject, published in the British Empire. It is administered by the Poet Laureate, advised by a committee.

Queen's Printer: the printer to whom is accorded by Letters Patent the sole right of printing for a number of years any specified work or group of works issued by or belonging to the reigning monarch. At the time the office was created by Henry VII in 1504 the King claimed the right to issue Acts, almanacs, Bibles, grammars and law-books; these groups were subdivided among printers, each being entitled to style himself King's Printer. The present holder of the office is the firm of Eyre & Spottiswoode.

See also *Bible printing, privilege* and *Bible printing in England*, addenda, page 51.

Quentell, Heinrich, fl. 1478–1509: a native of Strasbourg who established himself as a printer in Cologne. His most important work was the folio picture Bible, *c.* 1478, with more than a hundred illustrations.

His son Peter, fl. 1520–46, developed the business into one of the leading establishments of Cologne. His extensive publishing activities led him to commission such other printers as Hieronymous Fuchs.

Peter's son Johann continued to print until his death in 1551.

query: the symbol ?, used by the printer's reader in proof margins when the author is required to check some detail.

quick-drying inks: printing inks to which driers have been added to speed up the conversion of the varnish in the ink into a solid film.

Quick-S: the proprietary name of a mechanical alternative to *page-cord,* q.v. It consists of four pieces of zinc alloy, 12·8-point thick, which form a frame about a page or any other piece of setting where page-cord would otherwise be used. Each piece or section is extendible and self-adjusting, tension being maintained by recessed coil-springs. Corner fitting is by pegs and holes.

Quick-S, which is a modern Norwegian invention, is available in England in pica units; elsewhere in cicero sizes. It permits quicker and safer handling of type, easier correction and quicker lock-up, finer register for colour-proofing, and safer storage of type. Quick-S becomes part of the forme and is not removed until the type is distributed.

quick-set inks: printing inks in which the vehicle contains both a thin mineral oil and a stout varnish. When printed, the thin oil is quickly absorbed into the paper, leaving the pigment and varnish on the surface. The sheets can be handled sooner than if normal linseed oil-based inks have been used. As the final setting of the varnish is slower, the surface remains receptive longer to subsequent printings in multi-colour work.

quinternion: a gathering made up of five sheets.

See also *quaternion.*

quire: 1. twenty-four sheets of paper (and one 'outside'); the twentieth of a ream.

See also *cording quires, insides, mill ream, mille, printer's ream, ream, retree.*

2. a *gathering, section,* or *signature,* qq.v., particularly when unfolded. A quire was originally a gathering of four sheets forming eight leaves or sixteen pages after one fold had been made. It was thus synonymous with *quaternion.* The low-Latin word *quaternum* was shortened to 'quair' or 'quaer'. In the days of parchment books quires of four sheets would make a gathering convenient for sewing; when the use of paper spread it was possible to use from five to seven sheets without forming too thick a gathering for the binder. Thus the original association of quire with four became obscured.

See also *in quires.*

quirewise: the manner of gathering the leaves of a booklet by folding them and placing them one in another. They are then stitched.

quoins: metal or wooden wedges which are placed between the outer furniture and the sides of the chase in order to lock the type and blocks in it during printing. Metal quoins, of which there are various patent designs, are adjusted with a key until the required tension is attained.

At first wedges were used for this purpose, later wedge quoins and French quoins of different designs, but now screw quoins, or combined screw and wedge quoins, are most used. Quoins are also used inside a forme when it is desirable that some parts should be movable in relation to others, e.g. in colour printing.

Iron quoins were introduced in 1863 by Hippolyte Marinoni of Paris. (G.U.)

quotations: printers' spacing material, cast with hollowed centres, and used for 'whiting out'. They are cast by the typefounder and can also be cast on the Monotype Super Caster. An alternative name is *quotes.*

quotes: see *punctuation marks, quotations.*

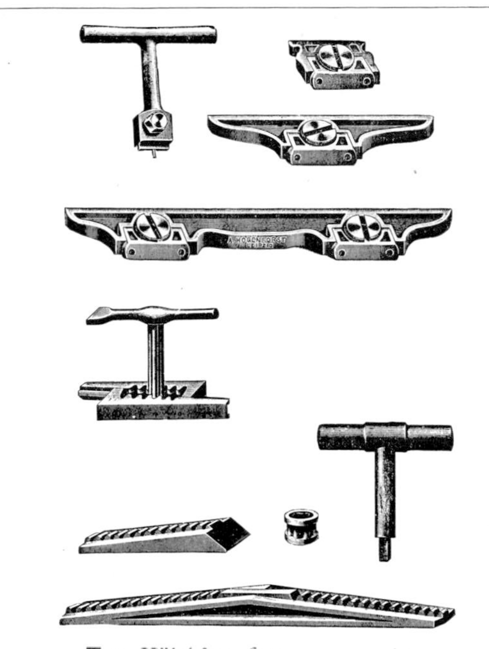

Top, Hölzle's safety screw quoins.
Centre, Hempel's wedge quoin.
Bottom, Marinoni or roll quoins (French quoins)

The 'Speed' quoin operates on its whole length, and its adjustment can be read. (Challenge Mach. Co., U.S.A.)

quousque tandem abutere: see *specimen sheet.*

q.v.: an abbreviation for the Latin 'quod vide', i.e. which see. The abbreviation for the plural form 'quae vide' is qq.v.

R

rag cutter: in paper-making, a special machine having revolving blades and sharp prongs, which tears and chops the rags into small pieces of uniform size. (M.L.)

rag paper: the finest quality paper, made from linen or rag pulp. This has been used since the 11th century. In 'The Spectator', May 1st, 1712, Joseph Addison wrote: 'It is pleasant enough to consider the Changes that a Linnen Fragment undergoes. . . . The finest Pieces of Holland, when worn to Tatters, assume a new Whiteness more beautiful than their first, and often return in the Shape of Letters to their Native Country. A Lady's Shift may be metamorphosed into Billets doux, and come into her Possession a second time. A Beau may peruse his Cravat after it is worn out with greater Pleasure and Advantage than ever he did in a Glass. In a Word, a Piece of Cloth, after having officiated for some Years as a Towel or a Napkin, may by this Means be raised from a Dung-hill, and become the most Valuable Piece of Furniture in a Prince's Cabinet.'

See also *paper-making*.

raised bands: ridges on the spine of a book where the leather of the cover is nipped up over the cords to which the sections have been secured by *flexible sewing*, q.v. When the book has not been sewn on raised cords the bands may be built up with thin strips of card or board, the leather being nipped up as at first described. See also *nipping up*.

The first books to be produced in Europe *without* raised bands were from the bindery of Aldus Manutius, though in Persia this had been common practice much earlier and it was probably craftsmen from the Middle East who introduced the idea to Venice.

raised printing: a process of printing from type or line engravings in relief on ordinary platen or cylinder presses. A special ink is used, and impressions are made on the stock as in ordinary printing. The lines are not so sharp and clean as in genuine steel-die embossing and copperplate engraving. (M.L.)

Ramage press: a hand-press, first made entirely of wood, later of iron, by Adam Ramage of Philadelphia. Said to be the first press made in the U.S.A. (M.L.)

random: the sloping work-top of a composing frame. Also known as *bank*.

ranging figures (or **lining figures**): the numerals of modern type-faces which all extend from the base line to the cap line. E.g. the Times New Roman figures 1, 2, 3, 4, 5, 6, 7, 8, 9, 0. Cf. *hanging figures*.

Rastell, John, fl. 1527–30: a London printer who mostly issued legal works, his first being 'An abridgment of the statutes', 1527. His best-known book is 'The pastyme of people; the cronycles of divers realmys', 1529, which he both wrote and printed.

Ratdolt, Erhard, *c.* 1447–*c.* 1527: a distinguished and enterprising German printer who, from 1476–86, worked in Venice, and from 1486 in his native Augsburg, where the same year he issued the first-known specimen sheet. At first he worked with Peter Löslein (probably as editor and proof reader) and Bernard Maler (as designer of border decorations). He printed numerous Missals and Breviaries for such widely scattered places as Melk, Passau, Salzburg, and Regensburg. He devoted much thought to the ornamentation of his books, using *entrelac initials*, q.v., and such embellishments as dedications printed in gold ink. In his edition of Euclid's 'Elementa geometriae', 1482, appear over 400 of the first printed mathematical diagrams: this was the first printed Euclid. In 1476 he printed the first proper *title-page*, q.v., and in 1491 a woodcut in five colours.

See also *label title, lapidary type*.

Raven Press: a private printing press established in 1931 by R. A. Maynard and H. W. Bray, both of whom executed wood engravings for their early publications. Notable were editions of Milton's 'Samson Agonistes' and Shakespeare's 'Venus and Adonis'.

Rawlinson, Richard, 1690–1755: a traveller, scholar, and benefactor of the Bodleian Library. He amassed a collection rich in heraldry, genealogy, topography, as well as deeds, charters, and general antiquities.

On his death about 1900 printed books and over 6000 manuscripts passed to the Bodleian.

Ray Society: a society instituted in London, in 1844, for the publication of works on natural history. (M.L.)

reader: one who reads and corrects the printer's proofs, comparing them with the original manuscript.
See also *Association of Correctors of the Press, proof.*

reader's box: the room in a printing establishment set aside for the reading of proofs. There may be several readers with attendant copy-boys or women working simultaneously, ideally separated by partitions or screens into boxes. Reading rooms should have good lighting and be reasonably quiet, but in nineteenth-century England (and sometimes today) they were often little more than cupboards, dim and airless.

reading copies: copies of a book sent by a publisher to selected booksellers as part of their sales promotion.
See also *advance copies, review copies.*

ream: originally twenty quires or 480 sheets of paper. Reams of book paper are now standardized at 500 sheets.
See also *long ream, mill ream, mille, perfect, printers' ream, quire, short ream.*

re-backed: said of a book having the spine re-covered in a style or material approximating the old. Cf. *backed.*

recension: a revised version of a text: the term implies critical editing.

recess printing: processes in which the ink for printing is contained in recesses in the printing plate or cylinder, e.g. *photogravure,* q.v.

recto: 1. the front of a single printed unfolded sheet.
2. the right-hand pages of a book, bearing the odd numbers.

Redman, Robert, fl. 1525–40: a London printer of lawbooks, and, in 1525, an edition of 'Magna Carta'. He moved into Pynson's premises in Fleet Street on the latter's death, and also used his device.

reducing apparatus: an apparatus used in lithographic work for altering the dimensions of a transferred picture. The apparatus consists of a rubber cloth in a strong frame, so fixed that the cloth can be stretched in different directions. Prints from an original lithograph are made in a multi-transferring machine on the rubber cloth which is then given the required shape by regulating the stretching device, after which the picture is transferred on to stone, plates, or transfer paper. The square reducing apparatus holding the rectangular rubber cloth is fastened on

Reducing apparatus

four rails which can be shifted along the fixed outer frame by screws or other means. Other constructions embody a circular cloth secured to the outer frame by radially fastened wires which can be tightened by winding on spindles. The apparatus can be used for both reducing and enlarging in one or more directions. (G.U.)

reduction: 1. the use of silver solvents in photography to reduce the density of the silver image on a dry plate. Three types of reducer are used for continuous tone negatives and positives—subtractive, proportional, and super-proportional. The first group will increase the contrast of a negative by attacking the shadow areas rather than the highlights; an example is Farmer's reducer. Proportional reducers exert a uniform action on the negative, thus preserving the tone, and among those used is the Kodak combining potassium permanganate, sulphuric acid, ammonium persulphate, and water. The third group is used to flatten off the scale of tones by first attacking the highlight areas: a typical formula combines ammonium persulphate, sulphuric acid, and water.
Other reducers are used for various photographic purposes.
Cf. *intensification.*
2. when reproducing an original image on a reduced scale a figure is used which shows the linear degree of reduction. A 2/3 reduction indicates that 3 cm. in the original are 2 cm. in the reproduction; a reduction to 75% means that 100 cm. become 75 cm. In maps the scale of reduction is indicated by a scale fraction, e.g. 1:100,000 which means that 1 km. (or 100,000 cm.) in the landscape is depicted as 1 cm. on the map. The area scale is the square of the longitudinal scale; in an original depicted in half-scale a certain area in the reproduction is one-quarter of it in size. (G.U.)
See also *intensification.*

reel-fed: said of a printing press which takes paper from a reel instead of a pile of single sheets, as on rotary presses. (M.L.)

reel stand: a device in a rotary press for positioning paper reels. A stand holds three reels, placed at an angle of 120° to each other, at one time. Paper unwinds from one reel, while the other two are kept in reserve. When the first reel comes to the end of its operating length the stand is turned (by motor power if necessary) so that the next reel is brought into the operating position. (G.U.)

For illustration see *rotary press*.

The Reference Catalogue of Current Literature: a handbook for the British book trade. The first edition, 1874, consisted of 135 publishers' catalogues of uniform size, bound in two volumes, with a separate index of 35,000 entries. The work continued in this form, at three- or four-year intervals, until 1932. From 1936–40 it appeared at two-year intervals, and was increased in scope by giving fuller bibliographical details of each book. The 1957 edition (issued 1958) records the books in print in Britain at the end of 1956. The listing of all works in print makes the catalogue unique among book-trade tools; and its useful features include an annotated list of publishers, a directory of directors, and the listing of works issued in publishers' series (in Vol. II. Titles).

'The Reference Catalogue' is published by J. Whitaker & Sons Ltd., 13 Bedford Square, London, W.C.1.

reference marks: signs inserted in the text of a work to direct the attention of the reader to footnotes. In order of use these are:

* asterisk, or star
† dagger
‡ double dagger
§ section
|| parallel
¶ paragraph

If more are needed they are printed in pairs. *Superior figures*, q.v., are preferable since they clearly indicate the order of the notes.

reflex printing: a means of reproducing documents or books without setting up type. The principle was discovered by Albrecht Beyer about 1839, since when several patented applications of it have been made. The original to be copied consists in most cases of a sheet of paper printed on both sides; this is placed with the side to be reproduced against sensitized material. It is exposed to light which first passes through the sensitized film and then strikes the paper surface. Where the paper is blank a large part of the light is reflected, so that it again strikes the sensitized film, while the dark parts of the image absorb the light. Thus the sensitized material is exposed on those parts which do not form the image to almost twice as much light as the parts forming it. By a suitable choice of sensitized material and developer prints can be obtained of sufficient contrast to be used even directly for printing plates by one of the usual methods of process work.

In Ullman's *Manul process* chromate gelatine on glass is the sensitized material. After developing in water the gelatine film is coloured and can then be used as a negative in offset printing. By having an intermediate layer between the gelatine and glass the film can be made removable, so that it can be used as a film negative. In this way it is also reversible.

The *Typon process*, originally introduced by Baltisch Papier-Industrie A.G., uses a special paper or film with a yellow filter inserted between the light and the printing material. (G.U.)

Regiomontanus, Johannes, 1436–76: a German scientist and printer of Königsberg (after which city he changed his birth name of Johannes Müller). After living in Vienna and Hungary he settled in Nuremberg where, financed by a patron, he established a printing press, a workshop, and an observatory. He issued a few astronomical works written by himself and his friends, notable being George Purbach's 'Theoricae planetarum novae', *c.* 1472. His printing activities were really an adjunct to his more important work as an astronomer.

It was in an edition of his 'Calendarium', Venice, 1476, that Erhard Ratdolt printed a notable early example of the modern title-page.

register: 1. the precise superimposing of the separate plates in an illustration printed in two or more colours. Careless work is said to be 'out of register'.

See also *lock-up table*.

2. the exact correspondence in position of the printed area on the two sides of a leaf.

See also *cut to register*.

3. a *signet*, q.v.

4. a list of signatures appearing at the end of early printed books as a guide to the binder. They were mostly used in Italy *c.* 1470–1600, the first being in the 'Epistolae Hieronymi', printed by Sixtus Riessinger, Rome, 1470, though examples do occur in English books. The list was usually headed *registrum foliorum* or *registrum chartarum*, and the first word of each signature would be given as an alternative to a letter.

register sheet: the sheet used to obtain correct register or position of the printed page.

See also *shining*.

register table: a table with an opaque-glass top, and a white-washed interior under it fitted with lights. This is used in the gravure planning department to

A register table

position negatives or positives, and any accompanying type matter, on a layout sheet. It is also used for register work in colour printing and for other purposes.

Also known as *lining-up table* or *shining-up table*.

registrum chartarum : see *register* (4).

registrum foliorum: see *register* (4).

reglets: strips of oil-soaked wood used as inter-linear spacing material, ¾ in. high and from 6- to 18-point thick. (6-point and 12-point are known as nonpareil and pica reglet respectively.)

See also *clumps*.

reimposition: the rearrangement of pages in a forme made necessary when it is desired to add additional text to matter already arranged in pages, or to use a different folding machine. Cf. *double setting*.

Reiner, Imre: an eminent graphic artist and typographer, born in Hungary, who is known for the imaginative and technically advanced wood engravings with which he has illustrated books, and also for his writings on typography.

Types designed by him include Corvinus, 1929–35 (for Bauersche Giesserei), and Matura, 1938 (for Monotype).

reinforced binding: a strengthened binding, i.e. at the joints, for public library use.

reinforced signatures: signatures which have had cambric pasted around or in the fold for the purpose of strengthening the paper and binding; this is often done on the first and last signatures of a book because of the extra strain at those points. (M. L.)

re-issue: 1. a new impression of a work, usually from standing type or plates.

2. said of what should properly be termed a new edition, e.g. 'Re-issued in the Malvern Library' or 'Re-issued in pocket form'.

relative humidity: the percentage of moisture present in the atmosphere compared with the amount which would be present were the atmosphere fully saturated with water vapour at the same temperature. Saturated air has an R.H. factor of 100%; in printing offices it is not unusual for this to vary from 30% to 90%.

Like all fibres of organic origin paper is hygroscopic and absorbs or emits water to adjust its moisture content to that of the air in which it is stored. While the R.H. factor varies with different kinds of fibre it remains constant for the same kind of fibre or fibre pulp, i.e. for the same quality of paper. The moisture content of paper affects its weight and printing properties and thus its R.H. must be known; it is measured by reading a sword hygrometer inserted in a stack of paper.

R.H. of the air	Corresponding water content of equal weights of a cellulose fibre
30%	5%
40%	6%
50%	7%
60%	8·5%
70%	10%
80%	13%

Any changes in the water content of a fibre immediately manifest themselves as changes in its dimensions, especially diagonally. The fibre diameter undergoes a considerable change, and the swelling in this direction at increased moisture content brings about a stretching of the paper. Other properties of the paper are also affected, but from the graphic point of view changes in size are the most significant. The absorption and emission of moisture require a certain time, the former taking place more rapidly than the latter in most cases. When paper is stored in a pile or roll it is the edges of the sheets or rolls which come into contact with the atmosphere, and it is these which will first be exposed to changes in humidity. If the air is, comparatively speaking, damper than the paper the edges will tend to buckle, while drying the edges may cause undulations in the middle of the pile. In order to avoid such changes in the dimensions of the paper it is often customary to allow it to 'hang' before printing commences. (See also *conditioning*.) Paper conditioning is of course more valuable when combined with the air conditioning of the printing premises. In offset printing establishments, where attention must be paid to the moisture transmissible to the paper direct from the damped plates (by way of the rubber cloth), a relative humidity of approximately 60% has proved suitable for register purposes, while in other printing offices and paper-handling concerns a lower moisture content may be more advantageous. (G. U.)

release: the sliding of the matrix out of the matrix magazine after the keys on Linotype and Intertype machines have been struck. Hence the *release mechanism* is the mechanism in the lower part of the matrix magazine which prevents the stored matrices from sliding out of their channels in the sloping magazine, expelling only the lowest matrix into a channel after a key had been struck. (G. U.)

See also *Intertype*, *Linotype*.

relief block: a line or half-tone printing block mounted to type height for letterpress printing.

relief printing: printing from surfaces which are raised to a certain height so that ink is deposited only on these. Relief printing is also referred to as *letterpress printing* and includes printing from stereos, electros, photoengraved plates, hand- and machine-set type and slugs, also half-tone, line block, linocut, woodcut, and wood engraving.

See also *anastatic printing*.

remainder binding: see *remainders*.

remainders: copies of a book which has ceased to sell well and of which the publisher or booksellers have large stocks. Disposal may be by reducing the price; by selling unbound copies or unfolded sheets to a wholesaler (who then markets them in a cheap *remainder binding*); or by pulping. A remaindered work is not necessarily a poor one: it may have been priced too high, or the edition (often a reprint of a successful book) may have been too large. It is not unknown for publishers, on finding a demand for a book at its reduced price, to print further copies as a *remaindered edition*.

A publisher proposing to remainder a title will insert an announcement in the weekly trade journals 'The Bookseller' and 'The Publishers' Circular'.

See also *terms*.

The practice of remaindering books was considerably developed by James Lackington (1746–1815) of the 'Temple of Muses' bookshop in London. During the 19th century certain dealers came to specialize almost exclusively in this branch of bookselling.

remelting pot: a pot for melting metal from type-setting and stereotype machines. It can either be a separate apparatus for remelting metal and casting ingots for type-setting machines and flat stereotypes, or it can be combined with a type-setting or stereo casting machine (casting pot). Remelters are usually heated by gas or electricity, and large models can hold up to 7½ tons. (G. U.)

removes: quotations or notes set at the foot of a page and in smaller type than that of the text. Thus a book set in 12-point may have notes set in 10-point.

Repertorium bibliographicum ad annum 1500: originally, an alphabetically arranged author list of 16,311 incunabula, based on the collection of what is now the Bavarian State Library, Munich. This was compiled by Ludwig F. T. Hain (1781–1836), and published by J. F. Cotta, 4 vols., Stuttgart, 1826–38.

An English bibliographer, Walter Arthur Copinger (1847–1910), published a supplement, 3 vols., 1895–1902, in which he corrected 7000 entries and described a further 6619 incunabula. An index to Hain was prepared by Konrad Burger, 1891, and a further 1921 incunabula were described in Dietrich Reichling's series of appendices, Munich, 1905–14.

A reprint of the 'Repertorium' was published in Milan, 1948.

Replika process: the trade name for a method of photo-litho facsimile printing practised by Percy Lund, Humphries & Co. of Bradford. The main use is for printing out-of-print books when standing type is not available; corrections can be made before photographing the original and it is especially economical when this includes tabular work, symbols, etc. By keeping, to the publisher's order, the photographic negatives of the reprints the firm can make further issues at any time without bulky storage problems. A further use of the process is its adaptation to the reproduction of line illustrations, typescript catalogues, brochures, etc. When preparing the manuscript for tabular matter an outline of the framework is drawn and photo-printed on to carbon-backed typing paper. The figures are typed in. After correction, the typed sheets may need to go to the composing department for the addition of pagination, prelims, etc. The book or booklet is then ready for photographing and machining. An advantage is that the typescript to be reproduced can either be prepared by the printer or in the customer's office, thus eliminating post-printing proofing and reading.

repped: said of a paper which has been given a ribbed effect by impressing it with steel rollers. (M. L.)

reprint: 1. a reproduction in print of any matter already printed.

2. a reissue of a work using the same type or plates employed in the original, with the text unchanged except for the correction of minor errors.

3. printed matter used as copy to be set up and printed again.

reproduction camera: see *camera.*

reproduction proof: a carefully pulled proof, showing all details of the type, used for reproduction purposes.

republication: a reprint of a book without corrections.

resin: see *size.*

resist: a coating of glue, enamel, or shellac, given to a plate when etching to protect non-printing areas from acid corrosion.

See also *cold enamel, fish-glue enamel, polyvinyl alcohol enamel.*

Restoration bindings: English bindings, made by various craftsmen at the time of the restoration of the English monarchy, 1660. The best known are those done in the workshop of *Samuel Mearne,* q.v., the Court binder.

ret: the second side of a sheet of paper.

retail bookseller: one whose main business is to sell books to the public at the full English net published price. In addition to private individuals the term 'public' embraces schools, public libraries, university libraries, and institutions wherever situated, and officials of such bodies.

See also *terms* (1 and 2).

retention: the percentage of loading remaining in the sheet as it forms on the wire. Factors affecting this are the other ingredients of the stock, the amount of beating, and the speed of the Fourdrinier. Cf. *back-water.*

retouching: 1. the skilled treatment of an original photograph prior to making a block. Process black and white are applied by brush in order to accentuate the high lights, deepen the dark tones and cover any unwanted parts; if the latter are at all extensive an airbrush is used.

2. the hand-correcting of colour separations in the photoengraving and photo-lithographic processes. This is known in America as *dot-etching.*

retransfer: an impression taken from a lithographic surface, usually in special ink and on special paper, for the sole purpose of duplicating this original lithographic image onto another lithographic surface. It is thus distinguishable from a *lithographic transfer* which is a surfaced paper bearing an inked image taken from any impression on a *non*-lithographic surface, and then transferred to a lithographic plate. Cf. *transfer.*

retree: the paper-maker's term for the slightly damaged sheets of several reams: this damage is limited to slight specks and minor defects. Outsides, or broken sheets, are marked XXX; 10% less than

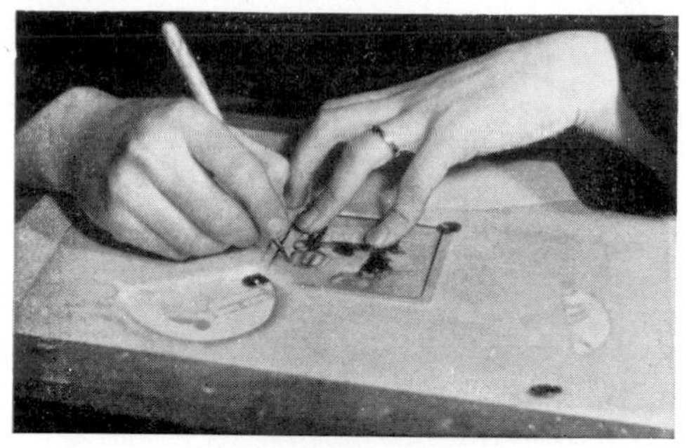

Retouching by hand

With an airbrush

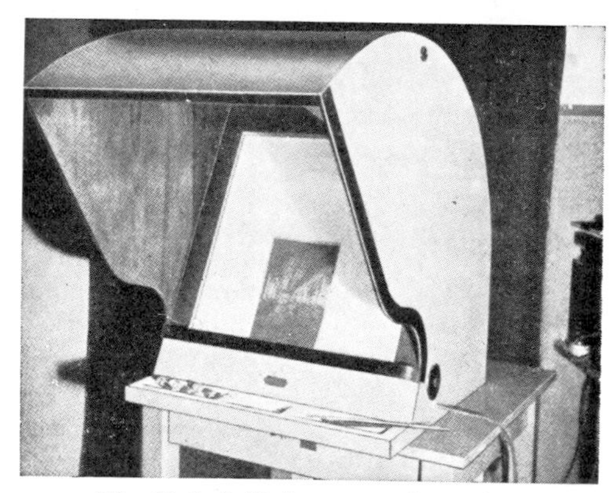

The Hoh & Hahne retouching desk

good are marked XX. Quires of retree are often sold separately with the latter marking.

retroussage: the passing of a folded gauze rag with a rocking motion across the surface of a copper printing plate to draw out the ink from the recesses so that it tends to spread over the surrounding areas. This treatment of a hand-inked plate is done to soften the outlines of the image, or to make dark tones appear still darker. (G. U.)

return on full credit: said of books supplied to a bookseller of which unsold copies may be returned should they become outdated. The publisher will not refund the bookseller's money, but will supply from his list other titles to the same value.

returns: books, supplied to a bookseller on sale or consignment, which are returned unsold to the publisher.

reversal developing: developing by which the material exposed in the camera shows a positive picture on the conclusion of the process instead of a negative one. Developing (first time) proceeds as for an ordinary negative, a negative silver picture appearing. Instead of fixing this, the developed plate or film is put in a bleaching bath which dissolves the silver reduced by the developer, but leaves the silver bromide unchanged. Then the whole of the material is exposed all over to light, and is again developed, only the silver bromide left after the first developing being blackened. A positive picture is thus obtained. Reversal developing is used extensively in direct colour photography, in amateur film photography, and for producing duplicate negatives, etc.

Reversal developing in connection with copying is used in many forms of process work, e.g. in copying positive originals or photographic positives on lithographic printing plates. (G. U.)

See also *deep-etch process*.

reverse aquatint: see *aquatint*.

reversing: an expression used in blockmaking for reversing black to white or left to right. The image on a letterpress block, i.e. one that is to be transferred to an offset plate, must be reversed for the impression in the offset press to appear correctly. A reversing apparatus built on the offset principle is used to do this. (G. U.)

Reversing apparatus

reverso: see *verso*.

review copies: copies of a book in its final form sent to reviewers before the publication date. They are thus not quite the same as *advance copies*, q.v.

revise: a further proof embodying corrections made by the author and/or reader to the first proof.

revised edition: an edition of a work bearing changes to the text as previously published. The new matter may be embodied in the text or added as a supplement. Also known, if sometimes inaccurately, as an *enlarged edition*. Publishers are required to inform the book trade of proposed revised editions by inserting notices in 'The Bookseller' and 'The Publishers' Circular'. Cf. *re-issue*.

Reynes, John, fl. 1521: a London stationer whose name is associated with the early use in England of gold tooling.

R.H.: see *relative humidity*.

Rhys Memorial Prize: see *John Llewelyn Rhys Memorial Prize*.

Riccardi Press: the name used since 1909 for the publications of the Medici Society, London. Herbert P. Horne, who founded the press, designed the Riccardi type in 1909, E. P. Prince cut the punches, and printing was done by the Chiswick Press.

Ricci, Seymour de, 1881–1942: a scholar and bibliographer who evolved an entirely new type of bibliographical study, the enumeration of all known examples of a given book. His first work of this kind was the 'Census of Caxtons', Bibliographical Society, 1909; similarly in 1911 he listed all known examples of Gutenberg's printing in 'Catalogue raisonné des premières impressions de Mayence', Gutenberg Gesellschaft. His sixth edition of Henry Cohen's 'Guide de l'amateur de livres à vignettes du XVIIIe siècle', Paris, 1870, appeared as 'Guide de l'amateur de livres à gravures du 18e siècle', Paris, 1912, and is known as Cohen–Ricci by bibliographers and librarians.

Ricci's 'The Book Collector's Guide', 1921, listed over 2000 first editions of authors from Chaucer to Swinburne. He gave the Sandars Lecture for 1929, published as 'English Collectors of Books and MSS., 1530–1930', C.U.P., 1930.

Richardson, Samuel: 1689–1771: author and printer. In 1706 he was apprenticed to the London printer John Wilde, setting up his own business in 1719. By the mid-century his trade was already extensive and he employed forty workmen. In addition to printing his own novels he printed the first edition of the 'Journals' of the House of Commons in twenty-six volumes (in 1753). He was also made Master of the Stationers' Company in 1754.

Richel, Bernhard, fl. 1474–82: an important printer of Basle. He issued the first dated book printed in Basle, the 'Sachsenspiegel' of 1474, and also the city's first illustrated book, the 'Spiegel des menschlichen Behältnisses', 1476, in which the woodcuts appear to derive from earlier blockbooks. The same blocks were used in 1478 when Martin Huss printed the work under the title 'Mirouer de la Rédemption'.

Richel worked for a time in association with Michael Wenssler. After his death, Richel's wife and son-in-law, Nicolaus Kessler, continued the business.

Ricketts, Charles de Sousy, 1866–1931: the founder of the Vale Press (1896–1904) for which he cut borders and initials, designed types, and planned the bindings.

Rinco process: the trade name of a gravure printing process. Negatives of the illustrations to be reproduced are made on bromide paper, the accompanying type matter being printed in white ink on black paper. They are assembled together and photographed to produce gravure positives of type and illustrations complete.

rising: the stage in making an *electrotype*, q.v., after wax moulding, in which the height of those parts of the mould corresponding with the white areas of the original is raised. This is done by an operator using a heated poker and a stick of hard wax.

Rittenhouse, William, 1654–1708: a German paper-maker (born Wilhelm Rittinghausen) from Mülheim who, in 1690, built on behalf of *William Bradford*, q.v., and Samuel Carpenter the first American paper-mill: this was at Germantown, Pa.

Rittenhouse and his family appear later to have assumed full control of the business which may be said to have established the supremacy of Pennsylvania as a paper-making centre.

Rituale: a book containing the form and order to be used at religious services.

rivers: unsightly white channels running through the lines of a printed page, caused when interword spacing material is set too wide.

Riverside Press: an American private press founded in 1888 by Henry O. Houghton in Cambridge, Mass., as a subsidiary of the publishing firm Houghton, Mifflin & Company, Boston. D. B. Updike was an employee of the press for two years, having previously worked in the publishing house. In 1896 *Bruce Rogers*, q.v., was appointed director of the press which, until it closed in 1911, issued some sixty books.

Rivière, Robert, 1808–82: a London bookbinder of French descent, who was commissioned by the Queen and leading bibliophiles. In 1829 he was working in Bath, the move to London taking place about 1840: here his business expanded to become the leading bookbinding firm of his day. His craftsmanship was of the highest standard, and he was entrusted with the restoration and binding of the Domesday Book in the Record Office.

Rizzi paper: hand-blocked pattern papers suitable for end-papers or book covers. They are the product of an Italian family who first issued them at Varese in the 17th century.

roan: a thin, soft *sheepskin*, q.v., tanned in sumach, dyed, and given a dark finish with a smooth grain for use in bookbinding, often as a substitute for morocco. It is not durable.

See also *skivers.*

Rob Roy type tray: a post-war system of type storage, invented in America by Professor Robert H. Roy. The British adaptation is known as the *Multifont type tray*, q.v.

Robert, Nicolas Louis, 1761–1828: the pioneer inventor of the paper-making machine. While working as an overseer in the Didot paper-mill at Essonnes, near his birthplace of Paris, he tried to evolve a paper-making machine. After some years, assisted by the mill-owner, St Léger Didot, he accomplished this, and in 1798 made the model of a machine for which he was awarded a State grant in order to construct a demonstration model for the Conservatoire des Arts, Paris. In 1799 he patented his invention, an endless wire machine: couch rolls were added by Perrier in 1801.

Robert sold his patent to Didot, who persuaded an English relative, John Gamble, to interest an English paper-maker in a scheme for building the machine in England. (No French capital for this project was available.) Gamble approached the London stationery firm Walker, Bloxam & Fourdrinier whose leading partners were the brothers Henry and Sealy Fourdrinier. Gamble himself took out the first English patents in 1801 and 1803. For the subsequent development of the machine see under *Bryan Donkin* and *Fourdrinier*. (With G.U.)

Robert of Jumièges: see *Sacramentary of Robert of Jumièges.*

Robert Southey Literary Prize: an award of £350 made by the Brazilian Government for the best book on any aspect of Brazilian culture written in English by a British subject domiciled in the U.K. and first published during the five years prior to December 21st, 1952.

Rochel paper: a high-quality printing paper imported into England from the Angoumois during the 16th and 17th centuries.

Rochester Press: a private printing press established in 1858 by Edwin Roffe, a steel engraver, at Somers Town, London. He issued small editions of several volumes of miscellaneous diaries, notes, and reminiscences. 'He was evidently a true bibliomaniac, and his notes upon his favourite books are full of the unction with which the real book-lover dilates upon his cherished treasures.' (B. Dobell.)

He appears to have ceased printing about 1872. The curious may examine examples of his work in the British Museum.

rocker: see *cradle.*

rocking-cylinder press: a cylinder machine in which the cylinder revolves in one direction during the forward movement of the bed, reversing and swinging back to its original position during the return of the bed. Some rocking-cylinder machines are so constructed that printing is done during both movements; in this case the press must have double feeding and delivery arrangements for the paper.

See also *letterpress machines.* (G.U.)

Rodker, John, d. 1956: see *Ovid Press.*

Rogers, Bruce, 1870–1957: a distinguished American typographer and printer who directed the Riverside Press of G. H. Mifflin at Cambridge, Mass. As a typographer he worked from 1917–19 in England at the Cambridge University Press, from 1929–31 with Sir Emery Walker, and later at the Oxford University Press on the Lectern Bible, 1935.

Famous types designed by him are Montaigne 1901, and the widely used Centaur 1915, which may be considered a refinement of the former: both are based on Jenson's roman of 1470. Centaur was cut by Monotype in 1929 and used in the Lectern Bible. His World Folio Bible is considered the finest Bible produced in America.

Rogers Prize: an irregularly made award of £100 for an essay on a medical or surgical subject written by any person on the Medical Register. The University of London chooses the subject and awards the prize.

roll: 1. a manuscript written on a sheet of parchment or vellum which is kept rolled, not folded. Official records of a Court or Government were often so preserved.

2. a binder's revolving tool for impressing either a line or a repeating pattern. The tool is a brass wheel, *c.* 3 in. diameter, with a long handle which rests on the shoulder during use.

3. the design impressed by (2) above.

roller: a roller for inking up the printing forme, or for rolling ink to its correct consistency and distributing it to other rollers which ink the forme.

See *composition-, distributor-, glazed-, ink-, nap roller.*

In letterpress work hand-rollers are used in connection with small proof presses, the composition roller being held between a fork-like tool. Narrow 'line-inking rollers' can be used for inking up single lines.

In the inking device of printing presses machine-rollers of greater length are used, with consequently greater need for durability and strength of the core and composition. A distinction is made between *distributing rollers* that roll the ink to correct consistency, carry and distribute it evenly, and *forme rollers* which rest against the forme. The former are made entirely of metal, or are cast in the same way as forme rollers which have a rubber or composition surface and an iron core. Cast composition rollers are of particular importance owing to the elasticity and absorbent capacity of their surface. This is, however, very sensitive to changes of moisture and temperature, and has little mechanical strength, and troubles occur. In rapid rotary presses high temperatures may cause the rollers to melt or buckle, so rubber is preferable. The latter, unlike composition, is not capable of keeping the forme clean and giving a first-class reproduction of illustrations. Experiments have been made in Holland and U.S.A. to combine the two by having a rubber roller which is given a thin gelatine coating; this is easily renewed. (G.U.)

roller washing: the rollers in a printing press must have the ink removed after printing, and often during it, by washing up (preferably with photogen in the case of composition rollers). In rotary presses, and especially in offset machines with their complicated inking devices, this washing is mostly done mechanically by attachments to the machine which consist in principle of a rubber blade which runs along one of the rollers and wipes off the mixture of ink and a washing solution which is fed to it; the inking system is allowed to revolve while this is done. In addition to such automatic washers, simpler apparatus is used for washing when the rollers are off the machine. (G.U.)

See also *washing up.*

Rollins, Carl P.: the founder of the *Montague Press,* q.v.

romain du roi Louis XIV: a type-face with precise, condensed letters having thin, flat, unbracketed serifs, designed by Philippe Grandjean for use under royal monopoly in the French *Imprimerie Royale*, q.v. The first book printed with this type (apart from a specimen book) appeared in 1702 and was 'Médailles sur les événements du règne de Louis-le-Grand'. Work on the fount was continued by Grandjean's pupil, Jean Alexandre, and the latter's son-in-law *Louis Luce*, q.v., who completed it in 1745.

See also *modern face*.

roman: ordinary vertical type as distinct from black letter or italic, so named because the letters were first used as manuscript forms in Rome. The first roman types were those of Adolf Rusch, Strasbourg, 1467; and, in purer form, Wendelin da Spira, Venice, 1469, and Nicolas Jenson, Venice, 1470. Francesco Griffo cut a roman face for Aldus Manutius which later led to that of Claude Garamond.

In France roman letters were used for the first work printed at the Sorbonne, 1470. In the Netherlands Johannes de Westfalia introduced roman types about 1472. In Spain Lambert Palmart used them in 1474. In Switzerland Johann Froben was a distinguished user of this face.

The first English book set wholly in roman type was the 'Oratio in pace nuperrime composita' of Richard Pace, printed in 1518 by *Richard Pynson*, q.v., who had, however, made occasional use of it from 1509.

roman à clef: a novel in which characters are based on real persons but with their names changed.

roman notation: the method of recording dates in the colophons or on the title-pages of some early printed books, e.g.

M iiiiC iiiiXX Viij
i.e. $1{,}000 + 4 \times 100 + 4 \times 20 + 8 = 1488$

roman numerals: forms of these are:—I = 1, II = 2, III = 3, IV = 4, V = 5, VI = 6, VII = 7, VIII = 8, IX = 9, X = 10, XI = 11, etc., L = 50, C = 100, D or IƆ = 500, DC or IƆC = 600, CM or DCCCC or IƆCCCC = 900, M or CIƆ = 1000. XL = 40, XLIV = 44. LX = 60, LXIV = 64.

Thus MCMLVIII = 1958.

Romanesque illumination: the art of the manuscript painter in 12th-century England was characterized by dignity and severity, suggesting the remoteness of the Almighty. A favourite subject was Christ on a rainbow, symbolic of His power; the Virgin and Child were also introduced.

Very large initials of coiled stems and leaf motifs were carefully drawn and painted in brilliant colours against a gold background. The solemn figures were curiously elongated or contorted, the swirling draperies which clad them tending to divide the body into oval shapes. Naturalism was often subordinated to rhythmic pattern, and the symbolism owed much to Byzantine art. The use of highly burnished gold for large background surfaces is also characteristic of Romanesque illumination.

It was during this era that complete Bibles and Psalters were widely produced, an outstanding example of the former being the Winchester Bible. Popular also were *bestiaries*, q.v.

See also *Canterbury School*, *Salisbury School*, *Winchester School*.

Romney Street Press: a hand-printing press founded by Francis (now Sir Francis) Meynell in 1915 at 67 Romney Street, Westminster. The aims were to publish books, pamphlets, and single sheets of poetry. Only two works, in editions of fifty copies each, appear to have been issued for sale before 1918.

See also *Meynell, Sir Francis*, *Nonesuch Press*, *Pelican Press*.

ronde: a script type-design based on a French manuscript hand and having the appearance of upright handwriting.

Rood, Theodoric: the printer from Cologne who in 1478 printed for the *Oxford University Press*, q.v.

Rosart: see *music printing*.

Rose Mary Crawshay Prize: a prize founded in 1888 by R. M. Crawshay as an annual award for writings on Byron, Keats, or Shelley. Since 1915 the scheme has been administered by the British Academy, and the scope altered: it is awarded to a woman writer of any nationality for a work on English literature written or published within three years preceding the date of the award. (Preference is still given to a work on Byron, Keats, or Shelley.)

Rosenbach, Abraham S. Wolf, 1876–1952: a scholar, bibliophile, and antiquarian bookseller who was a partner, with his elder brother, in the Rosenbach Company of Philadelphia and New York. During the 'twenties his activities on behalf of American collectors brought him to the more important European book sales for such acquisitions as Shakespeare Folios, a Gutenberg Bible (from Melk), and the rarest incunabula, illuminated manuscripts, and first editions of English literature. During the years Dr. Rosenbach assembled the major collection of Shakespeariana which in 1952 was bought by *Dr. Martin Bodmer*, q.v.

Rosenbach, Johann, fl. 1490–1530: an early printer of Barcelona whence he came from Heidelberg. He printed in several towns, his work being characterized by woodcut borders and illustrations, and best known for the letter in which Columbus described his crossing of the Atlantic.

Rosenwald, Lessing J.: a contemporary American bibliophile whose major collection of about 2000 illustrated books of all periods was presented to the Library of Congress in 1943. For the term of the donor's life, however, the books are housed in his library at Jenkintown, Penn. Notable among the 400 or so incunables are works printed by Gutenberg, Fust and Schöffer, Jenson, Zainer, Caxton, Sorg, and Verard; also here are the Laurentii 'Monte Santo di Dio', 1477, the Morgiani and Petri 'Epistolae et evangalia', Florence, 1495, and the Plannck edition of Turrecremata's 'Meditationes', Rome, 1484. Notable bindings include three Groliers, a Canevari, and examples of 'à la fanfare'.

Röslein: the German name for printers' ornaments or flowers.

rotary press: a machine for printing from a revolving cylindrical forme to which paper is usually fed from a reel. If printing is done on sheets the term *sheet-fed rotary* is used. Modern presses for intaglio and lithographic offset printing are always built on the rotary principle; for letterpress work rotary presses are mainly used for newspapers and periodicals, printing being done from cylindrical stereos. Sometimes printing is done from the original flat forme on an endless web of paper, a *flat-bed web press.*

For early forms of letterpress rotary machines see *letterpress machine.* The Bullock press (1866) and the Walter press (1868) were the first reel-fed rotary machines used to any great extent, especially for

Bullock's rotary press of 1865, *from a contemporary illustration*

newspapers. Early rotary presses were not equipped with folders, and the web was cut into sheets either before or after printing.

A modern letterpress rotary machine consists of one or more units in which the actual printing is done; a *folder* in which the printed matter is cut from the continuous web and folded; arrangements for conditioning the paper reels and controlling their speed; a number of conducting rollers for guiding the web through the press; and sometimes circular knives for cutting the web longitudinally. Their mutual position varies and is often adapted to the premises in which the press is installed. Small presses, on the contrary, are fairly standardized. A typical modern press is shown in the illustration.

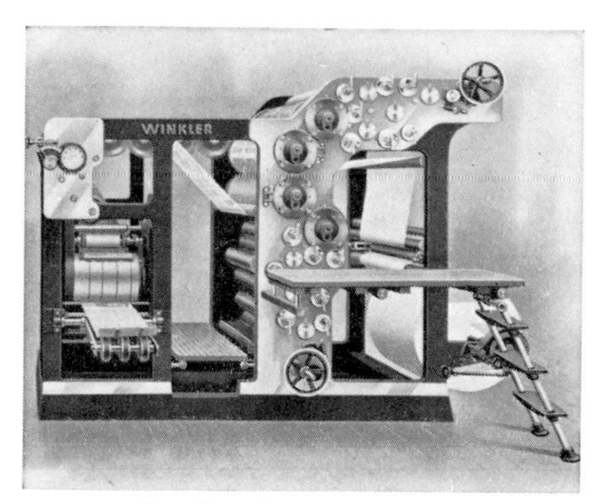

Small modern rotary press

Rotary presses may be over 150 feet long, but should then be regarded as a series of machines built tandem-fashion, from which the printed matter is taken out at various points. While theoretically an unlimited number of pages can be printed at a time, the upper limit is determined by the folder. A book of 256 pages can be printed in a single operation (Crabtree press). When premises are sufficiently lofty the press is then built on three decks. The lowest is for conditioning the paper reels and controlling their speed; on the middle one the printing units and folders are placed; while the top deck contains guiding rollers, cutting devices, and, when required, gumming apparatus. In this way the main deck, where the most highly skilled work of operating the press, distributing ink, etc., is carried out, is free from transporting paper and finished matter. The press illustrated is an excellent example of this modern type, and the diagram of the same press gives a good idea of the practical arrangement of a *composite machine.* (See page 353.)

The next illustration shows the basic design of a still more modern press, designed in 1946 and completed in 1948. The main difference between the two is the division of the motors into several units and their position above the press, so that the floor of the paper store is free, and in the vertical placing of the turner bars above the folder.

Paper is fed into a rotary press from a *reel stand.* On presses other than composite machines the reel stand consists of a simple storage device at one end of the press in which the reel is conditioned after being secured to an iron axle. In presses working on the deck principle, in which the units are placed one

Eight-page rotary press, 1884

Sixteen-page press, 1901

Sixty-four-page press, 1915

Crabtree press, 1935, *for double-width newspaper printing. Bottom deck, paper store; middle deck, printing units; top deck, main driving axle, slitters, conducting rollers, pasting apparatus*

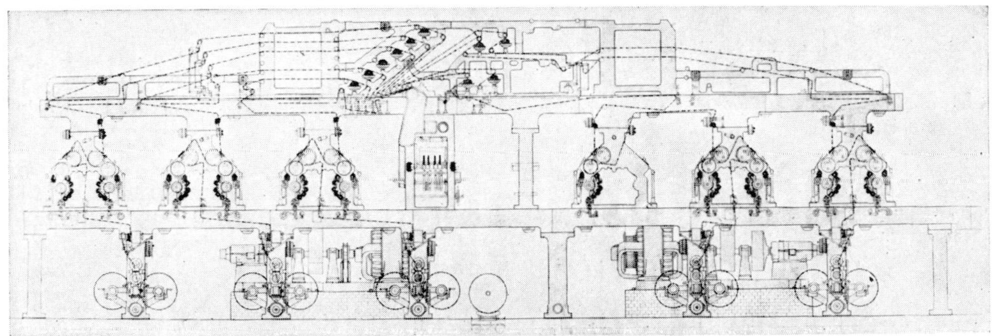

Diagrammatic drawing of Crabtree press, 1935

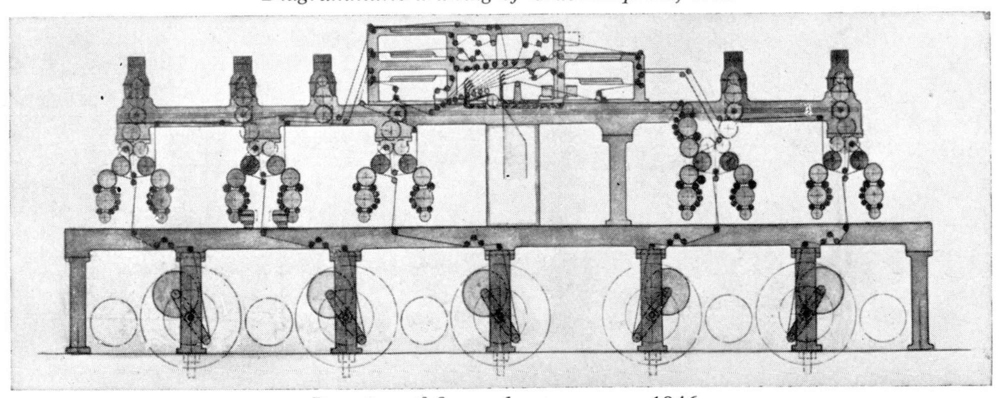

Drawing of five-reel rotary press, 1946

Rotary press with unit and reel stand on several decks

Reel stand of rotary press. Left, mechanical band-brake and electro-magnetic emergency brake installed on the same axle as the dowel which is equipped to engage the cardboard case of the reel

above the other, lifts for the reels are used. Composite machines have stands on the lowest deck either for two reels or three. Axles are not used, the reels being suspended on dowels, one of which is conical and smooth and the other cylindrical and provided with expanding spurs which penetrate into the cardboard wrapper of the reel. The two-reel and three-reel stands can be moved a few cm. in the transverse direction of the press to regulate the width of the margin: this is done by a motor operated by push-buttons. A special kind of reel stand, known as a *flying paster*, enables a reel to be changed at full speed or only slightly slower: this expensive device is only of profit in the case of large newspaper printing.

The paper reel in a rotary press cannot be used up to the innermost layer. The remnants of the reel can be preserved by re-winding in a special machine. A re-winding machine is illustrated below.

To regulate the tension in thc wcb each reel is provided with a brake. In its simplest form a reel brake is a steel band fixed round the reel of paper and fastened to a wire rope loaded with weights, or it consists of a hand-operated band- or shoe-brake

Reel stand in modern composite press. On the central column, from below, the motor with gear for tilting the stand; at the top, an automatic brake relay for constant paper tension

Re-winding machine for remains of old reels

Fitting an old reel

Part of the superstructure of a rotary press, showing a draw-in roller with ratchet wheels and circular cutter

Close-up of a cutter operating on a notch in a draw-in roller

working against the axle which supports the reel during printing. Opinions differ as to the advantages of brakes being on the reel or on the axle: Continental manufacturers favour the former, British and American users the latter. The degree of tension required on the web is estimated by the pressman. Immediately after starting up, the brakes on the different reels are adjusted, after which constant tension is automatically kept until the reel is finished. A regulating mechanism for an automatic brake is illustrated.

The printing unit is adapted for perfecting the web at one operation. It is composed of two pairs of cylinders, each with its own inking device and drive.

Automatic reel-brake for constant paper tension

Printing unit of a composite press

In modern composite machines the two pairs of cylinders and the inkers are placed symmetrically (see illustration). One of the cylinders in each pair carries the printing forme (stereotype plates) and is known as the *plate* or *forme cylinder*, the other is the *impression*

Driving system of printing unit

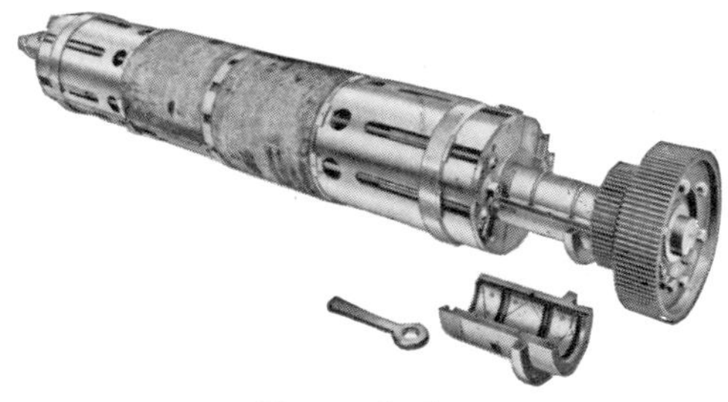

Plate cylinder

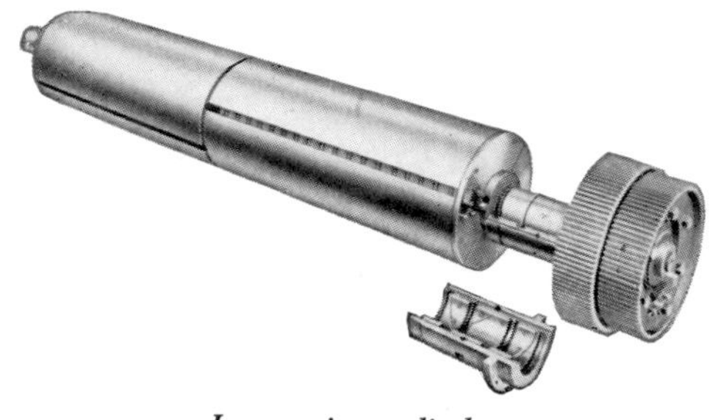

Impression cylinder

End of plate cylinder, showing clamping device, bearing, and driving gear

Stereo plate in Goss's Unitube press

Plate-dog

Safety arrangements for reducing damage if the web bursts. Crabtree's anti-winder device

Motors for sectional working, placed above press

Operating desk

cylinder. The forme cylinder has a fixed ring in the middle, movable rings at the ends (each embracing half of the circumference), and loose plate-clips in grooves for securing the plates. In the longitudinal direction of the cylinder are fixed supporting strips which prevent the sheets from sliding along the circumference. A method of increasing the durability of the plates and fastenings, and thereby the maximum speed of the press, was tried by Goss who built a Unitube press for plates embracing the whole circumference of the cylinder (see illustration).

The impression cylinder is usually made of heavy steel with a tympan clamp for fastening the packing. In recent presses, however, impression cylinders are made of special cast iron with the durability of steel but better able to moderate the vibration. The impression cylinder is on roller bearings resting on eccentric bushes, by turning which it can be moved nearer to or farther from the forme cylinder in order to regulate the depth of the impression. There is usually an indicator at each bearing of the impression cylinder to indicate its position in relation to the forme cylinder.

Presses for colour work vary in design; two colours can be printed on the same impression cylinder, but as a rule separate units are preferred for each colour with register adjustment by hand or photo-electric means.

There are various electric safety devices on the units for stopping the press in the event of a web breaking. This can be done from top speed in a few seconds, and is necessary in view of the risk of the paper winding itself round cylinders and inkers and breaking the bearings or even bending the axles.

Although letterpress work is most generally associated with rotary printing on reels, lithographic offset and intaglio work can also be done. The delivery of the paper through the press, the arrangement and driving of the units, folders, etc., are mainly the same as for rotary letterpress printing but with the differences inherent in the nature of the printing processes (see *intaglio*, *offset press*, *offset printing*). (G. U.)

rotary printing: printing from a forme fitted to the surface of a revolving cylinder. Rotary printing is used for intaglio, lithographic, and letterpress work, and for printing on sheets or paper reels; as a rule the term refers to the latter (see rotary press).

Given moderate pressure between the cylinders on a rotary press it can be considered that the plate does not experience any compression at all at the place where it is exposed to pressure, whereas the packing on the impression cylinder is considerably compressed: just how much depends on the force of the pressure and the hardness of the packing. From the illustration it will be seen that contact between the cylinders is not along a line, but along a surface the width of which grows as the packing is compressed. It is evident that perfect rolling cannot occur along the whole contact strip, and that there is a certain amount of slipping at some places. A narrow contact strip and comparatively slight compression, i.e. hard packing, should therefore give the sharpest impression. In theory the packing should be of such dimensions that perfect rolling is secured where the compression is greatest, and slipping where it is less. The circumference of the impression cylinder, measured outside the packing, should thus be slightly larger than the measure of the plate cylinder outside the plates.

The whole object of rotary printing is a high output. For various reasons (durability of plates, quality of paper, etc.) the presses cannot be worked at any speed desired. Arrangements must therefore be made for working at a maximum speed as long as possible, and for seeing that interruptions are reduced to a minimum. Careful interlay, devices for changing the reels without stopping the machine, steps for reducing the unavoidable breaks of paper, and proper care of the paper during transport and storage are steps in this direction.

In rotary printing both sides of the paper are impressed in quick succession without an opportunity for drying. As the paper passes into the second pair of cylinders some ink from the first printing is deposited on the packing of the impression cylinder. If the impression of type, screen dots, etc., in subsequent copies of these pages does not strike the ink on the packing with perfect accuracy, part of the ink returns to the clean paper quite close to the type or dot and appears as a shadow. The defect is due to jolts in the web from paper reels which are not quite round. This can be counteracted by careful handling of the paper. Another method is to use a *set-off reel*. A special web is conducted between the web to be

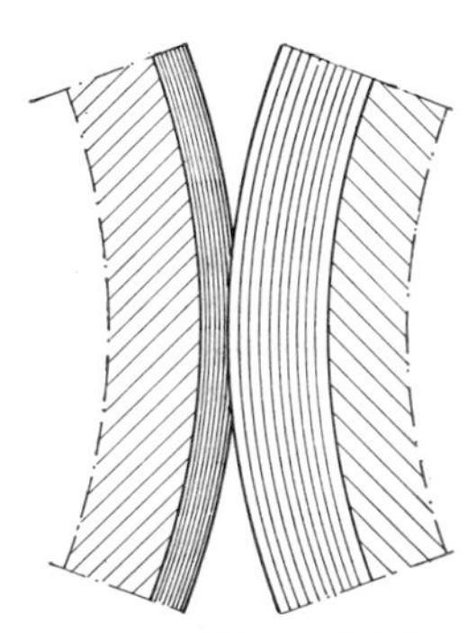

Contact between forme cylinder (right) and impression cylinder (left) in a high-pressure rotary press

printed and the packing on the second pair of cylinders, and then the set-off reel is wound up again: it can be passed through the press in this way several dozen times. Recently a packing was produced in America which is said not to absorb any ink at all, so that displacement is totally eliminated. Its surface is covered with very small glass beads, about 8000 per sq. cm. Quick-set inks which dry on surface contact with the paper open up fresh possibilities.

In modern lithographic (offset) printing as well as in (doctor-blade) intaglio printing, rotary printing is the rule, even for small runs when rotary presses are used for sheets. When, in offset printing and at times in intaglio printing, the printing formes are made as flat plates to be bent round the surface of the cylinders in the press, the deformation of the image by bending the plate should be taken into account (the same applies when bending the matrix in stereotyping). If the thickness of the plate is T and the diameter of the cylinder D, a distance L in the direction along the circumference of the cylinder will be increased in bending by $\frac{T}{D} \times L$. If the ratio of speed on the periphery is wrong, so that the peripheral speed of the cylinder surfaces pressing against each other is different, this will affect both the sharpness of the printed image and its size. This circumstance is sometimes utilized intentionally, e.g. when the thickness of the base for plates or rubber cloth is varied in register work. In intaglio printing patents have been taken out with regard to the possibility of maintaining different speeds on the forme cylinder and the surface of the paper in carbonizing, in order thereby to counterbalance the influence of the screen. (G. U.)

Rotofoto photo-setting machine: this consists of four units: 1. a standard Monotype keyboard; 2. a single-character projector which, instead of the metal-casting equipment and matrices of (1), has a master negative of each of the normal characters: these are photographed by a camera which moves to build up the lines and columns; 3. a proofing machine in which each line of the film produced in (2) is projected on to sensitized paper to produce a print for correcting; 4. a make-up machine in which the lines on the film produced in (2) are projected on to a second film to make whole-page transparencies. The product of (4) can be a roll of film containing several complete pages ready for imposing on glass for photogravure, or on plates for lithography, or etching on to a copper cylinder for rotary presses, or the product can be a number of flat plates or films, one per page. The image can be either positive or negative. The machine will produce arabic or similar characters in addition to the usual roman. It is the invention of George Westover of London, and was announced in 1948. (See 'Illustrated London News', December 18th, 1948, page 697.)

rotograph: a photograph of a book page or manuscript made by exposing it via a lense and prism on to sensitized paper.

rotogravure: printing from photogravure cylinders on a web-fed rotary press. Suitable for long runs.
See also *intaglio, photogravure.*

rotogravure paper: the main requirements are for smoothness and, when colour work is being reproduced, whiteness and a certain degree of absorbency. Esparto is one of the best papers for gravure, but good results are possible on super-calendered and imitation arts.

rotunda: the round black-letter or gothic type-face of the 15th century.
See also *letters—forms and styles.*

rough gilt: uncut edges are occasionally gilded before sewing, fore-edge first. When this is to be done the overlap paper is trimmed, but sufficient short sheets are left as binding proof. The finish is left dull. (The book must be interleaved with thick paper to produce a solid working surface.)
The head may be cut in the plough, and gilded after the boards have been attached. It will be polished. Cf. *antique gold edges.*

rough proof: a first or galley proof which has not been read or corrected by the printer's reader before it is sent to the publisher.

rough pull: a proof taken on rough paper without underlay or overlay. Also called *flat pull.*

rounce: the handle at the side of early printing presses used to turn a roller to which were affixed the ends of two leather straps. The other ends of the straps were secured to the sliding carriage bearing the forme. Turning the rounce thus drew the carriage under and out of the press. Some authorities define rounce as including both the handle and the roller.

rounding: the process of giving a book back a convex shape, after first gluing, and before casing. This is done by machine or by the forwarder who uses a round-headed hammer. In Britain and America books are rounded and backed to provide joints (see diagram under *backing*). In most European countries it is customary to round the book only without joints.
See also *backing.*

Rounding

router: a machine for working metal (or wood) by means of a rotating cutter. Such machines are used when preparing blocks and stereos since by their aid the outlines of an image can be followed with accuracy and, for example, any superfluous parts of a half-tone can be cut away, or when preparing line blocks the mechanical shaping of the metal can be a partial substitute for deep etching.
For the working of stereos many types of plane and round routers are in use; there are also jet routers for removing the jet from cast stereos, etc.
See also *blockmaking, stereotype.* (G.U.)

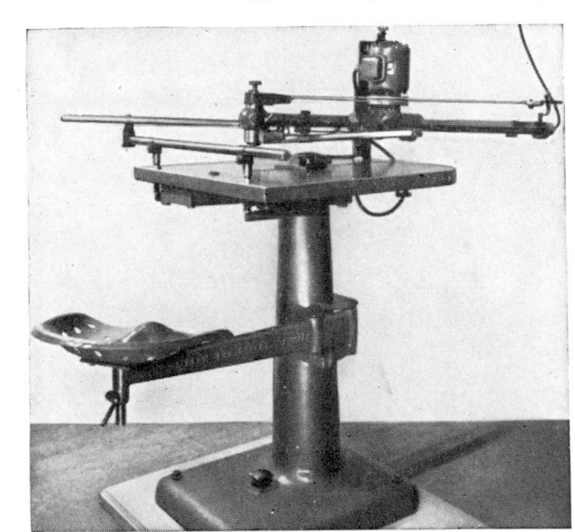

Block and stereo router

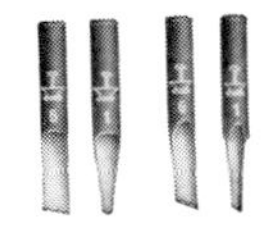

Flat and hollow routing cutters of various sizes

routing machine: a machine for cutting away the non-printing parts of stereotype plates. Cf. *plate-boring machine.* (G.U.)
See also *router.*

Routing machine for curved plates

Routledge, Thomas: see *esparto.*

Roxburghe, John Ker, third Duke of, 1740–1804: a nobleman and bibliophile who inherited and developed a library so rich in rarities that no one today could hope to assemble its equal. In this note it is only possible to outline its main groups: the manuscripts and printed editions of the Arthurian and other romances, numerous works printed by Caxton, de Worde, Pynson, and an extensive collection of Elizabethan and Jacobean drama. Many books were bound specially for him.

At the sale by auction in 1812 the Roxburghe collection realized £23,341.

See also *Roxburghe Club.*

Roxburghe binding: a style of binding in which a book is quarter-bound in brown or green roan, and has cloth or paper sides; the top is often gilded, side edges and bottoms being untrimmed. The style was used for the publications of the *Roxburghe Club*, q.v.

Roxburghe Club: a club formed in London in 1812, after the sale of the third Duke of Roxburghe's library, by prominent bibliophiles who met in St Alban's Tavern (Dibdin, Lord Spencer, and others). The club's purpose was the printing or reprinting of rare works, tracts, etc., for the benefit of the thirty-one (later forty) members.

royal: a standard size of printing paper, 25 in. by 20 in.

Royal Literary Fund: a fund established in 1788 as the 'Literary Fund' by the Rev. David Williams. It was incorporated in 1818, and in 1842 became the Royal Literary Fund, Stationers' Hall, London. Grants are made to authors who are British nationals or foreigners resident in the U.K. whose work is of approved literary merit.

royalties: payments made at regular intervals by a publisher to an author for the right of publishing and selling his work, the amount usually being a mutually agreed percentage of the published price and paid only in respect of copies sold. The reader should refer to 'Guide to Royalty Agreements', Publishers Association, London.

See also *publishers' agreements.*

Roycroft Press: a private press and bindery founded in 1893 by Elbert Hubbard at East Aurora, U.S.A. This hand-press was noted for the careful printing and fine bindings issued from it. Between 1894–1909 the 'Little Journey Books' were produced monthly and had such popularity that machines were installed to print editions. However, in 1903 the Irish poet W. B. Yeats wrote that the Roycroft books were 'eccentric, restless, and thoroughly decadent'.

R-printer: see *Rusch, Adolf.*

rubber-back binding: a method of binding a book by cutting off the folds and dipping the back in rubber solution. The method is now little used and was a stage in the development of *unsewn binding*, q.v.

rubber stereo: the usual name for a rubber stereotype produced by casting or pressing rubber on to a matrix. Rubber stereos are used to a large extent for aniline printing and for printing on unglazed paper, as well as in the form of rubber dies. A matrix of plaster or flong (see *stereotype*) or of lead (see *electrotype*) is made from an original forme (type, wood or lead engraving, zinc block, etc.). Ordinary paper matrices

Rubber stereo being removed from the matrix

can be used, but stronger, specially prepared matrix cardboard is preferable, sometimes with the addition of water-glass to the paste used for preparing the cardboard. After dusting with talcum on both sides, the rubber plate is pressed against the matrix in a moulding press; this is heated to about 150° C, pressure being slowly increased. By heating, the rubber is vulcanized at the same time. There are many patent varieties of rubber stereo, e.g. *Semperit*, q.v. (G.U.)

Rubel, Ira W.: a lithographer of New York who commercially developed *offset printing* on paper in 1904. The discovery is said to have been made when a rubber cloth was accidentally used as a cylinder covering in a lithographic press. Due to the negligence of the operator an impression was made on the rubber cloth, and when the next sheet of paper went through the press a very sharp impression was obtained on the back of it. The first offset press built on the 'American' system was constructed in accordance with Rubel's instructions. (G.U.)

See also *offset printing*.

rubric: 1. the heading, printed in red ink, of a chapter, section, or other division of a book, the rest of the text being printed in black. Such a book is said to be *rubricated.*

2. a direction for the conducting of Divine Service, which, in books of liturgy, is often printed in red ink.

rubric posts: wooden posts found outside booksellers' shops in 17th- and 18th-century England. They were used as a form of advertisement to display title-pages, of which extra copies were always made, a fact which may account for the detailed address of the printer and bookseller being printed on them.

rubricator: the artist employed by early printers to insert decorative initial letters, often in red, at the beginning of chapters. Spaces for these were left blank when printing the text, with possibly a *guide letter*, q.v., inserted.

During the 15th and 16th centuries Latin was read universally, and most books were written in it. This led to a flourishing export trade in books from the various centres of printing. Books were sent in sheets packed in barrels. Rubricating was done after the book was assembled by the receiving bookseller.

See also *illumination, untouched.*

ruby: the former name for a size of type, approximately 5½-point.

Ruette, Macé, fl. 1598–1644: a Parisian binder and bookseller who in 1635 succeeded Clovis Eve as Court binder. He developed the art of *marbling* and *pointillé*, qq.v.

Rui Barbosa Prize: a prize of £350 awarded every fifth year by the British Government to the Brazilian national who, during the preceding five years, has written the best book on any aspect of British national culture. It is the British counterpart to the *Robert Southey Prize*, q.v.

rule: strips of brass or type metal, type high, cast in point sizes and to various lengths.

See also *brass rule, mitred* (2), *multiple rule, Oxford corners, setting rule, swelled rules.*

rule-curving machine: a machine for curving lead or brass rule. A strip is placed between a concave and a convex steel block; pressure is applied. Interchangable blocks for different degrees of curve are used. (G.U.)

Rule-curving machine

rums: a slang term, used by 18th-century London booksellers, for a large assortment of unsaleable books. The suggested explanation that 'rums' were barrels of such books shipped to Jamaica in exchange for rum cannot be confirmed.

run: a machinist's term for the number of impressions taken from a forme at one time.

run-in sheets: the sheets of paper passed through a press at the beginning of a run, and rejected by the pressman as spoils until he considers ink colour and quality of impression to be satisfactory.

run on: an indication to the printer that a new paragraph is not to be made. This instruction is marked in copy and proofs by a line joining the end of one piece of matter to the beginning of the next.

See also *break-line, end a break, end even.*

run on chapters: chapters which do not begin on a fresh page but which are set on the same page as the conclusion of the preceding chapter. A style found in cheap bookwork.

run out and indented: type with the first line set to full measure; the next and succeeding lines of the same paragraph are indented.

run round: said of an illustration set in a page of text which has been indented to allow for it.

runners: small figures printed for reference purposes in page margins, e.g. in school texts of plays, or in long poems.

running heads: see *headline.*

run-up spine: said of the spine of a book when part of the decoration tooled on it consists of twin lines running up the edge of the two joints and across the spine, thus forming panels. A two-line roll and pallet are used.

Ruppel, Berthold, fl. 1460: probably a pupil of Gutenberg who may have set up the first press in Basle (part of the German Empire until 1501).

Rupprecht-Presse: a private printing press founded in Munich in 1914 by *Fritz Helmut Ehmcke,* q.v. In 1922 the press became part of the Beck'sche Verlagsbuchhandlung. Poetry, philosophy, and belles-lettres were the principal publications, all printed in types designed by Ehmcke.

Rusch, Adolf, d. 1489: a printer, paper-merchant, and publisher of Strasbourg where he worked with Johann Mentelin, later marrying the latter's daughter and taking over his business in 1478. He is known as the 'R-printer' due to his use of a curious capital letter R which he used in books not identifiable by his name. He was the first printer in Germany to use roman types (1474).

russia cowhide: an inferior russia leather in which cowhide is used and given a straight grain.
Also known as *American russia.*

russia leather: a hard-wearing reddish brown leather made from calf and used for binding. The skin is impregnated with birch-bark oil. Its use in England as a material for book covers dates from *c.* 1730, but it is not often employed today as it tends to dry and disintegrate.

rustic capitals: the roman alphabet as adapted from *square capitals,* q.v., by early scribes and used as a book hand from the 2nd–6th centuries. The letters were lighter and less formal than square capitals, giving a more condensed effect on the page. Also known as *scriptura actuaria.*
See also *letters—forms and styles.*

Rutland: the trade name for a fine-quality sheepskin used in bookbinding.

ruttier book: a 16th-century term for a book of sea-charts, tides, courses, etc.
See also *portolano.*

Ryland, William Wynne, 1732–83: the Royal engraver to George III who brought from Paris to England the art of *stipple engraving,* q.v., later to be made famous by his pupil Francesco Bartolozzi.

ADDENDA

roll-coated paper: a good-quality coated paper, made in various grades. The coating unit is an integral part of the paper-making machine. At a particular stage, the newly-made web of dried plain paper is brought into contact with rubber-covered rollers which deposit a liquid coating of china clay and other substances upon it. The moving web is immediately heat-dried, super-calendered, and reeled.

Being less costly than *art paper*, which involves the brush coating of a previously made body paper, and better quality than *imitation art*, for which the clay and starch which give the finished surface are added to the pulp, roll-coated papers are an extensively used alternative.

See also *cast coated paper*.

Rowfant Club: a club for bibliophiles, established in Cleveland, Ohio, in 1895. Books for members are occasionally published.

S

Sabin, Joseph, 1821–81: a bibliophile, publisher, and antiquarian of New York and Philadelphia. He wrote 'A Bibliography of Bibliography', 1877, and compiled the most comprehensive bibliography of Americana, 'Bibliotheca Americana, a bibliography of books relating to America from its discovery to the present time', 29 vols., New York, Bibliographical Society of America, 1868–1936. The first thirteen volumes were issued in Sabin's lifetime, Wilberforce Eames and R. W. G. Vail continuing and completing the work.

Sacramentary: a *Missal*, q.v., without Epistles and Gospels.

Sacramentary of Robert of Jumièges: a famous Missal (properly, Sacramentary) lavishly illuminated by artists of the *Winchester School*, q.v., probably between 1013–17, though whether at Winchester, Ely, or Peterborough has not been established. Before his banishment from England, Abbot Robert of Jumièges was Bishop of London (1044–50) and Archbishop of Canterbury (1055).

The work is illustrated with thirteen scenes from the New Testament and lives of the Saints; these are enclosed in the elaborate borders typical of the School. Since 1791 the Sacramentary has been in the Municipal Library of Rouen.

saddle stitch: a method of stitching brochures or pamphlets by placing them open astride a saddle-shaped support and stitching through the back.

Safavid bindings: 16th-century Persian bindings. Patterns were either contained in medallions or filled the whole cover, flowers, birds, and arabesques being usual motifs. The designs were impressed from large engraved plates of copper or steel. While pressing the design and gilding were normally combined in one operation, the leather was sometimes gilded before being pressed with the heated die. Such bindings had doublures often excelling in the splendour of their decoration that on the outer cover; delicate filigrees of leather or gold paper were placed on backgrounds of various coloured leathers. Persian bindings mostly had a protecting flap which formed part of the back cover and extended round the fore-edge to lie on the front cover.

St Aethelwold, Benedictional of: see *Benedictional of St Aethelwold.*

St Albans School: an important 13th-century school of English manuscript illumination. By 1236 *Matthew Paris*, q.v., royal historiographer, was head scribe. He revived tinted outline drawings, avoiding the lavish use of bold colours. His draperies were notable for their soft, natural folds.

The *Apocalypse*, q.v., was a favourite work for copying at St Albans.

St Bride Foundation: the most important technical library in Britain for the printing and allied trades. Until 1958 it was directed by W. Turner Berry, Esq., who supplied this note.

The collections of William Blades, Talbot Baines Reed, and works purchased with money donated by J. Passmore Edwards formed the nucleus of the stock of the library which was opened in 1895 by Sir Walter Besant. The 35,000 volumes and pamphlets cover in scope all branches of typographical history, inventions, general histories of printing, private presses, famous printers, publishing, binding, etc. There is a valuable collection of type specimens.

The premises are open daily, Monday to Friday, from 10.00–17.30. Most books are available for loan through the National Central Library. There is also a small lending library of text-books for London students.

St Chad Gospels: an 8th-century manuscript, written by an Irish monk, characterized by the simple severity of its pen drawings, the figures represented being almost symbols. The work is now in Lichfield Cathedral.

St Dominic's Press: a private press founded in 1915 by *Eric Gill*, q.v., and H. D. C. Pepler (until 1916 under the name Hammersmith Workshops). As can be imagined, wood engravings featured in many of the books issued.

The name was later changed to *Ditchling Press*, and Gill was joined by René Hague.

St Gall Gospels: an 8th-century manuscript of the Gospels made either in Ireland or at the monastery of St Gall.

Two Irish monks, Gall and Columban, left Bangor *c.* 590. They journeyed through France and Germany until *c.* 613, when Columban founded Bobbio monastery in Italy, and Gall founded St Gall on the Steinbach in Switzerland. Both places were centres of illumination.

St Omer Psalter: an early 14th-century Psalter of Norfolk origin, completed, however, in the 15th century. The principal decorative feature is a series of marginal miniatures of domestic animals and scenes of rural life. The work is now in the British Museum.

Sale Hill Press: a private printing press founded in 1904 by G. A. Hammond of Sheffield, but later moved to London. Until it closed in 1909 this hand-press was used for very small editions of privately circulated works.

Salisbury School: an important centre of illumination in the mid-13th century was Salisbury. Work was typified by the deep emotion shown in the faces (e.g. the tenderness of the Madonna and the agony of Christ); by the use of white hatching on garments; by the delicacy and strength of line; and by the rippling draperies. An example may be seen in the John Rylands Library, Manchester.

salle: a well-lighted room in a paper-mill where the paper is examined sheet by sheet, sorted, counted and put up in reams.
See also *look through*, *opacity*, *outsides*, *retree*.

Salomon, Bernard, fl. 1545–61: the woodcutter of Lyons who worked with Jean de Tournes, for whom he designed arabesques, cut blocks, and is thought to have experimented with *flowers*, q.v. He illustrated the Lyons edition of Alciati's 'Emblemata libellus' and several editions of the Bible.

Saltire Award: an annual award, established in 1956 but first made in 1957, of an inscribed silver quaich, for an outstanding contribution to Scottish literature. The award is made by the Saltire Society of Edinburgh for a book published in the preceding year from the following categories: history and biography, poetry, drama, fiction, and belles-lettres.

Saltire Society: a society formed in Edinburgh in 1936 with the object of encouraging Scottish art, literature, and music. The Society's publications are distributed by Oliver & Boyd of Edinburgh.

Salzburg School: from the 8th to the 12th century the Benedictine Monastery at Salzburg was an important centre of German illumination. A notable early work was the Cuthbert Gospels, *c.* 770. This was written by St Cuthbert, but whether in England or Salzburg is not known. The miniatures are similar in style to Canterbury work, with a strong Byzantine influence.
The two finest works of the 12th century are the 'Admonter Riesenbibel' and the Antiphony of St Peter. The latter is decorated with fourteen whole-page illuminations in gold and colours, and over four hundred initials drawn in ink on coloured grounds.
The works noted above are in the Österreichische Nationalbibliothek, Vienna.
Salzburg continued to be a centre of illumination until the end of the 15th century, the emphasis being more on secular work and even including grammars of Donatus.

Samurai Press: a press founded at Ranworth, Norfolk, by F. M. Browne, H. Monro, and others in 1907, but in the same year moved to Cranleigh, Surrey, where A. K. Sabin, of the *Temple Sheen Press*, q.v., managed its affairs. Among the small editions, mostly of poetry, produced by the press before it ceased activity in 1909, was an edition of Drinkwater.

Sangorski, Francis, and Sutcliffe, George: the founders, in 1901, of the leading British firm of craftsmen binders. Before their association they studied binding with *Douglas Cockerell*, q.v.
Among the most important of the firm's recent work was the binding of the Coronation Bible in 1953, to the design of Lynton Lamb.

sanserif: type-faces without serifs, originally known as gothic. Modern examples are Airport, Futura, Gill, Granby, Nobel, Vogue, and others.
See also *grotesque*.

sarsanet: a lining material made of stiffened cotton.

Sarum use: the book of Divine Service as used in the diocese of Salisbury from the 11th century to the Reformation.

Sauer: an important family of printers and type-founders in Colonial America. The founder of the business, Christopher I (1694–1758), settled in Germantown, Pa., in 1724. In 1738 he established a press to make more effective his religious propaganda among the local German colony. Most important was the Sauer Bible, 1743; this was a 12,000-copy edition of Luther's translation.
Christopher II (1722–84) expanded the business, and in 1771 he added a type-foundry with German matrices and moulds. In a copy of his religious periodical 'Ein geistliches Magazien' (est. 1764) he claimed that it was 'Gedruckt mit der ersten Schrift die jemals in Amerika gegossen worden', i.e. printed from the first types to be cast in America. He cast

black-face types. His two employees Justus Fox and Jacob Bay (or Bey) later set up their own premises and one of them probably cast the first commercially successful roman letter to be made in America. (It was not until 1781 that the roman face designed, cut, and cast in 1769 by Abel Buell of Killingworth, Conn., was made in quantity.) In the war of Independence Sauer's property was auctioned and he ended his days as a bookbinder.

Christopher III (1754–99) took over the firm in 1774, expanding it still further, and adding an ink mill to the premises.

Savage, William, 1770–1843: a London printer and engraver who did much to improve the quality of ink used for printing engravings. He is also remembered for his 'Dictionary of the Art of Printing', London, 1840–41.

Savile, Sir Henry, 1549–1622: a scholar of Oxford where, in 1619, he founded two lectureships (in geometry and astronomy). It was for the use of Readers here that Savile gave an important collection of Latin and Greek astronomical and mathematical manuscripts, as well as printed books on the sciences. He encouraged professors to enrich this library by donating additions. One holder of the Chair of Astronomy was Sir Christopher Wren (1661–73) who left a collection of works on geometry and astronomy.

In 1607 Savile sponsored the printing of his edition of the Greek text of St Chrysostom's works. This was issued in eight volumes, printed at Eton by John Norton, 1610–12 (13).

The administration of the Savile library was taken over by the Bodleian in 1884.

sawn-in back: the back of a book in which grooves have been sawn for the placing of the cords to which the sections are sewn. This is done for all leather bindings of calf or vellum which require a *hollow back*, q.v.; for books printed on very stiff paper; also for morocco or pigskin books which are given a *tight back*, q.v.

The practice of making saw-backs was popularized in 18th-century France by Nicholas Derome, but embroidered books were made in this way in England during the 17th century.

Sawn-in sewing is inferior to *flexible sewing*, q.v.

Saxton, Christopher, fl. 1570–96: the principal cartographer of his day whose maps were engraved by Augustine Ryther, Reynolds, and others. His most famous work was 'Britannia Insularum', 1583, on twenty-one sheets; these were widely copied.

S.C.: the abbreviation for *super-calendered paper*, q.v.

sc.: an abbreviation for the Latin 'scilicet', i.e. namely.

Scan-a-Graver: an electronic photoengraving machine, introduced by the Fairchild Camera & Instrument Corporation, U.S.A., in 1948, for making an engraved plastic half-tone plate from which printing can be done direct, or from which a stereo can be made.

Briefly, a stroboscopic microscope is first used to check the brightness of the original and pre-set the tonal levels. A revolving shaft bears two cylinders: to one of these the original is fitted; to the second a plastic sheet (8½ in. by 11 in. by 0·02 in. thick). When the machine is working a beam of light directed on the original gives off reflections which are picked up by a photoelectric cell. The reflections are transmitted to an electrically heated stylus needle having a pyramidal point. This thrusts into the plastic plate, burning a square hole of a depth proportionate to the brightness of the original dot at the moment of reflection. Screen rulings range from 65 to 120; and up to 600,000 impressions can be taken from a *Scan plate* without loss of image.

In 1954 Fairchild announced a *Variable Response Unit* for attaching to the Scan-a-Graver. This permits flexible control of the electronic response of the engraver to the scanning of the copy, enabling the machine to produce plates with tonal qualities and contrasts, hitherto the work of retouching by the photoengraver.

Also in 1954 came the *Scan-a-Sizer*. This is a device for enlarging or reducing copy on an 85- or 120-line screen block. The original can be 18 in. by 22 in. when laid flat, and the largest block size is 14 in. by 11 in. The enlargement or reduction ratio can be varied from 1 to 1 up to 4½ to 1 or down to 1 to 4½.

Printing from Scan plates involves no special attention; they can be set up with type for letterpress formes, or fitted to the cylinders of reel-fed rotaries.

scan plates: the name approved by the Federation of Master Process Engravers, London, for any plate made on an *electronic photoengraving machine*, q.v.

scanner: the part of an *electronic photoengraving machine*, q.v., where a beam of light is shone on an original image as it revolves on a cylinder, or is moved to and fro underneath it.

Schäufelein, Hans Leonhard, fl. 1505–38: a German book illustrator whose early style suggests his tuition by Dürer. He was commissioned mostly by publishers in Augsburg, but also in Basle, Hagenau, and Nördlingen. His twenty woodcuts for the 'Theuerdank', printed by Schönsperger in 1517; illustrations for Luther's 'Neue Testament', 1522; and for translations of the classics published by Heinrich Steiner, are among his best works.

Schedel, Hartmann, 1440–1514: a Nuremberg physician and bibliophile, remembered for his edition of 'Die Weltchronik', printed by Anton Koberger in 1493 (Hain 14508). This was in Latin; a German translation by Georg Alt was issued in the same year (Hain 14510). The fame of the work rests on the 1809 woodcuts by Michael Wolgemut and Wilhelm Pleydenwurff which made it the most lavishly illustrated German book of the period.

Schedel's personal library, which included 300 manuscripts and many incunabula, is now in the Bavarian State Library, Munich.

Schmaedel, J. von: see *Meisenbach, Georg.*

Schöffer, Peter, fl. 1449–1502: the partner in Mainz of *Johann Fust,* q.v. About 1450 he was working in Paris as a calligrapher. Some years later he came to Mainz and married Fust's daughter Christine about 1455. When Fust acquired Gutenberg's printing equipment Schöffer designed and cast types, and they began printing. The two issued one of the most beautiful of all incunabula, the Psalter of 1457, although much of the preparatory work on this must have been done by Gutenberg himself. Other important works issued jointly before the death of Fust in 1466 were editions in 1465 and 1466 of Cicero's 'De officiis', and the 'Liber sextus decretalium', 1465, for Boniface VIII. The last work known to have been printed by Schöffer was a Mainz Psalter in 1502.

He was succeeded by his son Johann (*c.* 1456–1531) whose extensive list included works by Erasmus and other Humanists, in addition to editiones principes of the classics (e.g. Livy). Ivo Schöffer (probably a son) continued the business until 1555. He was a distinguished citizen of the city and founded the University Press of Mainz.

See H. Lehmann-Haupt, 'Peter Schoeffer of Gernsheim and Mainz', New York, Hart, 1950.

scholium: a short marginal note, by a grammarian or professional writer, explaining an adjacent text, or interpreting or criticizing the author's treatment of his theme. Usage of the term is limited to works written before 1450. In some manuscripts the scholium would be a note by the owner of the codex, or a quotation from an earlier scholar's writings.

See also *adversaria, gloss.*

Schön, Erhard, *c.* 1491–1542: a German woodcut designer and pupil of Dürer who, between 1514 and 1540, was commissioned by most printers in his native Nuremberg. Notable were his illustrations for a New Testament printed by Peypus in 1524.

Schönsperger, Johann, fl. 1481–1524: an important printer of Augsburg. He issued many books with woodcut illustrations, and also printed editions of several works of note in German literary history ('Sachsenspiegel', 1482; 'Narrenschiff', 1494; 'Die Weltchronik', 1496; 'Theuerdank', 1517, etc.).

He attracted the attention of Maximilian I, and it was in his service that the first true example of German Fraktur type was used: its design, based on court hand, was once attributed to Vinzenz Rockner, head of Maximilian's Chancery, but later research assigns it to the Benedictine scribe Leonhard Wagner.

Schönsperger was for some years assisted by his son of the same name.

school edition: an issue of a book printed from the original plates but usually in a different format or style of binding, and probably with the addition of notes.

Schoolmaster of St Albans: the anonymous printer who established the first press at St Albans. He appears to have worked between 1480 and 1486, and copies of eight works from his press survive. It is thought that he used Caxton's second type and that some connection may have existed between the two printers.

Schopper-Dalen apparatus: see *paper-testing.*

Schwabacher: a later form of bastarda, used in Germany and Switzerland from *c.* 1480 until 1550. Schöffer's 'Hortus sanitatis', Mainz, 1485, is printed with such a type.

See also *letters—forms and styles.*

Schweitzer Prize: see *Albert Schweitzer Buchpreis.*

Scinzenzeler, Ulrich, fl. 1477–1500: a German printer working in Milan, remembered as the printer of the first illustrated book in that city (Hain 7159). He was at one time partnered by Leonhard Pachel, and was commissioned by other publishers. He issued independently theological and legal books, also several works in Italian.

scorcher: the machine which heats and curves stereo matrices for use on rotary presses.

scoring: the making of a crease in paper or card so that it will not be damaged by folding.

Scot, John, fl. 1552–71: a printer of St Andrews and Edinburgh. Very few of his publications survive, due partly to their ephemeral or controversial nature. For printing a Catholic tract by Winzet in 1562, Scot was imprisoned and lost his stock and press.

Scottish bindings: a style of bookbinding practised in Scotland from 1725–75. Usually the central design on the front cover was a large wheel with radiating spokes, floral and leaf motifs filling the rest of the panel up to an enclosing border of leaf patterns. An alternative design had a central vertical stem with

see page 370

Details in the picture are made up of screen dots of varying size

30° *angle between screen systems, insignificant moiré effect*

12° *angle, strong moiré effect*

In the screen reproduction of half-tones, or of a regular network of lines or squares, and in combined printing of two or more screen formes, certain mutual positions may cause a disturbing moiré effect

(*Screen process work*)

65-*line screen for use on newsprint*

85-*line screen for use on machine-finished paper*

100-*line screen for use on super-calendered paper*

120-*line screen for use on MF machine coated or imitation art paper*

133-*line screen for use on art or matt art paper*

150-*line screen for use on the finest glossy art paper*

HALF-TONE SCREENS OF DIFFERING DENSITIES

(illustration: *The Religions of Tibet*, H. Hoffman, George Allen & Unwin)

branching ornaments. The books often had gilded end-papers with embossed floral ornament.

Scottish Text Society: a society founded in 1882 'for the purpose of publishing works illustrative of the Scottish language, literature and history prior to the Union'.

scraper: a small hand-tool with a hardened cutting edge, for use in the graphic arts.

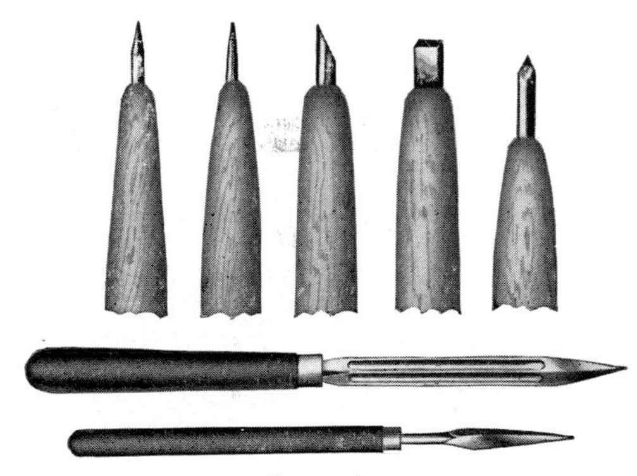

Scrapers

scraperboard: an illustration process for reproducing, with gradations of tone, photographs in line, or original drawings. The latter may be either black lines on a white surface, or white lines on a black background. The process is much used in commercial art.

scratted paper: a 17th-century form of marbled paper, made by splashing colours in small blobs on to the sheet, and used for end-papers.

screamer: a composing room term for an exclamation mark.

screen: 1. *half-tone.* A cross-line half-tone screen is used in process work for converting compact 'genuine' half-tones into 'false' half-tones which consist of dots of the same density (degree of colouring) but varying size, and so small as a rule that they are indistinguishable to the naked eye. This screen can be inserted immediately in front of the negative material, when exposing in the camera, or with similar effect in front of the printing layer in those (older) methods of production in which diffusion by the screen is only carried out in connection with the printing. Early experiments with screens in process work date from the mid-19th century when printing was done through gauze cloth. For the success of the half-tone process, however, the regular line-screen was necessary. This consisted of a glass plate in which a system of parallel, opaque lines was drawn, all at equal intervals. The next step in the development of the screen was that it was turned 90° during exposure. After further experiments the rectangular network screen was evolved and still occupies the leading position in screen process work. (See *Meisenbach, Georg.*)

Screen production was later perfected by Max Levy in the U.S.A. The engraved *original screens* in general use consist of two glass plates, cemented together, in the inner surfaces of which lines are engraved and blackened. In each plate all lines are absolutely parallel and of the same width; in modern screens the spaces which separate the lines are usually of the same width as the thickness of the lines. The two sets of lines must form an exact angle of 90°. Although screens are produced by machinery, the work is exacting and often results in failure, so that engraved screens are very expensive, especially in larger sizes. Attempts to substitute cheaper, photographically printed screens for reproduction work have not been successful. Network screens are usually rectangular with lines drawn at an angle of 45° to the edges. For colour work *pairs of screens* are also used, i.e. two connected screens, one at an angle of 45° and the other with a network of squares turned 30° in relation to the first. By inserting this

Normal 45° *screen*

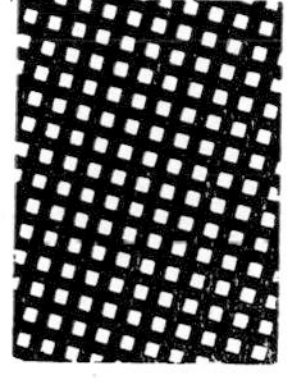

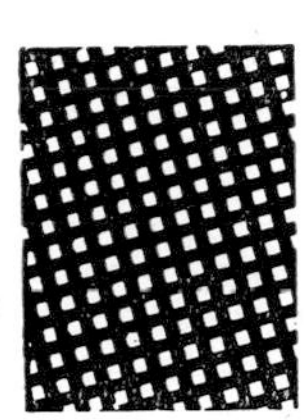

A 15° *screen can be put reversed in the camera, giving two possible screen positions with a difference in angle of* 30°. *With the* 45° *screen it forms a pair for three-colour reproduction*

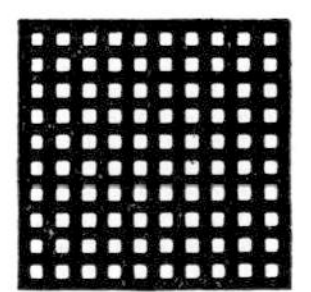

A set of screens for four-colour printing includes one with lines at right-angles to the edges

Circular screen in a reproduction camera. By precise graduation of the angles along the frame of the screen focusing can be done for positions suitable for reproducing colour

screen, reversed, in the camera a further position is obtained, so that with these two screens three positions can be obtained, all forming an angle of 30° to each other.

Circular screens afford still greater possibilities in this respect, utilizing better the size of the camera than single rectangular screens placed in a movable holder, but not equalling the capacity of pairs of screens.

In addition to the usual rectangular screen network oblique-angled (rhomboidal) networks, single-line screens, and grained screens are used for special purposes. See also *Erwin screen.*

To protect the edges of the glass plates and prevent the formation of air bubbles when cementing, the edges are often enclosed in a metal binding. The thickness of the plates must be known in process work, so that this can be taken into consideration when adjusting the distance of the screen. As a rule it is 2 mm. to 3 mm. The closeness of the lines varies: e.g. 50–65 lines per inch for newsprint, 120–150 for coated stock.

2. *photogravure.* A screen for printing-in the network for doctor-blade photogravure or intaglio. These screens generally have lines considerably narrower than the spaces which separate them; a proportion of 1 : 3 or 2 : 5 is usual. In contrast to half-tone screens the lines in intaglio screens are transparent and the squares are blackened. Photogravure screens are made as follows. A 'master-

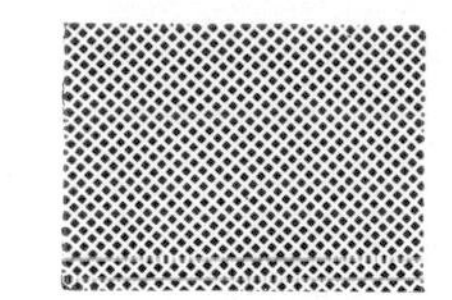

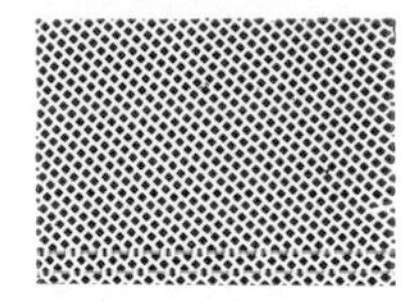

Photogravure screens: left, standard square screen; right, 'Backstein' screen

Bassani screen-holder

screen' is engraved by machinery, so that the two rectangular sets of lines are incised in the glass and then blackened. From this master-screen the working screen can be produced in various ways. The best 'original screens' are obtained by printing the master-screen on coated glass which is developed and etched in such a way that the squares are sunk and can be blackened. Working screens printed on sensitized film are simpler and cheaper. In photogravure screens the closeness of the lines is usually about 175 per inch. A variant of the checked network screen is provided by the *brick screen* in which the squares are disposed approximately like bricks in a wall. Irregular grain screens are also used. (G.U.)

screen process work: 1. the reproduction of half-tones by means of exposure through a screen in a camera. Screen process work is the basis of the half-tone process and modern offset reproduction. The screen is a shield with small, narrow openings which is placed in front of the sensitized material in the camera. Each little opening may be said to serve as a pinhole camera inside the larger camera, and draws a small, dull image of the diaphragm on the negative material. Adjacent screen openings, however, co-operate when these small pinpoint images appear in the negative, and the diffusion of light in such a point is rather similar to the picture in a rectangular diaphragm. The centre is strongly exposed, sufficiently for blackening the negative. The intensity of exposure decreases outwards, and the extent of the area remaining as a blackened surface after developing the negative depends on the quantity of light the diaphragm allows to pass in the direction of that part of the negative; in other words, the quantity of light reflected from that part of the original image which is reproduced at a particular point. The lighter the tone in the original image, the larger will be the blackened negative dots in the negative. For very light tones the negative dots will almost run into each other, and quite small dots will appear on the print from this negative, in which only the intervals between the dots are visible. In this way the half-tones of the original image are transformed into dot tones of a corresponding brightness. The image will be built up of dots of varying extent. Thus it is possible to produce a forme for those printing processes which require a uniformly thick layer of ink on all printing surfaces. In order that the formation of dots should be as intended in the reproduction, certain definite proportions are essential between the *screen distance* (the distance between the screen network and the negative material), the *screen opening* (which varies according to the screen ruling), the *diaphragm*, and the *extension* of the camera. Screen process work affords great opportunities for influencing the gradation of the picture. If the rule cited is

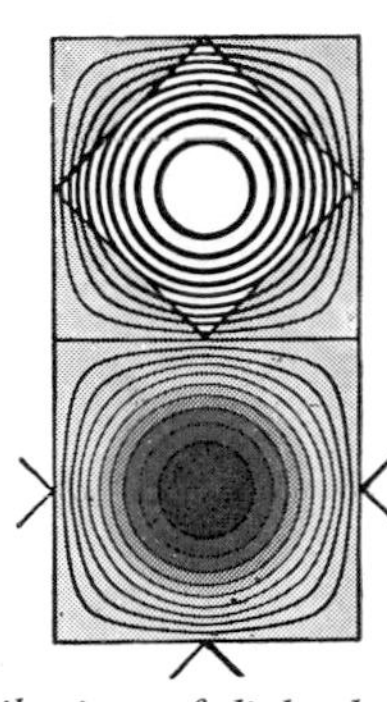

Distribution of light behind a screen opening (above), and behind the lines of the screen (according to Delville)

A print of the screen negative shows small black dots in the light parts. In the dark parts the black dots merge, leaving only small white dots between them. In the intermediate tones the black and white dots are about equal in size

not observed, and an exposure is made with a proportionately larger diaphragm, a different diffusion of light is obtained in the negative dot and this results in proportionately larger blackened dots in the light areas. On the other hand the greatest importance of a reduction of the diaphragm diameter is in regard to the shadows. It therefore happens that a photographer makes three or more successive exposures on the same negative, using different diaphragms, and seeks in this way to secure the most favourable dot formation for the different tones of the picture. If it is thought desirable in making blocks that a small white dot should be obtained in the darkest parts of the picture, a so-called flash exposure is sometimes resorted to, the additional exposure being made before or after the actual exposure of the picture, with a very small diaphragm and with the original covered by white paper. All these niceties of exposing were mainly intended, however, for silver iodide collodion plates and are less extensively used in working with silver bromide gelatine emulsions.

During the years various designs for diaphragms have been invented to take the place of repeated exposures, e.g. Brandweiner's iris diaphragm, worked by a clock mechanism, which changed continuously during the exposure, or Schumacher's vignetted diaphragm (star diaphragm). The coincidence diaphragm should also be mentioned, its main object being to shorten the time of exposure which is otherwise rather long. Attempts have been made by means of screens which move during exposure to secure a better reproduction of the tones of the original (the screen dot in the reproduction corresponds not only to a certain dot in the original picture, but to a small area surrounding it), and by regulating the motion the shape of the dot in the picture can be influenced. In offset reproduction in particular exposure is sometimes done in stages, revolving the screen between each.

Grain screens are used especially when the formation of patterns is to be avoided in multi-coloured reproductions. As the screen openings are quite irregular, the dot formation is worse and more difficult to control.

An exposed screen negative is developed, reduced and strengthened in such a way that as opaque dots as possible are obtained, separated by clear spaces. In some cases, especially in connection with offset process work, screen process work is moving in another direction. The Müller method aims at producing a screen negative with 'veil-like' dots which lend themselves to retouching.

2. Screen process work can be done by the contact printing of a half-tone negative on a photographic film by means of a special screen with *vignetted dots*. In this way a screen transparency is obtained which

can be used for offset printing, etc. (see *deep-etch process, offset printing*). This method was first introduced by Kodak in 1941. Later, Kodak introduced a method of producing screen negatives in the camera on a similar principle. (G.U.)
See also *contact screen.*

scribal copy: a manuscript written by a copyist as distinct from that written or dictated by the author.
See also *scriptorium.*

scribe: the manuscript copyists were called scribes; a professional or public penman. (M.L.)

scribing: the removal with a stylus of the coating from a sheet of coated foil as in the *Astrascribe Process,* q.v.

scrim: see *mull.*

script: type-faces designed to reproduce hand-writing.

scriptorium: the room in a monastery in which manuscripts were copied: the form varied, in some cases being a large room, in others a room divided into small cells by partitions. An armarius was responsible for administering the strict rules which governed conduct in these work-rooms. Artificial light was excluded to minimize the risk of fire, and absolute silence prevailed, a system of gestures being used for communication.
See also *illumination.*

scriptura actuaria: see *rustic capitals.*

scrittura umanistica: Carolingian minuscule as revived in the 15th century by Italian renaissance scholars.
See also *humanistic.*

scroll: a roll of parchment or paper, usually hand-written or illuminated.

Scudder, Wilbur Stephen: the inventor of the *Monoline* type-setting machine, q.v.

seal: the skin of the Newfoundland seal prepared for bookbinding, usually for limp covers.

second lining: see *lining.*

secondary binding: a difference in the *publisher's binding,* q.v., between copies of the same printing of a work may occur when the sales potentiality of a book cannot be foreseen, and the publisher deems it better for the sheets to be bound up in batches, a process which may be spread over a period of years. The colour or material first used may no longer be available, or the spinal lettering may be altered. While such binding variants are secondary bindings, it is necessary to establish which binding was first put on sale before applying the term. *Remainder bindings* are not secondary bindings.
Cf. *primary binding.*

secretary: a cursive black letter used about 1550 for legal documents.
See also *bastarda.*

section: 1. the reference mark § inserted in the text of a work to direct the attention of the reader to a footnote. This conjoined 's' symbol was used by 12th-century scribes as a paragraph mark.
2. a folded printed sheet, inclusive of *plates* and *inserts,* if any, and thus ready for *gathering* and *sewing,* qq.v. The term is not entirely synonymous with *signature,* as a signature does not become a section until plates and the like have been added to it, should they be needed. (L.K.)

see copy: a proof mark indicating an omission too long to be written on the proof. The copy is attached and the omission indicated for the compositor's guidance. Also a mark indicating to the author that the reader is unsure about something on the copy.

see safe: said of books bought by a bookseller from a publisher, and paid for, but with the understanding that at some future date the publisher may be asked to exchange the bookseller's surplus for copies of another title. Cf. *half see safe.*
See also *terms.*

Selden, John, 1584–1654: a jurist, parliamentarian, and Oriental scholar who assembled a library of works on theology, law, history, Hebrew literature and studies, as well as an important array of Oriental manuscripts. Some 8000 items from his collection passed to the Bodleian Library in 1659.

selectasine: a colour-printing process in which a single silk screen is used for all the colours.

semé (or **semis**): see *powdered.*

semi-uncial: see *half-uncial.*

Semperit block: a rubber stereotype devised by the Semperit Rubber Factory of Vienna. Printing formes are pressed, under heat, on a special Semperit matrix material, and from the matrix obtained a block is made which consists of several layers of artificial rubber and cardboard; the uppermost layer, bearing the impression, is of fairly hard rubber. Such blocks retain their shape well, resist oil, and owing to their flexibility can be used for rotary printing. (G.U.)

Senefelder, Aloysius, 1771–1834: the inventor of *lithography,* q.v. His father was an actor in Munich, and in his youth Aloysius wrote some comedies. As he had difficulty in getting his plays printed he tried to do the work himself. He made various experiments, including engraving and etching on copper, and printed his works in a primitive copperplate press. In trying to find a cheaper material for the formes he also tried plates of limestone slate. According to his own statement he happened to write a laundry bill on a polished stone which was at hand, and the writing was done with a mixture of ink which he used as an etching base on his plates. Later, the idea occurred to him of using script on stone for printing purposes, and when he etched this with spirit of nitre he obtained a printing forme with raised script which lent itself to inking in and printing. This was the origin of stone printing (1796), although done at first on the principle of relief printing. The inking up of the low image in relief, without affecting the intermediate surfaces, gave Senefelder trouble, and he found that for this purpose he had to use a flat board on which the ink had been ground with an ink-ball. By chance, however, he discovered that it was not necessary to etch the stone in relief, but that a usable printing forme could be obtained by damping the stone with diluted etching liquid, after inscribing it, and inking it in before it dried. He found that the limestone from Solnhofen was the most suitable material, and this has remained the only one for practical use in actual stone printing.

Senefelder soon discovered that a copperplate press was unsuitable for stone printing, and in 1796 he built a rod or cross-beam press which was improved in the next year and became the model for the lithographic hand-press still in use. (For illustration see *hand-press*.) In 1798 he experimented with methods of stone engraving and transferring (including a kind of anastatic printing), in 1799 with autographic printing and crayon drawing, and in 1805 with lithographic printing from zinc. The Elector of Bavaria gave him support, and in 1799 granted him a privilege for all lithographic printing; but when his first attempts to keep the process secret failed he was obliged, in order to raise money, to instruct others in the craft. Philipp André, a music publisher of Offenbach, offered Senefelder 2000 florins to establish a press for him and train workmen in its use. André also brought Senefelder to London to secure British patents (granted in 1801), the first book in England to show specimens being printed in 1803. He was not long in England.

In 1809 Senefelder obtained an appointment as inspector at the Kataster Printing Works in Munich and thus had a fixed income. He continued his experiments, and in 1813 invented a substitute for the heavy stone in the form of a substance which was spread on paper or cloth. In 1817 he built an automatic inking, damping, and printing stone press, and in 1826 he announced the invention of an original printing process in which the forme consisted of very small ink reservoirs placed close together; this did not require inking between each impression (mosaic printing).

Senefelder seems to have envisaged most of the developments and possibilities of his invention. In 1818 he published his manual on the subject 'Vollständiges Lehrbuch der Steindruckerei' (in German, simultaneously by Thienemann of Munich and Gerold of Vienna; an English translation published by Ackermann appeared in 1819, and in the same year a French translation was issued by Treuttel & Wärtz of Strasbourg). The illustrations to the various editions were the work of nationals of each country. (With G.U.)

Sensenschmidt, Johann, fl. 1470–91: the founder in 1470 of the first printing press in Nuremberg. He worked at first with Heinrich Kefer (or Keffer), an associate of Gutenberg. Their first joint work was the 'Pantheologia' of Rainerius de Pisis, 1473.

From 1481 Sensenschmidt worked in Bamberg, both alone and with Heinrich Petzensteiner, where he issued many liturgical works.

separate: an article reprinted from a periodical and issued separately. Also known as an *off-print*.

separation negative records: see *colour separation*.

serial: 1. a book published in parts appearing at regular intervals, a form often used in the 19th century for fiction.

2. a periodical.

serial rights: the author's or publisher's right to arrange the newspaper or magazine publication in serial form of a book.

series: 1. a set of type-founts based on one design and graded in size. Thus the type in which this book is set is known as Monotype Times New Roman, Series 327. It is available in composition founts ranging from $4\frac{3}{4}$-point to 14-point, and in display founts from 14- to 72-point for hand-setting.

See also *family*, *fount*.

2. see *fiction-*, *publisher's-*, *subject series*.

serif: the short finishing stroke set across or projecting from the end of a letter stem. There are several varieties of serif, those on old-face types are *bracketed* and curve from the stroke to a point; on modern faces they are flat *hair-lines* set at right-angles to the main strokes of letters; most egyptian faces have thick *slab* serifs, while such types as Clarendon have *slab bracketed*. Of all these the serifs of old face are more patently part of the basic letter design, and less of an addition of it.

Service books: see *Antiphonary, Book of Hours, Breviary, Collectarium, directory* (1), *enchiridion, Exultet roll, Gospel, Gradual, Legenda, Manuale, Missal, Missale plenarium, Penitential, Pentateuch, Pontifical, Portiforium, Primer, Processionale, Psalter, Pye-book* (1), *Rituale, Sacramentary, Sarum use, Totum, Troper.*

set: 1. the width of a type body.
2. a figure used to indicate the comparative width of a Monotype type design. 12-point, 10½ set is narrower generally than 12-point, 12 set.
3. to compose type.

set flush: matter set up without any indented lines.

set hand: the individual and formal style of handwriting used by each of the various Courts, or departments, in medieval England. This ensured a degree of uniformity within the Court. Cf. *free hand.*

set-off: a printing fault caused by the transference of ink from the freshly inked impression on a printed sheet to the underside of the next sheet to be laid upon it in the pile. This can be checked by printing with quick-set inks or using an *anti-set-off sprayer*, q.v.

set-off reel: a paper reel with a set-off sheet, used in reel-fed rotary presses to prevent ink from the first forme setting off on the packing of the impression cylinder. The set-off reel is wound off the reel at the same speed as the printing paper, passing between the latter and the packing of the cylinder, and then being wound up automatically. One set-off reel can be used in this way many times. (G.U.)

set solid: matter set without leads between the lines. Cf. *leaded.*

setting rule: a thin strip of brass, type high, about three points thick, and made in various lengths. It is placed in the composing stick before setting the first line; a lip projecting at one end enables it to be removed when a line is completed and placed in position for the setting of the next.

sewing: the fastening together of the sections of a book by means of thread. The operation may be by machine or hand. There are various styles of sewing, such as french, with tapes, sewn-in cords, raised cords, etc. Factors determining the style to be used are the size of the book, the paper, the thickness of sections, the style of binding, and the use to be made of the book. Cf. *unsewn binding.*
See also *all along, flexible sewing, french sewing, kettle-stitch, machine-sewing, overcasting, two sheets on.*

sewing thread: the linen thread for sewing books bound by hand, the linen or cotton thread for machine-sewing, also nylon or other synthetic materials. The thickness of the thread is usually stated in English units which indicate the number of skeins of thread, 300 yards (274·3 m.) long, which make an English pound (453·6 g.): 36–50 are the most usual thicknesses for sewing-machine thread; 20–30 for hand-sewing. The threads can be double or treble. (G.U.)

sewn flexible: see *flexible sewing.*

sextern: a gathering of six sheets, folded once, in which form some bound manuscripts and early printed books were assembled.
See also *quaternion.*

sexto-decimo: see *sixteenmo.*

Seybold: the name of cutting machines and other paper-making machinery manufactured by the Seybold Machinery Co., Dayton, Ohio, U.S.A., now affiliated to the Harris-Seybold Co. (G.U.)

sgraffito: a woodcut technique in which the design appears in white on a black or red ground. Ratdolt of Augsburg printed examples.
See also *woodcut.*

shaded letters: display and jobbing work letters in which a white line running at one side of the main strokes gives the effect of shadow caused by a light.
Cf. *outline letters.*

shake: the lateral oscillation applied to the moving wire of a paper-making machine to induce the interlocking of the fibres.

Shakespeare Head Press: the press founded in 1904 by Arthur Henry Bullen, with the object of producing a scholarly edition of Shakespeare's works. This he did in ten volumes in a series entitled the 'Stratford Town Shakespeare'. Bullen was an eminent Elizabethan scholar and issued other works of the period in limited editions until his death in 1920. The press was then taken over by Basil Blackwell of Oxford who appointed B. H. Newdigate as typographer. Under the latter's direction the standard of production was much improved.

sheepskin: prepared sheepskins were first used in England for bookbinding about 1400; the boards they covered were usually of oak.
See also *Alaska seal, law sheep, roan, Rutland, skivers, Smyrna morocco.*

sheet: any single piece of paper, either plain or printed.

sheet fed: a printing machine into which sheets are fed singly. Cf. *web fed.*

sheet stock: unbound printed sheets held in stock pending binding. Such stock is normally held by the printer or binder on behalf of the publisher. Synonymous with *quire stock*. (L.K.)

See also *in quires*.

sheet work: book printing in which one forme is used for one side of the paper and another forme for backing up. This is essential when printing on a perfector press. The forme for the first side printed bears the signature mark and is known as the *outer forme* and the backing up is printed from the *inner forme*. Cf. *work and turn*. (L.K.)

shelf back: the spine of a book.

Sherborne Missal: a work originally made, *c.* 1400, for Sherborne Abbey by John Siferwas, illuminator, and John Whas, scribe. It is now regarded as one of the last great examples of English illumination. While having ornamentation similar to that of the *East Anglian School*, q.v., the frame or page-border itself was more prominent. Siferwas included portrait medallions, named birds, black- or red-winged angels, and figures standing in architectural niches.

It is now owned by the Duke of Northumberland.

shifting tympan: an impression surface which shifts automatically. Also called *travelling tympam.* (M.L.)

shiners: mineral impurities in a sheet of paper seen as shining specks on the surface.

shining: the holding up to light of printed sheets, when folding, to ensure they are in register.

shining-up table: see *register table*.

shoo flies: the mechanism on a printing cylinder which raises the front edge of a printed sheet so that it passes over the edge of the stripper fingers and on to the delivery tapes.

shooting stick: a tool of metal or hardened wood used to secure wooden quoins against the sides of a chase when tightening the forme.

short ream: 480 sheets of paper.

Short-Title Catalogue: the standard British reference guide to early printed books. It was compiled by A. W. Pollard and G. R. Redgrave, and published in 1926 by the Bibliographical Society as 'A Short-title catalogue of books printed in England, Scotland and Ireland, and of English books printed abroad, 1475–1640'. It is an author list with appropriate group headings for some anonymous works. Locations of items in certain British libraries, and if rare, elsewhere, are given. Every entry is numbered, and these numbers, preceded by the letters *STC*, are used by librarians, booksellers, and others in catalogues and lists. Reprints of the STC appeared in 1946 and 1950, and a revised edition is in preparation. Users were handicapped by the lack of an index until 1950, when one by Paul G. Morrison was published in the U.S.A., by the University of Virginia Bibliographical Society.

A continuation of STC is D. Wing's 'Short-title catalogue of books printed in England, Scotland, Ireland, Wales and British America and of English books printed in other countries, 1641–1700', 3 vols., New York, Columbia University Press, 1945–51. This author catalogue has entries for anonymous works made mostly under the first word of the title not an article; others are under group headings. Locations are given. The work is referred to as *Wing*.

shoulder: the platform of a shank of type from which the face rises, i.e. the non-printing area surrounding the face.

shoulder-heads: headings to mark the second division of text within a chapter, subsidiary to *cross-heads*, q.v. They are set in caps., large or small, or in italics, and are set flush to the left-hand margin, often being separated by a line of leading from the first line of the paragraph which follows.

See also *side-heads*.

shoulder-notes: marginal notes placed at the top outer corners of pages.

shoulders: the name given in etching a line plate to the steps of metal allowed to remain until the final bath.

show side: the side of a material which is to show in the finished article, the other side being hidden, for instance, by pasting. Used especially of book cloths.

show through: a fault in which the printed impression on one side of a leaf is visible through the paper when reading the other side; caused by using ink and paper which are not suited to each other.

Siberch, John: the printer, born John Lair of Siegburg near Cologne, who, in 1521, established in Cambridge the first press there. His first work was Galen's 'Pergamensis de temperamentis et de inaequali intemperie libri tres, T. Linacro interprete', 1521. Less than a dozen items have been identified with certainty as having been printed by him, and after 1522–23 there was a period of sixty years when no book is recorded as having emanated from a Cambridge press.

The press of Siberch is regarded as the foundation of the *Cambridge University Press*, q.v.

See E. P. Goldschmidt, 'The first Cambridge Press in its European setting', C.U.P., 1955.

Sicoplast: the trade name of a thermoplastic material made by the Parisian firm Deberny & Peignot for the production of letterpress printing plates. These plates, which can be hard, medium hard, or flexible, will retain the finest screen or line details, yet will print runs of over a million without appreciable loss of image quality.

Printing inks, cleaning solutions, and rough handling cause no damage, and the plates can be stored indefinitely without deterioration.

side-cutters: the trimming knives on the Linotype and Intertype machines, adaptable to various bodies, between which the cast metal slug passes and is trimmed to the accurate body size before it enters the slug galley. (G.U.)

See also *slug-casting machine.*

side-heads: headings to mark the third division of text within a chapter, subsidiary to *shoulder-heads,* q.v. They are set in caps., large and small, in bold or in italics, at the beginning of a paragraph with the matter running on.

See also *shoulder-heads.*

side lay: see *lay edges.*

side marks: the fixed marks on a printing machine to which sheets are placed, or laid, to ensure uniformity of margins.

See also *lay edges.*

side notes: see *marginal notes.*

side sorts: the less frequently used characters of a fount, e.g. j, q, z, etc., kept in the small boxes at the side of the case. (M.L.)

side-stitch: to bind a pamphlet by wiring or sewing the sheets together sideways. (M.L.)

sides: the front and rear boards of a book.

sidestick: a long wedge of wood or metal placed along the length of pages when locking them up, and secured in position in the chase by quoins.

See also *footstick.*

siding: a term for fitting and gluing to the boards the paper or cloth sides of a half- or quarter-bound book.

Siegen, Ludwig von, 1609–80: the inventor, in 1642, of *mezzotint,* q.v.

Siferwas, John, fl. 1396–1407: the Benedictine monk who illuminated the *Sherborne Missal,* q.v., now owned by the Duke of Northumberland.

sig.: an abbreviation of *signature,* q.v.

Sigl, Georg, 1811–77: a Viennese engineer who in 1851 built the first machine for lithographic printing.

See also *lithography.*

sigla: a word meaning symbols which is sometimes printed at the head of a table of these.

signature: a book section, either in the flat or folded, to which a *signature mark,* q.v., has been given. The term is not entirely synonymous with *sheet* as a sheet as printed may contain more than one signature (see *folding*) and in the case of a *half-sheet,* q.v., constitute a signature of less pages than its fellows. Thus books consist of many signatures but all the signatures will not necessarily consist of the same number of pages.

Among bibliophiles, but not in the trade, the terms *gathering, quire,* and *section* are often used to denote *signature.* (L.K.)

See also *section.*

signature mark: letters of the alphabet, or numbers, printed at the left tail margin of the first page of each section of a book. The letters or numbers are assigned in sequence to the successive sections, thus providing a guide to the correct *gathering* of a book.

If letters are used, J, V, and W are omitted; this derives from the custom in manuscripts and incunabula of using the Latin alphabet in which I includes J, V includes U, and there is no W. If one sequence of the alphabet does not suffice, it is commenced again but doubled, thus AA, BB, or, if necessary, trebled, thus AAA, BBB. In speech these signatures are dubbed *two A, three A,* etc.

Where sections are systematically inserted (see *insert*) the outer unit will bear the signature mark, e.g. B, and the inserted unit will have the same signature plus a star, thus B*.

If a book is printed without the title as a *running headline,* it is important to add to the signature mark initials indicating the title, e.g. B—GL.B., to ensure identification. Similarly, it may be essential to add the volume number.

Signature marks were first printed, instead of being hand-written after printing the sheet, in Nider's 'Praeceptorium Divinae legis', issued by Johann Koelhoff of Cologne in 1472. (L.K.)

signet: a silk ribbon secured at the head of a book as a page-marker. These were frequently used by 16th-century French binders and were often lavishly ornamented with precious stones.

Also known as *register.*

Simon, Oliver, 1895–1956: one of Britain's leading typographers who began his career in 1920 when he studied printing under Harold Curwen of the Curwen Press, Plaistow. Simon was later Chairman of this firm, the work issued being of the highest standard.

At one time Oliver Simon edited 'The Fleuron', and later 'Signature'; both journals dealt with typography and the graphic arts.

Simon's 'Introduction to Typography', Faber, 1945, was issued as a Pelican Book in 1954, being one of the most attractive books in this series ever to appear.

See 'Printer and Playground', by Oliver Simon. Faber, 1956.

See also *Curwen Press.*

single-line half-tone: a half-tone plate in the making of which a screen bearing parallel lines of uniform width is used as an alternative to the normal glass screen bearing lines ruled at right-angles.

See also *half-tone screen.*

single quotes: see *punctuation marks.*

single-revolution machine: a cylinder machine in which the cylinder rotates at a constant speed and in such a way that during the first half-rotation the bed moves forward and the impression is made, while the bed returns during the second half-rotation. There are, however, single-revolution presses with varying speeds for the bed and/or cylinder, e.g. the Heidelberg cylinder. (G.U.)

See also *letterpress machines.*

sixteenmo: written 16mo. A book size resulting from folding a sheet of paper with four right-angle folds, thus giving a page size one-sixteenth the size of the sheet and forming a 32-page section. To define fully the size the paper size also must be stated, e.g. Crown 16mo.

Also known as *decimo-sexto* or *sexto-decimo.* (L.K.)

sixty-fourmo: written 64mo. A book size resulting from (notionally) folding a sheet of paper with six right-angle folds, thus giving a page size one sixty-fourth of the sheet. In practice paper cannot conveniently be folded more than four times, thus a quarter sheet folded four times would be used. From Crown paper the resulting page size would be $2\frac{1}{2}$ in. × $1\frac{7}{8}$ in., viz. Crown 64mo. (L.K.)

size: 1. a glutinous substance made by boiling the hide and bones of animals. It is thus purer than *glue* which is made by boiling the hide, bones, and occasionally other parts of animals.

See also *adhesives.*

2. resin added to paper stock when in the beater so that the finished paper will be non-absorbent; the discovery of its suitability for this purpose being attributed to Moritz Friedrich Illig of Darmstadt in 1806. Starch, casein, or animal glue may also be added as alternatives.

In hand-made paper-making sheets of waterleaf are soaked in a tub of gelatine and dried.

The degree of sizing is indicated as *hard sized*—notepaper, offset paper; *three-quarter sized*—lithographic printing paper; *soft sized*—half-tone printing paper; *quarter sized* to *unsized*—copperplate printing paper, duplicating paper. Newsprint is made without size but has a slightly sized appearance due to the resin content of the pulp. (With G.U.)

See also *animal-sized, engine-sized, tub-sized.*

size copy: see *dummy.*

size of books: see *book sizes.*

size of paper: see *paper sizes.*

size water: an alternative name for *backwater*, q.v.

skeletonizing: taking a job apart and rebuilding it so that its various parts may be printed in different colours. (M.L.)

skewings: a term used for waste gold leaf arising in the course of gold blocking and sent to gold refiners for recovery of the gold. (L.K.)

Skira, Albert: a 20th-century Swiss publisher of superbly printed art books, of which he has issued about 100 during the last twenty-five years. For some of them he sends teams of photographers and technicians to such places as Istanbul, Chios, Yugoslavia, and Pompeii to photograph mosaics, murals, and originals. He also commissioned such artists as Matisse (for 'Poésies' by Mallarmé, and 'Florilège des Amours de Ronsard', 1948) and Picasso (for 'Metamorphoses' of Ovid, 1931). He has offices in Paris, Geneva, and New York.

skivers: split *sheepskins*, q.v., used for bindings; they are not durable.

See also *roan.*

Skot, John, fl. 1521–37: a printer of London who may have been an apprentice of Wynkyn de Worde. Very few of his publications are known.

slab serifs: square serifs of almost the same thickness as the strokes on which they are placed.

See also *egyptian.*

slabbing: the process of rolling and hammering an electro or stereo after casting in order to obtain a level surface.

slice: 1. in paper-making, a long flat plate, set vertically, by which the depth and even distribution of pulp are controlled as it flows on to the moving wire belt from the head-box.

2. see *ink slice.*

slice boy: the layerman's assistant in a hand-made paper-making establishment. The removal of still moist sheets of very thin paper after pressure in the *post*, q.v., calls for care and skill. The layerman strips the top sheet off the post and lays it on a felt-covered zinc plate where a *pack* of about 230 sheets will be built up. As the next sheet is laid the boy steadies it on to the pile with a smooth wooden slice. He then holds the slice in position ready to assist in the laying of the next and subsequent sheets.

See also *layerman*.

slip case: a box to contain a book, or set of books, with one side open so that the spine of the book is visible. Its function is to protect the edges from soiling until purchased.

See also *solander*.

slip proof: see *galley proof*.

slip sheeting: the placing of rough paper as interleaving between freshly printed sheets to prevent *set-off*, q.v.

slips: the loose ends of the cords which, after sewing, extend at the sides of a book. They must be frayed with a bodkin, leaving them soft and pliable, before attaching the boards.

Fraying the slips

Sloane, Sir Hans, 1660–1753: a traveller, scientist, and physician, born in Ireland, who, in addition to making large botanical, zoological, and other collections, assembled a library. At the time of his death this included 347 volumes of drawings and illuminated works, 3516 volumes of manuscripts and books of prints, and some 46,800 printed books. The library was rich in 16th- and 17th-century works on botany, medicine, and natural history.

Hans Sloane made the contents of his library and museum available to scholars. In accordance with his wish the whole was offered to the nation, and authority to purchase was granted by an Act of 1753. The Sloane, Harleian, and Cottonian libraries were the foundation stock of the British Museum, opened in 1759.

See 'Sir Hans Sloane and the British Museum', by G. R. de Beer. O.U.P., 1953.

slug: a metal bar of the length and width of a line of type characters, to print an entire line. It has the appearance of a solid line of type and serves the same purpose.

See also *slug-casting machines*.

slug-casting machines: machines for producing set-up type in the form of cast lines or slugs. Modern slug-casting machines include the *Intertype*, *Italtype*, *Linograph*, *Linotype*, and *Typograph*, qq.v.

slug saw: a saw for cutting off cast slug lines. There are detached slug saws of different kinds as well as saws built into the casting machines which saw off blank parts of lines automatically, if the lines are cast to a greater length than the width of the type, e.g. in case of a cut-in.

The saw may be adjusted by hand with a wheel and scale, or may be connected with the assembler mechanism, being automatically adjusted by the latter. Long-lasting blades with tungsten carbide tips are available. Two cuts are often made, a primary and a trim. (G.U.)

slur: a letterpress machine printing fault in which irregular movement between the paper and the forme causes the dots of a half-tone to be distorted, or letters to show a double impression. Usual causes on a cylinder machine are an incorrectly packed cylinder, faulty make-ready, or a mechanical defect.

On a platen machine the frisket should be examined, the quoins should be readjusted, and the paper may need conditioning.

slurry: see *stuff*.

small capitals: capital letters set smaller than the upper-case letters of the fount to which they belong, e.g. ZEKI; indicated in manuscripts and proofs by two lines underneath the letters concerned.

small pica: the former name for a size of type, now standardized as 11-point.

smashing: the pressing of a book in a machine, after sewing, to compress the pages and expel air from between them. Also known as *nipping*.

Smith, Richard, 1590–1673: an early English bibliophile whose library of about 20,000 volumes was renowned in his day. It was particularly rich in English history. A movement to buy it by public subscription was started after his death, but as this failed it passed to the London bookseller Richard Chiswell who sold it by auction in 1682. Prices paid were not high and we learn that a Latin Psalter written on vellum in 1383 went for 2/10; Higden's 'Polychronicon' written on vellum, 2/6; Caxton's 'Game of chess', 1474, 13/2, and his 'Mirrour of the world', 1480, for 5/–.

smooth calf: an untooled calf binding.

smoothness: the smoothness of paper is affected by the fibres and loading used, also the treatment during manufacture of the surface. Coated papers have a surface coating over the fibres. Imitation art papers may have 25% loading added to the pulp. Various devices are available to measure the smoothness of the finished sheet. Cf. *gloss*.

See also *paper-testing*.

smooting: said of printers working for more than one employer at the same time.

Smyrna morocco: a sheepskin finished with a grain to represent morocco.

Smyth, David M.: one of the pioneers in constructing bookbinding machinery, including the first wire-stitching machine completed in 1878–79. The Smyth Manufacturing Co., Hartford, Conn., U.S.A., was established on the basis of his inventions. In Europe the firm is represented by Smyth-Horne Ltd., well known as suppliers of bookbinding machinery.

Snell, Johann, fl. 1480: a printer of Rostock, then Lübeck, whence he was invited in 1482 to Denmark to print a Breviary for the diocese of Odense, the first book to be printed in Denmark. In 1483 he went to Stockholm where, in addition to a large Missal for Uppsala, he printed a small collection of fables 'Dialogus creatorum moralizatus', the first dated book printed in Sweden. He issued other minor works in Sweden before returning to Lübeck where he then worked for Hans von Ghetelen. (G.U.)

Société des Bibliophiles françois: founded in Paris, 1820, to publish unknown works and revive the traditions of former French printers.

The Society of Antiquarian Booksellers' Employees: a society founded in London in 1951. Its aims are social, educational, and benevolent. Membership is open to all men and women, other than principals, employed in the antiquarian book trade. The society is popularly known as the *Bibliomites*.

The Society of Authors: a society founded in 1884 by Sir Walter Besant to advise its author members and protect their interests. Legal aid and representation in any part of the world are further benefits.

The society also administers several literary awards and prizes as noted elsewhere in this glossary.

The Society of Bookmen: a society of authors, publishers, critics, librarians, booksellers, etc., founded in 1921 by Sir Hugh Walpole. Membership is limited and is by election. The society meets monthly for dinner and formal but outspoken discussion of some important topical problem in the creation and distribution of books. The proceedings are never reported. The society has no power but considerable influence. It has among other things initiated the National Book Council (now the National Book League) and Book Tokens, and fostered the National Book Sale.

The Society of Indexers: a Society formed in London in 1957 with the aims of improving the standard of indexing and securing a measure of uniformity in technique. It was planned to issue occasional papers and notes on the subject, and to establish a panel of indexers, specializing in various fields, for the assistance of authors, publishers, and others. Advice will be given on the qualifications and remuneration of indexers.

Membership of the Society is open to bona fide indexers, librarians, cataloguers, archivists, and others interested in promoting its objects.

The address is 4 Fitzroy Street, London, W.1.

The Society of Young Publishers: an unofficial body which holds monthly meetings of its members at the National Book League, London, with a view to improving the knowledge about book publishing and kindred matters of those younger people in publishing who are likely to be the publishing executives of the future.

soft-ground etching: see *etching*.

soft paper: paper which has a soft surface and body, and little or no sizing, requiring relatively little pressure for printing; cheap book paper. (M.L.)

solander: a box, made in the form of a book, for containing loose plates or maps. It was devised by Daniel Charles Solander (1736–82).

solid dot Braille: see *Braille*.

solid matter: type set without interlinear leads.

Somerset Maugham Trust Fund: an annual award of about £400 made to a British subject under thirty-five years of age for a literary work, in English, which shows originality and promise. The prize is to enable the winner to travel, thus enriching his experience and extending the influence of modern English literature. Authors may submit their own works to the Society of Authors, London.

Sorensen, Christian: see *type-setting machine*.

sorts: specific letters as distinct from complete founts.

Sotheby & Co.: the senior firm of book auctioneers in London. It was in the 17th century that dealers discovered by degrees that consignments of books imported from the Continent could be disposed of more expeditiously and equally well by the auction method than by ordinary retail outlets, or even by exhibition and tender. (See *book auction*.) For some years, however, they were only a by-product of a dealer's business, and it was not until 1744 that Samuel Baker of Russell Street, Covent Garden (the D.N.B. states York Street, Covent Garden), held the first of a continuous series of sales of books, manuscripts, and prints, which constitute him the first professional book or art auctioneer, and entitle his firm, since known as Sotheby's, to claim the senior status in that business in London. Baker did not take a partner until he was joined by George Leigh in 1767 (D.N.B. dates this event 1774). Baker died in 1778 and his nephew, John Sotheby (1740–1807), joined Leigh in partnership about this time. He was the first of three generations of Sothebys who between them carried on the firm for nearly 100 years.

John Sotheby's nephew, Samuel Sotheby (1771–1842), directed the firm after Leigh's death in 1815. Both he and his son, Samuel Leigh Sotheby (1805–61), who also entered the firm, were authorities on typographical history. Thirty-six folio volumes of their writings are in the British Museum, while the sales catalogues they issued became of great importance to librarians and bibliographers everywhere.

At the time of his death in 1861 S. L. Sotheby was in partnership with John Wilkinson (1803–94). The latter was joined in 1864 by Edward Gross Hodge whose son, Tom Hodge, was left as sole partner in 1909, the point from which the modern history of the firm begins.

Hodge sold the business to a group of friends. They were Montagu Barlow, who secured a seat in Parliament in 1910, entered the Cabinet as Minister of Labour in 1922–23, and retired from Sotheby's in 1928; Geoffrey D. Hobson, a scholar and leading expert on bookbindings, who died in 1949; and Felix Warre, who successfully controlled the finances of Sotheby's, and died in 1953.

The business the 1909 syndicate had acquired conducted the sale of almost every British library of importance to come in the market for at least two generations, as well as such foreign collections as those of Talleyrand and Napoleon I. Within a few years they had three sales which realized over £1,000,000: the Huth Library (sold 1911–22 for £278,498); the Britwell Library (sold 1916–27 for £650,000); and the Yates Thompson manuscripts (sold 1919–21 for £135,349).

After the Great War the firm developed their handling of art sales, and within twenty years books were accounting for no more than 10% of the annual turnover.

Since the Second World War fewer great libraries have come up for disposal, but mention should be made of the Dyson Perrins illustrated books which realized £148,000 including £22,000 for only one of the two volumes of a Gutenberg Bible.

The book department is now (1956) directed by A. R. A. Hobson who joined the firm in 1947. He is the son of the late G. D. Hobson mentioned above.

Southey Literary Prize: see *Robert Southey Literary Prize.*

spacebands: the interword spacing material of the Linotype machine, being steel wedges mechanically inserted between the matrices when in the assembler box. After the line is set the justification block forces the wedges between the matrices until they occupy the full measure. Also used on Intertype machines.

spaces: type less than type height, cast in point sizes, and used as interword spacing material. They are cast smaller than an em quad, usual sizes being 3-em, 4-em, and 5-em space, i.e. a third, quarter, or fifth of an em.

See also *hair-spaces.*

spacing: the aesthetically satisfying distribution of printed matter on a printed page or pair of pages. It relates to the distance between letters, words, lines, and any illustrative or decorative matter.

spacing material: see *hair-spaces* (interletter), *spaces* and *quads* (interword), *leads* and *clumps* (interlinear), *quotations* and *furniture* (for whiting out pages having only a few lines of type). Type metal, wood, duralumin, lead, and plastic are among some of the materials which may be used.

Spalding Club: a club founded in Aberdeen in 1839 'for the printing of the historical, ecclesiastical, genealogical, typographical, and literary remains of the north-eastern counties of Scotland'. It ceased activity in 1871 but was reconstituted in 1886 as the New Spalding Club issuing, among other works, the first county bibliography to be published in Scotland.

Spanish calf: a light calf on which brilliant colour effects can be produced by staining.

Spanish illumination: the Spanish contribution to Renaissance illumination schools was slight, Christian influences being modified by the Islamic avoidance of natural forms.

Widely copied, however, from the 9th–12th centuries, especially in French Benedictine houses, was the important Spanish work 'Commentaria in Apocalypsin' written by Bishop Beatus of Liebana, *c.* 776.

special edition: an issue of a standard work with added notes, illustrations, or an appendix.

special sorts: types required for mixed composition or matter which is not straight composition.

See also *accents, astronomical symbols, botanical*

symbols, chessmen, cross, Domesday characters, medical symbols, meteorological symbols, peculiars, punctuation marks, split fractions.

specifications: the instructions sent to a printer with a typescript relating to size, type, paper, specimen page, etc.

specimen page: printed pages, usually four, and including chapter opening with any sub-headings, submitted by the printer to show the proposed style of setting.

specimen sheet: the sheet, usually in broadside form, on which printers displayed the range of founts, alphabets, ornaments, etc., available in their presses; type-founders issued similar sheets.

Fust and Schöffer probably originated the idea when, in 1469, they issued a broadsheet announcement of their books bearing the words 'hec est littera psalterij' as a specimen of their Psalter type. An early Continental example of a sheet devoted solely to specimens of type was printed by Erhard Ratdolt in 1486; on it were shown ten sizes of black letter, three of roman, and one of greek. The earliest English example is that of Nicholas Nicholls dated 1665, but William Caslon's of 1734 is probably the most famous.

The first *specimen book* known to have been issued by a printer is that of Christopher Plantin, 1567. The first in England was Caslon's of 1763.

A surprising number of 18th-century printers in England and elsewhere used as a text for display the passage from Cicero 'Quousque tandem abutere, Catilina, patientia nostra? . . .', a custom begun by Caslon in 1734.

Speed, John, 1552–1629: the first English publisher of a printed general atlas, 'Prospect of the Most Famous Parts of the World', 1627; and now particularly remembered for his 'Theatre of the Empire of Great Britaine', 1611.

Spencer, Charles, third Earl of Sunderland, 1674–1722: a statesman and bibliophile who began to found his library at Althorp when only nineteen. He was a sale-room rival of *Harley*, q.v.

It was George John Spencer (1758–1834), however, who made the library the most splendid of his age. In 1807 he retired from public life to devote his attention to book-collecting. From 1805 his librarian was Thomas Frognall Dibdin (1776–1847), one of the most famous English bibliographers.

The Althorp library included fifty-seven Caxtons, Manutius and Elzevier collections, first printed editions of the classics, and 108 books printed on vellum. The library remained at Althorp until 1892 when it was bought by Mrs. H. A. Rylands for £250,000; with it she established the John Rylands Library in Manchester.

Spenser Society: a society founded in 1866 for the printing of the lesser-known poetry of the 16th and 17th centuries. It ceased activity in 1894.

spike: see *bodkin.*

Spilman, Sir John, fl. 1580–1626: a German paper-maker who, *c.* 1588, had a paper-mill at Dartford, Kent. He was granted a monopoly in 1589. Paper continued to be made in this mill until 1739.

spine: the portion of the outer cover of a book which protects and encloses the *back*, q.v., and is usually lettered with the title, author's and publisher's name.

See also *flat backs, lettering on the spine.*

Spira, Johannes da: the German printer of the first book printed in Venice, where he established his press in 1469; in this year he issued two editions of Cicero's 'Epistolae ad familiares' and Pliny's 'Historia naturalis'. For these editions of 300 copies he used a roman type. He died in the same year and was succeeded by his brother Wendelin da Spira, fl. 1469–77, who printed classical texts, also Dante, and several law-books, the latter in gothic types. *Catchwords*, q.v., were first printed by Wendelin da Spira: this was in an edition of Tacitus, 1470.

spiral-laid dandy roll: see *dandy roll.*

spirex binding: a means of securing a number of leaves without using glue or thread. A spiral wire is run through holes punched in their inner margins. A tendency to tear makes the style unsuitable for general bookwork.

splash manner: a method used in lithography for obtaining a grained tone on a smooth surface.

See *autolithography.*

Splash manner

split boards: boards for use as book covers, made of a thin strawboard and a millboard, pasted into a unit, but leaving an unpasted marginal border on one side. After pressing and drying out the split marginal border is used for the insertion of the sewing tapes.
See also *boards* (1).

split-duct printing: simultaneous printing in two or more colours from one forme on a single-colour press. This involves the division of the ink duct into two or more sections, with a different colour in each, and ensuring they do not mix on the rollers where the lateral oscillation of the distributors would cause colour spoilage during the run if not prevented. This has hitherto meant cutting the distributor and forme rollers to leave a gap. Such a step is expensive unless the volume of work is considerable, and a modern American alternative is the *Dayco Color Separator* made by the Dayton Rubber Company who also make an effective ink-duct divider. The Separator is a device fitted to the tie-bar which runs across the press. The unit has a steel roller, from $\frac{1}{2}$ to $1\frac{1}{2}$ in. wide, which is positioned against one of the distributor rollers at a point where two colours of ink meet. As the ink is transferred to the steel roller a scraper guides it into a trough from which it is emptied at intervals. The Dayton Separator can be fitted to most leading makes of flat-bed, rotary letterpress, and offset-litho machines, and it is claimed that up to six colours can be printed from one forme with a single working.

split fractions: type for setting fractions, cast in two parts. One sort bears the upper figure, the lower figure and the dividing line being cast on the other. Fractions may be set diagonally ($^3/_4$) or horizontally ($\frac{3}{4}$).

spoils: sheets bearing imperfections; it is to allow for these that overs are issued to the printer.

Spottiswoode Society: a society instituted at Edinburgh, in 1843, which published ecclesiastical works until 1851. (M.L.)

spray-gun: see *anti-set-off sprayer*.

spray lithography: a means of obtaining delicate grained tones on a smooth surface by spraying it with litho ink from an airbrush. Sand-spraying with a special airbrush is also done in some lithographic work. (G.U.)
See also *autolithography*.

spraying: a defect which may occur with type-setting machines when molten metal spurts from behind the mould wheel. This is due to some obstacle preventing the matrix line, mould, and mouthpiece from fitting flush. (G.U.)

spring: when a forme is locked in the chase and any part of the type or furniture rises slightly from the imposing surface, it is said to spring; not in a proper condition for printing. (M.L.)

Spray lithography. Slugs hold a mask in position about the area to be treated

Springdale Colour Scanner: an American electronic photoengraving apparatus which produces a set of four separation continuous tone negatives for colour printing. The machine was built for the Time-Life Publishing Corporation who in 1955 owned the only model.

sprinkled calf: calfskin, used for book covers, having a speckled surface made by sprinkling acid on it. This was sometimes done in the 17th century, but the work was not durable as the acid rotted the skins.

sprinkled edges: the cut edges of a book which have been sprinkled with coloured ink to make the soiling of usage less noticeable. This alternative to gilding has been a feature of bookbinding from the 16th century to the present day.

squabble: a printing fault which occurs when one or more letters in a line are pushed into an adjacent line.

square capitals: the alphabet as adapted from the Roman lapidary capitals and used as a book hand from the 3rd–5th centuries. The letters were finished with wide square serifs instead of being sharply pointed as were those cut in stone. Square capitals were also known as *capitales quadrata*.
See also *letters—forms and styles*.

square folding: the method of folding a printed sheet in which the second fold is at right-angles to the first, the third to the second, etc.
See also *folding*.

squared up: an illustration printed within right-angled corners as distinct from illustrations of irregular shape. Cf. *vignette* (1).

squares: the margins of the cover of a book which extend beyond the pages and protect them. When a book is cased equal margins of cover are formed on the three edges. Cf. *cut flush.*

squash: said of ink which spreads beyond the area of contact between type and paper.

S.R.: the abbreviation for the Register of the *Stationers' Company*, q.v.

stabbing: 1. wire stitching a closed section or pamphlet near the back edge. Two staples may be used. This is cheap but not satisfactory since the pamphlet cannot be opened flat.

2. the piercing of a book section prior to stitching or sewing.

stacking tray: a tray made of battens of wood used in printing presses without pile feeders to receive from the press the printed sheets. Such trays are provided with raised edges at two opposite ends so that they can be stacked in piles to form shelves. (With G.U.)

staging out: the first step in the fine etching of a half-tone plate. The darker tones of the plate are painted with an acid-resisting enamel, so that the dots forming the middle tones and highlights can be further etched as required.

See also *fine etching.*

stained calf: calf that has been stained brown (only).

stained edges: see *coloured tops.*

Stamperia Valdonega: see *Officina Bodoni.*

Stamperia Vaticana: the official printing press of the Roman Catholic Church, founded in 1587 by Pope Sextus V under the practical direction (from 1590) of Aldus Manutius II and Domenico Basa. Special types were cut for the press by Robert Granjon, jun., of Paris.

Standard Cost-finding System: a system of record forms designed by a committee, the American Cost Commission, appointed in 1909 by the First Printers' Cost Congress in Chicago, to compile a practical system for obtaining accurate costs for the various departments of printing. (M.L.)

See also *chargeable time, Federation Costing System.*

standing formes: see *standing type.*

standing press: a large hand-operated vertical press standing on the floor and principally used by book-binders. The pressure is applied by a platen which is screwed down by the aid of a crow-bar. A small model of such presses standing on the work bench is much used but it is usual to term such a press *bench press.* Cf. *lying press.* (L.K.)

Small bench presses, table size, with different wheel and screw arrangement

Pressing cased books in a standing press

standing type: type which has been printed and which, instead of being distributed after use, is kept in store for reprints. Also known as *live matter* or *standing formes.*

The rules of the Stationers' Company forbade the keeping of standing type except for such works as ABC's, primers, almanacs, etc., and even for these the formes were to be distributed once a year. This, of course, was to create employment.

Cf. *dead matter.*

Stanhope press: the first all-iron printing press in England, which was introduced by the third Earl Stanhope about 1800 at the office of Bulmer's 'Shakspeare Press'. It employed the screw principle combined with a system of leverage for impressing, and two men could pull 200 impressions an hour on sheets twice as large as those used on former wooden presses.

Earl Stanhope was also largely responsible for the development of *stereotype*, q.v.

Star-chamber: the Court of the Star-chamber, an offshoot of the Privy Council, issued a decree in 1586 which empowered the Archbishop of Canterbury and the Bishop of London (as principal members of the Court of High Commission) to determine the number of presses, master printers, and apprentices in London, Oxford, and Cambridge (the only places in England where presses were allowed). Names for approval were submitted by the Court of the Stationers' Company. The Star-chamber, which in effect established Government control of printing and bookselling, was abolished in 1641.

See also *privilege, Stationers' Company.*

star signature: see *insert.*

start: a binding fault in which one section has been thrown forward from the others, much weakening the binding. This may occur particularly in books with a large number of sections.

starting charge: the term used by publishers' binders for the amount included in their prices to cover the costs incidental to starting to bind an order, and in particular those costs relating to the preparation of the machines. (L.K.)

state: part of an edition; being certain copies of a book differing from other copies of the same printing by alterations in the make-up or type-setting, either made during the running off of the sheets or at any subsequent stage before first publication. Such alterations may be additions, corrections, deletions or transpositions.

The 16th- and 17th-century custom of allowing authors to visit printing workshops while their works were being run off, and to make insertions or deletions, was often responsible for 'states' in books of the period.

See also *issue.*

static electricity: a phenomenon occurring in paper. In the paper warehouse this may be due to circumstances connected with its manufacture, such as evaporation, friction against the cylinder and the felt during the shrinkage which takes place when drying, or its passage through the machine glazer or calenders, etc. It also occurs when the paper is on the printing press or other machines where it is handled. The electricity causes the sheets of paper to adhere to each other or to machine parts, and may be very troublesome. The drier the paper the more easily it retains any electricity generated by its handling, so that moistening the air in the warehouse and storing the paper under carefully controlled conditions in an atmosphere of 65 to 70% relative humidity are helpful. The latter tends to be expensive due to the special equipment required.

There exist methods to free the paper course from static electricity in the paper-machine or printing press by conducting it through electric fields or by having earthed netting or trailing wires by the paper course. The principle here is that if the air round the paper web is ionized the current in the paper will be neutralized. The Croxted Manufacturing Co. in Britain make special equipment for combating static electricity. (G.U.)

stationarii: persons appointed by English and Continental universities in medieval times to supervise the distribution of books to students, and also to be responsible for their binding and repair. There was a stationarius at Oxford as early as 1308, and at Cambridge in 1310.

Stationers' Company: the authority established in 1557 by a Royal Charter from Queen Mary to regulate and organize printing and the book trade in England. It was created a livery company in 1560. Members were the booksellers, printers, and bookbinders of London (i.e. the 'stationers' as the word was then used).

On July 12th, 1403, 'the reputable men of the Craft of Writers of Text Letters those commonly called scriveners and other good folks citizens of London who were wont to bind and sell books' petitioned the Lord Mayor to form them into a guild. This was done in 1404. When scriveners were superseded by printers, who often disposed of their sheets to stationers who bound and sold them, the stationers became the more numerous and powerful body, and the guild was known as the Guild or Company of Stationers. Members were required to enter in the clerk's book details of every book or copy they claimed as their property. After 1557 this practice continued in the Register in which all works other than Bibles, almanacs, and certain other privileged books were to be entered. This was not always done, nor was entry in the Register necessarily more than a printer's claim to the rights of printing or publishing a work; entry should not be accepted as evidence of publication date in the case of undated books.

The Stationers' Company drew up strict rules to control all aspects of the book trade, and searchers were employed to ensure their observance, a practice which continued until at least 1677. Until the passing of the Copyright Act of 1842 apprentices to the printing trade were obliged to serve a member of the Company, and the number of apprentices an establishment might employ was limited. The former

STEEL ENGRAVING

Collotype reproduction of steel engraving by W. H. Egleton from a drawing by Pierre Staal, c. 1850.

statement 'Entered at Stationers' Hall' which was printed in books as proof of their registration is no longer necessary.

See also *English Stock*, *privilege*, *Star-chamber*.

Statute book: a book containing the laws made by the legislative body of a nation or state.

statutory copies: copies of any published work which publishers are required by law to supply free, within one month of publication, to the British Museum; and, if requested within twelve months, to the Bodleian Library, Oxford; the University Library, Cambridge; the National Library of Scotland in Edinburgh; and the Library of Trinity College, Dublin, Eire. The National Library of Wales comes in a slightly different category and there are restrictions on publishers' liability. Under the National Library of Wales (Delivery of Books) Regulations, 1924, publishers were not required to deliver to the Library a copy of certain classes of books except where these were of particular Welsh or Celtic interest. Two of these classes were 1. where the number of copies in the published edition does not exceed 400 and the published price of each volume exceeds £5, and 2. where the number of copies does not exceed 600 and the published price exceeds £10. An Amendment Regulation published in 1956 raised the price limits to £10 and £20 respectively. See the Copyright Act, 1911, Section 15.

An alternative name is *deposit copies*.

Forerunners of statutory copies date from the 16th century when Francis I of France ordered his Royal Printer, Conrad Néobar, to provide for the Royal Library a copy of every Greek book he printed, and Sir Thomas Bodley's arrangement in 1610 for the presentation to his library of a copy of every book printed by members of the Stationers' Company.

STC: the abbreviation for 'A Short-title catalogue of books printed in England, Scotland, and Ireland and of English books printed abroad, 1475–1640', by A. W. Pollard and G. R. Redgrave. London, Bibliographical Society, 1926.

Steamset: the trade name for a protected process in publishers' bookbinding, announced in 1956 by G. &. J. Kitcat Ltd. of London, whereby the back of the book is lined with an *expandable cloth*, prior to *rounding* and *backing*, qq.v. The lining and the adhesive on the back are softened by the application of steam, the rounding and backing being performed while the components are in the softened state. Full rounding with good joint formation together with durability and free opening are claimed for the process. (L.K.)

steel engraving: a print from an engraved steel plate. Copperplate engraving, which was the main method of printing illustrations in the 17th and 18th centuries, lost much of its importance when the new woodcut technique of end-grain cutting was developed by Bewick. Copperplate engraving was too delicate for printing large editions, and the method of printing was too involved and costly for most purposes. Independent invention of steel engraving is claimed for Charles Heath in England and J. Perkins in America; the two met and collaborated in 1818. They sought to infuse new life into the engraving process by adapting the technique to a material with greater strength. But if steel offered greater resistance to wear it was often to the detriment of artistic creation: steel engravings are characterized by a certain stiffness, particularly when such devices as ruling machines and pantographs are employed, even though technically they may be skilfully done with extraordinarily fine lines. Lithography, which came into prominence at the same time, overshadowed steel engraving for book illustration. (G.U.)

Stempel, David, 1869–1927: the founder, in 1895, of the Frankfurt type-founding business which today trades as Schriftgiesserei D. Stempel A.G. Since 1900 the firm has cut matrices for the German branch of Linotype & Machinery Ltd.

The acquisition of various type-foundries in Offenbach, Leipzig, Vienna, Basle, and Budapest during the period 1898–1920 furthered Stempel's ambition to become one of the largest type-founding concerns in Europe.

Among world-famous designers who have been commissioned by Stempel are Warren Chappell, F. H. Ehmcke, F. W. Kleukens, Rudolph Koch, Paul Renner, and Hermann Zapf. In 1951 Stempel established the *Trajanus-Presse*, q.v.

stencil process: see *pochoir*.

step-and-repeat machine: an apparatus for multiple copying (on offset plates, etc.) with devices for the precise adjustment of each copy. These machines are intended especially for reproduction in colour, in which the printing plates for yellow, red, etc., must be precisely superimposed in printing.

The first machines for this purpose were used in lithographic printing works about 1920. In the American *Ogden* machine the negative is fixed in a horizontal table lit from below by a copying lamp. The sensitized plate, with the layer on the lower side, is pasted on a disc hanging in a frame which can be moved in two directions at right-angles to each other above the fixed table with the negative. Movements of the frame are made by screw spindles, and their adjustment is read on scales with a precision of

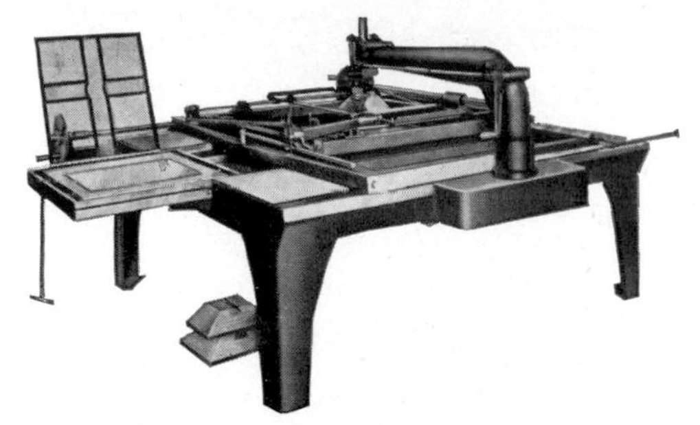

The Ogden step-and-repeat machine (American Machine & Foundry Co., Brooklyn). The negative is positioned on the extended plate by means of the transparent plate (shown here open) in which a hair cross is cut. The clamps by which pressure is exerted are changed according to the size of the negative.

1/50 mm. After each movement, the disc with the plate suspended beneath it is pressed down on the negative before exposing is done. The largest Ogden model is entirely automatic, with motor-driven movement of the negative. Other step-and-repeat machines in extensive use include the Dutch *Repetex* and the English *Printex* in which the prepared side of the plate is uppermost, while the negative hangs in a frame combined with the copying lamp, the frame being movable along a graduated scale. Modern American step-and-repeat machines usually work with a vertical plate, e.g. Monotype-Huebner's *MH-photo-composing machine*. In the *Rutherford* machine, invented by Harry C. Jones, the printing plate is suspended on a vertical disc which moves sideways, while the negative and the lamp can be

The Rutherford step-and-repeat machine (Fuchs & Lang Manufacturing Co., Rutherford, U.S.A.). The lamp is turned aside so that the negative frame with the suction device is visible. Later models are of a different form, but are on the same principle

The Mannotex copying frame (George Mann & Co., London)

The Printex Junior step-and-repeat machine (Pictorial Machinery Co., London)

The Krause step-and-repeat machine, model M 100 K, with mechanical pressure between the plate resting on the table and the negative which forms the base of the hood covering the arc lamp. Model L works with a vacuum for making contact between the negative and plate. It can hold negatives of larger sizes

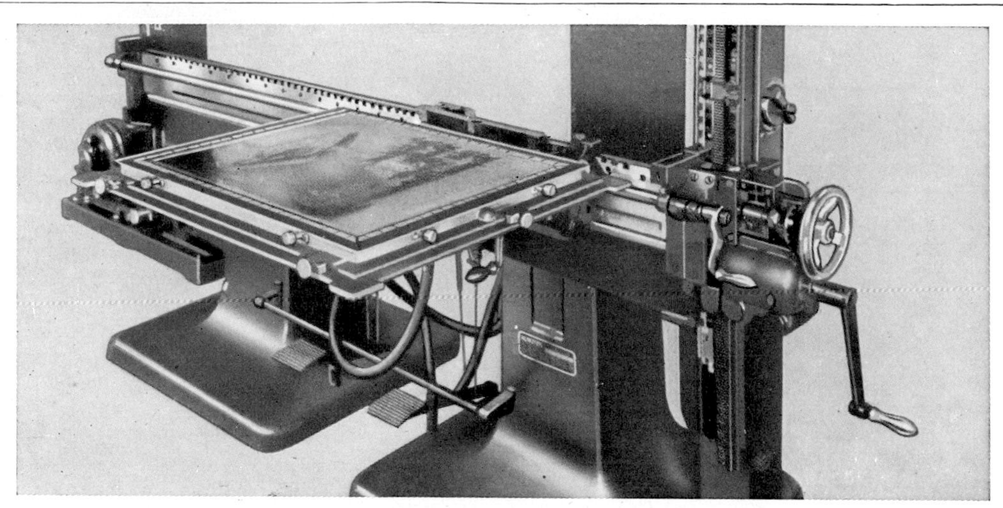

The Monotype-Huebner photo-composing machine is so constructed that negatives can be unmasked, etc., without disturbing the adjustment

moved up and down. Contact is established by means of a vacuum.

Among German machines are the *Variocombinex* and the *Krause*, both widely used. The plate in the latter lies on a fixed table above which the negative frame and copying lamp are moved. The Swedish *Multinex*, 1954, is a fully automatic electronically controlled machine producing contact negatives on film or glass from negative or positive film.

Something between step-and-repeat machines and the simple *vacuum frame*, q.v., consists of copying frames in which the negative (and lamp) are moved by hand but are adjusted by means of marks on graduated scales (the British *Mannotex*, etc.). (G.U.)

Stephenson Blake & Co.: a type-founding firm of Sheffield, established in 1819 by James Blake, John Stephenson, and William Garnett. In the same year they acquired the foundry of William Caslon IV, transferring the plant to Sheffield. The original trading name, Blake Garnett & Co., was changed to Blake and Stephenson in 1830, and to its present form in 1841. London premises were opened in 1865. In 1905 the firm bought the foundry of Sir Charles Reed & Sons Ltd., in this way acquiring types designed by Dr. Edmund Fry and William Thorowgood.

From 1907 a separate works was operated for the manufacture of furniture and other composing room equipment. In 1937 the firm acquired the goodwill of the type-foundry business of H. W. Caslon & Co. Ltd., and some of the matrices and punches, and in 1951 some of the proprietary types of Miller & Richard.

The range of display types marketed by Stephenson Blake & Co. is known and used all over the world: included are Chisel, Playbill, Windsor, Verona, Fry's Ornamented, Elongated Roman, Keyboard, and Marina Script.

stereotype (or **stereo**): a printing plate made by taking an impression from set-up type, or another plate, in a mould of plaster of Paris, papier mâché, or flong. Stereotype metal (an alloy of tin, antimony, and lead) is then poured into the matrix, as the impression-bearing mould is known, the surface of the resulting stereo being made more durable by nickelling. English stereos are usually 12-point thick; American are 10-point.

The process, which saves wearing the original types and the delays caused by their working loose, was invented in 1727 by William Ged of Edinburgh.

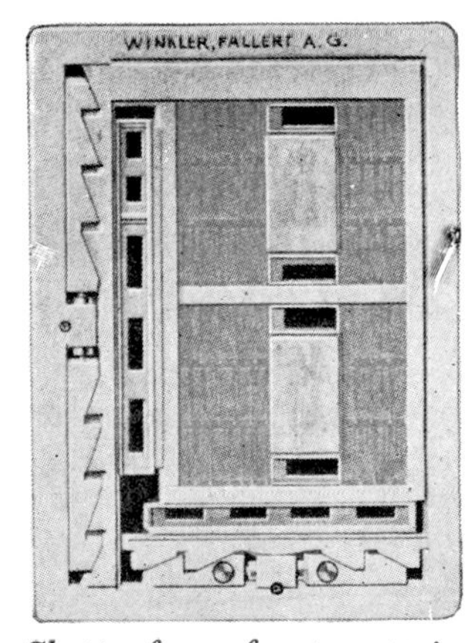

Shutter frame for stereotyping

(A Frenchman, Gabriel Valleyre, is said to have invented the process independently in 1730.) The name 'stereotype' was given about 1794 by Firmin Didot who experimented with Ged's invention, and also a similar invention by Johann Müller of Leyden in 1701 whereby pages of type were fused into a solid mass by soldering their bases. The first book produced by Ged was an edition of Sallust, 1744, but printers of the day opposed his development of the process. In 1784 Foulis and Tilloch of Glasgow patented a new stereotype process from which, in 1804, Earl Stanhope developed his plaster method at Cambridge University. Paper matrices are said to have been used towards the end of the 18th century in Nuremberg, but in 1830 the Parisian compositor Claude Genoux originated the papier mâché method now in use; other experiments in this direction were made in 1846 by the Italian Vanoni. The idea of fitting curved stereos to printing cylinders dates from 1816 when William Nicholson made attempts; it was not until the middle of the century, however, that they were in general production and use.

Plaster moulding process. When duplicating the finest half-tone blocks (200-line screen) for three- and four-colour printing, plaster-cast stereos are made. A plaster of 4 parts gypsum, 4 parts kaolin, 1 part dextrin, and 1 part talcum is stirred into a pulp immediately before use, and poured on to a backing paper. The layer of plaster is levelled to a predetermined thickness with a steel ruler, and left to stand for a few minutes. In the meantime the forme is oiled with photogen and covered with a thin cloth and a sheet of Japan paper. The frame containing the plaster is now laid face downwards on the forme. The whole is put into a press, covered with layers of absorbent paper, and pressed cold under light pressure until the matter has been impressed between 1½

Device for checking the position of blocks, etc., in the forme before stereotyping for multicolour printing

Beating the flong

and 3 mm. Then the forme is taken out of the press, the matrix frame lifted, and the cloth removed. The forme is again oiled and covered with a fresh sheet of Japan paper, prior to re-stamping, this time to a further depth of ½ mm. to 1 mm. After about ten minutes the solidified matrix is taken out, air-dried for half an hour, and baked in an oven where it is heated slowly to about 120° C. It is then ready for casting. Gypsum stereotyping cannot damage the original forme and the material is cheap, but the work is highly skilled and takes a comparatively long time. Disadvantages are that only one casting can be made from each matrix, and castings cannot be curved for rotary press use.

Wet and dry flong. Formerly the material for the matrix always consisted of *wet flong*, often made by the stereotypers themselves. This is composed of two sheets of strong mounting paper to which alternate layers of blotting paper and tough tissue-paper are pasted by a special starch paste. (Recipes for flong vary from foundry to foundry.) It is about 0·5 to 0·6 mm. thick. Flong is rolled to expel air bubbles. It is dampened and placed, tissue side down, on to the forme and beaten in with a brush (see illustration). It is then removed and dried in a heated press under pressure. A quicker and increasingly used material is *dry flong*. For coarse screen half-tones it can be used quire dry; otherwise it is slightly dampened. It is stored in a humidor until required as the matrix must be sufficiently soft to receive a precise impression of all details of the forme; the ductility must be so great that no cracks occur during moulding; the surface must be smooth and not vary more than 0·03 mm. at the most in thickness; the surface must withstand

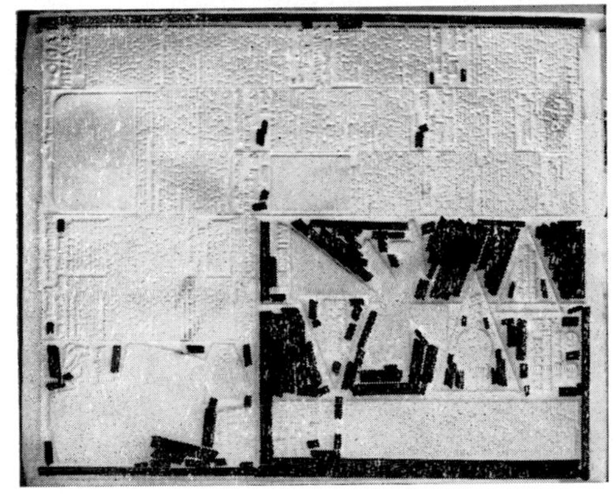

Both sides of a matrix. Upper, the face, showing the impression. Below, the obverse, packed out with card

350° to 375° C without scorching; and the matrix must be so strong that it will not tear when the mould is opened and the plate is separated from it.

Whether the finished mould is made of plaster or flong it must be packed out before casting (see illustration). This is done on the back of the matrix where any depressions are filled up with gummed strips of cardboard, shaped as required. This card acts as a support to prevent the blank areas on the face of the matrix being flattened out by the molten metal during casting. If packing out is not done the corresponding parts of the cast plate must be milled or routed off so that they will not take up ink and print.

Any moisture left in a flong matrix must be dried out before *casting*, q.v. Before placing it in the casting box strips of brown paper are pasted to the side of the mould which will be uppermost: these project from the mouth of the box and indicate to the operator where the molten metal must be poured. The casting metal should be poured at a temperature of 300° C (a pyrometer measures this).

If a flat stereo has been cast, it must be finished

Matrix dryer in which suction draws moisture through the cover

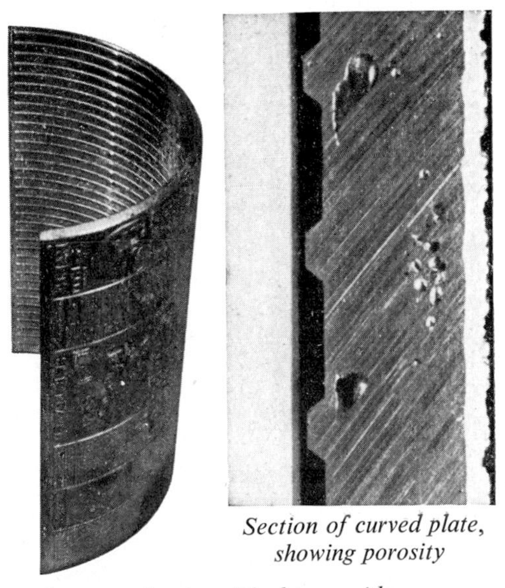

Section of curved plate, showing porosity

Curved stereo, showing ribbed inner side

after cooling off. This is done by squaring up and planing in a machine which shaves it to a uniform thickness of 12-point (10-point in U.S.A.). Any surplus shoulders of metal, which may take up ink, must be cut off in a *routing machine*, q.v. (a skilled task), and finally holes are punched in the margins for securing the plate to its mounting block.

Curved plates are made in a similar way to flat ones, but cast in a curved casting box (see illustration). They are finished off in a *boring machine*, q.v. The plate must fit closely to the carrying cylinder of the press, and should have an inner diameter slightly less than that of the plate cylinder. When the plate leaves the casting box its outer surface is hotter than the inner, due to the insulating effect of the matrix. As the temperature evens in cooling the diameter will increase, and the cylinder in the casting box must, therefore, be considerably smaller than the plate cylinder of the press. (The difference should be about

American matrix dryer, with vertical revolving drum

Patching can be done on the beaten damp flong matrix before fitting on the covering sheet and drying

Gas-heated drying table for hand-beaten matrices

Casting with a ladle in a flat caster. The tail, wedges, and part of the covering paper are seen at the top

4 mm.) During *boring* a shaving is simultaneously cut from all the supporting ribs. If the inner side of the plate is smooth, a revolving steel borer moves on a worm thread through the plate, cutting away the core.

Various defects which may occur in cast plates should be mentioned. *Hollows* may appear if the composition of the metal is such that it contracts in solidifying and the surface cools too quickly. When the molten metal behind the thin solidified outer layer contracts, the latter also does in places, and the temperature of the cooled plate should be raised 10° to 15°. A *grained surface* is generally due to the metal being too hot and burning the surface of the matrix, so that small gas bubbles are formed. The temperature should be lowered at least 30°. *Porous* plates occur if the air in the casting box cannot escape before the metal solidifies. The temperature of the metal should be raised or the quantity of cooling water reduced, so that the period of cooling is prolonged. *Cup-shaped type* is due to changes of shape in the matrix caused by the metal being too hot. *Badly finished half-tones* are obtained when the metal has not flowed into the hollows of the screen dots, either due to a low tin content of the metal or too low a temperature.

Sometimes, instead of stereotyping half-tones set in the letterpress, original blocks are cast into the stereo. It is more usual, however, in such cases to replace the block by a dummy while making the cast, and to reduce the finished stereo at this place with a routing machine to a height which will serve as underlay for the block when positioned later. This procedure is also adopted in rotary stereotyping with blocks specially made of zinc which can easily be bent. (With G.U.)

See also *autoplate machine*, *electrotype*, *flong*, *papier mâché*, *plate-boring machine*, *scorcher*.

stereotype metal: an alloy of tin, antimony, and lead for casting stereos. Lead is the main ingredient, about 80%. Tin makes the alloy tough and improves the sharpness of the cast. Antimony gives further hardness and also counteracts contraction in solidifying, so that the plate is as faithful a casting of the matrix as possible. Antimony by itself expands when it solidifies, whereas the other two metals contract. A stereo metal correctly constituted will neither expand nor contract in solidifying. The commonest alloy is 5% tin, 14% antimony, and 81% lead, but for fine screen work and durability the proportion of tin is raised to about 10%. The above alloy is cast at 300° C and solidifies at a temperature ranging between 260° and 230°. In passing through this range, crystals of tin-antimony are precipitated, and grow larger the more slowly cooling proceeds. In order to obtain

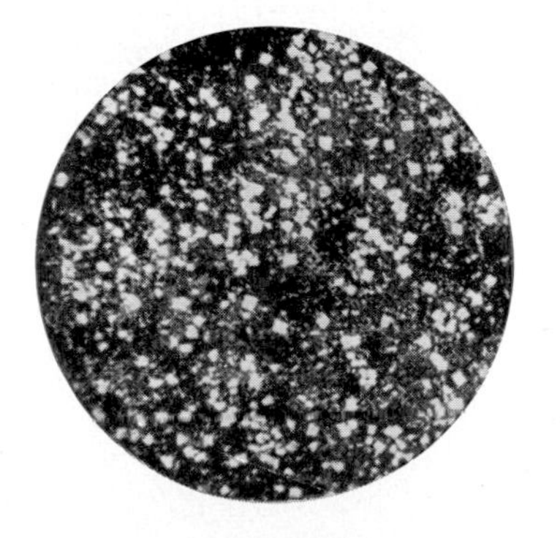

Microphotograph, enlarged 100 *times, of stereo metal with* 8% *tin and* 17% *antimony: above, rapidly cooled; below, slowly cooled*

fine-grained metal this temperature range must be passed through rapidly (see diagram).

When the metal in the melting pot comes into contact with air, oxidation occurs. The tin is oxidized most easily, which causes loss of tin, so that more must be added from time to time. The oxide floats above the metal and forms, to some extent, a

Broken surface of rapidly and slowly cooled metal; 10% *tin,* 15% *antimony*

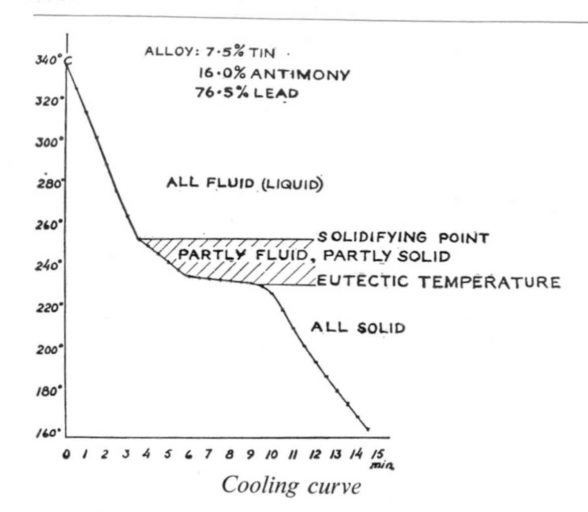

Cooling curve

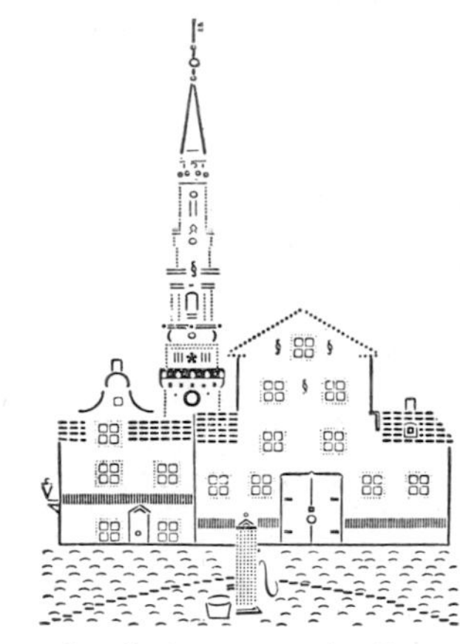
An example of stigmatypy, by E. H. Berling

protective layer. As a further protection against continued oxidation a layer of crushed charcoal can be laid over the surface of the metal. The oxide, which should be skimmed off once a week, can be treated with reducing agents to recover the metal. By stirring the metal in the pot impurities will rise to the surface, when they can be skimmed off with the oxide.

See also *type metal.* (G. U.)

stet: a word meaning 'let it stand' which is written marginally in proofs to cancel a previously marked correction. Dots are written under the word or words concerned.

stick: see *composing stick.*

sticking: sheets of paper may stick together either before or after printing. The former is due to incorrect storage of the paper or to cutting the sheets with a blunt knife which forces the edges into a solid pack. Sticking after printing is due to ink remaining wet on the paper, especially hard-surface papers.

Static electricity, q.v., is also a possible cause of sticking.

stiffened and cut flush: see *flush boards.*

stigmatypy: the printing of a design or portrait built up from small type-units. (G. U.)

stillage: a low platform on which paper is stored in the warehouse. It is made of battens of wood, strengthened by metal angle-bars. Advantages from its use are that damp floors do not affect the paper, air circulates around it, and the stillage and paper can be moved by hand truck or a fork-lift truck. Cf. *pallet.*

stilted covers: said of a book bound in extra large covers so that it will appear uniform on a shelf with volumes of larger size.

stipple engraving: a combination of *etching* and *engraving,* qq.v. The outline of the design is made with a needle on a grained plate which is then etched. With further use of a graver small dots are made; these give effects of light and shade in imitation of pencil shading. This form of engraving was first made popular in the 18th century by *Francesco Bartolozzi,* an Italian painter and engraver who came from Venice to London in 1764, where he worked for *John Boydell,* q.v.; it had, however, been used earlier by W. W. Ryland (1732–83) the Royal engraver.

stitching: a term implying that the thread or wire passes through the whole contents of the book in one hit. If the book is in gathered sections the stitching will pass from side to side about ⅛ in. from the back. If all sections are inserted the stitching is made through the back fold. Cf. *sewing,* which implies the individual sewing of each section to its neighbours. (L. K.)

stock: 1. the printing trade term for paper.

2. the wet pulp of mixed ingredients before it enters the paper-making machine to be formed into paper. Also known as *stuff.*

stockholding book wholesaler: a book wholesaler who carries in stock a substantial representation of bound books available for sale to the retail trade.

stone: the table bearing an iron plate (formerly a stone slab) on which the printer imposes set-up type, i.e. arranges the pages into the proper order for printing.

stone engraving: engraving on lithographic stone, a hand process used chiefly for script and line drawings in which sharpness and precision of line are more important than artistic expression, e.g. for maps. For stone engraving only blue and grey lithographic stones are used. The surface is prepared by grinding with pumice stone and polishing with snakestone. A solution of concentrated oxalic acid is applied until all the pores are closed and the surface is smooth and shiny. It is then coated with a thin layer of ink made of soot in a solution of gum. This is to help the lithographer to judge his work. Outlines are traced and then deeply scored with a steel or diamond pen so that they stand out against the dark ground. Engraving is completed by gradually deepening the lines. Broader lines can be incised to about 0·2 mm., while the thinnest are not more than 0·06 mm. deep. Fatty ink is dabbed into the finished engraving, and the black ground is washed off. Printing can be done in a transfer press.

An alternative method is to give the stone a ground of the kind used when etching on metal. The image is cut in the ground and then the lines are deepened with dilute nitric or acetic acid. If not all the lines are to be equally deep, etching is done in stages, painting out with a solution of asphalt or indian ink in between each.

Printing from a stone engraving can only be done in a hand-press, and normally editions are small. It is most usual, therefore, for a stone engraving to be made as an original for transferring to a plate for use in a printing press. (G.U.)

A stone engraver at work. As the engraving will be transferred to an offset plate it is face upwards on the stone

stone grinding: a lithographic stone must be given treatment to make its surface receptive to an image; the surface must be clean and completely flat. Grinding machines are used in which the surface is ground with fine sand and water by means of revolving flat plates; or grinding may be done by hand by laying a second stone on the first, or by using a *levigator*, q.v. (G.U.)

Stone-grinding machine

stone-hand: the craftsman in a printing establishment who imposes type matter in the chase.

stone printing: 1. Chinese stone printing. About A.D. 175 Ts'ai Yung suggested that the six holy books of Confucius should be engraved on stone slabs to preserve them for posterity. According to tradition the oldest stone printing was done from these slabs. Since the 9th century this idea was adapted for printing pictures. A thin sheet of tough paper was laid on the engraved stone, thoroughly soaked, and pressed into the engraving with a brush or felt and hammer, so that it covered the stone like a skin. Indian ink was spread over the paper, care being taken that it did not penetrate into the depressions. When the paper dried it could be prised off the stone to reveal a light script or image on a dark ground.

2. Printing from stone on which an image had been made with thick ink was the original form of lithographic printing. Stone printing is still used, but the term lithography is extended to include printing from grained zinc or aluminium plates. (See *lithography, Senefelder.*)

A stone to be used for lithographic work must first be ground, whether it be a new stone or one previously used. In the latter case the grinding must be sufficiently deep to remove traces of the previous preparation and any remaining ink. With time the thick ink penetrates deeply into the stone, and an old image may require prolonged grinding to remove it entirely. (See *stone grinding.*) After rough grinding, fine grinding is done with pumice stone. If the stone is for crayon drawing it must be grained with moist fine sand and a piece of lithographic stone. When the image has been imposed on the stone surface by direct drawing (in reverse), transfer, or copying (though the latter is rare on stone) it must be intensified, and the non-image areas must be made water-absorbent before the stone can be used for printing. This is done by *etching* the stone, preferably with diluted nitric acid, followed by coating the whole stone with a solution of gum arabic and water.

After grinding, the pores of the stone are to a large extent closed and the newly formed surface affords an excellent foundation for lithographing (a still better ground is obtained by pouring a semi-saturated solution of alum on the stone as this separates the finely distributed plaster in the pores). On the other hand this surface tends less to absorb and retain the solution of gum which forms one of the components in lithographic printing. Acids which form easily soluble calcium salts dissolve the finest particles of lime and open the pores in the stone surface. Lithographic crayons and indian ink, with which lithographing is done, contain soap. During the etching the soap dissolves, enabling its fat to sink into the pores. After etching the stone must therefore be washed, but must be allowed to dry. When it is essential to remove the etching slime before it has dried, the crayon may run off. It is therefore necessary to cover the stone with gum and dry it quickly, after which the fatty image is intensified by washing out. The washing out is done with asphalt and fat in a solution of turpentine which is rubbed into the gummed and dried surface. By this procedure the fatty substance which contains soap is exchanged for fatty substances insoluble in water, while the addition of turpentine promotes the absorption of the fat in the pores of the stone. The fatty image can be further intensified with powdered resin or asphalt which is ground into the thick ink and melted with a spirit flame or blowpipe. Prior to this the powder must be carefully removed from the non-image areas by means of dusting, which is made easier if talcum has been mixed with the powder. When the fatty ground has been intensified the stone can be etched more vigorously, and the etching can be carried so far that the stone becomes *relief etched* which facilitates printing on hard paper.

After etching, the stone is *gummed* with a solution of gum arabic and fanned dry. When the gum dries it is not dissolved by cold water but swells to an aqueous, fat-resisting layer. If this has to be removed the stone can be re-prepared with an acid which dissolves the lime and the layer of gum adhering to it, or by using an alum solution which hardens the gum, making it fat-absorbent. The soap contained in a layer of indian ink also acts destructively on the layer of gum, and it is thus possible to lithograph with indian ink on a stone which is etched and gummed and then merely washed with water.

In the machine press the humidity of the stone is maintained by a damping unit, in a hand-press by damping with a sponge and a cloth. Inking up is done by an inking device or a hand-roller. Ink used must be insoluble in water and contain linseed oil, wax compounds, reducers, and litho varnish. Rubber-attacking substances must be excluded from litho-offset inks.

Hand-fed sheet press for printing from stone

Due to the high price and difficulty of handling a lithographic stone a substitute was sought. Senefelder tried metal plates, and various attempts were made to give them a suitable surface. Efforts were also made to bind stone-dust to other bases, but it was not until the end of the 19th century that methods were worked out for grinding and etching aluminium and zinc plates to give a surface which could be dealt with by the methods used in lithographing on stone by hand (though not stone engraving), and could be printed in a stone-printing press. When rotary printing was introduced (zinc rotary and offset) actual stone printing was largely superseded. (G.U.)

See also *lithographic press.*

Stonyhurst Gospel: a version of the Gospel of St John, written in Northumbria in an uncial script. It is not decorated. The ninety surviving leaves, in a binding which is thought by some to be 7th-century work, are preserved in Stonyhurst College, Lancashire.

stop-cylinder press: a cylinder machine in which the paper-carrying cylinder stops after completing one revolution (in some older models one-half or one-third of a revolution), and is stationary during the return of the bed bearing the forme. During this pause fresh paper is fed. The cylinder is driven by gear racks on the bed which mesh with corresponding gears on the cylinder during printing. When the bed passes the cylinder, the outermost tooth of the gear rim loses contact with the gear rails of the bed and the rotary movement of the cylinder is intercepted by the pawl clutch which, with the cylinder brake, stops it. The pawl clutch also re-starts the cylinder when the bed is at its extreme end.

König's first cylinder machine (1812) was a stop-cylinder machine, and the main principles of his model have survived to the present day. (See illustration under *letterpress machines*.) A diagram below shows how paper was conveyed through a stop-cylinder machine of the type built from the 1860's to the automatic printing machine of the present time.

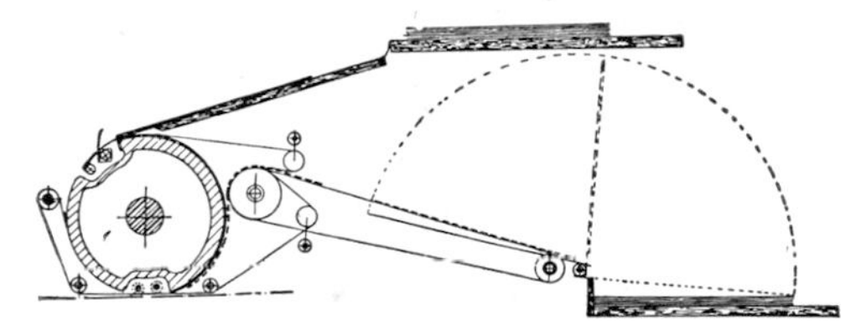

Passage of the sheet through a stop-cylinder press; a typical construction since the 1860'*s with tape conveyor and rack delivery*

From the feeding table above the press the sheet was fed down to the stationary cylinder where the front edge was seized by grippers. During the rotation of the cylinder the sheet was held in position by the lower travelling tape. By means of this and the upper travelling tape stretched round the cylinder, the printed sheet was conveyed to delivery tapes. Such delivery does not permit high speeds.

Modern stop-cylinder machines are arranged for pile delivery, with space for a delivery table which can be lowered automatically as the pile increases. The best known English model is the *Wharfedale*

König & Bauer press, late 19*th century*

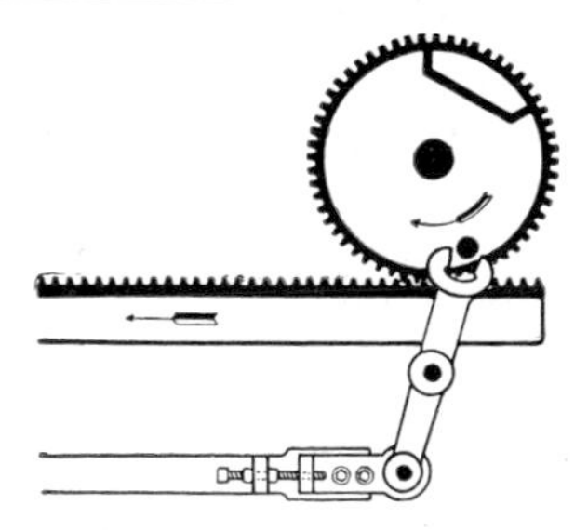

Pawl clutch on stop-cylinder press

Modern stop-cylinder press. Planeta automatic cylinder FD

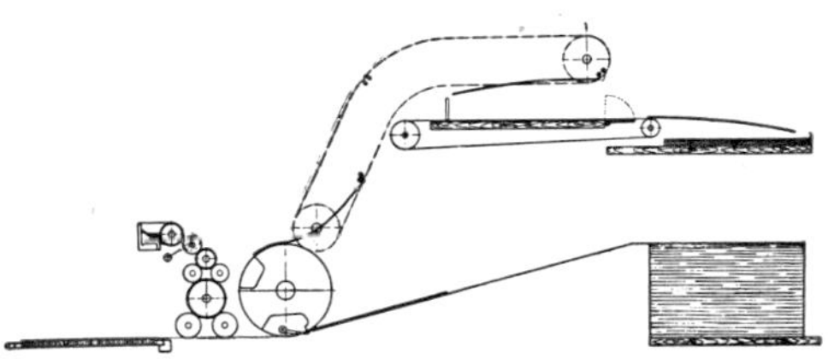

Passage of the paper through a Planeta FD

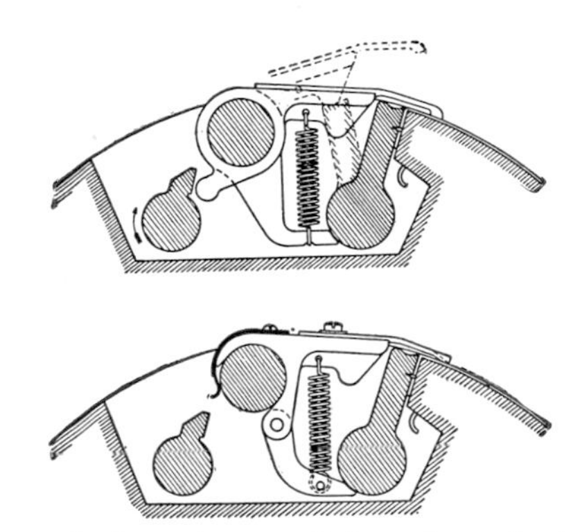

Above, cylinder grippers. Below, front feed guides. Planeta stop-cylinder press

machine q.v. Recent machines have automatic feed and extended pile delivery, with a printing speed of 3600 sheets an hour.

Among modern rapid automatic stop-cylinder presses the Miehle vertical is well known and unique in construction. The bed is vertical, moving up and down, while the cylinder moves in the opposite direction to the bed. (See illustration under *Miehle*.) (G.U.)

stopping out: covering with varnish such parts of an etching plate as are not to be further etched by acid during its repeated dipping in the acid bath. Cf. *staging out*.

Stowe MSS.: a valuable collection of nearly 1000 volumes of historical papers, works on heraldry, genealogy, topography, Anglo-Saxon charters, King Alfred's Psalter, etc. The majority were assembled in the late 18th century by the palaeographer and antiquary, Thomas Astle (1735–1803), Keeper of the Records in the Tower. In accordance with his will the collection was offered for £500 to George Grenville, first Marquis of Buckingham, of Stowe House. The collection was there enlarged by the acquisition of the Essex Papers and the Irish manuscripts of C. O'Connor.

In 1849 the Stowe MSS. were sold to the Earl of Ashburnham. After his death they were bought by the Government for £50,000; the important Irish works went to the Royal Academy in Dublin, the remainder to the British Museum.

straight-grain morocco: skins which are moistened and rolled or 'boarded' to make the grain run in straight lines. Roger Payne (1739–97) is believed to have originated the style.

straight matter: a normal piece of type-setting which does not contain display or tabular matter.

Strawberry Hill Press: the press, also known as 'Officina Arbutucana', established in 1757 by Horace Walpole, with William Robinson and Thomas Kirgate as successive printers. Caslon types were used. Walpole died in 1797.

See A. T. Hazen, 'A Bibliography of the Strawberry Hill Press', New Haven, Yale U.P.: O.U.P., 1942.

strawboards: cheap boards made from pulped straw and used for book covers, not, however, by hand-binders who prefer *millboards*, q.v.

stream feeder: see *feeder*.

strike: a piece of polished copper into which a steel punch (bearing an engraved character) has been struck by the typefounder. After *justification*, q.v., the strike is known as a *matrix*, and from it type is cast. An alternative name is *drive*.

strike-through: the name of a fault in printing in which ink printed on one side of a sheet penetrates to the other. Cf. *show through*.

striking off: 1. the making by hand of stereotype matrices.

2. the production of proofs from relief printing formes without using a printing press. A stiff beating brush is employed to strike the damp paper against the inked forme. The result is known as *strike off*. (G.U.)

Stringertype: a type-setting machine constructed in 1902 by an Englishman, Gilbert Stringer. It was something between a Linotype and a Monotype machine. As in the Linotype, matrices of brass were released from a magazine, but the matrices had a type-face cut into their broad side, and types were cast singly. Measure and justification were based on the Monotype system with space units in relation to the em quad. After many modifications the machine was last exhibited at the Wembley Exhibition in 1924 under the name of *Supertype*.

stripping: the removal of a negative from its original wet plate for mounting on a larger glass sheet. This is a stage in the *iodized collodion process*, q.v., when combining line and half-tone work, or doing fine line work alone. The dried negative is coated with a stripping lacquer (e.g. methyl cellulose in toluene, with castor-oil as a plasticizer), and when dry the film can be easily removed.

Other methods and solutions are in use.

stub: 1. the first column of matter set in tabular form.

2. the narrow margin which remains in a book when a cancel has been removed, and on to which a corrected leaf is fixed.

stuff: the wet pulp of mixed ingredients which is ready to be flowed on to the wire of the paper-making machine. Also known as *slurry* or *stock*.

See also *half-stuff*.

style of the house: the customary style of spelling, punctuation, spacing, etc., used in a printing house. The compositor will follow house rules and style in setting up type unless contrary instructions are specified by the publisher. Cf. *follow copy*.

stylus: a sharp instrument for writing, for scratching on a surface covered with a film of wax or similar substance, or for writing on carbon manifold sheets. (M.L.)

sub-heads: headings for the divisions of a chapter: size of type, position in relation to the text, and leading are factors to be considered when setting them.

See also *cross-heads, side-heads, shoulder-heads, cut-in heads.*

subject series: a number of books, often written by different authors, but which are uniform in format, scope, and method. They are usually published under the name of a general editor, e.g. the 'Complete Engineer' Series, ed. by E. Molloy. London, Newnes.

subscribing a book: the showing by a publisher's traveller of new books to booksellers and wholesalers prior to publication.

See also *advance copies, subscription terms.*

subscription terms: specially favourable terms (often $33\frac{1}{3}\%$) offered by a publisher to booksellers on orders placed for a book prior to first publication. This is a compensation for the extra risk they take in stocking copies of a work before its sales possibilities have been tested.

See also *terms* (1).

subscription works: books which, due to the unlikelihood of their cost being a sound business venture, are only published when a number of subscribers or guarantors has been found. The idea originated in the 17th century, early examples being 'Guide into tongues', privately printed for its compiler, John Minsheu, in 1617, and a polyglot Bible in six folio volumes printed by Thomas Roycroft, 1653–57, for Brian Walton, the Bishop of Chester.

See also *Chapter books, privately printed, privately published, subscription terms.*

subsidiaries: parts of a book excluding the preliminaries and text, viz.: appendix, notes, glossary, bibliography, index, plates and maps (when appearing at the end), colophon, end-papers. Also known as *end-matter.*

substance: a weight reference used in describing paper to help comparison between different sizes.

subtitle: an added phrase, usually explanatory, which follows the title.

subtractive colour synthesis: see *colour photography.*

sulphate pulp: a pulp used in making paper in which wood is boiled in a digester with sodium sulphate. Paper so made is strong, and is often used unbleached, but it can be bleached to a very white colour.

sulphite pulp: pulp used in making paper in which chipped wood is boiled with bisulphite of lime to separate the fibres. Such pulps are clean and bleach easily. A form of the process was devised in 1866 by two Americans, the brothers B. C. and R. Tilghmann. Commercial development by a Swede, C. D. Ekman, followed in 1872: he came to England and in 1886 established the Northfleet Paper & Pulp Co. in Kent.

summa: a collection of theological treatises.

sunk joints: see *french joints.*

sunken flexible: a manner of sewing the sections of a book in which grooves are sawn in them as far as the innermost fold. The thin cords which lie in these grooves are then completely encircled with the sewing thread, not crossed. The result is a *saw back* or *sawn-in back.*

super: the American term for *mull,* q.v.

super royal: a standard size of printing paper, $20\frac{1}{2}$ in. by $27\frac{1}{2}$ in.

super-calender: a calender which is separate from the paper-making machine. It consists of a stack of from five to sixteen rolls. These may be of cast iron, or of heated burnished iron and compressed paper (or cotton) rolls arranged alternately, with two paper rolls together in the middle. Only one roll is power-driven, friction driving the others. Paper is passed through under pressure to be given a highly glazed finish.

See also *bowls, calender, crown* (2), *finish.*

super-calendered paper: paper which has been given an extra smooth finish in a *super-calender,* q.v.

superior figures: small figures or letters printed above a word, e.g. to draw the reader's attention to a footnote. They are cast above the mean line and often on the same body as the type with which they appear.

See also *inferior figures, reference marks.*

Supertype: see *Stringertype.*

supplement: matter forming part of a work already published and either printed immediately following the text pages of a new edition or issued with its own title-page and covers.

See also *addendum.*

surface papers: see *coated papers.*

surface printing: see *planographic printing.*

Surtees Society: a society founded in Durham in 1834 for the purpose of printing for the historian early inedited manuscripts on the history, sociology and topography of Northumbria. Its last publication was in 1864.

Swan, Sir Joseph Wilson, 1828–1914: an English physicist (originally a chemist in Newcastle) who, as early as 1860, invented a carbon filament lamp. He improved electric accumulators and photographic dry plates, and worked out several galvanic methods. In 1862 he patented an improved carbon print process, and is regarded as the inventor of carbon tissue. Swan founded the Autotype Co., London, for the manufacture of carbon tissue.

See also *photogravure*. (G.U.)

The Swan Press: a small press which was developed, about 1921, by Sidney Matthewman as a branch of his father's jobbing printing establishment in Leeds. Although the press mostly issued pamphlet editions of verse by local writers, works by Laurence Binyon, Arthur Symons, and Swinburne were also published.

swash letters: ornamental italic capitals with decorative tails and flourishes, e.g. some letters of the Caslon Old Face italic and similar founts.

swelled rules: ornamental rules for the division of matter on the title-page and elsewhere. Their use developed in the 18th century, when proprietary designs were supplied by brass-founders. Modern examples are shown.

Sweynheym, Conrad, fl. 1465–77: the German printer who, with his colleague Arnold Pannartz, introduced into Italy the craft of printing. Their first press was established in 1465 at the Benedictine house Santa Scolastica, Subiaco near Rome, whence came the first book printed in Italy to bear a date; this was 'De Divinis institutionibus' of Lactantius. (A Donatus was their first work but no copy survives.) Two years later they moved to Rome. The type they used shows the influence of humanistic script, and was a forerunner of the pure roman letter of Venice. A modern derivation of their type was cut in 1902 for the Ashendene Press.

The two printers are also remembered as the publishers of the first printed Bible in the Italian language, 1471.

Swiney Prize: a prize of £100 cash, and a cup of the same value, awarded quinquennially for a published essay on jurisprudence. The Royal Society of Arts administers a sum of money left for this purpose by George Swiney (*c.* 1786–1844).

Sydenham Society: a printing society instituted in London, in 1843, for reprinting standard English medical works and annotated translations of foreign authors. It was dissolved in 1858 and succeeded by the New Sydenham Society, which continued to publish until 1863. (M.L.)

Sympson, Benjamin, fl. 1597: a Londoner, and the first independent letter-founder in England of whom records exist (viz. his bond in 1597 to the Stationers' Company). In general, English printers used letters cast in their printing shops, and the Star Chamber Decree of 1637 only allowed four independent Founders of Letters to practise their trade. In France, type-founding had been legally recognized as a separate trade in 1539.

Syndics: the governors of the Cambridge University Press, being a syndicate of senior members appointed by the Senate for a period of years to approve, on behalf of the University, every manuscript accepted for publication. Governors to the Press were first appointed in 1698, the first syndicate in 1737.

See also *Cambridge University Press, Curatores Praeli Typographici.*

synopsis: a concise version of any piece of writing in which only the essential matter of the original is retained.

Dialogue de la vie et de
La Mort, Composé en Toscan par
Maistre Innocent Ringhiere
Gentilhomme Boulongnois.

Nouuellement traduit en Francoys par Jehan
Louueau Recteur de Chastillon de Dombes.

A Lyon.
De l'Imprimerie de Robert Granjon.
Mil. Vc. L vij.

Robert Granjon 1557

D. JUNII

JUVENALIS

ET

AULI

PERSII FLACCI

SATYRAE.

BIRMINGHAMIAE:
Typis JOHANNIS BASKERVILLE.
MDCCLXI.

1761

THE

HOLY BIBLE

Containing the Old and New
Testaments: Translated out
of the Original Tongues and
with the former Translations
diligently compared and revised by His Majesty's special
Command

Appointed to be read in Churches

OXFORD
Printed at the University Press
1935

Bruce Rogers

FINNEGANS
WAKE

by
James Joyce

London
Faber and Faber Limited

1939

T

table book: 1. an obsolete term for a note-book. (Mentioned in Pepys's Diary, May 10th, 1667.)

2. an elaborately decorated edition of a book, often covered in silk or velvet, for drawing-room display. Popular in the 19th century.

table press: a small platen printing press which could be placed on a table. Although formerly not uncommon, these machines are now limited to small jobs.

Table press

tabular work: matter set in columns, either with or without rules.

tack marks: small dots incorporated in imposing schemes for sheets printed *work and turn*, q.v. One dot is used for the first side printed and two dots for the second side printed. Tack marks are also used to indicate the printer's *side lay*, in which case the dot is placed on the edge of the paper and bleeds off. (L. K.)

tail: 1. the *margin*, q.v., at the foot of the page.

2. the bottom edge of a book.

3. the curved terminal stroke of such letters as Q, R, K.

tail cap: the nipped-over fold of leather at the foot of the spine where it forms a protecting cover for the tailband.

tailband: the correct name for a *headband*, q.v., when this is affixed also to the foot of a book, although in modern usage 'headbands' includes both head and foot.

tail-piece: a decorative device printed in the blank space which follows a chapter. Designs may be specially drawn or built up from flowers. Cf. *head-piece.*

taille-douce: the French term for a copperplate engraving.

take: the amount of copy taken by a compositor to set up in type at one time.

take down: to prepare a book for re-binding. Taking down includes removing the cover, boards, end papers, all sewing threads and lining, cleaning, bleaching, and repairing any damage. When the book is reduced to its original separate sections it is said to be *pulled* or *taken down.*

taking out turns: inserting correct types where the twin black footmarks on a galley proof indicate that a turned sort has been used.

Talbot, William Henry Fox, 1800–77: a British scientist and inventor of several important photographic and reproduction methods. He devoted himself at an early age to mathematical and physical studies. In 1839 he published his invention of a negative-positive process. In 1841 he patented the *calotype* process, q.v., in which the negative was produced on iodized silver paper developed with gallic acid. Printing was done on silver chloride paper. Talbot used calotype for illustrating several books, and D. O. Hill, 'the father of artistic photography', used the same method in the 1840's for his famous masterpieces. In 1852 Talbot discovered the sensitivity to light of a compound of dichromate and gelatine; this gave rise to several valuable methods of reproduction. He also worked on photogravure or heliogravure and invented etching with ferric chloride. He was one of the pioneers of the screen distribution of half-tones.

See also *chromate process.* (G. U.)

Talbot Press: a private press founded in Dublin by W. G. Lyon in 1912. He proposed to publish books by Irish authors, or on Ireland.

talking books: gramophone records of books, made for use by the blind. Twelve-inch discs are used, each side playing for twenty-five minutes. The National

Institute for the Blind maintains a lending library of discs.

tall copy: a book having slightly larger head and foot margins than other copies from the same printing.
See also *narrow copy.*

Tallone, Alberto, 1898– : a Parisian printer-publisher, born at Bergamo. After working in the bookselling trade in Italy he settled in Paris in 1930 with the ambition of making well-produced books at modest prices. Tallone is his own typographer, and has designed a type-face (cut for him by Charles Malin) which was first used in 1950 for an edition of Shakespeare's sonnets. He at one time observed the curious practice of never hyphenating a word at the end of a line.

tampon: the dabber used for inking a lithographic or copper printing plate.

tapes: strips of closely woven cotton material, about ½ in. wide, on to which the sections of a book may be sewn. Two are usually used, but there can be as many as five. The use of tapes is diminishing in publishers' binding.

Tate, John: see *paper-making.*

tawing: the treatment of leather with salts of iron or chromium and alum; the skins are rendered white and supple. For bookbinding purposes tawed leather is not as durable as tanned leather.
Tawed leather is also known as *Hungarian leather.*

Tchemerzine, Avenir, *c.* 1870– : a Russian colonel who came to Paris during the 1917 Revolution. Here he compiled several studies on French printing. Important are his 'Bibliographie d'éditions originales ou rares d'auteurs français des XVe, XVIe, XVIIe et XVIIIe siècles, contenant 6000 fac-similés de titres et de gravures', 10 vols., Paris, 1927–33; and 'Répertoire de livres à figures rares et précieux édités en France au XVIIe siècle' (in the Versailles Library), Paris, Catin, 1933.
Incomplete are a bibliography of science and one of medicine.

t.e.g.: the abbreviation for *top edge gilt,* q.v.

teletypesetting: a semi-automatic system of type-setting by remote control. It combines a typewriter-style keyboard, named 'multiface perforator', with the teleprinter principle, and an operating unit which is used on Linotype and Intertype casters fitted with 'adaptor' keyboards. The Teletypesetter was invented in America by Walter Morey in the early 1930's.

As copy is tapped off on the perforator keyboard, a strip of tough paper ⅞ in. wide is punched with perforations which are based on a six-unit code; there are sixty-four possible combinations. The tape can be used immediately in the same office as the perforator by feeding into a mechanical operating unit attached to the line-casting machine: this automatically operates the keyboard and sends away the line of matrices for casting the type in justified lines. Alternatively, the tape can be used for transmission of electrical impulses, by radio or wire, to a receiver or reperforator which will convert them into a duplicate of the original tape. Thus compositors in the House of Commons tap off the text of Parliamentary reports on keyboards which operate Linotype Teletypesetters in 'The Times' office. For the simultaneous production of newspapers or periodicals such transmissions can be sent to several offices over a wide area.

There is also a page printer machine, with (or without) a keyboard, which transmits and receives typewritten copy in upper and lower case. This enables a proof to be read and a correction tape made before casting begins.

The 'multiface perforator', suitable for newspaper or bookwork, is an independent portable unit with an electric motor, and comprises keyboard, perforating, counting, and justifying mechanisms. It will accommodate any fount of standard matrices from 4¾- to 30-point. For each fount a different counting magazine is used. Character values are based on the em quad which is divided into thirty-two equal parts, and the counting magazine computes matrix width from $\frac{5}{32}$ to $\frac{32}{32}$ of the particular fount em quad. Although special keyboard layouts with extra sorts have been developed for bookwork, the problem of using together two faces with different alphabet lengths, as in mixed setting, has not been solved. As tapping proceeds a pointer shows on a scale the cumulative width of the characters in a line. When the line is in the justification area of the scale, and is complete, the operator strikes the 'return' and 'elevate' keys before proceeding with the next line.

The finished tape is fed into an operating unit attached to a Linotype or Intertype. The code on the tape is automatically interpreted into the mechanical actions necessary to set matrix lines for casting. The operating unit can be switched off should supplementary manual operation be required.

While all post-war Linotypes and Intertypes can be adapted for TTS, new machines have been designed. *The High-Speed Fleet* 54 *Linotype* with four magazines, similar to the standard Model 48, is specially designed for the extra rapid movements made (ten or twelve lines a minute), and certain new features have been included. A Thermo-Blo mould cooler and automatic metal feeder are fitted.

The High-Speed Intertype, which basically resembles Model C, may also be operated with TTS equipment. This model allows the setting of any regular text face; while four main magazines can be fitted. Some moving parts are hydraulically cushioned, the mould is cooled by a thermostatically controlled fan, and various mould arrangements are possible. The *Intertype Fotosetter* can also be arranged for TTS, a combination which may have great possibilities for bookwork.

Production of up to 25,000 ens an hour has been obtained on TTS operated machines.

The advantages of the TTS in bookwork may be summarized as the increased composing machine output, a saving in proofing costs, and the elimination of standing type or plate storage charges.

Temple Sheen Press: a hand-press founded by Arthur K. Sabin at East Sheen in 1911, but moved to Bethnal Green in 1922. Editions were very small, sometimes for private circulation only, but produced with careful craftsmanship.

See also *Samurai Press*.

Tenison Psalter: see *Psalter of Alphonso*.

tensile strength: in testing paper for strength, the weight necessary to apply to a given strip of paper to break it. (M.L.)

Term catalogues: the name given to the 17th-century catalogues of new books of which the pioneer was 'Mercurius Librarius', first issued at the end of Michaelmas Term, 1668, by John Starkey and Robert Clavell, who issued numerous classified lists of current literature. As their name implies, Term catalogues were issued four times a year.

terms: 1. for the terms offered by publishers to booksellers see *half see safe, journey terms, on sale or return, partial remainders, remainders, return on full credit, returns, see safe, subscription terms, trade terms*.

2. for general terms and conditions of supply, discounts, etc., see *courtesy terms, Library Licence Scheme, Net Book Agreement, net net, non-net books, Quantity Book-Buying Scheme*.

ternion: a gathering made of up three sheets, folded once, in which form some manuscripts and early printed books were assembled.

See also *quaternion*.

tetralogy: a group of four related dramatic works, especially said of three Greek tragedies and a satiric comedy.

tetraevangelium: a book containing the four Gospels.

Texoderm: the trade name of an imitation leather fabric; strong and durable, it is also water-, stain-, and bug-proof. (M.L.)

Texoprint: a process for reproducing letterpress. When type matter has been carefully freed from all traces of printing ink, it is sprayed with dull black varnish which is then removed from the printing surfaces. In this way the image of the letters will stand out brightly against a dull black ground. Upon photographing it a transparent positive is obtained which can be used for photogravure printing. Agfa's Texoprint film is developed, fixed in hot water, and results in a gelatine relief which can be inked in an ink bath. (G.U.)

text: 1. the main body of a book, excluding the preliminaries and subsidiaries.

2. paper which has been slightly calendered to give it a smooth surface, but not sufficiently to destroy its rough-textured nature.

text-book: a book published primarily for study purposes.

text hand: the style of large, formal script used in the Middle Ages for aesthetic, literary, religious, and scientific books, headings of documents, etc. Cf. *book hand, Court hand*.

text illustrations: illustrations in the text pages as distinct from separate plates or insets. Also known as *figures* or *cuts*.

text letter: a type-face which originated in the style of handwriting used for manuscripts. Also known as *black letter* or *gothic*.

textile binding: a Renaissance binding style which, in England, was popular in the 18th century. Books were bound in ornate fabrics, sometimes satin and velvet, embellished with embroidery of coloured silk, gold or silver threads.

Textur: the German name for *lettre de forme*, q.v.

textus: a formal Gothic script used in the 12th and 13th centuries for liturgical books. The two main varieties were *textus prescissus*, in which most of the letters rested horizontally on the line, and *textus quadratus*, in which most of the letters were finished with a diamond-shaped dot. It was the latter which became the basis of 15th-century black-letter types.

See also *letters—forms and styles*.

thermoplastic binder: a machine for use in *unsewn binding*, q.v. The 'Flexiback' model made by the Book Machinery Co., of London, in one continuous operation removes the folds and roughens the page edges at the back, applies three flows of glue (between each leaf, on the roughened back, on the lining), and welds the book into a unit. Rounding and backing follow, and it is claimed that such books open quite flat.

thermoplastic plates: printing plates made from any plastic which becomes soft in heating and sets again when cooled, in contrast to thermosetting material which is relatively soft when received, but becomes hard when heated and remains hard whether hot or cold. It is usual to make moulds from type or blocks using thermosetting material, e.g. bakelite, and from these moulds to make thermoplastic plates.

See also *plastic plates*, *Sicoplast*.

thesaurus: literally, a treasury or storehouse of knowledge; a term now especially associated with P. M. Roget's 'Thesaurus of English Words and Phrases . . .', Longmans, 1852, which is still issued in revised editions.

thickening: a term used in lithography when printing ink tends to spread from the image areas.

thickness copy: a publisher's dummy of a book made up of the actual number of pages it will require, and using the same paper that will be employed for printing. Among other purposes it is used for designing the jacket and planning lettering for the spine.

See also *dummy*.

thirty-twomo: written 32mo. A book size resulting from (notionally) folding a sheet of paper with five right-angle folds, thus giving a page size of one thirty-second of the sheet. In practice it is seldom practicable to fold paper more than four times, thus a half sheet folded four times would normally be used. From Crown paper the resulting size would be $3\frac{3}{4}$ in × $2\frac{1}{2}$ in. viz. Crown 32mo. Also called trigesimo-secundo. (L.K.)

Thomas Forman Scholarship: a scholarship of up to £250 per annum, tenable at the University of Nottingham, awarded to an approved candidate who, at the time it is made, is employed in the printing industry (but not in the ancillary trades). Particulars can be obtained from the Registrar of the University.

Thomas Harrison Memorial Award: a series of prizes totalling fifty guineas awarded to students of craft bookbinding. In 1955 a fund was launched in London to finance a memorial, in the form of an annual award, to Thomas Harrison (1876–1955). He was an influential craftsman-binder who, after working with several London firms, gained a considerable reputation for his free-lance work. He lectured to trade audiences in London and elsewhere, and in 1946 his services to bookbinding were recognized by the award of the O.B.E.

The first memorial award was made in 1957.

Thomason, George, *c.* 1601–66: a London bookseller who, between 1640 and 1661, assembled a unique and important collection of pamphlets, newspapers, and fugitive pieces dealing with daily events in those troubled years.

The Thomason Tracts, as the 22,000 or more pieces are known, were given to the British Museum by George III in 1762.

Thompson, Henry Yates, 1838–1928: an English bibliophile. In 1880 he acquired the 'Pall Mall Gazette' from his father-in-law, George Smith. Thompson's main interests as a bibliophile were illuminated manuscripts and books printed on parchment. In 1897 he bought for £30,000 part of the Ashburnham collection, and in 1902 items from John Ruskin's library. At a series of auction sales (1919–21) he sold about a hundred works for £150,000. His widow is still in possession of part of his library.

Thorne, Robert, fl. 1794–1820: a London typefounder who was apprenticed to *Thomas Cottrell*, q.v., and whose foundry he acquired in 1794. He is remembered for his fat-face jobbing founts, the popularity of which he did much to further. His skill led the Imprimerie Nationale, Paris, to commission a fount of fat face from his foundry.

Thorne's Fann Street Foundry was subsequently bought by *William Thorowgood*, q.v.

Thorowgood, William, fl. 1820–49: a London typefounder whose first connection with the craft was the purchase in 1820 of the Fann Street Foundry of *Robert Thorne*, q.v., yet within two years he was appointed Letter-Founder to George IV. In 1828 he acquired the foundry of Dr. Edmund Fry, and with it an important collection of oriental and greek founts. About 1838 he took Robert Besley (1794–1876) into partnership. Thorowgood retired in 1849 and the firm operated as Robert Besley & Co. Besley's partner, Benjamin Fox, was in 1845 responsible for the heavy egyptian face known as *Clarendon*. In 1861 the firm was joined by the printer Charles Reed (1819–81).

On the death of Fox in 1877 the name was changed to Sir Charles Reed & Sons (one of whom was the type historian and writer Talbot Baines Reed). The firm was sold in 1905 to *Stephenson Blake & Co.*, q.v., of Sheffield.

Thouvenin, Joseph, 1790–1834: a famous Parisian binder and pupil of *Bozérian*, q.v. Thouvenin was noted for his revival of past styles, especially *fanfare*, q.v. His annual output of *c.* 3000 volumes was bound for wealthy English and Russian patrons.

thread: see *sewing thread.*

three-colour reproduction: almost all colour can be reproduced by the superimposing of three colours: yellow, blue green (cyan) and magenta (red). Such plates are obtained by photography through filters of the complementary colours, i.e. red for cyan, blue for yellow and green for magenta ('red'). The possibility of three-colour reproduction is dependent upon the nature of human colour vision. This provides a convenient and economical method for colour printing. The use of a fourth, black printer, is not a technical necessity, but in practice makes it much easier to retain good quality. The eye is very sensitive to slight changes of hue such as may occur due to slight variations of one of three colours. The use of a black printing makes it easier to obtain neutral shadows and brightens the picture by making the dense shadows more intense. It is still difficult to make a perfect black plate and perfect four-colour reproduction would make use of the following facts: a dull green in three colours would be obtained by use of nearly solid yellow and cyan printings with an appreciable magenta printing. The same result could be obtained by use of black instead of the magenta and slightly less yellow and blue. If this could be carried out easily, although four printings were used, in any one spot no more than three would be present and in the brightest places only two. Brown would consist of yellow and magenta with a little black and so on.

Not only is it theoretically possible to match any colour with three printings out of the four mentioned above, but unless the colour is an exceptionally bright one the hues of ink are not critical, although to match a particular colour the duller the three primary inks the less black will be required. Until recently it has in fact been the custom to use inks which depart some way from the theoretically desirable. The yellow, although not always the same, was not markedly wrong, but the magenta was often red and the cyan often redder and darker than theory would require. In fact, these colour errors were less serious than might be expected and only caused practical difficulty when bright greens or bright purples were required. As the techniques of colour reproduction still involved a large amount of retouching or fine etching according to the process used there were no added difficulties in obtaining good colour reproduction, except for the bright colours mentioned above. Few scenes in nature and few great paintings contain any of these very bright colours.

The reasons for using such inks were partly lack of good pigments, but probably mostly due to a failure to understand the theoretical requirement. The use of the words 'red' and 'blue' rather than 'magenta' and 'cyan' does emphasize the misunderstanding. It was common to vary the exact hue to suit the subjects. This did not matter when single subjects were printed, but caused serious difficulty when several subjects were printed together.

Today, when rapid scientific development is taking place in colour correction by masking or electronic methods, and when it is normal practice to print many subjects together, the use of standard colours is even more important than the use of theoretically correct colours. Colour letterpress and colour lithographic inks are both standardized in a number of countries including Britain and Germany. The use of the brighter and more correct inks makes much cleaner greens, purples and blues possible, but it also makes even inking more important for the printer, as slight variations in any one ink will cause greater variation in the resultant colour.

The eye, although very critical in its judgement of two objects side by side is, in other respects, very tolerant. It is well known that the eye adapts itself easily to different lighting systems, e.g. daylight or incandescent, but it is also true that two subjects printed together will require much more careful colour correction and printing than if seen separately, even if the nature of the subject is quite different. The fact that one has a greenish cast and the other a reddish cast may only be obvious when they are side by side. The measurement of colour by physical instruments is still not easily carried out with an accuracy which would satisfy an ordinary man with ordinary colour vision. The critic must realize that the scientific reproduction of colour has still some way to go before it can reproduce all colour accurately and his own judgement may in fact be at fault sometimes, owing to conditions in which he is viewing the reproduction. The use of black or white or coloured surrounds will each cause the picture to appear different.

Although to the layman colour accuracy may seem the most important factor, it is probably true that tone accuracy or good choice of tone separation is even more important. One reproduction may be correct in colour, but seem dead as compared with another which is less accurate in colour. A typical example is the reproduction of an oil painting with dense glossy shadows.

Colours, too, affect each other. A colour adjacent to white appears paler than one adjacent to black; red and green each appear much brighter than if side by side. These and other changes can be noticeable enough to cause the same colour to appear markedly different in hue and strength.

See also *colour photography, colour systems, colour vision, two-colour reproduction, and plate.* (H. J. J.)

three-decker novel: three small octavo volumes which, in the early 19th century, became the standard form for publishing fiction. They usually had paper-covered boards and a paper label bearing the title, and were not illustrated. While their format improved in the mid-century, when cloth boards were used, their production declined in the nineties.

See also *fiction series, yellow-backs.*

3M Brand photo offset plates: the trade name of presensitized aluminium offset-litho plates introduced in 1953 by the Minnesota Mining & Manufacturing Co. of America. As their name suggests, the plates come from the makers ready for exposure. Grained aluminium plates are given a coating of a diazo-resin compound. After exposure under an arc lamp the plate is developed by applying 3M Process Gum and Rapid Desensitizer to the whole surface. A patent image developer is then sponged on until a deep red image appears; washing follows, prior to a final coating with the process gum. After mounting on the press the gum is washed off.

The plates are dimensionally stable, of great strength, and are not affected by oxidation, press-room temperature, or humidity. Half-tone reproductions of up to 300-line screens can be printed with good results.

three-quarter binding: a binding style with the spine and a generous portion of the sides covered in leather or cloth, the rest of the sides being in another coloured cloth or paper.

thrown out: said of a folded map or plan printed with a page-width guard. The opened map can thus be seen while the text is being read.

thumb index: an alphabetical or subject index cut into the fore-edge of a book to facilitate quick reference.

Thurston, John, 1774–1822: a distinguished book illustrator of his time, much of whose work, in the form of wood engravings, appeared in editions of verse and prose published by the *Chiswick Press,* q.v. He also did the designs for Ackermann's 'Religious Emblems', 1809, for which *Clennel, Nesbit,* qq.v., and others engraved the blocks.

ticket: a small paper label bearing the printed or engraved name of a bookbinder. Such tickets are usually found at the head or foot of the front or rear paste-down. This means of signing a binding occurs in English and French work of the early 18th century, and is still practised. Booksellers also use similar tickets.

Tickhill Psalter: an English Psalter of the early 14th century written, according to an inscription in it (but not universally accepted as genuine), by John Tickyll, Prior of Worksop, Notts. It is thought more probable that he merely applied and burnished the gold. It was skilfully illuminated by others. Features of the illustrations are scrolls which form the basis of nearly every page; the scenes depicted are based on the Old Testament. The figures are characterized by a certain simplicity, and drawings from nature of flowers also appear. The work is now in the New York Public Library.

tied letters: see *ligature.*

Tiemann, Walter, 1876–1951: a German book illustrator and typographer. From 1920–45 he directed the Staatliche Akademie für graphische Künste, Leipzig. Tiemann illustrated books for the Insel-Verlag, and designed at least sixteen type-faces for *Klingspor,* q.v. He was associated with Carl Ernst Poeschel in founding the *Janus-Presse,* q.v.

(With G.U.)

ties: 1. tapes fixed to the front edges of a book cover to facilitate handling and to secure a volume of unbound plates. Their use is common with vellum bindings which tend to warp.

2. terminations to lines tooled on each side of raised bands on the spine of a book, which are continued on to the covers as an ornamental feature.

tight back: a book cover which is glued to the body of the book at the back, a style used for flexibly sewn and library bindings. No supporting hollow is formed when the book is opened. A weakness is that the spinal lettering tends to crack with use. Cf. *hollow back.*

See also *sawn-in back.*

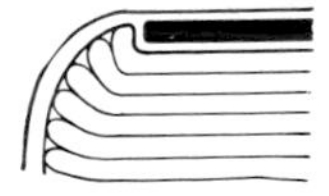

Tight back

Tilghmann, Benjamin Chew: see *sulphite pulp.*

timework: the system of wage payment whereby the amount earned is based upon the hours worked. Cf. *piecework.* (L.K.)

tint blocks: blocks for printing flat background colours; they may be engraved in various patterns or stipples to give an illusion of colour, depth, or tone.

See also *mechanical tints.*

tip: a thin flat brush consisting of a few camel or squirrel hairs fixed between two pieces of card. It is used for taking up gold leaf and applying it to a surface to be gilded.

tipped in: said of separately printed illustrations or maps which are cut to the size of the book, the inner margins being pasted into the text before gathering. An illustration so affixed is also known as a *paste in.*

tipping machine: a bookbinding machine for the gluing of end-papers or single plates on to folded sheets. There are various models. Usually the folded section and end-paper or plate are fed in separately from left to right, edged with paste along the back edge, and pressed together. (G.U.)

Tipping machine

tissued plate: see *interleaved* (2).

title-page: the page at the beginning of a book giving the title and sub-title, the author's name and his qualifications, the publisher's imprint, and sometimes a colophon and the date of publication. The reverse often states the edition or impression, printer's name, statement of copyright, and occasionally typographical information.

The development of the title-page was gradual and may be said to have begun with 'Bulla cruciatae contra turcos . . .' printed by Fust and Schöffer in 1463; this, however, was a *label title*, q.v. A further approach to the title-page proper was in the 'Kalendarius' of Johannes Müller, called Regiomontanus, issued in 1476 at Venice by Ratdolt and Maler; the introductory verse on the first page was surrounded by a graceful woodcut border of flower and leaf designs while the printers, place of printing, and date were stated. The first book to include on its title-page the information now customary (see above) was printed by Wolfgang Stöckel of Leipzig in 1500.

The first English book with a title-page was Canutus's 'A passing gode lityll boke . . . agenst the pestilence', printed by W. de Machlinia, *c.* 1490.

The possibilities of the title-page for decorative display were realized quite early in the 16th century. Not a few 16th-century title-pages had as the basic element of their design the Roman columned portico, the lettering being printed between the pillars. This was common to books printed in all European countries where printing was then practised, and may be thought to signify that by reading the succeeding pages one entered the classical world (it will be remembered that most books of the period were classics or written in Latin). An important subsidiary decorative feature was the medallion, based on Roman coins. Early Spanish title-pages in particular are typified by large heraldic emblems.

The colophon, which from ancient Egyptian times had supplied the author's name and title, gradually fell into disuse.

See also *incipit, initia, label title.*

title-page border: the frame, being a pattern built up from type ornaments, set round the matter on the title-page.

title signature: a signature mark is not printed on the first sheet of a book, this being termed the *title sheet*, thus the term *signature A* (*or* 1) is not used. The second sheet, however, is printed with the mark *B* (*or* 2), thereby indicating that there is a section to precede it. (L.K.)

titling alphabet: a fount of capital letters cast without shoulders so that the strokes of the character extend to the limits of the body, there being no beard. This is done to balance the space between lines. Ranging numerals and punctuation marks are included, but not lower-case letters.

Tom-Gallon Trust: an award made in alternate years by the administrators of the trust, the Society of Authors, being about £100 a year for two years paid to a fiction writer of modest means.

tonal colour: the effect of lightness or heaviness which a printed page gives. Among factors affecting this are the type-face used, e.g. Caslon and Perpetua have light faces, Bodoni and Plantin dark; the use of leads will increase the apparent lightness, and the surface of the paper is important, e.g. an antique paper will make type appear darker.

See also *full colour.*

tone engraving: see *wood engraving.*

toned paper: printing paper, pale buff or deep cream.

Tonson, Jacob: an eminent Restoration printer-publisher by whom works of Dryden, Congreve, and Pope were issued. He published the first illustrated Shakespeare in 1709-10, and an important edition of Caesar, edited by Samuel Clarke, in 1712. He was succeeded by descendants bearing the same name.

tooling: the impressing by hand on book covers of decoration and lettering, for which brass letters, dies, pallets, and rolls are used. Cloth bindings are given little decoration, often only the title on the spine, and tooling refers principally to work on leather covers: the craftsman who does the work is known as the *finisher*.

Blind tooling is done without leaf or foil; for *gold tooling*, q.v., gold in leaf or spool form is used. The use of a press and large dies is known as *blocking*.

The main stages of tooling are: (*a*) preparing, which includes marking with a bone folder the position of the chief lines, *blinding in*, the object being to enable the priming to be done at the precise place for the decoration, washing over with very thin paste and water to fill the pores before *priming* with glair, and rubbing over with vaseline; (*b*) laying-on, which means applying the leaf so that there is an unbroken layer of gold over the whole surface to be decorated; (*c*) pressing the gold with heated tools (which should just cease to hiss before use), whereupon the albumen in the glair coagulates and fixes the gold to the leather; (*d*) cleaning and polishing, the surplus gold being wiped off with a rubber from which it is later recovered, any vaseline is wiped off with petrol and cottonwool, and the finished decoration is cleaned, polished and pressed between polished nickel plates. (With G.U.)

See also *skewings*.

Tooling a doublure (with a roll)

The leather joint between the book and its cover is also visible.

top edge gilt: a book having only the top edge gilded, the fore and foot edges being left plain. Abbreviated *t.e.g.*

tops and tails: an expression used in some printing offices for preliminary and subsidiary matter.

Torresano, Andrea, fl. 1481–1529: a printer of Venice who, in 1481, bought the punches, matrices, and types of Jenson on the latter's decease. About 1500 his daughter married Aldus Manutius, and the two businesses were combined. Upon the death in 1515 of Aldus the Aldine press was directed by Torresano.

Tory, Geofroy, *c.* 1480–1533: of Bourges, a famous

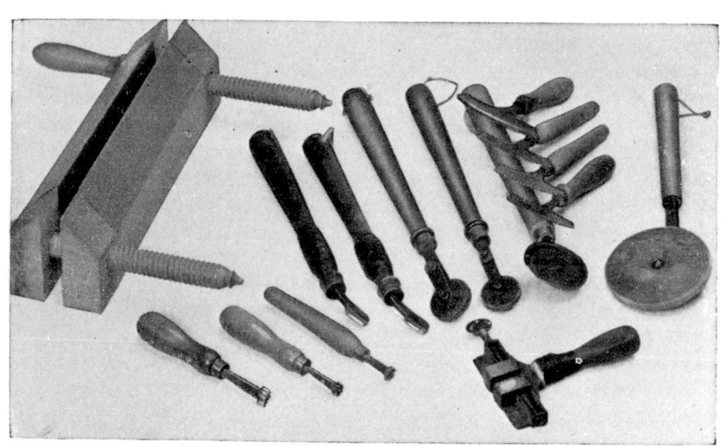

The finisher's hand-tools

Top, book clamp, two irons, three rolls, four pallets, and a laying-on wheel. Below, three small decorative dies and a pallet for holding a line of brass lettering

The finisher at work

The book is held in a clamp while decoration on the spine is impressed with a heated iron

French typographer, bookseller, engraver, and printer. Before opening his shop in Paris, *c.* 1522, he edited Latin texts for Parisian printers. His studies in Italy undoubtedly inspired his designs for roman faces, also the characteristic border decorations of his title-pages; these were light outlines on white backgrounds. His actual printing from his own press is thought to date from 1529, in which year his 'Champ Fleury' appeared: this is a work of importance to all students of letter design.

See also *entrelac initials, pot cassé.*

Tottel, Richard, fl. 1553–94: a London printer and stationer. He was an original member of the Stationers' Company, in which he held various high offices.

He held a patent for all common law books, but his importance for us stems from his literary publications. Notable were More's 'Dialogue of comfort', 1553; Lydgate's 'Fall of princes', 1554; and Grimald's translation of Cicero's 'De officiis', 1556. In June 1557 he brought out his famous 'Miscellany' of 271 poems: included were the poems of Sir Thomas Wyatt and Henry Howard, Earl of Surrey—the only form in which their verse survived for posterity. Wyatt developed the Elizabethan sonnet, and Surrey was the first to use blank verse. The Miscellany, entitled 'Songes and sonettes, written by Henry Haward late Earle Surrey, and other' (STC 13860), was thus a book of great significance in our literature. The first edition survives in a single copy: this is in the Bodleian Library. It was republished with additions and deletions in the same year and later.

Totum: a complete Roman Breviary.

Toy, Robert, fl. 1540–56: a London printer. From his press in St Paul's Churchyard he issued several theological works, Matthew's folio Bible, 1551, and a reprint of Thynne's Chaucer in 1555. He was a member and benefactor of the Stationers' Company.

His son, Humphrey (*c.* 1540–77), succeeded to the business, and was occasionally an official of the Company. He printed works in Welsh, and also William Salusbury's 'Playne and Familiar Introduction, teaching how to pronounce the Letters in the Brytishe Tongue, now commonly called Welshe', 1567.

tract: 1. a book or pamphlet devoted to one subject, usually religious or political. Also known as *tractate.*

2. a pamphlet made from a single sheet imposed in pages.

trade binding: 1. the plain calf or sheep bindings in which books were sold in England from the 15th–18th centuries: they only rarely bore spinal lettering. As an alternative, and until the 19th century, the purchaser usually bought the book unbound, or enclosed in wrappers, to be specially bound to his order.

2. another name for publisher's binding.

Trade books: see *Chapter books.*

trade catalogues: lists of books, systematically arranged by author or subject, and issued by publishers for the use of booksellers, or by booksellers for making their stocks known to the public. Georg Willer, an Augsburg bookseller, issued the first-known catalogue of this kind; this was a subject list of 256 titles, dated 1564. Catalogues were also issued at the great German book trade fairs of Leipzig (the first was by Henning Gross, 1595) and Frankfurt (1564): the fairs are still held.

In England, Andrew Maunsell (*d.* 1596), a bookseller of St Paul's, was the first publisher of an important alphabetical trade list of books. His earliest was a list of religious works; his second, medical and scientific.

See also *Term catalogues.*

trade edition: copies of a standard work which are regularly printed and supplied to booksellers at wholesale rates.

trade sales: auction sales of publishers' remainders at which only booksellers were invited to bid. The practice of disposing in this way of surplus stocks may have begun in late 17th-century Britain. After 1820 such sales also took place in Philadelphia and Boston, U.S.A.

The practice of holding large-scale auctions for the trade appears to have ceased about 1870.

trade terms: publishers' discount scales and payment dates allowed to booksellers.

See also *returns, see safe.*

Trajanus-Presse: the private press of the Frankfurt typefounding firm D. Stempel A.G. It was established in 1951 for the production of news-letters, type specimens, etc., in addition to occasional books. Their excellence and high standard has made these items sought as collectors' pieces by typophiles and others.

tranchefile: extra wires parallel to the chains at each end of the paper-making mould, and spaced a short distance from them. They leave an impression in the paper about half-way between the outer chain lines and the edges of the sheet. These are particularly noticeable in certain French papers.

transfer: a surfaced paper bearing a thickly inked image taken from an impression on a non-lithographic surface for transferring to a lithographic plate or stone. Lithographic transfers can be made from engraved plates, music on pewter plates, letterpress (including half-tone blocks) and drawings made with lithographic crayons or ink on transfer papers or on hard-sized papers. A transfer made from an existing lithographic forme is properly termed a *retransfer*, q.v.

A transfer worker's tools for a hand-press: fan, dabber, sponge, pumice stone, pins, leather roller

The original forme is inked with special transfer ink, and the impression is taken on prepared transfer paper, usually in a hand-press; should the impression be taken from a stone or plate a scraper press is used. If the illustration is to be placed in the new forme at right-angles to its position in the original, which is often the case in transfers for offset, it can be turned; it is more usual, however, in such cases not to take a direct impression on the transfer paper, but via a rubber cloth and a reversing apparatus, a reducing apparatus, or an offset hand-press.

When the impressions which together are to make up the new illustration have been taken, they are mounted by stabbing on a sheet which has been marked up in readiness for this. The impressions are fixed to the support by small stabs with the stabbing pin, and the mounted sheet is laid with the transfer paper towards the slightly damped surface of a lithographic stone or plate. A smooth plate or glossy cardboard is laid over the sheet and the whole is run through a transfer press of larger size. After running down, the transfer paper adheres to the surface of the stone or plate and the stabbing sheet may be removed. The backs of the remaining transfer papers are damped, some sheets of waste paper are laid on top, and the papers are again run through the press. Finally, greater damping with water is done, by which means the layer of transfer paper is released and can be removed, leaving the thick illustration on the new forme. This is finished off by gumming, rubbing with ink-turpentine, and powdering with resin, or by washing with bitumen on the dry or damp gum, and finally by etching (in the lithographic sense).

It is also possible by means of the transfer process to transfer an illustration from an old impression made by letterpress or lithographic printing, an *anastatic transfer*. (G.U.)

transfer paper: the paper on which an inked impression is brought to a lithographic surface where it then becomes the printing forme. It is usually a fairly thin, semi-gummed paper bearing a surface coating of substances soluble in water: there are many varieties. A common type of transfer paper is made by giving the sheet an undercoating of starch paste, gelatine, and some glycerine. This undercoating is soluble in water. The main layer now superimposed on it is rather less soluble and consists of a mixture of gelatine, starch, barium sulphate, and glycerine (among alternative ingredients for such layers are gum arabic, plaster of Paris, and flour). When dried the paper has a dull surface with great power of suction, but must be damped before use by laying it between damp waste paper. If such paper is given a further layer of albumen *Berlin paper* is obtained; this has a glossy, close surface, so that the ink has less tendency to penetrate into the layer. This paper, which is particularly suitable for half-tones, is used in a dry state, but in making transfers the plate or stone which is to receive the transfer must first be damped.

Another kind of transfer paper, known as *Everdamp*, is permanently moist due to its high glycerine content; this remains so moist that it can be used without further damping. In addition to glycerine the layer contains starch, gum arabic, and often chrome yellow (lead chromate) or gamboge.

Ordinary paper, not specially treated, can also be used as transfer paper, especially if it is heavily gummed and polished. (G.U.)

transfer press: a lithographic hand-press in which pressure is exerted by means of a scraper, i.e. a narrow disc standing on edge, usually of hard wood covered with leather. The scraper is placed against the plate or sheet of cardboard which covers the transfer paper resting on the flat forme; the bed is then rolled forward under the scraper. Hand or motor power may be used. Presses of larger size, intended for transferring on to large machine plates, sometimes have a steel roller instead of a scraper (see illustration). Space is saved if the scraper or roller is moved across a stationary bed, or if both the bed and roller move laterally. (G.U.)

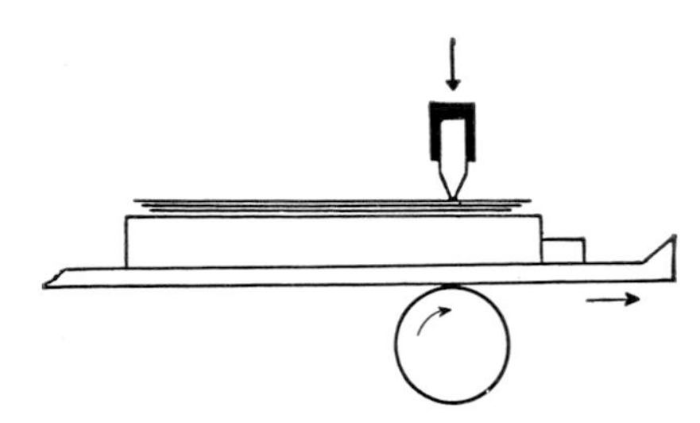

Principle of the scraper press. Pressure is adjustable; the transfer paper resting on the movable bed is protected by a plate which is lubricated to facilitate its motion under the scraper

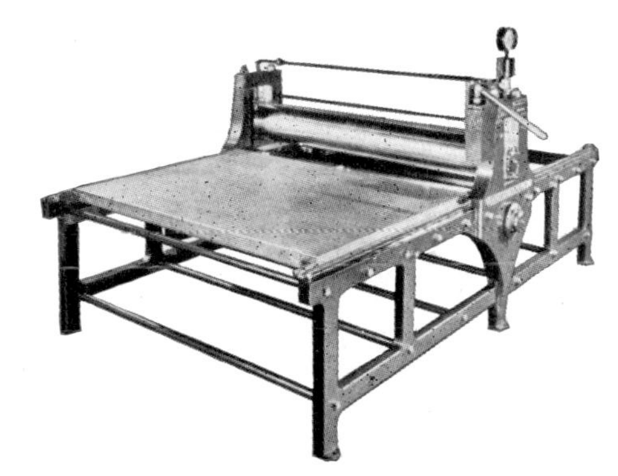

Hydraulic transfer press. The dial indicates the hydraulic pressure in lb. per sq. in. The bed rolls between the steel pressure cylinder (visible in illustration) and the driving cylinder (of which only the bearing is visible). (*Harris–Seybold*)

transitional: a name sometimes given to the type-face designed by John Baskerville, and its derivatives. While retaining the bracketed serifs of old face it suggests in its precision the engraved quality of modern-face types.

transliterate: to render the letters or characters of one alphabet by those of another so as to represent the same sound.

transparency (transparent positive): an exposed and developed film intended to be looked at against light, or projected through a projector. Transparent positives are produced as an intermediate stage in a number of reproduction processes. (G.U.)

transparent bindings: books covered with vellum which has been treated with pearl ash to make it transparent. This process was patented by *Edwards of Halifax*, q.v., in 1785.

transpose: the instruction written in the margin of proofs as *trs.* to indicate that the order of lines, words or letters must be changed.

Trattner, Johann Thomas, 1717–98: a Viennese printer and publisher who also developed his type-foundry into a prosperous business. Trattner published several books on the history of printing. He cut an extensive range of ornaments of which his celebrated 'angel' is shown under *flowers*, q.v.

Trautz, Georges, 1808–79: a German bookbinder who settled in Paris in 1830. He worked as a gilder for his father-in-law, *Antoine Bauzonnet*, q.v. Bindings made prior to 1851 were signed Bauzonnet–Trautz, but in possibly this year Trautz took over the business and rapidly became the leading French bookbinder of the century: work was signed Trautz–Bauzonnet. Many books were bound in the style of Joseph Thouvenin, all were sumptuous, costly, and commissioned by none but the wealthiest bibliophiles of Europe and America.

traveller's samples: certain signatures of a book, case-bound and jacketed, for submission to prospective buyers. Cf. *blad.*

travelling tympan: see *shifting tympan.*

tree-calf: calf book covers treated in a manner similar to *mottled* or *sprinkled calf*, qq.v., in which a sponge dipped in acid is used to stain the design of a tree. This was a feature of some 19th-century English bindings, but as the acid was ultimately damaging to the skin its use was not extensive.

See also *Etruscan bindings.*

Trevecca Press: a printing press established about 1770 at Trevecca, near Talgarth in Wales, as part of the Methodist revival there. The press appears to have been erected at the instigation of Howell Harris who led the Methodist community. The name of the first printer is unknown, but Thomas Roberts, his apprentice, was printer until *c.* 1796. 'E. Roberts & Co.' and 'Hughes & Co.' were subsequent imprints until 1805 when the press was moved to Talgarth, remaining in operation until at least 1829.

Many of the hundred or so works issued between 1770 and 1805 were Welsh hymn-books, religious propaganda, and elegies (marwnadau). Small pica and long primer were the two sizes of type used, and there was a case of ornaments for borders, initials, and tailpieces.

A collection of Trevecca Press publications is in Cardiff Public Library.

Treveris, Peter, fl. 1522–32: a printer of Southwark, London. He is remembered for several small grammatical tracts; an edition of Robert Whittinton's 'Syntaxis', 1522; a 'Grete herball', 1526 (STC 13176); and John de Trevisa's translation into English of Higden's 'Polychronicon', 1527.

trigesimo-secundo: see *thirty-twomo.*

Tridentine Index: an alternative name for the *Index librorum prohibitorum*, q.v.

trimmed edges: properly, said of a book having a cut top edge, and with only the larger projecting leaves of the tail and fore-edge trimmed down; they are thus left with a rough appearance. Cf. *cut edges.*

trimmed flush: see *cut flush.*

trimmers: various tools for planing and cutting used when casting types, stereos, or making blocks, etc., to ensure that adjacent surfaces will all be at right-angles and fit flush. Also known as *dressers.* (G.U.)

trimming: the bookbinding process of cutting away about ⅛ in. from each edge of a sewn book: the folds are thereby removed.

triple lining: a method of *lining up*, q.v., used for better-quality cased books. The work is done mechanically in seven stages. Briefly, these are the first coating of the back with glue; application of a strip of mull, inset slightly from the top and bottom edges of the back; second gluing; application of a broad strip of three-taped mull which has a carry-over on either side of the back for securing to the case; third gluing; positioning and securing of a crêpe manila lining, with head- and tailbands if required; and rubbing down with pneumatic rollers.

Troper: a book containing the musical interpolations or tropes. Tropes were the words or verses of embellishment to the text of a Mass, and they were discontinued at the revision of the Roman Missal under Pope Pius V in the 16th century.

trs.: the proof-corrector's abbreviation for *transpose*, q.v.

ts.: *typescript*, q.v.

T.S.: the abbreviation for *tub-sized*, q.v.

Tschichold, Jan, 1902– : one of Europe's leading calligraphers and typographers. When only eighteen he taught the first subject in the evening classes at the Graphic Arts Academy of his native Leipzig. As in his own case, he claims that a successful typographer should first study calligraphy. His many writings on the two subjects have had a considerable influence in western Europe.

At one period he worked in England as typographical adviser to Penguin Books Ltd.

Types designed by him include Transito, 1931, a display type cut for the Amsterdam Typefoundry; and Saskia, 1932, for Schelter & Giesecke.

tub-sized: said of hand-made sheets of waterleaf which have been dipped into a tub of animal glue, gelatine, or a prepared starch (or a combination of these). The sheets are dried on cow-hair ropes or hessian. They are then glazed. If machine-made papers are to be tub-sized, the roll coming from the paper machine is unwound and fed into a tub of size from which it emerges to be rolled, dried, and calendered. Tub-sized paper is strong and has a high resistance to moisture. Abbreviated as *T.S.* Cf. *animal-sized, engine-sized.*

tumbler scheme: the method of perfecting sheets to be printed from a forme imposed in the oblong or landscape manner. To obtain correct page sequence, the sheet must be turned, or tumbled, in its short direction.

See also *work and tumble.*

tung: a wood oil used as an alternative to linseed oil in printing ink.

Turkey leather: skins prepared with oil before the hair was removed, and after further processing which included staining in a distinctive shade of red, used for bookbinding.

Turkey morocco: originally, a goatskin that came from Turkey. Now, the texture is imitated by using goatskins finished with a fine, hard grain, or a bold cross-grain.

turned chain lines: abnormally placed chain lines, e.g. horizontal in folios, have been explained by the use of half-sheets of paper double the normal size. Also due to paper being made two sheets at a time on a divided mould. (M.L.)

turned sort: type letter used foot uppermost for one not to hand or not known, e.g. page number.

See also *taking out turns.*

turning-in corners: the binding stage when the leather or cloth is stretched over the corner of the cover by means of a corner iron. (G.U.)

Turning-in corners with a corner iron

twelvemo: written 12mo. The book size resulting from folding a sheet into twelve leaves (twenty-four pages) by means of right-angle folds. To define fully the size, the size of the paper must also be stated, e.g. Royal 12mo. Also called *duodecimo.* (L.K.)

twenty-fourmo: written 24mo. The book size resulting from folding a sheet into twenty-four leaves (forty-eight pages) by means of right-angle folds. To define fully the size, the size of the paper must also be stated, e.g. Royal 24mo. Also called *vigesimo-quarto.* (L. K.)

twin-wire paper: paper made on twin wire belts so that by bringing the two wet webs together, wire side innermost, a single sheet is formed with two top, or felt, sides. Such paper is eminently suitable for offset printing. Also known as *duplex paper.*

two-colour press: a machine printing two colours at one time. Most offset printing today is carried out on two-colour machines as the construction of a rotary two-colour machine is a straightforward engineering proposition, although the actual cylinder arrangements vary considerably in different makes.

two-colour reproduction can often resemble full three-colour printing. The colours used are generally green or blue, and orange. The economy of using only two colours is obvious, but subjects must be chosen carefully, as results can sometimes be crude (see plate).

two-line letters: capital letters having a body depth extending over two lines of the type with which they are used, e.g. as an initial capital for the first word of a chapter.

two-magazine mixer: a name given to any Linotype or Intertype machine in which the matrices from two magazines can be mixed and set in one line. (G.U.)

A Miller Major two-revolution press with swing-out feeder. (Miller Printing Machinery Co., Pittsburgh)

two-revolution press: a flat-bed cylinder machine in which the cylinder which carries the paper makes two revolutions for each impression. Printing is done during the first revolution, the bed with the forme returning during the second (the cylinder being kept raised), also during this second revolution the sheet is delivered. The cylinder revolves at a constant speed on early models; however, on recent models of both two-revolution and single-revolution machines this principle is abandoned, the aim being to allow

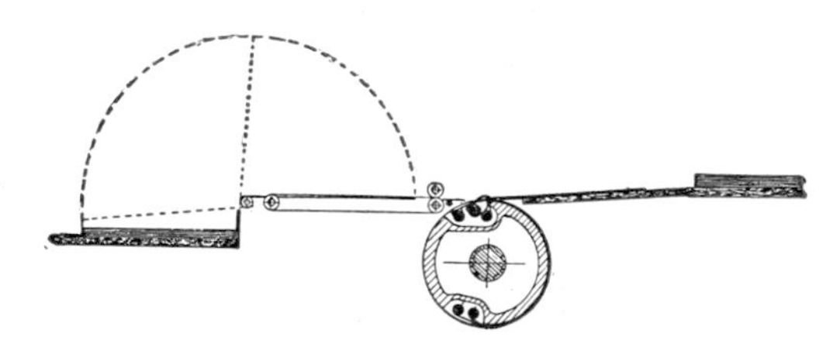

The earliest two-revolution presses had rack delivery

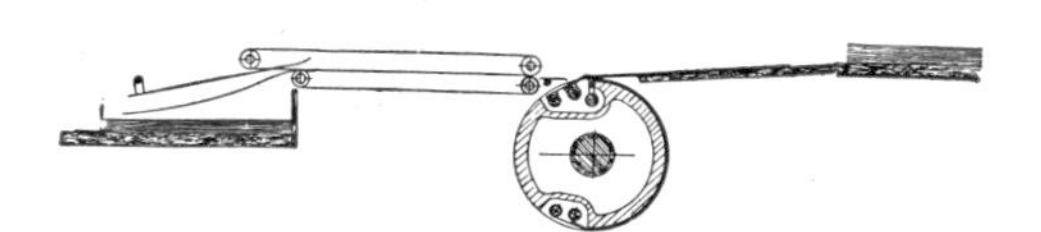

Scheme for frontal delivery, the sheet with the impression side uppermost

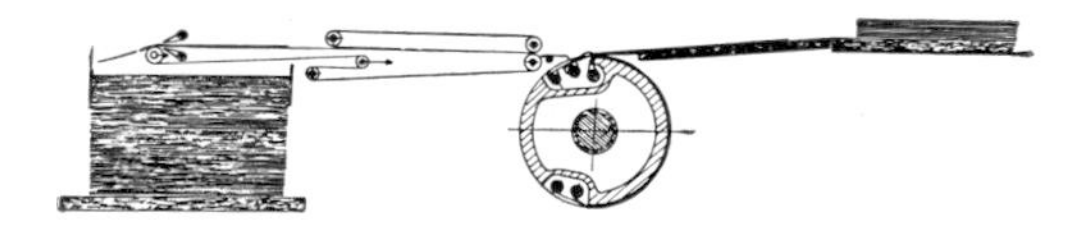

Babcock's frontal delivery scheme. The tape conveyor moves to and fro

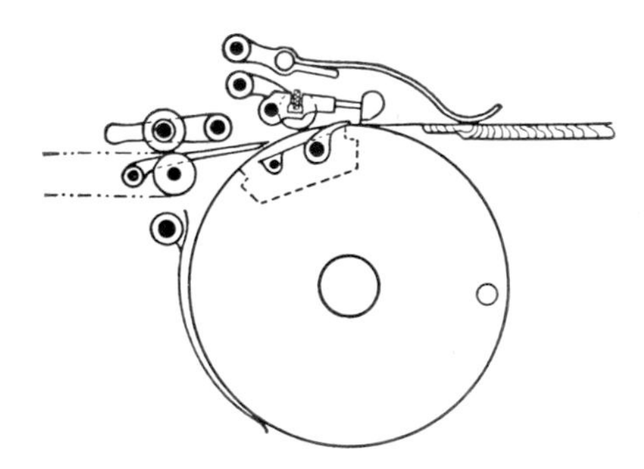

Impression cylinder. From the right: feeding table with sheet holder; guide or lay; gripper in the cylinder hollow; between them (partly visible on the left of the gripper) the shoo fly which raises the sheet when the grippers release it so that it slides out on to the bridge and over to the tapes. Below, left, the sheet band for keeping the sheet stretched round the cylinder

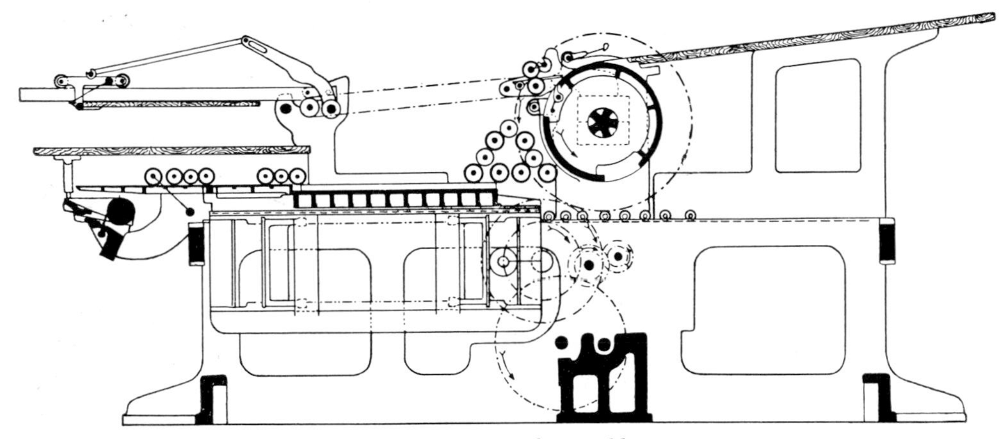

Diagram of a Miehle

longer time for the actual printing while quickening the return of the bed, in some cases with a varying cylinder speed in consequence. The Miehle 29 is an example.

Early two-revolution presses were constructed by König in 1814 and David Napier in 1828. As the

Driving gears on a Planeta two-revolution press

cylinder makes two revolutions between each impression, the feeding can be done from one side of it and delivery off the other; it was some time, however, before machines were built with the advantage of front delivery, and on the first models delivery was arranged approximately as in the old stop-cylinder machines. Flyer-stick (rack) delivery (see diagram), by which the sheet is turned so that the printed side is underneath, can be arranged; or, by using tapes, as illustrated, delivery is done with the printed side uppermost which is preferable since the quality of the impression can be watched. The sheet is allowed to drop freely on the table at the speed given by the

The sheet-holders on a Miehle

tape transporter. The delivery constructed by Babcock is in general use, with tapes running over a pair of rollers (see diagram). The tape carrier conveys the sheet forward over the delivery table, and as the carrier moves away the tapes unroll so that the sheet lays itself on the table or on the pile which is lowered automatically. (See *printing press*.)

The inking system in a two-revolution machine is by a pyramid of rollers, a duct, and a slab (see *inking device*). The forme is taken in on the bed under the feeding table. The cylinder is usually set in motion by a gear driven directly from the main axle, while the carriage with the bed is driven by a double shuttle action, i.e. a toothed wheel revolving at a constant speed operates alternately an upper and lower gear track on the under-side of the bed. The moving bed is slowed, stopped, and reversed by a crank drive; this arrangement was conceived by Robert Miehle, 1883–88, and he is regarded as the real originator of the modern two-revolution press. Air-buffers are often fitted to assist braking.

The cylinder is equipped with grippers and stretching devices for securing the packing. In order to maintain a high speed, two-revolution machines are equipped with swinging lays which grip the sheet lying on the feeding table and give it a speed which coincides with the speed of the cylinder grippers at the moment when it is gripped by the latter. The periphery speed of the cylinder must, at the moment of printing, be the same as the speed of the bed. (See *peripheral speed relationship*.)

To ensure precise correspondence in the mutual position of cylinder and forme, which is especially important in colour printing, the cylinder is equipped with register fingers and the bed with an adjustable register rack which come into operation immediately before the moment of impression. Correct setting of the register rack is of paramount importance. (G. U.)

two-set: the setting of two jobs in one forme so that each impression of the type gives two signatures.

two sheets on: a method of hand-sewing a book made up of thin sections. Two sections are treated as a unit and one length of thread attaches them to the tapes or cords. Undue bulk at the back is thereby avoided but the book is not so strong as when sewn normally.

The work is best done in a sewing press.

two-up: the processing of two books as a single unit from the forme through all binding stages until they are separated by the trimmer. This method is sometimes used for the mass-production of paper-backed books.

tying up: the securing of type which has been made up into pages by tying each page with cord. This remains in position until the page is surrounded with furniture on the imposing stone.

tympan and packing: in letterpress printing tympan is the name given to the packing on the platen; packing is also used on cylinder presses. This usually consists of a number of sheets of paper, and its purpose is to secure an even impression over the whole forme and to provide a suitable foundation for the paper when printing.

The tympan of a platen press consists of a bottom packing and a top packing. In a cylinder press the bottom packing usually consists of one or two sheets of hard cardboard and a sheet of sulphite paper (known as a draw sheet) which is drawn tightly over the whole by the first draw-rod. In the event of unevenness in the iron cylinder this bottom packing may be given a vantage sheet next to the cylinder. The bottom packing remains fixed during repeated use, and may not require renewal more than twice a year. The top packing varies with the nature of the job in hand. In most cases it comprises ten to twelve sheets

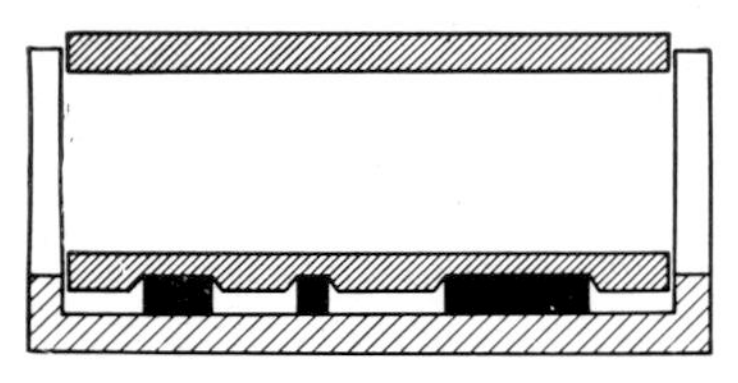

In a cylinder press the cylinder bearers rest against the foundation rails. For correct impression it is necessary that all the forme elements be of equal height with the supporting rails. The cylinder with packing (inclusive of printing paper) is of a larger diameter than the bearers, which implies that the packing is compressed. The degree of compression and the elasticity of the packing determine the printing pressure obtained between forme and packing, i.e. between forme and paper

Diagram to show the compression of the tympan by two equal-pressure elements at varying distances. The area of the packing, which is compressed in proportion to the supporting printing surface, reaches its maximum in the centre diagram, where the pressure per square mm. is greater than in the other two examples

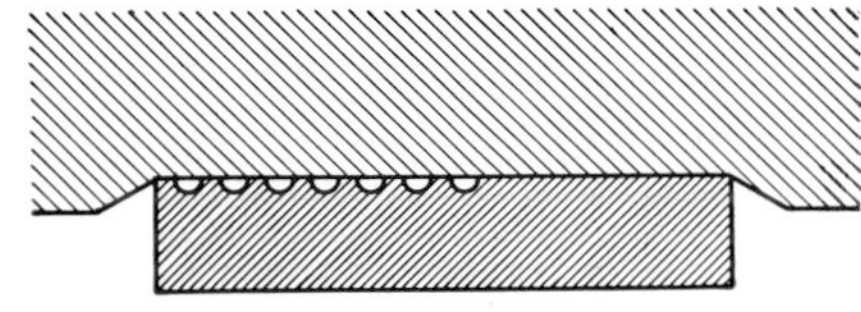

A corresponding diagram of a half-tone block shows that the pressure per square mm. is greater in the highlights (left) than in the dark (black) areas of the plate, assuming that no make-ready has been used

see page 405

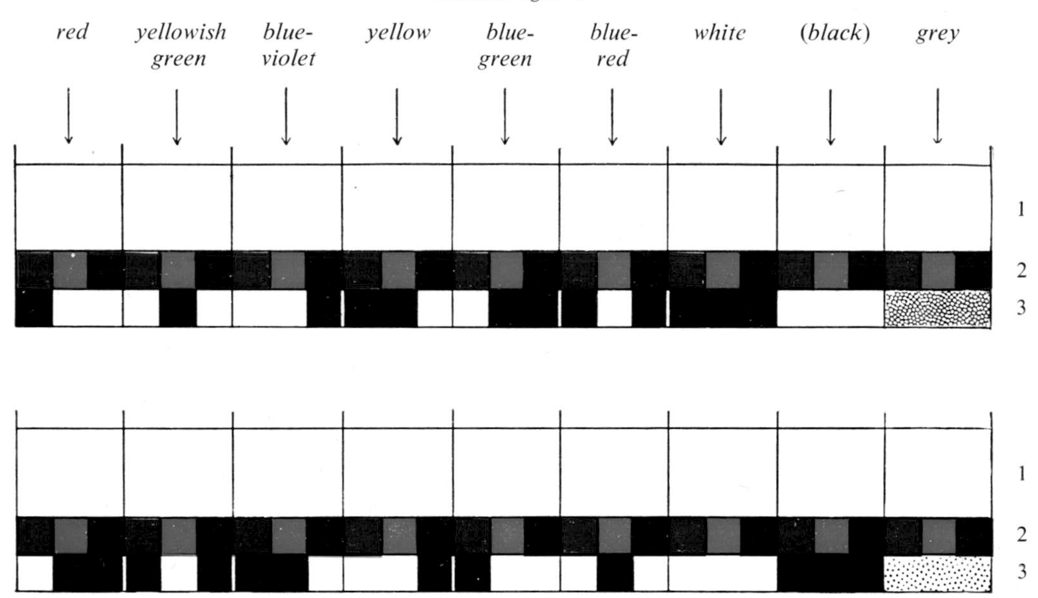

The lower illustration shows how a negative image is converted into a positive. In transmitting a white light, only such rays penetrate in the respective parts as correspond to the tone of the original light

The principle of the three-colour screen

1—*glass or film base* 2—*colour screen* 3—*photographic film*

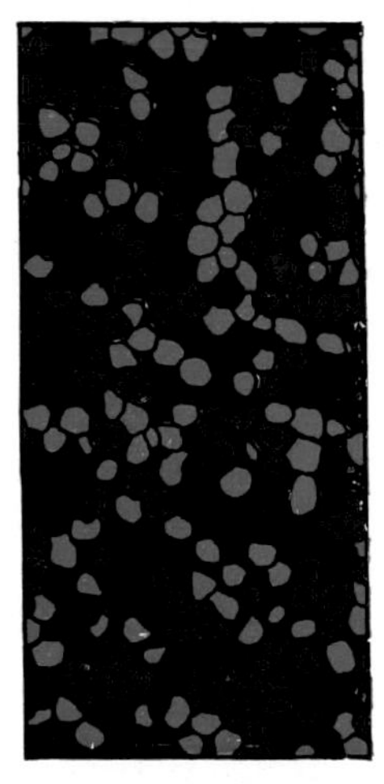

Colour screen in Lumière's autochrome plates and in the earliest Agfa material

Colour screen of the Dufaycolor process

THREE-COLOUR ANALYSIS

by colour screen methods

(*Three-colour analysis*)
see page 405

Original picture (= completed reproduction)

Blue filter absorbs yellow (green + yellow + red light causing yellow parts of picture to appear black

In the top row the original coloured picture is represented, then its appearance through the blue, green, and red filters. As the eye is much less sensitive to blue than to the rest of the spectrum, the blue filter appears very dark. For the same reason the yellow printing, which only absorbs blue and reflects the other colours, appears very light

Positive image obtained from the negative exposed through a blue filter

Yellow and magenta plates superimposed

The above printed in yellow (minus blue)

(*Three-colour analysis*)

see page 405

Green filter absorbs magenta (blue + red) light; red parts of picture appear black

Red filter absorbs cyan light (blue + green)

The same exposed through a green filter

The same exposed through a red filter

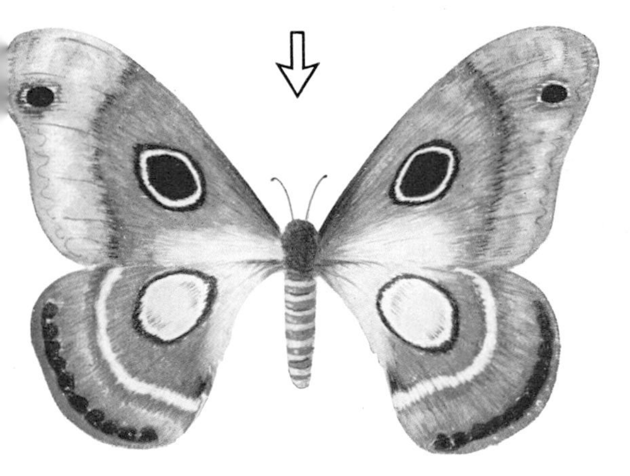

The above printed in 'red' (magenta = minus green)

The above printed in 'blue' (cyan = minus red)

(Three-colour reproduction)
see page 405

THREE-COLOUR REPRODUCTION

Made by photographic three-colour analysis of a natural subject, three-colour block printed in letterpress on art paper

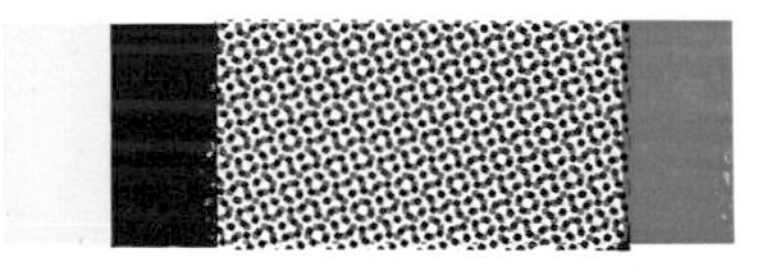

Enlargement of the colour elements which build up the reproduction above

of printing paper with a draw sheet held fast at the rear edge of the second draw-rod. All the sheets are pasted or drawn tight to the gripper edge, while only the outer draw sheet is secured at the rear edge by a draw-rod or pasting. In the top packing the number of sheets is reduced as sheets are added during *make-ready*, q.v., since the thickness must remain constant to ensure correct impression. On the other hand the hardness of the packing may be varied. A harder packing gives a sharper and cleaner impression but requires more careful make-ready. The elasticity of the packing is of fundamental importance for improving the quality of the printing, but this circumstance has been studied in detail only in recent years. Material used for packing includes rubber, impregnated tissue, Cellophane, plastic, or combinations of these. When perfecting follows immediately after printing the first forme it may be necessary to fix an oiled sheet (or specially prepared Antimacule) to avoid smearing; paper or tissue surfaced with glass beads, mineral powder, etc., are alternatives for this.

The tympan in a platen press is made up in a similar but simpler manner, the need for accurate thickness being less than with a cylinder press. In a newspaper rotary press, where a minimum time can be spent on the make-up, a soft packing is used; it mostly comprises a resilient bottom packing of cork or rubber and a top packing covered with a layer of waxed cloth for wear and tear. The more expensive bottom packing is used for several months, while the top is replaced every few weeks. (G. U.)

See also *frisket*.

tympan paper: a cheap paper, glazed or unglazed, used as packing for the tympan. (G. U.)

Typar: see *typewriter composing machine*.

type: a rectangular piece of metal on the top of which any one of the characters used in letterpress is cast. The main groups of type are venetian, old face, modern, and jobbing, each with their respective italics.

See also *exotic types*, *fount*, *parts of type*, *peculiars*.

type-casting: the casting by a typefounder of type for hand-composition. This was probably the essential contribution of Gutenberg to printing. His first mould for casting type was probably somewhat primitive, but since the 16th century designs have changed little in principle up to the present day (though mechanical casting has made them obsolete). The mould generally used in the 18th and 19th centuries was made up of two halves, each consisting of a bottom piece with a sliding core fixed on top, a side-piece, and other details, all made of brass or iron (see diagram). When the mould is assembled the surfaces of the bottom pieces and cores, turned inwards and smoothly ground, form the space in which a type is cast. Its body dimension is determined by the thickness of the core, and its width by the distance between the two cores. The casting space is closed at one end by the *matrix*, tightly held in the mould between adjustable sidepieces, so that the image of the character in the matrix is in the centre of

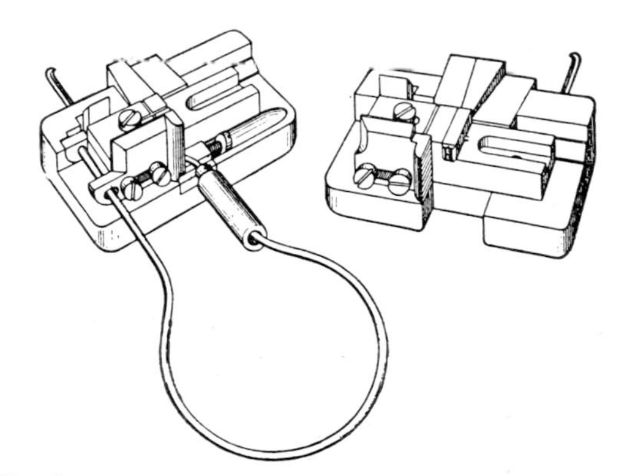

Hand-casting mould. Left, back; right, front. In the middle of the latter is the cast type (H) with its jet

the width of the type. In the second place adjustment is made by means of the movable back gauge against which one end of the matrix rests. The back gauge and its regulating screw are on that half of the mould which supports the *spring*, a steel wire of horseshoe shape for holding the matrix to the mould. On the bottom piece of either half of the mould, on the side opposite the matrix, pieces of metal are fitted so shaped that they form a funnel-like opening (or jet) through which the metal is poured. They slide, so that the width of the casting hole can be varied according to the size of type. By placing partitions between them and the bottom piece the height of the type can be altered. To enable the founder to handle the halves of the mould at high temperatures they are encased in wooden covers. On either half of the lining is a pointed steel hook, a means of removing the cast type from the mould.

Matrices consist of metal plates, about 40 mm. long and 9 mm. thick, with a smoothly ground surface into which the image of the character is struck with a steel punch. A *counter-punch* bearing the inner enclosed portions of a letter is first made. This is cut by hand with the inner shape of a letter, e.g. the bowl of an o, q, p, etc., or the space between the strokes of an n, m, h, etc., and then hardened. After punching with a counter-punch on the end of a steel shank the inside contour of a letter, the outside is filed and cut away, and the steel tempered.

Both halves of the mould are put together and the

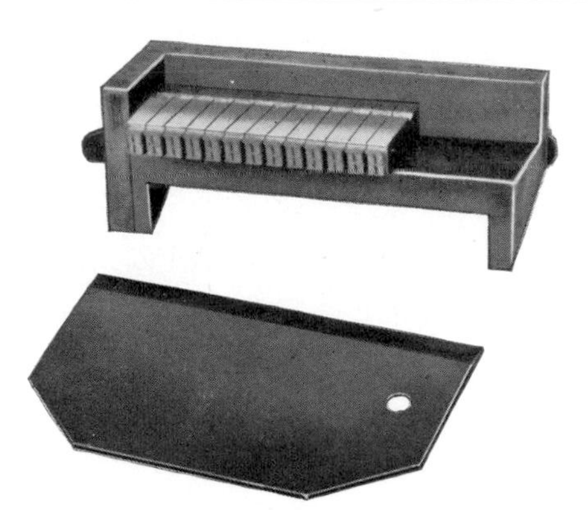

Dressing stick

matrix placed between the sidepieces where it is held firmly by means of the spring. The founder holds the mould in one hand and lifts the type metal in a casting ladle from a crucible with the other, and applies it to the mouth of the mould. By giving the mould a jerk at the moment of casting the metal penetrates all parts of it. Enough metal is poured in to fill the opening, and a *jet* is formed. When the mould is opened, the solidified type is released. The exact adjustment of mould and matrix must be checked by trial castings.

By tradition, letters 'm' and 'o' were cast first as a standard for adjusting the engraving on the type. A good founder could make about 5000 units a day.

In finishing the cast type the jet is first broken off, after which the body sides are ground by hand. The types are arranged in a wooden composing stick, face downwards, for the *dresser* to plane off the jet-break at the foot of the types and ensure they are of standard type height. The channel on the side of the type, which serves as a *nick* in type-setting, can also be made here if not already done when casting. After any necessary planing of the type shoulders, the sides are scraped in a scraping stick.

The metal used for type-casting seems, from the time of Gutenberg, to have been an alloy of lead and tin. In the 16th century bismuth was added as a hardening ingredient, and was later replaced by antimony. (See *type metal.*)

In the 15th century printers cast their own type, and handwriting was the model they sought to imitate in print. But casting and type-setting methods necessitated a certain system in shaping typographical material, and there could be little question of uniformity when every printer considered it an advantage to have type differing from that of other printers, if only to reduce the risk of theft and plagiarism: thus it was that heights varied. By degrees, however, type-foundries were established which had no direct connection with the printing trade. The first independent foundry in Germany was founded in 1571 at Frankfurt by Jakob Sabon, and in France by Guillaume Le Bé (died 1598), whose foundry passed to the Fournier family in the 18th century. Later it became more and more usual for printers to buy their type from special type-foundries, and the demand thus grew both for a uniform scale of sizes and a productive capacity which could not be satisfied by hand-casting tools. In 1819 Henri Didot of Paris invented a casting tool in which, by using a matrix bar and a trough mould, several units of type could be cast simultaneously at the rate of from 300 to 400 a minute.

An early mechanical type-caster was invented by *William Church*, q.v.

See also *logography.*

In 1830 G. W. Bower and H. A. Bacon of Sheffield

Steel die (punch)

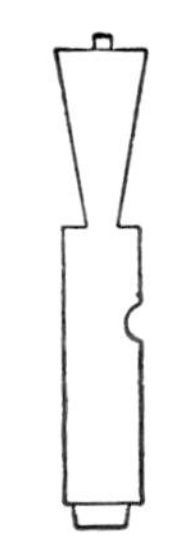

Type, showing nick and jet

Machine for engraving binders' brasses

invented a pumping device for the metal-pot, so that the metal could be forced into the mould under pressure.

About 1838 David Bruce of New York and the Dane Laurids Brandt invented a hand-casting machine which, after a single adjustment, required only a few simple manipulations for casting a large number of types in rapid succession. A model was probably used in the Edinburgh foundry of James Marr & Co. The finishing of type was still carried out in the old way until 1859 when John Robert Johnson and John Staines Atkinson constructed the first machine for dressing types after casting: this was improved in 1862. In 1881 an improved casting machine

Engraving a matrix in a boring machine

was built for the Bauersche Giesserei by John Mair Hepburn, but it was not until 1883 that the first complete casting machine appeared which delivered entirely finished type which required no further work at all. It was built by Foucher frères, who exhibited a double casting machine of still greater capacity in Paris in 1894. In many private foundries type is cast for use in Monotype casting machines; the output is from 6000 to 10,000 units an hour according to size.

As already mentioned, matrices were formerly produced by striking with a steel punch engraved by hand. The material generally consisted of copper, but also of lead, especially for larger sizes. After the introduction of electrotyping with a galvanic battery in 1838 this method was employed, about 1845, for making matrices from cast type. Both electrotype and nickeltype were used. Nowadays the original type for this purpose is made by engraving in a boring machine. Original matrices are also engraved directly in a similar machine. A punch-cutting machine was invented in 1885 by Linn Boyd Benton in Milwaukee. In principle it consists of a vertical pantograph with a revolving cutting tool at the upper end, and a pilot pin (the follower) which is guided around the outline of an enlarged metal pattern at the lower end.

When a new script has been designed the type-face is cut or engraved in one standard size (see *fusible*). After samples of type have been cast, and the stencils finally established for this size of type, they cannot immediately be used for other sizes. Diminution and enlargement of the image may affect the balance and proportions of the character. Only three or four sizes of matrices are therefore engraved from one set of stencils, while for others new designs and new stencils must be made. (G. U.)

type-casting machine: originally, a machine for the mechanical casting of single type units which were then set up in a stick by hand. *Type-setting machines*, q.v., were also invented which did not cast the type they set.

Such modern machines as the *Intertype*, *Italtype*, *Linotype*, *Monotype*, *Typograph*, and also the *teletype-setting* process, qq.v., both set and cast.

See also *photo-composing machine*, *typewriter composing machine*.

type composing: see *hand composition*.

type-composing machine: see *type-setting machine*.

type-face: see *face*.

type family: see *fount*.

type height: 1. the height of a type from the feet on which it rests to the printing surface, i.e. 0·918 in.

2. the height to which a printing plate is mounted on a wooden block for use in letterpress work, i.e. 0·918 in.

type-height gauge: a precision tool for testing the height and body size of type. The model made by Hawthorn Baker of Dunstable has a dial calibrated in thousandths and half-thousandths of an inch.

type-holder: see *pallet*.

type metal: an alloy of varying composition, used for typographic material. The basic metal is lead with different admixtures of tin and antimony, as well as such other metals as copper at times. Metal alloys were already in use in Gutenberg's day for type-casting

Lead by itself is too soft and too difficult to melt to be of great use. By the addition of antimony lead becomes harder, and by that of tin more easily melted, although both these substances affect the end product.

A molten blend of several metals has generally no definite temperature of solidification, but in continued cooling a pulpy mass first forms consisting of isolated crystals in the liquid mass. When the temperature falls below a certain point this solidifies into a blend of metals and metal combinations that is not homogeneous. A fixed solidifying point is obtained only in the case of certain definite proportions between the metals which form an alloy, and only then will the solidified mass display a uniform structure. Such an alloy is called *eutectic*. In the case of lead-antimony the eutectic alloy is formed by 13% antimony and 87% lead: this will solidify at 245° C. An alloy of 62% tin and 38% lead has a solidifying point of about 180° C. An alloy of all the three metals is eutectic when it consists of 4% (more precisely 3·8%) of tin, 12% (11·8%) of antimony, and 84% of lead. This alloy, with a melting point of 239° C (463° F), has the best possible properties for casting, and is the standard alloy for slug-casting machines. It solidifies with a bright, smooth or slightly ruffled surface, whereas non-eutectic alloys have a crystalline grey surface. If the proportion of tin is increased, the antimony content must be reduced to prevent the formation of too many white crystals of tin-antimony after solidifying, which reduces the suitability for casting. These small crystals, in cube form, and clearly distinguishable under a microscope, are harder than the rest of the mass and give strength and durability to the alloy.

Relatively large additions of antimony are often made to typefounders' type, and copper is also added to increase the hardness. Such type contains up to 24% antimony, up to 12% of tin, 1% copper, and 63% lead. *Stereotype metal*, q.v., has normally between 5% tin with 14% antinomy or 7% tin with 18% antimony. For rotary stereotype up to 12% tin is used, but antimony should not exceed 15%.

Stephenson Blake & Co. Ltd., of Sheffield, use 26% antimony, 25% tin, 1% copper, and 48% lead for their type alloy.

For Monotype casting machines proportions are from 6 to 10 % tin, and 15 to 19% antimony, the balance of lead. For spacing, metal with a low tin content can be used, while the antimony content is kept high to maintain resistance to wear and tear (3% tin with 18% antimony is usual.)

Certain impurities may be found in type metal. Arsenic and bismuth occur and are undesirable, but zinc and aluminium are more dangerous. Shavings of zinc from blocks can find their way in when type is being dispersed for re-melting. These impurities give the molten metal a higher surface tension which prevents good casting. In addition, copper and brass matrices are attacked, to which metal is liable to fasten, as also to iron surfaces. Molten metal with an impurity of 0·1% zinc acquires a distinctive bluish-grey tinge.

When molten metal comes into contact with air, oxides are formed, principally of tin and antimony, thus the proportion of these substances is not maintained on repeated re-melting. They must be replenished by adding alloys with 20 to 30% tin, 20 to 30% antimony, and the balance of lead. Metal oxides are inclined to dissolve colloidally in the molten metal, appreciably reducing its casting properties. By powerful stirring, possibly adding organic matter (potatoes, wood chips, etc.) or chemicals (cleaning powder), during the melting, the oxides can be made to form into a layer above the molten metal, whence they can be skimmed as 'type ash' or 'dross'. This has a large amount of tin and antimony in it which can be extracted. (See *metal feeder*.)

During re-melting and adding fresh metal the composition must be checked by analysis. (G.U.)

See 'Sampling and fluxing of Typemetals', PATRA, 1956; and 'Printing metals: their production, nature and use', 5th ed., Pass Printing Metals (London) Ltd., 1955.

type ornaments: see *brace ends*, *bracket*, *brass rule*, *cock*, *corners*, *dash*, *entrelac initials*, *flowers*, *head-piece*, *hooks*, *morisques*, *Oxford corners*, *parentheses*, *swelled rules*, *tail-piece*, *title-page border*.

type parts: see *parts of type*.

type-setting machine: a machine for the selection, assembling, and spacing of typefounders' letterpress printing types, these being stored and arranged in channels instead of cases. About 200 experimental models of such machines were patented between 1820 and 1883, mostly in America. The basic idea was a keyboard connected with the storage channels in such a way that by each stroke of a key a single type was ejected and carried to an assembly point; here the types were lined up. In most of the machines type was assembled in an endless row which an operator made up and justified into lines of the required measure. A third worker was often needed to replenish the type channels. As the compositor needed two assistants such type-setting by machinery was hardly more economical than setting by hand.

See also *Church, William*.

Distributing machines were also constructed, notable being that of the Dane Christian Sörensen,

c. 1850, who gave the various types special nicks by which they slid automatically down channels with corresponding mouths on the outside of a revolving cylinder; his machine was shown in the Great Exhibition of 1851. It was not until the 1880's that inventors solved the problem of justification: the Americans James W. Paige and Alexander Dow were among others to succeed, and, with a simpler system, Paul Cox. The latter used quad material of corrugated lead which, at the stroke of a key for each inter-word space, was cut off from a long rolled strip of lead. The line was set rather wider than required and then compressed to the measure.

The most successful type-setting machine was the Simplex or Unitype which required only one operator. It was constructed by Joseph Thorne who built a prototype in 1880 which included several earlier ideas, especially those of Sörensen. After various improvements and alterations the Thorne machine was given the name Simplex, and large numbers were sold about the year 1900. In 1898 it was combined with an improved spacing system by Cox and appeared under the name of Unitype, 1903. The Simplex machine consisted of two vertical cylinders placed above one another; vertical channels were let into their surfaces, and the shape of the channel mouths leading to the lower cylinder corresponded to special nicks on the back of the type, thus each type could only enter its correct channel. The matter to be distributed was placed in the channels of the upper cylinder, so that the type lay horizontally. During type-setting the upper cylinder revolved step by step, causing the channels on the upper and lower cylinders to meet in turn, so that the type was made to drop in this way into its proper channel from which it was released for subsequent setting by depressing a key. 10,000 types could be set in an hour. (G.U.)

See also *type-casting machine.*

type sizes: from the early years of printing until the late 19th century various names were used to describe type sizes and faces. It is thought that their association with a particular class of work determined the choice.

Names used in English foundries are listed here with their approximate equivalents in *point*, q.v.:

Canon, Four-line Pica	48	
Two-line Double Pica	44	
Two-line Great Primer	36	
Two-line English	28	
Two-line Pica	24	
Double Pica	22	
Paragon	20	
Great Primer	18	
Two-line Brevier (Columbian in U.S.A.)	16	
English	14	
Pica	12	(72)
Small Pica	11	(82–83·2)
Long Primer	10	(89–92)
Bourgeois	9	(102–103)
Brevier	8	(108½–112)
Minion	7	(120)
Emerald	6½	(128–138½)
Nonpareil	6	(144)
Ruby-nonpareil		(160–162)
Ruby (Agate in U.S.A.)	5½	(163 166)
Pearl	5	(178–184)
Diamond	4½	(204–210)
Gem	4	(222)
Brilliant, Half-minion	3½	(238)
Minikin, Semi-nonpareil	3	(288)

(The figure in parentheses gives the approximate number per foot.)

type-specimen book: see *specimen sheet.*

typescript: an author's original typed manuscript, or a professionally typed copy of it which he or his publisher may commission. Abbreviated as *ts.*

typewriter composing machine: a type-setting machine for producing an impression of letterpress on material suitable for photographic reproduction. With a view to simplifying the production of letterpress for offset and intaglio reproduction attempts in two ways were made to construct type-setting machines, the photographic type-setting machine and the typewriter composing machine. The wide use of small lithographic machines often suggested the economy of the typewriter as an original source for lettering instead of conventional type-setting methods. In addition to ordinary typewriters a number of special machines have been introduced. The *Varityper* is perhaps the best known. In this the type is on two semi-circular clips which may be removed and substituted by other type-faces, mathematical symbols, foreign alphabets, etc. In the later models the type is of variable width, i.e. unlike the ordinary typewriter the i is much narrower than the w, as with printers' type. There is also the possibility of varying the width of the spacing, and this can be used to justify the lines so that they range at both left and right-hand margins. This can, however, only be carried out by a second typing; the first typing being used to determine the amount by which spacing must be used to fill out the line.

The *IBM* typewriter has a variable width letter and also variable spacing, so that with the second typing justification is possible. Olivetti have also introduced a typewriter with variable-width letters.

The *Justowriter*, q.v., consists of two machines. Typing is carried out on the first, providing a perforated tape. This is transferred to the second machine which automatically types out with justified spacing. This machine also has variable-width letters, but the letters cannot be changed.

See also *near-print*. (H. J. J.)

Typograph: a slug-casting type-setting machine consisting of two main parts: the upper is a magazine unit comprising the matrices and keyboard, the lower contains the spacing and casting mechanism. It was constructed in 1890 at Cleveland, U.S.A., by John R. Rogers and Fred E. Bright.

The keyboard contains eighty-four keys arranged in a manner similar to those on a Remington typewriter. As the keyboard is placed rather high the operator must stand to work. Behind the keyboard, on a higher plane, is a frame from which guide wires descend to a point of junction below the keyboard. At the upper end of the wires hang the matrices consisting of steel shanks with an eyelet, and brass bodies bearing the

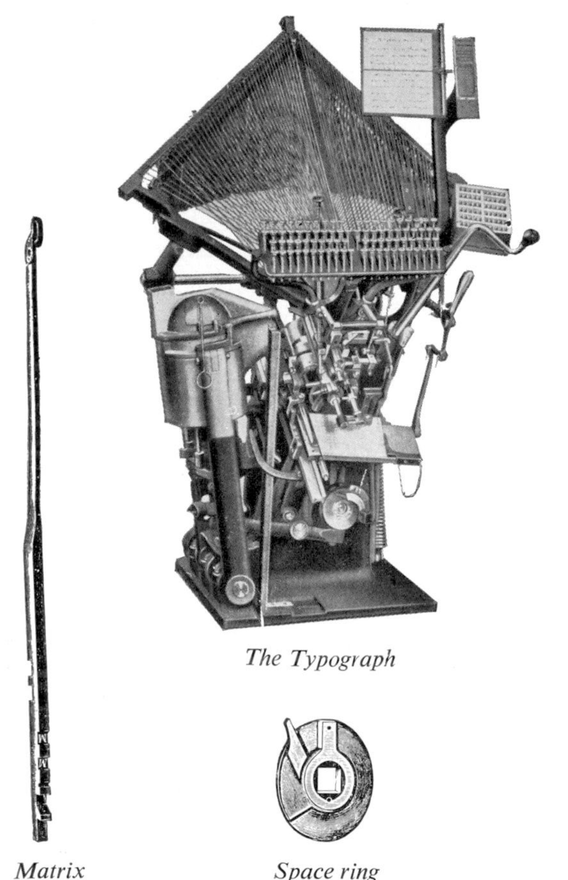

The Typograph

Matrix

Space ring

Matrices and guide wires

characters. Black letter and roman or gothic can be mixed as wished. The matrices are prevented from sliding down the guide wires by blocking forks. The depression of a key lifts its corresponding fork and releases a matrix down a wire into the assembling channel, while the remaining matrices of the same letter are held back by a rear blocking fork. By striking a spacing key a spacing ring is released; this is a disc with a tapered edge. A wedge-shaped tongue is connected with the disc which has a square hole (see diagram). Spacing rings slide on a square axle. When the line of type and spaces is almost complete and the casting mechanism has been started, the matrix line is held between two jaws while a rail guides them into line. The square axle turns the spacing rings, thereby increasing the spaces between words until the line is justified. The mould, supported by levers, now swings forward towards the matrix line, and a metal plate shoots in between the metal-pot and the mould into which the metal is now pumped in a single broad stream (cf. *Linotype*).

After casting, the Typograph slug is already finished and need not be trimmed with knives at the sides or base. The jet is broken off slightly above the base by the intermediate plate, after which the line is pressed out of the mould by spring pressure and is drawn to the slug galley, situated in front under the keyboard. Slugs and hand-set matter can be mixed in the galley.

The matrices are distributed by tipping backwards the frame with the guide wires.

Due to a lost law case concerning its patent the Typograph could not be built in America and its manufacture was transferred first to Canada and then to Germany (Loewe & Co., Berlin, now Typograph G.m.b.H.). There some details were altered, and early in the present century a large number of machines was installed in Europe. In 1908 a two-letter matrix was devised, and in 1914 the Universal model appeared with facilities for the rapid exchange of matrices and moulds; in 1928 the mould was improved. The machine is simple, cheap, and reliable, producing excellent matter. (G.U.)

typographer: one qualified by his taste and knowledge of types, their possibilities and limitations, to plan layouts of a proposed printed work in a manner suited to the subject and purpose of it as well as to the materials and processes to be used.

The definition of John Moxon in 1683 is not without point today: '. . . one who by his own judgement, from solid reasoning within himself, can either perform, or direct others to perform from the beginning to the end, all the handy-works and physical operations relating to typographie.'

typographia: relating to typography and its kindred subjects: used as a title for books and journals on printing, and as the name of a society of printers. (M.L.)

The Typographical Association: the trade union of the provincial letterpress printing industry in Britain, established in 1849. There had been other unions of printers in the early 19th century, notably the Northern Typographical Union (est. 1830), the Scottish Typographical Association (est. 1836), the Irish Typographical Union (est. 1836), and the London Union of Compositors (est. 1834).

The chief aims of these unions had been to regulate the number of hours worked and wages paid; to limit the number of apprentices so that they were not used as a source of cheap labour; to lay down a policy with regard to the various new mechanical printing presses and composing machines which were developed in the early 19th century; to give financial assistance to members during strikes; to discourage 'unfair' printing offices which paid less than the established ('stab) rates and employed non-union journeymen; and to help unemployed printers who tramped the country seeking work (this assistance was known as 'tramp relief' and was a sum of money varying from 9d. to 5/–).

There had been an earlier attempt at a general union of typographical societies in 1844 under the name National Typographical Association; this had covered the whole United Kingdom. Its objects were 'to advance the interests of the typographical profession, and to improve the social conditions of its members'. This union was dissolved in 1848 due to financial difficulties brought about by the payment of unemployment and strike benefits at a rate not covered by the income. As a result the London Society of Compositors was re-established in 1848; the Provincial Typographical Association was formed in 1849 (the former Northern Union); and the Scottish Typographical Association was formed in 1852–53.

In 1877 the name of the Provincial Typographical Association was shortened to the Typographical Association. Headquarters were opened in Manchester, and branches formed in many parts of Britain, but not, for a time, in the London area where the London Society of Compositors held sway.

See A. E. Musson, 'The Typographical Association: Origins and History up to 1949', O.U.P., 1954.

typography: 1. the craft of printing; embracing composition, imposition, and presswork.

2. the planning of a printed work, i.e. the choice of paper, type-face and size, positioning of illustrations, diagrams, etc., to make a balanced and attractive whole.

Typon process: a means of reproducing out-of-print books and other rare material. A sensitized sheet is forced against the page to be reproduced, the action of light turning this into a photographic negative of the page.

See also *reflex printing*.

Typopress: a typewriter composing machine developed in the 1950's by Andreas Goy of Budapest. It uses especially made types proportionally spaced in eight different widths. The machine as yet only exists in prototype form.

ADDENDA

TAGA (Technical Association of Graphic Arts): an American society for the printing and allied trades. Their annual report is in technical and scientific terms, but is an important guide to new technical ideas in the U.S.A.

Thames board: a British-made board much used in edition binding. Each side is lined with brown kraft paper to give equal surface tension, and thus rigidity, as well as a firm smooth exterior.

3M Brand make-ready process: the trade name of a make-ready process developed in America by the Minnesota Mining & Manufacturing Company. Briefly, a plastic powder is dusted on to an inked impression of the printing surface. This is heated and swells considerably in proportion to the ink, giving a simple method of make-ready of letterpress half-tone plates.

U

u.c.: the abbreviation for *upper case*, q.v.

Uhertype: a photo-composing machine built in 1928 by the Hungarian Edmund Uher, at first under the name *Luminotype*. The first of its three sections is a typewriter keyboard. After setting this to measure, keys are struck which release from their magazine steel balls, each ball marked with a type. The balls come to rest in the separate holes of a narrow metal strip, there being ninety holes in all. On completing the line the compositor strikes a spacing key (he is warned by a bell when this is necessary). This causes the balls to release a row of contacts which allow a ray of light to be directed against the types assembled. The types are projected on a sensitized master film about 4 mm. wide, this being shifted for interword spacing. Corrections can be done at this stage.

The exposed film is developed, fixed, and dried for conveying to the second section, the make-up machine. Here the strip of text is projected on to a second film band, line by line. The projector is set for the required size of type and width of line, and justification is completed. The film is now developed as a negative for photogravure work, or as a positive for offset litho.

The third unit is a Metteur photo-jobbing machine, used for display work. (With G.U.)

unauthorized edition: an edition printed without the consent of the owner of the copyright.

uncials: a term of disputed origin for the majuscule form of writing used as a book hand for the Christian Church from the 4th to 6th centuries, after which it declined, being superseded by the *half-uncial*, q.v.

Distinctive features are rounded forms of a, d, e, m, and u, also the minuscule forms of h, l, and q. The shapes of uncials are held to have been influenced by Byzantine art.

See also *letters—forms and styles.*

uncut: a book is said to be uncut if the edges of the paper have not been cut with the plough or guillotine. Cf. *unopened.*

See also *binding proof.*

undercutting: the faulty etching of a block by which the metal carrying the lines or dots of the image is pitted from the side. This gives the block poor strength in printing, and makes it difficult or impossible to take from it matrices for stereotypes or electrotypes. (G.U.)

underlaying: the placing of a sheet or sheets of paper or thin card under the forme and under the mounts of blocks to bring them to the required level for printing evenly.

See also *make-ready.*

ungrained plates: zinc plates for use in lithographic printing which, while not quite smooth, are considerably less rough than normal plates surfaced in a graining machine.

Ungrained deep-etch zinc plates are designed to increase the range of darker tones in a reproduction, and to improve the overall merging of tones (this is particularly important for the successful rendering of half-tone dots).

It is the graining on normal lithographic plates which holds the water in the non-image areas and the ink for printing; if the graining is largely to be dispensed with the condition of water/grease repellency must be achieved by other means. One of these is to treat the image areas of the deep-etch plate with a non-blinding lacquer to increase their ink-receptivity, thus making greater the contrast with the non-image area which is desensitized with cellulose gum.

A second method is to use pre-sensitized plates in which chemically treated aluminium foil is applied as a base and water-absorbent area, with a diazo-type coating as the image area. A third method is to use bi-metallic plates with copper as the ink-receptive image area, and aluminium, chromium, or stainless steel for the non-image area. If such a plate is immersed in a bath of phosphoric acid (20%) the above properties will result. Such plates are costly, but suitable for long runs.

Ungrained plates require more care on the press in such matters as roller adjustment, pressure, and ink consistency (it should be stiff). Smooth or coated stock are recommended as being the most suitable.

Unicorn Press: a private press founded in 1895 by Ernest Oldmeadow and the Rev. Joseph Dawson of London. The output was only small, and the press closed in 1905. Unicorn Press was strictly a publishing imprint since commercial firms were commissioned to do the printing.

uniform edition: a set or series of books all composed, bound, and jacketed in the same style.

Union Typographical Européene: see *International Typographical Union.*

Universal Composing Machine: see *typewriter composing machine.*

Universal Copyright Convention: a convention on copyright organized in 1952, by UNESCO, at which thirty-six countries signed their agreement with its conclusions. The most important article is perhaps No. II which provides that published works of nationals of any contracting State, and works first published in that State, shall enjoy in each other contracting State the same protection that other State accords to works of its nationals first published in its own territory.

Britain ratified the convention in 1957.

See also *Berne Convention, Copyright Act.*

Universal machine: a printing machine of the *platen* type, q.v.

unopened: a book of which the bolts are uncut, to be hand-slit with a paper-knife. When this has been done they are said to be opened. Cf. *uncut.*

unsewn binding: a method of machine-binding books without sewing or stitching their sections. There are many makes of machine but the principle in all is the same. The books are gathered and fed to the machine one by one where they are clamped and carried against a rotating cutter which shears off the back folds, leaving the book as a clamped block of single sheets. The sheared back is carried across gluing mechanism and a piece of lining cloth is applied, its overlapping edges being turned over the sides of the book. A flexible adhesive is essential and if a polyvinyl is used it is claimed to be possible to round and back the books and subsequently case up in the usual manner. Such books open quite flat.

In some machines provision is made to stick on a paper cover in place of the lining cloth and thus produce a paper-wrappered book which is subsequently cut flush. A disadvantage is that unsewn books cannot be satisfactorily rebound by sewing but only by the further shearing of the back margins; nor can books printed on coated stock be so bound. An alternative name is *perfect binding.* (L.K.)

See also *thermoplastic binder.*

untouched: a term limited to incunabula indicating a work which has not been rubricated or illuminated.

untouched edges: a bookbinding term for edges which are neither trimmed nor cut. The leaves have to be opened with a paper-knife by the reader. Synonymous with *unopened.* Cf. *uncut.* (L.K.)

Updike, Daniel Berkeley, 1860–1941: an eminent American printer and type historian whose 'Printing Types: their History, Forms and Use', 1922, is still a standard text-book.

From 1880–93 he worked for the Boston publishers Houghton, Mifflin & Co., the last two years being spent at their Riverside Press, Cambridge. In 1893 he set up the Merrymount Press 'to make work better for its purpose than was commonly thought worth while'. His associate John Bianchi was taken into partnership in 1915. Among the special types used were the Merrymount, designed by Bertram G. Goodhue (*c.* 1895), and the Montallegro, designed by Herbert P. Horne and cut by E. P. Prince (*c.* 1905).

The press was in no sense a private press, but achieved a reputation for the extraordinary care taken over details; it was said that every printed sheet issued was examined by one of the two partners before being delivered to the customer.

Upham cylinder: an arrangement for printing simultaneously in two colours (or four if divided rollers are used) on a two-revolution press by using an additional forme cylinder and inking device. The extra forme cylinder is placed close to the impression cylinder, so that the paper comes into contact with this revolving forme immediately after the flat forme has given its impression. This cylinder is intersected by threaded channels used for fixing the revolving forme; these are curved blocks or stereos. By means of a special Upham process the blocks for colour printing can be curved, while retaining register with the flat ones used on the normal bed of the press. The additional inking device has a smaller number of rollers than the regular one, but as the additional cylinder makes four revolutions, and is inked up

The Upham-Miehle with the extra cylindrical forme

twice for each impression, comparatively good inking and grinding are obtained. The illustration shows this cylinder on an Upham-Miehle. (G.U.)

upper case: the compositor's type case in which capital letters, reference marks, and accents are kept. Abbreviated as *u.c.*

upper end boy: the boy who assists the coucher (in a hand-made paper works) when the vat is on a very long sort. The boy helps to put the long felt on the *post*, q.v., and lightly squeezes down the mould as it is being couched. The upper end of the mould is that farthest from the coucher.

Utrecht Psalter: a manuscript of the Gallican version of the Psalms, written and illustrated by line-drawings at Rheims, about 840. It was brought to Canterbury where copies were made about 1000 (now in the British Museum), 1150 (the Eadwine Psalter, Trinity College, Cambridge), and about 1200 (Bibliothèque Nationale, Paris).

Figures and scenes are drawn among the text against landscape backgrounds. Colouring is used in the copies but not the original.

Utterson, Edward Vernon, *c.* 1776–1856: an antiquary and bibliophile, also an original member of the Roxburghe Club. About 1840 he established the *Beldornie Press*, q.v.

ADDENDUM

ultrasonic cleaning of type: a method of cleaning dried ink from letterpress printing type and plates which obviates the damage done by normal methods of brushing and lye washing. It was announced in 1958 in 'The British Printer'. The equipment, known as 'Soniclean', is made by Dawe Instruments Ltd., and consists essentially of a generator which produces an ultrasonic signal, transducers which convert the electrical signal into mechanical vibrations, and a stainless steel tank (of varying size) to contain the agitated solvent. The generator operates in the frequency range from 36 to 40 kilocycles per second, giving a succession of up to 40,000 pressure waves every second.

Briefly, it works as follows. Electrical signals from the generator cause the transducer to expand and contract at the frequency of the current supplied to it. If put in a tank of liquid, the constant expansion and contraction in the transducer will cause rapid pressure changes in the surrounding fluid. The result is the rapid generation and collapse of millions of tiny vapour bubbles. Bubbles tend to form round any nearby solid surface (this is known as cavitation), thus when a printing plate is immersed in the tank the bubbles will penetrate the smallest type or the finest line blocks where their agitation will dislodge caked dirt and dried ink. Warm solvent is more efficient than cold, and solvents containing cresol, e.g. Magnasol, give best results. Type or plates are finally removed from the tank and rinsed in warm tap water.

It should be borne in mind that plates mounted by adhesive foil will be loosened by the bubbles unless their edges are first sealed.

See also *washing up*.

V

vacuum frame: a copying frame used in process engraving for *printing down*, q.v. It may be vertical or horizontal and consists of a rubber-covered flat base. On this is laid a sensitized metal plate with the negative to be copied on top. Next comes a glass plate. The air between the rubber and glass is withdrawn by a pump, causing a vacuum in which the metal and negative are pressed together. Several plates of varying thickness and their accompanying negatives can be put in the frame at one time. (With G.U.)

See also *photo-lithographic plate.*

Vacuum frame

Val de Lagat: a French village, famous for its paper-mill, operating now as it did when built in the 13th century. (M.L.)

Vale Press: a press founded in 1894 by Charles Ricketts and Charles Hazelwood Shannon with the object of producing fine editions of the English classics. They had from 1889 collaborated to produce 'The Dial', a journal. Ricketts supervised the printing by Ballantyne & Hanson of the books he designed; special types used were the Vale, King's, and Avon. Ricketts also embellished and illustrated many of the books with wood engravings which he drew and cut.

'The Early Poems of John Milton', 1896, was the first Vale Press book to be printed in their special type. Rodenberg, in 'Deutsche Pressen', 1925, lists 'Daphnis and Chloë', 1893, as the first book to bear the Vale imprint. The press closed in 1904.

Valleyre, Gabriel: see *stereotype.*

Van Dijck, Christoffel: see *Dijck, Christoffel van.*

Van Gelder: one of the most famous of all hand-made papers, produced for a century or more in Holland and said to contain 100% rag. It is used by artists and publishers of fine editions.

Van Krimpen, Jan: see *Krimpen, Jan van.*

vanity publishing: publishing on behalf of and at the expense of an author who pays for the production and often for the marketing of his book. Also known as *subsidy publishing.*

vantage: a set of types, blocks, stereos, etc., which can be freed for future printing, i.e. need not be distributed. (G.U.)

variant: 1. (in MSS.), a difference in the text of a handwritten manuscript and copies made from it. Such variants resulted from careless copying.

2. (in books), a textual variation noticed in two copies of the same impression of a work. This is the result of correcting a minor mistake noticed when printing; only the later sheets bear the corrections, the earlier ones being issued without alteration. Cf. *state.* The variant can also be caused accidentally.

3. see *binding variants.*

variorum edition: an issue of a work containing the notes and opinions of various editors or commentators.

Varityper: see *typewriter composing machine.*

varnish: a general description of liquid substances which dry as hard films, insoluble in water, when applied in thin layers to various surfaces. Of special importance in the graphic industries are varieties of thick, viscous, linseed oil varnish, which form the binding agents in inks for letterpress and lithographic printing; while for gravure and aniline printing are varnishes made of resins contained in evaporating solvents. (G.U.)

vat paper: an alternative name for *hand-made paper*, q.v.

vatman: the craftsman who dips the mould into a vat of pulp and skilfully shakes it into a sheet of paper.

vehicle: the medium in which the pigment of a printing ink is dispersed. Vegetable oils (chiefly linseed) are the most used, but synthetic resins, which allow more control in drying, provide an alternative.

Veldener, John, fl. 1473: the first printer of Louvain, where he issued Cicero's letters in 1475.

vélin: the French term for wove paper. Also known as *vergé*.

vellum: the skin of the newly born calf, kid, or lamb prepared for writing by stretching and polishing with alum. It can also be used for binding but will tend to warp.
See also *Japanese vellum, ties*.

velvet bindings: bindings having velvet as the covering material. In England these belong to the era 1500–1650, often being used for prayer-books.

Venetian bindings: see *Ducali bindings*.

venetian types: the roman type-faces cut in Venice in the late 15th century with outlines based on humanistic hands of 15th-century Italy. Bold serifs gave a balanced squareness to the capitals, lower-case letters had a wide set, and there was no italic. The chief Venetian printers to use these types were Wendelin da Spira, Nicolas Jenson, and Aldus Manutius.

Venge, Edward, fl. 1590–1605: the operator of a secret press near Bishop's Hall, Stepney. In 1578 he had been apprenticed to Henry Carre, and on being freed in 1588 (Arber, Vol. II, 703) had his legitimate business in Fleet Street. The piratical printing and selling of privileged books was very profitable in London at this time, and secret presses were numerous in spite of the risks of seizure and confiscation. Apparently Venge took these risks, printing 'prymers, catechismes, and almanacks, contrarye to her Maiesties prohibicōn . . .', and in 1596 his secret press was seized. The entry, quoted from the Stationers' Register, appears to refer to one book only, an edition of the 'Primmer' which contains the primer, the catechism, and an almanac.

Venge continued to print until 1605, very few of his books being known.

Vérard, Antoine: fl. 1485–1514: an important figure in the early Parisian book trade, who maintained a scriptorium, and was also appointed Bookseller to Louis XII. He published *Books of Hours*, q.v., and numerous illustrated vernacular texts. It has not been finally established whether Vérard had his own printing premises or commissioned work from other printers; certainly the first work he issued, an edition in French of Boccaccio's 'Decameron', was printed by Jean du Pré, 1485.

verbatim et literatim: a Latin phrase meaning word for word, letter for letter; a literal translation.

vernis mou: an alternative name for *soft-ground etching*.
See *etching*.

versals: ornamented capital letters written marginally or partly in the text to mark the beginnings of paragraphs, verses, or important passages in a manuscript. In earlier examples the ornamentation was simple, being mostly flourishes, dotted outlines, or a contrasting colour. In the 15th century they became much more elaborate and developed into illuminated initials. Versals ranged over several lines of text but the top of the capital was approximately aligned with the minuscles of the word to which it belonged.
See also *illumination*.

versificator regis: see *Poet Laureate*.

verso: 1. the reverse of a single printed unfolded sheet.
2. the left-hand pages of a book, bearing the even numbers. Cf. *recto*.

vertical camera: a reproduction camera with a horizontal copyboard and the camera permanently focused for photographing through a prism. The lens is usually in a fixed position, and the copyboard and back of the camera (the position of the dark plate) are movable, their movements being correlated for automatic focusing. (G. U.)

vertical press: a printing press in which the forme is moved up and down instead of to and fro. Among several well-known makes are the *Miehle* and *Harrison*, qq.v.

Verulam Society: a society established in London in 1846, for the publication of cheap Law Reports. The project was abandoned after the production of a few numbers. (M. L.)

Vienna Dioscorides: a Greek herbal, being a parchment codex of 491 folios written in uncial script and illustrated with coloured drawings of plants, animals, and birds. There are 392 whole-page pictures and eighty-seven in the text. Most of the book is an alphabetically arranged sequence of drawings of plants with a description of each, and the text was largely the work of a Greek physician Pedanios

Dioscorides, fl. A.D. 54–68, who came from Anazarba in Cilicia (South Turkey), but writings of Claudius Galen and Krateuas are also included.

The scribe and artist(s) responsible for this great Byzantine manuscript are unknown, but it was completed before 513 since one of the pictures bears an inscription of dedication to Princess Anicia Juliana in gratitude for the building of a church at Honoratae, a suburb of Byzantium. Ecclesiastical historians say the church was completed about 512–13, thus establishing the date of the codex with some certainty. The pictures of plants are mostly copied from 1st-century B.C. originals.

The codex was rebound by Johannes Chortasmenos in 1406. It passed to the Turks after 1453 when Arabic and Turkish plant-names were entered in arabic script. In the 16th century Hebraic transcriptions were added, probably by Hamon, the Jewish doctor to Suleiman II. In 1569 the son of this doctor sold the book for 100 gold ducats to Augerius Ghislain von Busbeck who brought it from Constantinople to Kaiser Maxmilian II in Vienna, where it may now be seen in the Österreichische Nationalbibliothek (Codex Vindobonensis, Med. graec. 1.)

The first Latin translation, by Petrus Paduanensis, was published at Colle in 1478, and Aldus Manutius issued the first printed Greek edition in 1499. An English translation by John Goodyer in 1655 was not printed until 1934 when R. T. Gunther edited and privately published it.

Vienna Genesis: the book of Genesis as depicted in a series of forty-eight pictures painted on twenty-four parchment leaves (there were originally about ninety-six) in the late 6th century, probably at Antioch (Antakya, South Turkey). The work of eight artists can be traced. The leaves are of a dark purple-brown, but the colours of the paintings are still remarkably fresh.

From notes on some of the leaves the work is known to have been in Italy during the Middle Ages; since 1664 it has been in the Imperial Library, Vienna (now Österreichische Nationalbibliothek.)

For a contemporary work see also *Codex Rossanensis.*

vigesimo-quarto: see *twenty-fourmo.*

vignette: 1. an illustration in which the edges of the picture shade off into the surrounding paper, there being no rigid border or frame. Title-pages and chapter-heads of 18th- and 19th-century books were often illustrated with engravings printed in this form. For a modern vignetted half-tone see under *block* (1).

See also *livres à vignettes.*

2. an initial letter in illuminated manuscripts decorated with vine-leaves and tendrils.

Viktoria press: a German adaptation of the Universal press. (M. L.)

Village Press: see *Goudy, Frederic W.*

viz.: an abbreviation for the Latin 'videlicet', i.e. namely.

Vizlant, Jakob, *d.* 1475: a German merchant who financed the setting up of one of the early printing presses in Valencia, Spain. He employed John of Salzburg and Paul Hurus of Constance to operate it; this was in 1474. A year later the two printers set up the first press in Barcelona.

vocabulary: a systematically arranged list of words with explanations of their meanings. The term mostly applies to lists in books for studying a contemporary language, and is less comprehensive than a *dictionary*, q.v. A vocabulary differs from a *glossary*, q.v., which explains the words of a particular subject or a classical language.

Vollard, Ambroise: a 20th-century French publisher of limited and de luxe editions of illustrated works to which the text is often mostly subordinate.

volume: any work published with its own title-page and enclosed in covers. In German, *Band*; in French, *tome.*

volumen: a papyrus roll bearing columns of writing, which, when not being read, was wound round a stick which served as a handle. Each roll was identified when closed by a ticket. (The name 'volumen' is the Latin word for 'a thing rolled up'.)

Vox, Maximilien: a distinguished contemporary French publisher, typographer, and graphic artist. He devised a classification for existing type-faces, using nine groups: Manuaires, Humanes, Garaldes, Réales, Didones, Mécanes, Linéales, Incises, and Scriptes. A brief description of each group follows:

Manuaires. Black-letter types and those based on manuscript hands, and also formal unjoined pen or brush letters (as distinct from scripts). E.g. Linotype Old English, Monotype Mercurius.

Humanes. Revivals or derivatives of the roman letter of the late 15th century, and of the monumental capitals of classical Rome. E.g. Monotype Lutetia, Linotype Minerva.

Garaldes. Most old-face types fall in this group. E.g. Monotype Bembo, Stephenson Blake Caslon.

Réales. Faces with vertical shading, bracketed serifs, and medium contrast between the weight of strokes. E.g. Linotype Baskerville, Monotype Perpetua.

Didones. Types with distinct contrast between

thick and thin strokes and vertical shading. Usually with unbracketed serifs. E.g. Intertype Bodoni, Stephenson Blake Chisel.

Mécanes. Types with strokes of almost even thickness and slab serifs. E.g. Intertype Cairo, Nebiolo Egizio Nero Tondo.

Linéales. Types without serifs. E.g. Monotype Gill Sans, Intertype Vogue.

Incises. Types with a chiselled effect and a slightly thickened effect at the ends of strokes. E.g. Monotype Albertus, Bauersche Weiss Lapidar.

Scriptes. Calligraphic faces, either with joined letters as in most copperplate scripts, or with unjoined letters. E.g. Stephenson Blake Invitation, Olive Mistral.

Should a type not fit clearly into one category a double name could be used, thus Ashley Script could be described as Manuaire Scripte. A number of European founders are using the classification as the basis of their catalogues, notable being the Typefoundry Amsterdam.

M. Vox also organizes the annual École de Lure where graphic artists meet to discuss current printing and allied problems.

Vulgate: the Latin version of the Bible as translated by St Jerome *c.* 380–405. Of surviving manuscript copies the *Codex Amiatinus*, q.v., is perhaps most important. Various recensions have been prepared for the Catholic Church, notable being those authorized by Pope Sixtus V (1585–90) and Clement VIII (1592–1605).

ADDENDUM

Vapco: the trade name of an aluminium stamping foil made by George M. Whiley Ltd. of Ruislip. Its manufacture involves the continuous evaporation in a vacuum of the metal to produce a silverlike foil which does not tarnish. It is much used in Britain for blocking publishers' cases.

A recent development introduced by the same firm has been coloured aluminium foils for which chemical dyes are used. They are sold under the name *Newvap*.

Walbaum, Justus Erich, 1768–1839: a German engraver and metal-founder who in 1799 acquired the type-foundry of Kircher, a printer of Goslar, removing in 1803 to Weimar. In 1836 he sold his types to F. A. Brockhaus of Leipzig where they remained until they were bought in 1919 by the Berthold foundry of Berlin. The Monotype Walbaum Series 375 was cut in 1934.

Waldegrave, Robert, *c.* 1554–1604: at one time a printer for the secret Marprelate Press which in the 1580's issued Puritan tracts (thereby necessitating its removal from place to place). In 1590 he was appointed King's Scottish Printer to James I, and for some years issued mostly theological works from his Edinburgh press.

Walker, Sir Emery, 1851–1933: an English engraver and printer associated with the printing revival started by William Morris and continued by Cobden-Sanderson and Bruce Rogers. Walker worked with all three.

wallet edged: said of a limp-bound book when the back cover is extended to enclose the fore-edge and fasten into a slot in the front cover.

Walter press: an early rotary press for printing on rolls of paper. It was constructed at the instigation of J. Walter, the owner of 'The Times', by J. C. MacDonald and J. Calverley, 1866, and was later given a folding device. The reel of paper was moistened on both sides before printing, and the press could deliver 12,000 copies of the newspaper an hour. In the 1870's models were in use throughout Europe.

See also *Applegath press.* (G. U.)

Wanley, Humphrey, 1672–1726: the librarian and palaeographer who developed the library of *Robert Harley*, q.v. In the diary which Wanley kept intermittently between 1715 and 1726 we get an interesting account of 18th-century book-collecting, with such items as 'March 20th 1722–3. Mr. Elliot came and I delivered to him a parcel to bind, and 3 more of my Lord's Morocco Skins.'

warehousing: the storing by the binder of books in sheet or bound form, or by the printer in sheet form.

warping: the distortion of book covers after binding whereby they do not lie flat. Research has shown that this is due to the differing expansion and contraction of the various components of the cover, viz. cloth, boards, end-papers, and to a lesser extent the films of adhesive. On the newly bound book these causes are at work due to the drying out of the adhesives, and later further stresses may occur due to climatic changes. Among practical means of minimizing warping are the use of well-matured boards, end-papers having the grain running from head to tail, the use of adhesives with a minimum water content, and adequate pressing of the books after casing. (L. K.)

wash-drawing: a brush-drawing which contains grey tones in addition to blacks and whites.

washing up: 1. the removal of ink from the forme, inking system, or offset rubber blanket. Normally petrol or benzol is used for washing up the forme, photogen for cleaning the inking device with or without subsequent washing with petrol, and petrol or special washing solutions containing sulphur for the offset rubber blanket.

Remains of ink are removed from a forme on completing printing by washing with lye (wooden-based blocks must be taken out first). Steam for removing grease is also used, and latterly, baths of such detergent solutions as sodium sesquisilicate in water, heated by steam, have been found satisfactory. After some time in such a bath the forme is thoroughly washed in clean water, dried, and lightly oiled. The great disadvantage of the once popular caustic soda was its tendency to leave a film on the metal, quite apart from its offensive smell.

A fountain brush is available for forme cleaning: this contains its own fluid, released by pressing a button.

2. in binding, lightly sponging cases with glair to assist in the adherance of gold in gold blocking and the like. (L. K.)

water-colour inks: thin, transparent inks, made without oil, which may be used when printing in colours from a rubber surface. As they remain soluble when printed their impression would be spoiled by accidental wetting as, for example, on a jacket.

water finish: heavily loaded paper which is given a high finish by alternately damping each side of the roll of paper with water and passing it through heated rolls. The process is used when making *imitation art paper*, q.v.

water lines: another name for the laid and chain lines of *laid paper*, q.v.

watered silk: silk with a wavy or damask-like pattern: it is sometimes used for doublures.

waterleaf: sheets of unsized paper which are semi-absorbent and require sizing before use.

See *size* (1).

watermark: a distinguishing mark, lettering, or design made on paper during manufacture, and visible when the sheet is held up to light. Watermarks were used in Italy during the 13th century, being made from wire twisted into simple geometric shapes. While originally used as trade-marks, in the course of time they developed into designations of size, hence *pott* had a jug as watermark, *foolscap* had a cap and bells, *post* had a post-horn, etc.

In hand-made paper the wire design is sewn to the mould on which the sheet of paper is formed, causing the fibres to lie thinner where they touch it. In machine-made papers the design is sewn to the dandy roll and presses itself on the moist sheet after the web has been formed.

Watermarks are of considerable help when tracing the date and place of a manuscript, and reference should be made to Briquet's 'Les Filigranes' which reproduces 16,000 watermarks of the period 1282–1600.

Writing in 'The Library', Vol. 1, p. 220, William Blades advises how the watermark can guide the bibliographer in assigning the correct size to a book when writing a description of it (he should have said in deciding how the sheet was folded). He points out that in all paper made prior to 1750 it is a fixed rule that the chain-lines run from top to bottom of the unfolded sheet, the laid lines across it, with the watermark so placed that when the sheet is folded in half it appears about the centre of the right-hand half. He deduces: 1. 'In any old book, if the chain-lines run down, and the watermark is found about the centre of the page, that book must be *folio*.' 2. If the chain-lines run across, and the watermark appears in the middle of the last leaf of a section, that book is *quarto*. 3. If the chain-lines run down, and the watermark is found at the top edge of a leaf, that book must be *octavo*.

See also *impressed watermark*.

wax-engraving process: a method of making electros for the printing of maps in letterpress work. The outline is drawn on to a surface of wax, lettering being impressed by hand. A copper shell is then deposited on this.

waygoose: originally, an annual entertainment given by a master printer for his journeymen and apprentices. Writing in 1683 Moxon stated 'These Way-gooses are always kept about Bartholomew-tide. And till the Master-Printer have given this Way-goose, the Journey-men do not use to Work by Candle Light.'

The term has now come to describe the annual outing or dinner held by or for the members of a printing works. This word of obscure origin is also spelled *Wayzgoose*.

web fed: a printing machine into which the paper is fed from a reel. Cf. *sheet fed*.

See also *rotary press*.

web perfecting press: a rotary press which prints consecutively both sides of a continuous reel of paper.

Webb, H. G.: the founder of the *Caradoc Press*, q.v.

Weiss, Emil Rudolf, 1875–1942: a distinguished German type-designer who worked for the *Bauersche Giesserei*, q.v.

well closed: said of paper which, when examined, is found to have the stuff properly shaken into a sheet, with parallel, clump-free fibres.

Wellcome, Sir Henry, 1853–1936: an American by birth who settled in Britain in 1880 and founded the firm of pharmaceutical chemists, Burroughs Wellcome. Early in his career he began to collect books and objects to illustrate the history of medical thought, and at the time of his death he had 300,000 volumes. They were then organized into what became the Wellcome Historical Medical Library, opened in London in 1949 for the use of the medical profession, scholars, and approved students. A catalogue of the incunabula, published by the O.U.P. in 1954, describes 632 items. A further 10,000 books printed before 1641 are described in a second catalogue. Subsequent volumes (including some for the 10,000 manuscripts) will complete this major bibliography.

Welsh Manuscript Society: a society instituted at Abergavenny in 1837, 'for the publication of Bardic and historical remains of Wales, with English translations and notes'. (M. L.)

Welsh printing and publishing: the pioneers of the Welsh press were Englishmen working in London. The first Welsh book, a collection of prayers known by its incipit as 'Yny Lhyvyr hwnny' (in this book), was published by Edward Whitchurch in 1546, and the deputies of Christopher Barker printed the first Welsh Bible in 1588. During the 17th and 18th centuries printers at Oxford and Shrewsbury supplied the Welsh market. The first press in Wales of which we know was set up at Montgomery about 1648. It was one of the presses that followed the army, recording its doings in a broadsheet, usually called a 'Mercurie'.

Welsh books were occasionally printed on the Continent, as, for example, Griffith Roberts's 'Dosparth byrr arràmadeg cymraeg', Milan, 1567, and Rosier Smyth's translation of Petrus Canisius's 'Cathechisme', Paris, 1609.

It is believed that Isaac Carter set up the first press at which books were printed. This was in 1719 at Trefhedyn, and the first book was 'Eglurhad o Gatechism byrraf y Gymmanfa'. He later moved to Carmarthen which became the centre of the Welsh book trade.

Early Welsh printers were often Englishmen and of little skill; while due to the generally low level of education in Wales at that time there was little demand for their products. John Ross, fl. 1743, of Carmarthen, was a London printer who took the trouble to learn Welsh. He described himself in his imprints as 'the only printer in these parts properly brought up to the trade'.

An early Welsh private press was that of Thomas Johnes, established on his estate at Hafod. (See *Hafod Press.*)

Printing and publishing were more vigorously practised in the 19th century, but regionalism and denominationalism still circumscribed the areas of sales. Dissenting author-ministers would often arrange lengthy preaching tours, selling copies of their works after speaking.

Wernerian Club: a printing society established in 1844 'for the re-publication of standard works of scientific authors of old date'. (M. L.)

Westminster Press: a printing press founded by Lord Archibald Douglas in 1878, and from 1899 managed by *Gerard Meynell*, q.v. In 1913 the press issued 'The Imprint', a journal on printing. About the same time poster printing was undertaken, in addition to the normal book production commissioned by various publishers.

Westover, George: the inventor of the British *Rotofoto photo-setting machine*, q.v.

wet end: the part of a Fourdrinier where the paper is formed, and extending to the first drying cylinder. Cf. *dry end.*

wet-on-wet printing: printing in two or more colours where the ink film of the first colour to be printed is still wet when the paper receives a second or subsequent impression. The consistency of the successive inks must be progressively less tacky.

wet plate: a photographic plate made by coating a piece of glass with collodion and sensitizing it by immersion in a solution of silver nitrate. Plates so made are always exposed wet, hence their name.

wet-plate method: the name given to photographic negative emulsion materials used in the *iodized collodion process*, q.v. (G. U.)

wet printing process inks: quick-drying inks for use in multi-colour printing. The ink of the last colour to be printed binds them all.

wet strength: a property of certain papers for which 15% or more of melamine or urea-formaldehyde has been added to the stuff in the beater. This gives increased strength for the moist conditions of lithographic printing, and such paper is used for map printing.

Weyden, Rogier van der, fl. 1430–60: a painter of Tournai who, about 1435, established his atelier at Brussels where it became one of the most famous of the time. From 1439 his principal patron was Philip, Duke of Burgundy. His best-known work (within the scope of this book) is to be seen in the copy of Wauquelin's translation of the 'Chronique du Hainaut' where a splendid presentation miniature shows Philip, surrounded by his knights of the Golden Fleece, receiving the work. The composition, portraiture, and colouring skilfully combine to make this picture of knightly chivalry a document of historical importance. The work was completed in 1446. It is now in the Royal Library, Brussels.

w.f.: an abbreviation for *wrong fount*, q.v.

Wharfedale machine: a stop-cylinder printing machine (as distinct from a two-revolution cylinder which turns twice to each printing) originally devised about 1858 by William Dawson and David Payne of Otley in Wharfedale, Yorkshire, and in a developed form still in production. The first model was built for a Glasgow printer. The type was carried on a travelling flat bed which passed under inkers to the paper-bearing cylinder.

Whatman, James, 1741–98: paper-maker, of Turkey Mill, near Maidstone. His father, James Whatman I (1702–59), acquired the co-tenancy of Turkey Mill in 1740; a paper-mill since 1693. He developed the business until he was one of England's leading paper-makers. The first manufacture in Europe of *wove paper*, q.v., is attributed to him, and he may have invented the wove-wire mould about 1756.

James Whatman II continued his father's traditions. He made paper for such important customers as the Fourdriniers and Grosvenor Chater. To him was apprenticed William Balston in 1774. In 1794 Whatman retired and sold the mill to Thomas and Finch Hollingworth. Balston remained at the mill and became a partner. The business operated as Hollingworths & Balston. The partnership was dissolved in 1806, but the Hollingworths used the countermark 'J. Whatman, Turkey Mill' on their hand-made papers until 1859.

See T. Balston, 'James Whatman, father and son', Methuen, 1957.

Whatman paper: a fine-quality English hand-made wove paper which was first made by James Whatman at Maidstone, *c.* 1770. It is used by artists as well as publishers of fine editions (it was used by *John Boydell*, q.v.).

In recent years much of the paper has been made on a mould machine by W. & R. Balston Ltd., the successors of Whatman's business.

whipstitching: a method of stitching books consisting of single leaves or plates. (See *overcasting.*)

whirler: an apparatus for spreading evenly a sensitized layer on to metal plates or lithographic stones used for printing in reproduction process work. The plate revolves horizontally about an axle. The preparation solution is distributed evenly over the surface by

Preparing an offset plate in a horizontal whirler

Vertical whirler. (*Hoh & Hahne, Leipzig*)

rotation. Heating devices are installed for drying the layer.

In addition to horizontal whirlers there are vertical models in which the solution is applied with a spray. The speed of rotation can usually be controlled, and varies, as required, between 50 and 250 revs. per minute. (G. U.)

Whitaker's Cumulative Book List: since 1924, quarterly and annual cumulations of the trade lists of British books which are published weekly in 'The Bookseller'. There are also occasional larger volumes covering a number of years.

Whitchurch, Edward, fl. 1537–60: a London publisher and printer who, with Richard Grafton, in 1537 sponsored the sale in England of the first complete version of the Bible to be printed in English (printed in Antwerp) and also of Coverdale's 'New Testament' 1538 (printed in Paris). The Great Bible of 1539 was the first important work they printed in London.

white letter: the name occasionally given by early English printers to roman types.

white line: see *blank line.*

white out: to open out composed type with spacing or blanks to improve the appearance or fill an allotted area.

White Paper: an official British Government statement issued with a white paper cover.

white paper: the warehouse term for all unprinted paper stock, no matter what colour.

white water: an alternative name for *backwater*, q.v.

Whittingham, Charles, 1767–1840: the London printer who founded the *Chiswick Press*, q.v., in 1811. He did much to improve the standards of printing illustrated books by paying great attention to the materials he used, and perfecting make-ready. He was one of the first printers to use machine-made paper and the *Stanhope press*, q.v.

In 1840 he was succeeded by his nephew Charles (1795–1876), who is noted for the excellence of his typography and for his association with *William Pickering*, q.v.; this commenced in 1829 at an establishment set up by Charles, jun., in Chancery Lane.

Whittinton, Robert: a schoolmaster of Lichfield, remembered now since it was in a grammar of his that *Wynkyn de Worde*, q.v., first printed in England some greek characters, cut in wooden blocks. A collection of his epigrams was bound up as the earliest English binding with gilt decoration. This was a brown calf volume having two panel stamps, (i) St George and the dragon, (ii) Tudor emblems, and was made about 1519 for presentation to Cardinal Wolsey.

Writing in 'The Library', Vol. VII, No. 2, p. 121, H. M. Nixon suggests that heated panels were blocked without gold; glair was painted over the impressions, and gold leaf laid on before it dried. The cold block was lightly pressed again, causing the gold to adhere clearly. The work is now in the Bodleian Library, MS. 523.

whole bound: see *full bound.*

wholesale bookseller: one whose main business is to supply retail booksellers.

Wickersham quoins: expanding steel quoins, adjusted with a key, which are inserted together with furniture at the side and foot of a chase.

Wiegendruck: the German term for *incunabulum*, q.v.

Wiener Genesis: see *Vienna Genesis.*

Winchester Bible: a fine example of English late Romanesque illumination, *c.* 1140–90, or later. The superbly painted initials were done at different periods and by various artists. Sumptuous colours, and the flowing draperies which divide the curving bodies of their wearers into ovals, typify the earlier work. The extensive use of purple, a diapered background to one of the pictures, and simpler garments for the restrained figures which also show more character in their faces, are later, and some may be early 13th-century work: with gold backgrounds, they reveal the influence of Byzantium.

See 'Artists of the Winchester Bible', by Walter Oakeshott, Faber, 1945.

Winchester School: a name given to the style of illumination characteristic of manuscripts originating in southern England during the era 950–1100.

In 954 Aethelwold founded a monastery at Abingdon where he gathered around him skilled monks whose influence on contemporary illumination resulted in the finest development of this art in Anglo-Saxon England. As Bishop of Winchester, 963–84, he continued his patronage.

Elaborate borders of acanthus leaves within two gold lines, brilliant initials filled with interlaced foliage and occasional animal heads, and figures with fluttering draperies are perhaps the main features of an art which sought to refine the barbaric traditions of Northumbria with the softer graces of classical painting, and make the page a splendid pattern of colour rather than merely a decoration. A Continental influence is suggested by the first use in England of Caroline minuscule, and features of Rheims and Metz work.

The Charter of the New Minster at Winchester, 966, is the earliest important work in the new style, while the *Benedictional of St Aethelwold*, q.v., is held to be the finest.

The special features of *Romanesque illumination*, q.v., characterized a second school of painting at Winchester, of which the finest survivals are the three-volume *Winchester Bible*, q.v., and a Psalter (B.M., *Nero*, C. iv). The latter, made for Henry of Blois (Bishop of Winchester, 1129–71), includes thirty-six whole-page scenes from the Old and New Testaments, a Jesse tree, and other scenes.

See also *Canterbury School.*

Wing, D.: see *Short-Title Catalogue.*

winter: the stout horizontal beam forming the principal support and strengthener of the *cheeks*, q.v., on a wooden hand-printing press.

wipe: a fault in letterpress printing in which the ink is pushed right across the forme instead of being deposited as a thin, even film; it thus forms a thin ridge at the edge of type. It is caused by using too thin an ink, too greasy an ink, or incorrectly set rollers (especially on platen machines).

wiper: an alternative name for the *doctor blade* (1), q.v.

wire: the continuous band of phosphor-bronze wire gauze which forms the moulding unit of a paper-making machine. It is supported at one end by the breast roll and at the other by the couch roll.

The under, or wire, side of the paper is less smooth than the upper, or felt, side.

See also *twin-wire paper.*

wire-mark: the impression made by the wire gauze of a paper-making machine on the underside of the web of paper as the sheet is formed. This side may be thought to offer a less satisfactory surface for printing upon, and an alternative is to use *twin-wire paper*, q.v.

See also *felt side*.

wire stabbing: the process of machine stitching by means of one or more wire staples through a number of leaves or sections, normally from back to front. (Adapted, with permission, from British Standard 1544: 1949, 'Bound account and manuscript books'.)

wire stitching: the process of machine stitching by means of one or more wire staples through the back of a folded section. (From B.S. 1544: 1949.) Also known as *block stitching*.

In bookbinding wire-stitching machines the sheets are fed open (by hand) inserted one inside the other. The tin-plated steel wire passes automatically from a reel to the stitching head which clips the wire, bends it into a staple, and pushes it through the paper. The

Wire-stitching machine. (*Brehmer, Leipzig*)

staple is then closed on the other side by a head cup. The machines are sometimes built with several stitching heads, and the design of the table for placing the sheets between the stitching head and head cup also varies. The tables are often interchangeable for stapling from the inside, from the back, or from the side (flat stitching). (With G.U.)

Wise, Thomas J., 1859–1937: a British bibliophile, bibliographer, biblioklept, and literary forger. Concentrating on first editions of Romantic and Victorian writers of poetry and drama, he assembled a major library which after his death was sold to the British Museum for £66,000. He named his collection the Ashley Library after the road in Crouch Hill, London, where he once lived. Wise made a serious study of the writers he collected and published an important series of bibliographies as well as several catalogues of his own library. He was a President of the Bibliographical Society and a member of the Roxburghe Club.

For his forgeries he had the ingenious idea of printing in pamphlet form part of an already published edition and giving it an earlier date, thus creating first editions for profitable sale to trusting bibliophiles and libraries. More than fifty examples were exposed as frauds by John Carter and Graham Pollard in 1934. Best known, and most lucrative, was an edition of Elizabeth Barrett Browning's 'Sonnets from the Portuguese' which he dated 'Reading, 1847', whereas records prove they were unknown to Robert Browning before 1849.

See W. Partington, 'Thomas J. Wise in the Original Cloth', Hale, 1946.

witness: 1. bibliography. A term for the particular version of a manuscript or incunabulum which is accepted by scholars as authoritative.

2. printing and binding. Said of a book with fore-edges so slightly trimmed that some of these are still rough. Also known as *binding proof*.

See also *uncut*.

Wodhull, Michael, 1740–1816: a wealthy bibliophile who collected incunabula and first printed editions of the classics. Many works in his library were bound by Roger Payne. Wodhull is also remembered as the first translator into English verse of the writings of Euripides (published in 1782).

Wolfe, John, fl. 1580–1601: a son of R. Wolfe whose business he subsequently inherited. John Wolfe was a printer from the Fishmongers' Company who achieved a certain notoriety by his agitation against the granting of privileges by Queen Elizabeth. Later, however, he became a member of the Stationers' Company and printer to the City of London.

He printed the first edition of John Stow's 'Survey of London', 1598, Greene's 'Quip for an upstart courtier', and many voyages and travels.

He is more important for the edition of John Hayward's 'Life and raigne of King Henrie IIII' which he printed in 1599 and dedicated to the Earl of Essex. The book sold well, about 1200 copies of the first two printings within a month, but owing to certain passages which were held to be treasonable Wolfe and Hayward were imprisoned, and the innocent association of Essex with the dedication was later held against him.

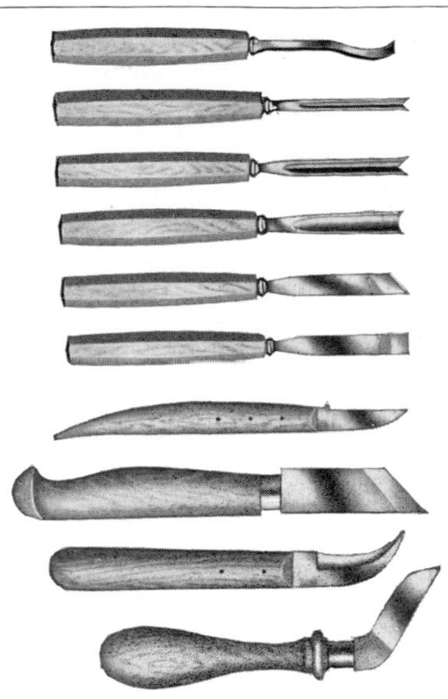

Tools for wood and linoleum cutting and engraving

Wolfe, Reginald (or **Reyner**), fl. 1536–73: a native of Strasbourg who about 1536 settled in England and was several times Master of the Stationers' Company. He was King's Printer for Latin, Greek, and Hebrew to Edward VI.

Wolgemut, Michael, 1434–1519: a Nuremberg painter, famous for his designs for woodcuts. His finest achievement was a series of illustrations for 'Schatzbehalter der wahren Reichtümer des Heils und der ewigen Seligkeit', 1491 (Hain 14507), which had ninety-six full-page cuts and is considered outstanding for the period. Another great work was the equally famous 'Die Weltchronik' (Nuremberg Chronicle) of Hartmann Schedel and Georg Alt,

From Holbein's 'Dance of Death', drawn in 1523–26, and cut by Lützelburger. The work was printed at Lyons in 1538 by Gaspar and Melchior Treschel. Reproduced here in original size

Full-scale reproduction of a woodcut from the first book printed with illustrations 'Der Edelstein' (Fables) by Boner, printed in 1461 by Albrecht Pfister of Bamberg. The original was hand-coloured

printed by Anton Koberger (in Latin, 1493, and German, 1493, Hain 14508 and 14510). His stepson Wilhelm Pleydenwurff collaborated with Wolgemut on the 1809 woodcuts for this last work. Albrecht Dürer was a pupil of Wolgemut (whose name is sometimes spelled Wohlgemuth. (With G. U.)

Wolpe, Berthold, 1905– : an eminent engraver and type-designer, born in Germany where he studied with *Rudolph Koch*, q.v. In 1932 Wolpe came to England, and has for many years been associated with Faber and Faber Ltd. He is widely known for the Albertus family of titling and display types, of which the earliest, Albertus Titling, was cut in 1934 and issued by the Monotype Corporation in the following year.

wood engraving: an impression from an inked forme cut in wood. White lines depict the image on a black background, and the medium can interpret tones and textures, according to the skill of the engraver, in a manner not fundamental to the *woodcut*, q.v. Inch-thick pieces of end-grain box wood are used, the design being cut with a graver and gouge. To give a tighter surface a saccharine solution can be coated over and burnt in: the surface is then treated with a solution of zinc white in gum arabic before outlining the design. Wood engraving permitted finer work, and could be carried out to advantage as *tone engraving*, which meant that the picture was washed on the block in tones of varying strength, after which it was left to the technical skill of the block cutter to reproduce them in lines and dots. Wood engraving in this way became an important means of illustration during the 19th century, especially when photography was used to transfer the picture to the prepared block.

The skill of *Thomas Bewick*, q.v., was responsible for the development and popularity of this medium (1775); he demonstrated that a more durable block could be made by cutting into an end-grain section rather than along the grain, and he introduced the white line technique. The adaptation of wood engraving for colour work dates from 1843.

(With G. U.)

wood free: paper made without mechanical wood pulp. *Chemical wood* pulp paper, q.v., is wood free. An alternative name, often preferred, is *pure*.

wood pulp: the principal ingredient in many kinds of paper. The two classes of wood pulps are mechanical or ground wood as used in newsprint, and chemical pulp produced by various methods including the sulphite, soda, and sulphate processes. The use of wood for paper dates from 1843 when it was discovered in Germany by Friedrich Gottlob Keller.

Woodburytype: 1. an intaglio illustration process in which the design on a film of gelatine in relief, taken from a photographic negative, is pressed on to a metal printing plate. It was devised in 1866 by W. B. Woodbury.

2. a print taken from such a plate.

woodcut: the earliest form of printed illustration in which an impression is taken from an inked forme cut in wood. Bold black lines or areas depict a design against a white background. The block for printing is made of soft, smooth-grained wood, usually type high, the design being drawn or transferred on to it for cutting with wood-carving tools along the plank grain; the non-image areas are cut away leaving the lines in relief.

The art is of very ancient origin, in China at least before the birth of Christ. In Europe it was practised by monks in the late 14th century for producing the figures of saints, but the oldest dated sheet known is from 1418. The best known of early dated European woodcuts is the Buxheim 'Saint

Detail from a wooden block of an ancient Chinese woodcut

An early Bewick engraving. Original size

Wood engraving by Harald Sallberg, emphasizing the effect of white lines on a dark ground. Reproduced from 'Rid i natt', 1942. *Original size*

Mechanically engraved shading. Original size

Wood engraving by F. Pierdon from a drawing by Gustave Doré. Detail of an illustration for 'Atala' by F. A. de Chateaubriand. Swedish edition of 1882

Detail from one of Dürer's Apocalypse series woodcuts, 1498. *In this full-scale reproduction the great advance which Dürer's art represented, both technically and artistically, is easily seen when compared with 'Der Edelstein'*

Christopher', 1423, and one of the first books to be so illustrated was Ulrich Boner's 'Fables' printed in 1461 by *Pfister* of Bamberg, q.v. At the time of Boner the text was printed first, and then the illustrations in spaces left for them; it was not for a few years that the idea of cutting the blocks to type height was conceived, permitting text and illustrations to be printed together.

Blocks of pear tree were used at first, cut along the length of the tree. The design was drawn or traced in reverse on the planed surface of the block, after which the white areas were cut away leaving the design in relief. The woodcutter used various knives and fine chisels as tools. The block was inked by hand with a dabber, and then a damp sheet of paper was laid over it and pressed to the block with a leather ball stuffed with horsehair. The wooden block was later printed with type in a hand-press. Colouring was also done by hand until the beginning of the 16th century when separate blocks for the different colours were used.

The artist's work had to be adapted to the technique, and very often the cutting of the block was done by another person (Ger. Formschneider) whose task it was to cut the details of the drawing in wood with the greatest possible accuracy, line by line.

Artistic woodcutting may be said to have developed with Michael Wolgemut, Albrecht Dürer, and their successors in the 16th century. In the 17th century the only truly famous craftsman was Christoffel Jegher (1596–1652), a German-Dutchman, remembered for his woodcuts of Rubens's paintings, emblem books, initials, and printers' devices. Owing to the increased popularity of *copper engraving*, q.v., woodcutting declined in the 18th century, to be revived, however, in the 19th under the influence of the Japanese woodcut. The Japanese worked mainly in many colours, preferably printed, so that the grain of the wood stood out. Colour was put on the block with a paint-brush which made toning possible. Water-colours with different vehicles were mostly used, and printing was done in a simple hand-press or by means of grinding with a suitable tool. Japanese mulberry paper is highly absorbent and was used in both a damp and dry state. Modern European engravers, too, are fond of using Japan paper and Japanese water-colours for their original wood engravings, i.e., engravings drawn, cut, and printed by the artist.

As wood blocks will only stand the printing of comparatively small editions, it is usual to make stereos or electros which are set up with type as ordinary blocks; in England the use of stereos for this purpose dates from the 1830's. (With G.U.)

See also *Colonna, Florentine woodcuts, Formschneider, wood engraving.*

Woodrow Society: a society instituted at Edinburgh, in 1841, for the publication of the early writers of the Reformed Church of Scotland. (M.L.)

word division: see *division of words.*

Worde, Wynkyn de, fl. 1477–1530: the assistant of William Caxton who, on the latter's death in 1491, continued the business, largely in his master's traditions. An edition of 'Liber festivalis', 1493, was the first book to bear his name. He issued about 800 publications (including broadsheets and reprints), of which his finest is perhaps 'De proprietatibus rerum' of Bartholomaeus, *c.* 1495.

While mostly using black letter he sometimes employed roman for scholastic works, and was the first printer in England to use italic; this last was in a translation of Lucian's 'Complures dialogi', 1528. In 1517 he printed some Greek words, from wooden blocks, in 'De concinitate grammatices' of *Robert Whittinton*, q.v. De Worde died in 1534.

work and tumble: the method of perfecting a sheet by feeding the opposite long edge to the grippers for the second impression from the same forme. Cf. *sheetwork, work and turn.*

work and turn: a method of printing whereby the matter for both sides of a sheet is set in one forme. Paper, double the size of the sheet required, is first printed on one side and then turned over end for end and backed up from the same forme. In the result each sheet as printed contains two perfected impressions of half its size, both halves being similar to each other. The two halves are separated either by slitting in the printing machine or in a guillotine. See also *half sheets, tack marks.* (L.K.)

work in progress: said of work in hand at the printer's. It is customary to make a periodical report to the publisher under this head.

work off: to print the paper.

work up: said of a lead space which has risen to the height of type causing a 'black'.

working: any forme which is on the press and being run off.

worm-eaten books: to fumigate worm-eaten books put a jar of paradichlorobenzine with the books into a tin; seal it, and leave for a week. Books infested with silver fish or mites require the same treatment. Lacquer paint containing Dieldrin should be used to paint bookshelves: it will remain toxic for three years, even if scrubbed.

worm hole: the damage to paper or bindings made by the larvae of various beetles.

wove paper: paper which when held up to light is seen to have an even or regular pattern of fine mesh, but with none of the lines which distinguish *laid paper*, q.v. This is caused by the weave of the dandy roll. Variations in the quality of wove paper are due to the mesh; 60 to 65 strands per inch of screen for newsprint, and 70 to 80 for other printing papers being usual.

James Whatman was probably the first manufacturer, if not the inventor, of wove paper. Its first-known use for bookwork was in 1757 when John Baskerville printed his Virgil upon it.

wrapped round: see *insert*.

wrapper: see *jacket*.

Wright, Edward, *c.* 1558–1615: an English cartographer, particularly noted for his world map for 'Hakluyt's Voyages', 1600.

writings: paper sized to take writing ink and usually stocked in sizes known as writing sizes, as distinct from *printings* which may not be suitable for writing upon and are stocked in an entirely different range of sizes.

wrong fount: a mistake in composition in which a letter of the wrong size or face is set. When proof correcting, the letters 'w.f.' are written marginally to draw attention to such faults.

Wyer, Robert, fl. 1529–56: an enterprising if undistinguished printer and bookseller living near Charing Cross, London, who developed a market for short, cheap books on popular scientific subjects, in addition to medical and religious works. These were mostly issued as roughly printed brochures, illustrated with simple woodcuts, and he was essentially a printer for the general public. Notable works were a translation by Whitford of 'De Imitatione Christi', *c.* 1531, and William Marshall's 'Defence of Peace', 1535.

In assigning dates to his undated publications it is a help to remember that imprints which include the words 'Bishop of Norwiches Rentes' must be dated before 1536, since in that year the Bishop sold the property to Henry VIII who assigned it to the Duke of Suffolk. Wyer's books imprinted 'in the Duke of Sufolkes Rentes' are thus post 1536.

Wynkyn de Worde Society: founded in London in 1957, being a social group instituted for the meeting at luncheon and other gatherings of persons associated with the creation and production of 'print', the promotion of mutual understanding, and the exchange and dissemination of information on printing and allied subjects.

ADDENDUM

weight: 'the degree of blackness of a typeface' (B.S. 2961: 1958). Types in a *family*, q.v., may vary in weight, e.g. extra-light, light, semi-light, medium, semi-bold, bold, extra-bold, ultra-bold. Paper, ink, and method of printing are factors to be considered when choosing a weight of type.

JAPANESE WOODCUT

Collotype reproduction from a coloured woodcut by Utagawa Toyokuni (1768–1825).

x-height: the height of lower-case letters (excluding ascenders and descenders), i.e., the height of a lower-case x; a term used to describe the apparent size of a type. In a 12-point type this may vary from 0·056 in. to 0·080 in. Walbaum, Perpetua, and Centaur have small x-heights, Times and Plantin have large.

Xerography: the name given to a process invented in the United States and developed commercially since about 1946 for electrically reproducing or copying an original without the use of ink, pressure or rollers.

Briefly, a selenium-coated surface is given a positive electrostatic charge and an image is then exposed to it through a camera. Where light is reflected the charge will be dissipated, leaving the positive charge in the image areas. When a negatively-charged black resinous powder is cascaded over the selenium it is attracted to the charged areas. If paper is now placed over the selenium and charged positively the powder image will be transferred to it, and the image can then be made permanent by heat and vapour fusing.

The process is of considerable importance, among other uses, for the reproduction of out-of-print books. For this purpose, the Copyflo machine is used. In America this is made by Haloid Xerox Inc., of Rochester, New York: in Britain (and for all world markets outside North America) by Rank-XeroX Limited, London. Pioneering the use of the Copyflo for reproducing out-of-print books are University Microfilms of Ann Arbor, Michigan, and of 44 Great Queen Street, London, W.C.2. Books reproduced by this method are referred to as 'Xerocopies'.

Procedure is briefly as follows. The book or document to be reproduced is photographed on to 35 mm. film. Each frame consists of a double page opening. The film is developed. It is then fed into the Copyflo machine which contains a 2,000 foot roll of non-sensitized paper and the powder. A current of 2,000 volts is used. As the machine operates a continuous roll of paper emerges, bearing upon it a book-size positive enlargement of the microfilmed matter. Only one side of the paper is used, the other remaining blank. The paper is next cut, folded, and glued up in a form of perfect binding, the outside folds forming the edges of each pair of printed pages. Top and bottom edges are trimmed but not the fore-edge which, by being closed, gives the effect of a Chinese book (see *orihon*).

Diagrams and line drawings reproduce well, but the system is not suitable for half-tones.

xylograph: 1. a wood engraving.
2. a block book.

Y

Yapp: a style of limp-leather binding with overlapping flaps or edges on three sides. Named after William Yapp who, between 1854 and 1875, had a Bible warehouse in London. He designed a limp binding suitable for Bibles to be carried in the pocket. This was made for him by Samuel Bagster, through whose catalogues the description and style 'Yapp binding' became known.

See also *circuit edges.*

Ye Sette of Odd Volumes: a London dining society founded in 1878 by Bernard Quaritch. The forty-two members meet to dine and read papers on literary, artistic, and scientific subjects. Some of these have been printed, and R. Straus has compiled 'An Odd Bibliography' listing those which appeared between 1878 and 1924.

year book: a book or pamphlet published once a year, in which a record of events, statistics, and other information relating to some work or subject is put into convenient form for reference. Also called *annual.* (M. L.)

yellow-backs: a cheap form of publishing novels, popular in mid-Victorian England, with boards covered in yellow paper, and bearing pictorial designs on the front.

See also *fiction series, three-decker novel.*

Young-Delcambre: a composing machine made in Belgium in 1840. It was designed by (Sir) Henry Bessemer, but the patent was taken out by J. H. Young and A. Delcambre of Lille.

Young Master Printers: a nationally organised body of management trainees and young Master Printers, officially recognised in 1931, but tracing its origins to the Junior Master Printers of 1925. Members meet annually for a Summer School (first held in 1934), since 1954 replaced by a Spring School at which technical developments and management subjects are discussed. There is also a National Conference (annually since 1946).

Z

Zaehnsdorf, Joseph, 1816–86: an Austro-Hungarian craftsman-binder (born in Budapest) who learned his craft in Stuttgart and Vienna. In 1842 he founded in London the firm of hand-binders still renowned for fine bindings. His forwarding and finishing were of the highest order, and a further speciality of the business was, and is, the restoration of valuable old books.

Zainer, Günther, fl. 1468–78: the printer from Strasbourg who, about 1468, erected the first press in Augsburg, later one of the most important centres of printing in 15th- and 16th-century Germany. In 1468 he issued the first dated book in that city, the 'Meditationes de vita Christi' of S. Bonaventura. He is noted for his extensive use of woodcuts.

Zainer encountered opposition from local wood-carvers and playing-card makers who thought the new craft would destroy their business, but Melchior von Stamhaim, the Abbot of St Ulrich, offered him room for his press. Two years later the Abbot bought five printing presses and, under Zainer's direction, established the first monastic printing press.

Zainer, Johann, fl. 1472–93: a native of Reutlingen who, in 1472, established the first printing press at Ulm. His first important work was Boccaccio's 'De claris mulieribus' (Famous Women), 1473, which appeared in a Latin and German edition; both were illustrated with eighty excellent woodcuts derived from French manuscript prototypes. These in turn were widely copied throughout northern Europe. Zainer was one of the first among several publisher-printers at this time to seek the aid of scholars to edit their productions, and he found in Dr. Heinrich Steinhöwel a learned collaborator. Among other important works issued in 1473 were Francesco Petrarca's 'Griseldis' (Patient Grissel) and Steinhöwel's own 'Regimen Sanitatis.'

In 1493 the claims of Zainer's creditors forced him to flee the city, but he is thought to have returned and continued his work from 1496–1523.

Zell, Ulrich: a priest of Mainz, where he learned printing and later established the first press in Cologne in 1465. He issued mostly theological works.

He is memorable for his statement in the 'Cronica van der hilliger Stat van Coellen' (Cologne Chronicle), issued from 1499 by Koelhoff, jun., that printing was invented by Johan Gudenburch van Mentz (Johann Gutenberg of Mainz.)

zig-zag guard: an alternative name for *continuous guard*, q.v.

Zilverdistel Press: the first modern Dutch private press, founded at The Hague, and directed from 1910 by J. F. van Royen. His early books show the influence of the British private press movement. Special types designed for the press were the Zilver type of de Roos, 1915, and the Distel type of Lucien Pissarro, 1917.

In 1923 the name was changed to *Kunera Press.*

zinco: 1. an abbreviation for *zincograph*, q.v.

2. a cheap alternative to the *binder's brass*, q.v. It is less durable, and the impression made with it lacks sharpness.

zincograph: a zinc etching.

See also *line block.*

Zip-a-tone: a series of mechanical tints printed on Cellophane. They are used by an artist or draughtsman when preparing originals for line engravings. The tints are available in various textures, and the Cellophane can be cut to any desired shape for combining with the artist's pen lines. This enables him to control the design to an extent not possible where tint laying is left to the blockmaker.

Zip-a-tone tints were invented in the U.S.A., and are made in Britain under licence.

zodiacal signs: see *astronomical symbols.*

APPENDIX A

SOME TYPE SPECIMENS

A Selection by Ronald Eames

See also the entry on *Letter forms*

GOTHIC FACES (BLACK LETTER)

Caxton Black

An imitation of the original Caxton face. V. J. Figgins 1904. 10 pt

ABCDEFGHIJKLMNOPQR
STUVWXYZ abcdefghijklmnopqrst
uvwxyz 1234567890

Fraktur

Monotype 1904. 12 pt

ABCDEFGHIJKLMNOPQRSTUVW
XYZÄÖÜ& 1234567890
abcdefghijklmnopqrſtuvwxyzäöüchck
ſſiſlllsſſſiſtßtz

Old English Text No. 2

Monotype 1934. 12 pt

ABCDEFGHIJKLMNOPQRST
UVWXYZ& abcdefghijklmnopqrst
uvwxyzæœ fiflffifflffächckllſſiſtſſtzß
1234567890

Schwabacher

Monotype 1910. 12 pt

ABCDEFGHIJKLMNOPQRSTUVWXYZ
ÄÖÜ&
abcdefghijklmnopqrſtuvwxyzäöü chckfiffflllſi
sſſſtßtz 1234567890

VENETIAN FACES

Centaur

Designed by Bruce Rogers. Based on Jenson's original. Monotype 1929. 12 pt

ABCDEFGHIJKLMNOPQRSTUVWXYZ
abcdefghijklmnopqrstuvwxyzææ 1234567890
ABCDEFGHIJKLMNOPQRSTUVWXYZ
abcdefghijklmnopqrstuvwxyzææ 1234567890
ABCDEFGHIJKLMNOPQRSTUVWXYZÆŒ

Cloister Old Style

Designed by Morris Benton. Monotype 1914. 12 pt

ABCDEFGHIJKLMNOPQRSTUVWXYZ
& abcdefghijklmnopqrstuvwxyz 1234567890
ABCDEFGHIJKLMNOPQRSTUVWXYZ 1234567890
ABCDEFGHIJKLMNOPQRSTUVWXYZ
abcdefghijklmnopqrstuvwxyzææ 1234567890
1234567890

Goudy Old Style

Designed by F. W. Goudy. American Typefounders 1928; Monotype. 14 pt

ABCDEFGHIJKLMNOPQ
RSTUVWXYZ abcdefghijkl
mnopqrstuvwxyz 1234567890
ABCDEFGHIJKLMNOPQ
RSTUVWXYZ abcdefghijklm
nopqrstuvwxyz 1234567890

OLD FACES

Bembo

Griffo's roman originally cut for Aldus Manutius and first used in Cardinal Bembo's *De Aetna*. Monotype 1929. 12 pt

ABCDEFGHIJKLMNOPQRSTUV WXYZ abcdefghijklmnopqrstuvwxyz 1234567890
ABCDEFGHIJKLMNOPQRSTU VWXYZ abcdefghijklmnopqrstuvwxyz 1234567890
ABCDEFGHIJKLMNOPQRSTUVWXYZ
ABCDEFGHIJKLMNOPQRST UVWXYZ abcdefghijklmnopqrs tuvwxyz 1234567890

Caslon Old Face

Once the most popular English Old Face. Introduced by William Caslon in 1725. Caslon. 12 pt

ABCDEFGHIJKLMNOPQRS TUVWXYZ abcdefghijklmnopqr stuvwxyz 1234567890
ABCDEFGHIJKLMNOPQRST UVWXYZ abcdefghijklmnopqrstu vwxyz
ABCDEFGHIJKLMNOPQRSTUVWXYZ
ABCDEFGHIJKLMNOPQR STUVWXYZ abcdefghijklmn opqrstuvwxyz 1234567890

Ehrhardt

A narrow face originating in Leipzig at the end of the 17th century. Monotype 1938. 12 pt

ABCDEFGHIJKLMNOPQRSTUV WXYZ&
ABCDEFGHIJKLMNOPQRSTUVWXYZ
abcdefghijklmnopqrstuvwxyz
1234567890 1234567890
ABCDEFGHIJKLMNOPQRSTUVWX YZ& ÆŒabcdefghijklmnopqrstuvwxyzæœ 1234567890
ABCDEFGHIJKLMNOPQRSTUV WXYZ&ÆŒ abcdefghijklmnopqrst uvwxyz 1234567890

Garamond

Based on types of the Imprimerie Nationale, not in fact cut by Garamond but by Jean Jannon (Mrs. B. Warde *Fleuron* No. 5) Monotype 1922. 12 pt

ABCDEFGHIJKLMNOPQRST UVWXYZ abcdefghijklmnopqrs tuvwxyz 1234567890
ABCDEFGHIJKLMNOPQRS TUVWXYZ abcdefghijklmnopqrst uvwxyz 1234567890
ABCDEFGHIJKLMNOPQRSTUVWXYZ
ABCDEFGHIJKLMNOPQRSTU VWXYZ&ÆŒ abcdefghijklmnopq rstuvwxyzæœfiflffiffifff 1234567890

Janson

Another of the types from the Ehrhardt foundry, Leipzig, associated with Anton Janson. Linotype 1934. 12 pt

ABCDEFGHIJKLMNOPQRSTU VWXYZ abcdefghijklmnopqrstu vwxyz 1234567890
ABCDEFGHIJKLMNOPQRSTU VWXYZ abcdefghijklmnopqrstu vwxyz 1234567890
ABCDEFGHIJKLMNOPQRSTUVWXYZ

Plantin

Named after the 16th-century printer, not in fact used by him but in use during his lifetime. Monotype 1914. 12 pt

ABCDEFGHIJKLMNOPQRS TUVWXYZ abcdefghijklmnopqr stuvwxyz 1234567890
ABCDEFGHIJKLMNOPQRS TUVWXYZ abcdefghijklmnopqrs tuvwxyz 1234567890
ABCDEFGHIJKLMNOPQRSTUVWXYZ
ABCDEFGHIJKLMNOPQRSTU VWXYZ& abcdefghijklmnopqrstuvwxyz 1234567890 1234567890

Van Dijck

Based, under the guidance of J. van Krimpen, on old types in the possession of the Enschedé foundry. Caslon used a Van Dijck model for his Old Face. Monotype 1935. 12 pt

ABCDEFGHIJKLMNOPQRSTUVWX YZ&
abcdefghijklmnopqrstuvwxyzæœ
1234567890
ABCDEFGHIJKLMNOPQRSTUVW XYZ&
abcdefghijklmnopqrstuvwxyzæœ
1234567890
ABCDEFGHIJKLMNOPQRSTUVWXYZ

Fournier

Based on the new roman designed by Pierre-Simon Fournier in the 1740's, under the influence of the 'romains du roi'. Monotype 1925. 12 pt

ABCDEFGHIJKLMNOPQRSTU VWXYZ abcdefghijklmnopqrstuvwx yz 1234567890
ABCDEFGHIJKLMNOPQRST UVWXYZ abcdefghijklmnopqrstuvw xyz 1234567890
ABCDEFGHIJKLMNOPQRSTUVWXYZ

TRANSITIONAL FACES

Baskerville

The English 18th-century face cut by John Baskerville. The original punches are now in the possession of Cambridge University Press. Monotype 1923. 12 pt

ABCDEFGHIJKLMNOPQRS TUVWXYZ abcdefghijklmnopq rstuvwxyz 1234567890
ABCDEFGHIJKLMNOPQRST UVWXYZ abcdefghijklmnopqrstuv wxyz 1234567890
ABCDEFGHIJKLMNOPQRSTUVWXYZ
ABCDEFGHIJKLMNOPQRST UVWXYZ
abcdefghijklmnopqrstuvwxyz

Bell

Cut by Richard Austin in 1788. Monotype 1931. 12 pt

ABCDEFGHIJKLMNOPQRST UVWXYZ abcdefghijklmnopqrst uvwxyz 1234567890
ABCDEFGHIJKLMNOPQRS TUVWXYZ abcdefghijklmnopqrst uvwxyz 1234567890
ABCDEFGHIJKLMNOPQRSTUVWXYZ

MODERN FACES

Bodoni

The Modern of Giambattista Bodoni. Now offered by most founders in many weights for book and display purposes. Monotype. 12 pt

ABCDEFGHIJKLMNOPQRST UVWXYZ abcdefghijklmnopqrs tuvwxyz 1234567890
ABCDEFGHIJKLMNOPQRS TUVWXYZ abcdefghijklmnopqr stuvwxyz 1234567890
ABCDEFGHIJKLMNOPQRSTUVWXYZ
ABCDEFGHIJKLMNOPQRSTU VWXYZ abcdefghijklmnopqrstuv wxyz 1234567890

De Vinne

Intertype 1914. 12 pt

ABCDEFGHIJKLMNOPQR STUVWXYZ abcdefghijklm nopqrstuvwxyz 1234567890
ABCDEFGHIJKLMNOPQR STUVWXYZ abcdefghijklm nopqrstuvwxyz 1234567890
ABCDEFGHIJKLMNOPQRSTUVWXYZ

Appendix A

Walbaum

A German version of Didot, introduced into England by the Curwen Press in 1925. Monotype 1934. 11 pt. (Didot)

ABCDEFGHIJKLMNOPQRSTU VWXYZ abcdefghijklmnopqrstuv wxyz 1234567890

ABCDEFGHIJKLMNOPQRST UVWXYZ abcdefghijklmnopqrstu vwxyz

ABCDEFGHIJKLMNOPQRSTUVWXYZ

ABCDEFGHIJKLMNOPQRSTUVWX YZ

abcdefghijklmnopqrstuvwxyzæœ

1234567890

CONTEMPORARY FACES

Caledonia

Designed by W. A. Dwiggins. Inspired by Scotch Roman and also types made by William Martin about 1790. Linotype 1949. 12 pt

ABCDEFGHIJKLMNOPQRSTU VWXYZ abcdefghijklmnopqrstu vwxyz 1234567890

ABCDEFGHIJKLMNOPQRSTU VWXYZ abcdefghijklmnopqrstu vwxyz 1234567890

ABCDEFGHIJKLMNOPQRSTUVWXYZ

ABCDEFGHIJKLMNOPQRSTU VWXYZ abcdefghijklmnopqrstu vwxyz 1234567890

Cornell

Designed by George F. Trenholm. Intertype 1935. 12 pt

ABCDEFGHIJKLMNOPQRSTU VWXYZ abcdefghijklmnopqrst uvwxyz 1234567890

ABCDEFGHIJKLMNOPQRSTU VWXYZ abcdefghijklmnopqrst uvwxyz 1234567890

ABCDEFGHIJKLMNOPQRSTUVWXYZ

Dante

Designed by Giovanni Mardersteig and cut by Charles Malin for use at the Officina Bodoni in 1954. Now generally available. Monotype 1958. 12 pt

ABCDEFGHIJKLMNOPQRSTUVW XYZ&

abcdefghijklmnopqrstuvwxyzæœ

1234567890

ABCDEFGHIJKLMNOPQRSTUVWXYZ&

abcdefghijklmnopqrstuvwxyzæœ

1234567890

ABCDEFGHIJKLMNOPQRSTUVWXYZ

Egmont

Designed by S. H. De Roos. Intertype 1937. 10 pt

ABCDEFGHIJKLMNOPQRSTUV WXYZ abcdefghijklmnopqrstuvwxyz 1234567890 1234567890

ABCDEFGHIJKLMNOPQRSTUV WXYZ abcdefghijklmnopqrstuvwxyz 1234567890 1234567890

ABCDEFGHIJKLMNOPQRSTUVWXYZ

ABCDEFGHIJKLMNOPQRSTUV WXYZ abcdefghijklmnopqrstuvwxyz 1234567890

ABCDEFGHIJKLMNOPQRSTUVWXYZ

ABCDEFGHIJKLMNOPQRSTUV WXYZ abcdefghijklmnopqrstuvwxyz 1234567890

ABCDEFGHIJKLMNOPQRSTUVWXYZ

Imprint

Modelled on an 18th-century Old Face to the instructions of J. H. Mason and Gerard Meynell specifically for *The Imprint* but now in general use. Monotype 1912. 12 pt

ABCDEFGHIJKLMNOPQRS TUVWXYZ abcdefghijklmnopqr stuvwxyz 1234567890

ABCDEFGHIJKLMNOPQRS TUVWXYZ abcdefghijklmnopqr stuvwxyz

ABCDEFGHIJKLMNOPQRSTUVWXYZ

ABCDEFGHIJKLMNOPQRSTUV WXYZ

abcdefghijklmnopqrstuvwxyz

1234567890

Juliana

A new narrow face designed by S. L. Hartz. Linotype 1958. 12 pt

ABCDEFGHIJKLMNOPQRSTU VWXYZ abcdefghijklmnopqrstu vwxyz 1234567890

ABCDEFGHIJKLMNOPQRSTU VWXYZ abcdefghijklmnopqrstu vwxyz 1234567890

ABCDEFGHIJKLMNOPQRSTUVWXYZ

Perpetua

Most popular of Eric Gill's Roman faces. Monotype 1929–30. 12 pt

ABCDEFGHIJKLMNOPQRSTUV WXYZ abcdefghijklmnopqrstuvwxyz 1234567890

ABCDEFGHIJKLMNOPQRSTUVW XYZ abcdefghijklmnopqrstuvwxyz 1234567890

ABCDEFGHIJKLMNOPQRSTUVWXYZ

ABCDEFGHIJKLMNOPQRSTUV WXYZ abcdefghijklmnopqrstuv wxyz 1234567890

Pilgrim

Designed by Eric Gill for a book published by The Limited Editions Club, New York. Now in general use. Linotype 1953. 12 pt

ABCDEFGHIJKLMNOPQRSTUVW XYZ abcdefghijklmnopqrstuvwx yz 1234567890

ABCDEFGHIJKLMNOPQRSTUVW XYZ abcdefghijklmnopqrstuvwx yz 1234567890

ABCDEFGHIJKLMNOPQRSTUVWXYZ

ABCDEFGHIJKLMNOPQRSTUVWXYZ

Spectrum

Designed by Jan van Krimpen. Enschedé 1952; Monotype 1956. 12 pt

ABCDEFGHIJKLMNOPQRSTUV WXYZ abcdefghijklmnopqrstuvw xyz 1234567890

ABCDEFGHIJKLMNOPQRSTUV WXYZ abcdefghijklmnopqrstuvwxyz 1234567890

ABCDEFGHIJKLMNOPQRSTUVWXYZ

Times New Roman

Designed under the direction of Stanley Morison for the restyling of *The Times* newspaper, but universally adopted for book use. Monotype, Linotype 1932. 12 pt

ABCDEFGHIJKLMNOPQRS TUVWXYZ abcdefghijklmnopq rstuvwxyz 1234567890

ABCDEFGHIJKLMNOPQRST UVWXYZ abcdefghijklmnopqrst uvwxyz 1234567890

ABCDEFGHIJKLMNOPQRSTUVWXYZ

ABCDEFGHIJKLMNOPQRS TUVWXYZ abcdefghijklmnopqr stuvwxyz 1234567890

Times Cyrillic

1956

АБВГДЕЖЗИКЛМНОПРСТУФ ХЦЧШЩЪЫЬЭЮЯѢЖЂЈЉЊЋ Џ абвгдежзиклмнопрстуфхцчшщ ъыьэюяѣжђђјљњћџ

Times Greek

1956

ΑΒΓΔΕΖΗΘΙΚΛΜΝΞΟΠΡΣΤΥΦΧ ΨΩϚ αβγδεζηθικλμνξοπρστυφχψως

SANS SERIF

Gill Sans

Designed by Eric Gill. Available in many variations and four different weights. Monotype 1928–30. 12 pt

ABCDEFGHIJKLMNOPQRSTUVW
XYZ abcdefghijklmnopqrstuvwxyz
1234567890
ABCDEFGHIJKLMNOPQRSTUVWXYZ
abcdefghijklmnopqrstuvwxyz
1234567890

Headline Bold

1956. 12 pt

ABCDEFGHIJKLMNOPQRSTUVWXYZ
ÆŒ abcdefghijklmnopqrstuvwxyz&
1234567890
ABCDEFGHIJKLMNOPQRSTUVW
XYZ& abcdefghijklmnopqrstuvwxyz
1234567890

Vogue

Designed originally for *Vogue* magazine. Intertype 1932. 12 pt

ABCDEFGHIJKLMNOPQRSTUV
WXYZ abcdefghijklmnopqrstuv
wxyz 1234567890
ABCDEFGHIJKLMNOPQRSTUV
WXYZ abcdefghijklmnopqrstuv
wxyz 1234567890

EGYPTIAN

Cairo

Intertype 1933. 12 pt

ABCDEFGHIJKLMNOPQRSTU
VWXYZ abcdefghijklmnopqr
stuvwxyz 1234567890
ABCDEFGHIJKLMNOPQRSTU
VWXYZ abcdefghijklmnopqr
stuvwxyz 1234567890

Rockwell

In four weights with condensed and shadow versions. Monotype 1934. 12 pt

ABCDEFGHIJKLMNOPQRSTUV
WXYZ
abcdefghijklmnopqrstuvwxyz
1234567890
ABCDEFGHIJKLMNOPQRSTUVWX
YZ abcdefghijklmnopqrstuvwxyz
1234567890

FAT FACE

Ultra Bodoni

American Typefounders 1928, Monotype 1936. 14 pt

ABCDEFGHIJKLMNOP
QRSTUVWXYZ
abcdefghijklmnopqurstuvw
xyz
1234567890
ABCDEFGHIJKLMNOP
QRSTUVWXYZ
abcdefghijklmnopqrstuv
wxyz

EXOTIC

Arabic Naskh Accented

Monotype 1956. 24 pt (Didot)

لكثة تصث غف ّف أطذحب كل٣خخ ى ث ح
٨طشذو٦ع يقلمخل آ٥لكل قا ح ق ى م أغطالله غ
لك مى ب ضهذ ممه عظصة ى ة مزم ش٤ح مى غ لإ ت
ذغصدمع حّل ج م ق ج ں خ مى ق لك اعم هلاب
ل خطة بم ألك حو • خى ب ف ث لا مى تى ح

DISPLAY FACES

ALBERTUS Albertus
TITLING
Berthold Wolpe. Monotype 1932–40

Ashley Script
Ashley Havinden. Monotype 1955

CASTELLAR
Designed by John Peters. Monotype 1957

Chisel
Stephenson Blake 1939

Colonna
Monotype 1927

CONSORT
Stephenson Blake 1956

CORVINUS SKYLINE
Bauersche Giesserei 1929–34

EGMONT
INLINE
De Roos. Typefoundry Amsterdam 1937

Egyptian
Condensed
Expanded
Monotype (expanded Stephenson Blake)

ERBAR Light
Ludwig and Mayer 1922–30

FESTIVAL
Phillip Boydell. Monotype 1951

Francesca Ronde
Stephenson Blake 1948

GILL TITLING
Bold Condensed
Extra bold, Line
SHADOW TITLING
Eric Gill. Monotype 1928–30

GRAVURE OPEN
Typefoundry Amsterdam

Grotesque (No. 9)
Stephenson Blake

Imprint Shadow
Monotype

Klang
Will Carter. Monotype 1955

LIBRA
De Roos. Typefoundry Amsterdam 1938

Marina
Stephenson Blake 1936

MINERVA *Italic* **Bold**
Reynolds Stone. Linotype 1955

ONYX
Gerry Powell. American Typefounders 1937

OTHELLO
Monotype

PROFIL
Eugen Lenz. Haas'sche Schriftgiesserei 1943

Rockwell
Bold
Italic
Bold Condensed
Monotype 1934

SANS SERIF SHADED
Stephenson Blake 1948

SELECT
Typefoundry Amsterdam 1936

Society Script
Stephenson Blake

Swing Bold
Monotype

Temple Script
Monotype 1937

THORNE SHADED
Stephenson Blake 1936

Thorowgood ***Thorowgood***
Robert Thorne. Stephenson Blake

TIMES HEAVY TITLING
Monotype

Trafton Script
Bauersche 1933

Ultra Bodoni ***Italic***
Monotype

Union Pearl
Oldest English decorated type. 18th century.
Stephenson Blake

APPENDIX B

LATIN PLACE NAMES AS USED IN THE IMPRINTS OF EARLY PRINTED BOOKS

Both the Latin and English forms of a place name are used as entry words in the single alphabetical sequence which follows, the former being printed in capitals. Where, however, this would result in the two entries for a place being adjacent, only the Latin into English is given. While Latin names usually occurred in the locative case, adjectival or possessive forms are not uncommon.

Aachen	AQUISGRANUM
ABBATISVILLA	Abbeville
ABREDONIA	Aberdeen
ALBANI VILLA	St Albans
Alcalà de Henares	COMPLUTUM
AMSTELODAMUM	Amsterdam
ANEDA	Edinburgh
ANDREAPOLIS	St Andrews
ANTUERPIA	Antwerp
AQUISGRANUM	Aachen
ARGENTINA	Strasbourg
ARGENTORATUM	Strasbourg
ASCULUM PICENUM	Ascoli Piceno
ASTURICA	Astorga (Spain)
ATHENAE RAURACAE	Basle
Augsburg	AUGUSTA VINDELICORUM
AUGUSTA PERUSIA	Perugia
AUGUSTA TIBERII	Regensburg
AUGUSTA TRINOBANTUM	London
AUGUSTA VINDELICORUM	Augsburg
AURELIA ALLOBROGUM	Geneva
AURELIACUM	Orleans
AVENIO	Avignon
BABENBERGA	Bamberg
Bamberg	GRAVIONATIUM
BARCHINO	Barcelona
BASILEA	Basle
Basle	ATHENAE RAURACAE
Basle	BASILEA
Basle	COLONIA MUNATIANA
BEROLINUM	Berlin
Besançon	VESUNTIO
BISUNTIA	Besançon
BONONIA	Bologna
BORBETOMAGUS	Worms
Breslau	VRATISLAVIA
BRIXIA	Brescia
CADOMUM	Caen
CANTABRIGIA	Cambridge
Canterbury	DUROVERNUM
Chester	DEVA
Chichester	REGUM
Cologne	UBII
COLONIA AGRIPPINA	Cologne
COLONIA ALLOBROGUM	Geneva
COLONIA CLAUDIA	Cologne
COLONIA MUNATIANA	Basle
COLONIA UBIORUM	Cologne
COMPLUTUM	Alcalà de Henares
Copenhagen	HAFNIA
Copenhagen	HAVNIA
COSMOPOLIS	a fictitious imprint
DANTISCUM	Danzig
DEVA	Chester
DIVIO	Dijon
DORDRACUM	Dordrecht
DUACUM	Douai
Dublin	EBLANA
DUNELMIA	Durham
DUROBRIVAE	Rochester
DUROCORTORUM	Rheims
DUROVERNUM	Canterbury
EBLANA	Dublin
EBORACUM	York
Edinburgh	ANEDA
EDINBURGUM	Edinburgh
ELEUTHEROPOLIS	a 'free city', usually an illegal book
ELVETIORUM ARGENTINA	Strasbourg
ERFORDIA	Erfurt
ERIDANIUM	Milan
Exeter	ISCA
Foligno	FULGENTIUM
FRANCOFURTUM AD MOENUM	Frankfurt am Main
Frankfurt am Main	HELENOPOLIS
Frankfurt am Oder	TRAJECTUM AD VIADRUM
FULGENTIUM	Foligno

GANDAVUM	Ghent
GEBENNA	Geneva
GENABUM	Orleans
Geneva	AURELIA ALLOBROGUM
Geneva	COLONIA ALLOBROGUM
Geneva	GEBENNA
Genoa	IANUA
Ghent	GANDAVUM
GIPPESWICUM	Ipswich
GLASCUA	Glasgow
GOTORUM	Lund
GRAVIONATIUM	Bamberg
HAFNIA	Copenhagen
HAGA COMITUM	The Hague
HAMMONA	Hamburg
HAVNIA	Copenhagen
HELENOPOLIS	Frankfurt am Main
HERBIPOLIS	Würzburg
HISPALIS	Seville
IANUA	Genoa
Ipswich	GIPPESWICUM
ISCA	Exeter
Langres	LINGONENSIS, CIVITAS
Leghorn	LIBURNUM
LEIDA	Leiden
Leiden	LUGDUNUM BATAVORUM
Leipzig	LIPSIA
LEMOVICENSE CASTRUM	Limoges
LEODIUM	Liège
Liège	LEODIUM
Limoges	LEMOVICENSE CASTRUM
LINGONENSIS, CIVITAS	Langres
LIPSIA	Leipzig
Lisbon	OLYSSIPO
Lisbon	ULYSSIPO
LONDINIUM	London
LONDINIUM SCANORUM	Lund
London	AUGUSTA TRINOBANTUM
London	LONDINIUM
LOVANIUM	Louvain
LUBICENSIS	Lübeck
LUGDUNUM	Lyons
LUGDUNUM BATAVORUM	Leiden
Lund	GOTORUM
Lund	LONDINIUM SCANORUM
LUTETIA	Paris
Lyons	LUGDUNUM
Madrid	MANTUA CARPETANORUM
MAGUNTIA	Mainz
Mainz	MOGUNTIA
MANTUA CARPETANORUM	Madrid
MEDIOLANUM	Milan
Milan	ERIDANIUM
Milan	MEDIOLANUM
Modena	MUTINA
MOGUNTIA	Mainz
MONACHIUM	Munich
Munich	MONACHIUM
MUTINA	Modena
NANNETES	Nantes
Naples	PARTHENOPE
NEAPOLIS	Naples
NICAEA	Nice
NORDOVICUM	Norwich
NORICA	Nuremberg
NORIMBERGA	Nuremberg
Norwich	NORDOVICUM
OLYSSIPO	Lisbon
Orleans	AURELIACUM
Orleans	GENABUM
Oxford (1st) University Press	THEATRUM (SHELDONIANUM)
OXONIA	Oxford
Padua	PATAVIUM
PANORMUM	Palermo
PAPIA	Pavia
Paris	LUTETIA
PARISIIS	Paris
PARISIUS	Paris
PARTHENOPE	Naples
PATAVIA	Passau
PATAVIUM	Padua
Pavia	PAPIA
Perugia	AUGUSTA PERUSIA
PETRIBURGUM	Peterborough
PISAE	Pisa
RATISBONA	Regensburg
ROTOMAGUS	Rouen
Regensburg	AUGUSTA TIBERII
Regensburg	RATISBONA
REGUM	Chichester
Rheims	DUROCORTORUM
Rochester	DUROBRIVAE
ROTHOMAGUM	Rouen
Rouen	ROTOMAGUS
SAENA	Siena
St Albans	ALBANI VILLA
St Albans	VILLA SANCTA ALBANI
St Andrews	ANDREAPOLIS
SALISBURIA	Salzburg
SARUM	Salisbury
SENAE	Siena
Seville	HISPALIS
Siena	SAENA
Siena	SENAE
Strasbourg	ARGENTINA
Strasbourg	ARGENTORATUM
Strasbourg	ELVETIORUM ARGENTINA
Strasbourg	TRIBBOCCORUM
SUBLACENSE MONASTERIUM	Subiaco
TAURINUM	Turin

THEATRUM (SHELDONIANUM)	Oxford (1st) University Press
THOLOSA	Toulouse
TIGURUM	Zürich
Tours	TURONIS
TRAJECTUM AD RHENUM	Utrecht
TRAJECTUM AD VIADRUM	Frankfurt am Oder
TRAJECTUM INFERIUS	Utrecht
TREVIRI	Trier
TRIBBOCCORUM	Strasbourg
Trier	TREVIRI
TURIGUM	Zürich
Turin	TAURINUM
TURONIS	Tours
UBII	Cologne
ULTRAJECTUM	Utrecht
ULYSSIPO	Lisbon
Utrecht	TRAJECTUM AD RHENUM
Utrecht	TRAJECTUM INFERIUS
Utrecht	ULTRAJECTUM
VARSAVIA	Warsaw
VENETIAE	Venice
VENTA BELGARUM	Winchester
VESUNTIO	Besançon
VICENTIA	Vicenza
VILLA SANCTA ALBANI	St Albans
VINDOBONA	Vienna
VIRCEBURGUM	Würzburg
VORMATIA	Worms
VRATISLAVIA	Breslau
Warsaw	VARSAVIA
WESTMONASTERIUM	Westminster
WIGORNUM	Worcester
Winchester	VENTA BELGARUM
Worcester	WIGORNUM
Worms	BORBETOMAGUS
Worms	VORMATIA
Würzburg	HERBIPOLIS
Würzburg	VIRCEBURGUM
York	EBORACUM
Zürich	TIGURUM
Zürich	TURIGUM

APPENDIX C

THE CONTEMPORARY PRIVATE PRESS

by John Ryder

The typographical adventure of William Morris and the publishing enterprise of Francis Meynell's Nonesuch Press might have been said, thirty years ago, to describe the two kinds of private presses. But at the present time, in the middle of the century, the field of private printing is a good deal too wide to be defined by any (or collectively, all) of the definitions given in Will Ransom's 'Private Presses and Their Books'. At least five main groups of private presses are to be distinguished and, although there will be problems of overlapping, the main function of a press will usually suggest one of these groups.

Presses may be considered under three headings:

[A] Commercial
[B] Official
[C] Private

The presses under the third heading are our present concern and may be subdivided into five groups:

[I] Publishing
[II] Teaching
[III] Experimental
[IV] Printing
[V] Clandestine

The second of these groups may again be subdivided into three sections:

[II] a. Handicraft
b. Typography and graphic design
c. Bibliography

With this plan in mind private presses as they exist today may be examined.

* * *

[I] The first group will contain all those presses which continue the pattern established in Emery Walker's time. Typical prototypes are Kelmscott and Doves and the group will include all presses of this kind whether or not they own printing equipment or use proprietary types. They set by hand or by machine (or revise machine settings by hand), print by hand or machine on (usually) hand-made paper. Their products, bound by hand in expensive materials or by machine in a variety of materials, are publicized and offered for sale. Their editions, numbered and sometimes signed, are generally limited to a thousand or fewer copies. Their texts, although varied to a high degree, make no essential innovations but the greatest importance must be attributed to their completely new attitude to illustrations. The moribund pages of the Morris–Burne-Jones 'Chaucer' have acted as a stern warning. Instead of type and illustrations suffocating each other they now exist side by side, in harmony or in contrast, surrounded by and infiltrated with light which has given the purchaser the chance to read.

Examples of Group [I]

GREAT BRITAIN:

Ark Press, Marazion
Cupid Press, Ipswich
Folio Society, London
Golden Cockerel Press, Leominster
Nonesuch Press, London
Rampant Lions Press, Cambridge
Signet Press, Greenock
Vine Press, Hemingford Grey

AMERICA:

Black Cat Press, Chicago
Book Club of California, San Francisco
Grabhorn Press, San Francisco
Gravesend Press, Lexington, Ky.
Limited Editions Club, New York
Peter Pauper Press, Mount Vernon, N.Y.
Private Press of the Indiana Kid, Nappanee, Ind.

[II] The second group, school presses, is probably the largest and may well become the most important subdivision of the private press. It will be necessary to divide again this group into three sections according to the didactic functions they perform:

a. Handicraft
b. Typography and graphic design
c. Bibliography

Appendix C

[IIa] Presses of this first subdivision will differ in accordance with the kind of instruction given. At one end of the scale is the press run by the school art master as an extension of the art department where typographical practices are subservient to the cutting and printing of blocks. At the other end of the scale typography becomes the object of the exercise and the students set and print according to more or less professional instructions. The work may be done on an experimental basis or the press, used in this way to teach a handicraft, may function as a jobbing printer. Or again the output of the press may be limited to school stationery and programmes. Most school presses grouped in this subdivision are of a kind somewhere between these two extremes.

Examples of group [IIa]

ENGLAND:
Bromsgrove School
Bushey Grammar School
Dartington Hall School, Totnes
King's College School, London
Kingswood School, Bath
Marlborough College

[IIb] The second subdivision contains the majority of school presses and is by far the most important group. It includes not only all trade printing schools but also those outside the trade where advanced typography and the handling of type is taught to students of graphic design. Such a private press, controlled by the department of graphic design in a college of art, has, under suitable direction, every opportunity of achieving fame. The Lion and Unicorn Press (of the Royal College of Art) already appears in the front rank of school presses and has, on limited subscription, issued books to the public during the last three years. Some of these books will deservedly go down in the annals of fine production.

Examples of group [IIb]

GREAT BRITAIN:
Birmingham College of Art
Bournemouth College of Art
Bradford Regional College of Art
Bristol College of Art
Camberwell School of Arts and Crafts
Canterbury College of Art
Central School of Arts and Crafts, London
Colchester School of Art
Edinburgh College of Art
Exeter College of Art
Gloucester College of Art
Guildford School of Art
Heriot-Watt College, Edinburgh
Hornsey School of Art, London
Leeds College of Technology
Leicester College of Art
Lion and Unicorn Press, London
London School of Printing and Graphic Arts
Maidstone College of Art
Medway College of Art, Rochester
Norwich City College and School of Art
Southampton College of Art
Stow College of Printing, Glasgow
Tunbridge Wells School of Art
Twickenham Technical College
Watford Technical College
Wolverhampton College of Art

[IIc] The third subdivision contains only three presses (according to present information) all of which function in a very special way. In 1913 R. B. McKerrow suggested that students of bibliography should set up and print pages of books in the styles and with the techniques of the originals they were studying in order to understand bibliographical problems exactly. Some years later, in 1934, Professor Hugh Smith (University College, London) established a press in the college. Professor Wilson and Mr Herbert Davis set up a similar press at Oxford in 1949, and in 1953 Mr Philip Gaskell established the Water Lane Press in King's College, Cambridge. Apart from the invaluable aid to bibliographical studies these presses have exercised considerable influence over their student printers and some have already set up their own private presses.

The presses in group [IIc]

Oxford University
University College, London
Water Lane Press, Cambridge

[III] The third group of presses, the most private of all those considered here, consists of small workshops from which there is usually no issue either for publication or for private circulation and often no issue retained even by the printer himself. The essential equipment is therefore a small hand-press often accompanied by a large selection of types and ornaments and sometimes by a great variety of papers and inks. But it is not uncommon for such a press to base its experiments exclusively on a single design of typeface. All the printers in this group, whatever their equipment may consist of, will be persons dedicated to typography. They will be

SOME PRIVATE PRESS MARKS

and their designers

OFFICINA BODONI
Emil Pretorius (?)

HAMMER CREEK
Oriental design

NONESUCH
Agnes Miller Parker

MINIATURE
Christopher Chamberlain

GRAVESEND
Fritz Kredel

LION & UNICORN
David Gentleman

TUINWIJKPERS
Sem Hartz

RAMPANT LIONS
Reynolds Stone

SHOESTRING
Ben Sands

mentally well-equipped for continual research and experiment. They will be persons who have discovered for themselves the truth of Dr Mardersteig's words: 'The mere fact that the hand-press is an ideal instrument for experiment is of incalculable value. Without experiment, without the constant examination of all the given possibilities, the perfect solution of a typographic problem can never be obtained.'

Examples of group [III]

ENGLAND:

Christopher Bradshaw, London
Geoffrey Dowding, Richmond
Martindale Press, London
Miniature Press, Richmond
Walter Tracy, London

EUROPE:

Tuinwijkpers (S. L. Hartz), Haarlem
Officina Bodoni, Verona (*see below*)

[IV] The fourth group is also of a private nature and is related to group **[III]** since its main interest lies in printing rather than in publishing. But presses of this fourth group are not maintained for experiment, although many have such tendencies, but for printing small editions of whatever may appeal to their owners. The writing or compiling, designing, printing, and usually binding, are done for the satisfaction of the doing and the issue is distributed by the printer amongst a few like-minded friends. The fact that some copies of certain items are offered for sale does not affect the classification provided that the mainstream of issue is directed without sale into strictly private circulation. It is not uncommon for the distribution of printed material from this group (and sometimes from certain presses in group **[III]** where an issue of proofs is established) to be conducted on an exchange basis.

Examples of group [IV]

EUROPE:

Capivard Press, London
Crickets Press, Totnes
Kit-Cat Press, Bushey
La Vis Press, Geneva
Piccolo Press, Stroud
Shoestring Press, London

AMERICA:

Ampersand Press, Baltimore
Between-Hours Press, New York
Endgrain Press, New York
Ralph Green, Chicago
Hammer Creek Press, New York
Hippogryph Press, Massachusetts
Katydid Press, Pennsylvania
Mermaid Press, New York
Molehill Press, Chicago
Pastime Printer, Front Royal, Virginia
Quattrocci Press, New Jersey
Rob Run Press, Detroit
Serendipity Press, New York

[V] To conclude, there is still one easily definable group of private presses to be mentioned although no list can ever be compiled. Because of their particular mode of action the presses in this fifth group, clandestine presses, remain secret until they are confiscated or disbanded. At the present time, in this country, political and religious freedom greatly reduce the number of clandestine presses. Only two kinds flourish and neither has anything like a cause with which society might have a little sympathy—the one kind concerns itself with pornography and the other kind with forgery.

* * *

One press of the highest importance has still to be mentioned—the Officina Bodoni. This press, directed by Giovanni Mardersteig at Verona, raises an important question of classification. It is impossible to place certain presses in any particular group and when the main functions of the Officina Bodoni are examined it will be seen that several definitions apply. In the first place it could be grouped with commercial presses **[A]** since many books have been printed for publishers in Italy, France, England, and America. It could also be grouped with official presses **[B]** since the Italian Government granted Dr Mardersteig exclusive use of Giambattista Bodoni's original punches and matrices. Within the private press group **[C]** it could be placed under **[I]** since many books have been published by the Officina Bodoni. But because books and specimens have been issued privately it could also be placed under **[IV]**. And yet the most important function of this press has still to be described, namely, as a private experimental workshop **[III]** which not only concerns itself with the design of books but also with the design of new type-faces. Dr Mardersteig has made three type-designs: Zeno, Griffo, and Dante. The last of these has been adopted by the Monotype Corporation (Series 952).

Thus, Officina Bodoni may be defined as **[A]**, **[B]**, **[I]**, **[III]**, and **[IV]**, and the fact that Giovanni Mardersteig excels in all these functions places the press in an extremely prominent position. According to many eminent typographers it is the most important contemporary press.

Other presses, commercial, official, and private, present similar problems of definition but usually there is one main function and some occasional subsidiary ones. University presses are normally official and commercial with only occasional private issue as when the printer to the university sends out gift books to his friends. The official business of the university press entitles it to **[B]** classification.

The printing departments of typefoundries (Monotype, Linotype, Stempel, Enschedé, Bauer, etc.) are akin to private presses **[IV]** but their special function, industrial publicity, makes them commercial **[A]** with a proviso that they do not offer their printing facilities to the public.

Many commercial presses **[A]** print items for private circulation. Their type specimens should be regarded in the same way as the publicity from foundry presses but the occasional issue of a book not about types or printing or even about the printer's own history can only be described as private press activity **[IV]**. This does not affect the category of the press if printing to order remains its main function. A good example of this kind of printing for private distribution is a little book called 'An Essex Dozen' printed in 1953 by Benham's of Colchester.

See also the entry on Private presses

NOTE

The short list of examples accompanying each section of the definition makes no pretence to completeness—except perhaps in the case of group **[IIc]**. It is doubtful if such a list could ever be prepared although an attempt has recently been made by The Signet Press to acquire and publish a check-list of contemporary private presses in the English-speaking world. Much research has gone into this work but, as John Ryder has pointed out in the foregoing Appendix, some presses, particularly in group **[III]**, are difficult to find and occasionally their owners do not wish any publicity.

In addition to The Signet Press publication detailed illustrated accounts of certain presses of importance appear from time to time in *Book Design and Production* (q.v.).

APPENDIX D

PROOF CORRECTION SYMBOLS

The British Standards Institution has very kindly authorized the reprinting here of an extract from B.S. 1219: 1958 'Printers' and Authors' Proof Corrections'.

Wherever possible all corrections should be made in the margin; only such marks being made in the text as are required to indicate the place to which the correction refers.

When three or more corrections occur in one line, the corrections should be divided between the left and right margins, the order being always from left to right.

When an alteration is desired in a letter, word or words, the existing letter, etc., should be struck through and the letter or matter to be substituted should be written in the margin, followed by /.

(Words printed in italics in the marginal mark column below are instructions and not part of the marks.)

No.	Instruction	Textual mark	Marginal mark
1	Correction is concluded	None	/
2	Insert in text the matter indicated in margin	⋏	*New matter followed by* /
3	Delete	Strike through characters to be deleted	₰
4	Delete and close up	Strike through characters to be deleted and use mark 21	₰ (with close-up mark)
5	Leave as printed	. . . . under characters to remain	stet
6	Change to italic	—— under characters to be altered	ital

No.	Instruction	Textual mark	Marginal mark
7	Change to even small capitals	═ under characters to be altered	s.c.
8	Change to capital letters	≡ under characters to be altered	caps
9	Use capital letters for initial letters and small capitals for rest of words	≡ under initial letters and ═ under the rest of the words	c.& s.c.
10	Change to bold type	~ under characters to be altered	bold
11	Change to lower case	Encircle characters to be altered	l.c.
12	Change to roman type	Encircle characters to be altered	rom
13	Wrong fount. Replace by letter of correct fount	Encircle character to be altered	w.f.
14	Invert type	Encircle character to be altered	9
15	Change damaged character(s)	Encircle character(s) to be altered	X
16	Substitute or insert character(s) under which this mark is placed, in 'superior' position	/ through character or ⋏ where required	⋎ *under character* (e.g. $\overset{x}{⋎}$)
17	Substitute or insert character(s) over which this mark is placed, in 'inferior' position	/ through character or ⋏ where required	⋀ *over character* (e.g. $\underset{x}{⋀}$)
18	Underline word or words	—— under words affected	underline
19	Use ligature (e.g. ffi) or diphthong (e.g. œ)	⁀‿ enclosing letters to be altered	⁀‿ *enclosing ligature or diphthong required*

No.	Instruction	Textual mark	Marginal mark
20	Substitute separate letters for ligature or diphthong	/ through ligature or diphthong to be altered	*write out separate letters followed by* /
21	Close up—delete space between characters	⁀‿ linking characters	⁀‿
22	Insert space*	⅄	#
23	Insert space between lines or paragraphs*	> between lines to be spaced	#
24	Reduce space between lines*	(connecting lines to be closed up	less #
25	Make space appear equal between words	| between words	eq #
26	Reduce space between words*	| between words	less #
27	Add space between letters*	ı ı ı ı ı ı between tops of letters requiring space	letter #
28	Transpose	⊔⊓ between characters or words, numbered when necessary	trs
29	Place in centre of line	Indicate position with ┌ ┐	centre
30	Indent one em	⊏	□
31	Indent two ems	⊏	□□
32	Move matter to right	⊏ at left side of group to be moved	⊏
33	Move matter to left	⊐ at right side of group to be moved	⊐

* Amount of space and/or length of re-spaced line may be indicated.

No.	Instruction	Textual mark	Marginal mark
34	Move matter to position indicated	[ ] at limits of required position	*move*
35	Take over character(s) or line to next line, column or page	⊏	*take over*
36	Take back character(s) or line to previous line, column or page	⊐	*take back*
37	Raise lines*	⊼ over lines to be moved ⌐___⌐ under lines to be moved	*raise*
38	Lower lines*	⌐‾‾‾⌐ over lines to be moved ⊻ under lines to be moved	*lower*
39	Correct the vertical alignment	||	||
40	Straighten lines	═ through lines to be straightened	═
41	Push down space	Encircle space affected	⊥
42	Begin a new paragraph	[before first word of new paragraph	*n.p.*
43	No fresh paragraph here	⌒ between paragraphs	*run on*
44	Spell out the abbreviation or figure in full	Encircle words or figures to be altered	*spell out*
45	Insert omitted portion of copy NOTE. The relevant section of the copy should be returned with the proof, the omitted portion being clearly indicated.	⋏	*out see copy*
46	Substitute or insert comma	/ through character or ⋏ where required	,/
47	Substitute or insert semi-colon	/ through character or ⋏ where required	;/

*Amount of space and/or length of line may be included.

No.	Instruction	Textual mark	Marginal mark
48	Substitute or insert full stop	/ through character or ⋏ where required	⊙
49	Substitute or insert colon	/ through character or ⋏ where required	(:)
50	Substitute or insert interrogation mark	/ through character or ⋏ where required	?/
51	Substitute or insert exclamation mark	/ through character or ⋏ where required	!/
52	Insert parentheses	⋏ or ⋏ ⋏	(/)/
53	Insert (square) brackets	⋏ or ⋏ ⋏	[/]/
54	Insert hyphen	⋏	|-|
55	Insert en (half-em) rule	⋏	en
56	Insert one-em rule	⋏	em
57	Insert two-em rule	⋏	2 em
58	Insert apostrophe	⋏	'/
59	Insert single quotation marks	⋏ or ⋏ ⋏	'/ '/
60	Insert double quotation marks	⋏ or ⋏ ⋏	"/ "/
61	Insert ellipsis*	⋏	.../
62	Insert leader	⋏	(...)
63	Insert shilling stroke	⋏	(/)
64	Refer to appropriate authority anything of doubtful accuracy	Encircle words, etc. affected	(?)

* See notes on use of symbols.

NOTE. When fresh matter not in copy is to be inserted, the caret mark is to be used in the text and 'Take in A' (B, C, etc., as the case may be) written in the margin, the additional matter, whether written on the proof, or on attached slips, being lettered to correspond. In the case of large insertions, a horizontal arrow in the margin pointing between the lines replaces the caret mark.

APPENDIX E

A SHORT READING LIST

This reading list is limited to works consulted in the preparation of the Glossary, the editions being those which were available to me and not necessarily the most recent. Works mentioned in the Glossary are not repeated here.

Arrangement of the Sections

General Reference Books

AMERICAN LIBRARY ASSOCIATION. *Glossary of library terms.* U.S.A., A.L.A., 1943.

AVIS, F. C. *The Bookman's concise dictionary.* Avis, 1956.

BATESON, F. W. *ed. The Cambridge bibliography of English literature.* 4 vols. C.U.P., 1940.

BIGMORE, E. C., AND WYMAN, C. W. H. *Bibliography of printing.* 2nd ed. New York, Duschnes, 1945.

BINNS, N. E. *Introduction to historical bibliography.* Association of Assistant Librarians, 1953.

BOOK COLLECTOR. Shenval Press. Quarterly.

BOWKER AND CO. *Bookman's glossary.* 3rd ed. New York, Bowker & Co., 1951.

CAMBRIDGE UNIVERSITY PRESS. *Preparation of manuscripts and correction of proofs.* C.U.P., 1951.

CARTER, JOHN. *A B C for book-collectors.* Hart-Davis, 1952.

CARTER, JOHN. *Books and book-collectors.* London: Hart-Davis, 1956. *New York World*, 1957.

CHAMBERS'S ENCYCLOPAEDIA. Chambers, 1950.

CHAMBERS'S TECHNICAL DICTIONARY. Chambers, 1958.

COLLINS, F. H. *ed. Authors' and printers' dictionary.* 10th ed. O.U.P., 1956.

COWLEY, J. D. *Bibliographical description and cataloguing.* Grafton, 1939.

ENCYCLOPAEDIA BRITANNICA. 14th ed. 1947.

ESDAILE, ARUNDEL. *A Student's manual of bibliography.* 3rd ed. Allen & Unwin, 1954.

HARRISON, FREDERICK. *A Book about books.* Murray, 1943.

HARROD, L. M. *A Librarian's glossary.* Grafton, 1938.

HART, HORACE. *Rules for compositors and readers at the University Press, Oxford.* 36th ed. O.U.P., 1952. Reprinted with alterations, 1957.

HAZLITT, W. C. *The Book-collector.* Redway, 1904.

HOSTETTLER, R., AND OTHERS. *The Printer's terms.* Redman, 1905.

JACOBI, C. T. *The Printers' vocabulary.* Whittingham, 1887–9.

KIRCHNER, JOACHIM. *Lexikon des Buchwesens.* 4 vols. 2nd ed. Stuttgart, Hiersemann, 1952–6.

LANGWELL, W. H. *The Conservation of books and documents*. Pitman, 1957.

LEHMANN-HAUPT, H. *One hundred books about bookmaking*. U.S.A., Columbia U.P.: O.U.P., 1949.

MCKERROW, RONALD B. *An Introduction to bibliography for literary students*. O.U.P., 1927.

NATIONAL BOOK LEAGUE. *Books about books*. (Catalogue.) C.U.P., 1955.

NATIONAL BOOK LEAGUE. *The Book series*. 6 parts. C.U.P., 1955.

THORNTON, J. L., AND TULLY, R. I. J. *Scientific books, libraries and collectors*. Library Association, 1954.

History of Printing and the Book

ALDIS, H. G. *A List of books printed in Scotland before 1700, including those printed furth of the realm for Scottish booksellers*. Edinburgh, Edinburgh Bibliographical Society, 1904.

ALDIS, H. G. *The Printed book*. 3rd ed. by J. Carter & B. Crutchley. C.U.P., 1951.

BIBLIOTHÈQUE NATIONALE. *Le livre anglais: trésors des collections anglaises*. (Catalogue.) Paris, B.N., 1951.

BOSANQUET, E. F. *Notes and further addenda to English printed almanacks and prognostications to 1600*. Bibliographical Society, 1937.

BRITISH MUSEUM. *A Guide to the exhibition in the King's Library, illustrating the history of printing, music printing, and bookbinding*. B.M., 1939.

DIRINGER, D. *The Hand-produced book*. Hutchinson, 1953.

DUFF, E. G. *Early printed books*. Kegan Paul, 1893.

EYRE, F. *20th century children's books*. British Council, 1952.

GOLDSCHMIDT, E. P. *The Printed book of the Renaissance*. C.U.P., 1950.

GREG, W. W., AND BOSWELL, E. *ed. Records of the Court of the Stationers' Company: 1576–1602—from Register B*. Bibliographical Society, 1930.

HIGGINS, F. R. *Progress in Irish printing*. Dublin, 1936.

JACKSON, H. *The Printing of books: essays on English printing since 1800*. Cassell, 1938.

JONES, J. I. *A History of printing and printers in Wales to 1810, and of successive and related printers to 1923*. Cardiff, Lewis, 1925.

KENYON, SIR FREDERICK G. *Books and readers in ancient Greece and Rome*. O.U.P., 1932.

KNIGHT, C. *The Old printers and the modern press*. Murray, 1854.

LEJARD, A. *ed. The Art of the French book from early manuscripts to the present time*. Elek, 1947.

MCLEAN, RUARI. *Modern book design*. Faber, 1959.

MCMURTRIE, D. C. *The Book: the story of printing and bookmaking*. 3rd ed. O.U.P., 1943.

MEYNELL, SIR FRANCIS. *English printed books*. Collins, 1946.

NATIONAL BOOK LEAGUE. *The Italian book, 1465–1900*. (Catalogue.) 1953.

OSWALD, J. C. *A History of printing: its development during five hundred years*. New York, Appleton, 1928.

PEDDIE, R. A. *ed. Printing: a short history of the art*. Grafton, 1927.

PLOMER, H. R. *A Short history of English printing, 1476–1901*. Kegan Paul, 1927.

POLLARD, A. W. *Fine books*. Methuen, 1912.

PROCTOR, ROBERT. *The Printing of Greek in the fifteenth century*. Bibliographical Society Monographs No. 4. 1900.

PUTNAM, G. H. *Authors and their public in ancient times*. Putnam, 1893.

ROSNER, CHARLES. *Printer's progress, 1851–1951*. Sylvan Press, 1951.

SADLEIR, M. *ed. Bibliographia: a series of studies in book history and book construction, 1750–1900*. Constable, 1930.

WINSHIP, G. P. *Gutenberg to Plantin*. O.U.P., 1926.

Printing—General Books

CORRIGAN, A. J. *A Printer and his world*. Faber, 1946.

JACKSON, H., AND MORISON, S. *A Brief survey of printing history and practice*. Fleuron, 1923.

JACKSON, H. E. *26 lead soldiers: a textbook of printing types, methods, and processes for journalism students*. U.S.A., Stanford U.P., 1937.

JACOBI, C. T. *Some notes on books and printing: a guide for authors, publishers and others*. Chiswick Press, 1903.

JENNETT, S. *The Making of books*. Faber, 1951.

MORISON, STANLEY. *The Art of printing*. British Academy Annual Lecture on Aspects of Art, 1937.

PENROSE ANNUAL. Edited by Alan Delafons, Lund Humphries, annually.

POLLARD, A. W. *The Trained printer and the amateur*. Monotype Corporation, 1929.

SIMON, O., AND RODENBERG, J. *Printing of today*. Davies, 1928.

TARR, J. C. *Printing today*. O.U.P., 1948.

THE TIMES. Printing supplement. July, 1955.

WARDE, B. L. *Printing should be invisible*. Chiswick Press, 1936.

WILLIAMSON, H. *Methods of book design: the practice of an industrial craft*. O.U.P., 1956.

Printing—Practical Handbooks and Technology

ASHWORTH, J. *Operation and mechanism of the Linotype and Intertype*. 2 vols. Staples, 1955.

BRITISH FEDERATION OF MASTER PRINTERS. *Book impositions*. 4th ed. 1956.

BRITISH PRINTER. Monthly.
COVENEY, C. E. *The Compositors' and printers' handbook.* London Society of Compositors, 1926.
JACKSON, H. E. *Printing primer.* U.S.A., Stanford U.P.: O.U.P., 1949.
JACOBI, C. T. *Printing: a practical treatise.* 6th ed. Bell, 1919.
L. & M. NEWS. Linotype & Machinery Ltd. Six per year.
MONOTYPE RECORDER. Monotype Corporation. Irregular issues.
POLK, R. W. *The Practice of printing.* U.S.A., Peoria, Manual Arts Press, 1926.
PRINT IN BRITAIN. Monthly.
PRINTING NEWS. Weekly.
PRINTING REVIEW. Quarterly.
RADFORD, R. G. *Letterpress machine work.* 2 vols. Staples, 1951.
SOUTHWARD, J. *Modern printing.* 2 vols. Leicester, De Montfort Press, 1950–54.
TARR, J. C. *ed. Printing theory and practice.* Pitman. (A series).
WHETTON, H. *ed. Practical printing and binding.* 2nd ed. Odhams, 1954.

Printing—Illustration Processes

AUER, A. *Die Entdeckung des Naturselbstdruckes.* Wien, Staatsdruckerei, 1854.
BARBER, T. S. *Photo-engraving.* 2 vols. Pitman, 1947.
BIGGS, J. R. *Illustration and reproduction.* Blandford Press, 1950 (i.e. 1951).
BISKEBORN, H. *Photogravure machine printing.* Pitman, 1949.
BLAND DAVID. *The Illustration of books.* London: Faber, 1951. New York: *World Publishing Co.*
BLUNT, WILFRID. *The Art of botanical illustration.* Collins, 1950.
BRINKLEY, J. *Design for print: a handbook of design and reproduction processes.* Sylvan Press, 1949.
BRITISH FEDERATION OF MASTER PRINTERS. *A Selected list of graphic arts literature: books and periodicals.* 1948.
BRITISH MUSEUM. *A Guide to the processes and schools of engraving, with notes on some of the most important masters.* B.M., 1933.
BUCKLAND-WRIGHT, J. *Etching and engraving: techniques and the modern trend.* Studio, 1953.
CUMMING, D. *A Handbook of lithography.* 3rd ed. by C. Parkinson. Black, 1932.
CURWEN, H. *Processes of graphic reproduction.* Faber, 1946.
FLADER, L., AND MERTLE, J. S. *Modern photoengraving.* U.S.A., Chicago, Modern Photoengraving Publishers, 1948.
GAMBLE, C. W. *Modern illustration processes.* 3rd ed. Pitman, 1950.
GREENWOOD, H. W. *Document photography.* 2nd ed. O.U.P., 1943.
HALPERN, B. R. *Color correction for offset lithography.* New York, Lithographic Technical Foundation, 1956.
HILL, T. G. *Essentials of illustration.* Wesley, 1915.
HILLIER, J. *Japanese masters of the colour print.* Phaidon, 1954.
HIND, A. M. *An Introduction to a history of woodcuts, with a detailed survey of work done in the 15th century.* Constable, 1936.
JAMES, PHILIP. *English book illustration: 1800–1900.* Penguin, 1947.
LEWIS, JOHN. *A Handbook of type and illustration.* Faber, 1956.
LEWIS, J., AND BRINKLEY, J. *Graphic design.* Routledge, 1954.
PICHON, L. *Modern French book illustration.* Studio, 1927.
POLLARD, A. W. *Early illustrated books: a history of the decoration and illustration of books in the 15th and 16th centuries.* Kegan Paul, 1926.
SMITH, JANET ADAM. *Children's illustrated books.* Collins, 1948.
SMITH, W. J., AND OTHERS. *Photo-engraving in relief.* Pitman, 1948.
TIEFDRUCKAUSSTELLUNG veranstaltet zur Ehrung des Erfinders Karl Klíč. Prague, Kunstgewerbemuseum der Handels und Gewerbekammer, 1929.
TORY, B. E. *Photolithography.* Sydney, Associated General Publications, 1953.
ULLYETT, K. *Pictorial printing processes.* Pitman, 1949.
WOOD, FRANKLIN. *Photogravure.* Pitman, 1949.

Printing—Ink and its manufacture

APPS, E. *Printing ink technology.* Hill, 1957.
BURNS, R. *Printing inks.* Pitman, 1948.
ELLIS, C. *Printing inks.* Chapman & Hall, 1940.
GAMBLE, W. B. *Chemistry and manufacture of writing and printing inks.* New York. N.Y. Public Library Bulletin, 1925.

Printing—Office and Works Management

AUSTEN-LEIGH, R. A. *ed. The Master Printer's Annual and Typographical Year Book.* Spottiswoode, Ballantyne. Annually.
BOARD OF TRADE. Council for Art and Industry. (Scottish Committee). *Printing and allied trades in Scotland.* Edinburgh, 1937.
BRITISH FEDERATION OF MASTER PRINTERS. *The British Master Printers Federation costing system: explanation and specimen forms.* 1940.
BRITISH FEDERATION OF MASTER PRINTERS. *Salesmanship for printers.* 1936.

FORSAITH, J. W. *Organization and management for master printers*. Staples, 1949.

HAZELL, W. H. *Estimating for printers*. B.F.M.P., 1936.

HOWE, ELLIC. *The London compositor, documents relating to wages, working conditions and customs of the London printing trade, 1785–1900*. Bibliographical Society & O.U.P., 1947.

JOWETT, W. *Simple lessons on estimating for printers*. Pitman, 1939.

KARCH, R. R. *Printing and the allied trades*. Pitman, 1939.

MILLS, H. *The Printer's estimator*. Sidgwick & Jackson, 1938.

MONTAGUE, NOEL. *Printing management*. Sylvan Press, 1947.

Printing—Presses and Printers

BARNES, G. R. *A List of books printed in Cambridge at the University Press, 1521–1800*. C.U.P., 1935.

BASKERVILLE, JOHN. *Letters of the famous 18th-century printer, John Baskerville of Birmingham, together with a bibliography of works printed by him at Birmingham*. 1932.

BEILENSON, P. *ed. Updike: American printer, and his Merrymount Press*. American Institute of Graphic Arts, 1947.

BENNETT, W. *John Baskerville, the Birmingham printer: his press, relations and friends*. 1937.

BENNETT, W. *William Caslon, 1692–1766, ornamental engraver, typefounder, and music lover*. City of Birmingham School of Printing, 1935.

BLADES, W. *The biography and typography of William Caxton*. . . . Trubner, 1882.

BLAKEY, D. *The Minerva Press, 1790–1820*. Bibliographical Society, 1939.

CAVE, T. *John Baskerville: the printer, 1706–1775: his ancestry*. 1936.

CLAUDIN, A. *The First Paris press . . . , 1470–1472*. Bibliographical Society, 1898.

CRUTCHLEY, E. A. *A History and description of the Pitt Press, erected for the use of the University Printing Press, A.D. 1833, altered and restored A.D. 1937*. C.U.P., 1938.

CURWEN PRESS. *Catalogue raisonné of books printed at the Curwen Press, 1920–1923*. Medici Society, 1924.

DOVES PRESS. *A List of books printed and in preparation by T. J. Cobden-Sanderson and Emery Walker at the Doves Press*. 1901. 1906.

GILL, ERIC. *Letters*. Cape, 1948.

GOLDEN COCKEREL PRESS. *Chanticleer: a bibliography of the Golden Cockerel Press, April 1921–August 1936*. 1936.

GOLDEN COCKEREL PRESS. *Pertelote: a sequel to 'Chanticleer', being a bibliography, October 1936–April 1943*. 1943.

GOLDEN COCKEREL PRESS. *Cockalorum: a sequel to 'Chanticleer' and 'Pertelote', being a bibliography, June 1943–December 1948*. 1950.

GOLDSCHMIDT, E. P. *The First Cambridge press in its European setting*. C.U.P., 1955.

HINDLEY, C. *History of the Catnach Press*. 1886.

HORNBY, C. H. ST J. *A Descriptive bibliography of the books printed at the Ashendene Press, MDCCCXCV–MCMXXXV*. Ashendene Press, 1935.

JOHNSON, J., AND GIBSON, S. *Print and privilege at Oxford to the year 1700*. O.U.P., 1946.

KEEFE, H. J. *A Century in print: the story of Hazell's, 1839–1939*. Hazell, Watson & Viney, 1939.

MACLEHOSE, JAMES. *The Glasgow University Press, 1638–1931*. Glasgow U.P., 1931.

MARSTON, E. *Cambridge University Press: notes on its history and development*. C.U.P., 1930.

MURRIE, E. *Notes on the printers and publishers of English songbooks, 1651–1702*. Edinburgh Bibliographical Society Transactions. Vol 1. 1938.

NONESUCH PRESS. *The Nonesuch century: an appraisal, a personal note and a bibliography of the first hundred books issued by the Press, 1923–1934*. 1936.

OXFORD UNIVERSITY PRESS. *Some account of the Oxford University Press, 1468–1921*. O.U.P., 1922.

PEPLER, H. D. C. *Hand press*. Ditchling Press, 1953.

RANSOM, WILL. *Private presses and their books*. New York, Bowker, 1929.

REDGRAVE, G. R. *Erhard Ratdolt and his work at Venice*. Bibliographical Society, 1894.

ROBERTS, S. C. *History of the Cambridge University Press, 1521–1921*. C.U.P., 1921.

RODENBERG, J. *Deutsche Pressen: eine Bibliographie*. Wien, Amalthea, 1925.

ROGERS, BRUCE. *An Account of the making of the Oxford Lectern Bible*. Monotype Corporation, 1936.

SHEPPARD, L. A. *The Printers of the Coverdale Bible, 1535*. Bibliographical Society, 1935.

SPARLING, H. H. *The Kelmscott Press and William Morris, master craftsman*. Macmillan, 1924.

STRAUS, R., AND DENT, K. R. *John Baskerville: a memoir*. Chatto, 1907.

THORNTON, J. C. *A Tour of the Temple Press: an account of printing and binding books at the works of J. M. Dent & Sons*. Dent, 1935.

TIMPERLEY, C. H. *A Dictionary of printers and printing*. Johnson, 1839.

TOMKINSON, G. S. *A Select bibliography of the principal modern presses, public and private, in Great Britain and Ireland*. First Edition Club, 1928.

WARDE, B. *Thirty-two outstanding dates in the history of printing*. Guildford, School of Art, 1949.

WILLIAMS, H. *Book clubs and printing societies of Great Britain and Ireland.* First Edition Club, 1929.

Printing—Typography and Fine Printing

BALDING AND MANSELL. *Type: principles and application.* n.d.

BASTIEN, A. *Type lettering: some contemporary alphabets.* Bastien, 1950.

BERRY, W. TURNER, AND JOHNSON, ALFRED FORBES. *ed. Catalogue of specimens of printing types by English and Scottish printers and founders, 1665–1830.* O.U.P., 1935.

BIGGS, J. R. *An Approach to type.* Blandford, 1949.

BIGGS, J. R. *Use of type: the practice of typography.* Blandford, 1954.

DE VINNE, THEODORE L. *Plain printing types.* New York, 1902.

DOWDING, GEOFFREY. *Factors in the choice of type faces.* Wace & Co., 1957.

EHRLICH, F. *The New typography and modern layouts.* Chapman & Hall, 1934.

GILL, ERIC. *Essay on typography.* Sheed & Ward, 1936.

GRAY, NICOLETTE. *XIXth century ornamented types and title pages.* Faber, 1938.

GUPPY, H. *Stepping-stones to the art of typography.* Longmans, Green, 1928.

ISAAC, F. S. *English printers' types of the sixteenth century.* O.U.P., 1936.

JOHNSON, ALFRED FORBES. *A Catalogue of Italian engraved title-pages in the sixteenth century.* O.U.P., 1936.

JOHNSON, ALFRED FORBES. *Type designs, their history and development.* Grafton, 1934.

JOHNSON, J. *Typographia.* 2 vols. Longmans and others, 1824.

JONES, HERBERT. *Type in action.* Sidgwick & Jackson, 1938.

LEGROS, L., AND GRANT, J. C. *Typographical printing surfaces.* Longmans, 1916.

MCKERROW, RONALD B., AND FERGUSON, F. S. *Title page borders used in England and Scotland, 1485–1640.* Bibliographical Society Illustrated Monographs No. 21.

MCKERROW, RONALD B. *Printers' and publishers' devices in England and Scotland, 1485–1640.* Bibliographical Society, 1913.

MONOTYPE CORPORATION. *Leaves out of books: brought together as examples of 20 classic 'Monotype' faces at work.* 1938.

MORE, E. R. *Dissertation upon English typographical founders and foundries.* Nichols, 1779.

MORISON, STANLEY. *First principles of typography.* C.U.P., 1951.

MORISON, STANLEY. *Four centuries of fine printing.* 2nd ed. Benn, 1949.

MORISON, STANLEY. *Modern fine printing.* Benn, 1925.

MORISON, STANLEY. *The Art of the printer.* Benn, 1925.

MORISON, STANLEY. *Type designs of the past and present.* Fleuron, 1926.

MORISON, STANLEY. *The Typographic arts.* Sylvan Press, 1949.

REED, TALBOT BAINES. *A History of the old English letter-foundries.* New ed. by A. F. Johnson. Faber, 1952.

REPORT of the Committee Appointed to Select the Best Face of Type and Modes of Display for Government Printing. H.M.S.O., 1922.

ROGERS, BERNARD. *Elementary typography.* Pitman, 1948.

SIGNATURE: a quadrimestrial of typography and graphic arts. Ed. by Oliver Simon. New series, 1946–54.

SIMON, OLIVER. *Introduction to typography.* Faber, 1945.

TARR, J. C. *How to plan print.* Crosby Lockwood, 1950.

TARR, J. C. *Style book for the guidance of letterpress students.* Chiswick, 1936.

THOMAS, D. *Type for print.* 2nd ed. Whitaker, 1939.

THOMAS, D. B. *A Book of printed alphabets.* Sidgwick & Jackson, 1937.

UPDIKE, DANIEL BERKELEY. *Printing types: their history, forms and use.* 2 vols. Harvard U.P.: O.U.P., 1922.

WARDE, BEATRICE. *The Crystal goblet: an invitation to typography.* Sylvan Press, 1947.

WARDE, BEATRICE. *Typography in art education.* A paper read at the annual conference, 1945, of the National Society for Art Education, 1946.

Printing—Type-Specimen Books

BALDING AND MANSELL, Wisbech. *Ars typographica.* 1930 & 1940.

BERRY, W. TURNER, AND JOHNSON, ALFRED FORBES. *Encyclopaedia of type faces.* Blandford, 1953.

CLOISTER PRESS, Heaton Mersey. *A Specimen book of types and ornaments.* 1935.

COLLINS, WILLIAM. *Fontana: specimens of a new type face for books designed by Hans Mardersteig for the exclusive use of the House of Collins.* 1936.

COWELL, Ipswich. *A Book of typefaces.* 1952.

COWELL, Ipswich. *A Handbook of printing types, with notes on the style of composition and graphic processes used by Cowells, Ipswich.* 1947.

CURWEN PRESS, London. *A Specimen book of types and ornaments in use at the Curwen Press.* 1928.

FANFARE PRESS, London. *A Book of Fanfare ornaments, with an introduction by James Laver.* 1939.

HARRISON AND SONS, London. *Type specimen book.* 1933.

HAZELL, WATSON AND VINEY, Aylesbury. *Type faces.* 1925 & 1940.

JARROLD AND SONS, Norwich. *Specimen types and pages*. 1934.
KYNOCH PRESS, Birmingham. *Specimens of types in use at the Kynoch Press*. 1934.
KYNOCH PRESS, Birmingham. *The Kynoch Press book of type specimens*. 1927.
LINOTYPE AND MACHINERY LTD. *The Printed word*. 1938.
LINOTYPE AND MACHINERY LTD. *Specimens of faces*. 1953.
MORISON, STANLEY. *On type faces*. Medici Society & The Fleuron, 1923.
MORRISON AND GIBB, Edinburgh. *Type faces*. 1937.
PELICAN PRESS, London. *Typography*. Compiled by Francis Meynell. 1923.
PERCY LUND, HUMPHRIES, Bradford. *Type index: a utilitarian specimen book*. 1929.
RICHARD CLAY, Bungay. *A Book of printing types and ornaments used by Richard Clay & Sons at the Chaucer Press*. 1930.
SHENVAL PRESS, Hertford. *A Handbook of printing types, rules, printer's flowers and typographical decorations available for use at the Shenval Press*. 1939.
SPOTTISWOODE, BALLANTYNE AND CO., London. *Printing types*. 1924 & 1939.
TAYLOR'S FOREIGN PRESS. *Typographia: a treatise on English, oriental and foreign type faces in use at Taylor's Foreign Press*. 1936.
TILLOTSONS (BOLTON) LTD. *Type specimen book*. 2nd ed. 1952.
WESTERN TYPESETTING CO., Bristol. *A Catalogue of type faces, ornaments, borders, rules*. 1939.
WESTMINSTER PRESS, London. *Faces, borders and ornaments*. 1929.
WILLIAM CLOWES, Beccles. *Book types*. 1936.

Manuscripts—The Alphabet, Calligraphy and Illumination; Map-making

BAINS, D. *A Supplement to Notae Latinae: abbreviations in Latin MSS of 850 to 1050 A.D.* C.U.P., 1936.
BOASE, T. S. R. *English art, 1100–1216*. O.U.P., 1953.
BODLEIAN LIBRARY. *English Romanesque illumination*. Oxford, 1951.
BODLEIAN LIBRARY. *Italian illuminated manuscripts from 1400 to 1550*. (Catalogue.) Oxford, 1948.
BOECKLER, ALBERT. *Deutsche Buchmalerei vorgotischer Zeit*. Königstein im Taunus, Langewiesche Verlag, 1952.
BRITISH MUSEUM. *Schools of illumination*. 6 parts. 1914–30.
CHRISTOPHER, H. G. T. *Palaeography and archives: a manual for the librarian, archivist and student*. Grafton, 1938.
CRONE, G. R. *Maps and their makers*. Hutchinson, 1953.
DIRINGER, D. *The Alphabet*. 2nd ed. Hutchinson, 1949.
DIRINGER, D. *The Illuminated book*. Faber, 1958.
DIRINGER, D. *Staples alphabet exhibition*. (Handbook.) 1953.
EVANS, JOAN. *Art in mediaeval France, 987–1498*. O.U.P., 1948.
EVANS, JOAN. *English art: 1307–1461*. O.U.P., 1949.
HASELDEN, R. B. *Scientific aids for the study of manuscripts*. Oxford, 1935. (Supplement to the Bibliographical Society's Transactions No. 10.)
HERBERT, J. A. *Illuminated manuscripts*. Methuen, 1911.
JOHNSON, CHARLES, AND JENKINSON, CHARLES HILARY. *English court hand, A.D. 1066–1500: illustrated chiefly from the Public Records*. 2 vols. O.U.P., 1915.
JOHNSTON, EDWARD. *Writing and illuminating, and lettering*. Pitman, 1939.
JOHNSTON, W. AND A. K. *One hundred years of map-making*. Johnston, 1925.
KENDRICK, T. D. *Anglo-Saxon art to A.D. 900*. Methuen, 1938.
KENDRICK, T. D. *Late Saxon and Viking art*. Methuen, 1949.
LAMB, C. M. *ed. The Calligrapher's handbook*. Faber, 1956.
LYNAM, E. *The Mapmaker's art*. Batchworth, 1953.
MADAN, FALCONER. *Books in manuscript*. 2nd ed. Kegan Paul, 1920.
MITCHELL, C. A. *Documents and their scientific examination*. Griffin, 1935.
MOÉ, E. A. VAN. *Illuminated initials in mediaeval manuscripts*. Thames & Hudson, 1950.
OAKESHOTT, WALTER. *The Artists of the Winchester Bible*. Faber, 1945.
OAKESHOTT, WALTER. *The Sequence of English medieval art: illustrated chiefly from illuminated MSS, 650–1450*. Faber, 1950.
ÖSTERREICHISCHE NATIONALBIBLIOTHEK. *Abendländische Buchmalerei*. (Catalogue.) Wien, 1952.
ÖSTERREICHISCHE NATIONALBIBLIOTHEK. *Buchkunst des Morgenlandes*. (Catalogue.) Wien, 1953.
PÄCHT, OTTO. *The Master of Mary of Burgundy*. Faber, 1948.
RICE, D. T. *English art, 871–1100*. O.U.P., 1952.
RICKERT, MARGARET. *Painting in Britain: the Middle Ages*. Penguin, 1954.
SAUNDERS, O. E. *English art in the Middle Ages*. O.U.P., 1932.
SAUNDERS, O. E. *English illumination*. 2 vols. Florence, Pantheon, n.d.
STANDARD, PAUL. *Calligraphy's flowering, decay and restauration*. Sylvan Press.
SULLIVAN, SIR EDWARD. *Book of Kells*. 5th ed. Studio, 1952.

TOOLEY, R. V. *Maps and map-makers*. Batsford, 1949.

TSCHICHOLD, JAN. *An Illustrated history of writing and lettering*. Zwemmer, 1946.

Bookbinding

BLADES, W. *Books in chains*. Stock, 1892.

BRASSINGTON, W. SALT. *ed. A History of the art of bookbinding, with some account of the books of the ancients*. Elliot Stock, 1894.

BRITISH STANDARDS INSTITUTION. *Glossary of leather terms*. (B.S. 2780: 1956.)

CARTER, JOHN. *Publisher's cloth: an outline history of publisher's binding in England, 1820–1900*. Constable, 1935.

COBHAM, VISCOUNT, *ed. The Society of Arts report on leather for bookbinding*. Bell, 1905.

COCKERELL, DOUGLAS. *Bookbinding, and the care of books*. 5th ed. Pitman, 1953.

COCKERELL, DOUGLAS. *Some notes on bookbinding*. O.U.P., 1948.

DAVENPORT, CYRIL. *Decorative bookbinding*. Journal of the Society of Arts, 1898.

DIEHL, E. *Bookbinding: its background and technique*. 2 vols. New York, Rinehart, 1946.

DIMAND, M. S. *Handbook of Muhammadan art*. 2nd ed. New York, Hartsdale House, 1947.

DUTTON, M. K. *Historical sketch of bookbinding as an art*. U.S.A., Norwood, Holliston Mills, 1926.

FLETCHER, W. Y. *Bookbindings in the British Museum*. 1895–6.

HARTHAN, J. P. *Bookbindings*. Victoria & Albert Museum, 1950.

HOBSON, A. R. A. *The Literature of bookbinding*. C.U.P., 1954.

HOBSON, G. D. *Blind-stamped panels in the English book-trade, c. 1485–1555*. Bibliographical Society, 1944.

HOBSON, G. D. *Maioli, Canevari and others*. Benn, 1926.

HOBSON, G. D. *Les Reliures à la fanfare: le problème de l's fermé*. Chiswick Press, 1935.

HOWE, ELLIC. *London bookbinders, 1780–1806*. Dropmore, 1950.

HOWE, ELLIC, AND CHILD, J. *The Society of London Bookbinders, 1780–1951*. Sylvan Press, 1952.

HULME, E. W., AND OTHERS. *Leather for libraries*. Library Supply Co., 1905.

LEIGHTON, D. *Modern bookbinding: a survey and a prospect*. Dent, 1935.

MASON, JOHN. *A Practical course in bookcraft and bookbinding*. Leicester, Backus, 1947.

MASON, JOHN. *Edition case binding*. Pitman, 1948.

MASON, JOHN. *Letterpress bookbinding*. Pitman, 1948.

MITCHELL, W. S. *A History of Scottish bookbinding, 1432–1650*. University of Aberdeen, 1955.

PHILIP, ALEX J. *The Business of bookbinding for librarians, publishers, students, binders, and the general reader*. Gravesend, Philip, 1935.

PLENDERLEITH, H. J. *The Preservation of leather bookbindings*. B.M., 1946.

RAMSDEN, CHARLES. *French bookbinders, 1789–1848*. Lund, Humphries, for the author, 1950.

RYE, R. A., AND QUINN, M. S. *Catalogue of historical and armorial bookbindings exhibited in the University Library*. University of London, 1937.

STEPHEN, G. A. *Commercial bookbinding: a description of the processes and the various machines used*. London, Stonehill, 1910.

THOMAS, H. *Early Spanish bookbindings: IX–XI centuries*. Bibliographical Society, 1939.

TOWN, L. *Bookbinding by hand*. Faber, 1951.

VAUGHAN, A. J. *Modern bookbinding*. Raithby, Lawrence, 1946.

WATERER, J. W. *Leather in life, art and industry*. Faber, 1946.

Paper-making

ASSOCIATION OF MAKERS OF ESPARTO PAPERS. *Esparto paper*. Neame, 1956.

BOWATER PAPERS. Bowater Paper Corporation. Irregular issues.

BRIQUET, C. M. *Les filigranes*. 4 vols. Leipzig, 1923.

BROWN, T. *Introducing paper: a guide for the newcomer to the paper trade*. Whitaker, 1939.

CHURCHILL, W. A. *Watermarks in paper in Holland, England, France, etc., in the XVII and XVIII centuries, and their interconnection*. Amsterdam, 1935.

CLAPPERTON, R. H., AND HENDERSON, W. *Modern paper-making*. 3rd ed. Blackwell, 1947.

CLAPPERTON, R. H. *Paper: an historical account of its making by hand from the earliest times down to the present day*. Shakespeare Head Press, 1934.

DAWE, E. A. *Paper and its uses*. 2 vols. Crosby Lockwood, 1929.

DAWE, E. A. *Paper for printers*. Pitman, 1949.

DAY, F. T. *Paper converting and usage*. Trade Journals, 1954.

EVEREST, A. B. *Nickel alloys in the paper-making industry*. Paper Makers Association of Great Britain and Ireland, 1935.

GILMOUR, S. C. *Paper: its making, merchanting, and usage*. National Association of Paper Merchants, 1955.

GREEN, J. B. *Notes on the manufacture of hand-made paper*. London School of Printing, 1936.

GREEN, J. B. *Paper-making by hand in 1953*. Phillips, 1953.

HUNTER, D. *Paper-making: the history and technique of an ancient craft*. 2nd ed. Cresset, 1957.

LABARRE, E. J. *Dictionary of paper and paper-making terms.* 2nd ed. O.U.P., 1952.

LORING, R. B. *Decorated book papers.* 2nd ed. Cambridge (Mass.), Harvard U.P., 1952.

MADDOX, H. A. *Paper, its history, sources and manufacture.* 6th ed. Pitman, 1945.

PAPER MAKERS ASSOCIATION. *Standard method for the determination of the thickness and bulk of paper.* 1936.

SPALDING AND HODGE. *Paper terminology.* 1954.

Publishing and the Book Trade

ARBER, EDWARD. *List, based on the Registers of the Stationers' Company, of 837 London publishers between 1553 and 1640 A.D.* Birmingham, 1890.

BARKER, R. E. *Books for all.* UNESCO, 1956.

BENNETT, H. S. *English books and their readers, 1475–1557.* C.U.P., 1952.

BRITISH BOOK TRADE ORGANIZATION: a report on the work of the Joint Committee, 1939.

GRANNIS, C. B. *What happens in book publishing.* U.S.A., Columbia U.P.: O.U.P., 1957.

GREG, W. W. *Some aspects and problems of London publishing between 1550 and 1650.* O.U.P., 1956.

HAMPDEN, JOHN. *The Book world today.* Allen & Unwin, 1957.

HODGSON, S. *The Worshipful Company of Stationers and Newspaper Makers: notes on its origin and history.* Stationers' Hall, 1953.

HYDE, SYDNEY. *Sales on a shoestring.* Deutsch, 1956.

JOY, THOMAS. *Bookselling.* Pitman, 1952.

KNIGHT, C. *Shadows of the old booksellers.* Bell, 1865.

MUMBY, F. A. *Publishing and bookselling: a history from the earliest times to the present day.* 4th ed. Cape, 1956.

PENGUIN BOOKS LTD. *The Penguin story, MCMXXXV–MCMLVI.* London, 1956.

PLANT, MARJORIE. *The English book trade: an economic history of the making and sale of books.* Allen & Unwin, 1939.

ROBERTS, S. C. *The Evolution of Cambridge publishing.* C.U.P., 1956.

UNWIN, SIR STANLEY. *The Truth about publishing.* 7th ed. Allen & Unwin, 1960.

UNWIN, SIR STANLEY. *The Truth about a publisher.* Allen & Unwin. 1960.

Additional titles

BIGGS, JOHN. *Woodcuts.* Blandford, 1958.

BOOK DESIGN AND PRODUCTION. Quarterly.

BRITISH STANDARDS INSTITUTION. *Typeface nomenclature.* (B.S. 2961: 1958.)

CARTER, HARRY. *Wolvercote Mill.* O.U.P., 1957.

DAVIS, G. R. C. *Medieval cartularies of Great Britain: a short catalogue.* Longmans, 1958.

FEBVRE, LUCIEN, AND MARTIN, HENRI-JEAN. *L'Apparition du livre.* Paris, Michel, 1958.

GREAT BRITAIN. Treasury. *Official publications.* H.M.S.O., 1958.

HANDOVER, P. M. *Printing in London.* 1960.

HEWITT, R. A. *Style for print and proof-correcting.* Blandford, 1958.

JARRETT, JAMES. *Printing Style.* Allen & Unwin, 1960.

LETOUZEY, V. *Colour and colour measurement in the graphic industries.* Pitman, 1958.

MOTIF. Quarterly.

NIXON, HOWARD. *Broxbourne Library: styles and designs of bookbindings from the 12th to the 20th century.* Maggs, 1950.

NORTON, F. J. *Italian printers, 1501–1520.* Bowes, 1958.

PISSARRO, L. *Notes on the Eragny Press,* ed. A. Fern. (Privately printed.) C.U.P., 1957.

PRINTING, PRESS AND PUBLISHING NEWS. Weekly.

WEBBER. R. B. *The Book of pH.* Newnes, 1958.